He Flies through the Air
with the Greatest of Ease

He Flies through the Air with the Greatest of Ease

A William Saroyan Reader

Edited by William E. Justice

Great Valley Books
Heyday Books, Berkeley, California

This book was made possible in part by generous grants from the William Saroyan Foundation and the James Irvine Foundation.

Library of Congress Cataloging-in-Publication Data

Saroyan, William, 1908–1981.
　[Selections. 2008]
　He flies through the air with the greatest of ease : a William Saroyan reader / edited by William E. Justice ; foreword by Herbert Gold.
　　p. cm.
　Includes bibliographical references.
　ISBN-13: 978-1-59714-089-8 (hardcover : alk. paper)
　ISBN-13: 978-1-59714-090-4 (pbk.: alk. paper)
　I. Justice, William E. II. Title.
　PS3537.A826A6 2008
　818'.5209--dc22 2007048249

Cover Art and Design: Lorraine Rath
Interior Design/Typesetting: Leigh McLellan Design
Printing and Binding: Thomson-Shore, Dexter, MI

Orders, inquiries, and correspondence should be addressed to:
　　Heyday Books
　　P.O. Box 9145, Berkeley, CA 94709
　　(510) 549-3564, Fax (510) 549-1889
　　www.heydaybooks.com

Printed in the United States of America

10 9 8 7 6 5 4 3 2 1

green press
INITIATIVE

Heyday Books is committed to preserving ancient forests and natural resources. We elected to print *He Flies Through The Air With The Greatest Of Ease* on 50% post consumer recycled paper, processed chlorine free. As a result, for this printing, we have saved:

　33 Trees (40' tall and 6-8" diameter)
　　13,892 Gallons of Wastewater
　5,587 Kilowatt Hours of Electricity
　　1,531 Pounds of Solid Waste
　3,008 Pounds of Greenhouse Gases

Heyday Books made this paper choice because our printer, Thomson-Shore, Inc., is a member of Green Press Initiative, a nonprofit program dedicated to supporting authors, publishers, and suppliers in their efforts to reduce their use of fiber obtained from endangered forests.

For more information, visit www.greenpressinitiative.org

3δ

Contents

Short Stories

from *The Daring Young Man on the Flying Trapeze*

from *Inhale and Exhale*

The Daring Old Man on the Flying Trapeze

by Herbert Gold

Evidently pilfered from his house after his death, a broken cardboard box labeled WM SAROYAN, MAN, sat on a shelf in a used bookshop in San Francisco. It was a photocopy of the unpublished manuscript of *More Obituaries*, the book Saroyan was writing as he was dying.

The bookseller said, "Ten bucks okay with you? Anything else here catch your fancy?"

My sixth-grade English teacher in Lakewood, Ohio, put her nicotine-stained fingers on my shoulder at the drinking fountain and said, (a) my composition would have gotten a top grade, but the word "grewsome" should be spelled "gruesome," and (b) I really ought to read a certain story about a starving writer in San Francisco. "The Daring Young Man on the Flying Trapeze" was written by a handsome, dark-haired young Armenian. I, too, might someday become a starving, dark-haired young writer in San Francisco, even without being handsome and Armenian.

Saroyan's voice, insistent, overflowing with humor, overcoming melancholy, wielding the American language with the freedom of a boy abandoned to a home for orphans, who read merely everything, listened to the babble of voices in Fresno and San Francisco, in the fields and barbershops, the streets, taverns, and short-order joints, fully intended to take charge of his world, which was the only world that mattered. He would make it matter to all within earshot. Like Mark Twain and Henry Miller, he was an American sport, hiding the necessary suspicion of monstrousness under his yelling love and optimism. He was merry and bright. Life handed him deep griefs, as it does to most of us.

I didn't see all that at age twelve. I grew some.

More than a few years later, in the sixties, I found myself a writer in San Francisco, but had not yet succeeded in starving, darn it. One afternoon I was brooding alone in the San Francisco Museum of Art, then still in the Veterans Memorial Building on Van Ness, when I heard a voice booming, saw that strong-featured, heavy Armenian face, now with a bristling mustache, lecturing to two children about the meaning of the paintings nearby, and incidentally also lecturing—hectoring, nagging, informing, bragging—about the meaning of life and their proper place in the world. The children were his son and daughter. The rich baritone was that of a Personage, a father, a man speaking from the depths of imperativeness and soul.

"Mr. Saroyan, I presume."

He may have been pleased to find an admirer here on a gray weekday afternoon. It's not unusual for writers to be pleased to meet admirers. The son, Aram, and the daughter, Lucy, were happy to have the meaning of life interrupted for ice cream and cookies.

Somehow lonely William Saroyan, adrift after a bitter pair of divorces from the same woman, and idle Herbert Gold, also divorced with two children, new to San Francisco on a gray November day, became instant coconspirators. He didn't mind my telling him that the teacher with the nicotine-stained fingers had both sent me to his first stories and also initiated my closest friend into sex. I got the best of the deal, although my friend got the bragging rights.

I asked Bill if he might like to spend an evening with a pair of adventurous Mills College girls. (We were younger then; in 1961, people still called young women "girls.") For once, he was at a loss for words—for about five seconds; and then: *"When?"*

The young women arrived at my flat (also known as a beatnik pad). I lit the kindling in my fireplace. Bill lumbered up the stairs. I opened the door and the draft sent the fire leaping out into the room. Bill said, "The tiger is in the fireplace!" and we all sootily pushed flames back where they belonged.

Then he took a sharp look at the young women, literature majors at a college for sometimes well-behaved daughters, and instantly transformed himself from a beaky Armenian eagle into a nurturing Armenian uncle. We walked down Russian Hill to North Beach, a family-style

Basque dinner at the Hotel du Midi, a lecture about the history of the International Settlement and the Barbary Coast, a reminiscence about his days as a telegraph messenger boy. He was sending us swift spiritual telegrams: LET ME BE YOUR GUIDE. He seemed deeply shocked that we hadn't yet attended to Turk Murphy and his Dixieland band, so a visit to Earthquake McGoon's was next on the program. IN THE TIME OF YOUR LIFE, LIVE. That was an order.

The evening ended late. And then we all swore a solemn oath to meet again as soon as possible.

My woman friend's roommate still regrets, nearly fifty years later, that all she got from William Saroyan was laughter, literature, history, undying memories. Okay, there was a touch of romance, but nothing that called for the early-sixties cream and diaphragm, which she confesses having tucked into her purse.

Discovering that Saroyan badly needed money in those days, after his bouts of divorce, gambling ("It isn't gambling if you win," he said), drinking, and neglect of the income tax laws, I invited him to dinner at the Brighton Express in North Beach, along with Mark Schorer, chairman of the English department at the University of California, Berkeley. Bill was likely to charm Professor Schorer, and he did. He improvised a play, casting the people in the little restaurant. He invaded the kitchen to interview the Japanese American cook as the ingénue love interest. He decided God should be played by a horse, the only actor not on the premises.

Mark Schorer offered a large lecture fee and pulled out his notebook to schedule it. Saroyan was enthusiastic. Schorer proposed a date. Bill wasn't sure he would be available. Mark asked him to name another date. Bill gave the matter some deep thought, and wondered if God absolutely needed to be played by a horse. "A lecture," Mark reminded him. "When? I need to schedule and request the funds."

"Tell you what, Mark," Bill said. "I might be driving west from New York, on my way back from Paris because the melons are in season in Fresno, and I'll send you a postcard and say I'm on my way."

"No, that won't work. We need to schedule in advance."

"It'll work fine, Mark. I'll say, Hey Mark, how about next Thursday?"

"No. Bill."

Saroyan shrugged. He thought hard. "You think we can get a horse to behave like God, or do we have to dress up a couple of my cousins in Fresno?"

Again my matchmaking was fruitless. But Bill managed to take a gig at Purdue University, which didn't require finicky advance planning. Instead of lecturing, he directed an improvised play with students he enlisted on the spot. It was West Lafayette, Indiana's finest theatrical experience of the year. In the off-Indianapolis theatrical market.

> Herbert Gold, trying to make polite conversation with a not-brilliant Armenian young woman: "Is it true, as someone said, that William Saroyan is the most famous Armenian who ever lived?"
>
> Not-brilliant Armenian young woman, after careful consideration: "I think that's because he's well-known."

In Paris, a French publisher with a fine Left Bank house and a cook—assets more common among publishers than among writers—suggested that I invite some Americans-in-Paris to dinner. I thought of Mary McCarthy, the tight-lipped wit, and William Saroyan, the loose-lipped jokester. There were only two problems. Mary McCarthy said, "He doesn't like me." William Saroyan said, "She hates me."

"Come anyway," I said. "Good chow."

It sounded like a normal Paris dinner party. Unfortunately, Bill arrived four hours early, announcing that he had changed his mind about dinner, but we could go for a walk instead. We strolled to George Whitman's Shakespeare & Company bookshop, looked for Bill's books and mine, scheduled a reading for Bill at some Sunday yet to be determined. Then, for variety, we visited another bookshop. The statue of Diderot poking his finger at the church of St.-Germain-des-Prés. A beer at Chez Lipp. A sit in the little garden of the Russian church at the corner of the Boulevard St.-Germain and the rue des Saints-Pères. A few complaints about ex-wives. A discussion of the melons that grow near Fresno and the red wine and cheese which grow all over Paris…Bill decided to walk me back to the publisher's house. He entered. He smelled the cooking in progress.

He didn't ask permission to visit the kitchen and lift the tops of the pots, peer within, sniff approvingly. "Maybe I'll have dinner," he said. A great writer has the right to change his mind. Tolstoy, Herman Melville, and Ross Bagdasarian were known to have done so. What is hatred between two writers at opposite ends of the literary spectrum compared with a fine meal of lamb, couscous, *haricots verts*, and beverages not easily available in Fresno, although the best melons grow there?

Mary McCarthy arrived, a bit bustling and nervous. I, too, had enjoyed a quarrel with her, although since then we had danced and made up. Even Bill seemed edgy.

So he began to talk. His voice was booming, rich, and cadenced. His stories, recounted in long, loping run-on sentences, filled with melon juice and red wine, love of family, and gaiety about disaster, sometimes ended with his personal version of Samuel Beckett's despair. "It's terrible. It's okay. It's *verrry interesting.*"

His partial deafness did not prevent his noticing Mary's laughter. Once she clapped her hands with glee, like Alice in Wonderland, although an Alice-Mary with a mouth full of sharkish teeth. She was happy. The publisher and I were happy. Bill was happy. Dissatisfied with his children, exasperated by the rhythm of his decline on the literary stock exchange, where fickleness of esteem competes with irrelevance of opinion, lonely without a lover, aging, sometimes weary, his heart was still in the highlands.

Mary stayed till one a.m. After she left, Bill stayed for another nightcap, then a post-nightcap nightcap, and rolled down the stairs prudently before dawn. It had turned out to be a perfect evening. All I needed for breakfast was a container of plain yogurt and two aspirin.

Bill decided not to do the reading at Shakespeare & Company, but then showed up anyway and did a reading. I'm not sure if Mary McCarthy attended.

Passionate living is not easy living. The stress of being a long-term effervescent boy was wearing the man down. I decided to take my son Ari, aged nine, to visit William Saroyan in Fresno; and if he was too tired to see us, we'd just visit an Armenian restaurant, buy a few melons, take sightseeing walks among microwaved burritos, practice breathing the smog of California's Central Valley. But Bill said come on, come on, come on-a my house. This was the refrain of a traditional folk song he had adapted with his cousin, Ross Bagdasarian.

We went onna his house. He showed Ari his manual typewriter, his long legal-sized sheets of manuscript, his rock collection, his sketches, and lectured him about the duties and glory of being a writer. He asked Ari about his family heritage, Jewish and Wasp, and suggested that his own children also had a *verrry interesting* bloodline, Armenian and Jewish. "But everyone has a verrry interesting bloodline!"

Then he heard from Ari that there was a twin brother. "Verrry interesting!" he proclaimed, and announced that he would visit San Francisco soon to meet the verrry interesting brother-younger-by-five-minutes. A photograph shows Bill, Ari, Ethan, and Herb, poking our heads through the sunroof of my battered Fiat.

One of Bill's complaints about his beloved, hated, twice-married-to-him, twice-divorced wife, Carol, was that she was an addict of the social ramble: too much drinking, too much partying, and therefore the next morning he couldn't write enough good words. Then followed another evening, another party, and consequently not enough words, even if they were good ones. And then another, and maybe only one or two hundred good words. "But they were good words! But only a hundred good words," he roared. "That's not enough!"

In his last weeks, he was still writing. Dying of prostate cancer, he would need to be rushed to the hospital to be catheterized. And then, relieved, he would come back home to finish the day's writing. Bladder wrecked, he was still the soulful singer of his undaunted songs of yearning. The words in the manuscript of *More Obituaries*, labeled MAN, which I found in that used bookstore, were still warm-hearted, questing, generous, boiling with life, the death-defying rushing song of the old man still soaring and plunging on his flying trapeze.

There are peaks and valleys in every writing writer's work. William Saroyan was one of the writingest of writers. In his massive oeuvre, there are times when he is merely poking and prodding his voice. But when he finds it, there are high moments of humor, generosity, vivid storytelling, evocations of pain and pleasure. For example, his shame and grief over a troubled relationship with his son can touch any parent; his transparent rage at his wife and at himself in connection with her should evoke fellow feeling in all who know that the path of spousedom is a rocky one. For me, three short pages, Chapter 106, of one of his late books, *Obituaries*, the rhythm, sly humor, and shrugged-off grief, the sad recapitulation of the pleasures of simple existence, the exalted awareness of mortality, an offhand but measured conviction of moral responsibility are a peak of Saroyan's long meditation on the sense and responsibility of life. These three pages, which I've sometimes read aloud to would-be writers, remind me of "Euthyphro," Plato's dialogue on the responsibility of fathers and sons—but with Saroyan's unique wise-ass sideswipes at the whole deal. "Reader, take my advice, don't die, just don't die, that's all, it doesn't pay…"

After evoking the sourdough bread and the tea and the good sweet butter, which are some of the good reasons for avoiding death, he ambles to the point: His friend Johnny Mercer was a great songwriter, a singer of them, a wealthy man—but what was really important about him was that, after his father died, Johnny Mercer paid his father's debts. "A great living member of the human race died, and he is gone, and don't you do it—"

Reader, read this chapter aloud. It is full of fun and grief, tricks and utter sincerity. Beyond the words, Saroyan's sentence rhythms play like great music. If you have tears available, they will flow.

Elsewhere, not very far away, out of the same mellow, insistent, swift American voice, you will find occasions for laughter. Living through deep and permanent injuries, but supported by a metabolic joy in survival, Saroyan spun like a gyroscope to the edge of the earth; and discovering that the world is not flat and he wouldn't fall off, despite so much adverse opinion, he danced himself back into the crowded carnival midway which is human life.

Editor's Preface

William E. Justice

> In the critic's vocabulary, the word "precursor" is indispensable,
> but it should be cleansed of all connotations of polemic or rivalry.
> The fact is that every writer creates his own precursors. His work
> modifies our conception of the past, as it will modify the future.
> —*Jorge Luis Borges*

*T*o edit an obsession.

To tidy the hypergraphia of this man, this Saroyan, who, in order to become a writer, first learned to type.

To constrict what wants so forcefully to expand.

This is strange and unnatural work. A seedbed for hallucinations.

I dreamed of a Saroyan Ur-book. Each story, each play, every novel, every memoir, and even the essays, letters, and journals atomized. His prose in heaps where the sentences rise and fall on the air like downy feathers. Slowly, and guided by the poetry that is madness, the dissembled work is resurrected piecemeal and stitched together with heavy thread. In the end, on the desk before me, one uninterrupted cataract spanning the breach of a few thousand pages, roaring, the genius of the man, which was, as Blake knew, his shape: "*...the forms of all things are derived from their Genius, which by the Ancients was call'd an Angel & Spirit & Demon.*" The book would delineate the faces of Saroyan's Angel and chart the movements of his sizable, tangible Demon.

It begins thus:

> "Psychiatry, no," Dr. Pingitzer said. "People—little bit. Little, little,
> little bit. Every year, every day—less, less, less. Why? People is
> difficult. People is people. People is fun, play, imagination, magic.
> Ah ha. People is pain, people is sick, people is mad, people is hurt,
> people is hurt *people,* is kill, is kill self. Where is fun, where is play,

where is imagination, where is magic? Psychiatry I hate. People I love. Mad people, beautiful people, hurt people, sick people, broke people, in pieces people, I love, I love. Why? Why is lost from people fun, play, imagination, magic? What for? Ah ha. Money?" he smiled. "I think so. Money. Is love, this money. Is beauty, this money. Is fun, this money. Where is money? I don't know. No more fun. Work now. Work. Tiger. Tiger."

Then! Revealed, a network of associations and symbols no less complex than Proust, a spiritual struggle akin to Dostoevsky...

Thereafter, in the mad editor's monologue of comparative literary giantism, my dream through boredom dissolves and I am back at the task at hand. Winnow and thresh. Paring and plating the apple. Tiger. Tiger. The fever-dream is allegory after all. Saroyan should be read always with an eye on his pieces. Watch for watermelons, animals, bicycles, bits of song, children and old men. Here, something important is happening. These are his stories, his genius, and he cannot, must not cease their telling. The result of a *sane* edit, the volume laid out before you, contains twenty-seven short stories; the complete texts of the proto-novel *(My Name Is Aram)*, the Pulitzer-winning play *(The Time of Your Life)*, his unacknowledged masterpiece in novella *(Tracy's Tiger)*, and the first of his memoirs *(The Bicycle Rider in Beverley Hills)*; and a selection from his last work, the previously unpublished *More Obituaries*. Anyone reading this book with new eyes will be amply rewarded.

It is true that William Saroyan is not as widely read as he once was. The Critics are blamed for this so that they might be entreated, through the implied flattery, to aid in his rehabilitation. On the centennial of his birth, the William Saroyan Foundation has supported the creation of this large collection in the hopes that it will spur critics, reviewers, teachers, and readers to rectify this mistake. I am unconcerned. Perhaps it is his peculiar destiny to remain, for a while at least, a secret kind of writer, a writer whose books are passed from hand to hand, quietly, without the aid of the *New York* or other *Review of Books*. Or, his is a dream deferred.

The German Jewish essayist Walter Benjamin, writing in the 1930s of another neglected writer, Nikolai Leskov, saw the essential reasons so clearly that I must be careful not to let him hijack this entire preface. The trouble with Leskov, and I suggest Saroyan, is not the quality of his writing, but its category.

> Familiar though his name may be to us, the storyteller in his living
> immediacy is by no means a present force....To present someone...
> as a storyteller does not mean bringing him closer to us but, rather,
> increasing our distance from him.

The reasons Benjamin saw the storyteller in retreat were primarily economic and technological. Inheritors of the oral tradition, storytellers rely on artisans, on the working and domestic classes, in kitchens and workshops where harmony and handwork inspired the telling of stories and the art of listening to them as well. All move to the rhythm of work. The Fresno of Saroyan's childhood and the touchstone of his writing, agriculturally bound and immigrant crowded, created an oasis of the storytelling world and Saroyan was unbound from it.

Osip Mandelstam saw the disparity in similar terms.

> Literature is a social phenomenon while philology is domestic,
> intimate. Literature is a lecture, the street...philology is the
> family.

There are two strains of writing then. The storyteller reaches back to the epic and the folktale. He is a collector and a repeater. He distinguishes himself from his fellows through his style. The family. The kitchen.

The novelist is concerned in the creation of systems or puzzles and the dissemination of information. He seeks to be unrepeatable. His stories are meant to be heard alone, in silence. A lecture. The street. Alone in a room or alone in a crowd.

Saroyan's work is memorable for its leaps. The most workaday characters discuss the most mundane topics and then leap into pronouncements of brotherhood, the joy of being alive—which is different from the joy of "life"—but my god! These high and hard leaps—as if he suddenly saw a snake. I cannot help but see in each of these moments the Thing from which he leapt. Or, to borrow Benjamin again: "Death is the sanction of everything that the storyteller can tell. He has borrowed his authority from death."

To perceive in those leaps insights mawkish or sentimental is to read poorly.

Rejoining Borges, now that Saroyan is dead and was born a century ago, who are his created successors and precursors, and, to add another variable to Borges's equation, who are his created readers?

Precursors
Armenian oral tradition
folktales
Walt Whitman
William Blake

Successors
Kenneth Patchen*
Kurt Vonnegut
Hunter S. Thompson

Readers
The makers of things. Builders, bakers, guitar players.
Shipwrights, drivers of the combine harvester, quilters.
Whittlers, jam makers, painters. Those whose bodies
and hands retain the storytelling rhythms.

I write slowly and take walks often. Sometimes I forget to come back. I left my apartment where this preface is being composed, overdue, from the kitchen table—teapot, bouquet of sunflowers, empty candleholders—and walked, through a sunny day after the rains and before rains to come, to Cafe Ina, where I am friendly with the owner, Maria, and one of her employees, Melanie, who, when she is sweet, is called Melon, but when she is sour goes by Lemon. I drank my coffee with milk because I really shouldn't drink the stuff at all and addressed large questions of literature to the room. Maria was chopping turkey sausage for chili. She doesn't read much anymore but, before opening a cafe, liked science fiction. Melanie's reading is mostly contemporary. Tom Robbins and Anne Lamont. I couldn't hold them to my Big Questions very long and was pleased when the topics changed from books to film to music to food and to the strangeness of kids these days, our conversation in harmony with the quick rhythms of the cafe kitchen, Melanie working the espresso machine, Maria glazing apple turnovers. My head cleared. Saroyan, I thought, would like these people. On my way out I said, "I'll bring you in some Saroyan. I think you'll like him."

"Please do," said Maria and Melanie.

---

*A note on the beats. Though Kerouac & Co. owe much to Saroyan in style, there is not much storytelling in them.

Acknowledgments

I'd like to thank Robert Setrakian and Haig Mardikian from The Saroyan Foundation, whose commitment to Saroyan's legacy has demanded this work; Michael Murphy, Boyd Williamson, and Amanda Choi, who struggled with rotten copies of Saroyan's books and digitized them for little or no reward; Annette Keogh from Stanford University Libraries and Dickran Kouymjian, who assisted with the bibliography and images; the inimitable Lorraine Rath for the cover illustration; the writers David Kherdian and Aram Saroyan for their wisdom and advice; Gayle Wattawa for everything; Malcolm Margolin, who is the shepherd of this and so much more; and Herb Gold, who provided the unpublished *More Obituaries* manuscript and for remembering and writing so well of the man himself, William Saroyan.

Short Stories

from
*The Daring Young Man
on the Flying Trapeze*

The Daring Young Man
on the Flying Trapeze

I. Sleep

*H*orizontally wakeful amid universal widths, practicing laughter and mirth, satire, the end of all, of Rome and yes of Babylon, clenched teeth, remembrance, much warmth volcanic, the streets of Paris, the plains of Jericho, much gliding as of reptile in abstraction, a gallery of watercolors, the sea and the fish with eyes, symphony, a table in the corner of the Eiffel Tower, jazz at the opera house, alarm clock and the tapdancing of doom, conversation with a tree, the river Nile, Cadillac coupe to Kansas, the roar of Dostoyevsky, and the dark sun.

This earth, the face of one who lived, the form without the weight, weeping upon snow, white music, the magnified flower twice the size of the universe, black clouds, the caged panther staring, deathless space, Mr. Eliot with rolled sleeves baking bread, Flaubert and Guy de Maupassant, a wordless rhyme of early meaning, Finlandia, mathematics highly polished and slick as a green onion to the teeth, Jerusalem, the path to paradox.

The deep song of man, the sly whisper of someone unseen but vaguely known, hurricane in the cornfield, a game of chess, hush the queen, the king, Karl Franz, black Titanic, Mr. Chaplin weeping, Stalin, Hitler, a multitude of Jews, tomorrow is Monday, no dancing in the streets.

O swift moment of life: it is ended, the earth is again now.

II. Wakefulness

He (the living) dressed and shaved, grinning at himself in the mirror. Very unhandsome, he said; where is my tie? (He had but one.) Coffee and a gray sky, Pacific Ocean fog, the drone of a passing streetcar, people going to the city, time again, the day, prose and poetry. He moved swiftly down the stairs to the street and began to walk, thinking suddenly, *It is only in*

5

sleep that we may know that we live. There only, in that living death, do we meet ourselves and the far earth, God and the saints, the names of our fathers, the substance of remote moments; it is there that the centuries merge in the moment, that the vast becomes the tiny, tangible atom of eternity.

He walked into the day as alertly as might be, making a definite noise with his heels, perceiving with his eyes the superficial truth of streets and structures, the trivial truth of reality. Helplessly his mind sang, *He flies through the air with the greatest of ease; the daring young man on the flying trapeze*; then laughed with all the might of his being. It was really a splendid morning: gray, cold, and cheerless, a morning for inward vigor; ah, Edgar Guest, he said, how I long for your music.

In the gutter he saw a coin which proved to be a penny dated 1923, and placing it in the palm of his hand he examined it closely, remembering that year and thinking of Lincoln whose profile was stamped upon the coin. There was almost nothing man could do with a penny. I will purchase a motorcar, he thought. I will dress myself in the fashion of a fop, visit the hotel strumpets, drink and dine, and return to the quiet. Or I will drop the coin into a slot and weigh myself.

It was good to be poor, and the Communists—but it was dreadful to be hungry. What appetites they had, how fond they were of food! Empty stomachs. He remembered how greatly he needed food. Every meal was bread and coffee and cigarettes, and now he had no more bread. Coffee without bread could never honestly serve as supper, and there were no weeds in the park that could be cooked as spinach is cooked.

If the truth were known, he was half starved, and yet there was still no end of books he ought to read before he died. He remembered the young Italian in a Brooklyn hospital, a small sick clerk named Mollica, who had said desperately, I would like to see California once before I die. And he thought earnestly, I ought at least to read *Hamlet* once again; or perhaps *Huckleberry Finn*.

It was then that he became thoroughly awake: at the thought of dying. Now wakefulness was a state in the nature of a sustained shock. A young man could perish rather unostentatiously, he thought; and already he was very nearly starved. Water and prose were fine, they filled much inorganic space, but they were inadequate. If there were only some work he might do for money, some trivial labor in the name of commerce. If they would only allow him to sit at a desk all day and add trade figures, subtract and multiply and divide, then perhaps he would not die. He would buy food, all sorts of it: untasted delicacies from Norway, Italy, and France; all manner of beef, lamb, fish, cheese; grapes, figs, pears, apples, melons, which he would worship when he had satisfied his hunger. He would place a bunch of red grapes on a dish beside two black figs, a large yellow pear, and a green apple. He would hold a cut melon to his nostrils for hours. He would buy great brown loaves of French bread, vegetables of all sorts, meat; he would buy life.

From a hill he saw the city standing majestically in the east, great towers, dense with his kind, and there he was suddenly outside of it all, almost definitely certain that he should never gain admittance, almost positive that somehow he had ventured upon the wrong earth, or perhaps into the wrong age, and now a young man of twenty-two was to be permanently ejected from it. This thought was not saddening. He said to himself, sometime soon I must write *An Application for Permission to Live*. He accepted the thought of dying without pity for himself or for man, believing that he would at least sleep another night. His rent for another day was paid; there was yet another tomorrow. And after that he might go where other homeless men went. He might even visit the Salvation Army—sing to God and Jesus (unlover of my soul), be saved, eat and sleep. But he knew that he would not. His life was a private life. He did not wish to destroy this fact. Any other alternative would be better.

Through the air on the flying trapeze, his mind hummed. Amusing it was, astoundingly funny. A trapeze to God, or to nothing, a flying trapeze to some sort of eternity; he prayed objectively for strength to make the flight with grace.

I have one cent, he said. It is an American coin. In the evening I shall polish it until it glows like a sun and I shall study the words.

He was now walking in the city itself, among living men. There were one or two places to go. He saw his reflection in the plate-glass windows of stores and was disappointed with his appearance. . He seemed not at all as strong as he felt; he seemed, in fact, a trifle infirm in every part of his body, in his neck, his shoulders, arms, trunk, and knees. This will never do, he said, and with an effort he assembled all his disjointed parts and became tensely, artificially erect and solid.

He passed numerous restaurants with magnificent discipline, refusing even to glance into them, and at last reached a building which he entered. He rose in an elevator to the seventh floor, moved down a hall, and, opening a door, walked into the office of an employment agency. Already there were two dozen young men in the place; he found a corner where he stood waiting his turn to be interviewed. At length he was granted this great privilege and was questioned by a thin, scatterbrained miss of fifty.

Now tell me, she said; what can you do?

He was embarrassed. I can write, he said pathetically.

You mean your penmanship is good? Is that it? said the elderly maiden.

Well, yes, he replied. But I mean that I can write.

Write what? said the miss, almost with anger.

Prose, he said simply.

There was a pause. At last the lady said:

Can you use a typewriter?

Of course, said the young man.

All right, went on the miss, we have your address; we will get in touch with you. There is nothing this morning, nothing at all.

It was much the same at the other agency, except that he was questioned by a conceited young man who closely resembled a pig. From the agencies he went to the large department stores: there was a good deal of pomposity, some humiliation on his part, and finally the report that work was not available. He did not feel displeased, and strangely did not even feel that he was personally involved in all the foolishness. He was a living young man who was in need of money with which to go on being one, and there was no way of getting it except by working for it; and there was no work. It was purely an abstract problem which he wished for the last time to attempt to solve. Now he was pleased that the matter was closed.

He began to perceive the definiteness of the course of his life. Except for moments, it had been largely artless, but now at the last minute he was determined that there should be as little imprecision as possible.

He passed countless stores and restaurants on his way to the Y.M.C.A., where he helped himself to paper and ink and began to compose his *Application*. For an hour he worked on this document, then suddenly, owing to the bad air in the place and to hunger, he became faint. He seemed to be swimming away from himself with great strokes, and hurriedly left the building. In the Civic Center Park, across from the Public Library Building, he drank almost a quart of water and felt himself refreshed. An old man was standing in the center of the brick boulevard surrounded by sea gulls, pigeons, and robins. He was taking handfuls of bread crumbs from a large paper sack and tossing them to the birds with a gallant gesture.

Dimly he felt impelled to ask the old man for a portion of the crumbs, but he did not allow the thought even nearly to reach consciousness; he entered the Public Library and for an hour read Proust, then, feeling himself to be swimming away again, he rushed outdoors. He drank more water at the fountain in the park and began the long walk to his room.

I'll go and sleep some more, he said; there is nothing else to do. He knew now that he was much too tired and weak to deceive himself about being all right, and yet his mind seemed somehow still lithe and alert. It, as if it were a separate entity, persisted in articulating impertinent pleasantries about his very real physical suffering. He reached his room early in the afternoon and immediately prepared coffee on the small gas range. There was no milk in the can, and the half pound of sugar he had purchased a week before was all gone; he drank a cup of the hot black fluid, sitting on his bed and smiling.

From the Y.M.C.A. he had stolen a dozen sheets of letter paper upon which he hoped to complete his document, but now the very notion of writing was unpleasant to him. There was nothing to say. He began to polish the penny he had found in the morning, and this absurd act somehow afforded him great enjoyment. No American coin can be made to shine so brilliantly as a penny. How many pennies would he need to go on living? Wasn't there something more he might sell? He looked about the bare room. No. His watch was gone; also his books. All those fine books; nine of them for eighty-five cents. He felt ill and ashamed for having parted with his books. His best suit he had sold for two dollars, but that was all right. He didn't mind at all about clothes. But the books. That was different. It made him very angry to think that there was no respect for men who wrote.

He placed the shining penny on the table, looking upon it with the delight of a miser. How prettily it smiles, he said. Without reading them he looked at the words, *E Pluribus Unum One Cent United States Of America*, and turning the penny over, he saw Lincoln and the words, *In God We Trust Liberty 1923*. How beautiful it is, he said.

He became drowsy and felt a ghastly illness coming over his blood, a feeling of nausea and disintegration. Bewildered, he stood beside his bed, thinking *there is nothing to do but sleep*. Already he felt himself making great strides through the fluid of the earth, swimming away to the beginning. He fell face down upon the bed, saying, I ought first at least to give the coin to some child. A child could buy any number of things with a penny.

Then swiftly, neatly, with the grace of the young man on the trapeze, he was gone from his body. For an eternal moment he was all things at once: the bird, the fish, the rodent, the reptile, and man. An ocean of print undulated endlessly and darkly before him. The city burned. The herded crowd rioted. The earth circled away, and knowing that he did so, he turned his lost face to the empty sky and became dreamless, unalive, perfect.

Seventy Thousand Assyrians

I hadn't had a haircut in forty days and forty nights, and I was beginning to look like several violinists out of work. You know the look: genius gone to pot, and ready to join the Communist Party. We barbarians from Asia Minor are hairy people: when we need a haircut, we *need* a haircut. It was so bad, I had outgrown my only hat. (I am writing a very serious story, perhaps one of the most serious I shall ever write. That is why I am being flippant. Readers of Sherwood Anderson will begin to understand what I am saying after a while; they will know that my laughter is rather sad.) I was a young man in need of a haircut, so I went down to Third Street (San Francisco), to the Barber College, for a fifteen-cent haircut.

Third Street, below Harvard, is a district; think of the Bowery in New York, Main Street in Los Angeles: think of old men and boys, out of work, hanging around, smoking Bull Durham, talking about the government, waiting for something to turn up, simply waiting. It was a Monday morning in August and a lot of the tramps had come to the shop to brighten up a bit. The Japanese boy who was working over the free chair had a waiting list of eleven; all the other chairs were occupied. I sat down and began to wait. Outside, as Hemingway *(The Sun Also Rises; Farewell to Arms; Death in the Afternoon; Winner Take Nothing)* would say, haircuts were four bits. I had twenty cents and a half-pack of Bull Durham. I rolled a cigarette, handed the pack to one of my contemporaries who looked in need of nicotine, and inhaled the dry smoke, thinking of America, what was going on politically, economically, spiritually. My contemporary was a boy of sixteen. He looked Iowa; splendid potentially, a solid American, but down, greatly down in the mouth. Little sleep, no change of clothes for several days, a little fear, etc. I wanted very much to know his name. A writer is always wanting to get the reality of faces and figures. Iowa said, "I just got in from Salinas. No work in the lettuce fields. Going north now, to Portland; try to ship out." I wanted to tell him how it was with me: rejected story from *Scribner's,* rejected essay from *The Yale Review,* no money for decent cigarettes, worn shoes, old shirts, but I was afraid to make something of my own troubles.

A writer's troubles are always boring, a bit unreal. People are apt to feel, *Well, who asked you to write in the first place?* A man must pretend not to be a writer. I said, "Good luck, north." Iowa shook his head. "I know better. Give it a try, anyway. Nothing to lose." Fine boy, hope he isn't dead, hope he hasn't frozen, mighty cold these days (December, 1933), hope he hasn't gone down; he deserved to live. Iowa, I hope you got work in Portland; I hope you are earning money; I hope you have rented a clean room with a warm bed in it; I hope you are sleeping nights, eating regularly, walking along like a human being, being happy. Iowa, my good wishes are with you. I have said a number of prayers for you. (All the same, I think he is dead by this time. It was in him the day I saw him, the low malicious face of the beast, and at the same time all the theatres in America were showing, over and over again, an animated film-cartoon in which there was a song called "Who's Afraid of the Big Bad Wolf?", and that's what it amounts to; people with money laughing at the death that is crawling slyly into boys like young Iowa, pretending that it isn't there, laughing in warm theatres. I have prayed for Iowa, and I consider myself a coward. By this time he must be dead, and I am sitting in a small room, talking about him, only talking.)

I began to watch the Japanese boy who was learning to become a barber. He was shaving an old tramp who had a horrible face, one of those faces that emerge from years and years of evasive living, years of being unsettled, of not belonging anywhere, of owning nothing, and the Japanese boy was holding his nose back (his own nose) so that he would not smell the old tramp. A trivial point in a story, a bit of data with no place in a work of art, nevertheless, I put it down. A young writer is always afraid some significant fact may escape him. He is always wanting to put in everything he sees. I wanted to know the name of the Japanese boy. I am profoundly interested in names. I have found that those that are unknown are the most genuine. Take a big name like Andrew Mellon. I was watching the Japanese boy very closely. I wanted to understand from the way he was keeping his sense of smell away from the mouth and nostrils of the old man what he was thinking, how he was feeling. Years ago, when I was seventeen, I pruned vines in my uncle's vineyard, north of Sanger, in the San Joaquin Valley, and there were several Japanese working with me, Yoshio Enomoto, Hideo Suzuki, Katsumi Sujimoto, and one or two others. These Japanese taught me a few simple phrases, *hello, how are you, fine day, isn't it, good-bye*, and so on. I said in Japanese to the barber student, "How are you?" He said in

Japanese, "Very well, thank you." Then, in impeccable English, "Do you speak Japanese? Have you lived in Japan?" I said, "Unfortunately, no. I am able to speak only one or two words. I used to work with Yoshio Enomoto, Hideo Suzuki, Katsumi Sujimoto; do you know them?" He went on with his work, thinking of the names. He seemed to be whispering, "Enomoto, Suzuki, Sujimoto." He said, "Suzuki. Small man?" I said, "Yes." He said, "I know him. He lives in San Jose now. He is married now."

I want you to know that I am deeply interested in what people remember. A young writer goes out to places and talks to people. He tries to find out what they remember. I am not using great material for a short story. Nothing is going to happen in this work. I am not fabricating a fancy plot. I am not creating memorable characters. I am not using a slick style of writing. I am not building up a fine atmosphere. I have no desire to sell this story or any story to *The Saturday Evening Post* or to *Cosmopolitan* or to *Harper's*. I am not trying to compete with the great writers of short stories, men like Sinclair Lewis and Joseph Hergesheimer and Zane Grey, men who really know how to write, how to make up stories that will sell. Rich men, men who understand all the rules about plot and character and style and atmosphere and all that stuff. I have no desire for fame. I am not out to win the Pulitzer Prize or the Nobel Prize or any other prize. I am out here in the far West, in San Francisco, in a small room on Carl Street, writing a letter to common people, telling them in simple language things they already know. I am merely making a record, so if I wander around a little, it is because I am in no hurry and because I do not know the rules. If I have any desire at all, it is to show the brotherhood of man. This is a big statement and it sounds a little precious. Generally a man is ashamed to make such a statement. He is afraid sophisticated people will laugh at him. But I don't mind. I'm asking sophisticated people to laugh. That is what sophistication is for. I do not believe in races. I do not believe in governments. I see life as one life at one time, so many millions simultaneously, all over the earth. Babies who have not yet been taught to speak any language are the only race of the earth, the race of man: all the rest is pretense, what we call civilization, hatred, fear, desire for strength....But a baby is a baby. And the way they cry, there you have the brotherhood of man, babies crying. We grow up and we learn the words of a language and we see the universe through the language we know, we do not see it through all languages or through no language at all, through silence, for example, and we isolate ourselves in the language we know. Over here we isolate ourselves in English, or American as Mencken calls it. All the eternal things, in our words. If I want to do anything, I want to speak a more universal language. The heart of man, the unwritten part of man, that which is eternal and common to all races.

Now I am beginning to feel guilty and incompetent. I have used all this language and I am beginning to feel that I have said nothing. This is what drives a young writer out of his head, this feeling that nothing is being said. Any ordinary journalist would have been able to put the whole business into a three-word caption. Man is man, he would have said. Something clever, with any number of implications. But I want to use language that will create a single implication. I want the meaning to be precise, and perhaps that is why the language is so imprecise. I am walking around my subject, the impression I want to make, and I am trying to see it from all angles, so that I will have a whole picture, a picture of wholeness. It is the heart of man that I am trying to imply in this work.

Let me try again: I hadn't had a haircut in a long time and I was beginning to look seedy, so I went down to the Barber College on Third Street, and I sat in a chair. I said, "Leave it full in the back. I have a narrow head and if you do not leave it full in the back, I will go out of this place looking like a horse. Take as much as you like off the top. No lotion, no water, comb it dry." Reading makes a full man, writing a precise one, as you see. This is what happened. It doesn't make much of a story, and the reason is that I have left out the barber, the young man who gave me the haircut.

He was tall, he had a dark serious face, thick lips, on the verge of smiling but melancholy, thick lashes, sad eyes, a large nose. I saw his name on the card that was pasted on the mirror, Theodore Badal. A good name, genuine, a good young man, genuine. Theodore Badal began to work on my head. A good barber never speaks until he has been spoken to, no matter how full his heart may be.

"That name," I said, "Badal. Are you an Armenian?" I am an Armenian. I have mentioned this before. People look at me and begin to wonder, so I come right out and tell them. "I am an Armenian," I say. Or they read something I have written and begin to wonder, so I let them know. "I am an Armenian," I say. It is a meaningless remark, but they expect me to say it, so I do. I have no idea what it is like to be an Armenian or what it is like to be an Englishman or a Japanese or anything else. I have a faint idea what it is like to be alive. This is the only thing that interests me greatly. This and tennis. I hope some day to write a great philosophical work on tennis, something on the order of *Death in the Afternoon*, but I am aware that I am not yet ready to undertake such a work. I feel that the cultivation of tennis on a large scale among the peoples of the earth will do much to annihilate racial differences, prejudices, hatred, etc. Just as soon as I have perfected my drive and my lob, I hope to begin my outline of this great work. (It may seem to some sophisticated people that I am trying to make fun of Hemingway. I am not. *Death in the Afternoon* is a pretty sound piece of prose. I could never object to it as prose. I cannot even object to it as philosophy. I think it is finer philosophy than that of Will Durant and Walter Pitkin. Even when Hemingway is a fool, he is at least an accurate fool. He tells you what actually takes place and he doesn't allow the speed of an occurrence to make his exposition of it hasty. This is a lot. It is some sort of advancement for literature. To relate leisurely the nature and meaning of that which is very brief in duration.)

"Are you an Armenian?" I asked.

We are a small people and whenever one of us meets another, it is an event. We are always looking around for someone to talk to in our language. Our most ambitious political party estimates that there are nearly two million of us living on the earth, but most of us don't think so. Most of us sit down and take a pencil and a piece of paper and we take one section of the world at a time and imagine how many Armenians at the most are likely to be living in that section and we put the highest number on the paper, and then we go on to another section, India, Russia, Soviet Armenia, Egypt, Italy, Germany, France, America, South America, Australia, and so on, and after we add up our most hopeful figures the total comes to something a little less than a million. Then we start to think how big our families are, how high our birthrate and how low our death-rate (except in times of war when massacres increase the death-rate), and we begin to imagine how rapidly we will increase if we are left alone a quarter of a century, and we feel pretty happy. We always leave out earthquakes, wars, massacres, famines, etc., and it is a mistake. I remember the Near East Relief drives in my home town. My uncle used to be our orator and he used to make a whole auditorium full of Armenians weep. He was an attorney and he was a great orator. Well, at first the trouble was war. Our people were being destroyed by the enemy. Those who hadn't been killed were homeless and they were starving, *our own flesh and blood*, my uncle said, and we all wept. And we gathered money and sent it to our people in the old country. Then after the war, when I was a bigger boy, we had another Near East Relief drive and my uncle stood on the stage of the Civic Auditorium of my home town and he said, "Thank God this time it is not the enemy, but an earthquake. God has made us suffer.

15

We have worshipped Him through trial and tribulation, through suffering and disease and torture and horror and (my uncle began to weep, began to sob) through the madness of despair, and now he has done this thing, and still we praise Him, still we worship Him. We do not understand the ways of God." And after the drive I went to my uncle and I said, "Did you mean what you said about God?" And he said, "That was oratory. We've got to raise money. What God? It is nonsense." "And when you cried?" I asked, and my uncle said, "That was real. I could not help it. I had to cry. Why, for God's sake, why must we go through all this God damn hell? What have we done to deserve all this torture? Man won't let us alone. God won't let us alone. Have we done something? Aren't we supposed to be pious people? What is our sin? I am disgusted with God. I am sick of man. The only reason I am willing to get up and talk is that I don't dare keep my mouth shut. I can't bear the thought of more of our people dying. Jesus Christ, have we done something?"

I asked Theodore Badal if he was an Armenian.

He said, "I am an Assyrian."

Well, it was something. They, the Assyrians, came from our part of the world, they had noses like our noses, eyes like our eyes, hearts like our hearts. They had a different language. When they spoke we couldn't understand them, but they were a lot like us. It wasn't quite as pleasing as it would have been if Badal had been an Armenian, but it was something.

"I am an Armenian," I said. "I used to know some Assyrian boys in my home town, Joseph Sargis, Nito Ella, Tony Saleh. Do you know any of them?"

"Joseph Sargis, I know him," said Badal. "The others I do not know. We lived in New York until five years ago, then we came out west to Turlock. Then we moved up to San Francisco."

"Nito Elia," I said, "is a Captain in the Salvation Army." (I don't want anyone to imagine that I am making anything up, or that I am trying to be funny.) "Tony Saleh," I said, "was killed eight years ago. He was riding a horse and he was thrown and the horse began to run. Tony couldn't get himself free, he was caught by a leg, and the horse ran around and around for a half hour and then stopped, and when they went up to Tony he was dead. He was fourteen at the time. I used to go to school with him. Tony was a very clever boy, very good at arithmetic."

We began to talk about the Assyrian language and the Armenian language, about the old world, conditions over there, and so on. I was getting a fifteen-cent haircut and I was doing my best to learn something

16

at the same time, to acquire some new truth, some new appreciation of the wonder of life, the dignity of man. (Man has great dignity, do not imagine that he has not.)

Badal said, "I cannot read Assyrian. I was born in the old country, but I want to get over it."

He sounded tired, not physically but spiritually.

"Why?" I said. "Why do you want to get over it?"

"Well," he laughed, "simply because everything is washed up over there." I am repeating his words precisely, putting in nothing of my own. "We were a great people once," he went on. "But that was yesterday, the day before yesterday. Now we are a topic in ancient history. We had a great civilization. They're still admiring it. Now I am in America learning how to cut hair. We're washed up as a race, we're through, it's all over, why should I learn to read the language? We have no writers, we have no news—well, there is a little news: once in a while the English encourage the Arabs to massacre us, that is all. It's an old story, we know all about it. The news comes over to us through the Associated Press, anyway."

These remarks were very painful to me, an Armenian. I had always felt badly about my own people being destroyed. I had never heard an Assyrian speaking in English about such things. I felt great love for this young fellow. Don't get me wrong. There is a tendency these days to think in terms of pansies whenever a man says that he has affection for man. I think now that I have affection for all people, even for the enemies of Armenia, whom I have so tactfully not named. Everyone knows who they are. I have nothing against any of them because I think of them as one man living one life at a time, and I know, I am positive, that one man at a time is incapable of the monstrosities performed by mobs. My objection is to mobs only.

"Well," I said, "it is much the same with us. We, too, are old. We still have our church. We still have a few writers, Aharonian, Isahakian, a few others, but it is much the same."

"Yes," said the barber, "I know. We went in for the wrong things. We went in for the simple things, peace and quiet and families. We didn't go in for machinery and conquest and militarism. We didn't go in for diplomacy and deceit and the invention of machine-guns and poison gases. Well, there is no use in being disappointed. We had our day, I suppose."

"We are hopeful," I said. "There is no Armenian living who does not still dream of an independent Armenia."

"Dream?" said Badal. "Well, that is something. Assyrians cannot even dream any more. Why, do you know how many of us are left on earth?"

17

"Two or three million," I suggested.

"Seventy thousand," said Badal. "That is all. Seventy thousand Assyrians in the world, and the Arabs are still killing us. They killed seventy of us in a little uprising last month. There was a small paragraph in the paper. Seventy more of us destroyed. We'll be wiped out before long. My brother is married to an American girl and he has a son. There is no more hope. We are trying to forget Assyria. My father still reads a paper that comes from New York, but he is an old man. He will be dead soon."

Then his voice changed, he ceased speaking as an Assyrian and began to speak as a barber: "Have I taken enough off the top?" he asked.

The rest of the story is pointless. I said *so long* to the young Assyrian and left the shop. I walked across town, four miles, to my room on Carl Street. I thought about the whole business: Assyria and this Assyrian, Theodore Badal, learning to be a barber, the sadness of his voice, the hopelessness of his attitude. This was months ago, in August, but ever since I have been thinking about Assyria, and I have been wanting to say something about Theodore Badal, a son of an ancient race, himself youthful and alert, yet hopeless. Seventy thousand Assyrians, a mere seventy thousand of that great people, and all the others quiet in death and all the greatness crumbled and ignored, and a young man in America learning to be a barber, and a young man lamenting bitterly the course of history.

Why don't I make up plots and write beautiful love stories that can be made into motion pictures? Why don't I let these unimportant and boring matters go hang? Why don't I try to please the American reading public?

Well, I am an Armenian. Michael Arlen is an Armenian, too. He is pleasing the public. I have great admiration for him, and I think he has perfected a very fine style of writing and all that, but I don't want to write about the people he likes to write about. Those people were dead to begin with. You take Iowa and the Japanese boy and Theodore Badal, the Assyrian; well, they may go down physically, like Iowa, to death, or spiritually, like Badal, to death, but they are of the stuff that is eternal in man and it is this stuff that interests me. You don't find them in bright places, making witty remarks about sex and trivial remarks about art. You find them where I found them, and they will be there forever, the race of man, the part of man, of Assyria as much as of England, that cannot be destroyed, the part that massacre does not destroy, the part that earthquake and war and famine and madness and everything else cannot destroy.

This work is in tribute to Iowa, to Japan, to Assyria, to Armenia, to the race of man everywhere, to the dignity of that race, the brotherhood of things alive. I am not expecting Paramount Pictures to film this work. I am thinking of seventy thousand Assyrians, one at a time, alive, a great race. I am thinking of Theodore Badal, himself seventy thousand Assyrians and seventy million Assyrians, himself Assyria, and man, standing in a barber shop, in San Francisco, in 1933, and being, still, himself, the whole race.

Myself upon the Earth

A beginning is always difficult, for it is no simple matter to choose from language the one bright word which shall live forever; and every articulation of the solitary man is but a single word. Every poem, story, novel and essay, just as every dream is a word from that language we have not yet translated, that vast unspoken wisdom of night, that grammarless, lawless vocabulary of eternity. The earth is vast. And with the earth all things are vast, the skyscraper and the blade of grass. The eye will magnify if the mind and soul will allow. And the mind may destroy time, brother of death, and brother, let us remember, of life as well. Vastest of all is the ego, the germ of humanity, from which is born God and the universe, heaven and hell, the earth, the face of man, my face and your face; our eyes. For myself, I say with piety, rejoice.

I am a young man in an old city. It is morning and I am in a small room. I am standing over a bundle of yellow writing paper, the only sort of paper I can afford, the kind that sells at the rate of one hundred and seventy sheets for ten cents. All this paper is bare of language, clean and perfect, and I am a young writer about to begin my work. It is Monday...September 25, 1933...how glorious it is to be alive, to be still living. (I am an old man; I have walked along many streets, through many cities, through many days and many nights. And now I have come home to myself. Over me, on the wall of this small, disordered room, is the photograph of my dead father, and I have come up from the earth with his face and his eyes and I am writing in English what he would have written in our native tongue. And we are the same man, one dead and one alive.) Furiously I am smoking a cigarette, for the moment is one of great importance to me, and therefore of great importance to everyone. I am about to place language, my language, upon a clean sheet of paper, and I am trembling. It is so much of a responsibility to be a user of words. I do not want to say the wrong thing. I do not want to be clever. I am horribly afraid of this. I have never been clever in life, and now that I have come to a labor even more magnificent than living itself I do not want to utter a single false word. For months I have been telling

21

myself, "You must be humble. Above all things, you must be humble." I am determined not to lose my character.

I am a story-teller, and I have but a single story—man. I want to tell this simple story in my own way, forgetting the rules of rhetoric, the tricks of composition. I have something to say and I do not wish to speak like Balzac. I am not an artist; I do not really believe in civilization. I am not at all enthusiastic about progress. When a great bridge is built I do not cheer, and when airplanes cross the Atlantic I do not think, "What a marvelous age this is!" I am not interested in the destiny of nations, and history bores me. What do they mean by history, those who write it and believe in it? How has it happened that man, that humble and lovable creature, has been exploited for the purpose of monstrous documents? How has it happened that his solitude has been destroyed, his godliness herded into a hideous riot of murder and destruction? And I do not believe in commerce. I regard all machinery as junk, the adding-machine, the automobile, the railway engine, the airplane, yes, and the bicycle. And I do not believe in transportation, in going places with the body, and I would like to know where anyone has ever gone. Have you ever left yourself? Is any journey so vast and interesting as the journey of the mind through life? Is the end of any journey so beautiful as death?

I am interested only in man. Life I love, and before death I am humble. I cannot fear death because it is purely physical. Is it not true that today both I and my father are living, and that in my flesh is assembled all the past of man? But I despise violence and I hate bitterly those who perpetrate and practise it. The injury of a living man's small finger I regard as infinitely more disastrous and ghastly than his natural death. And when multitudes of men are hurt to death in wars I am driven to a grief which borders on insanity. I become impotent with rage. My only weapon is language, and while I know it is stronger than machine-guns, I despair because I cannot singlehanded annihilate the notion of destruction which propagandists awaken in men. I myself, however, am a propagandist, and in this very story I am trying to restore man to his natural dignity and gentleness. I want to restore man to himself. I want to send him from the mob to his own body and mind. I want to lift him from the nightmare of history to the calm dream of his own soul, the true chronicle of his kind. I want him to be himself. It is proper only to herd cattle. When the spirit of a single man is taken from him and he is made a member of a mob, the body of God suffers a ghastly pain, and therefore the act is a blasphemy.

I am opposed to mediocrity. If a man is an honest idiot, I can love him, but I cannot love a dishonest genius. All my life I have laughed at rules and mocked traditions, styles and mannerisms. How can a rule be applied to such a wonderful invention as man? Every life is a contradiction, a new truth, a new miracle, and even frauds are interesting. I am not a philosopher and I do not believe in philosophies; the word itself I look upon with suspicion. I believe in the right of man to contradict himself. For instance, did I not say that I look upon machinery as junk, and yet do I not worship the typewriter? Is it not the dearest possession I own?

And now I am coming to the little story I set out to tell. It is about myself and my typewriter, and it is perhaps a trivial story. You can turn to any of the national five-cent magazines and find much more artful stories, stories of love and passion and despair and ecstasy, stories about men called Elmer Fowler, Wilfred Diggens, and women called Florence Farwell, Agatha Hume, and so on.

If you turn to these magazines, you will find any number of perfect stories, full of plot, atmosphere, mood, style, character, and all those other things a good story is supposed to have, just as good mayonnaise is supposed to have so much pure olive oil, so much cream, and so much whipping. (Please do not imagine that I have forgotten myself and that I am trying to be clever. I am not laughing at these stories. I am not laughing at the people who read them. These words of prose and the men and women and children who read them constitute one of the most touching documents of our time, just as the motion pictures of Hollywood and those who spend the greatest portion of their secret lives watching them constitute one of the finest sources of material for the honest novelist. Invariably, let me explain, when I visit the theatre, and it is rarely that I have the price of admission, I am profoundly moved by the flood of emotion which surges from the crowd, and newsreels have always brought hot tears from my eyes. I cannot see floods, tornadoes, fires, wars and the faces of politicians without weeping. Even the tribulations of Mickey Mouse make my heart bleed, for I know that he, artificial as he may be, is actually a symbol of man.) Therefore, do not misunderstand me. I am not a satirist. There is actually nothing to satire, and everything pathetic or fraudulent contains its own mockery. I wish to point out merely that I am a writer, a story-teller. I go on writing as if all the periodicals in the country were clamoring for my work, offering me vast sums of money for anything I might choose to say. I sit in my room smoking one cigarette after another, writing this story of mine, which I know will never be able to meet the stiff competition of my more artful and talented contemporaries. Is it not strange? And why should I, a story-teller, be so attached to my typewriter? What earthly good is it to me? And what satisfaction do I get from writing stories?

Well, that is the story. Still, I do not want anyone to suppose that I am complaining. I do not want you to feel that I am a hero of some sort, or, on the other hand, that I am a sentimentalist. I am actually neither of these things. I have no objection to *The Saturday Evening Post*, and I do not believe the editor of *Scribner's* is a fool because he will not publish my tales. I know precisely what every magazine in the country wants. I know the sort of material *Secret Stories* is seeking, and the sort *The American Mercury* prefers, and the sort preferred by the literary journals like *Hound & Horn*, and all the rest. I read all magazines and I know what sort of stuff will sell. Still, I am seldom published and poor. Is it that I cannot write the sort of stuff for which money is paid? I assure you that it is not. I can write any sort of story you can think of. If Edgar Rice Burroughs were to die this morning, I could go on writing about Tarzan and the Apes. Or if I felt inclined, I could write like John Dos Passos or William Faulkner or James Joyce. (And so could you, for that matter.)

But I have said that I want to preserve my identity. Well, I mean it. If in doing this it is essential for me to remain unpublished, I am satisfied. I do not believe in fame. It is a form of fraudulence, and any famous man will tell you so. Any honest man, at any rate. How can one living man possibly be greater than another? And what difference does it make if one man writes great novels which are printed and another writes great novels which are not? What has the printing of novels to do with their greatness? What has money or the lack of it to do with the character of a man?

But I will confess that you've got to be proud and religious to be the sort of writer that I am. You've got to have an astounding amount of strength. And it takes years and years to become the sort of writer that I am, sometimes centuries. I wouldn't advise any young man with a talent for words to try to write the way I do. I would suggest that he study Theodore Dreiser or Sinclair Lewis. I would suggest even that, rather than attempt my method, he follow in the footsteps of O. Henry or the contributors to *The Woman's Home Companion*. Because, briefly, I am not a writer at all. I have been laughing at the rules of writing ever since I started to write, ten, maybe fifteen, years ago. I am simply a young man. I write because there is nothing more civilized or decent for me to do.

Do you know that I do not believe there is really such a thing as a poem-form, a story-form or a novel-form? I believe there is man only. The rest is trickery. I am trying to carry over into this story of mine the man that I am. And as much of my earth as I am able. I want more than anything else to be honest and fearless in my own way. Do you think I could not, if I chose, omit the remark I made about Dos Passos and Faulkner and Joyce, a remark which is both ridiculous and dangerous? Why, if someone were to say to me, "All right, you say you can write like Faulkner, well, then, let's see you do it." If someone were to say this to me, I would be positively stumped and I would have to admit timidly that I couldn't do the trick. Nevertheless, I make the statement and let it stand. And what is more, no one can prove that I am cracked; I could make the finest alienist in Vienna seem a raving maniac to his own disciples, or if I did not prefer this course, I could act as dull and stupid and sane as a judge of the Supreme Court. Didn't I say that in my flesh is gathered all the past of man? And surely there have been dolts in that past.

I do not know, but there may be a law of some sort against this kind of writing. It may be a misdemeanor. I hope so. It is impossible for me to smash a fly which has tickled my nose, or to step on an ant, or to hurt the feelings of any man, idiot or genius, but I cannot resist the temptation to mock any law which is designed to hamper the spirit of man. It is essential for me to stick pins in pompous balloons. I love to make small explosions with the inflated bags of moralists, cowards, and wise men. Listen and you will hear such a small explosion in this paragraph.

All this rambling may seem pointless and a waste of time, but it is not. There is absolutely no haste—I can walk the hundred yard dash in a full day—and anyone who prefers may toss this story aside and take up something in the *Cosmopolitan*. I am not asking anyone to stand by. I am not promising golden apples to all who are patient. I am sitting in my room, living my life, tapping my typewriter. I am sitting in the presence of my father, who has been gone from the earth so many years. Every two or three minutes I look up into his melancholy face to see how he is taking it all. It is like looking into a mirror, for I see myself. I am almost as old as he was when the photograph was taken and I am wearing the very same moustache he wore at the time. I worship this man. All my life I have worshipped him. When both of us lived on the earth I was much too young to exchange so much as a single word with him, consciously, but ever since I have come to consciousness and articulation we have had many long silent conversations. I say to him, "Ah, you melancholy

Armenian, you; how marvelous your life has been!" And he replies gently, "Be humble, my son. Seek God."

My father was a writer, too. He was an unpublished writer. I have all his great manuscripts, his great poems and stories, written in our native language, which I cannot read. Two or three times each year I bring out all my father's papers and stare for hours at his contribution to the literature of the world. Like myself, I am pleased to say, he was desperately poor; poverty trailed him like a hound, as the expression is. Most of his poems and stories were written on wrapping paper which he folded into small books. Only his journal is in English (which he spoke and wrote perfectly), and it is full of lamentations. In New York, according to this journal, my father had only two moods: *sad* and *very sad*. About thirty years ago he was alone in that city, and he was trying to earn enough money to pay for the passage of his wife and three children to the new world. He was a janitor. Why should I withhold this fact? There is nothing shameful about a great man's being a janitor in America. In the old country he was a man of honor, a professor, and he was called Agha, which means approximately lord. Unfortunately, he was also a revolutionist, as all good Armenians are. He wanted the handful of people of his race to be free. He wanted them to enjoy liberty, and so he was placed in jail every now and then. Finally, it got so bad that if he did not leave the old country, he would kill and be killed. He knew English, he had read Shakespeare and Swift in English, and so he came to this country. And they made a janitor of him. After a number of years of hard work his family joined him in New York. In California, according to my father's journal, matters for a while were slightly better for him; he mentioned sunshine and magnificent bunches of grapes. So he tried farming. At first he worked for other farmers, then he made a down payment on a small farm of his own. But he was a rotten farmer. He was a man of books, a professor; he loved good clothes. He loved leisure and comfort, and like myself he hated machinery.

My father's vineyard was about eleven miles east of the nearest town, and all the farmers nearby were in the habit of going to town once or twice a week on bicycles, which were the vogue at that time and a trifle faster than a horse and buggy. One hot afternoon in August a tall individual in very fine clothes was seen moving forward in long leisurely strides over a hot and dusty country road. It was my father. My people told me this story about the man, so that I might understand what a fool he was and not be like him. Someone saw my father. It was a neighbor farmer who was returning from the city on a bicycle. This man was amazed.

"Agha," he said, "where are you going?"

"To town," my father said.

"But, Agha," said the farmer, "you cannot do this thing. It is eleven miles to town and you look…People will laugh at you in such clothes."

"Let them laugh," my father said. "These are my clothes. They fit me."

"Yes, yes, of course they fit you," said the farmer, "but such clothes do not seem right out here, in this dust and heat. Everyone wears overalls out here, Agha."

"Nonsense," said my father. He went on walking.

The farmer followed my father, whom he now regarded as insane.

"At least, at least," he said, "if you insist on wearing those clothes, at least you will not humiliate yourself by *walking* to town. You will at least accept the use of my bicycle."

This farmer was a close friend of my father's family, and he had great respect for my father. He meant well, but my father was dumbfounded. He stared at the man with horror and disgust.

"What?" he shouted. "You ask me to mount one of those crazy contraptions? You ask me to tangle myself in that ungodly piece of junk?" (The Armenian equivalent of junk is a good deal more violent and horrible.) "Man was not made for such absurd inventions," my father said. "Man was not placed on the earth to tangle himself in junk. He was placed here to stand erect and to walk with his feet."

And away he went.

Ah, you can be sure that I worship this man. And now, alone in my room, thinking of these things, tapping out this story, I want to show you that I and my father are the same man.

I shall come soon to the matter of the typewriter, but there is no hurry. I am a story-teller, not an aviator. I am not carrying myself across the Atlantic in the cockpit of an airplane which moves at the rate of two hundred and fifty miles per hour.

It is Monday of this year, 1933, and I am trying to gather as much of eternity into this story as possible. When next this story is read I may be with my father in the earth we both love and I may have sons alive on the surface of this old earth, young fellows whom I shall ask to be humble, as my father has asked me to be humble.

In a moment a century may have elapsed, and I am doing what I can to keep this moment solid and alive.

Musicians have been known to weep at the loss of a musical instrument, or at its injury. To a great violinist his violin is a part of his identity.

27

I am a young man with a dark mind, and a dark way in general, a sullen and serious way. The earth is mine, but not the world. If I am taken away from language, if I am placed in the street, as one more living entity, I become nothing, not even a shadow. I have less honor than the grocer's clerk, less dignity than the doorman at the St. Francis Hotel, less identity than the driver of a taxi-cab.

And for the past six months I have been separated from my writing, and I have been nothing, or I have been walking about unalive, some indistinct shadow in a nightmare of the universe. It is simply that without conscious articulation, without words, without language, I do not exist as myself. I have no meaning, and I might just as well be dead and nameless. It is blasphemous for any living man to live in such a manner. It is an outrage to God. It means that we have got nowhere after all these years.

It is for this reason, now that I have my typewriter again, and have beside me a bundle of clean writing paper, and am sitting in my room, full of tobacco smoke, with my father's photograph watching over me—it is for this reason that I feel as if I have just been resurrected from the dead. I love and worship life, living senses, functioning minds. I love consciousness. I love precision. And life is to be created by every man who has the breath of God within him; and every man is to create his own consciousness, and his own precision, for these things do not exist of themselves. Only confusion and error and ugliness exist of themselves. I have said that I am deeply religious. I am. I believe that I live, and you've got to be religious to believe so miraculous a thing. And I am grateful and I am humble. I do live, so let the years repeat themselves eternally, for I am sitting in my room, stating in words the truth of my being, squeezing the fact from meaninglessness and imprecision. And the living of this moment can never be effaced. It is beyond time.

I despise commerce. I am a young man with no money. There are times when a young man can use a small sum of money to very good advantage, there are times when money to him, because of what it can purchase, is the most important thing of his life. I despise commerce, but I admit that I have some respect for money. It is, after all, pretty important, and it was the lack of it, year after year, that finally killed my father. It wasn't right for a man so poor to wear the sort of clothes he knew he deserved; so my father died. I would like to have enough money to enable me to live simply and to write my life. Years ago, when I labored in behalf of industry and progress and so on, I purchased a small portable typewriter, brand new, for sixty-five dollars. (And what an enormous lot of money that is, if you are poor.) At first this machine was strange to me and I was annoyed by the racket it made when it was in use; late at night this racket was unbearably distressing. It resembled more than anything else silence which has been magnified a thousand times, if such a thing can be. But after a year or two I began to feel a genuine attachment toward the machine, and loved it as a good pianist, who respects music, loves his piano. I never troubled to clean the machine and no matter how persistently I pounded upon it, the machine did not weaken and fall to pieces. I had great respect for it.

And then, in a fit of despondency, I placed this small machine in its case and carried it to the city. I left it in the establishment of a money-lender, and walked through the city with fifteen dollars in my pocket. I was sick of being poor.

I went first to a bootblack and had my shoes polished. When a bootblack is shining my shoes I place him in my place in the chair and I descend and polish his shoes. It is an experience in humility.

Then I went to a theatre. I sat among people to see myself in patterns of Hollywood. I sat and dreamed, looking into the faces of beautiful women. Then I went to a restaurant and sat at a table and ordered all the different kinds of food I ever thought I would like to eat. I ate two dollars' worth of food. The waiter thought I was out of my head, but I told him everything was going along first rate. I tipped the waiter. Then I went out into the city again and began walking along the dark streets, the streets where the women are. I was tired of being poor. I put my typewriter in hock and I began to spend the money. No one, not even the greatest writer, can go on being poor hour after hour, year after year. There is such a thing as saying to hell with art. That's what I said.

After a week I became a little more sober. After a month I got to be very sober and I began to want my typewriter again. I began to want to put words on paper again. To make another beginning. To say something and see if it was the right thing. But I had no money. Day after day I had this longing for my typewriter.

This is the whole story. I don't suppose this is a very artful ending, but it is the ending just the same. The point is this: *day after day I longed for my typewriter.*

This morning I got it back. It is before me now and I am tapping at it, and this is what I have written.

Aspirin Is a Member
of the N.R.A.

Remember above all things the blood, remember that man is flesh, that flesh suffers pain, and that the mind being caught in flesh suffers with it. Remember that the spirit is a form of the flesh, and the soul its shadow. Above all things humor and intelligence, and truth as the only beginning: not what is said or done, not obviousness: the truth of silences, the intelligence of nothing said, nothing done. The piety. Faces. Memory, our memory of the earth, this one and the other, the one which is now this and the one that was once another, what we saw, and the sun. It is our life and we have no other. Remember God, the multitudinous God.

Remember laughter.

There were nights, in New York, when my hair would freeze on my head, and I would awaken from sleeplessness and remember. I would remember stalking through print, the quiet oratory of some forgotten name, a quiet man who put something down on paper: *yea* and *yea* and *yea*. Something wordless but precise, my hair frozen, and the small attic room in the heart of Manhattan, across the street from the Paramount Building, and myself in the room, in the darkness, alone, waiting for morning. I used to leave my bed sometimes and smoke a cigarette in the darkness. The light I disliked, so I used to sit in the darkness, remembering.

One or two faces I saw coming across the Continent: the boy with a bad dose, riding in the bus, going home to his mother, taking a bad dose with him from a South American resort, talking about the girl, just a young kid and very beautiful, and God, what a pain, every moment and nothing to do about it. He was eighteen or nineteen, and he had gone down to South America to sleep with a girl, and now he had got it, where it hurt most, and he was drinking whisky and swallowing aspirin, to keep him going, to deaden the pain. York, Pennsylvania, a good town, and his people living there. Everything, he said, everything will be all right the minute I get home. And the sick girl, going back to Chicago, talking in her sleep. The language of fear, the articulation of death, no grammar, exclamations, one after another, the midnight grief, children emerging from the grown girl, talking.

And the faces of people in the streets, in the large cities and in the small towns, the sameness.

I used to get up in the middle of the night and remember. It was no use trying to sleep, because I was in a place that did not know me, and whenever I tried to sleep the room would declare its strangeness and I would sit up in bed and look into the darkness.

Sometimes the room would hear me laughing softly. I could never cry, because I was doing what I wanted to do, so I couldn't help laughing once in a while, and I would always feel the room listening. Strange fellow, this fellow, I would hear the room say; in this agony, he gets up, with his hair frozen, in the middle of the night, and he laughs.

There was enough pain everywhere, in everyone who lived. If you tried to live a godly life, it didn't make any difference, and in the end you came up with a dull pain in your body and a soul burning with a low fire, eating its substance slowly. I used to think about the pain and in the end all I could do was laugh. If there had been a war, it would have been much easier, more reasonable. The pain would have been explicable. We are fighting for high ideals, we are protecting our homes, we are protecting civilization, and all that. A tangible enemy, a reasonable opposition, and swift pain, so that you couldn't have time enough to think about it much: either it got you all the way, carrying you over into death and calm, or it didn't get you. Also, something tangible to hate, a precise enemy. But without a war it was different. You might try hating God, but in the end you couldn't do it. In the end you laughed softly or you prayed, using pious and blasphemous language.

I used to sit in the dark room, waiting for morning and the fellowship of passengers of the subway. The room had great strength. It belonged. It was part of the place. Fellows like me could come and go, they could die and be born again, but the room was steady and static, always there. I used to feel its indifference toward me, but I could never feel unfriendly toward it. It was part of the scheme, a small attic room in the heart of Manhattan, without an outside window, four dollars a week: me or the next fellow, any of us, it didn't matter. But whenever I laughed, the room would be puzzled, a bit annoyed. It would wonder what there was for me to laugh about, my hair frozen, and my spirit unable to rest.

Sometimes, during the day, shaving, I used to look into the small mirror and see the room in my face, trying to understand me. I would be laughing, looking at the room in the mirror, and it would be annoyed, wondering how I could laugh, what I saw in my life that was amusing.

It was the secrecy that amused me, the fact of my being one of the six million people in the city, living there, waiting to die. I could die in this room, I used to say to myself, and no one would ever understand what had happened, no one would ever say, Do you know that boy from California, the fellow who is studying the subway? Well, he died in a little room on Forty-fourth Street the other night, alone. They found him in the little room, dead. No one would be able to say anything about me if I died, no one knew I was from California and that I was studying the subway, making notes about the people riding in the subway. My presence in Manhattan was not known, so if I came to vanish, my vanishing would not be known. It was a secret, and it amused me. I used to get up in the middle of the night and laugh about it quietly, disturbing the room.

I used to make the room very angry, laughing, and one night it said to me, You are in a hurry but I am not: I shall witness your disintegration, but when you are destroyed I shall be standing here quietly. You will see.

It made me laugh. I knew it was the truth, but it was amusing to me. I couldn't help laughing at the room wanting to see me go down.

But there was an armistice: what happened was this: I moved away. I rented another room. It was a war without a victor. I packed my things and moved to the Mills Hotel.

But it isn't so easy to escape a war. A war has a way of following a man around, and my room in the Mills Hotel was even more malicious than the other. It was smaller and therefore its eloquence was considerably louder. Its walls used to fall in upon me, with the whiteness of madness, but I went on laughing. In the middle of the night I used to hear my neighbors, old and young men. I used to hear them speaking out against life from their sleep. I used to hear much weeping. That year many men were weeping from their sleep. I used to laugh about this. It was such a startling thing that I used to laugh. The worst that can happen to any of us, I used to laugh, is death. It is a small thing. Why are you men weeping?

It was because of remembrance, I suppose. Death is always in a man, but sometimes life is in him so strongly that it makes a sad remembrance and comes out in the form of weeping through sleep.

And it was because of the pain. Everybody was in pain. I was studying the subway and I could see the pain in the faces of everybody. I looked everywhere for one face that was not the mask of a pained life, but I did not find such a face. It was this that made my study of the subway so fascinating. After months of study I reached a decision about all of us in Manhattan. It was this: the subway is death, all of us are riding to death. No catastrophe, no horrible accident: only slow death, emerging from life. It was such a terrific fact that I had to laugh about it.

I lived in many rooms, in many sections of the city, East Side, West Side, downtown, uptown, Harlem, the Bronx, Brooklyn, all over the place. It was the same everywhere, my hair frozen at night, alien walls around me, and the smile of death in my eyes.

But I didn't mind. It was what I had wanted to do. I was a clerk in one of thousands of offices of a great national enterprise, doing my part to make America the most prosperous nation on earth, more millionaires per square inch than all the other nations put together, etc. I was paying cash for my sleeplessness, for the privilege of riding in the subway. I was eating in the Automats, renting vacant rooms all over the place, buying clothes, newspapers, aspirin.

I do not intend to leave aspirin out of this document. It is too important to leave out. It is the hero of this story, all of us six million people in New York, swallowing it, day after day. All of us in pain, needing it. Aspirin is an evasion. But so is life. The way we live it. You take aspirin in order to keep going. It deadens pain. It helps you to sleep. It keeps you aboard the subway. It is a substitute for the sun, for strong blood. It stifles remembrance, silences weeping.

It does not harm the heart. That is what the manufacturers say. They say it is absolutely harmless. Maybe it is. Death does not harm the heart either. Death is just as harmless as aspirin. I expect casket manufacturers to make this announcement in the near future. I expect to see a full page advertisement in *The Saturday Evening Post*, making a slogan on behalf of death. *Do not be deceived…die and see your dreams come true…death does not harm the heart…it is absolutely harmless…doctors everywhere recommend it…*and so on.

You hear a lot of sad talk about all the young men who died in the Great War. Well, what about this war? Is it less real because it destroys with less violence, with a ghastlier shock, with a more sustained pain?

The coming of snow in Manhattan is lovely. All the ugliness is softened by the pious whiteness. But with the snow comes the deadly cold. With the snow death comes a little closer to everyone. If you are pretty rich, it doesn't bother you much: you don't have to get up in the morning in a cold room and rush out to an Automat for a cup of coffee and then dive into the subway. If you are rich, the snow is only beautiful to you. You get up when you please, and there is nothing to do but sit in warm rooms and talk with other rich people. But if you aren't rich, if you are working to make America a nation of prosperous millionaires, then the snow is both beautiful and ghastly. And when the cold of the snow gets into your bones you are apt to forget that it is beautiful; you are apt to notice only that it is ghastly.

A few evenings ago I was listening to the radio, out here in San Francisco. Aspirin days are over for me. I depend on the sun these days. I was listening to a very good program, sponsored by one of America's most prosperous manufacturers of aspirin. You know the name. I do not intend to advertise the company. It does enough advertising of its own. The radio announcer said the cold and sore throat season had come, and of course it had. I could see snow falling over Manhattan, increasing the sales of aspirin all over the city. Then the announcer said, Aspirin is a member of the N.R.A.

It made me laugh to hear that. But it is the truth. Aspirin *is* a member of the N.R.A. It *is* helping everyone to evade fundamentals, it *is* helping to keep people going to work. Aspirin *is* helping to bring back prosperity. It *is* doing its part. It *is* sending millions of half-dead people to their jobs. It *is* doing a great deal to keep the spirit of this nation from disintegrating. It *is* deadening pain everywhere. It *isn't* preventing anything, but it is deadening pain.

What about the N.R.A.? Well, I leave that to you. Maybe the N.R.A. is a member of aspirin. Anyhow, together they make a pretty slick team. They are deadening a lot of pain, but they aren't preventing any pain. Everything is the same everywhere.

All I know is this: that if you keep on taking aspirin long enough it will cease to deaden pain.

And that is when the fun begins. That is when you begin to notice that snow isn't beautiful at all. That is when your hair begins to freeze and you begin to get up in the middle of the night, laughing quietly, waiting for the worst, remembering all the pain and not wanting to evade it any longer, not wanting any longer to be half-dead, wanting full death or full life. That is when you begin to be mad about the way things are going in this country, the way things are with life, with man. That is when, weak as you are, something old and savage and defiant in you comes up bitterly out of your illness and starts to smash things, making a path for you to

35

the sun, destroying cities, wrecking subways, pushing you into the sun, getting you away from evasions, dragging you by your neck to life.

It made me laugh, the way I used to laugh in New York, when I heard that radio announcer say that aspirin was a member of the N.R.A., and it made me remember. It made me want to say what I knew about aspirin.

A Cold Day

*D*ear M————,

I want you to know that it is very cold in San Francisco today, and that I am freezing. It is so cold in my room that every time I start to write a short story the cold stops me and I have to get up and do bending exercises. It means, I think, that something's got to be done about keeping short story writers warm. Sometimes when it is very cold I am able to do very good writing, but at other times I am not. It is the same when the weather is excessively pleasant. I very much dislike letting a day go by without writing a short story and that is why I am writing this letter: to let you know that I am very angry about the weather. Do not think that I am sitting in a nice warm room in sunny California, as they call it, and making up all this stuff about the cold. I am sitting in a very cold room and there is no sun anywhere, and the only thing I can talk about is the cold because it is the only thing going on today. I am freezing and my teeth are chattering. I would like to know what the Democratic party ever did for freezing short story writers. Everybody else gets heat. We've got to depend on the sun and in the winter the sun is undependable. That's the fix I am in: wanting to write and not being able to, because of the cold.

One winter day last year the sun came out and its light came into my room and fell across my table, warming my table and my room and warming me. So I did some brisk bending exercises and then sat down and began to write a short story. But it was a winter day and before I had written the first paragraph of the story the sun had fallen back behind clouds and there I was in my room, sitting in the cold, writing a story. It was such a good story that even though I knew it would never be printed I had to go on writing it, and as a result I was frozen stiff by the time I finished writing it. My face was blue and I could barely move my limbs, they were so cold and stiff. And my room was full of the smoke of a package of Chesterfield cigarettes, but even the smoke was frozen. There were clouds of it in my room, but my room was very cold just the same. Once, while I was writing, I thought of getting a tub and making a fire in it. What I intended to do was to burn a half-dozen of my books and keep warm, so that I could write my story. I found an old tub and I brought it to my room, but when I looked around for books to burn I couldn't find any. All of my books are old and cheap. I have about five hundred of them and I paid a nickel each for most of them, but when I looked around for titles to burn, I couldn't find any. There was a large heavy book in German on anatomy that would have made a swell fire, but when I opened it and read a line of that beautiful language, *sie bestehen aus zwei Hüftgelenkbeugemuskeln des Oberschenkels, von denen der eine breitere*, and so on, I couldn't do it. It was asking too much. I couldn't understand the language, I couldn't understand a word in the whole book, but it was somehow too eloquent to use for a fire. The book had cost me five cents two or three years ago, and it weighed about six pounds, so you see that even as fire wood it had been a bargain and I should have been able to tear out its pages and make a fire.

But I couldn't do it. There were over a thousand pages in the book and I planned to burn one page at a time and see the fire of each page, but when I thought of all that print being effaced by fire and all that accurate language being removed from my library, I couldn't do it, and I still have the book. When I get tired of reading great writers, I go to this book and read language that I cannot understand, *während der Kindheit ist sie von birnförmiger Gestalt und liegt vorzugsweise in der Bauchhöhle*. It is simply blasphemous to think of burning a thousand pages of such language. And of course I haven't so much as mentioned the marvelous illustrations.

Then I began to look around for cheap fiction.

And you know the world is chock full of such stuff. Nine books out of ten are cheap worthless fiction, inorganic stuff. I thought, well, there are at least a half-dozen of those books in my library and I can burn them and be warm and write my story. So I picked out six books and together they weighed about as much as the German anatomy book. The first was *Tom Brown At Oxford: A Sequel to School Days At Rugby,* Two Volumes in One. The first book had 378 pages, and the second 430, and all these pages would have made a small fire that would have lasted a pretty long time, but I had never read the book and it seemed to me that I had no right to burn a book I hadn't even read. It looked as if it ought to be a book of cheap prose, one worthy of being burned, but I couldn't do it. I read, *The belfry-tower rocked and reeled, as that peal rang out, now merry, now scornful, now plaintive, from those narrow belfry windows, into the bosom of the soft southwest wind, which was playing round the old gray tower of Englebourn church.* Now that isn't exactly tremendous prose, but it isn't such very bad prose either. So I put the book back on the shelf.

The next book was *Inez: A Tale of the Alamo*, and it was dedicated to The Texan Patriots. It was by the author of another book called *Beulah*, and yet another called *St. Elmo*. The only thing I knew about this writer or her books was that one day a girl at school had been severely reprimanded for bringing to class a book called *St. Elmo*. It was said to be the sort of book that would corrupt the morals of a young girl. Well, I opened the book and read, *I am dying; and, feeling as I do, that few hours are allotted me, I shall not hesitate to speak freely and candidly. Some might think me deviating from the delicacy of my sex; but, under the circumstances, I feel that I am not. I have loved you long, and to know that my love is returned, is a source of deep and unutterable joy to me.* And so on.

This was such bad writing that it was good, and I decided to read the whole book at my first opportunity. There is much for a young writer to learn from our poorest writers. It is very destructive to burn bad books, almost more destructive than to burn good ones.

The next book was *Ten Nights In A Bar Room, and What I Saw There* by T. S. Arthur. Well, even this book was too good to burn. The other three books were by Hall Caine, Brander Matthews, and Upton Sinclair. I had read only Mr. Sinclair's book, and while I didn't like it a lot as a piece of writing, I couldn't burn it because the print was so fine and the binding so good. Typographically it was one of my best books.

Anyway, I didn't burn a single page of a single book, and I went on freezing and writing. Every now and then I burned a match just to remind myself what a flame looked like, just to keep in touch with the idea of heat and warmth. It would be when I wanted to light another cigarette and instead of blowing out the flame I would let it burn all the way down to my fingers.

It is simply this: that if you have any respect for the mere idea of books, what they stand for in life, if you believe in paper and print, you cannot burn any page of any book. Even if you are freezing. Even if you are trying to do a bit of writing yourself. You can't do it. It is asking too much.

Today it is as cold in my room as the day I wanted to make a fire of books. I am sitting in the cold, smoking cigarettes, and trying to get this coldness onto paper so that when it becomes warm again in San Francisco I won't forget how it was on the cold days.

I have a small phonograph in my room and I play it when I want to exercise in order to keep warm. Well, when it gets to be very cold in my room this phonograph won't work. Something goes wrong inside, the grease freezes and the wheels won't turn, and I can't have music while I am bending and swinging my arms. I've got to do it without music. It is much more pleasant to exercise with jazz, but when it is very cold the phonograph won't work and I am in a hell of a fix. I have been in here since eight o'clock this morning and it is now a quarter to five, and I am in a hell of a mess. I hate to let a day go by without doing something about it, without saying something, and all day I have been in here with my books that I never read, trying to get started and I haven't gotten anywhere. Most of the time I have been walking up and down the room (two steps in any direction brings you to a wall) and bending and kicking and swinging my arms. That's practically all I have been doing. I tried the phonograph a half-dozen times to see if the temperature hadn't gone up a little, but it hadn't, and the phonograph wouldn't play music.

I thought I ought to tell you about this. It's nothing important. It's sort of silly, making so much of a little cold weather, but at the same time the cold is a fact today and it is the big thing right now and I am speaking of it. The thing that amazes and pleases me is that my typewriter hasn't once clogged today. Around Christmas when we had a very cold spell out here it was always clogging, and the more I oiled it the more it clogged. I couldn't do a thing with it. The reason was that I had been using the wrong kind of oil. But all this time that I have been writing about the cold my typewriter has been doing its work excellently, and this amazes and pleases me. To think that in spite of the cold this machine can go right on making the language I use is very fine. It encourages me to stick with it, whatever happens. If the machine will work, I tell myself, then you've got to work with it. That's what it amounts to. If you can't write a decent short story because of the cold, write something else. Write anything. Write a long letter to somebody. Tell them how cold you are. By the time the letter is received the sun will be out again and you will be warm again, but the letter will be there mentioning the cold. If it is so cold that you can't make up a little ordinary Tuesday prose, why, what the hell, say anything that comes along, just so it's the truth. Talk about your toes freezing, about the time you actually wanted to burn books to keep warm but couldn't do it, about the phonograph. Speak of the little unimportant things on a cold day, when your mind is numb and your feet and hands frozen. Mention the things you wanted to write but couldn't. This is what I have been telling myself.

After coffee this morning, I came here to write an important story. I was warm with the coffee and I didn't realize how really cold it was. I brought out paper and started to line up what I was going to say in this important story that will never be written because once I lose a thing I lose it forever, this story that is forever lost because of the cold that got into me and silenced me and made me jump up from my chair and do bending exercises. Well, I can tell you about it. I can give you an idea what it was to have been like. I remember that much about it, but I didn't write it and it is lost. It will give you something of an idea as to how I write.

I will tell you the things I was telling myself this morning while I was getting this story lined up in my mind:

Think of America, I told myself this morning. The whole thing. The cities, all the houses, all the people, the coming and going, the coming of children, the going of them, the coming and going of men and death, and life, the movement, the talk, the sound of machinery, the oratory, think of the pain in America and the fear and the deep inward longing of all things alive in America. Remember the great machines, wheels turning, smoke and fire, the mines and the men working them, the noise, the confusion. Remember the newspapers and the moving picture theatres and everything that is a part of this life. Let this be your purpose: to suggest this great country.

Then turn to the specific. Go out to some single person and dwell with him, within him, lovingly, seeking to understand the miracle of his being, and utter the truth of his existence and reveal the splendor of the mere fact of his being alive, and say it in great prose, simply, show that he is of the time, of the machines and the fire and smoke, the newspapers and the noise. Go with him to his secret and speak of it gently, showing that it is the secret of man. Do not deceive. Do not make up lies for the sake of pleasing anyone. No one need be killed in your story. Simply relate what is the great event of all history, of all time, the humble, artless truth of mere being. There is no greater theme: no one need be violent to help you with your art. There *is* violence. Mention it of course when it is time to mention it. Mention the war. Mention all ugliness, all waste. Do even this lovingly. But emphasize the glorious truth of mere being. It is the major theme. You do not have to create a triumphant climax. The man you write of need not perform some heroic or monstrous deed in order to make your prose great. Let him do what he has always done, day in and day out, continuing to live. Let him walk and talk and think and sleep and dream and awaken and walk again and talk again and move and be alive. It is enough. There is nothing else to write about. You have never seen a short story in life. The events of life have never fallen into the form of the short story or the form of the poem, or into any other form. Your own consciousness is the only form you need. Your own awareness is the only action you need. Speak of this man, recognize his existence. Speak of man.

Well, this is a poor idea of what the story was to have been like. I was warm with coffee when I was telling myself what and how to write, but now I am freezing, and this is the closest I can come to what I had in mind. It was to have been something fine, but now all that I have is this vague remembrance of the story. The least I can do is put into words this remembrance. Tomorrow I will write another story, a different story. I will look at the picture from a different viewpoint. I don't know for sure, but I may feel cocky and I may mock this country and the life that is lived here. It is possible. I can do it. I have done it before, and sometimes when I get mad about political parties and political graft I sit down and mock this great country of ours. I get mean and I make man out to be a rotten, worthless, unclean thing. It isn't man, but I make out as if it is. It's something else, something less tangible, but for mockery it is more convenient to make out that it is man. It's my business to get at the truth, but when you start to mock, you say to hell with the truth. Nobody's telling the truth, why should I? Everybody's telling nice lies, writing nice stories and novels, why should I worry about the truth. There is no truth. Only grammar, punctuation, and all that rot. But I know better. I can get mad at things and start to mock, but I know better. At its best, the whole business is pretty sad, pretty pathetic.

All day I have been in this room freezing, wanting to say something solid and clean about all of us who are alive. But it was so cold I couldn't do it. All I could do was swing my arms and smoke cigarettes and feel rotten.

Early this morning when I was warm with coffee I had this great story in my mind, ready to get into print, but it got away from me.

The most I can say now is that it is very cold in San Francisco today, and I am freezing.

42

Dear Greta Garbo

*D*ear Miss Garbo:

I hope you noticed me in the newsreel of the recent Detroit Riot in which my head was broken. I never worked for Ford but a friend of mine told me about the strike and as I had nothing to do that day I went over with him to the scene of the riot and we were standing around in small groups chewing the rag about this and that and there was a lot of radical talk, but I didn't pay any attention to it.

I didn't think anything was going to happen but when I saw the newsreel automobiles drive up, I figured, well, here's a chance for me to get into the movies like I always wanted to, so I stuck around waiting for my chance. I always knew I had the sort of face that would film well and look good on the screen and I was greatly pleased with my performance, although the little accident kept me in the hospital a week.

Just as soon as I got out, though, I went around to a little theatre in my neighborhood where I found out they were showing the newsreel in which I played a part, and I went into the theatre to see myself on the screen. It sure looked great, and if you noticed the newsreel carefully you couldn't have missed me because I am the young man in the blue-serge suit whose hat fell off when the running began. Remember? I turned around on purpose three or four times to have my face filmed and I guess you saw me smile. I wanted to see how my smile looked in the moving pictures and even if I do say so I think it looked pretty good.

My name is Felix Otria and I come from Italian people. I am a high school graduate and speak the language like a native as well as Italian. I look a little like Rudolph Valentino and Ronald Colman, and I sure would like to hear that Cecil B. De Mille or one of those other big shots noticed me and saw what good material I am for the movies.

The part of the riot that I missed because they knocked me out I saw in the newsreel and I mean to say it must have got to be a regular affair, what with the water hoses and the tear-gas bombs, and the rest of it. But I saw the newsreel eleven times in three days, and I can safely say no other man, civilian or police, stood out from the crowd the way I did, and I wonder if you will take this matter up with the company you work for and see if they won't send for me and give me a trial. I know I'll make good and I'll thank you to my dying day, Miss Garbo. I have a strong voice, and I can play the part of a lover very nicely, so I hope you will do me a little favor. Who knows, maybe some day in the near future I will be playing the hero in a picture with you.

Yours very truly,
Felix Otria.

Three Stories

I. Greenland

Monday or Tuesday morning each week the postman brings me the *Herald Tribune Books*, from New York, and it is about writing of all kinds, and all kinds of writers. Many are being printed, many more are not, and I would like to know of a single city block where there is not at least one writer, and if there is a small village of fifty people somewhere in which a writer does not live I would like to know of this village. I would like to go to such a village and try to find out why one of the fifty people is not trying to tell the story of man on earth. I would like to walk into the village some morning and go quietly down the main street and all around it, looking at the houses and studying the movements of the inhabitants, because fifty people are many people and the moments of their lives are many. I would like to know of such a village, but I am sure there isn't such a place, not even in Greenland, and if you think I am joking, all you have to do is go down to the public library and look up the literature of Greenland, and you will find that the country is full of poets and writers of prose, and very good ones too. It is Greenland, though, and this is what I am coming to. The poetry is Greenland, and the prose is Greenland. Our country, America, is large dimensionally, and we have many writers, mostly unprinted, and my own writing is San Francisco, and it is not all of San Francisco; it is the western part, from Carl Street to the Pacific Ocean. It is Greenland, and not some clever young man, and you can praise God that this is so; not cleverness but the place, not art exactly but inevitability, the only thing, Greenland.

I am of Frisco, the fog, the foghorns, the ocean, the hills, the sand dunes, the melancholy of the place, my beloved city, the place where I have moved across the earth, before daybreak and late at night, the city of my going and coming, and the place where I have my room and my books and my phonograph. Well, I love this city, and its ugliness is lovely to me. And the truth is that I am not at all a writer and it is the truth that I do not want to be a writer. I never try to say anything. I do not have to try. I say only what I cannot help saying, and I never use a dictionary, I never make things up. All the prose in the world is still outside of books and largely outside of language, and all I do is walk around in my city and keep my eyes open.

Each Monday or Tuesday I turn the pages of this paper that is brought to me from New York and I look at the pictures in the paper and now and then I read a few words here and there, the names of new books and the names of writers. I want to know what is being written by the men who are being printed, because when I know what is being printed I can understand what is not being printed, and I think the greatest prose of America is the prose that is secret, and everybody knows that for every book printed there are twenty or thirty or forty that are not printed: America, as it was Greenland, the same.

Myself, I am a very poor writer. It is because I have never read the works of great writers, or because I have never been to college, and it is because the place is more important to me than the person: it is more solid, and it does not talk, and printed writers talk very much, and it is largely nonsense. I would like to know this: Is there anything to talk about, as a writer? I know there is much to be silent about, as a writer. I know there is much to talk about, *not* as a writer, the weather especially, ah, lovely, lovely, the sun so lovely this morning, and so on, but of course in different words, meaning the same. And this is so: today is the fourth day of sunny loveliness, and it is the first day that I have stayed in my room. It has been too good and I have been too happy, and now I must stay in my room in spite of the clear and warm air. I must stay here and try to speak quietly of this city, and not as a writer.

What it amounts to is this: I would like to try to say what all the unprinted writers would be apt to try to say if they were here, if they had lived during these three days of fine weather. And I am certainly not trying to write a story. The story is here of course. It is impossible to omit the story. It is always present, even if you write about the manufacture of clocks or electric washing machines—always present. It is my city, San Francisco, and it is the sun, very bright, the place, and it is the air, very clear, and it is myself, alive, and it is the earth, Greenland, not cleverness, America, not talk. This is the first story, and if you do not like the style you can stop reading, because this is it, the whole thing, the place and the climate of the place, and what we think is less important than what we feel, and when the weather is this way we feel that we are alive, and this feeling is great prose and it is very important, being first the place and then ourselves, and it is everything, Greenland, America, my city, San Francisco, yourself and myself, breathing, knowing that we are alive, drinking water and wine, eating food, walking, seeing one another, and it is all the unnamed and unknown writers everywhere, and they are saying what I am saying: that all of us are alive and that we are breathing, so if the style is unpleasant to you you can read the evening newspaper instead, and to hell with you.

II. Vladimir

Vladimir Horowitz was here a number of days ago, and one evening at the San Francisco Opera House he played the piano, and rich ladies applauded, and it made conversation. They are still talking of Vladimir's hands, and much of the talk is nonsense, and apparently it is impossible to get away from talking nonsense.

Vladimir came to this city and on Tuesday evening, February 27, 1934, he played the piano, and all the fat and thin ladies of wealth applauded him, and he took his money and went away, to Los Angeles, I think, and the ladies are still talking of him, breathlessly, though of course unsexually, art being of the spirit and not of the flesh. Well, it is laughable, and I myself heard several of the ladies talking of Vladimir's hands, and the talk was not of the spirit, not by a long shot; but of course this is not the point, and everybody has heard rich ladies talking. It is pleasant in a way, and it may be just as well that the talk was not of the spirit, and even the rich are basically only alive, breathing. If they go to concerts in order to have something to talk about, something other than the climate, it is because they *are* rich and because it is considered, in the best circles, shameful to talk about the weather. And the ladies must talk about *something*, and they cannot go on talking about Russia forever. But the point is this: myself again. I must explain that nothing I ever say is purely autobiographical, and the fact is that I am always speaking and thinking of the place and of the time of the place, and that I myself am included in the thought because it is inevitable. It is not a question of pride, but a question of accuracy and truth. I do so objectively: myself, of this place, of this time.

The evening Vladimir played the piano for the rich ladies I sat alone in my room, listening to him. The concert began at 8:30 o'clock, and I was in my room an hour earlier. I have seen the outside of the San Francisco

Opera House many times, and I once sneaked in and saw the inside, at night, so I could see the place, sitting in my room. Around eight o'clock I began to see the big automobiles coming up to the Opera House, and I began to see the rich ladies alighting from the automobiles, and every lady was dressed in the most stylish mode. After a while the automobiles began to arrive in great numbers and special police began to blow whistles, getting the situation under hand.

Vladimir walked onto the stage and the ladies began to applaud; he played and bowed and played and bowed and the ladies applauded; then he took his money and went on to Los Angeles, and I sat in my room, smiling about it. What I hope is this: that Vladimir got a lot of money: this is the important thing.

From where I was in the city I could not hear the concert well, and as a matter of fact I could not hear it at all: I could only imagine Vladimir playing. Well, finally, at eleven o'clock at night I decided to listen to a concert of my own, and I walked swiftly to the beach, by the ocean: the beach is the place where hot dogs are sold and where you can ride the chutes and other things, and there is a merry-go-round at the beach: I went to the merry-go-round and listened to its music: this is the second story and it is probably a little more difficult than the first, and the whole point is this: that Vladimir did not play the merry-go-round music and the music of the merry-go-round happened mechanically and it was very bad but very splendid, being the music little children hear when they ride the merry-go-round horses and goats and lions and camels and it was the music of remembrance, so very bad, and so difficult to talk about, and still, it was very splendid and I sat alone listening to the concert and at midnight the music stopped and I applauded loudly and I said *bravo*, the second story, Vladimir and myself and the rich ladies.

III. An Old Woman Breathing

The third story I will not write, because it is not a story that can be written: this morning from my window I saw the old woman who is bent half way to the earth and she was out in the sunlight, walking and breathing, and she was in black as she always is, locomotor ataxia, scientifically, and she was walking through the sunlight and I knew it was a story I could not write, and I said, I will say only this: that the old woman was in the light this morning, she herself, still alive, breathing, the little old woman bent half way to the earth, breathing this place and this time, the place, not cleverness, Greenland and America, the moment of our breathing, our greatest literature, not writing, *being*, not talking. Vladimir himself, not conversation, and his playing, and the machine music of the merry-go-round, and no children there at midnight, only the ghosts of all children, and finally the latest moment, the moment of the walking and breathing of the old old woman in the sunlight, and myself at the window, myself finally, Vladimir and the rich ladies and the Opera House and the ocean and the writers here and there in the sun and the warmth of the sun and clear air and the old woman, myself writing great prose in the only language, the language of being, Greenland and America, the young Russian at the piano, the unturning merry-go-round, and forever the Pacific Ocean, my beloved city, San Francisco.

Love

A little before midnight the thick fog that had been falling over the city became rain, and, walking along Sixth Street, Max stepped out of the rain into a doorway, wiping the rain from his face with a handkerchief. We can get out of the rain here, he said to his friend Pat Ferraro. We can go upstairs and sit down until the rain stops.

O. K., said Pat, but no fooling around.

Max pressed the button, and promptly, a bit too promptly, the door swung open. Business must be rotten, Pat thought. At the top of the stairs they saw a plump, middle-aged colored maid. She was smiling, trying to seem pleased to see them.

Good evening, Pat said to her. How are you, anyway?

Good evening, boys, said the maid. Right up front. Take the front room.

They entered the small front room, closed the door, and sat down. The maid went down the hall to get the girls. The place was very quiet, and they could hear the maid going down the hall. There were three chairs in the room, and a low tea table with a colored tile surface and an ash tray on it. On two of the walls were amateur oils of nudes. The nudes looked unhappy, a bit lopsided. On the lower shelf of the tea table were three copies of a pulp paper magazine called *Love*. The room overlooked the street, but the blinds of the two windows were drawn. Looking out the window, Pat watched the rain falling to the street.

It's coming down pretty heavy now, he said. Good thing we got out of it.

He sat down again. Do you know these girls? he asked.

No, said Max. This is the first time I ever came to this place. All the small hotels along this street are like this. You can stop anywhere along this street when it rains. These hotels don't rent out rooms.

No fooling around, though, said Pat.

Sure, said Max. We'll just talk till the rain stops.

They heard the girls coming up the hall. The girls weren't talking, they weren't laughing, and somehow their coming sounded a bit sad to Pat. He lit a cigarette. I hope they don't make me feel sorry for them, he thought. I hope I don't go away from here worrying about them.

The door opened, and the girls entered, three of them, in the usual sort of clothes. At first it was their bodies that he noticed, but after a while this bored him and he began to look into their faces, watching their eyes and their lips, wanting to know how they felt.

Each of the girls uttered the usual invitation, to which neither Pat nor Max made any reply. Instead, they remained silent, smiling. Then the girls seemed to forget the business they were in, and stopped using trade language.

Raining, isn't it? said the smallest of the girls. She was about nineteen, and she looked about as frightened as anyone Pat had ever seen. He began immediately to want to destroy the fear in her, to give her the sort of support she could never get in such a place, to get himself inside of her, simply by being in her presence, extend his strength to her.

Yes, he replied simply. Come here. I want to talk to you.

He saw her amazement. Defensively, she made another trade remark, and sat on his knees. He did not touch her, but held her hand. It was cold and the nails were long and ugly, tinted red.

What's your name? he said. He knew she would not tell him her name, but he wanted to find out what name she had made up for herself, and he wanted to talk with her.

Martha, she replied. Come on, she said, let's go to a room and have a party.

Martha what? he said. You look Jewish.

Martha Blum, she replied. Come on, honey, let's go make whoopee.

Cut it, he said. How've you been?

All right, I guess.

Max entertained the other two girls. The largest, who was very large, actually fat, sat in his lap, and Max began to touch her. She liked it very much because she imagined that after a while Max would go with her to a room and it would make a good impression on the landlady.

My, said Max, what lovely features you have, and he fondled her breast. You'd make a great mother.

Come on, honey, said the fat girl, let's go get married, let's go be man and wife.

Sure, said the third girl, why don't you two go to a room and enjoy yourselves?

Apparently, Pat thought, business had been terribly bad, and it had gotten the girls down. Maybe they were going to lose their jobs. They looked worried. They sounded *very* worried. It was pathetic the way they were wanting to seem desirable.

My, said Max, what solid thighs you have.

He got up suddenly, lifting the fat girl with him, and went to the window. He became suddenly severe, ignoring the fat girl, and when he sat down again she was afraid to sit in his lap. She looked a bit dazed, a bit bewildered. Her big body, her thick lips, the sensuousness of her, and these fellows sitting around as if she was made of wood or something. Pat could see that she was deeply hurt, and when she began trying again to interest Max, Pat began to feel rotten.

This is wrong, he felt; this is lowdown and rotten, a dirty trick. This will make these girls feel rotten for weeks. They'll never get over this.

He looked across the room at Max. Come on, he said. Let's scram.

Don't talk nonsense, said Max. It's raining outside. It's not every night these girls can be touched by a couple of handsome young fellows like us.

Each of the girls tried to laugh, but their laughter sounded fake and pathetic.

Besides, said Max, if you girls are busy, you can run along. You don't *have* to stay with us. We won't mind sitting here without you.

Now is that nice? said the third girl. She sat in his lap, and Max put his arms around her.

Do you know, he said, you're not at all bad. There's something about you.

Then he made a sour face, as if he was smelling something unclean.

The fat girl stood in a corner, looking miserable. She was amazed. For Christ's sake, she said suddenly, you fellows ain't bulls, are you?

Don't excite yourself, said Max. Take it easy. My name is Max Kamm. I fight in the ring. Maybe you've heard of me. My friend's name is Pat Ferraro. He doesn't do anything. He plays the ponies and he cheats at poker. And it's raining outside. We're here to be out of the rain. Now if you want to run along, run along. If you want to stay and be sociable, stay.

Oh, said the girls.

Are you staying? said Max.

None of the girls got up to go. They seemed a bit relieved, but disappointed.

Fine, said Max. Now what shall we talk about?

He began to laugh and talk with the girls, and Pat lit a cigarette for the small Jewish girl. She inhaled deeply, looking at him sadly, making him feel sorry for her. He could feel himself liking the girl a lot and wanting to mean something to her, not the way it happened in these dumps, but really liking her, the girl herself, not her body and the convenience of performing the act with her, not to lie with her a few minutes and then go away, but to know her, inwardly, to be a part of that in her which seemed so admirable to him. It was foolish, but he was afraid he even loved her, really cared for her because of the deep sadness she could not hide, a girl who had to please anybody who happened to come to the place, old men and monsters. He was a bit amazed at what was going on in him, but he knew that if he had ever really loved a girl, if he had ever really cared for one, this was the girl. He began to speak with her quietly, while Max shouted at the other two girls, laughing with them, slapping their rumps, the rain splashing against the windows, sometimes impulsively with a sudden rush, sometimes softly, like weeping.

How do you really feel? he said.

She exhaled smoke, looking into his serious face, wondering if she could take him seriously, or if he was only kidding, killing time.

Oh, she said, expressing no specific emotion, I feel fine.

No, said Pat. Don't talk like a whore to me. Don't be like one with me. I really want to know. Is it driving you nuts? You look as if you were about ready to jump in the river. Is it really that bad?

She looked into his eyes again, and he could see that she thought he was simply talking, killing time like Max, waiting for the rain to stop.

I want to know, he said.

It's not so bad, she replied.

But you want to get out of it, don't you?

She looked toward the other girls to see if they were listening. Don't talk so loud, she said. If they tell the old woman what I've been saying, I'll lose my job.

Well, lose it, he said. To hell with it.

It isn't so funny, she said, if you can't get another job and you have no place to sleep and nothing to eat.

How long you been here? he asked.

Nine nights now, said the girl.

This girl, he thought. I'll get her out of here. I'll get a job and rent a small apartment and make her eat and sleep decently, and exercise. I won't touch her. I'll just stay with her until she gets on her feet again. I've got enough money for a week, and the first thing in the morning I'll go around to the employment agencies and look for a job. I've got to do this. I'd be a bastard not to try to help this girl.

He went on talking quietly with her, thinking about having her away from this life that was driving her nuts. He could tell now that she would go with him, anywhere. He could tell that she wanted to go with him.

He heard the doorbell ring, and someone coming up the stairs. Then he heard the maid opening and closing the door of a room, talking with a man. The maid came to the room, looking at the girls.

Number Eight, Martha, she said, and the girl got up from his knees, moving automatically.

He was stunned, and he got up with her, wanting to tell the maid to get the hell away from them, and leave them alone. He loved this girl. He didn't want her to be putting herself naked in front of some dirty punk with a stinking body and a putrid mind, and he would knock hell out of any bastard who tried to touch her. He would kill any man who tried to lay his dirty hands on her and drive her nuts, destroying the decency that was in her, that he alone could see in spite of the paint and in spite of the way she tried to talk, trying to be like a whore. He would break the whole God damn hotel to pieces and take this girl away with him, the bastards, making her want to die, scaring hell out of her.

He stood in front of the girl, staring at the maid.

Who wants to see her? he asked.

She's got to go, said the maid. There's a man out there who wants her. He was here last night.

Take me to the bastard, he said quietly. I'll kill him.

Max pushed aside the girl in his lap and grabbed Pat by the shoulders.

What the hell you talking about? he said, laughing. Let the girl go. What the hell's come over you, anyway? I never did see you talk this way before, and I *know* you're not drunk.

I'll kick hell out of anyone who tries to lay hands on her, he said. Nobody's going to touch this girl.

Jesus, said Max. You're nuts. He began to laugh at his friend. This *is* funny, he said. This *is* a gag.

Well, said the maid, if you want to go to a room with Martha first, you can go. I'll ask the other man to wait a little.

I don't want to go to a room with anybody, he said, and I don't want anybody to fool with this girl again.

Don't talk like an idiot, said Max.

I'll go get the landlady, said the maid.

Then he saw the girl, looking at him pathetically, run through the open door and down the hall. The maid left the room, closing the door, and he sat down.

Max was still laughing at him. For a minute, said Max, I thought you were serious.

The girls could think of nothing to say. Pat lit a cigarette. Well, he thought, that was funny, me acting that way over one of these girls. He began to laugh, inhaling and exhaling smoke. He went to the window and saw that the rain had stopped.

Let's scram, he said. Here, he said to the girls, buy yourselves a couple of drinks; and he handed each of the girls a silver dollar. Give them something, he said to Max.

Sure, said Max. Here's something for your girl. He placed a dollar on the table, and they left the room.

Walking down the hall, Pat saw room Number Eight, and he could feel the girl in the room, holding her job. He hurried down the stairs, thinking of the girl, feeling that he had been a coward not to have done what he had wanted to do, not to have busted the joint to pieces and taken the girl away; and at the same time he felt a little amused with himself, wondering how it had happened.

For a minute, Max said, I thought you were serious. I was ready to hit you on the chin and drag you out.

It was nothing, Pat said. These joints always depress me.

But he knew that he was lying, that it *had* been something, that if ever he had loved a girl, if ever he had really wanted to mean something to another person, it was the little Jewish girl, in the room, lying naked beside the man he should have knocked hell out of.

War

Karl the Prussian is five, a splendid Teuton with a military manner of walking over the sidewalk in front of his house, and a natural discipline of speech that is both admirable and refreshing, as if the child understood the essential dignity of mortal articulation and could not bear to misuse the gift, opening his mouth only rarely and then only to utter a phrase of no more than three or four words, wholly to the point and amazingly pertinent. He lives in a house across the street and is the pride of his grandfather, an erect man of fifty with a good German moustache whose picture appeared in a newspaper several years ago in connection with a political campaign. This man began teaching Karl to walk as soon as the boy was able to stand on his legs, and he could be seen with the small blond boy in blue overalls, moving up and down a half block of sidewalk, holding the child's hands and showing him how to step forward precisely and a bit pompously, in the German royalist manner, knees stiff, each step resembling an arrested kick.

Every morning for several months the old man and the little boy practised walking, and it was a very pleasant routine to watch. Karl's progress was rapid but hardly hurried, and he seemed to understand the quiet sternness of his grandfather, and even from across the street it was easy to see that he believed in the importance of being able to walk in a dignified manner, and wished to learn to do it the way his grandfather was teaching him to do it. Fundamentally, the little boy and the old man were the same, the only difference being the inevitable difference of age and experience, and Karl showed no signs of wishing to rebel against the discipline imposed upon him by the old man.

After a while the little boy was walking up and down the stretch of sidewalk in front of his house, unassisted by the old man, who watched him quietly from the steps of his house, smoking a pipe and looking upon the boy with an expression of severity which was at the same time an expression of pride, and the little boy kicked himself forward very nicely. The walk was certainly old-fashioned and certainly a little undemocratic, but everyone in this neighborhood liked Karl and regarded him as a very fine little man. There was something about a small boy walking that way that was satisfying. True Teutons appreciate the importance of such relatively automatic functions as breathing, walking and talking, and they are able to bother about these simple actions in a manner that is both reasonable and dignified. To them, apparently, breathing and walking and talking are related closely to living in general, and the fuss they make about these actions isn't therefore the least ridiculous.

People living in the houses of this block have been breeding well during the past six or seven years, and the street has a fair population of children, all of them healthy and interesting, to me extremely interesting. Karl is only one of the group, and he is mentioned first because he is perhaps the only one who has been taught a conscious racial technique of living. The other children belong to a number of races, and while the basic traits of each race is apparent in each child, these traits have not been emphasized and strengthened as they have been emphasized and strengthened in Karl. In other words, each child is of his race naturally and instinctively, and it is likely that except for the instruction of his grandfather, Karl himself would now be more like the other children, more artless and unrepressed. He would not have the military manner of walking which is the chief difference between him and the other children, and the mannerism which sometimes gets on the nerves of Josef, the Slovenian boy who lives in the flat downstairs.

Josef is almost a year older than Karl, and he is a lively boy whose every action suggests inward laughter. He has the bright and impish face of his father who is by trade a baker, and he is the sort of boy who talks a lot, who is interested in everything and everyone around him, and who is always asking questions. He wants to know the names of people, and his favorite question is *where have you been?* He asks this question in a way that suggests he is hoping you have just returned from some very strange and wonderful place, not like anything he has ever seen, and perhaps not like any place on earth, and I myself have always been embarrassed because I have had to tell him that I have come from a place no more wonderful than town, which he himself has seen at least a half-dozen times.

Karl hardly ever runs, while Josef hardly ever walks, and is almost always running or skipping or leaping, as if *going* from one place to another was a good deal more important to him than leaving one place and reaching another place, as if, I mean, the mere going was what pleased him, rather than any specific object in going. Josef plays, while Karl performs. The Slav is himself first and his race afterwards, while the Teuton is his race first and himself afterwards. I have been studying the children who live in this block for a number of years, and I hope no one will imagine that I am making up things about them in order to be able to write a little story, for I am not making up anything. The little episode of yesterday evening would be trivial and pointless if I had not watched the growth of these boys, and I only regret that I do not know more about Irving, the Jewish boy who cried so bitterly while Karl and Josef struck each other.

Irving came with his mother and father to this block last November, not quite four months ago, but I did not begin to see much of him until a month later when he began to appear in the street. He is a melancholy-looking boy, about Josef's age, and of the sort described generally as introspective, seeming to feel safer within himself. I suppose his parents are having him educated musically, for he has the appearance of someone who ought to develop into a pretty fine violinist or pianist, the large serious head, the slight body, and a delicate nervous system.

One evening, on the way to the grocer's, I saw Irving sitting on the steps of his house, apparently dreaming the unspeakably beautiful dream of a child bewildered by the strangeness of being, and I hoped to speak to him quietly and try to find out, if possible, what was going on in his mind, but when he saw me coming toward him, he got up swiftly and scrambled up the steps and into the house, looking startled and very much afraid. I would give my phonograph to know what Irving had been dreaming that evening, for I believe it would somehow make explicable his weeping last night.

Karl is solid and very sure of his stance, extremely certain of himself because of the fact that discipline prohibits undue speculation regarding circumstances unrelated to himself, while Josef, on the other hand, though no less certain of himself, is a good deal less solid because of the fact that a lively curiosity about all things impels him to keep in motion, and to do things without thinking. The presence of Irving on this street is solid enough, but there is something about his presence that is both amusing and saddening, as if he himself cannot figure it out and as if, for all he knows, he were somewhere else. Irving is not at all certain of himself. He is neither disciplined nor undisciplined, he is simply melancholy. Eventually, I suppose, he will come to have the fullest understanding of himself and his relation to all things, but at the moment he is much too bewildered to have any definite viewpoint on the matter.

Not long ago there were riots in Paris, and shortly afterwards a civil war developed in Austria. It is a well-known fact that Russia is preparing to defend herself against Japan, and everyone is aware of the fidgetiness which has come over all of Europe because of the nationalistic program of the present dictator of Germany.

I mention these facts because they have a bearing on the story I am telling. As Joyce would say, the earth haveth childers everywhere, and the little episode of last night is to me as significant as the larger episodes in Europe must be to the men who have grown up and become no longer children. At least, seemingly.

The day began yesterday with thick fog, followed by a brief shower. By three in the afternoon the sun was shining and the sky was clear except for a number of white clouds, the kind of clouds that indicate good weather, a clear moment, clean air, and so on. The weather changes this way in San Francisco. In the morning the weather is apt to be winter weather, and in the afternoon the winter weather is apt to change suddenly to spring weather, any season of the year. Hardly anyone is aware of seasons out here. We have all seasons all the year round.

When I left my room in the morning, none of the children of this street was outdoors, but when I returned in the evening, I saw Josef and Irving standing together on my side of the street, in front of Irving's house, talking. Karl was across the street, in front of his house, walking in the military manner I have described, looking pompous in an amusing sort of way and seeming to be very proud of himself. Farther down the street were five little girls, playing a hopping game on the sidewalk: Josef's big sister, two Irish girls who were sisters, and two Italian girls who were sisters.

After rain the air clears up and it is very pleasant to be abroad, and these children were playing in the street, in the sunlight. It was a very fine moment to be alive and to have love for all others alive in one's time, and I mention this to show that the occasional ugliness of the human heart is not necessarily the consequence of some similar ugliness in nature. And we know that when the European countryside was loveliest this had no effect on the progress of the last war, and that the rate of killing remained just as high as it had been during the bad weather, and that the only thing that happened as a consequence of the lovely weather was some touching poetry by young soldiers who wanted to create, who wanted wives and homes, and who did not want to be killed.

Walking past Josef and Irving, I heard Josef say, speaking of Karl: Look at him. Look at the way he's walking. Why does he walk that way?

I had known for some time that Josef resented the pompous certainty of Karl's manner of walking, and therefore his remarks did not surprise me. Besides, I have already said that he was naturally curious about all things that came within the range of his consciousness, and that he was always asking questions. It seemed to me that his interest in Karl's way of walking was largely aesthetic, and I didn't seem to detect any malice in his speech. I did not hear Irving make a reply, and I came directly to my room. I had a letter to write and I went to work on it, and when it was finished I stood at the window of my room, studying the street. The small girls had disappeared, but Karl was still across the street, and Josef and Irving were still together. It was beginning to be dusk, and the street was very quiet.

I do not know how it happened, but when Josef and Irving began crossing the street, going to Karl, I saw a whole nation moving the line of its army to the borders of another nation, and the little boys seemed so very innocent and likable, and whole nations seemed so much like the little boys that I could not avoid laughing to myself. Oh, I thought, there will probably be another war before long, and the children will make a great fuss in the world, but it will probably be very much like what is going to happen now. For I was certain that Josef and Karl were going to express their hatred for each other, the hatred that was stupid and wasteful and the result of ignorance and immaturity, by striking one another, as whole nations, through stupid hatred, seek to dominate or destroy one another.

It happened across the street, two small boys striking each other, a third small boy crying about it, whole nations at war on the earth. I did not hear what Josef said to Karl, or what Karl said to Josef, and I am not sure just how the fight started, but I have an idea that it started a long while before the two boys began to strike each other, a year ago perhaps, perhaps a century ago. I saw Josef touch Karl, each of them fine little boys, and I saw Karl shove Josef, and I saw the little Jewish boy watching them, horrified and silent, almost stunned. When the little Teuton and the little Slav began to strike each other in earnest, the little Jew began to weep. It was lovely—not the striking, but the weeping of the little Jew. The whole affair lasted only a moment or two, but the implication was whole, and the most enduring and refreshing part of it is this weeping I heard. Why did he cry? He was not involved. He was only a witness, as I was a witness. Why did he cry?

I wish I knew more about the little Jewish boy. I can only imagine that he cried because the existence of hatred and ugliness in the heart of man is a truth, and this is as far as I can go with the theory.

The Shepherd's Daughter

*I*t is the opinion of my grandmother, God bless her, that all men should labor, and at the table, a moment ago, she said to me: You must learn to do some good work, the making of some item useful to man, something out of clay, or out of wood, or metal, or cloth. It is not proper for a young man to be ignorant of an honorable craft. Is there anything you can make? Can you make a simple table, a chair, a plain dish, a rug, a coffee pot? Is there anything you can do?

And my grandmother looked at me with anger.

I know, she said, you are supposed to be a writer, and I suppose you are. You certainly smoke enough cigarettes to be anything, and the whole house is full of the smoke, but you must learn to make solid things, things that can be used, that can be seen and touched.

There was a king of the Persians, said my grandmother, and he had a son, and this boy fell in love with a shepherd's daughter. He went to his father and he said, My lord, I love a shepherd's daughter, and I would have her for my wife. And the king said, I am king and you are my son and when I die you shall be king, how can it be that you would marry the daughter of a shepherd? And the son said, My lord, I do not know but I know that I love this girl and would have her for my queen.

The king saw that his son's love for the girl was from God, and he said, I will send a message to her. And he called a messenger to him and he said, Go to the shepherd's daughter and say that my son loves her and would have her for his wife. And the messenger went to the girl and he said, The king's son loves you and would have you for his wife. And the girl said, What labor does he do? And the messenger said, Why, he is the son of the king; he does no labor. And the girl said, He must learn to do some labor. And the messenger returned to the king and spoke the words of the shepherd's daughter.

The king said to his son, The shepherd's daughter wishes you to learn some craft. Would you still have her for your wife? And the son said, Yes, I will learn to weave straw rugs. And the boy was taught to weave rugs of straw, in patterns and in colors and with ornamental designs, and at the end of three days he was making very fine straw rugs, and the messenger returned to the shepherd's daughter, and he said, These rugs of straw are the work of the king's son.

And the girl went with the messenger to the king's palace, and she became the wife of the king's son.

One day, said my grandmother, the king's son was walking through the streets of Bagdad, and he came upon an eating place which was so clean and cool that he entered it and sat at a table.

This place, said my grandmother, was a place of thieves and murderers, and they took the king's son and placed him in a large dungeon where many great men of the city were being held, and the thieves and murderers were killing the fattest of the men and feeding them to the leanest of them, and making sport of it. The king's son was of the leanest of the men, and it was not known that he was the son of the king of the Persians, so his life was spared, and he said to the thieves and murderers, I am a weaver of straw rugs and these rugs have great value. And they brought him straw and asked him to weave and in three days he weaved three rugs, and he said, Carry these rugs to the palace of the king of the Persians, and for each rug he will give you a hundred gold pieces of money. And the rugs were carried to the palace of the king, and when the king saw the rugs he saw that they were the work of his son and he took the rugs to the shepherd's daughter and he said, These rugs were brought to the palace and they are the work of my son who is lost. And the shepherd's daughter took each rug and looked at it closely and in the design of each rug she saw in the written language of the Persians a message from her husband, and she related this message to the king.

And the king, said my grandmother, sent many soldiers to the place of the thieves and murderers, and the soldiers rescued all the captives and killed all the thieves and murderers, and the king's son was returned safely to the palace of his father, and to the company of his wife, the little shepherd's daughter. And when the boy went into the palace and saw again his wife, he humbled himself before her and he embraced her feet, and he said, My love, it is because of you that I am alive, and the king was greatly pleased with the shepherd's daughter.

Now, said my grandmother, do you see why every man should learn an honorable craft?

I see very clearly, I said, and as soon as I earn enough money to buy a saw and a hammer and a piece of lumber I shall do my best to make a simple chair or a shelf for books.

from
Inhale and Exhale

Five Ripe Pears

*I*f old man Pollard is still alive I hope he reads this because I want him to know I am not a thief and never have been. Instead of making up a lie, which I could have done, I told the truth, and got a licking. I don't care about the licking because I got a lot of them in grammar school. It was part of my education. Some of them I deserved, and some I didn't. The licking Mr. Pollard gave me I didn't deserve, and I hope he reads this because I am going to tell him why. I couldn't tell him that day because I didn't know how to explain what I knew. I am glad I haven't forgotten, though, because it is pretty important.

It was about spring pears.

The trees grew in a yard protected by a spike fence, but some of the branches grew beyond the fence. I was six, but a logician. A fence, I reasoned, can protect only that which it encloses.

Therefore, I said, the pears growing on the branches beyond the fence are mine—if I can reach them.

And I couldn't. Love of pears, though, encouraged effort. I could see the pears, and I knew I wanted them. I did not want them only for eating, which would have been barbaric. I wanted them mostly for wanting them. I wanted pears, these being closest at the time and most desirable. More, though, I wanted wanting and getting, and I invented means.

It was during school recess, and the trees were two blocks from the school. I was thirsty for the sweet fluids of growing fruit, and for things less tangible. It is not stealing, I said.

It was adventure. Also art. Also religion, this sort of theft being a form of adoration. And it was exploration.

I told the Hebrew boy, Isaacs, I was going to the trees, and he said it was stealing. This meant nothing, or it meant that he was afraid to go with me. I did not bother at the time to investigate what it meant, and went running out of the school grounds, down the street. Peralta, I think it was. In minutes I did not know how long recess endured, but I knew it never endured long. Certainly never long *enough*. Recess should endure forever, was my opinion.

Running to pears as a boy of six is any number of classically beautiful things: music and poetry and maybe war. I reached the trees breathless but alert and smiling. The pears were fat and ready for eating, and for plucking from limbs. They were ready. The sun was warm. The moment was a moment of numerous clarities, air, body, and mind.

Among the leaves I saw the pears, fat and yellow and red, full of it, the stuff of life, from the sun, and I wanted. It was a thing they could not speak about in the second grade because they hadn't found words for it. They spoke only of the easiest things, but pears were basic and not easy to speak of except as pears. If they spoke of pears at all, they would speak of them only as pears, so much a dozen, not as shapes of living substance, miraculously; strange, exciting, and marvelous. They would think of them apart from the trees and apart from the earth and apart from the sun, which was stupid.

They were mine if I could reach them, but I couldn't. It was lovely enough only to see them, but I had been looking at them for weeks. I had seen the trees when they had been bare of leaf. I had seen the coming of leaves, the coming of blossoms. I had seen the blossoms falling away before the pressure of the hard green shapes of unripe pears.

Now the pears were ripe and ready, and I was ready. I had seen and the pears were mine, from God.

But it was not to eat. It was to touch and feel and know: *the pear*. Of life—the sum of it—which could decay. It was to know and to make immortal.

A thief can be both an artist and a philosopher, and probably should be both. I do not know whether I invented the philosophy to justify the theft, or whether I denied the existence of theft in order to invent the philosophy. I know I was deeply sincere about wanting the ripe pears, and I know I was determined to get them, and to remain innocent.

Afterwards, when they made a thief of me, I weakened and almost believed I *was* a thief, but it was not so.

I laughed, standing beneath the pear boughs, but it was not the laughter of one who destroys and wastes. It was the laughter of one who creates and preserves. An artist is one who looks and sees, and all who have vision are not unblind. I saw the pears. I saw them first with my eyes, and little by little I saw them with every part of my body, and with all of my heart. Therefore, they were mine.

Also, because they existed on branches growing beyond the fence.

A tragic misfortune of youth is that it is speechless when it has most to say, and a sadness of maturity is that it is garrulous when it has forgotten where to begin and what language to use. Oh, we have been well educated in error, all right. We at least know that we have forgotten.

I couldn't reach them, so I tried leaping, which was and is splendid. At first I leaped with the idea of reaching a branch and lowering it to myself, but after I had leaped two or three times I began to leap because it was splendid to leap.

It was like pears being more than pears. It was to get a little way off the earth, upward, inwardly and outwardly, and then to return suddenly to it, with a sound; to be flesh and more than flesh; full of it. And I leaped many times.

I was leaping when I heard the school bell ring, and I remember that at first it sickened me because I knew I was late. A moment afterwards, though, I thought nothing of being late, having as justification both the ripe pears and my discovery of leaping.

I knew it was a reasonable bargain. I forget what they were teaching that day in the second grade, but I believe it was hardly more important than my wanting and getting ripe pears, and finding out about leaping upward toward pear boughs.

Wholly speechless, though. I didn't stop to think they would ask me, and I would not have the words to say it. I only knew I knew.

I got five pears by using a dead tree twig. There were many more to have, but I chose only five, those that were most ready. One I ate. Four I took to class, arriving ten minutes late.

A normal man is no less naïve at six than at sixty, but few men are normal. Many are seemingly civilized. Four pears I took to class, showing them as the reason for lateness. I do not remember what I said, if I said anything, but the ripe pears I showed.

This caused an instantaneous misunderstanding, and I knew I was being taken for a thief, which was both embarrassing and annoying. I had nothing to say because I had the pears. They were both the evidence and the justification, and I felt bewildered because the pears to Miss Larkin were only the evidence. I had hoped she would have more sense, being a teacher and one who had lived long.

She was severe and said many things. I understood only that she was angry and inclined toward the opinion that I should be punished. The details are blurred, but I remember sitting in the school office, feeling somewhat a thief, waiting for Mr. Pollard, our principal.

The pears were on his table, now certainly only evidence. They were cheerless and I was frightened.

There was nothing else to do; so I ate a pear. It was sweet, sweeter than the one I had eaten by the tree. The core remained in my hand, lingering there in a foolish way. I could not invent an artful thing to do with the core and began fearfully to think: apple core—who for?—Baltimore. And so on. A core should be for throwing, but there were walls around me and windows.

I ate also the core, having only in my hand a number of seeds. These I pocketed, thinking of growing pear trees of my own.

One pear followed another because I was frightened and disliked feeling a thief. It was an unaesthetic experience because I felt no joy.

Mr. Pollard came at last. His coming was like the coming of doom, and when he coughed I thought the whole world shook. He coughed a number of times, looked at me severely a number of times, and then said: I hear you have been stealing pears. Where are they?

I imagined he wanted to eat a pear, and consequently felt very much ashamed of myself because I had none to give him, but I suppose he took it the other way around and believed I was ashamed because I was a thief who had been caught.

Then I knew I would be punished, because I could see him taking advantage of my shame.

It was not pleasant, either, to hear him say that I had stolen, because I hadn't. I saw the pears before they were pears. I saw the bare tree twigs. I saw the leaves and the blossoms, and I kept seeing the pears until they were ready. I *made* them. The ripe ones belonged to me.

I said: I ate them.

It is a pity I could not tell him I hadn't stolen the pears because I had created them, but I knew how to say only that which others expected me to say.

You *ate* the pears? he said. It seemed to me that he was angry. Nevertheless, I said: Yes, sir.

How many pears? he said.

Four, I said.

You *stole* four pears, he said, and then *ate* them? No, sir, I said. Five. One I ate by the tree.

Everything was tangled up, and I knew I wouldn't be able to get out of it. I couldn't think of a thing to say that was my own, and all I could do was answer questions in a way that would justify his punishing me, which he did.

He gave me a sound licking with a leather strap, and I cried for all I was worth. It didn't hurt so much as my crying made out that it hurt, but I *had* to cry because it seemed very strange to me that no one could even faintly understand why I picked the five pears and carried four of them to class when I could have eaten them instead and made up a lie about helping a stranger find a street, or something like that.

I know Miss Larkin is dead, but if old man Pollard is still alive I hope he reads this because I am writing it for him, saying now that I did *not* steal the pears, I created them, and took four to class because they were beautiful and I wanted others to see them as I saw them. No hard feelings, Mr. Pollard, but I thought I ought to tell you how it really was with me that day.

The Broken Wheel

We had a small house on Santa Clara Avenue, in the foreign district where everyone moved about freely and where conversations were carried on across yards and alleys and streets. This house had been the home of a man who had been in the business of roasting and marketing all kinds of nuts. We found small and large pieces of his machinery in the two barns, and in the cracks of the floors we sometimes found nut-shells and bits of nut-meats. The house had a clean wholesome smell. There were a number of crickets somewhere near the kitchen sink and quite a few house spiders, the kind that are called daddy-long-legs. There was also a cat. The cat was there when we moved into the house, so we took it for granted. It was a big black tom with a proud demeanor, an aristocratic air of superiority and indifference. At first it lived under the house in the dark, but later on when it got cold it moved into the house. We never bothered to give it a name, but referred to it simply as the *Gadou*, which is cat in Armenian.

Our trees were two sycamores at the side of the house, by the alley; an English walnut tree in the back yard that was perhaps twenty years old; a small olive tree; and three lilac trees that were growing close to the front porch. The porch was shaded by a thick honeysuckle plant. There were also geraniums and Bermuda grass and other weeds. After a while we planted two peach trees, a cactus tree, and a castor plant. The peach trees happened accidentally; we hadn't meant to plant them, we had only thrown peach-pits in the back yard and the trees had come up by themselves and we hadn't transplanted them. They were growing much too close to one another but they were either very lucky or very stubborn and after three years the leaves that fell from them in the fall were enough to rake into a pile and burn. They were growing just outside our yard but since we had no fence and no close neighbors except for the family immediately across the alley, we considered the peach trees our trees. It wasn't a question of fruit; we could buy peaches cheaper than they could be grown; it was rather a question of being responsible for the growth of something fine or perhaps a question of blossoms in the spring.

Once a year my sister Naomi would bring some of the pink blossoms into the house and place them in a black vase.

We used to see the blossoms in the black vase and suddenly we used to feel that it was all splendid. It seemed to mean that we were alive and we used to laugh about it. In the winter we laughed a great deal. We would be sullen and sorrowful for weeks at a time and then suddenly all of us would begin to laugh. We would laugh fifteen or twenty minutes and then we would be sullen and sorrowful again. It was all splendid and at the same time we felt that it must be pretty sad because it was in us to feel bewildered and futile.

My brother Krikor was responsible for the cactus tree. He came home one afternoon with a piece of thorny-cactus in his hand. He said to me, Did you know that all of this country was desert once and that cactus was growing everywhere?

Do you mean, I asked, no one was living here?

Yes, said Krikor. No one but the lizards, I guess, and the snakes and the horny-toads and the chicken-hawks and things like that. No people.

I thought of our valley without people and streets and houses and I thought it was very strange, very irregular.

Do you mean, I said, all the way to Selma and all the way to Clovis and away over to Kerman, past Skaggs Bridge?

I mean the whole valley, Krikor replied. I mean all this level land between the Coast Ranges and the Sierra Nevadas. All this country where the vineyards are growing now. It was dry here in those days, so they began to bring in the water in canals and irrigation ditches.

Krikor planted the cactus that afternoon and by the time I was ten it was producing splendid red blossoms and a fruit no one knew how to eat; and it was taller than a tall man.

The castor tree happened accidentally too. An old castor tree was growing in the yard of our neighbors across the alley and one summer some of its seeds got into our yard and the following summer we had a small castor tree of our own. It was a spurious sort of a tree, growing much too rapidly and being much too delicate for a tree. A small boy couldn't climb it and the least little storm that came along would tear some of its branches away. But it had a nice leaf and a clean growing-odor and it made a lot of shade. We hadn't planted it, but as long as it started to grow we were glad about it. Everyone hated castor-oil but we thought the tree itself was innocent enough.

In the summertime it would be very hot and we would have to get up early in the morning to feel a cool breeze. Every summer the city sent out a long tractor to plow into the tar of Santa Clara Avenue and improve the condition of the street. This tractor made a monotonous noise, pounding steadily and hollowly, approaching and going away from our house. In the morning we would begin to hear its far-away *boom-boom-boom* and as it came closer to our house we would hear the noise louder and louder and we used to think that this coming and going was like something in life but we couldn't tell just what. We used to say in Armenian, *Yegav noren*, Here it is again. We had no definite basis for our objection, but we sometimes asked what difference it made if the street was a little uneven. No one uses it, anyway, we said. Casparian, the man who sold watermelons each summer, passed over the street every afternoon with his old horse and his wobbly wagon, crying watermelon in Armenian, but there wasn't much other traffic. Those who wanted to get around in a hurry rode bicycles.

One year my uncle Vahan, then a young man, drove drown from San Francisco in a brand new Apperson roadster and stopped in front of our house.

How do you like it? he asked. There are only eleven Appersons in America and only one red one. His was the red one. We felt splendid and we all laughed and my uncle Vahan smoked cigarettes. He took his sister, my mother, for a ride to Roeding Park. It was her first ride in an automobile and she felt very proud of her brother. We all thought he was splendid. It wasn't only the Apperson, it was also his nervousness and his energy and the way he laughed and talked. When he came back with my mother he took my sisters, Lucy and Naomi, for a ride to town. My brother Krikor sat on the front porch with a book, waiting nervously for his turn to ride. Krikor said the automobile could go fifty miles per hour. Rouben, our neighbor, was sitting on the porch with us and he said his uncle Levon had a Cadillac which was a more expensive car than an Apperson and could go sixty miles an hour.

Yes, I said, but is it red? He admitted sadly that it was black. There is only one red Apperson in America, I said. It was like saying that one's great-grandfather had seen Lincoln or that one's ancestors had come over on the *Mayflower*; only it was more impressive. You knew that a great big piece of red junk on wheels would come around the corner, thundering, and stop before your house, and you felt that it was a big thing. This is the machine age, and *Over in Europe they are using machine-guns in the War*, and, *They are inventing all sorts of things that turn swiftly, saving time.*

My uncle Vahan came home with Lucy and Naomi and went inside for a cup of Turkish coffee. We could hear him telling his sister how splendidly he had been getting along in San Francisco. He had passed his Bar examination and was now an attorney-at-law, but he had made most of his money selling watermelons wholesale. Eventually he hoped to open an office in the Rowell Building right here at home. My mother was very happy about her young brother and we could hear her laughing with him and asking him questions.

Krikor was very ill at ease because his uncle Vahan had not offered to take him for a ride and because he was too proud or too polite to ask for a ride, but I felt, There is a lawyer in our family and he has a red Apperson. We are an enterprising people. I was so happy about this that I couldn't sit still and kept walking on the porch-railing and jumping down.

When my uncle Vahan came out of the house Krikor was standing a few feet from the automobile, admiring it. He was admiring it so humbly, with so much youthful adoration, that my uncle understood what it was that was eating him and said, Come on, you fellows. I'll give you a ride.

Our neighbor Rouben and Krikor got into the car first, and I sat on Krikor's lap. My uncle Vahan started the motor and we went off, making much smoke and a terrific noise. I remember that my mother and Lucy and Naomi stood on the front porch and waved to us. We had an exciting ride through town and felt very elated. When we returned, my mother had cut two cold watermelons and we all sat in the parlors eating watermelon and talking. It was very hot and we were all perspiring but it was a clear moment in our lives.

My uncle Vahan said, We do not know how fortunate we are to be in such a country as this. Opportunities are unlimited here. Every man is free and he can go as far as he is able. He spoke in Armenian because it was easier for him. He had been thirteen when he came to America and now he was twenty-two. He asked Krikor if he had yet decided on a career for himself and Krikor became embarrassed and began to eat watermelon very rapidly. I hope, my uncle Vahan said, you will decide to study law. And my mother replied, Of course. I thought, Krikor wants to be a musician because he told me, but I didn't say anything. In a day or two my uncle Vahan drove away in his red Apperson and we began to remember all the little details of his visit that we hadn't paid much attention to at first.

Everything was solid and permanent at our house and we didn't notice the time that was passing. One afternoon Krikor came home with a small black satchel. He placed the satchel on the table in our dining-room and we all gathered around to see what was in it. We never knew what Krikor was likely to do and we were always prepared for anything. Krikor was very excited and silent. He placed a small key into the key-hole of the satchel and turned it and opened the satchel, and we saw that it contained a cornet. My mother asked in Armenian, What is that, Krikor? and Krikor replied in Armenian that it was called a cornet.

As far back as I could remember we had always had a piano wherever we had lived. There would be times when no one would go near the piano for months and then suddenly all of us would be playing it. My sister Lucy had taken lessons and could play by note. She played serious music like the works of Chopin and Liszt and Mozart. Naomi played by ear and she played the songs that seemed to be without printed music and that seemed to be the songs of the people, *Keep the Home Fires Burning, I Love You, California, There's a Long Long Trail, Smiles, Dardanella, Oh, What a Pal Was Mary*, and songs like that. I couldn't play by note and I couldn't play by ear but I had managed to invent a few melodies from which it seemed I could never escape and to which I seemed always to be returning, a bit sullenly, as it were. In my despair I used to beat the keys of the piano, employing all the variations of tempo and volume I could devise, and I was always being driven away from the piano by one of my sisters. They said I played as if I were half-crazy. I didn't know why I had to try to play the piano but it seemed to me that I had to. We were all living and it seemed to me that something should happen. I believed this fiercely and when it always turned out that everything remained the same and we kept on doing things over and over again I would be frantic and I wouldn't know what to do with myself. And then once again we would all be laughing.

And now we were to have another musical instrument in our house. Krikor's cornet was a blunt and tangled affair, more a piece of plumbing than a musical instrument. He brought home a music stand and a book on how to play the cornet. By Christmas, he said, I'll be playing *Barcarole*. He blew into the horn and his lips became swollen and sore. Somehow he taught himself to play a very mediocre version of *America* and an even worse version of *My Old Kentucky Home*, and he always insisted that I stand up when he tried to play *America*.

He practiced a long time and we began to accept the horn as something permanent around the house, like the cat or the crickets or the English walnut tree; but he never learned to play *Barcarole*. Krikor had a very bad time of it from the beginning and gradually his ardor cooled and he began to be suspicious. He would fidget with his music and make a valiant effort to play only the printed notes and then suddenly he would go off and make all sorts of noises, and we knew that he could be heard as far south as the brewery and as far north as the Court House Park because we had been told. After a while he would be too tired to blow any more and he would sit down and look very miserable. He would say, I don't know what's the matter. I have done everything the book says to do and I have practiced regularly. He would look at the horn bitterly and ask, Do you think it's because this horn is so old or is it just that I haven't any talent for cornet-playing? I wouldn't know what to think but I would understand how he felt because I felt the same way. There was something to be done, something perfect and precise and graceful, but we hadn't found out what it was.

Everyone for blocks around knew that Krikor had a cornet and when he passed people in the street they would whisper to one another, There he goes. The boy who is making all that noise. He has a cornet and he is trying to learn to play. We thought it was those street cats, but cats don't make that noise in the daytime.

Each summer the long tractor came back and filled the days with its dismal hollow pounding, the nuts from the English walnut tree fell to earth and we gathered them into boxes. Imperceptibly the change was always going on and each spring my sister Naomi placed peach blossoms in the black vase.

One day Krikor said, I have decided to give up the cornet. I can't play it. He spoke deliberately and, I thought, bravely. Less than a week later he came home on a bicycle, riding under the cross-bar because he couldn't reach the pedals from the seat. He was almost twelve but he was small for his age. When my mother saw him coming up our street, pumping under the cross-bar, his body all out of shape, she ran down the front porch steps to the sidewalk. What is this you've brought home? she said. Get out of that crazy thing. Do you want to cripple yourself for life?

Krikor took the bicycle to the back yard and began trying to lower the seat. He worked hard and after a while he got the seat down as far as it would go, but even at that the bicycle was too big for him and he had to go on riding it from under the bar. My mother carried the bicycle into the house one evening and locked it in a closet. Your father, she told Krikor, was an erect man and your mother is an erect woman and I am sure I am not going to let you make a cripple of yourself. If you must ride a bicycle you had better get one you can ride from the top.

Krikor had been selling the *Evening Herald* after school almost two years and he had been saving money. My mother encouraged him to save his earnings but she did not object to his spending as much as he felt he ought to spend. On his twelfth birthday he came home with a cake which had cost him seven dollars and fifty cents. When we asked why he had gone to such an unreasonable expense and why he had brought home such a large cake when there were only five of us to eat it, he said, This was the first cake the baker showed me and I hadn't ever bought a birthday cake before. I thought it was about the right size. Is it too big?

Lucy said, Why, we couldn't eat this cake in a month.

We had cake at every meal for a whole week and we never stopped laughing about it.

So Krikor took the big bicycle back to the shop and traded it in for a smaller one. He had very little talent for making bargains and the only reason he had bought the big bicycle in the first place was that Kebo, the bicycle man, had insisted on selling it to him. He came home on a smaller bicycle, sitting on the seat where he belonged and my mother said, That's more like it. You look like something now.

It wasn't long before I was riding the bicycle more than Krikor was, and finally we got into a fight over it. We had had fights before, but this was our biggest fight because we had grown bigger. Krikor chased me around the house and then suddenly I turned and chased him around the other way. We were wrestling and doing everything we could to be properly angry and at the same time not really to hurt one another when my mother separated us and said that we could not have the bicycle at all if we could not keep from fighting over it. I knew, and I think Krikor knew, it wasn't the bicycle. We would have fought over something else. The bicycle just happened to be there. It was because we were brothers and because we loved one another and because we had been together through so many different things. One day when Krikor and I were fighting silently in the back yard old man Andreas, who was passing through the empty lot next to our house, ran up to our front door and cried in Armenian, Ester, Ester, your sons are killing one another.

Somehow we began to use the bicycle together, hiking one another. Sometimes I hiked Krikor but most of the time he hiked me. There were lots of brothers in the town who were doing this. We had made a path across the lot and at the end of the lot there was a steep bank of three or four feet. We used to start from our back yard and after picking up some speed we used to go down this bank.

One Sunday afternoon in November we decided to ride out to the County Fair Grounds. There was no Fair and no baseball game but we wanted to go out there and get on the dirt track with our bicycle. We had done this before and we had enjoyed being in the deserted Fair Grounds because it was different from being out there when all the people were there. It was finer and more private and we had lots more fun being alone. We liked the quiet and the enormity of the place, the strangeness of the empty grandstands. We used to take turns riding the bicycle around the mile track. Krikor had a watch and he would time me and then I would time him and we had a small book in which we kept a written record of our speed.

The castor plant had grown a lot and the peach trees had spread out. Easter and Christmas and Raisin Day had come around, we had thinned the honeysuckle plant to give it new life, we had bought new shoes and new clothes, we had got ill with the flu, but we hadn't noticed and we hadn't remembered. There were a few photographs of us in the family album, but to look at them it didn't seem as if we had changed. We had gone on quietly, sitting through the winter evenings, doing our school lessons, playing the piano, talking with one another, and laughing loudly for no reason. It had all happened and it was all there but we hadn't remembered about it and now we wanted to get on our bicycle and go out to the County Fair Grounds again.

I sat on the cross-bar and Krikor got on the seat and we went across the lot. Now for the big dip, Krikor said. We came to the bank and went down it but while we were going down it something happened. The fork of our bicycle cracked and broke and the front wheel sank on its side. It happened almost too slowly to be real and while it was happening, while the fork was cracking and the wheel was sinking, we seemed to be coming out of an endless dream and we seemed to feel that this trivial occurrence was a vast and a vital thing. It ought to have been amusing and we ought to have laughed about it, but it wasn't at all amusing and we didn't laugh. We walked back to the house without saying a word.

My mother had seen what had happened from the window of Naomi's room and when we went into the house, bewildered and frantically awake, she said, Don't you boys realize you've grown? You're much too big for one bicycle now.

We didn't speak of the matter all afternoon. We sat around the house trying to read, trying to feel that everything was the same and that only the fork of our bicycle had broken but we knew that everything was not the same. It seemed to me that we had forgotten our lives and that now because of this little incident we were remembering all the little details that marked the stages of our growth. I remembered the time Krikor and

I made a canoe of plaster laths and burlap and tar, because we wanted to go down a stream, and walked with it six miles to Thompson Ditch through a burning sun and saw it sink.

I remembered the time I nearly drowned in Kings River and Krikor swam after me shouting frantically in Armenian. The time Lucy lost her job at Woolworth's and cried for a week. The time Naomi was ill with pneumonia and we all prayed she wouldn't die. The time Krikor came home with a small phonograph and two records: *Barcarole* and *O Sole Mio*.

And I remembered with a sickening sensation the day my uncle Vahan came to our house in a soldier's uniform and played *Johnny Get Your Gun* on his violin; my mother's cheerfulness when he sat at our table and her sobbing when he went away in a train. I remembered all the days she sat in the parlor reading the *Asbarez* and telling us about the misery and the pain and the dying in the old country.

And I remembered the day we learned that my uncle Vahan had been killed in France and we all sat at the supper table and couldn't eat and went to bed and couldn't sleep because we were all crying and talking about him.

I remembered that I had run down to the *Herald* office each noon for the extra edition about the War and had run through the streets shouting. I remembered the day it ended and the *Herald* printed a front-page etching of our Lord and the words *Peace on Earth, Good Will Toward Men*. How I came home, hoarse from shouting and sick in my soul because it was all over and my uncle Vahan was out there dead. I remembered the times I had walked alone, seeing things and being alive and thinking of my uncle Vahan, and suddenly burst into tears because life was so bright and clean and fierce.

All afternoon and almost all evening there was no talking in our house. My sister Lucy played the piano for a few minutes and my sister Naomi hummed *Smiles* until she remembered that my mother had asked her never to hum that song because her brother Vahan had sung it. We all felt sullen and bewildered. We were getting ready to go to bed when Krikor said, Wasn't it funny the way the bicycle broke under us?

My mother and my sisters said it was the funniest sight they had ever seen and they began to laugh about it. They laughed softly at first. They would stop laughing for a moment and then remember how funny it had been and then they would start laughing again, only louder. Krikor began to laugh with them and it almost seemed as if everything in our world was all right and that we had nothing to feel sad about. I couldn't decide what to do and I didn't think the incident had been funny at all, but after a while I began to laugh, too. All those things had happened and yet we were still living together in our house and we still had our trees and in the summer the city would send out the long tractor again and we would hear it and old Casparian would pass before our house in his wagon, crying watermelon in Armenian. I didn't feel at all happy but I laughed until tears came from my eyes.

Then suddenly something strange happened; it happened inside of me, and at the same time it seemed to be happening all over the world, in the cities, on the surface of the earth everywhere, wherever there were men. I felt that at last I was a part of life, that at last I knew how all things ended. A strange, desolating sadness swept through the earth and for the first time in my life I was feeling it definitely, personally. It seemed as if I had just been born, that I had at that moment become aware of the earth, of man on it, of life, of the beauty and the pain, the joy and the fear and the ugliness. It was all very clear to me and I knew why I had always sat at the piano pounding the keys, why I had fought with my brother Krikor, and why we had laughed together. And because I had been laughing, and because tears had come from my eyes, I sat on my bed and began to cry.

Without saying a word, Krikor began to cry, and after him my sisters began to cry.

My mother said in Armenian, It is no use to cry. We have always had our disappointments and hardships and we have always come out of them and always shall.

When we were all supposed to be asleep, I got up from my bed and went to the door that opened on our parlor and opened it an inch or two. I saw that my mother had taken her brother's photograph from the piano. She had placed it before her on the table and I could hear her weeping softly, and I could see her swaying her head from side to side the way people from the old country do.

Antranik of Armenia

I didn't learn to speak Armenian until my grandmother came to our house
and every morning sang about Antranik the soldier until I knew he was
an Armenian, a mountain peasant on a black horse who with only a handful
of men was fighting the enemy. That was in 1915, the year of physical pain
and spiritual disintegration for the people of my country, and the people of
the world, but I was seven and I didn't know. From my own meaningless
grief I could imagine something was wrong in the world, but I didn't know
what. My grandmother sang in a way that made me begin to find out, singing mournfully and with great anger, in a strong voice, while she worked
in the house. I picked up the language in no time because it was in me in
the first place and all I needed to do was fit the words to the remembrance.
I was an Armenian. God damn the bastards who were making the trouble.
(That is the way it is when you are an Armenian, and it is wrong. There are
no bastards. The bitter feeling of the Armenian is also the bitter feeling of
the Turk. It is all absurd, but I did not know. I did not know the Turk is a
simple, amiable, helpless man who does what he is forced to do. I did not
know that hating him was the same as hating the Armenian since they were
the same. My grandmother didn't know either, and still does not know. I
know now, but I don't know what good it is going to do me because there is
still idiocy in the world and by idiocy I mean everything lousy, like ignorance
and, what is still worse, wilful blindness. Everybody in the world knows there
is no such thing as nationality, but look at them. Look at Germany, Italy,
France, England. Look at Russia even. Look at Poland. Just look at all the
crazy maniacs. I can't figure out why they won't open their eyes and see that
it is all idiocy. I can't figure out why they won't learn to use their strength
for life instead of death, but it looks as if they won't. My grandmother is
too old to learn, but how about all the people in the world who were born
less than thirty years ago? How about all those people? Are they too young
to learn? Or is it proper to work only for death?)

In 1915 General Antranik was part of the cause of the trouble in the
world, but it wasn't his fault. There was no other way out for him and

he was doing only what he had to do. The Turks were killing Armenians and General Antranik and his soldiers were killing Turks. He was killing fine, simple, amiable Turks, but he wasn't destroying any real criminal because every real criminal was far from the scene of fighting. An eye for an eye, but always the wrong eye. And my grandmother prayed for the triumph and safety of General Antranik, although she knew Turks were good people. She herself said they were.

General Antranik had the same job in Armenia and Turkey that Lawrence of Arabia had in Arabia: to harass the Turkish Army and keep it from being a menace to the armies of Italy and France and England. General Antranik was a simple Armenian peasant who believed the governments of England and France and Italy when these governments told him his people would be given their freedom for making trouble for the Turkish Army. He was not an adventurous and restless English writer who was trying to come to terms with himself as to what was valid in the world for him, and unlike Lawrence of Arabia General Antranik did not know that what he was doing was stupid and futile because after the trouble the governments of England and France and Italy would betray him. He did not know a strong government needs and seeks the friendship of another strong government, and after the war there was nothing in the world for him or the people of Armenia. The strong governments talked about doing something for Armenia, but they never did anything. And the war was over and General Antranik was only a soldier, not a soldier and a diplomat and a writer. He was only an Armenian. He didn't fight the Turkish Army because it would give him something to write about. He didn't write two words about the whole war. He fought the Turkish Army because he was an Armenian. When the war ended and the fine diplomatic negotiating began General Antranik was lost. The Turkish government looked upon him as a criminal and offered a large sum of money for his capture, dead or alive. General Antranik escaped to Bulgaria, but Turkish patriots followed him to Bulgaria, so he came to America.

General Antranik came to my home town. It looked as if all the Armenians in California were at the Southern Pacific depot the day he arrived. I climbed a telephone pole and saw him when he got off the train. He was a man of about fifty in a neat American suit of clothes. He was a little under six feet tall, very solid and very strong. He had an old-style Armenian moustache that was white. The expression of his face was both ferocious and kindly. The people swallowed him up and a committee got him into a great big Cadillac and drove away with him.

I got down from the telephone pole and ran all the way to my uncle's office. That was in 1919 or 1920, and I was eleven or twelve. Maybe it was a year or two later, it doesn't make any difference. Anyway, I was working in my uncle's office as office boy. All I used to do was go out and get him a cold watermelon once in a while which he used to cut in the office, right on his desk. He used to eat the big half and I used to eat the little half. If a client came to see him while he was eating watermelon, I would tell the client my uncle was very busy and ask him to wait in the reception room or come back in an hour. Those were the days for me and my uncle. He was a lawyer with a good practice and I was his nephew, his sister's son, as well as a reader of books. We used to talk in Armenian and English and spit the seeds into the cuspidor.

My uncle was sitting at his desk, all excited, smoking a cigarette.

Did you see Antranik? he said in Armenian.

In Armenian we never called him General Antranik, only in English. I saw him, I said.

My uncle was very excited. Here, he said. Here's a quarter. Go and get a big cold watermelon.

When I came back with the watermelon there were four men in the office, the editor of the *Asbarez*, another lawyer, and two clients, farmers. They were all smoking cigarettes and talking about Antranik. My uncle gave me a dollar and told me to go and get as many more watermelons as I could carry. I came back with a big watermelon under each arm and my uncle cut each melon in half and each of us had half a melon to eat. There were only two big spoons and one butter knife, so the two farmers ate with their fingers, and so did I.

My uncle represented one of the farmers, and the other lawyer represented the other. My uncle's client said he had loaned two hundred dollars to the other farmer three years ago but had neglected to get a note, and the other farmer said he had never borrowed a penny from anybody. That was the argument, but nobody was bothering about it now. We were all eating watermelon and being happy about Antranik. At last the other attorney said, About this little matter?

My uncle squirted some watermelon seeds from his mouth into the cuspidor and turned to the other lawyer's client.

Did Hovsep lend you two hundred dollars three years ago? he said.

Yes, that is true, said the other farmer.

He dug out a big chunk of the heart of the watermelon with his fingers and pushed it into his mouth.

But yesterday, said the other lawyer, you told me he didn't lend you a penny.

That was yesterday, said the farmer. Today I saw Antranik. I have no money now, but I will pay him just as soon as I sell my crop.

Brother, said the farmer named Hovsep to the other farmer, that's all I wanted to know. I loaned you two hundred dollars because you needed the money, and I wanted you to pay me so people wouldn't laugh at me for being a fool. Now it is different. I don't want you to pay me. It is a gift to you. I don't need the money.

No, brother, said the other farmer, a debt is a debt. I insist upon paying.

My uncle swallowed watermelon, listening to the two farmers.

I don't want the money, said the farmer named Hovsep.

I borrowed two hundred dollars from you, didn't I? said the other farmer.

Yes.

Then I must pay you back.

No, brother, I will not accept the money.

But you must.

No.

The other farmer turned to his lawyer bitterly. Can we take the case to court and make him take the money? he said.

The other lawyer looked at my uncle whose mouth was full of watermelon. He looked at my uncle in a way that was altogether comical and Armenian, meaning, Well, what the hell do you call this? and my uncle almost choked with laughter and watermelon and seeds.

Then all of us busted out laughing, even the two farmers.

Countrymen, said my uncle. Go home. Forget this unimportant matter. This is a great day for us. Our hero Antranik has come to us from Hairenik, our native land. Go home and be happy.

The two farmers went away, talking together about the great event.

Every Armenian in California was happy about the arrival of Antranik from the old country.

One day six or seven months later Antranik came to my uncle's office when I was there. I knew he had visited my uncle many times while I was away from the office, in school, but this was the first time I had seen him so closely, he himself, the man, our great national hero General Antranik, in the very room where I sat with my uncle. I felt very angry and sad because I could see how bewildered and bitter and disappointed he was.

Where was the glorious new Armenia he had dreamed of winning for his people? Where was the magnificent resurrection of the ancient race?

He came into the office quietly, almost shyly, as only a great man can be quiet and shy, and my uncle jumped up from his desk, loving him more than he loved any other man in the world, and through him loving the lost nation, the multitude dead, and the multitude living in every alien corner of the world. And I with my uncle, jumping up and loving him the same way, but him only, Antranik, the great man fallen to nothing, the soldier helpless in a world now full of cheap and false peace, he himself betrayed and his people betrayed, and Armenia only a memory.

He talked quietly for about an hour and then went away, and when I looked at my uncle I saw that tears were in his eyes and his mouth was twisting with agony like the mouth of a small boy who is in great pain but will not let himself cry.

That was what came of our little part in the bad business of 1915, and it will be the same with other nations, great and small, for many years to come because that way is the bad way, the wasteful way, and even if your nation is strong enough to win the war, death of one sort or another is the only ultimate consequence, death, not life, is the only end, and it is always people, not nations, because it is all one nation, the living, so why won't they change the way? Why do they want to go on fooling themselves? They know there are a lot of finer ways to be strong than to be strong in numbers, in war, so why don't they cut it out? What do they want to do to all the fine, amiable, simple people of every nation in the world? The Turk is the brother of the Armenian and they know it. The German and the Frenchman, the Russian and the Pole, the Japanese and the Chinese. They are all brothers. They are all small tragic entities of mortality. Why do they want them to kill one another? What good does it do anybody?

I like the swell exhilaration that comes from having one's body and mind in opposition to some strong force, but why should that force be one's own brothers instead of something less subject to the agonies of mortality? Why can't the God damn war be a nobler kind of war? Is every noble problem of man solved? Is there nothing more to do but kill? Everybody knows there are other things to do, so why won't they cut out the monkey business?

The governments of strong nations betrayed Antranik and Armenia after the war, but the soldiers of Armenia refused to betray themselves. It was no joke with them. It would be better to be dead, they said, than to be betrayed by their own intelligence into new submission. To fight was to be impractical, but not to fight was to be racially nullified. They knew it would be suicide because they had no friend in the world. The governments of strong nations were busy with complex diplomatic problems of their own. Their war was ended and the time had come for conversation. For the soldiers of Armenia the time had come for death or great good fortune, and the Armenian is too wise to believe in great good fortune.

These were the Nationalists, the *Tashnaks*, and they fought for Armenia, for the nation Armenia, because it was the only way they knew how to fight for life and dignity and race. The world had no other way. It was with guns only. The diplomats had no time for Armenia. It was the bad way, the God damn lousy way, but these men were great men and they did what they had to do, and any Armenian who despises these men is either ignorant or a traitor to his race. These men were dead wrong. I know they were dead wrong, but it was the only way. Well, they won the war. (No war is ever won: that is a technical term, used solely to save space and time.) Somehow or other the whole race was not annihilated. The people of Armenia were cold and hungry and ill, but these soldiers won their war and Armenia was a nation with a government, a political party, the *Tashnaks*. (That is so sad, that is so pathetic when you think of the thousands who were killed, but I honor the soldiers, those who died and those who still live. These I honor and love, and all who compromised I only love.) It was a ghastly mistake, but it was a noble mistake, and Armenia was Armenia. It was a very small nation of course, a very unimportant nation, surrounded on all sides by enemies, but for two years Armenia was Armenia, and the capital was Erivan. For the first time in thousands of years Armenia was Armenia.

I know how silly it is to be proud, but I cannot help it, I am proud.

The war was with the Turks of course. The other enemies were less active than the Turks, but watchful. When the time came one of these, in the name of love, not hate, accomplished in no time at all what the Turks, who were more honest, whose hatred was unconcealed, could not accomplish in hundreds of years. These were the Russians. The new ones. They were actually the old ones, but they had a new theory and they said their idea was brotherhood on earth. They made a brother of Armenia at the point of a gun, but even so, if brotherhood was really their idea, that's all right. They killed all the leaders of the Armenian soldiers, but nobody will hold that against them either. Very few of the Armenians of Armenia wanted to be brothers to the new Russians, but each of them was hungry and weary of the war and consequently the revolt against the new enemy was brief and tragic. It ended in no time at all. It looked like the world simply wouldn't let the Armenians have their own country, even after thousands of years, even after more than half of the Armenians of Asia Minor had been killed. They just didn't want the Armenians to have their nation. So it turned out that the leaders of the Armenian soldiers were criminals, so they were shot. That's all. The Russian brothers just shot them. Then they told the Armenians not to be afraid, the Turks wouldn't bother them any more. The brotherly Russian soldiers marched through the streets of the cities of Armenia and told everybody not to be afraid. Every soldier had a gun. There was a feeling of great brotherliness in Armenia.

Away out in California I sat in my uncle's office. To hell with it, I said. It's all over. We can begin to forget Armenia now. Antranik is dead. The nation is lost. The strong nations of the world are jumping with new problems. To hell with the whole God damn mess, I said. I'm no Armenian. I'm an American.

Well, the truth is I am both and neither. I love Armenia and I love America and I belong to both, but I am only this: an inhabitant of the earth, and so are you, whoever you are.

I tried to forget Armenia but I couldn't do it. My birthplace was California, but I couldn't forget Armenia, so what is one's country? Is it land of the earth, in a specific place? Rivers there? Lakes? The sky there? The way the moon comes up there? And the sun? Is one's country the trees, the vineyards, the grass, the birds, the rocks, the hills and mountains and valleys? Is it the temperature of the place in spring and summer and winter? Is it the animal rhythm of the living there? The huts and houses, the streets of cities, the tables and chairs, and the drinking of tea and talking? Is it the peach ripening in summer heat on the bough? Is it the dead in the earth there? The unborn of love beginning? Is it the sound of the spoken language in all the places of that country under the sky? The printed word of that language? The picture painted there? The song of that throat and heart? That dance? Is one's country their prayers of thanks for air and water and earth and fire and life? Is it their eyes? Their lips smiling? The grief?

Well, I do not know for sure, but I know it is all these things as remembrance in the blood. It is all these things within one's self, because I have been there, I have been to Armenia and I have seen with my own eyes, and I know. I have been to the place. Armenia. There is no nation there, but that is all the better. But I have been to that place, and I know this: that there is no nation in the world, no England and France and Italy, and no nation whatsoever. And I know that each who lives upon the earth is no more than a tragic entity of mortality, let him be king or beggar. I would like to see them awaken to this truth and stop killing one another because I believe there are other and finer ways to be great and brave and exhilarated. I believe there are ways whose ends are life instead of death. What difference does it make what the nation is or what political theory governs it? Does that in any way decrease for its subjects the pain and sorrow of mortality? Or in any way increase the strength and delight?

I went to see. To find out. To breathe that air. To be in that place.

The grapes of the Armenian vineyards were not yet ripe, but there were fresh green leaves, and the vines were exactly like the vines of California, and the faces of the Armenians of Armenia were exactly like the faces of the Armenians of California. The rivers Arax and Kura moved slowly through the fertile earth of Armenia in the same way that the rivers Kings and San Joaquin moved through the valley of my birthplace. And the sun was warm and kindly, no less than the sun of California.

And it was nowhere and everywhere. It was different and exactly the same, word for word, pebble for pebble, leaf for leaf, eye for eye and tooth for tooth. It was neither Armenia nor Russia. It was people alive in that place, and not people only, but all things alive there, animate and inanimate: the vines, the trees, the rocks, the rivers, the streets, the buildings, the whole place, urban and rural, nowhere and everywhere. The earth again. And it was sad. The automobile bounced over the dirt road to the ancient Armenian church at Aitchmiadzin, and the peasants, men and women and children, stood in bare feet on the ancient stone floor, looking up at the cross, bowing their heads, and believing. And the Armenian students of Marx laughed humbly and a little shamefully at the innocent unwisdom and foolish faith of their brothers. And the sadness of Armenia, my country, was so great in me that, sitting in the automobile, returning to Erivan, the only thing I could remember about Armenia was the quiet way General Antranik talked with my uncle many years ago and the tears in my uncle's eyes when he was gone, and the painful way my uncle's lips were twisting.

The International Song
of the Machine Gun

The theme is both musical and mathematical: there is a suggestion of science and a suggestion of religion: Mr. Maxim and our Lord: and the object is mortality: man: and godliness: through violent death.

There is only a moment of violence: this moment is followed by a moment of extraordinary grace: as of the dance: and during this moment of grace the mangled body acquires the deathless form of organic matter and performs movements of timelessness.

The substance of mortality is in motion: there is an abrupt and often screaming halt: the substance is shocked with pain: and the face of man is torn with horror: this comes before the moment of grace: it is the gruesome part: war pictures for the Hearst newspapers.

The idea first: metal: massed: perfected: and extremely precise: deadly with mathematics: having a function: to do: this or that: some special act: in this case to kill: and very swiftly: as a form of contemporary efficiency.

Then mortality: yourself.

If: assuming yourself to be: and swiftly not to be: quick effacement of thought and of faith and of hope for tomorrow: and a quality of absence seldom surpassed: now alive and now unalive: yourself: the face and the form: sudden blood in the earth: still warm: and certain noise: hardly symphonic but deadly with precision: the smashing Internationale: hail Africa: Albania: and Afghanistan.

Africa is a large continent: and the color of the mortality there is a dark color: and the structure is a lithe structure: it is said that the civilizations of this continent are no longer admirable: but this is an impertinent supposition: it is known that man inhabits the continent. The bodies of the blacks are hard yet supple: and the thought of the blacks is a quiet thought: falling suddenly before the precision of the machine the blacks bleed with pain: and they perish.

It is much the same with Albania: and with the nation of Afghans: with Arabs and with Armenians: with Austrians and Australians: very much the same: the functioning of the machine is also the same.

Death is a loveliness: it is a loveliness only when it is earned: and the earning is not simple: and it is slow: involving time and growth and much remembrance: the accumulation of yourself. However: it is best not to be philosophical in a practical age: Therefore: let the machine determine the philosophy of this moment: which is a quiet moment: I myself will tactfully tiptoe to the door and go away: whistling *Ave Maria*: I myself will say nothing. I will ask the machine to do all the talking. Speak clear and simple English: I will suggest.

There are books: there are books on all themes: covering all subjects related and unrelated to man: the theme of living and the theme of becoming unalive, etc. This is from a book devoted to the theme of becoming unalive: not you yourself: it is devoted to the theme of rendering unalive others: not yourself.

Still: there is another book in every other language of man devoted to the theme of rendering you yourself and others unalive: it is part of the idea: part of the precision: you (an American) are involved in the idea of rendering unalive others like yourself belonging to other groups: political and racial: and anything else you please.

You are not supposed to be destroyed by the precision of the machine: the book is in English and you are an American and you are supposed to do the destroying.

It is amusing: however.

Oftentimes you yourself are destroyed: it is not part of the plan but it happens. It is very sad when it is you yourself dancing the moment of timelessness. I do not know whether or not it is a memorable moment, for I have never been killed: and I cannot say. I can imagine that the moment is not unduly gruesome: I can imagine that it has something of a quality of fulfilment. You can decide for yourself.

The object of the precision of the machine is recorded in every language: therefore: all men shall be prepared to employ the machine for purposes of halting the motion of mortality: I am not a moralist: I am not preaching: this work is a small work of art: largely technical: in places flippant.

Note: (from the book: it is a small book: light in weight and having an aspect of innocence)

*The methods of Organization of Machine Gun Units and the
sequence of training set forth in this book are those that have been*

accepted for instructional purposes as a result of the experience of the last three years (1915, 1916, 1917). The book is written out of the experience of the author at the front and in instructing men for active service at the present war.

The author is a soldier: he does not pretend to be anything else: and I am certainly not concerned with his grammar: and I certainly do not mean to ridicule anyone: the machine created this man (necessarily nameless) and the machine created this book: and this is all that interests me.

MACHINE GUN PRACTICE AND TACTICS

Quietly: the words:
Machine: and
Gun: and
Practice: and
Tactics.
Page and print: forms of articulation: practicality: the theme is death.
I shall be obliged to hurry: being in certain circles an artist.

OBJECTS

1. Differentiate between training in Machine Gun and Automatic Rifle (latter is branch of Infantry).

In those days there was little time for ornate prose styles:

A. Thorough knowledge of gun and accessories, including proper sequence of instruction, with special attention to stoppages and remedies thereof.

A stoppage, I suppose, is a machine suddenly ineffectual: and I suppose only the dullest-minded person cannot see the man behind the gun. It is a graceless moment: the gun will not function: another group is in motion rapidly approaching the man behind the gun and somebody is likely to be killed. There are cures, however.
Under this head:

(a) *General description and names of parts.*

It is after all a form of art and a form of science: everything is named and all is orderly.

(b) *Action of Mechanism.*

Art again.

Swiftly to:

(f) *Stoppages: Immediate Action.*
     Causes.
     Remedies.
     Prevention.

It is 1934 and the war from which this book emerged is over.

There is a sort of peace everywhere: it is a rather fidgety sort of peace: Spengler says it is not peace at all: opinions vary: there is also a form of peace during major wars: it happens in the living and it happens in the dying: it is a sickening quiet and ghastly bodily dispersion.

    B. Drill: Necessary so that men will perform duties instinctively when in action.

This is rather splendid: after a fashion.

I shall have to do some emphasizing: first: the word *duties* must be carefully weighed in the mind: second: the phrase *instinctively when in action*.

The implication is precise: man must function with the machine as machine: man himself: performing his labor without thought: without remembrances of religion: without dreams of immortality.

    OBJECT: *To teach quickest and best method of doing things without unnecessary movement.*

Perhaps I am wrong: perhaps the author is something more than a soldier: the language is artful.

    2. Carrying and dragging gun and tripod, creeping, crawling over all sorts of ground, occupation of positions, etc.

I myself can see the performance: there is a war again and I can see a human being creeping, crawling, carrying the gun and tripod to a place from which the precision of the machine will not be wasteful.

    C. Firing on the Range.
    (a) *25 yd. range.*
       Holding.
       Grouping.
       Application.
       Traversing.

Vertical Searching.
Correction of Stoppages.

Emphasize vertical searching: I will swear the man is not only a writer but a poet. But it is hardly the man: it is always the machine: this poetry emerges from the machine: just as the man emerges from it. And the language belongs to the machine.

 E. General Theoretical.
 F. Tactical.
  (a) *Open Warfare.*
 Principles of use of Machine Gun in action: attack and defense.

Principles et cetera.

 Study of Ground.

Poetry again: the saddening studying of ground: of course I am thinking of terms unrelated to the art of warfare: I see a man looking fondly upon the earth: loving it: wanting it: wanting to remain for a long time to come related to it: wanting his feet upon it: I see a man looking sadly upon the earth: he is a soldier at the moment and he is involved in the function of a machine gun but he is not wholly a soldier and he is wholly a man and he desires more than to kill to live: he himself.

The war is beyond him: he is rather helpless: and he is looking fondly upon the earth.

 Study of Ground.

 4. SUPPLEMENTARY TRAINING FOR MACHINE GUNNERS.
  1. Automatic Rifle.
  2. Bombing.
  3. Bayonet Fighting.

No comment: bayonet fighting: your heart bleeding and across from you the face and form of your brother: of another race: speaking another language: seen for the first time: shocked with grief for you: and shocked with love: and your mouth bloody with inarticulation: and you know that it was not he who thrust the blade into your body and you would forgive him: there is a moment of seeing one another: you see your brother and he sees you and it is a moment of godliness: and you want to forgive him for doing this ugly thing but you cannot: you cannot speak the words of your articulation: and you fall on your face: and you are dead: and the remembrance of the shocked face of your brother is with you.

I have never been to a war. What I say about dying may be amusing to soldiers. The only wars I have seen have been the wars filmed in motion pictures. I am simply alive: and I am saying only what I cannot help saying. I am trying to understand how it would be with a decent man who has been stabbed by another decent man. I am not permitting the war to destroy the decency within each man. I am presuming that it is a quality beyond destruction. I may be a long distance from the truth: but this is a work of something in the nature of art. Still: it may be so: it may have been so: I am willing to believe it was so. You can think anything you like: you can have brothers hating one another at the last moment: you can have them cursing: I prefer to have them loving one another: and I prefer to have the dying one praying. It is more artful: and certainly more manly. A trivial thing stimulates cursing: and I do not suppose you can be trivial about having a bayonet thrust through your heart.

But let it go: suit yourself.

CHARACTERISTICS OF THE MACHINE GUN
A thorough knowledge of the characteristics of the machine gun is essential, for upon those characteristics is based the tactical employment of the gun.

You can be taught one thing as well as another.

1. Fixed Platform.

Our Little Brown Brothers
the Filipinos

I don't suppose you ever saw a two-hundred-and-fifty-pound Filipino. They don't come that size very often, but when they do, brother, look out. It's as bad as an earthquake or a hurricane. I guess I was just about the best friend Ramon Internationale had in the world, but do you think I could ever figure out what that crazy baboon was liable to do, especially in a wrestling match? I never could figure out anything. I used to sit in the little office on Columbus Avenue and worry about him all the time. He just wouldn't lose. He was the biggest and toughest and wildest gorilla that ever got out of the jungle into the world. The only difference between him and something goofy in a cage was that he could talk, and boy how he could talk. Perfect English. You know nothing, he used to say; you do not know anything.

Ramon Internationale? I said. Never heard of him.

Never heard of him? he said. Ever hear of Jimmy Londos, Strangler Lewis? Ever hear of Dempsey? Well, this baby was all of those guys in one large package. Not to mention Firpo. Where the hell were you two years ago?

I was right here in Frisco, I said.

Well, so was Internationale, he said. What were you doing, hiding? Didn't you ever read the papers? Don't you remember seeing his picture on the front page of every newspaper the day after he wrestled six policemen, one referee, two timekeepers, three reporters, and me?

No, I said. I don't remember. Who won the match?

Who won the match? Who else? Internationale won the match. The ligaments of my left leg were in a knot three weeks after that trouble. His heart was broken about that. He claimed he didn't know it was me. He said he thought it was some enemy of his people. He figured everybody in Frisco hated his people. Tom, he said, why didn't you stay out of that trouble? Who told you to jump in there when I was angry? I told him I had to do it to keep him from going to jail.

How come? I said.

I was his manager. That's how come. I couldn't let him mangle all them citizens without trying to quiet him down. The crowd thought it was the best wrestling match in the history of the game. That was the only thing that kept him from going to jail. The crowd was tickled to death because he knocked everybody out of the ring and then refused to move. He stood right in the middle of the ring and refused to move. The crowd was tickled to death. It was like some crazy giant challenging the whole world, and that's something that always goes over big with people who go to wrestling matches.

What started the trouble in the first place? I said.

What? he said. You don't mean what. You mean *who*. It wasn't *anything*. It was Internationale. He was supposed to lose a match to Vasili Ivanovitch, the Russian rock crusher, so Vasili wouldn't look like a punk. Vasili looked like a real tough guy, but Internationale could floor him in three minutes any day in the week. I agreed with Vasili's manager that Internationale should throw the match, but I didn't know very much about Internationale at the time. He didn't like the idea of losing to Vasili. He just didn't like the idea of losing at all. He couldn't understand such a thing. I had got five matches for him and he had won each of them easily because they weren't framed. This was his first big match, so of course it was framed. Well, he moped in the office four days in a row before the match. Tom, he said, I don't want to wrestle this Russian if I got to lose to him. I can floor that fellow in three minutes. I knew that. He didn't have to tell me, but the game has rules and if you don't want to starve you've got to play the game according to the rules. Internationale could floor any man in the world in three minutes, but that's no business. There's got to be a contest. The crowd likes it better when a strong man loses. I argued with him four days in a row and even then I didn't know for sure what he would do. I guess he himself didn't know. I guess he wanted to wait until he got into the ring with the Russian rock crusher before making up his mind. He was supposed to let Vasili floor him after eleven minutes the first time, and after seven minutes the second. Well, he let Vasili floor him the first time after fifty-seven minutes. He nearly killed that poor Russian in them fifty-seven minutes. Then he laid down in the middle of the ring, flat on his back, and Vasili sprawled all over him, trying to act tough. That was the first fall. It was two out of three.

Well, when they started the next one Vasili got a little careless with his facial expression, figuring he was going to win anyway, and he got Internationale sore, and Internationale floored the Russian in seven minutes.

I was scared stiff and when I went to Internationale in the dressing room I knew it was all over.

He was smoking a cigar. Tom, he said, you know nothing; you do not know anything.

What's the matter? I said.

That Russian fool thinks he's tough, he said. He thinks he can have fun with me.

No, I said. You're wrong, Ramon. He knows you can floor him in three minutes.

You know nothing, he said. You do not know how it is with me in the ring. It is not like out here, talking. When he starts thinking he is better than I am, I got to show him he's wrong. I got to lay him out.

Don't be like that, Internationale, I said. Lose this match, so we can get a return match at more money.

I don't want more money, he said.

Listen, Internationale, I said. Who was it took you out of the pea fields down in Salinas and brought you up to Frisco and made a great wrestler out of you? It was me, wasn't it? Well, you got to play ball. You got to do me this little favor. You got to lose this match to Vasili Ivanovitch because if you will, you and me both are just about through in this game. No manager in the country will give us another match.

Why? he said. I can floor any of their wrestlers. Why do I have to lay down for them?

Well, I said, that's the way the game is played, and we've got to play the game according to the rules.

So it was time to go back to the ring. The crowd was yelling for more, especially all the little Filipinos, not one of them more than a hundred ten pounds in weight, but every one of them dressed in purple and red and green clothes, every one of them smoking a long panetela cigar. There must have been a thousand of them, but it looked more like a million. Every one of them had bet money on Internationale to win, and me and Vasili's manager and a couple of cops and the referee and the timekeepers and the three newspaper reporters had bet on him to lose.

First Internationale took to throwing Vasili out of the ring, and Vasili kept rubbing his bruises and groaning and looking around at everybody to see why everything was going wrong. Internationale threw him out of the ring three times, and then Diamond Gates the referee figured he'd stop all the nonsense. Vasili was horsing around a little and Internationale fell on his back. He was getting up, holding Vasili by the nose, eyes, ears, and hair with one hand, and both feet with the other, all primed to throw him out of the ring again, when Diamond Gates patted Vasili on the back and called him the winner. Of course that was the only thing to do, but it was a mistake. Internationale threw Vasili out of the ring, and then he threw Diamond Gates out, and then the three reporters, who had been drinking a little, jumped into the ring, and Internationale threw them out, and then the cops jumped in, and the ones he didn't get to throw out, he knocked out, and then I jumped in. Less than ten seconds later I was sitting in Harry White's lap, away back in the tenth row. By the time my head cleared Internationale was standing alone in the center of the ring challenging the world. And the crowd was tickled to death.

Didn't you ever read about that in the papers? he said.

No, I said. I guess I missed that. But what happened? How did it end?

Well, he said, Internationale kept waving at Vasili to come back into the ring like a man and finish the match, but Vasili wouldn't think of it. Then Internationale asked the cops to come back, and the timekeepers, and the reporters, but nobody would come back, and then he made a speech. Boy, that was the craziest speech I ever heard. Everybody in Dreamland was yelling and laughing and whistling, but everybody heard what Internationale said in his little speech. There were two ladies in the crowd and Internationale said, Ladies and gentlemen, you know nothing; you do not know anything. The referee says I am the loser of this match, but you know nothing. I am the winner. I challenge Vasili Ivanovitch, the Russian rock crusher, to return to this ring, and I challenge anybody else in this audience to enter this ring, and I will not leave this ring until the referee declares that I am the winner.

The crowd cheered louder than ever, because Internationale *was* the winner.

From a safe distance Diamond Gates shouted, The winner of this match is Vasili Ivanovitch. The bout is over. Everybody go home.

Well, nobody got up and left the building, not one solitary soul. Then somebody ordered the lights to be turned out. That was a crazy mistake. The little Filipinos thought it was a plot, so in the darkness they started hitting people on the heads with pop bottles, and when the lights went on, everybody in the crowd was slugging somebody else, including the two ladies. And Internationale was still in the center of the ring, alone.

He wouldn't budge. About two hundred police arrived with sawed-off shotguns, tear-gas bombs, clubs, and horses. The horse cops rode right into Dreamland on their horses, because they were afraid to get off. They ordered everybody to get out of the building, and after a half hour or so the building was empty except for two hundred cops, fifty of them on horses, the three reporters, Diamond Gates, Vasili Ivanovitch, his manager Pat Connor, the two timekeepers, and me. The cops pointed shotguns at Internationale and told him to get out of the ring or they would shoot. I was scared stiff. I knew the cops wouldn't really shoot, but I was afraid one of them might get nervous and kill him accidentally. I didn't want anybody to hurt Ramon Internationale because I knew he was right. So I ran up to the ring and begged him to get out. He said he wouldn't leave the ring until he was declared the winner, or at least until Vasili returned and went on with the match. Vasili returned from the shower room dressed in his street clothes, smoking a cigar.

It was the worst affair I ever saw. Little by little the little Filipinos started coming back into the auditorium to see the finish of the fight, and the horse cops would turn their horses around and run them out, and five minutes later they would come back in, anxious to learn the final result of the match. Their countryman Ramon Internationale was still in the center of the ring and still alive, and they wanted to know how the match was going to turn out. About fifty of them sneaked up to the balcony where the horse cops couldn't go, and they locked the doors, so the other cops couldn't reach them. It was the craziest thing I ever saw. Then they started to cheer Internationale. The cops pointed sawed-off shotguns at them and threatened to mow them down, but these fifty little Filipinos wouldn't move. They were as stubborn as their hero Internationale. And then somebody fired into the ceiling, and one of the little Filipinos fainted. This made the other forty-nine Filipinos sore, so they started throwing pop bottles at the cops. A couple of horses got scared and busted loose, falling all over seats and crying out with pain. And Internationale wouldn't budge.

I almost cried, begging him to get out of the ring. You know nothing, he shouted at me; you do not know anything.

Outside, people from all over San Francisco were rushing to Dreamland in automobiles, by street car, and by foot, and although we didn't know it, there was a crowd of over three thousand people in the streets, and more arriving every minute. People love to see one man, especially someone dark-complected, challenging the whole world, and nine times out of ten they are for him. This crowd was certainly on Internationale's side. Most of the people hadn't seen the match, but from what they found out about it from people who had seen it, they were sure Internationale was the winner. They started guessing how long he'd be able to hold out against the police, and wondered how the police would finally get him out of the ring. They believed he would die before he'd get out, unless they declared him the winner. Even people who had never before heard of Internationale. They just knew he would stand there in the middle of the ring and let them kill him because that's exactly what they themselves would do if they were as big as he was, and as crazy. The part that bothered every one of them was his being a Filipino. They couldn't understand how a Filipino could grow to be two hundred and fifty pounds in weight, but everybody was glad it had happened. You know how happy the world was about the successful birth of the quintuplets.

They had to get the chief of police out of bed at midnight to ask him what they should do, and, boy, was he sore? It took them over twenty minutes to explain just what had happened and what was going on, and even then he didn't know for sure. Finally, he got out of bed and put on his clothes and came down to Dreamland in a red automobile traveling sixty miles an hour through heavy traffic, with a half-dozen motorcycle cops in front and a half-dozen behind. I remember how amazed he was when he walked into the auditorium and saw all the horse cops riding up and down the aisles, and Internationale in the middle of the ring, and the fifty little Filipinos in the balcony, throwing pop bottles. One of the bottles busted on the cement floor right beside him, and that's when he turned around and saw the little Filipinos up there. He was scared to death.

What the hell are all the well-dressed Filipinos doing up there? he said.

Ha ha, said the reporter from the *News*. They've locked themselves in, and they're throwing pop bottles. So let's see you get them out. Go ahead, you're chief of police. Get them out. Let's see you get Internationale out of the ring, too. You're a brave man. Go in there and throw him out.

The chief took one good look at Internationale and decided to argue it out. He said they wouldn't put Internationale in jail if he got out of the ring peacefully and went home, but if he refused to do so, they would gas him out and put him in jail for ten years. Internationale said, You know nothing: you do not know anything, and one of the little Filipinos in the balcony threw a pop bottle that hit another horse and the horse jumped from the sixth row into the ring. The cop on the horse took one big leap and landed in the fourth row because Internationale was moving toward him. The horse, however, was too stunned to move, so Internationale got into the saddle. It was the craziest thing in the history of wrestling. I was afraid he was going to throw the horse out of the ring, too, but

Internationale was too kind-hearted to do a dirty trick like that. He loved dumb animals.

Every once in a while we could hear the crowd outside booing, and we knew why, but the chief didn't. What the hell are they booing about? he said.

No cop would tell him, so the reporter from the *News* told him. Ha ha, he said, they're booing you and the cops, that's who. Every man, woman, and child out there is one hundred per cent for Internationale.

So the chief came over to me. He was disgusted.

You his manager? he said, and I said I was.

All right, he said. Get him out of there.

So I began begging Internationale to get out of the ring again. Well, this time that crazy frightened horse neighed at me. I nearly fell over. I guess the horse didn't want to get out of the ring either. Internationale said the same thing as before. You know nothing, he started to say, and I said, I know, I know, don't tell me again. I do not know anything. But for the love of Mike, Ramon, get the hell out of that ring.

He wouldn't budge.

So the chief and Vasili Ivanovitch and Vasili's manager and the referee and the timekeepers arid the reporters and two dozen cops held a little meeting. They decided to send Vasili back into the ring to finish the match, but he wouldn't hear of it. He began to stamp his feet like a baby, pointing at the horse, but that was only an alibi, he was scared to death. He said he had been declared the winner once and that was enough. Then the chief sat down and started to groan. He would be disgraced. The whole city would laugh at him.

He jumped up, looking furious. Gas him out, he said. He looked at the fifty little Filipinos in the balcony. Gas them all out, he said. Our little brown brothers the Filipinos, he said. Gas them all out.

How about the horse? somebody asked.

Gas the horse out, too, said the chief.

Then he heard the crowd outside booing, and he changed his mind.

Wait a minute, he said. Aren't there fifty able-bodied men among you who are willing to go into that ring and arrest him?

There wasn't one, let alone fifty.

The chief was disgusted. He telephoned the mayor, and the mayor swore at him for five minutes. Then the mayor told him to leave the Filipino wrestler on the horse in the ring, and the fifty little ones in the balcony, and clear the streets and let the Filipinos stay in the auditorium until they got sleepy or hungry and went home. The chief thought this was a great idea until he found out the people in the streets wouldn't go away and kept rushing into the auditorium and sitting down and cheering, at least five thousand of them. It was a clear night in August and everybody was feeling great and didn't want to go home.

The chief was panic-stricken. This was worse than a strike. It was ten times worse.

He telephoned the mayor again and talked a long time. Then he told Diamond Gates to go into the ring and declare Internationale the winner.

I can't do that, Diamond Gates said, and the chief said, Like hell you can't. You go on in there and declare that crazy Filipino the winner or there won't be any more wrestling matches in Frisco.

So Diamond Gates tried to get into the ring. Every time he ducked under the lower rope the frightened horse would stand on its hind legs and neigh very mournfully and Diamond Gates would run half way up the aisle, sweating and shivering. Finally he stood on a seat and declared Ramon Internationale the winner. Everybody in Dreamland cheered, especially the fifty little Filipinos in the balcony, and gradually the auditorium emptied. Then Internationale got off the horse and left the ring.

I never did find out how the horse got out of the ring. It was scared to death.

The Black Tartars

*I*n 1926 there were only twelve Black Tartars in Russia, and now, in 1935, there are only ten because of the deep love of Mago the soldier for Komi the daughter of Moyskan.

In 1926 Mago was nineteen years old. I met his brother and his brother's wife on the train from Kiev to Kharkov. Mago's brother Karachi is no soldier and he doesn't care if Black Tartars vanish from the world altogether because he believes it is wiser to live quietly than to live greatly and foolishly, and he would rather be a Russian, anyway. But Mago, no. He would live greatly.

Karachi spoke in Russian to the Jewish girl on her way to Tiflis and the Jewish girl translated his words to me. Karachi's wife was a Ukrainian girl. Karachi didn't care to marry a Black Tartar and preserve the race and the culture of the race. All he wanted was to live and have a girl near him when he didn't feel so good.

The Jewish girl translated and Karachi's wife smiled and moved closer to the young Black Tartar.

Moyskan, said Karachi in Russian to the Jewish girl and the girl in English to me, was an excellent singer. He not only sang the older Black Tartar songs but made new ones, especially when he was drunk. After beating his wife, his songs were full of lamentations and he would call on God to destroy him, and the next day he would complain bitterly to his friends, What can I do if God wills me to live?

Moyskan had five sons and one daughter. Three of the sons were killed in small wars or in banditry, one was in Siberia for no reason in the world, and the other was a worker in a Moscow tractor factory. Moyskan's daughter Komi was the most beautiful girl in the world, said Karachi. I fell in love with Komi, he said, my brother Mago fell in love with her, and all the officers and men of the Soviet Azerbaijan Army fell in love with her. Any man who saw Komi fell in love with her, he said.

He lit a Russian cigarette, inhaled deeply, and glanced impatiently at his wife and at the Jewish girl, and then said very politely, Komi was not like these, God forgive my crazy brother, wherever he may be. She was all beautiful things of the earth. Her heart was a dark sea. A black deep endless sea, and my brother wanted her for his wife.

Moyskan said *yes* with a new song. He sang the wedding of my brother Mago and his daughter Komi three days and three nights without stopping, except to drink.

Komi said to my brother Mago, said the young Black Tartar, I do not wish to love you.

My brother Mago stole a horse and brought it to her and again she spoke the same words.

It was a fine horse and any other girl would have loved my brother for stealing such a horse for her, but not Komi.

My poor brother stole a dress for Komi, and again she said she did not wish to love him. He stole a cow for her and Moyskan slaughtered it and ate it, and he stole a table for her, and still she did not wish to love him and he said he would steal an American automobile, for her, only he did not know how to drive an automobile.

I am a year younger than my brother Mago, said Karachi. An older brother speaks to a younger brother. A younger brother does not say to an older brother, You must not do this, you must do *this*.

It is not this way with Black Tartars only, he said. It is the same with many people. Is it so with Americans?

In a way, yes, I said.

My brother, said Karachi, wished to steal an American automobile for Komi because he loved her so much. I loved Komi, too, but when a sea is dark and wild only a great man will wish to swim across the sea, or a crazy man, or a man who is not afraid to die, or who wishes to die, and I did not wish to die. My brother was not sleeping at night and he was not sleeping during the day, and I could see in his eyes that he could destroy the world in order to love Komi, that he could kill her so that no other man could love her, that he could do *anything*. It is foolishness, said Karachi, but it is greatness, too. Only my brother Mago is a real Black Tartar. Only he is a fool and not ashamed to be a fool. Only he would steal an American automobile for Komi. The officers of the Army would not do it and the soldiers would not do it. They knew fear. To steal an American automobile that belongs to the government is to die.

Mago stole a Cadillac and drove it into a hotel, said Karachi.

He wished to take Komi an American automobile, but he did not know how to drive, and he drove into the New Europe Hotel on Malygin Street, in Baku.

Karachi got up from the bench and shook his head slowly and sadly.

My brother, he said. My crazy brother. My poor crazy brother Mago. To love so deeply.

He sat down again and remained silent for some time, remembering his brother, looking at the floor sullenly.

Ahkh ahkh ahkh ahkh, he whispered.

Do you understand such a thing in America? he asked.

Ask the American, he said to the Jewish girl, if they understand such a thing in America.

He wants to know if you can understand such a thing in America, said the Jewish girl.

Tell him yes, I said to the Jewish girl. Tell him it is the same everywhere. Tell him it has nothing to do with the form of government, Capitalist, Fascist, or proletarian, it is the same everywhere.

The Jewish girl translated what I said, and the young Black Tartar said in Russian to me, Da, da.

My brother, said Karachi, drove the American automobile through the door of the New Europe Hotel on Malygin Street in Baku. He broke the door down. He broke the glass window to a thousand pieces. He frightened all the people in the hotel. He arrived in the lobby of the hotel in the American automobile with his head bloody from pieces of broken glass. My brother Mago sat in the automobile and smoked a cigarette and everywhere around him ran a hundred people, shouting and screaming, and then two hundred people, and then came Moyskan, and then Komi.

My brother said, Komi, is there another soldier in the Azerbaijan Army who would do this for you? Is there another man in all the world who would do this for you?

This was in 1926, said Karachi. The years go by, he sighed. The landscape of life changes. (He says, said the Jewish girl, the landscape of life changes. I do not know how to translate his words.) The dead are forgotten by the living. My poor crazy brother killed Komi. My brother who loved her more than any other man in the whole Azerbaijan Army. My poor brother who is now in Irak [sic] or Afghanistan or dead. Ahkh ahkh.

Everybody said my brother would be shot in the morning. To steal an American automobile. To steal from the government.

To the New Europe Hotel they sent one officer of the Army and one hundred soldiers.

The officer said to Mago, What are you doing in this automobile?

I am sitting in this automobile, said Mago.

The officer said, Where did you get this automobile?

My brother said, I got this automobile on Narimanovskaya Street, in front of the building of the People's Commissars.

The officer said, You know this automobile belongs to the Central Executive Committee?

Yes, I know, said my crazy brother.

You stole this automobile? said the officer.

Yes, said Mago, I stole it.

My brother was brave and crazy, said Karachi.

Do you know what is the punishment for such a crime? said the officer.

Yes, I know, said my brother. It is death.

Ahkh, Mago, Mago, Mago, said Karachi.

He turned bitterly to the Jewish girl and asked many questions. I knew they were questions from the intonation of his voice and from the expression on his face.

What is he asking? I asked the Jewish girl.

He is asking if I am translating every word, said the Jewish girl. He wants to know if you understand the deep love of his brother. He does not believe any man who has not seen Komi can understand why his brother stole the American automobile and drove it into the New Europe Hotel.

Tell him I understand, I said.

Da? he asked me. Yes? You understand?

Yes, I said.

Everybody, he said, is listening carefully to the officer and my brother, and when my brother says the punishment is death, everybody is talking out loud and saying, Listen, listen to him, did you hear? the punishment is death, he knows, he is not afraid.

Then why did you steal this automobile? said the officer.

Because I love Komi, said my brother.

Then everybody is being very quiet, only one man is speaking. This man is a man with a hunchback. He is saying, The whole world is in love with Komi, even I. And somebody is putting a hand over his mouth because it is true and the people are ashamed. They are ashamed to love a girl so beautiful and they are proud that my brother Mago is not ashamed to love such a girl and to steal an American automobile for her and drive it into the New Europe Hotel.

The officer was in love with Komi too, said Karachi.

The officer did not make any reply. He understood.

So they took my brother Mago to the military jail in Baku. In the morning they began to ask him many questions. To every question he answered the truth.

They said, Did you steal a horse?

And my brother said, Yes, I stole a horse.

Did you steal a dress? Did you steal a cow? Did you steal a table? Yes. Yes. Yes.

Why did you steal these things?

I stole them for Komi.

The military Judge was a big Captain. He was an old man with a big moustache.

Who is Komi? said this man.

She is a Black Tartar girl, said Mago. She is the most beautiful girl in the world. I am a Black Tartar. I love Komi and I want to live in the same house with her. There are not many Black Tartars in the world. I do not wish to see the tribe of Black Tartars to end in the world. I wish to love Komi.

You do not look very black, said the Judge.

I have not been in the sun very much lately, said my brother. I am in the Azerbaijan Army and I work where it is shady, in the stable. A month in the sun and I am as black as Komi herself. It is the shade of the stable that has given me this sickly white color. In times of war I ride in the cavalry, but in times of peace I work in the stable.

I never heard of Black Tartars, said the Judge. I have seen many white Tartars. Who are the Black Tartars?

They are the ones who are black, said my brother.

Ah, said the Judge. How many Black Tartars are there in the world?

In the world I do not know, said my brother. In Baku there are only nine or ten. Thirty years ago a Black Tartar named Kotova went to America. He is now an American and his children are not black any longer and they live in Pittsburgh.

What language do you speak? said the Judge.

Mostly other languages, said my brother. Arabic, Kurdish, Turkish, and lately Russian.

Have you any language? said the Judge.

Yes, we have a language, said my brother.

Is it a written language? said the Judge.

Of course, said my brother. Only there is no Black Tartar in the world who can read or write in our language or in any other language.

Ah, said the Judge. What is your word for *sun*?

We have no word for *sun* in our language, said my brother.

Have you any words at all in your language? asked the Judge.

Oh, yes, said my brother. We have many words. They are Arabic and Kurdish and Turkish and Russian, only we speak these words in our own language, as Black Tartars.

How is that? asked the Judge.

We speak as Black Tartars, said my brother. We are Black Tartars and any words we use are in our language.

And you stole the official automobile of the Central Executive Committee in order to give it as a gift to this Black Tartar girl you love. Is that so? asked the Judge.

Yes, it is so, said my brother.

Please bring this girl to me, said the Judge.

In the afternoon of the same day they brought Komi to the room where they were asking my brother questions. The Judge was looking at papers when she entered the room. Then he began to read aloud, opening the trial. He was reaching aloud when he lifted his eyes and saw Komi. He stopped reading and stared at her.

Is this the girl? he said.

Yes, said my brother. This is Komi.

Give her a chair, said the Judge. He looked very excited. Why are you fools standing around? he said. Give her a chair.

After a while Komi stood before the Judge and he asked her some questions.

Do you understand what has happened? he asked.

No, said Komi.

This foolish young soldier, said the Judge, is in love with you. He has stolen a horse for you, a dress, a cow, a table, and finally the official automobile of the Central Executive Committee. Do you understand?

No, said Komi. Mago is my cousin.

Komi, said Mago. That is not so. I am not your cousin.

Silence, said the Judge. Do you realize you are on trial for your life?

I am not her cousin, said Mago. You can ask any Black Tartar in Baku.

Silence, said the Judge.

He turned to Komi, bending away over his desk in order to be closer to her.

Do you love this foolish young soldier? he said.

No, said Komi.

Now then, said the Judge, and he leaned way back in his chair.

Now then, he said, let me see.

You have stolen the official automobile of the Central Executive Committee, he said.

Yes, said Mago.

You were in love at the time, said the Judge.

Yes, said Mago. I am still in love. I shall always be in love with Komi.

Silence, said the Judge.

By law the punishment for such a monstrous crime, said the Judge, is immediate death.

He is my cousin, said Komi. You are not going to kill him, are you?

I am not afraid to die, said Mago.

Silence, said the Judge.

He turned to Komi again, leaning forward.

We shall do everything in our power to forgive this sorrowful misconduct of your cousin, he said. We shall examine his record and if he has murdered no man during the last five years, we shall return him to the ranks of the Army where his behavior will be closely watched.

Four days later, said Karachi, they returned Mago to the Army. Everybody in Baku was happy about this.

One evening my brother Mago saw Komi in an automobile with the Judge. The Judge was crowding over Komi, and Komi was laughing at him. The Judge was an old man and his children were older than Mago.

My brother Mago was very angry. First, he said, he would kill the Judge, then he would kill the Judge's wife, then each of his five children, the oldest first, the next oldest next, and so on down the line until all of them were killed.

Then he said he would not kill the Judge, he would steal two good horses, and tie Komi to one of the horses and take her into the hills where he would keep her until each of them died, either of old age, or starvation, or from loving one another too much and not wanting to be alive.

My brother Mago went to Komi and said, Why are you going around with this rotten old man?

Because I want to, said Komi.

He is not a Black Tartar, said Mago. If I see you with him again, I will kill him.

He saved your life, said Komi.

I will kill him, anyway, said Mago. You are a Black Tartar and you must love a Black Tartar.

I do not know what I am, said Komi. Maybe I am not a Black Tartar.

You are a Black Tartar, said Mago. I want you to live in the same house with me.

I do not wish to love you, said Komi.

You will love me, said Mago. You are a Black Tartar and I am a Black Tartar and you will love me.

Ahkh, ahkh, said Karachi. There are so many girls in the world. But my poor brother would not look at another girl as long as Komi was alive. Maybe you will understand this, but my poor crazy brother killed Komi and went away to Irak or Afghanistan, or maybe he killed himself, too. We do not know.

She would not love him, said Karachi. He was the one man in the world for her, and she would not love him. He drove the American automobile into the lobby of the New Europe Hotel for her and still she would not love him.

One morning before daybreak my brother Mago went to Moyskan's house with two of the finest horses from the stables of the Azerbaijan Army. He entered the house and tied Komi's arms and legs, kissing her lips and hands and hair. Moyskan helped him because he did not think it was good for Komi to go around with an old man, but Moyskan's wife cried and screamed until Moyskan knocked her down. Then my brother Mago tied Komi to one of the horses and took her with him into the hills.

Nobody knows what happened there, said Karachi.

No man in all the world loved a girl as deeply as my brother Mago loved Komi, he said.

They sent soldiers on horses into the hills. First ten soldiers, then twenty, then fifty, then a hundred, then the whole Azerbaijan Army.

The old Captain was very angry. He said, Shoot that foolish young soldier, but bring back the young girl unharmed. But the soldiers did not find my brother and Komi.

One morning they found Komi dead. My brother Mago had held her under the water of a shallow stream. He did not want her to live if she would not love him.

In America, said Karachi, does a man love a woman so deeply?

I don't think so, I said.

He turned to the Jewish girl again and began to talk to her very rapidly.

He is saying, said the Jewish girl, that he wants you to understand it was not a crime. It was not hate, it was love. You have never seen Komi, he is saying. He wants you to know his brother was a great man. He was a man who wanted to live greatly. That is why he did all those foolish things.

Tell him I know how it was, I said.

And the Jewish girl told him.

He did not speak for many minutes.

Then he said, Ahkh, Mago, Mago, Mago. And many other words in Russian which I did not understand.

What is he saying? I asked the Jewish girl.

He is saying, To kill such a girl as Komi. To kill her. To end the life of such a one as Komi. A man must love deeply to do such a thing.

Kharkov, Russia. June, 1935.

The Armenian and the Armenian

*I*n the city of Rostov I passed a beer parlor late at night and saw a waiter in a white coat who was surely an Armenian, so I went in and said in our language, How are you, God destroy your house, how are you? I don't know how I could tell he was an Armenian, but I could. It is not the dark complexion alone, nor the curve of nose, nor the thickness and abundance of hair, nor is it even the way the living eye is set within the head. There are many with the right complexion and the right curve of nose and the same kind of hair and eyes, but these are not Armenian. Our tribe is a remarkable one, and I was on my way to Armenia. Well, I am sorry. I am deeply sorry that Armenia is nowhere. It is mournful to me that there is no Armenia.

There is a small area of land in Asia Minor that is called Armenia, but it is not so. It is not Armenia. It is a place. There are plains and mountains and rivers and lakes and cities in this place, and it is all fine, it is all no less fine than all the other places of the world, but it is not Armenia. There are only Armenians, and these inhabit the earth, not Armenia, since there is no Armenia, gentlemen, there is no America and there is no England, and no France, and no Italy, there is only the earth, gentlemen.

So I went into the little Russian beer parlor to greet a countryman, an alien in a foreign land.

Vy, he said with that deliberate intonation of surprise which makes our language and our way of speech so full of comedy. You?

Meaning of course I, a stranger. My clothes, for instance. My hat, my shoes, and perhaps even the small reflection of America in my face.

How did you find this place?

Thief, I said with affection, I have been walking. What is your city? Where were you born? (In Armenian, Where did you enter the world?)

Moush, he said. Where are you going? What are you doing here? You are an American. I can tell from your clothes.

Moush. I love that city. I can love a place I have never seen, a place that no longer exists, whose inhabitants have been killed. It is the city my father sometimes visited as a young man.

Jesus, it was good to see this black Armenian from Moush. You have no idea how good it is for an Armenian to run into an Armenian in some far place of the world. And a guy in a beer parlor, at that. A place where men drink. Who cares about the rotten quality of the beer? Who cares about the flies? Who, for that matter, cares about dictatorship? It is simply impossible to change some things.

Vy, he said. Vy (slowly, with deliberate joy) vy. And you speak the language. It is amazing that you have not forgotten.

And he brought two glasses of the lousy Russian beer.

And the Armenian gestures, meaning so much. The slapping of the knee and roaring with laughter. The cursing. The subtle mockery of the world and its big ideas. The word in Armenian, the glance, the gesture, the smile, and through these things the swift rebirth of the race, timeless and again strong, though years have passed, though cities have been destroyed, fathers and brothers and sons killed, places forgotten, dreams violated, living hearts blackened with hate.

I should like to see any power of the world destroy this race, this small tribe of unimportant people, whose history is ended, whose wars have all been fought and lost, whose structures have crumbled, whose literature is unread, whose music is unheard, whose prayers are no longer uttered.

Go ahead, destroy this race. Let us say that it is again 1915. There is war in the world. Destroy Armenia. See if you can do it. Send them from their homes into the desert. Let them have neither bread nor water. Burn their houses and their churches. See if they will not live again. See if they will not laugh again. See if the race will not live again when two of them meet in a beer parlor, twenty years after, and laugh, and speak in their tongue. Go ahead, see if you can do anything about it. See if you can stop them from mocking the big ideas of the world, you sons of bitches, a couple of Armenians talking in the world, go ahead and try to destroy them.

New York. August, 1935.

from
The Trouble with Tigers

Sweetheart Sweetheart Sweetheart

One thing she *could* do was play the piano and sing. She couldn't cook or anything like that. Anyhow she didn't like to cook because she couldn't make pastry anyway and that's what she liked. She was something like the pastry she was always eating, big and soft and pink, and like a child although she was probably in her late thirties. She claimed she'd been on the stage. *I was an actress three seasons,* is what she told the boy's mother. His mother liked the neighbor but couldn't exactly figure her out. She was married and had no kids, that's what his mother couldn't figure out; and she spent all her time making dresses and putting them on and being very pretty.

Who for? his mother would ask his sister. She would be busy in the kitchen getting food cooked or making bread and in English, which she couldn't talk well but which she liked to talk when she was talking about the neighbor, she said, What for, she's so anxious to be pretty? And then in Italian she'd say, But my, how nice she plays the piano. She's a good neighbor to have.

They'd just moved from one side of town to the other, from Italian town to where the Americans were. This lady was one of them, an American, so his mother guessed that was the way they were, like fancy things to eat, sweet and creamy and soft and pink.

The neighbor used to come over a lot because, she said, it was so refreshing to be among real people.

You know, Mrs. Amendola, she used to say, it's a pleasure to have a neighbor like you. It's so wonderful the way you take care of all your wonderful children without a husband. All your fine growing girls and boys.

Oh, his mother used to laugh, the kids are good. I feed them and take care of them. Headache, toothache, trouble at school, I take care of everything; and his mother roared with laughter. Then his mother looked at the neighbor and said, They're my kids. We fight, we yell, we hit each other, but we like each other. You no got children?

119

No, the neighbor said. The boy became embarrassed. His mother was so boisterous and abrupt and direct. It was about the third time she'd asked if the neighbor had no children. What she meant, he knew, was, How come you haven't got any? A big woman like you, full of everything to make children?

The neighbor used to come over often when her husband was away. He covered the valley from Bakersfield to Sacramento, selling hardware. Sometimes his wife went with him, but most often not.

She preferred not to because travel was so difficult. And yet whenever she didn't go that meant that she would be in the house alone, and that made her lonely, so she used to visit the Italian family.

One night she came over sobbing and his mother put her arms around the neighbor as if she was one of his mother's kids, and comforted her.

But one thing he noticed that kind of puzzled him; she wasn't *really* crying. It wasn't honest-to-God crying; it was something else; she wasn't hurt or sorry or in pain or anything; it seemed like she just felt like crying, so she cried, just the same as if she might have felt like buying a dozen cream puffs and eating them. That's the impression he got.

Oh, Mrs. Amendola, she said. I was sitting all alone in the house when all of a sudden I began to remember all the years and then I got scared and started to cry. Oh, I feel so bad, she said and then smiled in a way that seemed awfully lovely to the boy and awfully strange. She looked around at his sister, and then, smiling, she looked at him and he didn't know what to do. She looked a long time. It wasn't a glance. And he knew right away something he didn't understand was going on. She was awfully lovely, big and soft and full of everything, and he felt embarrassed. Her arms were so full.

The little kids were all in bed, so it was only his mother and his sister and him. His mother said, You be all right. You sit with us and talk, you be fine. What's the matter?

I feel so sad, the neighbor said. When I remember all the years gone by, the times when I was a little girl, and then when I was almost grown-up at high school, and then on the stage, I feel so lonely.

Oh, you be all right, his mother said. You like a glass of wine?

His mother didn't wait for her to answer. She got out the bottle and poured two drinks, one for herself and one for the neighbor.

Drink wine, his mother said. Wine is good.

The neighbor sipped the wine.

Oh, it's wonderful, she said. You're a wonderful family, Mrs. Amendola. Won't you come to my house for a visit? I'd like to show you the house.

Oh, sure, his mother said. His mother wanted to see what her house looked like. So they all went to the house next door and room by room the neighbor showed them the house. It was just like her, like cream puffs. Soft and warm and pink, all except *his* room. He had his own room, bed and everything. There was something fishy somewhere, the boy thought. Americans were different from Italians, that's all he knew. If he slept in one bed and she in another, something was funny somewhere. Her room was like a place in another world. It was so like a woman that he felt ashamed to go in. He stood in the doorway while his mother and sister admired the beautiful room, and then the neighbor noticed him and took his hand. He felt excited and wished he was with her that way alone and in another world. The neighbor laughed and said, But I want *you* to admire my room, too, Tommy. You're such an intelligent and refined boy.

He didn't know for sure, maybe it was his imagination, but when she said he was intelligent and refined it seemed to him she squeezed his hand. He was awfully scared, almost sick. He didn't know about the Americans yet, and he didn't want to do anything wrong. Maybe she *had* squeezed his hand, but maybe it was as if she was just an older person, or a relative. Maybe it was because she was their neighbor, nothing else. He took his hand away as quickly as possible. He didn't speak about the room because he knew anything he'd say would be ridiculous. It was a place he'd like to get in and stay in forever, with her. And that was crazy. She was married. She was old enough to be his mother, although she was a lot younger than his mother. But that was what he wanted.

After they saw the house she cooked chocolate and brought them a cup each. The cups were very delicate and beautiful. There was a plate full of mixed pastry, all kinds of it. She made each of them eat a lot; anyway, for every one she ate, she made them eat one, too, so they each ate four, then there were two left. She laughed and said she could never get enough pastry, so she was going to take one of the last two, and since Tommy was the man present, he ought to take the other. She said that in a way that more than ever excited the boy. He became confused and deeply mournful about the whole thing. It was something new and out of the world. It was like wanting to get out of the world and never come back. To get into the strange region of warmth and beauty and ease and something else that she seemed to make him feel existed; by her voice and her way of laughing and the way she was, the way her house was, especially the way she looked at him.

He wondered if his mother and sister knew about it. He hoped they didn't. After the chocolate and pastry, his mother asked her to play the piano and sing and she was only too glad to. She played three songs; one for his mother; one for his sister; and then she said, This one for Tommy. She played and sang *Maytime*, the song that hollers or screams, *Sweetheart sweetheart sweetheart*. The boy was very flattered. He hoped his mother and sister didn't catch on, but that was silly because the first thing his mother said when they got home was, Tommy, I think you got a sweetheart now. And his mother roared with laughter.

She's crazy about you, his sister said.

His sister was three years older than him, seventeen, and she had a fellow. She didn't know yet if she was going to marry him.

She's just nice, the boy said. She was nice to all of us. That's the way she is.

Oh, no, his sister said. She was *nicer* to you than to us. She's falling in love with you, Tommy. Are you falling in love with her?

Aw, shut up, the boy said.

You see, Ma, his sister said. He is falling in love with her.

Tell her to cut it out, Ma, the boy said.

You leave my boy alone, his mother told his sister.

And then his mother roared with laughter. It was such a wonderful joke. His mother and his sister laughed until he had to laugh, too. Then all of a sudden their laughter became louder and heartier than ever. It was *too* loud.

Let's not laugh so loud, the boy said. Suppose she hears us? She'll think we're laughing at *her*.

He's in love, Ma, his sister said.

His mother shrugged her shoulders. He knew she was going to come out with one of her comic remarks and he hoped it wouldn't be too embarrassing.

She's a nice girl, his mother said, and his sister started laughing again.

He decided not to think about her any more. He knew if he did his mother and sister would know about it and make fun of him. It wasn't a thing you could make fun of. It was a thing like nothing else, most likely the best thing of all. He didn't want it to be made fun of. He couldn't explain to them but he felt they shouldn't laugh about it.

In the morning her piano-playing wakened him and he began to feel the way he'd felt last night when she'd taken his hand, only now it was worse. He didn't want to get up, or anything. What he wished was that they were together in a room like hers, out of the world, away from everybody, forever. She sang the song again, four choruses of it, *Sweetheart sweetheart sweetheart*.

His mother made him get up. What's the matter? she said. You'll be late for work. Are you sick?

No, he said. What time is it?

He jumped out of bed and got into his clothes and ate and got on his wheel and raced to the grocery store. He was only two minutes late.

The romance kept up the whole month, all of August. Her husband came home for two days about the middle of the month. He fooled around in the yard and then went away again.

The boy didn't know what would ever happen. She came over two or three times every week. She appeared in the yard when he was in the yard. She invited the family over to her house two or three times for chocolate and pastry. She woke him up almost every morning singing *Sweetheart sweetheart sweetheart.*

His mother and sister still kidded him about her every once in a while.

One night in September when he got home his sister and mother had a big laugh about him and the neighbor.

Too bad, his mother said. Here, eat your supper. Too bad.

We feel sorry for you, his sister said.

What are you talking about? the boy said.

It's too late now, his mother said.

Too late for *what?* the boy said.

You waited too long, his sister said.

Aw, cut it out, the boy said. What are you talking about?

She's got another sweetheart now, his sister said.

He felt stunned, disgusted, and ill, but tried to go on eating and tried not to show how he felt.

Who? he said.

Your sweetheart, his sister said. You know *who.*

He wasn't sorry. He was angry. Not at his sister and mother; at *her.* She was stupid. He tried to laugh it off.

Well, it's about time, he said.

He comes and gets her in his car, his sister said. It's a Cadillac.

What about her husband? the boy said. He felt foolish.

He don't know! his mother said. Maybe he don't *care.* He's dead, I think.

His mother roared with laughter, and then his sister, too, and then he, too. He was glad Italians laughed, anyway. That made him feel a little better. After supper, though, he was strangely ill all the time. She was a stupid, foolish woman.

Every night for a week his mother and sister told him about the man coming and getting her every afternoon, driving off with her in his Cadillac.

She's got no family, his mother said. She's right. What's the use being pretty for nothing?

He's an awful handsome man, his sister said.

The husband, his mother said, he's dead.

They told him about the neighbor and her lover every night for a week, and then one night she came over to pay another visit. She was lovelier than ever, and not sad any more. Not even make-believe sad.

He was afraid his mother would ask about the man, so he tried to keep her from doing so. He kept looking into his mother's eyes and telling her not to make any mistakes. It would be all right across the tracks, but not in this neighborhood. If *she* wanted to come out with it herself, *she* could tell them. She didn't, though. The boy waited five minutes and then he decided she wasn't going to say anything.

He got his cap and said, I'm going to the library, Ma.

All right, his mother said.

He didn't say good night to her. He didn't even look at her. She knew *why*, too.

After that she never played the piano in the mornings, and whenever she *did* play the piano she didn't play the song she'd said was for him.

The Brokenhearted Comedian
and the Girl Who Took the Place
of his Unfaithful Wife

Maybe you remember him. He was before your time, but maybe you saw him in pictures when you were a kid. He was one of the boys who used to throw pies in the old slap-stick comedies. Johnny Kilgore. He was a small guy who was funny. He used to wear a big mustache and his most famous business was to lift his eyebrows eight or nine times by way of flirting or being amazed.

His wife ran away with a guy whose name I won't mention because he's still alive. So is she. It was nothing. She just wanted to have an affair. She was around thirty-four and she was getting fat, so she figured she'd be unfaithful. I don't know what kind of an affair she had with the actor, but when she got back Johnny told her to get out and stay out.

Maybe he was in love with her. Anyhow, when she came back from this love affair he said out. It didn't do him any good.

He was pretty sad, although he kept on being funny. He kept everybody on the lot laughing. No place is sadder than a lot where they're shooting a comedy. It's no comedy shooting a comedy, it's a tragedy, but he kept them laughing all the time.

One day went to another and after a week Johnny phoned me and I went over.

Forget it, he said. All I want is some fun. Get me a girl.

All right. I'd get me one, too. I phoned Emma Dauber who used to be in pictures before she got fat and told her to send over two of her best girls.

She did. One of the girls was a red-head. Johnny just naturally let me have her. In fact, he insisted. Her name was Joyce. The other girl was the most serious-looking girl I'd ever seen, and very beautiful. She had a way of standing around helpless that made you like her. Johnny started acting for her. After she found out he wasn't making fun of her she started laughing. We had some drinks and she started laughing louder. She laughed beautifully.

Well, around three in the morning Joyce went home.

This other girl, Bess, though, didn't. She told Johnny she didn't want to go back. Johnny thought she was kidding, but she wasn't. She wouldn't take his money and she asked him if she couldn't stay with him.

Johnny told her to stay.

I've got to have somebody around, he said. It might as well be you.

Then he apologized and told her he loved her. I don't know, maybe he did. He apologized for talking to her that way and he said he loved her.

Then he asked her why she wanted to stay with him.

She said she wanted to stay near him because he made her laugh.

From that night on she was his girl. She liked being near him. She liked being near the humor. She was only a kid, not more than nineteen, and she liked being near somebody who was funny.

Johnny didn't stop being miserable, though.

He used to fly an airplane. When I say fly I mean he used to do everything in the world a pilot shouldn't do. Well, he was drunk most of the time. I guess that was the reason.

The girl was always afraid she'd lose him, so she'd never let him go away from her. Not far, anyhow. She'd always be right with him. It was because she didn't want to go back. It was wonderful being with Johnny.

I went up in the plane with them one day and I could see she was scared to death.

When the plane landed her face was the sickest color I ever saw.

Look, Bess, I said, you don't have to stay near him *all* the time.

Yes, I do, she said.

You know how they talk. She just knew she had to be near him and that was all there was to it. No two ways about it.

One night Johnny got drunk and hit her. I can't tell you about that. I was there, but I can't tell you what happened. She just smiled and before I knew it Johnny was crying.

She was lovely. I mean, she was just a kid and the whole thing had been something nobody could have made different, and then all of a sudden she met Johnny.

He cried like a baby. He couldn't understand how he could have hurt someone like her.

One day he took her up in his plane while he was cockeyed. He was cockeyed most of the time. He flew out around Catalina Island and then decided to land. He came down to land and then decided to have some fun, so he turned around and shot straight up and the motor died. He was turning to land and then the motor died. The plane dived straight into the ocean.

I mean, that's all. They didn't find him or her.

It used to scare her to death to get into the plane, but she just couldn't think of being away from him.

The Great Leapfrog Contest

Rosie Mahoney was a tough little Irish kid whose folks, through some miscalculation in directions, or out of an innate spirit of anarchy, had moved into the Russian-Italian-and-Greek neighborhood of my home town, across the Southern Pacific tracks, around G Street.

She wore a turtle-neck sweater, usually red. Her father was a bricklayer named Cull and a heavy drinker. Her mother's name was Mary. Mary Mahoney used to go to the Greek Orthodox Catholic Church on Kearny Boulevard every Sunday, because there was no Irish Church to go to anywhere in the neighborhood. The family seemed to be a happy one.

Rosie's three brothers had all grown up and gone to sea. Her two sisters had married. Rosie was the last of the clan. She had entered the world when her father had been close to sixty and her mother in her early fifties. For all that, she was hardly the studious or scholarly type.

Rosie had little use for girls, and as far as possible avoided them. She had less use for boys, but found it undesirable to avoid them. That is to say, she made it a point to take part in everything the boys did. She was always on hand, and always the first to take up any daring or crazy idea. Everybody felt awkward about her continuous presence, but it was no use trying to chase her away, because that meant a fight in which she asked no quarter, and gave none.

If she didn't whip every boy she fought, every fight was at least an honest draw, with a slight edge in Rosie's favor. She didn't fight girl-style, or cry if hurt. She fought the regular style and took advantage of every opening. It was very humiliating to be hurt by Rosie, so after a while any boy who thought of trying to chase her away, decided not to.

It was no use. She just wouldn't go. She didn't seem to like any of the boys especially, but she liked being in on any mischief they might have in mind, and she wanted to play on any teams they organized. She was an excellent baseball player, being as good as anybody else in the neighborhood at any position, and for her age an expert pitcher. She had a wicked

129

wing, too, and could throw a ball in from left field so that when it hit the catcher's mitt it made a nice sound.

She was extraordinarily swift on her feet and played a beautiful game of tin-can hockey.

At pee-wee, she seemed to have the most disgusting luck in the world.

At the game we invented and used to call *Horse* she was as good at *horse* as at *rider*, and she insisted on following the rules of the game. She insisted on being horse when it was her turn to be horse. This always embarrassed her partner, whoever he happened to be, because it didn't seem right for a boy to be getting up on the back of a girl.

She was an excellent football player too.

As a matter of fact, she was just naturally the equal of any boy in the neighborhood, and much the superior of many of them. Especially after she had lived in the neighborhood three years. It took her that long to make everybody understand that she had come to stay and that she was *going* to stay.

She did, too; even after the arrival of a boy named Rex Folger, who was from somewhere in the south of Texas. This boy Rex was a natural-born leader. Two months after his arrival in the neighborhood, it was understood by everyone that if Rex wasn't the leader of the gang, he was very nearly the leader. He had fought and licked every boy in the neighborhood who at one time or another had fancied himself leader. And he had done so without any noticeable ill-feeling, pride, or ambition.

As a matter of fact, no one could possibly have been more good-natured than Rex. Everybody resented him, just the same.

One winter, the whole neighborhood took to playing a game that had become popular on the other side of the tracks, in another slum neighborhood of the town: *Leapfrog*. The idea was for as many boys as cared to participate, to bend down and be leaped over by every other boy in the game, and then himself to get up and begin leaping over all the other boys, and then bend down again until all the boys had leaped over him again, and keep this up until all the other players had become exhausted. This didn't happen, sometimes, until the last two players had traveled a distance of three or four miles, while the other players walked along, watching and making bets.

Rosie, of course, was always in on the game. She was always one of the last to drop out, too. And she was the only person in the neighborhood Rex Folger hadn't fought and beaten.

He felt that that was much too humiliating even to think about. But inasmuch as she seemed to be a member of the gang, he felt that in some way or another he ought to prove his superiority.

One summer day during vacation, an argument between Rex and Rosie developed and Rosie pulled off her turtle-neck sweater and challenged him to a fight. Rex took a cigarette from his pocket, lighted it, inhaled, and told Rosie he wasn't in the habit of hitting women—where he came from that amounted to boxing your mother. On the other hand, he said, if Rosie cared to compete with him in any other sport, he would be glad to oblige her. Rex was a very calm and courteous conversationalist. He had poise. It was unconscious, of course, but he had it just the same. He was just naturally a man who couldn't be hurried, flustered, or excited.

So Rex and Rosie fought it out in this game Leapfrog. They got to leaping over one another, quickly, too, until the first thing we knew the whole gang of us was out on the State Highway going south towards Fowler. It was a very hot day. Rosie and Rex were in great shape, and it looked like one was tougher than the other and more stubborn. They talked a good deal, especially Rosie, who insisted that she would have to fall down unconscious before she'd give up to a guy like Rex.

He said he was sorry his opponent was a girl. It grieved him deeply to have to make a girl exert herself to the point of death, but it was just too bad. He had to, so he had to. They leaped and squatted, leaped and squatted, and we got out to Sam Day's vineyard. That was half-way to Fowler. It didn't seem like either Rosie or Rex were ever going to get tired. They hadn't even begun to show signs of growing tired, although each of them was sweating a great deal.

Naturally, we were sure Rex would win the contest. But that was because we hadn't taken into account the fact that he was a simple person, whereas Rosie was crafty and shrewd. Rosie knew how to figure angles. She had discovered how to jump over Rex Folger in a way that weakened him. And after a while, about three miles out of Fowler, we noticed that she was coming down on Rex's *neck*, instead of on his back. Naturally, this was hurting him and making the blood rush to his head. Rosie herself squatted in such a way that it was impossible, almost, for Rex to get anywhere near her neck with his hands.

Before long, we noticed that Rex was weakening. His head was getting closer and closer to the ground. About a half mile out of Fowler, we heard Rex's head bumping the ground every time Rosie leaped over him.

131

They were good loud bumps that we knew were painful, but Rex wasn't complaining. He was too proud to complain.

Rosie, on the other hand, knew she had her man, and she was giving him all she had. She was bumping his head on the ground as solidly as she could, because she knew she didn't have much more fight in her, and if she didn't lay him out cold, in the hot sun, in the next ten minutes or so, she would fall down exhausted herself, and lose the contest.

Suddenly, Rosie bumped Rex's head a real powerful one. He got up very dazed and very angry. It was the first time we had ever seen him fuming. By God, the girl was taking advantage of him, if he wasn't mistaken, and he didn't like it. Rosie was squatted in front of him. He came up groggy and paused a moment. Then he gave Rosie a very effective kick that sent her sprawling. Rosie jumped up and smacked Rex in the mouth. The gang jumped in and tried to establish order.

It was agreed that the Leapfrog contest must not change into a fight. Not any more. Not with Fowler only five or ten minutes away. The gang ruled further that Rex had had no right to kick Rosie and that in smacking him in the mouth Rosie had squared the matter, and the contest was to continue.

Rosie was very tired and sore; and so was Rex. They began leaping and squatting again; and again we saw Rosie coming down on Rex's neck so that his head was bumping the ground.

It looked pretty bad for the boy from Texas. We couldn't understand how he could take so much punishment. We all felt that Rex was getting what he had coming to him, but at the same time everybody seemed to feel badly about Rosie, a girl, doing the job instead of one of us. Of course, that was where we were wrong. Nobody but Rosie could have figured out that smart way of humiliating a very powerful and superior boy. It was probably the woman in her, which, less than five years later, came out to such an extent that she became one of the most beautiful girls in town, gave up tomboy activities, and married one of the wealthiest young men in Kings County, a college man named, if memory serves, Wallace Hadington Finlay VI.

Less than a hundred yards from the heart of Fowler, Rosie, with great and admirable artistry, finished the job.

That was where the dirt of the highway siding ended and the paved main street of Fowler began. This street was paved with cement, not asphalt. Asphalt, in that heat, would have been too soft to serve, but cement had exactly the right degree of brittleness. I think Rex, when he squatted over the hard cement, knew the game was up. But he was brave to the end. He squatted over the hard cement and waited for the worst. Behind him, Rosie Mahoney prepared to make the supreme effort. In this next leap, she intended to give her all, which she did.

She came down on Rex Folger's neck like a ton of bricks. His head banged against the hard cement, his body straightened out, and his arms and legs twitched.

He was out like a light.

Six paces in front of him, Rosie Mahoney squatted and waited. Jim Telesco counted twenty, which was the time allowed for each leap. Rex didn't get up during the count.

The contest was over. The winner of the contest was Rosie Mahoney.

Rex didn't get up by himself at all. He just stayed where he was until a half-dozen of us lifted him and carried him to a horse trough, where we splashed water on his face.

Rex was a confused young man all the way back. He was also a deeply humiliated one. He couldn't understand anything about anything. He just looked dazed and speechless. Every now and then we imagined he wanted to talk, and I guess he did, but after we'd all gotten ready to hear what he had to say, he couldn't speak. He made a gesture so tragic that tears came to the eyes of eleven members of the gang.

Rosie Mahoney, on the other hand, talked all the way home. She said everything.

I think it made a better man of Rex. More human. After that he was a gentler sort of soul. It may have been because he couldn't see very well for some time. At any rate, for weeks he seemed to be going around in a dream. His gaze would freeze on some insignificant object far away in the landscape, and half the time it seemed as if he didn't know where he was going, or why. He took little part in the activities of the gang, and the following winter he stayed away altogether. He came to school one day wearing glasses. He looked broken and pathetic.

That winter Rosie Mahoney stopped hanging around with the gang, too. She had a flair for making an exit at the right time.

Woof Woof

Money, in this country, is (1) the penny, (2) the nickel, (3) the dime, (4) the quarter, (5) the half-dollar, and (6) the dollar, woof woof.

Money is one cent, two cents, three cents, four cents, five cents, car-fare, cup of coffee, cheap cigar, telephone call. Six cents, seven cents, eight cents, nine cents, ten cents, hamburger, package of cheap cigarettes, two cheap cigars, two rides in the subway, two cups of coffee, woof woof. Eleven cents, twelve cents, thirteen cents, fourteen cents, fifteen cents, admission to a cheap movie, a hamburger and coffee, three telephone calls, a package of Chesterfields, Camels, Lucky Strikes, or Old Golds.

That's what money is. Forty-eight cents, forty-nine cents, woof woof, fifty cents, a cheap room in a decaying building on a mean street, a hard bed containing eighty-five, eighty-six, woof woof, lice.

Money. What is the stuff? Nothing; it's nothing, it's only twenty-three, twenty-four, pennies, minutes, hours, days. That's what money is in Capitalist countries and that's what it is in Communist countries, and that's what it always has been and that's most likely what it always will be, and if you've got a lot of it, it's nothing, and if you haven't got any of it, it's everything.

And if you haven't got any of it, you're just as good as fresh out of everything: food, shelter, time, place, space, the earth, hydrogen, oxygen, life. Comrade, you're just as good as dead.

Unless.

Unless, mind you.

Unless, Comrade, you've got more of one thing than another and less of one thing than another, such as having less of pride than anger, and more of impudence than despair, and then, Comrade, money, although still sixty-six, woof woof, and everything else, is not exactly everything, because if you've got more of impudence than the opposites of it, you've got at least nine good chances out of ten.

To do what?

Well, Comrade, to do one of any number of noble, magnificent, humiliating, splendid things: beg, steal, or, in more accurate terminology, demand, take, or, in even more accurate and scientific terminology, function.

Function?

That's it, woof woof.

If you beg as a beggar, it's humiliating. If you do it as a scholar and as a gentleman and as at least the equivalent of any king of any country who ever lived, it is not humiliating, it is noble, it is magnificent, and you are not a bum, you are a hero.

In their terminology, though, they may call you a bum, but if you begged as at least the scientific equivalent of any king in the world, then they are liars, and you are all right.

And if you robbed as a scholar and as a gentleman, you are all right. You are as great a hero as any soldier who ever destroyed an enemy.

They don't know about such things as one cent, two cents, three cents, one street, two streets, no house, no door, no room, no bed, twenty-four hours of accumulated hunger, thirst, weariness, anger. They don't know what a nickel is, what a dime is, what a nickel and a dime together are, what two dimes together are, they don't know anything, they don't know what the world is, what life is, what beauty there is in a cup of coffee at three in the morning, what renewal, what delight, eighty-six, woof woof, they don't know what delight a bed is to a tired body, they don't know anything at all.

They tremble with fear, and that's the old song and dance again, twenty-two, twenty-three, the enemy closing in, woof woof, the government spending one penny, two pennies, one million dollars, two million dollars, one billion dollars: rooms, beds, sleep: life. They are scared to death. The poor dopes think it's their money, and they're scared to death about the old international melody, woof woof, closing in on them, taking away from them, balancing, proportioning, leveling off. They are afraid because they know if it were left to God and nature and the universe, if they were exposed to the hard, brittle, cold, endless dangers of the world, they would die. They would disappear like nothing.

They?

Who the hell are they? Well, fellow-citizens, they are the ones with plenty of it, and to them it doesn't mean a thing because, ordinarily, there would be no end to it, but now that it seems as if there might be an end to it, now that it seems they might be exposed to the world, they are full of trembling, and they hate the guts of Mr. Roosevelt.

They hate the guts of the old melody closing in on them, the way it's *got* to close in on them, in spite of all their organizing, in spite of all their newspaper editorials and phony news items, in spite of all their oratory and all their plans. The numbers are piling up against them, one hundred million, one hundred million and one, one hundred million and two, and three, and four, and five, and six, woof woof, people, human beings, like themselves, only different in that they have none of it, and don't die, and so it's getting them down, because these are millions of humanity, the great public, the lousy great public, the awful masses, sixty-four, sixty-five, woof woof, living, not dying, closing in on them, and who the hell are they? They are only people too, only men and women and children, although with plenty of it, and wanting to keep plenty of it, so what's to be?

Well, you Comrades can call it dialectical materialism, revolution, or anything else you like, but it is actually nothing, it is certainly no more than the crazy melody, woof woof, and I'm in favor of it, although it doesn't mean a thing, and as far as I can tell never will.

Citizens of the Third Grade

T om Lucca was incredible. Only eight years old, he was perhaps the brightest pupil in the third grade, certainly the most alert, the most intellectually savage, and yet the most humane. Still, his attitude seemed sometimes vicious, as when Aduwa was taken and he came to class leering with pride, the morning newspaper in his pants pocket, as evidence, no doubt, and during recess made the Fascist salute and asked the colored Jefferson twins, Cain and Abel, what they thought of old King Haile Selassie now.

Same as before, Miss Gavit heard Abel say. You got no right to go into Africa.

And Tom, who wouldn't think of getting himself into a fist-fight since he was too intelligent, too neat and good-looking, laughed in that incredible Italian way that meant he knew everything, and said, We'll take Addis Ababa day after tomorrow.

Of course this was only a gag, one of Tom Lucca's frequent and generally innocent outbursts, but both Abel and Cain didn't like it, and Miss Gavit was sure there would be trouble pretty soon no matter what happened.

If General Bono *did* take Addis Ababa and Tom Lucca forgot himself and irritated Cain and Abel, there would surely be trouble between the colored boys in the Third Grade and the Italian boys, less brilliant perhaps than Tom Lucca, but more apt to accept trouble, and fight about it: Pat Ravenna, Willy Trentino, Carlo Gaeta, and the others. Enough of them certainly. And then there were the other grades. The older boys.

On the other hand, if Ras Desta Demtu, the son-in-law of Emperor Haile Selassie, turned back the Italian forces at Harar, Cain and Abel, somewhat sullenly, would be triumphant without saying a word, as when Joe Louis, the Brown Bomber of Detroit, knocked out and humiliated poor Maxie Baer, and Cain and Abel came to class whistling softly to themselves. Everybody, who normally didn't dislike the boys, quiet and easy-going as they were, deeply resented them that morning.

No matter what happened, Miss Gavit believed, there would be trouble at Cosmos Public School, and it seemed very strange that this should be so, since these events were taking place thousands of miles away from the school and did not concern her class of schoolchildren, each of whom was having a sad time with the new studies, fractions and English grammar.

Tom Lucca was impossible. He had no idea how dangerous his nervous and joyous behavior was getting to be. It was beginning to irritate Miss Gavit herself who, if anything, was in favor of having the ten million Ethiopians of Abyssinia under Italian care, which would do them much less harm than good and probably furnish some of the high government officials with shoes and perhaps European garments.

It was really amazing that many of the leaders of Abyssinia performed their duties bare-footed. How could anybody be serious without shoes on his feet, and five toes of each foot visible? And when they walked no important sound of moving about, as when Americans with shoes on their feet moved about.

Of course she hated the idea of going into an innocent and peaceful country and bombing little cities and killing all kinds of helpless people. She didn't like all the talk about poison gases and machine guns and liquid fire. She thought it was very cruel of the Italians to think of killing people in order to gain a little extra land in which to expand, as Mussolini said.

Miss Gavit just bet ten cents the Italians could do all the expanding they needed to do right at home, in the 119,000 square miles of Italy. She just bet ten cents with anybody that Mussolini didn't really need more land, all he wanted to do was show off and be a hero. It was dreadful the way some people wanted to be great, no matter how many people they killed. It wasn't as if the people of Abyssinia were pagans; they were Christians, just like the Italians: their church was the Christian church, and they worshiped Jesus, the same as Pope Pius.

(The Pope, though, was a man Miss Gavit didn't like. She saw him in a Paramount News Reel, and she didn't like his face. He looked sly for a holy man. She didn't think he was really holy. She thought he looked more like a scheming politician than like a man who was humble and good and would rather accept pain for himself than have it inflicted upon others. He was small and old and cautious. First he prayed for peace, and then Italy went right ahead and invaded Abyssinia. Then Pope Pius prayed for peace again, but it was war just the same. Who did he think he was fooling?

She guessed every important man in the world was afraid, the same as the Pope. Poor loud-mouthed Huey got his, and for what? What did poor

Huey want for the people except a million dollars for every family? What was wrong with that? Why did they have to kill a man like that, who really had the heart of a child, even if he did shout over the radio and irritate President Roosevelt by hinting that he, Huey Long of Louisiana, would be the next President of the United States? What did they want to invent guns for in the first place? What good did guns do the people of the world, except teach them to kill one another? First they worried about wild animals, and then Indians, and then they began worrying about one another, France worrying about Germany, Germany worrying about France and England and Russia, and Russia worrying about Japan, and Japan worrying about China.

Miss Gavit didn't know. Site couldn't quite understand the continuous mess of the world. When it was the World War she was a little girl in grammar school who thought she would be a nun in a convent, and then a little later, a singer in opera: that was after the San Carlo opera troupe came to town and gave a performance of *La Bohème* at the Hippodrome Theatre and Miss Gavit went home crying about poor consumptive Mimi. Then the war ended and the parades ended and she began to forget her wilder dreams, like the dream of some day meeting a fine man like William Farnum and being his wife, or the still more fantastic dream of suddenly learning from authoritative sources that she was the true descendant of some royal European family, a princess, and all the other wild dreams of sudden wealth and ease and fame and importance, sudden surpassing loveliness, the most beloved young lady of the world. And sobering with the years, with the small knowledge of each succeeding grade at school, she chose teaching as her profession, and finally, after much lonely studying, full of sudden clear-weather dreaming of love, she graduated from the normal school, twenty-two years old, and was a teacher, if she could get a job.

She was very lucky, and for the past five years had been at Cosmos Public School, in the foreign section of the city, west of the Southern Pacific tracks, where she herself was born and lived. Her father was very happy about this good luck. The money she earned helped buy new furniture, a radio, and later on a Ford, and send her little sister Ethel to the University of California. But she didn't know. So many things were happening all over the world she was afraid something dangerous would happen, and very often, walking home from school, late in the afternoon, she would suddenly feel the nearness of this danger with such force that she would unconsciously begin to walk faster and look about to see if anything were changed, and at the same time remember poignantly all the little boys and girls who had passed through her class and gone on to the higher grades, as if these young people were in terrible danger, as if their lives might suddenly end, with terrific physical pain.

And now, with this trouble between Italy and Abyssinia, Benito Mussolini, Dictator of Italy, and Haile Selassie, the Lion of Judah, Miss Gavit began, as Tom Lucca's joyousness increased, to feel great inward alarm about the little boy because she knew truthfully that he was very kind-hearted, and only intellectually mischievous. How many times had she seen him hugging Mrs. Amadio's little twenty-month-old daughter, chattering to the baby in the most energetic Italian, kissing it, shouting at Mrs. Amadio, and Mrs. Amadio guffawing in the loudest and most delightful manner imaginable, since Tom was such a wit, so full of innocent outspokenness, sometimes to the extent even of being almost vulgar. The Italians. That's the way they were, and it was not evil, it was a virtue. They were just innocent. They chattered about love and passion and child-birth and family quarrels as if it were nothing, just part of the day's experience. And how many times had she seen Tom Lucca giving sandwiches from his lunch to Johnny Budge whose father had no job and no money? And not doing it in a way that was self-righteous. She remembered the way Tom would say, Honest, Johnny, I can't eat another bite. Go ahead, I don't want this sandwich. I already ate three. I'll throw it away if you don't take it. And Johnny Budge would say, All right, Tom, if you're sure you don't want it. That was the strange part of it, the same little Italian boy being fine like that, giving away his lunch, and at the same time so crazy-proud about the taking of Aduwa, as if that little mud-city in Africa had anything to do with him, coming to class with the morning paper and leering at everybody, stirring the savage instincts of the Negro twins, Cain and Abel Jefferson.

Miss Gavit believed she would do something to stop all the nonsense. She wouldn't sit back and see something foolish and ugly happen right under her nose. She knew what she would do. She would keep Tom Lucca after school.

When the last pupil had left the room and the door was closing automatically and slowly, Miss Gavit began to feel how uneasy Tom was, sitting still but seeming to be moving about, looking up at her, and then at the clock, and then rolling his pencil on the desk. When the door clicked shut, she remembered all the little boys she had kept in after school during the five years at Cosmos and how it was the same with each of them, resentment at accusation, actual or implied, and dreadful impatience, agonized longing to be free, even if, as she knew, many of them really liked her, did not hate her as many pupils often hated many teachers, only wanting to be out of the atmosphere of petty crime and offense, wanting to be restored to innocence, the dozens and dozens of them. She wondered how she would be able to tell Tom why she had kept him after school and explain how she wanted his behavior, which was always subtle, to change, not in energy, but in impulse. How would she be able to tell him not to be so proud about what Mussolini was doing? Just be calm about the whole business until Italy annexed Abyssinia and everything became normal in the world again, at least more or less normal, and Cain and Abel Jefferson didn't go about the school grounds apart from everybody, letting their resentment grow in them.

What's the matter now? Tom said. He spoke very politely, though, the inflexion being humble, implying that it was *he* who was at fault: he was ready to admit this, and if his offense could be named he would try to be better. He didn't want any trouble.

Nothing's the matter, Miss Gavit said. I want to talk to you about the war, that's all.

Yes, ma'am, he said.

Well, said Miss Gavit, you've got to be careful about hurting the feelings of Cain and Abel Jefferson.

Hurting their feelings? he thought. Who the hell's hurting whose feelings? What kind of feelings get hurt so easily? What the hell did I ever say? The whole world is against the Italians and *our* feelings ain't hurt. They want to see them wild Africans kick hell out of our poor soft soldiers, two pairs of shoes each. How about our feelings? Everybody hates Mussolini. What for? Why don't they hate somebody else for a change?

He was really embarrassed, really troubled. He didn't understand, and Miss Gavit noticed how he began to tap the pencil on the desk.

I don't know, he began to say, and then began tapping the pencil swifter than before.

He gestured in a way that was very saddening to Miss Gavit and then looked up at her.

You are an American, said Miss Gavit, and so are Cain and Abel Jefferson. We are all Americans. This sort of quarreling will lead nowhere.

What quarreling? he thought. Everybody in the world hates us. Everybody calls us names. I guess Italians don't like that either.

He could think of nothing to say to Miss Gavit. He knew she was all right, a nice teacher, but he didn't know how to explain about everybody hating the Italians, because this feeling was in Italian and he couldn't translate it. At home it was different. Pa came home from the winery and sat at the table for supper and asked Mike, Tom's big brother in high school, what the afternoon paper said, and Ma listened carefully, and Mike told them exactly what was going on, about England and the ships in the Red Sea, and France, and the League of Nations, and Pa swallowed a lot of spaghetti and got up and spit in the sink, clearing his throat, and said in Italian, All right, all right, all right, let them try to murder Italy, them bastards, and Ma poured more wine in his cup and Pa said in American, God damn it, and Tom knew how the whole world was against Italy and he was glad about the good luck of the army in Africa, taking Aduwa, and all the rest of it, but now, at school, talking with Miss Gavit, he didn't know what to say.

Yes, ma'am, he said.

Miss Gavit thought it was wonderful the way he understood everything, and she laughed cheerfully, feeling that now nothing would happen.

All right, Tom, she said. Just be careful about what you say.

You may go now.

Jesus Christ, he thought. To hell with everybody.

He got up and walked to the door. Then he began walking home, talking to himself in Italian and cussing in American because everybody was against them.

Tom was very quiet at the supper table, but when Pa asked Mike how it was going in Abyssinia and Mike told him the Italians were moving forward very nicely and it looked like everything would turn out all right before the League would be able to clamp down on Italy, Tom said in Italian, We'll show them bastards. His father wondered what was eating the boy.

What's the matter, Tom? he said in American.

Aw, Tom said, they kept me in after school just because I talked about taking Aduwa. They don't like it.

His father laughed and spit in the sink and then became very serious.

They don't like it, hey? he said in Italian. They are sorry the Italian army isn't slaughtered? They hate us, don't they? Well, you talk all you like about the army. You tell them every day what the army is doing. Don't be afraid.

The next day Cain Jefferson swung at Tom Lucca and almost hit him in the eye. Willy Trentino then challenged Cain Jefferson to a fight after school, and on her way home Miss Gavit saw the gang of Italian and colored and Russian boys in the empty lot behind Gregg's Bakery. She knew for sure it was a fight about the war. She stood in the street staring at the boys, listening to their shouting, and all she could think was, This is terrible; they've got no right to make these little boys fight this way. What did they want to invent guns for in the first place?

She ran to the crowd of boys, trembling with anger. Everybody stopped shouting when Miss Gavit pushed to the center of the crowd where Willy Trentino and Cain Jefferson were fighting. Willy's face was bloody and Cain was so tired he could barely breathe or lift his arms. Miss Gavit clapped her hands as she did in class when she was angry and the two boys stopped fighting. They turned and stared at her, relieved and ashamed.

Stop this nonsense, she said, panting for breath from excitement and anger. I am ashamed of you, Willy. And you, Cain. What do you think you are fighting about?

Miss Gavit, said Cain Jefferson, they been laughing at us about the Ethiopians. All of them, teasing us every day.

How about you? said Willy. How about when Joe Louis knocked out Max Baer? How about when it looked like Abyssinia was going to win the war?

Then three or four Italian boys began to talk at once, and Miss Gavit didn't know what to think or do. She remembered a college movie in which two football players who loved the same girl and were fighting about her were asked to shake hands and make up by the girl herself, and Miss Gavit said, I want you boys to shake hands and be friends and go home and never fight again.

Miss Gavit was amazed when neither Willy Trentino nor Cain Jefferson offered to shake hands and make up, and she began to feel that this vicious war in Abyssinia, thousands of miles away, was going to bring about something very foolish and dangerous in the foreign section. In the crowd she saw Abel Jefferson, brooding sullenly and not speaking, a profound hate growing in him, and she saw Tom Lucca, his eyes blazing with excitement and delight, and she knew it was all very horrible because, after all, these were only little boys.

And then, instead of shaking hands and making up as she had asked them to do, Willy Trentino and Cain Jefferson, and all the other boys, began to move away, at first walking, and then, overcome with a sense of guilt, running, leaving the poor teacher standing in the empty lot, bewildered and amazed, tearing her handkerchief and crying. They hadn't shaken hands and made up. They hadn't obeyed her. They had run away.

She cried bitterly, but not even one small tear fell from her eyes. When old Paul Gregg stepped from the bakery into the lot and said, What's the trouble, Miss Gavit? the little teacher said, Nothing, Mr. Gregg. I want a loaf of bread. I thought I would come in through the back way.

When she got home she took the loaf of white bread out of the brown paper bag and placed it on the red and blue checkered table-cloth of the kitchen table and stared at it for a long time, thinking of a thousand things at one time and not knowing what it was she was thinking about, feeling very sorrowful, deeply hurt, angry with everybody in the world, the Italians, the Pope, Mussolini, the Ethiopians, the Lion of Judah, and England.

She remembered the faces of the boys who were fighting, and the boys who were watching. She breathed in the smell of the bread, and wondered what it was all about everywhere in the world, little Tom Lucca kissing Mrs. Amadio's baby and giving Johnny Budge his sandwich and leering at everybody because of the taking of Aduwa, the Negro twins joyous about Joe Louis and sullen about Abyssinia. The bread smelled delicious but sad and sickening, and Abel Jefferson watching his brother fighting Willy Trentino, and the *Morning Chronicle* with news of crime everywhere, and the *Evening Bee* with the same news, and the holy Pope coming out on the high balcony and making a holy sign and looking sly, and somebody shooting poor Huey Long, and none of her pupils being able to understand about English grammar and fractions, and her wild dreams of supreme loveliness, and her little sister at the University of California, and the day ending. She folded her arms on the table and hid her head. With her eyes closed she said to herself, They killed those boys, they killed them, and she knew they were killing everybody everywhere, and with her eyes shut the smell of the fresh loaf of bread was sickening and tragic, and she couldn't understand anything.

from
The Whole Voyald

A Writer's Declaration

On October 15, 1934, my first book, *The Daring Young Man on the Flying Trapeze and Other Stories*, was published. The year 1934 seems quite near, but the fact remains that it was twenty years ago, as I write. Many things happened in those twenty years, several of them to me.

I didn't earn one dollar by any means other than writing. I wrote short stories, plays, novels, essays, poems, book reviews, miscellaneous comment, letters to editors, private letters, and songs.

Nothing that I wrote was written to order, on assignment, or for money, although a good deal of what I wrote happened to earn money. If an editor liked a story as I had written it, he could buy it. If he wanted parts of it written over, I did not do that work. Nobody did it. One editor took liberties with a short piece about Christmas, and the writer of a cook book to which I had written a free Preface added a few lines by way of making me out a soldier-patriot. I protested to the editor and to the writer of the cook book, but of course the damage had been done. During the Second World War I wrote no propaganda of any kind, although I was invited several times to do so. The point is that for twenty years I have been an American writer who has been entirely free and independent.

I consider the past twenty years the first half of my life as a published writer, and the next twenty I consider the second half. At that time I shall be sixty-six years old, which can be very old, or not. I expect to be more creative in the next twenty years than I was in the first twenty, even though I start with a number of handicaps. To begin with, I owe so much in back taxes that it is very nearly impossible arithmetically to even the score by writing, and I have acquired other personal, moral, and financial responsibilities.

I have never been subsidized, I have never accepted money connected with a literary prize or award, I have never been endowed, and I have never received a grant or fellowship. A year or two after my first book was published I was urged by friends to file an application for a Guggenheim Fellowship. Against my better judgment I filed an application, which was necessarily if not deliberately haphazard. How should I know what I wanted to write, for instance? I couldn't possibly describe it. My application was turned down and I began to breathe freely again.

I am head over heels in debt. I expect to get out of debt by writing, or not at all. I have no savings account, no stocks or bonds, no real estate, no insurance, no cash, and no real property that is convertible into anything like a sum of money that might be useful. I simply have got to hustle for a living. I mention these matters impersonally, as facts, and not to arouse sympathy. I don't want any.

Had my nature been practical I might at this time know financial security, as it's called. There is nothing wrong with such security, I suppose, but I prefer another kind. I prefer to recognize the truth that I *must* work, and to believe that I *can*.

I squandered a great deal of money that I earned as a writer and I lost a lot of it gambling. It seems to have been my nature to squander and to gamble, that's all. I gave some away, perhaps a great deal. I am not unaware of the possible meaning of the discomfort I have felt when I have had money, and the compulsion I have had to get rid of it somehow or other. I think I have felt the need to be only a writer, a writing writer, and not a success of any kind.

The ability or compulsion to hoard money has always seemed to me a complicated if not offensive thing. And yet I have always had sympathy for those who have been experts at hoarding, at legal means by which not to pay taxes, at timely thrusts into new and profitable areas of money-making, such as investments, real estate, inventions, oil, uranium, government contracts, the backing of plays, manufacturing, and marketing. The noticeable shrewdness of such people has always amused me, even when I myself have been the party to be outwitted.

When I was in the Army, for instance, in the snow of Ohio, in the dead of winter, a very capable money-man who was quite rich and young and not in the Army flew from New York to Ohio to discuss with me changes he felt I ought to make in one of my plays on which he had paid me a thousand dollars in advance. I met him whenever the Army regulations permitted me to, and I heard him out, which took a great deal of time I would have preferred to keep to myself. The man talked around and around, and it suddenly occurred to me that what he was really trying to say but couldn't was that he didn't feel the play would be a hit, and that he was helpless not to do something about the thousand dollars. This did not astonish me. I took a check for a thousand dollars to his hotel and left it at the desk, along with a short note. I wanted to see if my hunch was right. It was. We were supposed to meet the following night. We didn't. He flew back to New York with the check, cashed it, and I never heard from him again. There was no legal, or even moral, reason for me to return the thousand dollars. I simply couldn't bear to see him so upset about the small sum of money, all the while pretending that he was concerned only about art.

At one of the biggest moving-picture factories in Hollywood, when I discovered that I had been hoodwinked into making a poor deal, I met the executives who had done the brilliant hoodwinking, I established that they *had* done it, and I got into my car and drove to San Francisco. I was informed several years later that I had left behind wages due me under the terms of the hoodwinking agreement that amounted to something between five and fifteen thousand dollars. I never investigated the matter. The factory and its chief beneficiaries were hoarding profits by the millions, working diligently and profitably with the government on shabby propaganda films, and yet six or seven of the executives found it absolutely necessary to act in unison and to outwit the writer of a story they wanted desperately, from which they acquired three or four more millions of dollars. I have no idea what they have done with their money, but I am sure it has been something cautious and useless.

Before my first book was published I was not a drinker, but soon after it came out I discovered the wisdom of drinking, and I think this is something worth looking into for a moment.

In 1935 I drank moderately, and traveled to Europe for the first time, but the following nine years, until I was drafted into the Army, I drank as much as I liked, and I frequently drank steadily for nine or ten hours at a time.

I was seldom drunk, however. I enjoyed the fun of drinking and talking loudly with friends—writers, painters, sculptors, newspapermen, and the girls and women we knew in San Francisco.

Drinking with good companions can be a good thing for a writer, but let a writer heed this humble and perhaps unnecessary warning: stop drinking when drinking tends to be an end in itself, for that is a useless end. I believe I have learned a lot while I have been drinking with friends, just as most of us may say we have learned a lot in sleep. There is, however, a recognizable limit to what may be learned by means of drinking.

In the writing that I have done during the past twenty years, what do I regret?

Nothing. Not one word.

Did I write enough?

No. No writer ever writes enough.

Might I have written differently? More intelligently, for instance?
No.

First, I always tried my best, as I understand trying. Second, I believe I was quite intelligent all the time. Then, what about the theory of certain critics and readers that my writing is unrealistic and sentimental? Well, I think they are mistaken. In writing that is *effective* I don't think *anything* is unrealistic. As for my own writing, I think it has always been profoundly realistic if not ever superficially so. I don't think my writing is sentimental either, although it is a very sentimental thing to be a human being.

As I write, I am back in San Francisco, where I lived when my first book was published, where I have not lived in six or seven years, and the day is the thirteenth of October. I drove up from Malibu two days ago for a visit of ten or eleven days while my house on the beach is being painted inside and out. I did not drive to San Francisco in order to be here on the twentieth anniversary of the publication of my first book, but I shall be here on that day nevertheless.

Already I have walked in the various neighborhoods of San Francisco I have known, to notice again the various houses in which I have lived: 348 Carl Street, 1707 Divisadero, 2378 Sutter, 123 Natoma: and the various places in which I worked before I had had a story published in a national magazine: various branch offices of the Postal Telegraph Company—on Market Street in the Palace Hotel Building, on Powell Street at Market, on Taylor at Market in the Golden Gate Theatre Building, and at 405 Brannan, near Third.

I was a clerk and teletype operator in the first three offices, but I was the manager of the office on Brannan. I have always been a little proud of that, for I was the youngest manager of a Postal Telegraph branch office in America, nineteen years old and without a high school diploma.

Yesterday I walked through the Crystal Palace Market and visited the stand at which I once hustled potatoes and tomatoes, the *Fiore d'Italia*.

I went into the building at Market and Sixth where the offices of the Cypress Lawn Cemetery Company are located. I worked there, too.

The vice-president said, "Do you intend to make Cypress Lawn your lifetime career?"

I said, "Yes, sir."

I got the job.

I quit a month later, but working there was a valuable experience. I remember the arrival of Christmas week and the vice-president's bitter complaint that owing to the absence of an epidemic of influenza the company's volume of business for December over the previous year had fallen twenty-two per cent.

I remarked, "But everybody will catch up eventually, won't they?"

The vice-president lifted his glasses from the bridge of his nose to his forehead in order to have another look at me.

"I'm a writer," I said. "Unpublished."

He asked me to look at some slogans he had composed for the company: *Inter here. A lot for your money.*

I said he had a flair.

I walked along the Embarcadero to the Dodd Warehouse, across from Pier 17, for I worked there a month, too. The trouble with that job was the floating crap games of the longshoremen every lunch hour in empty boxcars or behind piles of lumber on the docks. My take-home pay every week was nothing, although I made a friend of the great Negro crapshooter and game manager who was called Doughbelly. The sunlight down there on the waterfront during those lunch-hour crap games was wonderful, and as I walked there yesterday I could almost see the huge old man calling the points of the game, and I had to remember that whenever he noticed I wasn't betting he correctly surmised that I was fresh out of funds and slipped me a silver dollar or two so that I might get back into the action.

Once, when I stayed away from the games for three days running in the hope of having a few dollars in my pocket for Saturday night, Doughbelly kept asking everybody, "Where's that Abyssinian boy?"

I was in the Dodd Warehouse eating sandwiches and reading Jack London, that's where I was.

It was at 348 Carl Street twenty years ago on this day, October 13, that I opened a package from Random House and saw a copy of my first book. That was a hell of a moment. I was so excited I couldn't roll a Bull Durham cigarette. After three tries I finally made it, and began to inhale and exhale a little madly as I examined the preposterous and very nearly unbelievable object of art and merchandise. What a book, what a cover, what a title page, what words, what a photograph—now just watch the women swarm around. For a young writer *does* write in order to expect pretty women to swarm around.

Alas, the swarmers aren't often pretty. This is a mystery that continues to baffle me. Pretty women swarm around fat little men who own and operate small businesses. They swarm around chiropractors who are full of talk about some of their interesting cases and achievements. They swarm around young men who wear black shirts and have five buttons on the sleeves of their sport coats, who have no visible means of support, who spend hours chatting amiably about last night's preposterous trivia as if it were history.

Pretty women swarm around everybody but writers.

Plain, intelligent women *somewhat* swarm around writers.

But it wasn't only to have pretty women swarm around that I hustled my first book into print. It wasn't that alone by a long shot.

I also meant to revolutionize American writing.

In the early thirties the word revolutionize enjoyed popularity and was altogether respectable, but a special poll invented by a special statistician would be the only means today by which to measure my success in revolutionizing American writing. To pretend that my writing hasn't had any effect at all on American writing, however, would be inaccurate. The trouble is that for the most part my writing influenced unpublished writers who remained unpublished, and to measure that kind of an influence calls for a lot of imagination and daring. The good writers that my writing influenced were already published, some of them long published, but the truth is that my writing *did* influence their writing, too, for I began to notice the improvement almost immediately. And I didn't notice it in short stories alone, I noticed it in novels and plays, and even in movies.

What did my writing have that might be useful to writing in general? Freedom.

I think I demonstrated that if you have a writer, you have writing, and that the writer himself is of greater importance than his writing—until he quits, or is dead.

Thus, if you *are* a writer, you do not have to kill yourself every time you write a story, a play, or a novel.

But why did I want to revolutionize American writing?

I had to, because I didn't like it, and wanted to.

And why, as a writer, was I unwilling to act solemn? Didn't I know that unless I acted solemn the big critics would be afraid to write about my writing? I knew. I refused to act solemn because I didn't feel solemn. I didn't feel I *ought* to feel solemn, or even dignified, because I knew acting dignified was only a shadow removed from being pompous. Some writers are naturally solemn, dignified, or pompous, but that doesn't mean that they are also naturally great, or even effective.

There simply isn't any mysterious connection between solemnity and great writing. Some great writers had great solemnity, but most of them had almost none. They had something else.

What is this other thing?

I think it is an obsession to get to the probable truth about man, nature, and art, straight through everything to the very core of *one's own* being.

What is this probable truth?

It changes from day to day, certainly from year to year. You can measure the change from decade to decade, and the reason you can measure it is that there have been writers (and others) who have been obsessed about it, too.

To become free is the compulsion of our time—free of everything that is useless and false, however deeply established in man's fable. But this hope of freedom, this need of it, does not for a moment mean that man is to go berserk. Quite the contrary, since freedom, real freedom, true freedom, carries the life and fable of man nearer and nearer to order, beauty, grace, and meaning—all of which must always remain correctable in details—revised, improved, refined, enlarged, extended.

Intelligence *is* arriving into the fable of the life of man. It isn't necessarily welcome, though, certainly not in most quarters. In order to be a little less unwelcome it must be joined by humor, out of which the temporary best has always come. You simply cannot call the human race a dirty name unless you smile when you do so. The calling of the name may be necessary and the name itself may be temporarily accurate, but not to smile at the time is a blunder that nullifies usefulness, for without humor there is no hope, and man could no more live without hope than he could without the earth underfoot.

Life rules the world, impersonal and free life. The anonymous living tell their story every day, with the help of professional or amateur writers, but the greatest storyteller of all is time and change, or death. But death is not our doom and not our enemy. Next to birth it is our best gift, and next to truth it is our best friend.

I am back in San Francisco on the occasion of the twentieth anniversary of the publication of my first book—the beginning of my life as a writer, as a force in the life of my time, as a voting representative of my anonymous self and of any and all others whose aspirations parallel my own—to live creatively, to live honorably, to hurt no one insofar as possible, to enjoy mortality, to fear neither death nor immortality, to cherish fools and failures even more than wise men and saints since there are more of them, to believe, to hope, to work, and to do these things with humor.

To say yes, and not to say no.

What advice have I for the potential writer?

I have none, for anybody is a potential writer, and the writer who *is* a writer needs no advice and seeks none.

What about courses in writing in colleges and universities?

Useless, they are entirely useless.

The writer is a spiritual anarchist, as in the depth of his soul every man is. He is discontented with everything and everybody. The writer is everybody's best friend and only true enemy—the good and great enemy. He neither walks with the multitude nor cheers with them. The writer who is a writer is a rebel who never stops. He does not conform for the simple reason that there is nothing yet worth conforming to. When there is something half worth conforming to he will not conform to that, either, or half conform to it. He won't even rest or sleep as other people rest and sleep. When he's dead he'll probably be dead as others are dead, but while he is alive he is alive as no one else is, not even another writer. The writer who is a writer is also a fool. He is the easiest man in the world to belittle, ridicule, dismiss, and scorn: and that also is precisely as it should be. He is also mad, measurably so, but saner than all others, with the best sanity, the only sanity worth bothering about—the living, creative, vulnerable, valorous, unintimidated, and arrogant sanity of a free man.

I am a writer who is a writer, as I have been for twenty years, and expect to be for twenty more.

I am here to stay, and so is everybody else. No explosive is going to be employed by anybody on anybody. Knowing this, believing this, the writer who is a writer makes plans to watch his health casually, and to write his writing with more and more purposeful intelligence, humor, and love.

I am proud of my twenty years, undecorated as they may be. I am proud to be a writer, the writer I am, and I don't care what anybody else is proud of.

The Rescue of the Perishing

There was a chicken hiding under a parked car on Van Ness Avenue, in the heart of town, on the first rainless day after eleven days and nights of storm, after the floods. And three cars farther down the street, there was a small dog hiding under another car.

He'd never have noticed them on his way home from the public library if they hadn't been so upset about something. The chicken, a big hen with mottled black-and-white feathers, was making noises that were for all the world almost human. And the little dog, a common lost dog not more than twice the size of a cat, was whimpering the same way, making almost the same appeal.

He'd passed up the chicken, astonished that it was there at all and half believing it must belong to the owners of the car, and then he came upon the dog.

It was after six, the streets were almost deserted, he was late for supper. He'd been to the library, examining the whole place—not one book, not one shelf of them, but the whole library, looking into one book after another, as if he were in search of something and knew what it was but just couldn't find it.

Whenever he was at the public library and got to searching that way he forgot time and supper and everything else, sometimes feeling glad about his luck, about drawing nearer to what he was looking for, and sometimes feeling miserable, believing his search was hopeless.

One afternoon during the eleven-day storm he rode out to Skaggs Bridge on his bicycle in answer to a radio appeal, riding six miles in heavy rain. There he got on a truck with twenty others, none of them under sixteen. He was twelve, and eager to prove that twelve years are enough to help in a flood. The truck traveled over muddy roads until it came to where the river was nearest flooding over. The men all smoked in the truck, and the boy took a cigarette when it was offered and tried his best to smoke it. He stayed with the men from five in the afternoon until one in the morning, and worked as hard as any of them. He stopped for coffee and sandwiches only when the others did, and together they put up a high bank.

But when the truck got back to the country store at Skaggs Bridge where he'd left his bike, the bike was gone.

He asked the old man at the store about the bike, telling where he'd put it and the kind it was. It was one he'd bought from Paul Saydak, who'd been rebuilding bikes for twenty years, working in the barn behind his house on Oleander Avenue. It was a lean bike, and strong. Paul Saydak had let him have it for $27.50, although Paul had said it was worth $35.

The old man in the store, at half past one in the morning, hardly knew what the boy was talking about, but he understood that the boy's bike had been swiped, and he couldn't help feeling upset about it. He didn't understand the part about Paul Saydak, but he went outside and let the boy point out to him where he had put the bike. Then he told the boy he hadn't been at the store at five in the afternoon, so he hadn't seen the bike at all. He said he would ask about it, though. He went to the driver of the truck and asked him to get the boy home.

The next day the boy took a bus to school, and the next afternoon he hitchhiked to Skaggs Bridge to ask at the store about his bike. But nobody knew what he was talking about, and he himself felt he was making quite a lot of a $27.50 bike in weather like that, the river free in a dozen different places and millions of dollars lost in damages of all kinds. The bike was gone, that's all. And there wasn't a great deal of interest in the fact that it *was* gone, or in the circumstances under which he had given somebody the best chance in the world to take off with it. He'd listened to the radio appeal for help, he'd got on his bike, he'd gone as fast as he could go to where they'd asked him to go, and there somebody had swiped his bike.

"The radio appeal wasn't to *you*," his father said the night after the bike had been stolen.

"I thought it was," the boy said.

"No," his father said, "it was to *me*, and I didn't go. You might have known they'd steal your bike."

"I didn't think they would."

"Well, they did. And since they did, and since they had no right to, no right even to be *tempted* to steal it—anybody at the store should have taken it inside and put it away somewhere—well, I'm going to buy you a new bike. Any kind you want. Any time you want it. Tomorrow. You pick it out and I'll buy it."

"That's not it," the boy said. "I don't want a new bike."

"Well, you've lost the old one," the man said. "Pick out the one you want and I'll buy it."

"I liked my bike because I'd bought it with money I'd earned myself," the boy said. He was a little angry with his father for being so angry with whoever had stolen the bike, and with people in general. He knew his father was sympathetic and *did* want him to have a bike, but he didn't like to see his father so angry about people and things in general. The angrier his father got with people, the kinder he became with his family.

"Perhaps it's just as well," his mother said to his father. "So few boys nowadays ride bikes to school, and motorists are so careless. Perhaps it's just as well he's had it stolen. It's always made me worry. Must you have another bike?"

"Of course he must," his father said.

"No," the boy said, "I think I'd rather not have one."

"I'm sure he doesn't want a new bike," his mother said.

"Oh, *are* you?' his father said. He turned to the boy and said, "I leave it to you. Think about it and let me know."

He rode the bus to school after that. It wasn't half as much fun as riding his bike, but it was all right. He couldn't move as freely as he'd moved for a year—for the year he'd had the bike. And every now and then he forgot that the bike had been stolen, so that when he stepped out of the house or out of school he believed he was on his way to his bike and a quick ride to wherever he was going.

Five days after the bike had been stolen, he took the bus after school and rode to town and went to the public library.

He took the place shelf by shelf, forgetting the bike and his father's anger. He read parts of plays, short stories, novels, travel books, histories, biographies, and philosophy. Everything he read seemed fresh and good and new, but not quite what he wanted, not what he was searching for. He was in the public library for hours, sitting down at last to read a story, not knowing the name of the story or who the writer was, and not stopping until the story came to a description of a meal, making him hungry. He looked at the clock and saw that it was twenty past six. His father would be getting home in a few minutes, and supper would start in half an hour. He left the book open on the table and hurried out of the library to the street. The sky was clear and the air seemed clean and fresh, as if nobody had ever breathed it. If he waited for a bus, he might not get home any sooner than if he walked, so he decided to cut through town and enjoy a swift glance at anything he came to, and then get on home. It was a walk of about a mile and a half, but he felt like walking.

When he heard the chicken under the parked car on Van Ness Avenue, he couldn't imagine what it was that was making such a sorrowful appeal for help. Every day the paper was full of stories about strange things that had happened during the storm, so he felt the noise had something to do with it, too. But he didn't expect it to be a chicken, and he didn't expect it to be under a car.

He was some time finding out what it was and where it was, and when he saw that it *was* a chicken under a car he didn't feel that he ought to try to do something for it. It might just belong to the people who owned the car, and they might think he was stealing it. But when he came to the whimpering dog, he knew it belonged to no one, and he was sure he couldn't just leave it there. He called to the dog, but the dog was afraid of him. It took a good three or four minutes to stop the dog from being afraid. The dog crawled out from under the car, still struggling with its fear. The boy was very gentle with the dog, speaking softly and not touching it for some time. At last he began to stroke the dog's head. The dog got to its feet and barked, but all it could manage was one little sound that was more like a cough than a bark.

He picked it up and walked back to where the chicken was.

He set the dog down on the pavement and said, "Now, you just stand there. I'm going to take you home and give you some food and a warm place to sleep, but I've got to get this chicken, too."

The dog watched him and listened to his voice, but couldn't stand still and couldn't understand. It managed to bark again once. It ran off a little, whimpering, and then came back and asked if the boy wanted it to go away.

"Now, will you just stand there a minute while I see about the chicken?" the boy said. "There's a lost chicken under the car here that I've got to take home and take care of, too."

The dog seemed to understand a little, so the boy went around to the back of the car where the hen was sitting as if it were hatching. He began to talk to it, but a bird is a bird, even if it's a hen, and a bird, even if it's lost and sick, has *got* to be afraid of a human being. The hen got to its feet, but not all the way up: not because there wasn't room enough under the car, but because in fear all creatures, even men, do not rise to their full height: only in pride or exultation do they stand very tall, as men do when they are glad about themselves or as roosters do when they are overwhelmed about themselves and must push themselves to the limits of themselves, and then, half dying with joy, crow about who they are and what they can do. The lost hen wobbled to the next car, and then to a third car, the boy going after it slowly and speaking to it softly. He had to crawl under the third car to reach the hen and bring it out.

When the dog saw the hen it began to dance, growling softly—partly, perhaps, because it was a dog and the bird was a bird, and partly, perhaps, because another lost creature had been rescued.

"All right," the boy said to both of them. "Now we're going home."

The dog stayed close to the boy's heels, barking now and then, and the hen stopped being frightened. When the boy got home he picked up the dog and went in through the back door.

He stepped into the dining room, the dog under one arm, the chicken under the other, the eyes of both creatures open and unsure. Everybody at the table stared at the boy, the dog, and the hen.

"I found them," the boy said. "They were hiding under cars on Van Ness. They were both crying. I thought I'd better bring them home."

"Orphans of the storm, is that it?" the father said. "That's not a bad-looking dog."

"Can I keep them?" the boy asked.

"A dog and a chicken?" the mother said.

"They won't be any trouble," the boy said. "I'll fix up a small coop with a nest and a perch for the hen, and the dog can sleep in a box in the garage. Can I keep them?"

"Can he?" his father asked his mother.

"Can he?" the boy's kid brothers asked.

"Well," his mother said, "are you sure you *want* to? I mean, nobody keeps chickens in their yards any more, and dogs—*some* dogs—have a way of getting the people who own them into a lot of trouble."

"I'd like to keep them," the boy said.

"They were lost. Nobody wanted them. I found them. They were afraid of me. I had to talk to them. It wasn't easy, especially the hen. I didn't buy them, but I do feel they are mine, and I'd like to keep them."

"Well," his mother said. She turned to his father. "Are you sure it's all right?"

"I don't know why not," his father said.

"All right," his mother said. She got up. "I'll help you put them away until after you've had your supper."

"No," the boy said, "you go ahead. They're both hungry. I'll give the dog a little warm milk to start, and the hen maybe a little rice or something. I won't be a minute."

All the same, his mother went with him to the kitchen and warmed milk for the dog. The boy set the chicken on the floor, and his mother sprinkled rice in front of it, and soon both creatures began to eat and come alive in earnest.

After supper, the boy went to the garage with his younger brothers, and they fixed the hen a small coop with a perch and a nest, and the dog a little house, made out of a small box, with rags on the bottom for a bed.

While they were out in the garage, the boy's father and mother sat in the living room and talked.

"Well, so far he's said nothing about a new bike," the man said. "That bike meant everything in the world to him. You know it did."

"Yes," the woman said, "but *that* bike only. *His* bike. The bike bought with his own money. No other bike can take its place. Something else has got to."

"A stray dog and a tired old hen?" the man said.

"Well, yes," the woman said. "They're *his*. I don't think he'll ever have another bike. I don't think he'll ever want another one. The next time he saves up some money, he'll buy something else. But he did love his bike. It became part of him. He knows it's gone forever, though."

"Then I shouldn't surprise him and bring home a new one?" the man said.

"No," the woman said. "He wouldn't like it. Not *really*. Oh, he'd like it, of course, but it couldn't possibly be what his own bike was."

"Yes, I suppose so," the man said. "Well, it was quite a storm at that, wasn't it?"

"Yes," the woman said. "Everybody's talked of nothing else."

"I can't imagine," the man said, "why you allowed him to ride his bike all the way to Skaggs Bridge in the first place."

"Can you imagine my asking him *not* to?" the woman said. "He *wanted* to. It seemed silly, of course, but it wasn't silly to him, and he *did* help. I mean he did actually do the same work as everybody else."

The man saw the whole thing very clearly: he saw a boy on a bike riding to the rescue of the world, and he laughed, perhaps because it can't be done, perhaps because it must, perhaps because only a small boy can believe it's worth trying to do.

The woman laughed, too, and then both of them stopped quickly, to resume their expressions of earnestness, for they heard him down the hall with his kid brothers, all of them on their way to the living room, to report on what they had done in the brave business of rescuing the perishing.

A Visitor in the Piano Warehouse

I work in the warehouse of Sligo, Baylie on Bryant Street between First and Second, directly under the curve of the Fremont Street ramp of the Bay Bridge in San Francisco. The warehouse is one block long, and half a block wide. It is full of pianos.

Sligo, Baylie is an old San Francisco music store located at the corner of Grant Avenue and Geary Street, about two miles from the warehouse. It has been in business one hundred and eleven years. The company occupies its own building of six floors. It deals in everything pertaining to music, as well as in radios, televisions, refrigerators, deep-freeze boxes, stoves, sporting goods, and many other things. I have never met Lucander Sligo III, who owns and operates the business.

The first Lucander Sligo founded the company with Elton Baylie. The business was a piano business exclusively for quite a number of years. Baylie had no sons, but his daughter Eltonia went into the company. Baylie hoped she would marry the first Lucander's son, but Eltonia married a man named Spezzafly when she was forty-four and he was ten or eleven years younger. Eltonia's husband wasn't interested in pianos, if in fact he was interested in Eltonia. He certainly wasn't interested in their son. He left Eltonia before the boy was born.

The staff at the warehouse of Sligo, Baylie consists of Eltonia's son, Oliver Morgan Spezzafly, now sixty-nine, and myself, Ashland Clewpor, twenty-four.

I have been at the warehouse a year and a half.

I applied for work at the personnel department of Sligo, Baylie, on the sixth floor. The girl in charge was quite impressed with the facts of my background, but she regretted very much that there was no opening.

"Unless," she said, "you wouldn't mind working at the warehouse."

"What kind of work is it?"

She then told me about O.M. Spezzafly. She warned me that over the past twenty-five years nobody had worked for him for longer than a month.

"Why not?"

She tried to tell me as nicely as possible that O.M., as she called him, was certainly entitled to an important position with the firm, with an important yearly salary, but that it had been absolutely necessary twenty-five years ago to make him manager of the warehouse—or, to put it bluntly, to get him out of the way.

As manager of the warehouse, O.M. had asked for a staff, she said, and Lucander Sligo III had insisted on letting O.M. have a secretary, a bookkeeper, a janitor, and an all-around piano man, one who could tune and repair pianos. The secretary quit after a week, though, and the others within a month. Little by little O.M. became adjusted to the idea of having a staff of only one.

"What does the job pay?" I said.

"Sixty-five dollars a week to start. There is a five-dollar raise every month, however."

"For how long?"

"For as long as you keep the job."

"Suppose I keep it three years?"

"You will get a raise of five dollars every month."

"What are my duties?"

"O.M. will let you know."

"Can you give me an idea what they *might* be?"

"I'm afraid not," the girl said. "All I know is that you will be at the warehouse eight hours a day Monday through Friday. I'm afraid I can't urge you to take the job."

Half an hour later I was at the warehouse, knocking at the front door. I knocked because the door was locked. At last I heard footsteps, light and swift, and the door was swung open. I saw a tall man who wore a dark business suit. I introduced myself, and he asked me to come to his office, the door of which was only a few feet from the entrance to the warehouse.

Mr. Spezzafly's office was large and handsomely furnished. His desk was enormous and expensive. His chair was made of black leather. Behind his chair was a large portrait in oils of his grandfather Elton Baylie, and beside it a portrait of his mother Eltonia.

The interview was short, although Mr. Spezzafly examined the form I had filled out at the personnel department.

"Ashland Clewpor?"

"Yes, sir."

"Let me show you your office, Mr. Clewpor."

We walked through pianos of all kinds, but not through a path of any kind, to the far end of the warehouse where a fence had been put around a small area. The fence began two feet from the floor and stopped at five feet. We entered through swinging doors and I saw a small area entirely bare of anything except a plain flat-top desk and a plain unvarnished chair. There was a telephone on the desk. Nothing else.

"Sit down, please, Mr. Clewpor."

I sat at the desk.

"Very good," Mr. Spezzafly said, and left.

I sat at the desk without moving for about ten minutes, and then I drew open the drawers of the desk and found all six of them empty. The whole office was a desk and a chair, surrounded by a fence.

At a quarter to five I decided to use the telephone, more for something to do than somebody to talk to. I thought I would call Newbegin's and ask if they could recommend a good book on pianos. I began to dial Information for the number, but while I was doing so I heard somebody say, "Yes?"

It was Mr. Spezzafly.

"I thought I would telephone Newbegin's to see if they have a good history of the piano."

"O.M. Spezzafly speaking."

"Yes, sir."

"May I ask who's calling?"

"There must be something the matter with the phone, Mr. Spezzafly," I said. "This is Ashland Clewpor."

"What is it, Mr. Clewpor?"

"I was wondering if I might telephone Newbegin's."

"What is Newbegin's?"

"It's a bookstore, sir."

"I'll call you back," Mr. Spezzafly said.

I thought he meant in a few minutes.

He called me back on Friday at five minutes to five.

"Mr. Clewpor," he said, "on your way out please stop at my desk and pick up your check."

"Yes, sir."

The check was in a green plate that might have served as an ash tray.

"You'll find it there every Friday," Mr. Spezzafly said. "Yes, sir. Thank you."

I took the check and folded it, so that if there was anything he might wish to tell me there would be time for him to do so.

"Well done," he said. "That was a perfect fold."

I waited a moment in the hope that he would say something about what I might expect next week, but he said nothing.

Saturday morning I visited the personnel department of Sligo, Baylie, and the girl there said, "Well?"

"I was wondering if there is anything you might care to tell me about Mr. Spezzafly."

"You haven't come to quit?"

"No, I don't think I have."

"What did you do all week?"

"Nothing."

"What did he do?"

"I don't know."

"Do you think him odd?"

"He doesn't *look* odd."

"You plan to stay, then?"

"Is there an opening here?"

"Well," the girl said, "to be perfectly honest, there is, but it's in the stove department, and it's sixty-five a week, with no raises at all. Certainly not for a year or two. Would you like to meet the manager of the stove department?"

"Well, if I kept my job with Mr. Spezzafly for a year I'd be getting a salary of one hundred and twenty five dollars a week, wouldn't I?"

"Yes, that's right," the girl said.

"That's pretty good, isn't it?"

"Yes, it is."

"Well, I'm not married."

"Yes, I noticed that you're not when I read your application last Monday."

"Well, after a year with Mr. Spezzafly if I said to you will you be my wife, what would you say?"

"I'm married," the girl said. "Do you want to meet the manager of the stove department?"

"No," I said. "Is there anything you can tell me about Mr. Spezzafly? I mean, what are my duties?"

"Well," the girl said, "if you've decided to stay with Mr. Spezzafly another week, why not ask him Monday morning?"

Mr. Spezzafly was standing outside the door of his office at eight o'clock Monday morning.

"I appreciate punctuality," he said. "The time is one minute to eight. I am apt to be here at *ten* minutes to eight, but it is quite all right for you to be here at one minute to eight."

"Yes, sir."

"I also appreciate a good appearance. A man who comes to work Monday morning looking fit is a man who is going to look fit all week."

"Mr. Spezzafly, what are my duties?"

"My boy," Mr. Spezzafly said, "your work is waiting for you in your office."

He nodded courteously and went into his office. I walked through the pianos and went into my office. I expected to see a stack of papers on my desk, but there wasn't anything there. I sat down and tried to guess who she had married, but I couldn't. A girl who is married is married, that's all.

The second week went by exactly like the first. Friday afternoon at five I picked up my check and went home. Saturday morning I went back to the personnel department, because I had to see her again.

"There's an opening in the refrigerator department," she said. "Would you like to meet the manager of the refrigerator department?"

"Who is he?"

"Mr. Stavros."

"How much is the salary?"

"Sixty-five, but there's no promise of a raise. Aren't you happy at the warehouse?"

"I don't know what I'm supposed to do."

"Yes, that's how it goes."

"I made a path through the pianos."

"Did Mr. Spezzafly approve?"

"He didn't say."

"Did he *use* the path?"

"No, but the day I made the path he phoned at a quarter to five and said that whenever I answer the phone in the future I should say, 'Ashland speaking.' I *had* been saying 'Hello.'"

"I believe he likes the path you made."

"Do you mean I should go ahead and do things like that?"

"Yes, I think so."

"Shouldn't I try to *sell* a piano?"

"Has anybody asked for one?"

"No, but he keeps the front door locked."

"Well, it *is* a warehouse, not a salesroom."

"What are the pianos for?"

"People trade in old pianos for various modern things, and we put the old pianos in the warehouse, that's all."

"Do you ever take them out?"

"There isn't much demand for old pianos."

"We've got a hundred and twenty-three of them. I counted them."

"Do you like being among a lot of pianos?"

"Yes, I *do*. I like to see those pianos every morning. Of course, I see them all day, too, but I mean when I go in there every morning I *especially* enjoy seeing them. There they are, I mean. *All* of them. All kinds of them. Who did you marry?"

"My husband is an accountant at Wells, Fargo. The refrigerator department is full of laughter and jokes all day long, because Mr. Stavros is such a humorous man. Would you like to meet him?"

"No, but if you have a sister, I'd like to meet her."

"I don't have a sister. There are three rather attractive girls in the refrigerator department, though. Perhaps you ought to leave the warehouse."

"I never *expected* to work in a warehouse. My ambition has always been to be famous."

"A lot of people think Mr. Stavros would have been famous if he had gone on the stage." She scribbled something on a piece of paper with some mimeographed typing on it. She folded the piece of paper and held it out to me.

"What is it?"

"An introduction to Mr. Stavros."

"I don't think I want to leave the warehouse just yet."

Monday morning at one minute to eight Mr. Spezzafly was standing outside the door of his office.

"Ash," he said, "if you'll go straight to your office and sit at your desk, I'm going to try something."

I went to my office and sat at my desk, and after two or three minutes the telephone buzzed and I lifted the receiver.

"Ashland speaking," I said.

"Ash," Mr. Spezzafly said, "I'm thinking of leaving the front door unlatched, so that it can be opened from the street without a key. I thought I'd try that this morning, and possibly this afternoon."

"Yes, sir."

"If somebody comes in, I'll let you know by telephone."

"Yes, sir."

"In case I don't happen to notice, though, and you *do*—"

Mr. Spezzafly stopped. I waited a moment, and then I said, "Yes, sir?"

"Well, Ash, what I mean is, find out who it is."

"Yes, sir. Shall I let you know?"

"I don't think so, Ash. This is only an experiment."

"Yes, sir."

Nobody came in all day Monday. Tuesday morning at half past ten my telephone buzzed and Mr. Spezzafly said, "I just want you to know, Ash, that I've left the door unlatched again."

"Yes, sir."

"On second thought, if somebody comes in, give me a ring. Just say, 'Visitor in the warehouse.' I'll understand."

"Yes, sir. Visitor in the warehouse."

"Precisely."

Nobody came in, but at a quarter to five I thought I'd phone him to ask if he wanted me to try to sell a piano.

When he lifted the receiver he said, "Visitor in the warehouse, Ash?"

"No, sir."

"Dang."

"I called to ask if you'd like me to try to sell a piano."

"Ash," Mr. Spezzafly said, "let's just call when there's a visitor in the warehouse."

"Yes, sir."

There wasn't a visitor all week. Friday afternoon I picked up my check and went home, and Saturday morning I went up to the personnel department again, and the girl there said, "I've got a rather exciting position to offer you in the sporting goods department. Mr. Plattock wants a likely-looking man to demonstrate the rowing machine and the limbering-up bicycle. Would you like to meet Mr. Plattock?"

"I don't know."

"You will be permitted to wear sports clothing supplied by Sligo, Baylie, and I have an idea you will make an excellent impression."

She began to scribble on the small piece of paper again, but I just wasn't thinking about demonstrating a rowing machine or a limbering-up bicycle, I was thinking about having a visitor in the warehouse.

"Could you come to the warehouse next Monday during your lunch hour?"

"I *could*—of course," the girl said. "Is there a particular reason why I *should*, however?"

"Well, Mr. Spezzafly is trying out something new. He's leaving the front door unlatched, so that anybody who wants to come into the warehouse from Bryant Street can do so, but all last week nobody came in. I thought if you were to come in, I could telephone Mr. Spezzafly."

"I see."

"Afterwards, we could go to lunch at the place next to the S.P. depot."

"I generally have lunch with my husband at a little place next door to Wells, Fargo."

"Could you skip lunch with your husband on Monday?"

"You'd rather not meet Mr. Plattock, then?"

"I don't think so. You see, when I start something, I like to try to see it through."

"Oh? You feel you've started something, do you?"

"Yes, I do."

"What is it that you feel you've started?"

"I've started to understand Mr. Spezzafly."

"Really?"

"Yes, and a few other things, too."

"What else have you started to understand?"

"Well, being famous, for instance. Now, being famous the way famous people are famous is not *really* being famous, but being famous the way Mr. Spezzafly's famous, that's being really famous. And a few others I know."

"Everybody at Sligo, Baylie has known about Mr. Spezzafly's fame for years. Who are the others?"

"Well, the way *you're* famous seems to me to be a way that's more famous than the way the famous movie actresses are famous."

"Well, that's very nice of you, but hardly anybody in the whole world knows me."

"That's the part I'm beginning to understand. You're famous without very many people knowing you, but the ones who *do* know you, *they* know you're famous."

"How do you know they do?"

"Well, I hardly know you, and I know you're famous, so just imagine how it is with those who really know you, like your husband, or your children, if you've got any."

"I haven't got any."

"But if you had some, wouldn't they know how famous you are, though?"

"Yes, I suppose they would, at that."

"Will you visit the warehouse?"

"Well, perhaps not Monday, but perhaps Tuesday or Wednesday."

"You'll find the door unlatched. My office is in the back, on the right."

Monday I took my lunch and ate it under the Fremont Street ramp of the Bay Bridge, while Mr. Spezzafly ate his at his desk. I don't know why he eats his sandwiches in his office. I eat mine in the streets because I enjoy walking during my lunch hour.

I walk down First Street to Pier 38 or down Bryant Street to Pier 28 and I look at the ships down there, and think.

I think about the past, the present, and the future, but mainly about the future, although I can't forget the past, especially where I spent so many years in the homes of people who wanted to find out if they wanted to adopt me, and decided they didn't—about when I was fifteen, and ran away because I wanted to live my own life, and when I was eighteen and got in the Marines and went to Korea and got wounded but didn't get killed, the way three of my pals did, just spent a year in different hospitals, and got discharged in San Francisco when I was twenty-two.

Mostly, though, on the lunch-hour walks I think about the future.

At twelve o'clock on Tuesday I didn't leave my office, even though I had no lunch to eat. I just sat at my desk, listening. There wasn't anything to listen to, but there *might* be pretty soon, and I wanted to be ready for it. At a quarter after twelve I heard it.

It was a visitor in the warehouse.

The footsteps came closer, and then the swinging doors of my office opened.

I got on the phone.

"Visitor in the warehouse, Mr. Spezzafly."

"Who is it, Ash?"

"Girl here in a blue dress."

"Thank you, Ash."

Mr. Spezzafly hung up, I hung up, and the girl in the blue dress stepped up to my desk and held out a piece of folded paper to me. It was the introduction form of the personnel department of Sligo, Baylie, and it said: *Introducing Miss Stella Mayhew to Mr. Ashland Clewpor. P.S. Good luck.*

I walked around the desk and put my hand out, and Stella Mayhew and I shook hands.

"I'm happy to make your acquaintance," I said.

Stella seemed awful scared, but I was awful scared myself, because in the first place I had expected the visitor to be the girl in the personnel department, a married girl, and in the second place Stella was the first visitor in the warehouse, and in the third place I had never seen a girl I liked so much.

Stella opened her handbag quickly and brought out a folded application. I unfolded it and started reading the answers she had given to the questions.

I wanted to be as businesslike as possible, so after I had read a few answers I said, "I see." I read a few more answers and again I said, "I see."

And then—well, I just took her in my arms and kissed her. I knew I ought to try to be a little more businesslike, but I kept thinking about the past and the future. I kept seeing the past all smoothed out on account of her, and I kept seeing the future just the way I'd always wanted to see it—a little house of our own, both of us famous, and a famous son, and a little later on a famous daughter.

I was kissing Stella when the telephone buzzed.

"Ashland speaking."

"What's the visitor want, Ash?"

"I don't know, sir."

"Everything in order?"

"Yes, sir."

"All right, Ash. I'll have my lunch, then."

"Yes, sir."

Again Mr. Spezzafly hung up and I hung up.

I took my chair around the desk and asked Stella Mayhew to please sit down, because I wanted to talk to her. She sat down, and I told her about my whole life, past, present, and future, and then I said, "I mean, I'm not really a business executive or anything like that. I don't have a job to offer, but I've got a job myself, and I plan to keep it, especially if there's something nice and sensible I can do with the money I earn. I'd like to make a down payment on a new house somewhere, but I wouldn't care to do that unless I had somebody to move in there with, to be my wife. That's the only job I can offer you—if it's all right. I've read the application and I like everything in it. And of course I can *see* you. I mean, I'm glad you've been in San Francisco only a week, and I'm glad you don't have any people, either, because I don't, either, and people who don't have any people—well, when they have one another, I guess it means something. Is it all right?"

"Yes, sir," Stella Mayhew said.

I was kissing her again when I heard Mr. Spezzafly coming down the path I had made through the pianos, but I just couldn't stop. Mr. Spezzafly pushed the swinging doors open, and I said, "Mr. Spezzafly, may I present Miss Stella Mayhew?"

"How do you do, Miss Mayhew," Mr. Spezzafly said.

"Miss Mayhew," I said, "is the future Mrs. Ashland Clewpor."

"Well, Ash," Mr. Spezzafly said, "I think that's very nice. You couldn't have found a nicer girl if you had looked all over the world." He smiled at Stella. "And you couldn't find a nicer boy," he said.

"Thank you, sir," Stella said.

"Not at all," Mr. Spezzafly said. He left the office, and Stella and I listened to him walking up the path back to his office.

Then Stella told me everything she knew about her own life, past, present, and future. She tried not to cry a couple of times, and made it, too, but one time she didn't. I didn't, either.

The year and a half that I've been employed in the warehouse of Sligo, Baylie has been the happiest time of my whole life. I don't ever expect to quit, although I've asked the girl in the personnel department to stop giving me the five-dollar raise every month.

"Not yet," she says. "Plenty of time to stop the raises. How is Mr. Spezzafly?"

"Just famous, the same as ever."

"And how is your wife Stella?"

"Just famous, too, thank you."

"And how is your son?"

"My son is the most famous man in the world."

"I've got a rather attractive position in the television department I can offer you," the girl in the personnel department says, but she just says that for the fun of it, because she knows I don't want to leave the warehouse.

She knows that when I start something I like to see it through.

The Return to the Pomegranate Trees

There are journeys you take again and again, like books you read or music you listen to, faces you see or people you speak to, and each time something is changed and something is the same.

There are places I heard about when I was a kid, and never saw, like the town Goshen, near Fresno. Ever since, I've planned to go to Goshen, but so far I haven't, although I've been to all the other towns anywhere near Fresno. It may be that Goshen isn't a town at all, or if it is, it's one of those towns you never know is a town, a crossroads and a store with a hound on the porch and a rooster badgering two hens alongside.

Oleander's another place like Goshen, but even though I've been to Oleander I can't remember where it is or what it's like.

Fresno is in the center of the great valley that is named San Joaquin, which is pronounced Wahkeen, about which my pal Fat Khashkhash's brother Leo sang to a student body at Longfellow Junior High in 1919 or 1920:

> San Joaquin, valley green,
> You're the nicest place I've seen.
> Orange blossoms scent the air.
> The sun is shining everywhere.

In order to get from Fresno to the central and north coast of California, and the cities there, you've got to get through the Coast Ranges, either by way of Pacheco Pass, which begins at Los Banos and ends at Hollister and Gilroy, or by way of the cut-through after Tracy, which ends around Livermore just before you get to the outskirts of Oakland.

But there are other ways, too, and I took one of them in August once. You go to Kerman, on to Mendota, and then you are on a dirt road in low hills with nothing around except hawks and now and then a flock of sheep and a Basque shepherd with his dog.

Pretty soon, though, and for miles, for an hour at least—traveling twenty-five or thirty miles an hour because you don't want to drive any faster and oughtn't to anyhow since the road is unmarked and unfamiliar—there is nothing, and except for the car you're driving you might be in Spain, Italy, Greece, or Asia Minor, and you almost believe you are.

The one thought that occurs to you is, "They sure could put a lot of fine people in here and make this whole place over into orchards and vineyards and towns, couldn't they?"

Well, if they could, they haven't, and in any case it isn't easy. It takes doing, and the people might prefer to stay in New York, anyway.

The road I followed has a number and a name, but I know neither: it has history, too, which I also don't know. It's a fine drive, though, and I expect to make it again.

The drives from Fresno to San Francisco or Los Angeles, around two hundred miles each, or from San Francisco or Los Angeles to Fresno are commonplace, but exciting every time I take them. I guess it has to do with leaving one place and heading for another.

The drives around Fresno, to the familiar places, are always pleasant, and I make them again and again, but the drive I want to remember is this one:

The first short story I wrote in the collection that became the book called *My Name Is Aram* was called "The Pomegranate Trees."

When I wrote the story I was in San Francisco. The year was 1935 and I had been away from Fresno on and off since 1926, about nine years. The story itself concerned a still earlier time, when I was fifteen, so that I was writing about stuff that seemed at the time far away.

I didn't know "The Pomegranate Trees" was to become the first of a series of stories. I thought it was only another story. I sent it to *The Atlantic Monthly*, after it had been rejected by a dozen or more editors. *The Atlantic* took it, and Edward Weeks, the editor, suggested that I write more stories of that kind. As a matter of fact, I *had* written more of them by that time, but his letter put me to work in earnest.

The story concerned 640 acres of barren land that my mother's younger sister's husband Dikran had bought and planned to transform into a garden.

On a portion of this land Dikran planted pomegranate trees—twenty acres of them.

I worked on the land, and I planted the trees, working with a man named Nazaret Torossian who had been a wrestler at one time.

The project failed, the land reverted to its original owners, the pomegranate trees were abandoned, and Dikran moved along to other projects.

But while Nazaret and I were planting the trees (we worked for weeks, tending the trees after they had been planted) I couldn't help thinking I would some day return to the orchard and see the wonderful trees loaded with the wonderful fruit.

Years went by and whenever I happened to be in Fresno I remembered the pomegranate trees and where Nazaret and I had planted them, but I never drove out there.

The drive was out Ventura Avenue to where a right turn takes you to Sanger, but you make a left turn there and follow the road eight or nine miles, and then somewhere in that area is the land of the pomegranate trees.

One year, at last, I made the drive again.

With me was my son, at that time aged five, named Aram after the boy in *My Name Is Aram*.

The drive began with no destination in mind. It was just a drive in the summertime along the roads, among the vineyards and orchards around Fresno. I stopped many times, so the boy could get out and pick grapes or peaches, and eat them.

After a while, though, I began to drive and not stop, and pretty soon I was at the place on Ventura Avenue where if you turn right you go to Sanger.

My father's younger brother Levon and his four sons had vineyards near Sanger, and I suppose I had had in mind visiting them, but I turned left and began to speed down the road.

"Where we going?" Aram said.

"I planted some pomegranate trees down here about twenty-five years ago."

At the proper place I stopped the car, and my son and I got out and began to walk over the dry land, as I had walked over it a quarter of a century ago.

"Where's the trees?"

"Well, we planted them somewhere around here, but they're not here any more."

"Where are they?"

"Nowhere. They died."

The whole place was taken over again by the little burrowing animals, the horned toads, and the jack rabbits. It didn't seem wrong, either.

I believed I might find one tree hanging on, but I didn't.

My son and I went back to the car and drove off.

"What are they?" he said.

"The little animals?"

"No, what you planted."

"Pomegranates."

"I want to see one."

I drove him to my father's brother's place in Sanger, and in the family orchard adjoining the house I showed him an old pomegranate tree, and the pomegranates on it. They weren't ready yet, but I took one off the tree and handed it to him.

My father's brother came out of the house and took us in, and we visited him for an hour or more.

When we got back to the hotel in Fresno and up to the room we were sharing I saw my son bring the pomegranate out of his pocket. He looked at it a moment, then placed it on the bureau.

The following morning we drove back to San Francisco by way of Pacheco Pass.

When we got home he put his stuff away, and I saw him place the pomegranate on his bureau.

It stayed there a long time. After more than a month it got to looking pretty sad. His mother wanted to know if she ought to throw it out.

"No," he said, "I want it."

Several days later the whole family drove to Fresno and the boy said, "Let's drive out there again."

"Where?"

"Where you planted the trees."

So once again, twice in forty days or so, I drove to a place I hadn't driven to in twenty-five years.

When my son and I had walked a hundred yards or more into the dry land and I had stopped to light a cigarette, I saw him bring the pomegranate out of his pocket. He glanced at it, glanced around at the whole place, and then very carefully set it down on the earth.

I waited for him to say something, but since he didn't I didn't either, and after a moment we went back to the car and drove back to Fresno.

He never said anything about the pomegranate again.

I haven't tried to figure it out, because they are always doing things like that, and there's no telling why.

Novels

My Name Is Aram

The Summer of
the Beautiful White Horse

One day back there in the good old days when I was nine and the world was full of every imaginable kind of magnificence, and life was still a delightful and mysterious dream, my cousin Mourad, who was considered crazy by everybody who knew him except me, came to my house at four in the morning and woke me up by tapping on the window of my room.

Aram, he said.

I jumped out of bed and looked out the window.

I couldn't believe what I saw.

It wasn't morning yet, but it was summer and with daybreak not many minutes around the corner of the world it was light enough for me to know I wasn't dreaming.

My cousin Mourad was sitting on a beautiful white horse.

I stuck my head out of the window and rubbed my eyes.

Yes, he said in Armenian. It's a horse. You're not dreaming. Make it quick if you want to ride.

I knew my cousin Mourad enjoyed being alive more than anybody else who had ever fallen into the world by mistake, but this was more than even I could believe.

In the first place, my earliest memories had been memories of horses and my first longings had been longings to ride.

This was the wonderful part.

In the second place, we were poor.

This was the part that wouldn't permit me to believe what I saw.

We were poor. We had no money. Our whole tribe was poverty-stricken. Every branch of the Garoghlanian family was living in the most amazing and comical poverty in the world. Nobody could understand where we ever got money enough to keep us with food in our bellies, not even the old men of the family. Most important of all, though, we were famous for our honesty. We had been famous for our honesty for something like eleven centuries, even when we had been the wealthiest family in what we liked to think was the world. We were proud first, honest next, and after that we believed in right and wrong. None of us would take advantage of anybody in the world, let alone steal.

Consequently, even though I could *see* the horse, so magnificent; even though I could *smell* it, so lovely; even though I could *hear* it breathing,

185

so exciting; I couldn't *believe* the horse had anything to do with my cousin Mourad or with me or with any of the other members of our family, asleep or awake, because I *knew* my cousin Mourad couldn't have *bought* the horse, and if he couldn't have bought it he must have *stolen* it, and I refused to believe he had stolen it.

No member of the Garoghlanian family could be a thief.

I stared first at my cousin and then at the horse. There was a pious stillness and humor in each of them which on the one hand delighted me and on the other frightened me.

Mourad, I said, where did you steal this horse?

Leap out of the window, he said, if you want to ride.

It was true, then. He *had* stolen the horse. There was no question about it. He had, come to invite me to ride or not, as I chose.

Well, it seemed to me stealing a horse for a ride was not the same thing as stealing something else, such as money. For all I knew, maybe it wasn't stealing at all. If you were crazy about horses the way my cousin Mourad and I were, it wasn't stealing. It wouldn't become stealing until we offered to sell the horse, which of course I knew we would never do.

Let me put on some clothes, I said.

All right, he said, but hurry.

I leaped into my clothes.

I jumped down to the yard from the window and leaped up onto the horse behind my cousin Mourad.

That year we lived at the edge of town, on Walnut Avenue. Behind our house was the country: vineyards, orchards, irrigation ditches, and country roads. In less than three minutes we were on Olive Avenue, and then the horse began to trot. The air was new and lovely to breathe. The feel of the horse running was wonderful. My cousin Mourad who was considered one of the craziest members of our family began to sing. I mean, he began to roar.

Every family has a crazy streak in it somewhere, and my cousin Mourad was considered the natural descendant of the crazy streak in our tribe. Before him was our uncle Khosrove, an enormous man with a powerful head of black hair and the largest mustache in the San Joaquin Valley, a man so furious in temper, so irritable, so impatient that he stopped anyone from talking by roaring, *It is no harm; pay no attention to it.*

That was all, no matter what anybody happened to be talking about. Once it was his own son Arak running eight blocks to the barber shop where his father was having his mustache trimmed to tell him their house was on fire. This man Khosrove sat up in the chair and roared, It is no harm; pay no attention to it. The barber said, But the boy says your house is on fire. So Khosrove roared, Enough, it is no harm, I say.

My cousin Mourad was considered the natural descendant of this man, although Mourad's father was Zorab, who was practical and nothing else. That's how it was in our tribe. A man could be the father of his son's flesh, but that did not mean that he was also the father of his spirit. The distribution of the various kinds of spirit of our tribe had been from the beginning capricious and vagrant.

We rode and my cousin Mourad sang. For all anybody knew we were still in the old country where, at least according to some of our neighbors, we belonged. We let the horse run as long as it felt like running.

At last my cousin Mourad said, Get down. I want to ride alone.

Will you let me ride alone? I said.

That is up to the horse, my cousin said. Get down.

The *horse* will let me ride, I said.

We shall see, he said. Don't forget that I have a way with a horse.

Well, I said, any way you have with a horse, I have also.

For the sake of your safety, he said, let us hope so. Get down.

All right, I said, but remember you've got to let me try to ride alone.

I got down and my cousin Mourad kicked his heels into the horse and shouted, *Vazire*, run. The horse stood on its hind legs, snorted, and burst into a fury of speed that was the loveliest thing I had ever seen. My cousin Mourad raced the horse across a field of dry grass to an irrigation ditch, crossed the ditch on the horse, and five minutes later returned, dripping wet.

The sun was coming up.

Now it's my turn to ride, I said.

My cousin Mourad got off the horse.

Ride, he said.

I leaped to the back of the horse and for a moment knew the awfulest fear imaginable. The horse did not move.

Kick into his muscles, my cousin Mourad said. What are you waiting for? We've got to take him back before everybody in the world is up and about.

I kicked into the muscles of the horse. Once again it reared and snorted. Then it began to run. I didn't know what to do. Instead of running across the field to the irrigation ditch the horse ran down the road to the vineyard of Dikran Halabian where it began to leap over vines. The horse leaped over seven vines before I fell. Then it continued running.

My cousin Mourad came running down the road.

I'm not worried about you, he shouted. We've got to get that horse. You go this way and I'll go this way. If you come upon him, be kindly. I'll be near.

I continued down the road and my cousin Mourad went across the field toward the irrigation ditch.

It took him half an hour to find the horse and bring him back.

All right, he said, jump on. The whole world is awake now.

What will we do? I said.

Well, he said, we'll either take him back or hide him until tomorrow morning.

He didn't sound worried and I knew he'd hide him and not take him back. Not for a while, at any rate.

Where will we hide him? I said.

I know a place, he said.

How long ago did you steal this horse? I said.

It suddenly dawned on me that he had been taking these early morning rides for some time and had come for me this morning only because he knew how much I longed to ride.

Who said anything about stealing a horse? he said.

Anyhow, I said, how long ago did you begin riding every morning?

Not until this morning, he said.

Are you telling the truth? I said.

Of course not, he said, but if we are found out, that's what you're to say. I don't want both of us to be liars. All you know is that we started riding this morning.

All right, I said.

He walked the horse quietly to the barn of a deserted vineyard which at one time had been the pride of a farmer named Fetvajian. There were some oats and dry alfalfa in the barn.

We began walking home.

It wasn't easy, he said, to get the horse to behave so nicely. At first it wanted to run wild, but, as I've told you, I have a way with a horse. I can get it to want to do anything I want it to do. Horses understand me.

How do you do it? I said.

I have an understanding with a horse, he said,

Yes, but what sort of an understanding? I said.

A simple and honest one, he said.

Well, I said, I wish I knew how to reach an understanding like that with a horse.

You're still a small boy, he said. When you get to be thirteen you'll know how to do it.

I went home and ate a hearty breakfast.

That afternoon my uncle Khosrove came to our house for coffee and cigarettes. He sat in the parlor, sipping and smoking and remembering the old country. Then another visitor arrived, a farmer named John Byro, an Assyrian who, out of loneliness, had learned to speak Armenian. My mother brought the lonely visitor coffee and tobacco and he rolled a cigarette and sipped and smoked, and then at last, sighing sadly, he said, My white horse which was stolen last month is still gone. I cannot understand it.

My uncle Khosrove became very irritated and shouted, It's no harm. What is the loss of a horse? Haven't we all lost the homeland? What is this crying over a horse?

That may be all right for you, a city dweller, to say, John Byro said, but what of my surrey? What good is a surrey without a horse?

Pay no attention to it, my uncle Khosrove roared.

I walked ten miles to get here, John Byro said.

You have legs, my uncle Khosrove shouted.

My left leg pains me, the farmer said.

Pay no attention to it, my uncle Khosrove roared.

That horse cost me sixty dollars, the farmer said.

I spit on money, my uncle Khosrove said.

He got up and stalked out of the house, slamming the screen door.

My mother explained.

He has a gentle heart, she said. It is simply that he is homesick and such a large man.

The farmer went away and I ran over to my cousin Mourad's house.

He was sitting under a peach tree, trying to repair the hurt wing of a young robin which could not fly. He was talking to the bird.

What is it? he said.

The farmer, John Byro, I said. He visited our house. He wants his horse. You've had it a month. I want you to promise not to take it back until I learn to ride.

It will take you *a year* to learn to ride, my cousin Mourad said.

We could keep the horse a year, I said.

My cousin Mourad leaped to his feet.

What? he roared. Are you inviting a member of the Garoghlanian family to steal? The horse must go back to its true owner.

When? I said.

In six months at the latest, he said.

He threw the bird into the air. The bird tried hard, almost fell twice, but at last flew away, high and straight.

Early every morning for two weeks my cousin Mourad and I took the horse out of the barn of the deserted vineyard where we were hiding it and rode it, and every morning the horse, when it was my turn to ride alone, leaped over grape vines and small trees and threw me and ran away. Nevertheless, I hoped in time to learn to ride the way my cousin Mourad rode.

One morning on the way to Fetvajian's deserted vineyard we ran into the farmer John Byro who was on his way to town.

Let me do the talking, my cousin Mourad said. I have a way with farmers.

Good morning, John Byro, my cousin Mourad said to the farmer.

The farmer studied the horse eagerly.

Good morning, sons of my friends, he said. What is the name of your horse?

My Heart, my cousin Mourad said in Armenian.

A lovely name, John Byro said, for a lovely horse. I could swear it is the horse that was stolen from me many weeks ago. May I look into its mouth?

Of course, Mourad said.

The farmer looked into the mouth of the horse.

Tooth for tooth, he said. I would swear it is my horse if I didn't know your parents. The fame of your family for honesty is well known to me. Yet the horse is the twin of my horse. A suspicious man would believe his eyes instead of his heart. Good day, my young friends.

Good day, John Byro, my cousin Mourad said.

Early the following morning we took the horse to John Byro's vineyard and put it in the barn. The dogs followed us around without making a sound.

The dogs, I whispered to my cousin Mourad. I thought they would bark.

They would at somebody else, he said. I have a way with dogs.

My cousin Mourad put his arms around the horse, pressed his nose into the horse's nose, patted it, and then we went away.

That afternoon John Byro came to our house in his surrey and showed my mother the horse that had been stolen and returned.

I do not know what to think, he said. The horse is stronger than ever. Better-tempered, too. I thank God.

My uncle Khosrove, who was in the parlor, became irritated and shouted, Quiet, man, quiet. Your horse has been returned. Pay no attention to it.

The Journey to Hanford

The time came one year for my sad uncle Jorgi to fix his bicycle and ride twenty-seven miles to Hanford, where it seems there was a job. I went with him, although at first there was talk of sending my cousin Vask instead.

The family didn't want to complain about having among its members a fool like Jorgi, but at the same time it wanted a chance, in the summertime, to forget him for a while. If he went away and got himself a job in Hanford, in the watermelons, all would be well. Jorgi would earn a little money and at the same time be out of the way. That was the important thing—to get him out of the way.

To hell with him and his zither both, my grandfather said. When you read in a book that a man sits all day under a tree and plays a zither and sings, believe me, that writer is an impractical man. Money, that's the thing. Let him go and sweat under the sun for a while. Him and his zither both.

You say that now, my grandmother said, but wait a week. Wait till you begin to need music again.

That is nonsense, my grandfather said. When you read in a book that a man who sings is one who is truly a happy man, that writer is a dreamer, not a merchant in a thousand years. Let him go. It is twenty-seven miles to Hanford. That is a good intelligent distance.

You speak that way *now*, my grandmother said, but in three days you'll be a melancholy man. I shall see you walking about like a tiger. I am the one who shall see that. Seeing that, I am the one who shall laugh.

You are a woman, my grandfather said. When you read in a book with hundreds of pages of small print that a woman is truly a creature of wonder, that writer has turned his face from his wife and is dreaming. Let him go.

It is simply that you are not young any longer, my grandmother said. That is the thing that is making you roar.

Close your mouth, my grandfather said. Close it, or here comes the back of my hand.

My grandfather looked about the room at his children and grand-children.

I say he goes to Hanford on his bicycle, he said. What do you say?

Nobody spoke.

Then that's settled, my grandfather said. Now, who shall we send with him? Which of the uncouth of our children shall we punish by sending him with Jorgi to Hanford? When you read in a book that a journey to another city is a pleasant experience for a young man, that writer is probably a man of eighty or ninety who as a child once went in a wagon two miles from home. Who shall we punish? Vask? Shall Vask be the one? Step up here, boy.

My cousin Vask got up from the floor and stood in front of the old man, who looked down at him furiously, twisted his enormous mustaches, cleared his throat, and put his hand over the boy's face. His hand practically covered the whole head. Vask didn't move.

Shall you go with your uncle Jorgi to Hanford? my grandfather said.

If it pleases my grandfather, I shall, Vask said.

The old man began to make faces, thinking it over.

Let me think a moment, he said. Jorgi's spirit is the foolish one of our tribe. Yours is also. Is it wise to put two fools together?

He turned to the others.

Let me hear your spoken thoughts on this theme, he said. Is it wise to put a grown fool and a growing one together, of the same tribe? Will it profit anyone? Speak aloud so I may consider.

I think it would be the natural thing to do, my uncle Zorab said. A fool and a fool. The man to work, the boy to keep house and cook.

Perhaps, my grandfather said. Let's consider. A fool and a fool, one to work, the other to keep house and cook. Can you cook, boy?

Of course he can cook, my grandmother said. Rice, at least.

Is that true, boy, about the rice? my grandfather said. Four cups of water, one cup of rice, one teaspoonful of salt. Do you know about the trick of making it come out like food instead of swill, or are we dreaming?

Of course he can cook rice, my grandmother said.

The back of my hand is on its way to your mouth, my grandfather said. Let the boy speak for himself. He has a tongue. Can you do it, boy? When you read in a book that a boy answers an old man wisely, that writer is probably a Jew, bent on exaggeration. Can you make it come out like food, not swill?

I have cooked rice, Vask said. It came out like food.

Was there enough salt to it? my grandfather said. If you lie, remember my hand.

Vask hesitated a moment.

I understand, my grandfather said. You are embarrassed about the rice. What was wrong with it? Truth is all that pleases me. Speak up fearlessly. If it is the truth fearlessly, no man can demand more. What embarrasses you about the rice?

It was too salty, Vask said. We had to drink water all day and all night, it was so salty.

No elaboration, my grandfather said. Only what is true. The rice was too salty. Naturally you had to drink water all day and all night. We've all eaten that kind of rice. Don't think because you drank water all day and all night that you are the first Armenian who ever did that. Just tell me that it was too salty. I'm not here to learn. I *know*. Just say it was too salty and let me try to determine if you are the one to go.

My grandfather turned to the others. He began to make faces again.

I think this is the boy to go, he said, but speak up, if you have something to say. Salty is better than swill. Was it light in texture, boy?

It was light in texture, Vask said.

I believe this is the one to send, my grandfather said. The water is good for the gut. Shall it be this boy, Vask Garoghlanian, or who?

On second thought, my uncle Zorab said, two fools, out and out, perhaps not, although the rice is not swill. I nominate Aram. Perhaps he should go. He deserves to be punished.

Everybody looked at me.

Aram? my grandfather said. You mean the boy who laughs? You mean loud-laughing Aram Garoghlanian?

Who else would he mean? my grandmother said. You know very well who he means.

My grandfather turned slowly and for half a minute looked at my grandmother.

When you read in a book, he said, about some man who falls in love with a girl and marries her, that writer is truly referring to a very young man who has no idea she is going to talk out of turn right up to the time she is ready to go into the ground at the age of ninety-seven. That writer is thinking of a younger type of man.

Do you mean Aram? he said. Aram Garoghlanian?

Yes, my uncle Zorab said.

What has he done to deserve this awful punishment? my grandfather said.

He knows, my uncle Zorab said.

Aram Garoghlanian, my grandfather said.

I got up and stood in front of my grandfather. He put his big hand over my face and rubbed it. I knew he was not angry.

What have you done, boy? he said.

I began to laugh, remembering the things I had done. My grandfather listened a moment and then began laughing with me.

Only he and I laughed. The others didn't dare laugh. My grandfather had instructed them not to laugh unless they could laugh like him. I was the only other Garoghlanian in the world who laughed that way.

Aram Garoghlanian, my grandfather said, tell me. What have you done?

Which one? I said.

My grandfather turned to my uncle Zorab.

Which one? he said. Tell the boy which mischief to acknowledge. There appear to be several.

He knows which one, my uncle Zorab said.

Do you mean, I said, telling the neighbors you are crazy?

My uncle Zorab refused to speak.

Or do you mean, I said, going around talking the way you talk?

This is the boy to send with Jorgi, my uncle Zorab said.

Can you cook rice? my grandfather said.

He didn't care to go into detail about my making fun of my uncle Zorab. If I could cook rice, I should go with Jorgi to Hanford. That was what it came to. Of course I *wanted* to go, no matter what the writer was who wrote that it was a fine experience for a boy to travel. Fool or liar or anything else, I *wanted* to go.

I can cook rice, I said.

Salty or swill, or what? my grandfather said.

Sometimes salty, I said. Sometimes swill. Sometimes perfect.

Let's consider, my grandfather said.

He leaned against the wall, considering.

Three large glasses of water, he said to my grandmother.

My grandmother went to the kitchen and after a moment returned with three large glasses of water on a tray. My grandfather drank one glass after another, then turned to the others, making many thoughtful faces.

Sometimes salty, he said. Sometimes swill, Sometimes perfect. Is this the boy to send to Hanford?

Yes, my uncle Zorab said. The only one.

So be it, my grandfather said. That will be all. I wish to be alone.

I moved to go. My grandfather took me by the neck.

Stay a moment, he said.

When we were alone he said, Talk the way your uncle Zorab talks.

I did so and my grandfather roared with laughter.

Go to Hanford, he said. Go with the fool Jorgi and make it salty or make it swill or make it perfect.

In this manner I was assigned to be my uncle Jorgi's companion on his journey to Hanford.

We set out the following morning before daybreak. I sat on the crossbar of the bicycle and my uncle Jorgi on the seat, but when I got tired I got off and walked, and after a while my uncle Jorgi got off and walked, and I rode. We didn't reach Hanford till late that afternoon.

We were supposed to stay in Hanford till the job ended, after the watermelon season. That was the idea. We went around town looking for a house to stay in, a house with a stove in it, gas connections, and water. We didn't care about electricity, but we wanted gas and water. We saw six or seven houses and then we saw one my uncle Jorgi liked, so we moved in that night. It was an eleven-room house, with a gas stove, a sink with running water, and a room with a bed and a couch. The other rooms were all empty. My uncle Jorgi lighted a candle, brought out his zither, sat on the floor, and began to play and sing. It was beautiful. It was melancholy sometimes and sometimes funny, but it was always beautiful. I don't know how long he played and sang before he realized he was hungry, but all of a sudden he got up off the floor and said, Aram, I want rice.

I made a pot of rice that night that was both salty and swill, but my uncle Jorgi said, Aram, this is wonderful.

The birds got us up at daybreak.

The job, I said. You begin today, you know.

Today, my uncle Jorgi groaned.

He walked tragically out of the empty house and I looked around for a broom. There was no broom, so I went out and sat on the steps of the front porch. It seemed to be a nice region of the world in daylight. It was a street with only four houses. There was a church steeple in front of the house, two blocks away. I sat on the porch about an hour. My uncle Jorgi came up the street, on his bicycle, zigzagging with joy unconfined.

Not this year, thank God, he said.

He fell off his bicycle into a rose bush.

What? I said.

There is no job, he said. No job, thank God.

He smelled a rose.

No job? I said.

No job, thank our Heavenly Father, he said.

He looked at the rose, smiling.

Why not? I said.

The watermelons, he said.

What about them? I said.

The season is over, he said.

That isn't true, I said.

The season is over, my uncle Jorgi said. Believe me, it is over.

Your father will break your head, I said.

The season is over, he said. Praise God, the watermelons are all harvested.

Who said so? I said.

The farmer himself. The farmer himself said so, my uncle Jorgi said.

He just said that, I said. He didn't want to hurt your feelings. He just said that because he knew your heart wouldn't be in your work.

Praise God, my uncle Jorgi said, the whole season is over. All the fine, ripe watermelons have been harvested.

What are we going to do? I said. The season is just beginning.

It's ended, he said. We shall dwell in this house a month and then go home. We have paid six dollars rent and we have money enough for rice. We shall dream here a month and then go home.

With no money, I said.

But in good health, he said. Praise God, who ripened them so early this year.

My uncle Jorgi danced into the house to his zither, and before I could decide what to do about him he was playing and singing. It was so beautiful I didn't even get up and try to chase him out of the house. I just sat on the porch and listened.

We stayed in the house a month and then went home. My grandmother was the first to see us.

It's about time you two came home, she said. He's been raging like a tiger. Give me the money.

There is no money, I said.

Did he work? my grandmother said.

No, I said. He played and sang the whole month.

How did your rice turn out? she said.

Sometimes salty, I said. Sometimes swill. Sometimes perfect. But he didn't work.

His father mustn't know, she said. I have money.

She lifted her dress and got some currency out of a pocket in her pants and put it in my hands.

When he comes home, she said, give him this money.

She looked at me a moment, then added: *Aram Garoghlanian.*

I will do as you say, I said.

When my grandfather came home he began to roar.

Home already? he said. Is the season ended so soon? Where is the money he earned?

I gave him the money.

I won't have him singing all day, my grandfather roared. There is a limit to everything. When you read in a book that a father loves a foolish son more than his wise sons, that writer is a bachelor.

In the yard, under the almond tree, my uncle Jorgi began to play and sing. My grandfather came to a dead halt and began to listen. He sat down on the couch, took off his shoes, and began to make faces.

I went into the kitchen to get three or four glasses of water to quench the thirst from last night's rice. When I came back to the parlor the old man was stretched out on the couch, asleep and smiling, and his son Jorgi was singing hallelujah to the universe at the top of his beautiful, melancholy voice.

The Pomegranate Trees

My uncle Melik was just about the worst farmer that ever lived. He was too imaginative and poetic for his own good. What he wanted was beauty. He wanted to plant it and see it grow. I myself planted over one hundred pomegranate trees for my uncle one year back there in the good old days of poetry and youth in the world. I drove a John Deere tractor too, and so did my uncle. It was all pure esthetics, not agriculture. My uncle just liked the idea of planting trees and watching them grow.

Only they wouldn't grow. It was on account of the soil. The soil was desert soil. It was dry. My uncle waved at the six hundred and eighty acres of desert he had bought and he said in the most poetic Armenian anybody ever heard, Here in this awful desolation a garden shall flower, fountains of cold water shall bubble out of the earth, and all things of beauty shall come into being.

Yes, sir, I said.

I was the first and only relative to see the land he had bought. He knew I was a poet at heart, and he believed I would understand the magnificent impulse that was driving him to glorious ruin. I did. I knew as well as he that what he had purchased was worthless desert land. It was away over to hell and gone, at the foot of the Sierra Nevada Mountains. It was full of every kind of desert plant that ever sprang out of dry hot earth. It was overrun with prairie dogs, squirrels, horned toads, snakes, and a variety of smaller forms of life. The space over this land knew only the presence of hawks, eagles, and buzzards. It was a region of loneliness, emptiness, truth, and dignity. It was nature at its proudest, dryest, loneliest, and loveliest.

My uncle and I got out of the Ford roadster in the middle of his land and began to walk over the dry earth.

This land, he said, is my land.

He walked slowly, kicking into the dry soil. A horned toad scrambled over the earth at my uncle's feet. My uncle clutched my shoulder and came to a pious halt.

What is that animal? he said.

That little tiny lizard? I said.

That mouse with horns, my uncle said. What is it?

I don't know for sure, I said. We call them horny toads.

The horned toad came to a halt about three feet away and turned its head.

My uncle looked down at the small animal.

Is it poison? he said.

To eat? I said. Or if it bites you?

Either way, my uncle said.

I don't think it's good to eat, I said. I think it's harmless. I've caught many of them. They grow sad in captivity, but never bite. Shall I catch this one?

Please do, my uncle said.

I sneaked up on the horned toad, then sprang on it while my uncle looked on.

Careful, he said. Are you sure it isn't poison?

I've caught many of them, I said.

I took the horned toad to my uncle. He tried not to seem afraid.

A lovely little thing, isn't it? he said. His voice was unsteady.

Would you like to hold it? I said.

No, my uncle said. You hold it. I have never before been so close to such a thing as this. I see it has eyes. I suppose it can see us.

I suppose it can, I said. It's looking up at you now.

My uncle looked the horned toad straight in the eye. The horned toad looked my uncle straight in the eye. For fully half a minute they looked one another straight in the eye and then the horned toad turned its head aside and looked down at the ground. My uncle sighed with relief.

A thousand of them, he said, could kill a man, I suppose.

They never travel in great numbers, I said. You hardly ever see more than one at a time.

A big one, my uncle said, could probably bite a man to death.

They don't grow big, I said. This is as big as they grow.

They seem to have an awful eye for such small creatures, my uncle said. Are you sure they don't mind being picked up?

I suppose they forget all about it the minute you put them down, I said.

Do you really think so? my uncle said.

I don't think they have very good memories, I said.

My uncle straightened up, breathing deeply.

Put the little creature down, he said. Let us not be cruel to the innocent creations of Almighty God. If it is not poison and grows no larger than a mouse and does not travel in great numbers and has no memory to speak of, let the timid little thing return to the earth. Let us be gentle toward these small things which live on the earth with us.

Yes, sir, I said.

I placed the horned toad on the ground.

Gently now, my uncle said. Let no harm come to this strange dweller on my land.

The horned toad scrambled away.

These little things, I said, have been living on soil of this kind for centuries.

Centuries? my uncle said. Are you sure?

I'm not sure, I said, but I imagine they have. They're still here, anyway.

My uncle looked around at his land, at the cactus and brush growing out of it, at the sky overhead.

What have they been eating all this time? he shouted.

I don't know, I said.

What would you say they've been eating? he said.

Insects, I guess.

Insects? my uncle shouted. What sort of insects?

Little bugs, most likely, I said. I don't know their names. I can find out tomorrow at school.

We continued to walk over the dry land. When we came to some holes in the earth my uncle stood over them and said, What lives down there?

Prairie dogs, I said.

What are *they?* he said.

Well, I said, they're something like rats. They belong to the rodent family.

What are all these things doing on my land? my uncle said.

They don't know it's your land, I said. They've been living here a long while.

I don't suppose that horny toad ever looked a man in the eye before, my uncle said.

I don't think so, I said.

Do you think I scared it or anything? my uncle said.

I don't know for sure, I said.

If I did, my uncle said, I didn't mean to. I'm going to build a house here some day.

I didn't know that, I said.

Of course, my uncle said. I'm going to build a magnificent house.

It's pretty far away, I said.

It's only an hour from town, my uncle said.

If you go fifty miles an hour, I said.

It's not fifty miles to town, my uncle said. It's thirty-seven.

Well, you've got to take a little time out for rough roads, I said.

I'll build me the finest house in the world, my uncle said. What else lives on this land?

Well, I said, there are three or four kinds of snakes.

Poison or non-poison? my uncle said.

Mostly non-poison, I said. The rattlesnake is poison, though.

Do you mean to tell me there are *rattlesnakes* on this land? my uncle said.

This is the kind of land rattlesnakes usually live on, I said.

How many? my uncle said.

Per acre? I said. Or on the whole six hundred and eighty acres?

Per acre, my uncle said.

Well, I said, I'd say there are about three per acre, conservatively.

Three per acre? my uncle shouted. Conservatively?

Maybe only two, I said.

How many is that to the whole place? my uncle said.

Well, let's see, I said. Two per acre. Six hundred and eighty acres. About fifteen hundred of them.

Fifteen hundred of them? my uncle said.

An acre is pretty big, I said. Two rattlesnakes per acre isn't many. You don't often see them.

What else have we got around here that's poison? my uncle said.

I don't know of anything else, I said. All the other things are harmless. The rattlesnakes are pretty harmless too, unless you step on them.

All right, my uncle said. You walk ahead and watch where you're going. If you see a rattlesnake, don't step on it. I don't want you to die at the age of eleven.

Yes, sir, I said. I'll watch carefully.

We turned around and walked back to the Ford. I didn't see any rattlesnakes on the way back. We got into the car and my uncle lighted a cigarette.

I'm going to make a garden of this awful desolation, he said.

Yes, sir, I said.

I know what my problems are, my uncle said, and I know how to solve them.

How? I said.

Do you mean the horny toads or the rattlesnakes? my uncle said.

I mean the problems, I said.

Well, my uncle said, the first thing I'm going to do is hire some Mexicans and put them to work.

Doing what? I said.

Clearing the land, my uncle said. Then I'm going to have them dig for water.

Dig where? I said.

Straight down, my uncle said. After we get water, I'm going to have them plow the land and then I'm going to plant.

What are you going to plant? I said. Wheat?

Wheat? my uncle shouted. What do I want with wheat? Bread is five cents a loaf. I'm going to plant pomegranate trees.

How much are pomegranates? I said.

Pomegranates, my uncle said, are practically unknown in this country.

Is that all you're going to plant? I said.

I have in mind, my uncle said, planting several other kinds of trees.

Peach trees? I said.

About ten acres, my uncle said.

How about apricots? I said.

By all means, my uncle said. The apricot is a lovely fruit. Lovely in shape, with a glorious flavor and a most delightful pit. I shall plant about twenty acres of apricot trees.

I hope the Mexicans don't have any trouble finding water, I said. Is there water under this land?

Of course, my uncle said. The important thing is to get started. I shall instruct the men to watch out for rattlesnakes. Pomegranates, he said. Peaches. Apricots. What else?

Figs? I said.

Thirty acres of figs, my uncle said.

How about mulberries? I said. The mulberry tree is a very nice-looking tree.

Mulberries, my uncle said. He moved his tongue around in his mouth. A nice tree, he said. A tree I knew well in the old country. How many acres would you suggest?

About ten, I said.

All right, he said. What else?

Olive trees are nice, I said.

Yes, they are, my uncle said. One of the nicest. About ten acres of olive trees. What else?

Well, I said, I don't suppose apple trees would grow on this kind of land.

I suppose not, my uncle said. I don't like apples anyway.

He started the car and we drove off the dry land on to the dry road. The car bounced about slowly until we reached the road and then we began to travel at a higher rate of speed.

One thing, my uncle said. When we get home I would rather you didn't mention this farm to the folks.

Yes, sir, I said. *(Farm?* I thought. *What farm?)*

I want to surprise them, my uncle said. You know how your grandmother is. I'll go ahead with my plans and when everything is in order I'll take the whole family out to the farm and surprise them.

Yes, sir, I said.

Not a word to a living soul, my uncle said.

Yes, sir, I said.

Well, the Mexicans went to work and cleared the land. They cleared about ten acres of it in about two months. There were seven of them. They worked with shovels and hoes. They didn't understand anything about anything. It all seemed very strange, but they never complained. They were being paid and that was the thing that counted. They were two brothers and their sons. One day the older brother, Diego, very politely asked my uncle what it was they were supposed to be doing.

Señor, he said, please forgive me. Why are we cutting down the cactus?

I'm going to farm this land, my uncle said.

The other Mexicans asked Diego in Mexican what my uncle had said and Diego told them.

They didn't believe it was worth the trouble to tell my uncle he couldn't do it. They just went on cutting down the cactus.

The cactus, however, stayed down only for a short while. The land which had been first cleared was already rich again with fresh cactus and brush. My uncle made this observation with considerable amazement.

It takes deep plowing to get rid of cactus, I said. You've got to plow it out.

My uncle talked the matter over with Ryan, who had a farm-implement, business. Ryan told him not to fool with horses. The modern thing to do was to turn a good tractor loose on the land and do a year's work in a day.

So my uncle bought a John Deere tractor. It was beautiful. A mechanic from Ryan's taught Diego how to operate the tractor, and the next day when my uncle and I reached the land we could see the tractor away out in the desolation and we could hear it booming in the awful emptiness of the desert. It sounded pretty awful. It *was* awful. My uncle thought it was wonderful.

Progress, he said. There's the modern age for you. Ten thousand years ago, he said, it would have taken a hundred men a week to do what the tractor's done today.

Ten thousand years ago? I said. You mean yesterday.

Anyway, my uncle said, there's nothing like these modern conveniences.

The tractor isn't a convenience, I said.

What is it, then? my uncle said. Doesn't the driver sit?

He couldn't very well stand, I said.

Any time they let you sit, my uncle said, it's a convenience. Can you whistle?

Yes, sir, I said. What sort of a song would you like to hear?

Song? my uncle said. I don't want to hear any song. I want you to whistle at that Mexican on the tractor.

What for? I said.

Never mind what for, my uncle said. Just whistle. I want him to know we are here and that we are pleased with his work. He's probably plowed twenty acres.

Yes, sir, I said.

I put the second and third fingers of each hand into my mouth and blew with all my might. It was good and loud. Nevertheless, it didn't seem as if Diego had heard me. He was pretty far away. We were walking toward him anyway, so I couldn't figure out why my uncle wanted me to whistle at him.

Once again, he said.

I whistled once again, but Diego didn't hear.

Louder, my uncle said.

This next time I gave it all I had, and my uncle put his hands over his ears. My face got very red, too. The Mexican on the tractor heard the whistle this time. He slowed the tractor down, turned it around, and began plowing straight across the field toward us.

Do you want him to do that? I said.

It doesn't matter, my uncle said.

In less than a minute and a half the tractor and the Mexican arrived. The Mexican seemed very delighted. He wiped dirt and perspiration off his face and got down from the tractor.

Señor, he said, this is wonderful.

I'm glad you like it, my uncle said.

Would you like a ride? the Mexican asked my uncle.

My uncle didn't know for sure. He looked at me.

Go ahead, he said. Hop on. Have a little ride.

Diego got on the tractor and helped me on. He sat on the metal seat and I stood behind him, holding him. The tractor began to shake, then jumped, and then began to move. It moved swiftly and made a good deal of noise. The Mexican drove around in a big circle and brought the tractor back to my uncle. I jumped off.

All right, my uncle said to the Mexican. Go back to your work.

The Mexican drove the tractor back to where he was plowing.

My uncle didn't get water out of the land until many months later. He had wells dug all over the place, but no water came out of the wells. Of course he had motor pumps too, but even then no water came out. A water specialist named Roy came out from Texas with his two younger brothers and they began investigating the land. They told my uncle they'd get water for him. It took them three months and the water was muddy and there wasn't much of it. There was a trickle of muddy water. The specialist told my uncle matters would improve with time and went back to Texas.

Now half the land was cleared and plowed and there was water, so the time had come to plant.

We planted pomegranate trees. They were of the finest quality and very expensive. We planted about seven hundred of them. I myself planted a hundred. My uncle planted quite a few. We had a twenty-acre orchard of pomegranate trees away over to hell and gone in the strangest desolation anybody ever saw. It was the loveliest-looking absurdity imaginable and my uncle was crazy about it. The only trouble was his money was giving out. Instead of going ahead and trying to make a garden of the whole six hundred and eighty acres, he decided to devote all his time and energy and money to the pomegranate trees.

Only for the time being, he said. Until we begin to market the pomegranates and get our money back.

Yes, sir, I said.

I didn't know for sure, but I figured we wouldn't be getting any pomegranates to speak of off those little trees for two or three years at least, but I didn't say anything. My uncle got rid of the Mexican workers and he and I took over the farm. We had the tractor and a lot of land, so every now and then we drove out to the farm and drove the tractor around, plowing up cactus and turning over the soil between the pomegranate trees. This went on for three years.

One of these days, my uncle said, you'll see the loveliest garden in the world in this desert.

The water situation didn't improve with time, either. Every once in a while there would be a sudden generous spurt of water containing only a few pebbles and my uncle would be greatly pleased, but the next day it would be muddy again and there would be only a little trickle. The pomegranate trees fought bravely for life, but they never did get enough water to come out with any fruit.

There were blossoms after the fourth year. This was a great triumph for my uncle. He went out of his head with joy when he saw them.

Nothing much ever came of the blossoms, though. They were very beautiful, but that was about all. Purple and lonely.

That year my uncle harvested three small pomegranates.

I ate one, he ate one, and we kept the other one up in his office.

The following year I was fifteen. A lot of wonderful things had happened to me. I mean, I had read a number of good writers and I'd grown as tall as my uncle. The farm was still our secret. It had cost my uncle a lot of money, but he was always under the impression that very soon he was going to start marketing his pomegranates and get his money back and go on with his plan to make a garden in the desert.

The trees didn't fare very well. They grew a little, but it was hardly noticeable. Quite a few of them withered and died.

That's average, my uncle said. Twenty trees to an acre is only average. We won't plant new trees just now. We'll do that later.

He was still paying for the land, too.

The following year he harvested about two hundred pomegranates. He and I did the harvesting. They were pretty sad-looking pomegranates. We packed them in nice-looking boxes and my uncle shipped them to a wholesale produce house in Chicago. There were eleven boxes.

We didn't hear from the wholesale produce house for a month, so one night my uncle made a long-distance phone call. The produce man, D'Agostino, told my uncle nobody wanted pomegranates.

How much are you asking per box? my uncle shouted over the phone.

One dollar, D'Agostino shouted back.

That's not enough, my uncle shouted. I won't take a nickel less than five dollars a box.

They don't want them at one dollar a box, D'Agostino shouted.

Why not? my uncle shouted.

They don't know what they are, D'Agostino shouted.

What kind of a business man are you anyway? my uncle shouted. They're pomegranates. I want five dollars a box.

I can't sell them, the produce man shouted. I ate one myself and I don't see anything so wonderful about them.

You're crazy, my uncle shouted. There is no other fruit in the world like the pomegranate. Five dollars a box isn't half enough.

What shall I do with them? D'Agostino shouted. I can't sell them. I don't want them.

I see, my uncle whispered. Ship them back. Ship them back express collect.

The phone call cost my uncle about seventeen dollars.

So the eleven boxes came back.

My uncle and I ate most of the pomegranates.

The following year my uncle couldn't make any more payments on the land. He gave the papers back to the man who had sold him the land. I was in the office at the time.

Mr. Griffith, my uncle said, I've got to give you back your property, but I would like to ask a little favor. I've planted twenty acres of pomegranate trees out there on that land and I'd appreciate it very much if you'd let me take care of those trees.

Take care of them? Mr. Griffith said. What in the world for?

My uncle tried to explain, but couldn't. It was too much to try to explain to a man who wasn't sympathetic.

So my uncle lost the land, and the trees, too.

About three years later he and I drove out to the land and walked out to the pomegranate orchard. The trees were all dead. The soil was heavy again with cactus and desert brush. Except for the small dead pomegranate trees the place was exactly the way it had been all the years of the world.

We walked around in the orchard for a while and then went back to the car.

We got into the car and drove back to town.

We didn't say anything because there was such an awful lot to say, and no language to say it in.

One of Our Future Poets, You Might Say

When I was the fourteenth brightest pupil in the class of fifteen third-graders at Emerson School, the Board of Education took a day off one day to think things over.

This was years ago.

I was eight going on nine or at the most nine going on ten, and good-natured.

In those days the average Board of Education didn't make a fuss over the children of a small town and if some of the children seemed to be doltish, the average Board of Education assumed that this was natural and let it go at that.

Certain Presbyterian ministers, however, sometimes looked into a sea of young faces and said: You are the future leaders of America, the future captains of industry, the future statesmen, and, I might say, the future poets. This sort of talk always pleased me because I liked to imagine what sort of future captains of industry pals of mine like Jimmy Volta and Frankie Sousa were going to make.

I knew these boys.

They were great baseball players, but by nature idiots, or, in more scientific terminology, high-grade cretins: healthy, strong, and spirited. I didn't think they would be apt to develop into captains of industry and neither did they. If they were asked what career they intended to shape for themselves, they would honestly say, I don't know. Nothing, I guess.

Ordinarily, however, our Board of Education had no such glorious faith as this in the young hoodlums it was trying to teach to read and write.

Nevertheless, one day our Board of Education took a day off to think things over quietly and after seven hours of steady thinking decided to put every public school pupil through a thorough physical examination to solve, if possible, the mystery of health in the young inhabitants of the slums.

According to documentary proof, published and tabulated, all the inhabitants of my neighborhood should have had badly shaped heads, sunken chests, faulty bone structure, hollow voices, no energy, distemper, and six or seven other minor organic defects.

According to the evidence before each public school teacher, however, these ruffians from the slums had well-shaped heads, sound chests, handsome figures, loud voices, too much energy, and a continuous compulsion to behave mischievously.

Something was wrong somewhere.

Our Board of Education decided to try to find out what.

They *did* find out.

They found out that the published and tabulated documentary proof was wrong.

It was at this time that I first learned with joy and fury that I was a poet. I remember being in the Civic Auditorium of my home town at high noon with six hundred other future statesmen, and I remember hearing my name sung out by old Miss Ogilvie in a clear hysterical soprano.

The time had arrived for me to climb the seventeen steps to the stage, walk to the center of the stage, strip to the waist, inhale, exhale, and be measured all over.

There was a moment of confusion and indecision, followed quickly by a superhuman impulse to behave with style, which I did, to the horror and bewilderment of the whole Board of Education, three elderly doctors, a half-dozen registered nurses, and six hundred future captains of industry.

Instead of climbing the seventeen steps to the stage, I *leaped*.

I remember old Miss Ogilvie turning to Mr. Rickenbacker, Superintendent of Public Schools, and whispering fearfully: This is Garoghlanian—one of our future poets, I might say.

Mr. Rickenbacker took one quick look at me and said: Oh, I see. Who's he sore at?

Society, old Miss Ogilvie said.

Oh, I see, Mr. Rickenbacker said. So am I, but I'll be damned if I can jump like that. Let's say no more about it.

I flung off my shirt and stood stripped to the waist, a good deal of hair bristling on my chest.

You see? Miss Ogilvie said. A writer.

Inhale, Mr. Rickenbacker said.

For how long? I asked.

As long as possible, Mr. Rickenbacker said.

I began to inhale. Four minutes later I was still doing so. Naturally, the examining staff was a little amazed. They called a speedy meeting while I continued to inhale. After two minutes of heated debate the staff decided to ask me to stop inhaling. Miss Ogilvie explained that unless they *asked* me to stop I would be apt to go on inhaling all afternoon.

That will be enough for the present, Mr. Rickenbacker said.

Already? I said. I'm not even started.

Now exhale, he said.

For how long? I said.

My God! Mr. Rickenbacker said.

You'd better tell him, Miss Ogilvie said. Otherwise he'll exhale all afternoon.

Three or four minutes, Mr. Rickenbacker said.

I exhaled four minutes and was then asked to put on my shirt and go away.

How are things? I asked the staff. Am I in pretty good shape?

Let's say no more about it, Mr. Rickenbacker said. Please go away.

The following year our Board of Education decided to give no more physical examinations. The examinations went along all right as far as future captains of industry were concerned, and future statesmen, but when it came to future poets the examinations ran helter-skelter and amuck, and nobody knew what to do or think.

The Fifty-Yard Dash

After a certain letter came to me from New York the year I was twelve, I made up my mind to become the most powerful man in my neighborhood. The letter was from my friend Lionel Strongfort. I had clipped a coupon from *Argosy All-Story Magazine*, signed it, placed it in an envelope, and mailed it to him. He had written back promptly, with an enthusiasm bordering on pure delight, saying I was undoubtedly a man of uncommon intelligence, potentially a giant, and—unlike the average run-of-the-mill people of the world who were, in a manner of speaking, dreamwalkers and daydreamers—a person who would some day be somebody.

His opinion of me was very much like my own. It was pleasant, however, to have the opinion so emphatically corroborated, particularly by a man in New York—and a man with the greatest chest expansion in the world. With the letter came several photographic reproductions of Mr. Strongfort wearing nothing but a little bit of leopard skin. He was a tremendous man and claimed that at one time he had been puny. He was loaded all over with muscle and appeared to be somebody who could lift a 1920 Ford roadster and tip it over.

It was an honor to have him for a friend.

The only trouble was—I didn't have the money. I forget how much the exact figure was at the beginning of our acquaintanceship, but I haven't forgotten that it was an amount completely out of the question. While I was eager to be grateful to Mr. Strongfort for his enthusiasm, I didn't seem to be able to find words with which to explain about not having the money, without immediately appearing to be a dreamwalker and a daydreamer myself. So, while waiting from one day to another, looking everywhere for words that would not blight our friendship and degrade me to commonness, I talked the matter over with my uncle Gyko, who was studying Oriental philosophy at the time. He was amazed at my curious ambition, but quite pleased. He said the secret of greatness, according to Yoga, was the releasing within one's self of those mysterious vital forces which are in all men.

These strength, he said in English which he liked to affect when speaking to me, ease from God. I tell you, Aram, eat ease wonderful.

I told him I couldn't begin to become the powerful man I had decided to become until I sent Mr. Strongfort some money.

Mohney! my uncle said with contempt. I tell you, Aram, mohney is nawthing. You cannot bribe God.

Although my uncle Gyko wasn't exactly a puny man, he was certainly not the man Lionel Strongfort was. In a wrestling match I felt certain Mr. Strongfort would get a headlock or a half-nelson or a toe hold on my uncle and either make him give up or squeeze him to death. And then again, on the other hand, I wondered. My uncle was nowhere near as big as Mr. Strongfort, but neither was Mr. Strongfort as dynamically furious as my uncle. It seemed to me that, at best, Mr. Strongfort, in a match with my uncle, would have a great deal of unfamiliar trouble—I mean with the mysterious vital forces that were always getting released in my uncle, so that very often a swift glance from him would make a big man quail and turn away, or, if he had been speaking, stop quickly.

Long before I had discovered words with which to explain to Mr. Strongfort about the money, another letter came from him. It was as cordial as the first, and as a matter of fact, if anything, a little more cordial. I was delighted and ran about, releasing mysterious vital forces, turning handsprings, scrambling up trees, turning somersaults, trying to tip over 1920 Ford roadsters, challenging all comers to wrestle, and in many other ways alarming my relatives and irritating the neighbors.

Not only was Mr. Strongfort not sore at me, he had reduced the cost of the course. Even so, the money necessary was still more than I could get hold of. I was selling papers every day, but *that* money was for bread and stuff like that. For a while I got up very early every morning and went around town looking for a small satchel full of money. During six days of this adventuring I found a nickel and two pennies. I found also a woman's purse containing several foul-smelling cosmetic items, no money, and a slip of paper on which was written in an ignorant hand: Steve Hertwig, 3764 Ventura Avenue.

Three days after the arrival of Mr. Strongfort's second letter, his third letter came. From this time on our correspondence became one-sided. In fact, I didn't write at all. Mr. Strongfort's communications were overpowering and not at all easy to answer, without money. There was, in fact, almost nothing to say.

It was wintertime when the first letter came, and it was then that I made up my mind to become the most powerful man in my neighborhood and ultimately, for all I knew, one of the most powerful men in the world. I had ideas of my own as to how to go about getting that way, but I had also the warm friendship and high regard of Mr. Strongfort in New York, and the mystical and furious guardianship of my uncle Gyko, at home.

The letters from Mr. Strongfort continued to arrive every two or three days all winter and on into springtime. I remember, the day apricots were ripe enough to steal, the arrival of a most charming letter from my friend in New York. It was a hymn to newness on earth, the arrival of springtime, the time of youth in the heart, of renewal, fresh strength, fresh determination, and many other things. It was truly a beautiful epistle, probably as fine as any to the Romans or anybody else. It was full of the legend-quality, the world-feeling, and the dignity-of-strength-feeling so characteristic of Biblical days. The last paragraph of the lovely hymn brought up, apologetically, the coarse theme of money. The sum was six or seven times as little as it had been originally, and a new element had come into Mr. Strongfort's program of changing me over from a nobody to a giant of tremendous strength, and extreme attractiveness to women. Mr. Strongfort had decided, he said, to teach me everything in one fell swoop, or one sweep fall, or something of that sort. At any rate, for three dollars, he said, he would send me all his precious secrets in one envelope and the rest would be up to me, and history.

I took the matter up with my uncle Gyko, who by this time had reached the stage of fasting, meditating, walking for hours, and vibrating. We had had discussions two or three times a week all winter and he had told me in his own unique broken-English way all the secrets *he* had been learning from Yoga.

I tell you, Aram, he said, I can do *anything*. Eat ease wonderful.

I believed him, too, even though he had lost a lot of weight, couldn't sleep, and had a strange dynamic blaze in his eyes. He was very scornful of the world that year and was full of pity for the dumb beautiful animals that man was mistreating, killing, eating, domesticating, and teaching to do tricks.

I tell you, Aram, he said, eat ease creaminal to make the horses work. To keal the cows. To teach the dogs to jump, and the monkeys to smoke pipes.

I told him about the letter from Mr. Strongfort.

Mohney! he said. Always he wants mohney. I do not like heem.

My uncle was getting all his dope free from the theosophy-philosophy-astrology-and-miscellaneous shelf at the Public Library. He believed, however, that he was getting it straight from God. Before he took up Yoga he had been one of the boys around town and a good drinker of *rakhi*, but after the light began to come to him he gave up drinking. He said he was drinking liquor finer than *rakhi* or anything else.

What's that? I asked him.

Aram, he said, eat ease weasdom.

Anyhow, he had little use for Mr. Strongfort and regarded the man as a charlatan.

He's all right, I told my uncle.

But my uncle became furious, releasing mysterious vital forces, and said, I wheel break hease head, fooling all you leatle keads.

He ain't fooling, I said. He says he'll give me all his secrets for three dollars.

I tell you, Aram, my uncle Gyko said, he does not know any seacrets. He ease a liar.

I don't know, I said. I'd like to try that stuff out.

Eat ease creaminal, my uncle Gyko said, but I wheel geave you tree dollar.

My uncle Gyko gave me the necessary three dollars and I sent them along to Mr. Strongfort. The envelope came from New York, full of Mr. Strongfort's secrets. They were strangely simple. It was all stuff I had known anyhow but had been too lazy to pay any attention to. The idea was to get up early in the morning and for an hour or so to do various kinds of acrobatic exercises, which were illustrated. Also to drink plenty of water, get plenty of fresh air, eat good wholesome food, and keep it up until you were a giant.

I felt a little let down and sent Mr. Strongfort a short polite note saying so. He ignored the note and I never heard from him again. In the meantime, I had been following the rules and growing more powerful every day. When I say *in the meantime*, I mean for four days I followed the rules. On the fifth day I decided to sleep instead of getting up and filling the house with noise and getting my grandmother sore. She used to wake up in the darkness of early morning and shout that I was an impractical fool and would never be rich. She would go back to sleep for five minutes, wake up, and then shout that I would never buy and sell for a profit. She would sleep a little more, waken, and shout that there were once three sons of a king; one was wise like his father; the other was crazy about girls; and the third had less brains than a bird. Then she would get out of bed, and, shouting steadily, tell me the whole story while I did my exercises.

The story would usually warn me to be sensible and not go around waking her up before daybreak all the time. That would always be the moral, more or less, although the story itself would be about three sons of some king, or three brothers, each of them very wealthy and usually very greedy, or three daughters, or three proverbs, or three roads, or something else like that.

She was wasting her breath, though, because I wasn't enjoying the early-morning acrobatics any more than she was. In fact, I was beginning to feel that it was a lot of nonsense, and that my uncle Gyko had been right about Mr. Strongfort in the first place

So I gave up Mr. Strongfort's program and returned to my own, which was more or less as follows: to take it easy and grow to be the most powerful man in the neighborhood without any trouble or exercise. Which is what I did.

That spring Longfellow School announced that a track meet was to be held, one school to compete against another; *everybody* to participate.

Here, I believed, was my chance. In my opinion I would be first in every event.

Somehow or other, however, continuous meditation on the theme of athletics had the effect of growing into a fury of anticipation that continued all day and all night, so that before the day of the track meet I had run the fifty-yard dash any number of hundreds of times, had jumped the running broad jump, the standing broad jump, and the high jump, and in each event had made my competitors look like weaklings.

This tremendous inner activity, which was strictly Yoga, changed on the day of the track meet into fever.

The time came at last for me and three other athletes, one of them a Greek, to go to our marks, get set, and go; and I did, in a blind rush of speed which I knew had never before occurred in the history of athletics.

It seemed to me that never before had any living man moved so swiftly. Within myself I ran the fifty yards fifty times before I so much as opened my eyes to find out how far back I had left the other runners. I was very much amazed at what I saw.

Three boys were four yards ahead of me and going away.

It was incredible. It was unbelievable, but it was obviously the truth. There ought to be some mistake, but there wasn't. There they were, ahead of me, going away.

Well, it simply meant that I would have to overtake them, with my eyes open, and win the race. This I proceeded to do. They continued, incredibly, however, to go away, in spite of my intention. I became irritated and decided to put them in their places for the impertinence, and began releasing all the mysterious vital forces within myself that I had. Somehow or other, however, not even this seemed to bring me any closer to them and I felt that in some strange way I was being betrayed. If so, I decided, I would shame my betrayer by winning the race in spite of the betrayal, and once again I threw fresh life and energy into my running. There wasn't a great distance still to go, but I knew I would be able to do it.

Then I knew I wouldn't.

The race was over.

I was last, by ten yards.

Without the slightest hesitation I protested and challenged the runners to another race, same distance, back. They refused to consider the proposal, which proved, I knew, that they were afraid to race me. I told them they knew very well I could beat them.

It was very much the same in all the other events.

When I got home I was in high fever and very angry. I was delirious all night and sick three days. My grandmother took very good care of me and probably was responsible for my not dying. When my uncle Gyko came to visit me he was no longer hollow-checked. It seems he had finished his fast, which had been a long one—forty days or so; and nights too, I believe. He had stopped meditating, too, because he had practically exhausted the subject. He was again one of the boys around town, drinking, staying up all hours, and following the women.

I tell you, Aram, he said, we are a great family. We can do *anything*.

A Nice Old-Fashioned Romance, with Love Lyrics and Everything

My cousin Arak was a year and a half younger than me, round-faced, dark, and exceptionally elegant in manners. It was no pretense with him. His manners were just naturally that way, just as my manners were bad from the beginning. Where Arak would get around any sort of complication at school with a bland smile that showed his front upper teeth, separated, and melted the heart of stone of our teacher, Miss Daffney, I would go to the core of the complication and with noise and vigor prove that Miss Daffney or somebody else was the culprit, not me, and if need be, I would carry the case to the Supreme Court and prove my innocence.

I usually got sent to the office. In some cases I would get a strapping for debating the case in the office against Mr. Derringer, our principal, who was no earthly good at debates. The minute I got him cornered he got out his strap.

Arak was different; he didn't care to fight for justice. He wasn't anywhere near as bright as me, but even though he was a year and a half younger than me, he was in the same grade. That wouldn't be so bad if the grade wasn't the fifth. I usually won all my arguments with my teachers, but instead of being glad to get rid of me they refused to promote me, in the hope, I believe, of winning the following semester's arguments and getting even. That's how it happened that I came to be the oldest pupil in the fifth grade.

One day Miss Daffney tried to tell the world I was the author of the poem on the blackboard that said she was in love with Mr. Derringer, and ugly. The author of the poem was my cousin Arak, not me. Any poem I wrote wouldn't be about Miss Daffney, it would be about something worthwhile. Nevertheless, without mentioning any names, but with a ruler in her hand, Miss Daffney stood beside my desk and said, I am going to find out who is responsible for this horrible outrage on the blackboard and see that he is properly punished.

He? I said. How do you know it's a boy and not a girl?

Miss Daffney whacked me on the knuckles of my right hand. I jumped out of my seat and said, You can't go around whacking me on the knuckles. I'll report this.

Sit down, Miss Daffney said.

I did. She had me by the right ear, which was getting out of shape from being grabbed hold of by Miss Daffney and other teachers.

I sat down and quietly, almost inaudibly, said, You'll hear about this.

Hold your tongue, Miss Daffney said, and although I was sore as the devil, I stuck out my tongue and held it, while the little Mexican, Japanese, Armenian, Greek, Italian, Portuguese, and plain American boys and girls in the class, who looked to me for comedy, roared with laughter. Miss Daffney came down on my hand with the ruler, but this time the ruler grazed my nose. This to me was particularly insulting, inasmuch as my nose then, as now, was large. A small nose would not have been grazed, and I took Miss Daffney's whack as a subtle comment on the size of my nose.

I put my bruised hand over my hurt nose and again rose to my feet.

You told me to hold my tongue, I said, insisting that I had done no evil, had merely carried out her instructions, and was therefore innocent, utterly undeserving of the whacked hand and the grazed nose.

You be good now, Miss Daffney said. I won't stand any more of your nonsense. You be good.

I took my hand away from my nose and began to be good. I smiled like a boy bringing her a red apple. My audience roared with laughter and Miss Daffney dropped the ruler, reached for me, fell over the desk, got up, and began to chase me around the room.

There I go again, I kept saying to myself while Miss Daffney chased me around the room. There I go again getting in a mess like this that's sure to end in murder, while my cousin Arak, who is the guilty one, sits there and smiles. There's no justice anywhere.

When Miss Daffney finally caught me, as I knew she would unless I wanted even more severe punishment from Mr. Derringer, there was a sort of free-for-all during which she tried to gouge my eyes out, pull off my ears, fingers, and arms, and I, by argument, tried to keep her sweet and ladylike.

When she was exhausted, I went back to my seat, and the original crime of the day was taken up again: Who was the author of the love lyric on the blackboard?

Miss Daffney straightened her hair and her clothes, got her breath, demanded and got silence, and after several moments of peace during which the ticking of the clock was heard, she began to speak.

I am going to ask each of you by name if you wrote this awful— poem—on the blackboard and I shall expect you to tell the truth. If you lie, I shall find out anyway and your punishment will be all the worse.

She began to ask each of the boys and girls if they'd written the poem and of course they hadn't. Then she asked my cousin Arak and he also said he hadn't. Then she asked me and I said I hadn't, which was the truth.

You go to the office, she said. You liar.

I didn't write any poem on any blackboard, I said. And I'm not a liar.

Mr. Derringer received me with no delight. Two minutes later Susie Kokomoto arrived from our class with a message describing my crime. In fact, quoting it. Mr. Derringer read the message, made six or seven faces, smiled, snapped his suspenders, coughed and said, What made you write this little poem?

I didn't, I said.

Naturally, he said, you'd say you didn't, but why did you?

I *didn't* write it, I said.

Now don't be headstrong, Mr. Derringer said. That's a rather alarming rumor to be spreading. How do you *know* Miss Daffney's in love with me?

Is she? I said.

Well, Mr. Derringer said, that's what it says here. What gave you that impression? Have you noticed her looking at me with admiration or something?

I haven't noticed her looking at you with anything, I said. Are *you* in love with *her* or something?

That remains to be seen, Mr. Derringer said. It isn't a bad poem, up to a point. Do you really regard Miss Daffney as ugly?

I didn't write the poem, I said. I can prove it. I don't write that way.

You mean your handwriting isn't like the handwriting on the blackboard? Mr. Derringer said.

Yes, I said, and I don't write that kind of poetry either.

You *admit* writing poetry? Mr. Derringer said.

I write poetry, I said, but not *that* kind of poetry.

A rumor like that, Mr. Derringer said. I hope you know what you're about.

Well, I said, all I know is I didn't write it.

Personally, Mr. Derringer said, I think Miss Daffney is not only not ugly, but on the contrary attractive.

Well, that's all right, I said. The only thing I want is not to get into a lot of trouble over something I didn't do.

You *could* have written that poem, Mr. Derringer said.

Not *that* one, I said. I could have written a good one.

What do you mean, *good?* Mr. Derringer said. Beautiful? Or insulting?

I mean beautiful, I said, only it wouldn't be about Miss Daffney.

Up to this point, Mr. Derringer said, I was willing to entertain doubts as to your being the author of the poem, but no longer. I am convinced you wrote it. Therefore I must punish you.

I got up and started to debate.

You give me a strapping for something I didn't do, I said, and you'll hear about it.

So he gave me a strapping and *the whole school* heard about it. I went back to class limping. The poem had been erased. All was well again. The culprit had been duly punished, the poem effaced, and order re-established in the fifth grade. My cousin Arak sat quietly admiring Alice Bovard's brown curls.

First thing during recess I knocked him down and sat on him.

I got a strapping for that, I said, so don't write any more of them.

The next morning, however, there was another love lyric on the blackboard in my cousin Arak's unmistakable hand, and in his unmistakable style, and once again Miss Daffney wanted to weed out the culprit and have him punished. When I came into the room and saw the poem and the lay of the land I immediately began to object. My cousin Arak was going too far. In Armenian I began to swear at him. He, however, had become stone deaf, and Miss Daffney believed my talk was for her. Here, here, she said. Speak in a language everybody can understand if you've got something to say.

All I've got to say is I didn't write that poem, I said. And I didn't write yesterday's either. If I get into any more trouble on account of these poems, somebody's going to hear about it.

Sit down, Miss Daffney said.

After the roll call, Miss Daffney filled a whole sheet of paper with writing, including the new poem, and ordered me to take the message to the office.

Why *me?* I said. I didn't write the poem.

Do as you're told, Miss Daffney said.

I went to her desk, put out my hand to take the note, Miss Daffney gave it a whack, I jumped back three feet and shouted, I'm not going to be carrying love-letters for you.

This just naturally was the limit. There was a limit to everything. Miss Daffney leaped at me. I in turn was so sore at my cousin Arak that I turned around and jumped on him. He pretended to be very innocent, and offered no resistance. He was very deft, though, and instead of getting the worst of it, he got the least, while I fell all over the floor until Miss

Daffney caught up with me. After that it was all her fight. When I got to the office with the message, I had scratches and bruises all over my face and hands, and the love-letter from Miss Daffney to Mr. Derringer was crumpled and in places torn.

What's been keeping you? Mr. Derringer said. Here, let me see that message. What mischief have you been up to now?

He took the message, unfolded it, smoothed it out on his desk, and read it very slowly. He read it three or four times. He was delighted, and, as far as I could tell, in love. He turned with a huge smile on his face and was about to reprimand me again for saying that Miss Daffney was ugly.

I didn't write the poem, I said. I didn't write yesterday's either. All I want is a chance to get myself a little education and live and let live.

Now, now, Mr. Derringer said

He was quite pleased.

If you're in love with her, I said, that's your affair, but leave me out of it.

All I say is you could be a little more gracious about Miss Daffney's appearance, Mr. Derringer said. If she seems plain to you, perhaps she doesn't seem plain to someone else.

I was disgusted. It was just no use.

All right, I said. Tomorrow I'll be gracious.

Now that's better, Mr. Derringer said. Of course I must punish you.

He reached for the lower drawer of his desk where the strap was.

Oh, no, I said. If you punish me, then I won't be gracious.

Well, what about today's poem? Mr. Derringer said. I've got to punish you for that. Tomorrow's will be another story.

No, I said. Nothing doing.

Oh, all right, Mr. Derringer said, but see that you're gracious.

I will, I said. Can I go back now?

Yes, he said. Yes. Let me think this over.

I began to leave the office.

Wait a minute, he said. Everybody'll know something fishy's going on somewhere unless they hear you howl. Better come back here and howl ten times, and then go back.

Howl? I said. I can't howl unless I'm hurt.

Oh, sure you can, Mr. Derringer said. Just give out a big painful howl. You can do it.

I don't think I can, I said.

I'll hit this chair ten times with the strap, Mr. Derringer said, and you howl.

Do you think it'll work? I said.

Of course it'll work, he said. Come on.

Mr. Derringer hit the chair with the strap and I tried to howl the way I had howled yesterday, but it didn't sound real. It sounded fishy, somewhere.

We were going along that way when Miss Daffney herself came into the office, only we didn't know she'd come in, on account of the noise.

On the tenth one I turned to Mr. Derringer and said, That's ten.

Then I saw Miss Daffney. She was aghast and mouth-agape.

Just a few more, son, Mr. Derringer said, for good measure.

Before I could tell him Miss Daffney was in the office, he was whacking the chair again and I was howling.

It was disgusting.

Miss Daffney coughed and Mr. Derringer turned and saw her—his beloved.

Miss Daffney didn't speak. She *couldn't*. Mr. Derringer smiled. He was very embarrassed and began swinging the strap around.

I'm punishing the boy, he said.

I understand, Miss Daffney said.

She didn't either. Not altogether anyway.

I'll not have any pupil of this school being impertinent, Mr. Derringer said.

He was madly in love with her and was swinging the strap around and trying to put over a little personality. Miss Daffney, however, just didn't think very much of his punishing the boy by hitting a chair, while the boy howled, the man and the boy together making a mockery of justice and true love. She gave him a very dirty look.

Oh! Mr. Derringer said. You mean about my hitting the chair? We were just rehearsing, weren't we, son?

No, we weren't, I said.

Miss Daffney, infuriated, turned and fled, and Mr. Derringer sat down.

Now look what you've done, he said.

Well, I said, if you're going to have a romance with her, have it, but don't mess me up in it.

Well, Mr. Derringer said, I guess that's that.

He was a very sad man.

All right, he said, go back to your class.

I want you to know I didn't write them poems, I said.

That's got nothing to do with it, Mr. Derringer said.

I thought you might want to know, I said.

It's too late now, he said. She'll never admire me any more.

Why don't you write a poem to her yourself? I said.

I can't write poems, Mr. Derringer said.

Well, I said, figure it out some way.

When I went back to class Miss Daffney was very polite. So was I. She knew I knew and she knew if she got funny I'd either ruin the romance or make her marry him, so she was very friendly. In two weeks school closed and when school opened again Miss Daffney didn't show up. Either Mr. Derringer didn't write her a poem, or did and it was no good; or he didn't tell her he loved her, or did and she didn't care; or else he proposed to her and she turned him down, *because I knew*, and got herself transferred to another school so she could get over her broken heart.

Something like that.

My Cousin Dikran, the Orator

Twenty years ago, in the San Joaquin Valley, the Armenians used to regard oratory as the greatest, the noblest, the most important, one might say the *only*, art. About ninety-two per cent of the vineyardists around Fresno, by actual count, believed that any man who could make a speech was a cultured man. This was so, I imagine after all these years, because the vineyardists themselves were so ineffective at speechmaking, so self-conscious about it, so embarrassed, and so profoundly impressed by public speakers who could get up on a platform, adjust spectacles on their noses, look at their pocket watches, cough politely, and, beginning quietly, lift their voices to a roar that shook the farmers to the roots and made them know the speaker was educated.

What language! What energy! What wisdom! What magnificent roaring! the farmers said to themselves.

The farmers, assembled in the basement of one or another of the three churches, or in the Civic Auditorium, trembled with awe, wiped the tears from their eyes, blew their noses, and, momentarily overcome, donated as much money as they could afford. On some occasions, such as when money was being raised for some especially intimate cause, the farmers, in donating money, would stand up in the auditorium and cry out, Mgerdich Kasabian, his wife Araxie, his three sons, Gourken, Sirak, and Toumas—fifty cents! and sit down amid thunderous applause, not so much for the sum of money donated as for the magnificent manner of speaking, and the excellent and dramatic pronunciation of the fine old-country names: Mgerdich, Araxie, Gourken, Sirak, Toumas.

In this matter of speaking and donating money, the farmers competed with one another. If a farmer did not get up and publicly make his announcement like a man—well, then, the poor fellow! Neither money nor the heart to get up fearlessly and throw away the trembling in his soul! Because of this competition, a farmer unable to donate money (but with every impulse in the world to help the cause), would sit nervously in shame year after year, and then finally, with the arrival of better days, leap to his feet, look about the auditorium furiously, and shout, Gone are the days of poverty for this tribe from the lovely city of Dikranagert—the five Pampalonian brothers—twenty-five cents! and go home with his head high, and his heart higher. Poor? In the old days, yes. But no more. (And the five enormous men would look at one another with family pride, and push their sons before them—with affection, of course; that strange Near-Eastern, Oriental affection that came from delight in no longer being humiliated in the eyes of one's countrymen.)

No farmer was prouder, however, than when his son, at school, at church, at a picnic, or anywhere, got up and made a speech.

The boy! the farmer would shout at his eighty-eight-year-old father. Listen to him! It's Vahan, my son, *your* grandson—eleven years old. He's talking about Europe.

The grandfather would shake his head and wonder what it was all about, a boy of eleven so serious and so well-informed, talking about Europe. The old man scarcely would know where Europe was, although he would know he had visited Havre, in France, on his way to America. Perhaps Havre—perhaps that was it. *Yevroba.* Europe. But what in the world could be the matter with Havre suddenly—to make the boy so tense and excited? Ahkh, the old man would groan, it is all beyond me. I don't remember. It was a pleasant city on the sea, with ships.

The women would be overjoyed and full of amazement at themselves, the mothers. They would look about at one another, nodding, shaking their heads, and after ten minutes of the boy's talking in English, which they couldn't understand, they would burst into sweet silent tears because it was all so amazing and wonderful—little Berjie, only yesterday a baby who couldn't speak two words of Armenian, let alone English, on a platform, speaking, swinging his arms, pointing a finger, now at the ceiling, now west, now south, now north, and occasionally at his heart.

It was inevitable under these circumstances for the Garoghlanians to produce an orator too, even though the Old Man regarded speechmakers as fools and frauds.

When you hear a small man with spectacles on his face shouting from the bottom of his bowels, let me tell you that that man is either a jackass or a liar.

He was always impatient with any kind of talk, except the most direct and pertinent. He wanted to know what he didn't know, and that was all. He wanted no talk for talk's sake. He used to go to all the public meetings, but they never failed to sicken him. Every speaker would watch his face to learn how displeased the Old Man was, and when they saw his lips moving with silent curses they would calm down and try to talk sense, or, if they had talked to him in private and learned how stupid he regarded them, they would try to get even with him by shouting louder than ever and occasionally coming forth with, We know there are those among us who scoff at us, who ridicule our efforts, who even, out of fantastic pride of heart, regard us as fools, but this has always been the cross we have had to carry, and carry it we will.

Here the Old Man would tap his sons on their heads, these in turn would tap their sons on their heads, these would nudge one another, the women would look about, and together the Garoghlanians, numbering thirty-seven or thirty-eight, would rise and walk out, with the Old Man looking about furiously at the poor farmers and saying, They're carrying the cross again—let's go.

In spite of all this, I say, it was inevitable for the Garoghlanians to produce an orator. It was the style, the will of the people, and some member of the Garoghlanian tribe would naturally find it essential to enter the field and show everybody what oratory could really be—what, in fact, it really was, if the truth were known.

This Garoghlanian turned out to be my little cousin Dikran, my uncle Zorab's second son, who was nine years old when the war ended, a year younger than myself, but so much smaller in size that I regarded him as somebody to ignore.

From the beginning this boy was one of those very bright boys who have precious little real understanding, no humor at all, and the disgraceful and insulting attitude that all knowledge comes from the outside—disgraceful particularly to the Garoghlanians, who for centuries had come by all their wisdom naturally, from within. It was the boast of the Old Man that any real Garoghlanian could spot a crook in one glance, and would have the instinctive good sense to know how to deal with the man.

When you look at a man who hides behind his face, the Old Man used to say, let me tell you that that man is no good. He is either a spy or a swindler. On the other hand, if you look at a man whose glance tells you, *Brother, I am your brother*—watch out. That man carries a knife on his person somewhere.

With instruction of this sort, beginning practically at birth, it was only natural for the average Garoghlanian to grow up in wisdom of the world and its strange inhabitants.

The only Garoghlanian who couldn't catch on, however, was this cousin of mine, Dikran. He was strictly a book-reader, a type of human being extremely contemptible to the Old Man, unless he could perceive definite improvement in the character of the reader—of necessity a child, as who else would read a book? In the case of Dikran, the Old Man could perceive no improvement; on the contrary, a continuous decline in understanding, until at last, when the boy was eleven, the Old Man was informed that Dikran was the brightest pupil at Longfellow School, the pride of his teachers, and an accomplished public speaker.

When this news was brought to the Old Man by the boy's mother, the Old Man, who was lying on the couch in the parlor, turned his face to the wall and groaned, Too bad. What a waste. What's eating the boy?

Why, he's the brightest boy in the whole school, the mother said.

The Old Man sat up and said, When you hear of a boy of eleven being the brightest boy in a school of five hundred boys—pay no attention to it. For the love of God, what's he bright about? Isn't he eleven? What bright? Who wants a child to burden himself with such a pathetic sense of importance? You have been a poor mother, I must tell you. Drive the poor boy out of the house into the fields. Let him go swimming with his cousins. The poor fellow doesn't even know how to laugh. And you come here in the afternoon to tell me he is bright. Well, go away.

In spite of even this, I say, the boy moved steadily forward, turning the pages of books day and night, Sundays and holidays and picnic days, until finally, on top of everything else, it was necessary to fit glasses to his face—which made him all the more miserable-looking, so that every time there was a family gathering the Old Man would look about, see the boy, and groan, My God, the philosopher! All right, boy, come here.

The boy would get up and stand in front of the Old Man.

Well, the Old Man would say, you read books. That's fine. You are now eleven years old. Thank God for that. Now tell me—what do you know? What have you learned?

I can't tell you in Armenian, the boy would say.

I see, the Old Man would say. Well, tell me in English.

Here everything would go beautifully haywire. This little cousin of mine, eleven years old, would really begin to make a speech about all the wonderful things he had found out from the books. They *were* wonderful, too. He knew all the dates, all the reasons, all the names, all the places, and what the consequences were likely to be.

It was very beautiful in a minor, melancholy way.

Suddenly the Old Man would stop the boy's speech, shouting, What are you—a parrot?

Even so, it seemed to me that the Old Man was fond of this strange arrival among the Garoghlanians. Book-readers were fools—and so were orators—but at any rate *our* book-reader and orator was not by any means a run-of-the-mill book-reader and orator. He was at any rate something special. For one thing he was younger than the others who imagined they had learned many things from books, and for another he spoke a lot more clearly than the others.

For these reasons, and because of the evident determination in the boy to follow his own inclination, he was accepted by all of us as the Garoghlanian scholar and orator, and permitted to occupy his time and develop whatever mind he may have been born with as he pleased.

In 1920, Longfellow School announced an evening program consisting of (1) Glee Club Singing, (2) a performance of *Julius Caesar*, and (3) a speech by Dikran Garoghlanian—a speech entitled *Was the World War Fought in Vain?* At the proper time the Garoghlanians seated themselves in the school auditorium, listened to the awful singing, watched the horrible performance of *Julius Caesar*, and then listened to the one and only Garoghlanian orator—Dikran, the second son of Zorab.

The speech was flawless: dramatic, well-uttered, intelligent, and terribly convincing—the conclusion being that the World War had *not* been fought in vain, that Democracy *had* saved the world. Everybody in the auditorium was stricken with awe, and applauded the speech wildly. It was really too much, though—I mean for the Old Man. In the midst of the thunderous applause, he burst out laughing. The speech was really splendid, in a way. It was at least the best thing of its kind—the best of the worst kind of thing. There was some occasion for pride in this, even.

That evening at home the Old Man called the boy to him and said, I listened to your speech. It's all right. I understand you spoke about a war in which several million men were killed. I understand you *proved* the war was not fought in vain. I must tell you I am rather pleased. A statement as large and as beautiful as that deserves to come only from the lips of a boy of eleven—from one who believes what he is saying. From a grown man, I must tell you, the horror of that remark would be just a little too much for me to endure. Continue your investigation of the world from books, and I am sure, if you are diligent and your eyes hold out, that by the time you are sixty-seven you will know the awful foolishness of that remark—so innocently uttered by yourself tonight, in such a pure flow of soprano English. In a way I am as proud of you as of any other member of this tribe. You may all go now. I want to sleep. I am not eleven years old. I am sixty-seven.

Everybody got up and went away, except me. I stayed behind long enough to see the old man take off his shoes and hear him sigh, These crazy wonderful children of this crazy wonderful world!

The Presbyterian Choir Singers

One of the many curious and delightful things about our country is the ease with which our good people move from one religion to another, or from no particular religion at all to any religion that happens to come along, without experiencing any particular loss or gain, and go right on being innocent anyhow.

Myself, I was born, for instance, a kind of Catholic, although I was not baptized until I was thirteen, a circumstance which, I remember clearly, irritated the priest very much and impelled him to ask my people if they were crazy, to which my people replied, We have been away.

Thirteen years old and not baptized! the priest shouted. What kind of people are you?

For the most part, my uncle Melik replied, we are an agricultural people, although we have had our brilliant men, too.

It was a Saturday afternoon. The whole thing took no more than seven minutes, but even after I was baptized it was impossible for me to feel any change.

Well, my grandmother said, you are now baptized. Do you feel any better?

For some months, I believe I ought to explain, I had been feeling intelligent, which led my grandmother to suspect that I was ill with some mysterious illness or that I was losing my mind.

I think I feel the same, I said.

Do you believe now? she shouted. Or do you still have doubts?

I can easily *say* I believe, I said, but to tell you the truth I don't know for sure. I want to be a Christian of course.

Well, just believe then, my grandmother said, and go about your business.

My business was in some ways quaint and in other ways incredible.

I sang in the Boys Choir at the Presbyterian Church on Tulare Street. For doing so I received one dollar a week from an elderly Christian lady named Balaifal who lived in sorrow and solitude in the small ivy-covered house next to the house in which my friend Pandro Kolkhozian lived.

This boy, like myself, was loud in speech. That is to say, we swore a good deal—in all innocence of course—and by doing so grieved Miss or Mrs. Balaifal so much that she sought to save us while there was still time. To be saved was a thing I for one had no occasion to resent.

Miss Balaifal (I shall call her that from now on, since while I knew her she was certainly single, and since I do not know for sure if she ever married, or for that matter if she ever thought of marrying, or if she ever so much as fell in love—earlier in life of course, and no doubt with a scoundrel who took the whole matter with a grain of salt)—Miss Balaifal, as I began to say, was a cultured woman, a reader of the poems of Robert Browning and other poets and a woman of great sensitivity, so that coming out on the porch of her house to hear us talk she could stand so much and no more, and when the limit had been reached, cried out, Boys, boys. You must not use profane language.

Pandro Kolkhozian, on the one hand, seemed to be the most uncouth boy in the world and on the other—and this was the quality in him which endeared him to me—the most courteous and thoughtful.

Yes, Miss Balaifum, he said.

Balaifal, the lady corrected him. Please come here. Both of you.

We went to Miss Balaifal and asked what she wanted.

What do you want, Miss Balaifum? Pandro said.

Miss Balaifal went into her coat pocket and brought out a sheaf of pamphlets, and without looking at them handed one to each of us. My pamphlet was entitled *Redemption, The Story of a Drunkard*. Pandro's was entitled *Peace at Last, The Story of a Drunkard*.

What's this for? Pandro said.

I want you boys to read those pamphlets and try to be good, Miss Balaifal said. I want you to stop using profane language.

It doesn't say anything here about profane language, Pandro said.

There's a good lesson for each of you in those pamphlets, the lady said. Read them and don't use profane language any more.

Yes, ma'am, I said. Is that all?

One thing more, Miss Balaifal said. I wonder if you boys would help me move the organ from the dining room to the parlor?

Sure, Miss Balaifum, Pandro said. Any time.

So we went into the lady's house and, while she instructed us in just how to do it without damaging the instrument or ourselves, we moved it, by slow degrees, from the dining room to the parlor.

Now read those pamphlets, Miss Balaifal said.

Yes, ma'am, Pandro said. Is that all?

Well, now, the lady said. I want you to sing while I play the organ.

I can't sing, Miss Balaifum, Pandro said.

Nonsense, the lady said. Of course you can sing, Pedro.

Pandro, not Pedro, Pandro said. Pedro is my cousin's name.

As a matter of fact Pandro's name was Pantalo, which in Armenian means pants. When he had started to school his teacher hadn't cared for, or hadn't liked the sound of, the name, so she had written down on his card Pandro. As for his cousin's name, it was Bedros, with the *b* soft, which in turn had been changed at school to Pedro. It was all quite all right of course, and no harm to anybody.

Without answering him, the elderly lady sat on the stool, adjusted her feet on the pedals of the organ, and without any instructions to us, began to play a song which, from its dullness, was obviously religious. After a moment she herself began to sing. Pandro, in a soft voice, uttered a very profane, if not vulgar, word, which fortunately Miss Balaifal did not hear. Miss Balaifal's voice was, if anything, not impressive. The pedals squeaked a good deal louder than she sang, the tones of the organ were not any too clear, but even so, it was possible to know that Miss Balaifal's voice was not delightful.

Galilee, bright Galilee, she sang.

She turned to us, nodded, and said, Now sing. Sing, boys.

We knew neither the words nor the music, but it seemed that common courtesy demanded at least an honest effort, which we made, trying as far as possible to follow the music coming out of the organ and the dramatic words coming out of Miss Balaifal.

Ruler of the storm was He, on the raging Galilee, she sang.

In all, we tried to sing three songs. After each song, Pandro would say, Thank you very much, Miss Balaifum. Can we go now?

At last she got up from the organ and said, I'm sure you're the better for it. If evil friends invite you to drink, turn away.

We'll turn away, Miss Balaifum, Pandro said. Won't we, Aram?

I will, I said.

I will too, Pandro said. Can we go now, Miss Balaifum?

Read the pamphlets, she said. It's not too late.

We'll read them, Pandro said. Just as soon as we get time.

We left the lady's house and went back to the front yard of Pandro's house and began to read the pamphlets. Before we were half through reading, the lady came out on the porch and in a very high and excited voice said, Which of you was it?

Which of us was *what?* Pandro said.

He was very bewildered.

Which of you was it that *sang?* Miss Balaifal said.

We both sang, I said.

No, Miss Balaifal said. Only one of you sang. One of you has a beautiful Christian voice.

Not me, Pandro said.

You, Miss Balaifal said to me. Eugene. Was it you?

Aram, I said. Not Eugene. No, I don't think it was me either.

Boys, come here, Miss Balaifal said.

Who? Pandro said.

Both of you, the lady said.

When we were in the house and Miss Balaifal was seated at the organ again Pandro said, I don't want to sing. I don't like to sing.

You sing, the lady said to me.

I sang.

Miss Balaifal leaped to her feet.

You are the one, she said. You must sing at church.

I won't, I said.

You mustn't use profane language, she said.

I'm not using profane language, I said, and I promise not to use profane language again as long as I live, but I won't sing in church.

Your voice is the most Christian voice I have ever heard, Miss Balaifal said.

It isn't, I said.

Yes, it is, she said.

Well, I won't sing anyway, I said.

You must, you must, Miss Balaifal said.

Thanks very much, Miss Balaifum, Pandro said. Can we go now? He doesn't want to sing in church.

He must, he must, the lady insisted.

Why? Pandro said.

For the good of his soul, the lady said.

Pandro whispered the profane word again.

Now tell me, the lady said. What is your name?

I told her.

You are a Christian of course? she said.

I guess so, I said.

A Presbyterian of course, she said.

I don't know about that, I said.

You are, the lady said. Of course you are. I want you to sing in the Tulare Street Presbyterian Church—in the Boys' Choir—next Sunday.

Why? Pandro said again.

We need voices, the lady explained. We must have young voices. We must have singers. He must sing next Sunday.

I don't like to sing, I said. I don't like to go to church either.

Boys, Miss Balaifal said. Sit down. I want to talk to you.

We sat down. Miss Balaifal talked to us for at least thirty minutes.

We didn't believe a word of it, although out of courtesy we kept answering her questions the way we knew she wanted us to answer them, but when she asked us to get down on our knees with her while she prayed, we wouldn't do it. Miss Balaifal argued this point for some time and then decided to let us have our way—for a moment. Then she tried again, but we wouldn't do it. Pandro said we'd move the organ any time, or anything else like that, but we wouldn't get down on our knees.

Well, Miss Balaifal said, will you close your eyes?

What for? Pandro said.

It's customary for everybody to close his eyes while someone is praying, Miss Balaifal said.

Who's praying? Pandro said.

No one, *yet*, Miss Balaifal said. But if you'll promise to close your eyes, *I'll* pray, but you've got to promise to close your eyes.

What do you want to pray for? Pandro said.

I want to pray for you boys, she said.

What for? Pandro said.

A little prayer for you won't do any harm, Miss Balaifal said. Will you close your eyes?

Oh! all right, Pandro said.

We closed our eyes and Miss Balaifal prayed.

It wasn't a little prayer by a long shot.

Amen, she said. Now, boys, don't you feel better?

In all truth, we didn't.

Yes, we do, Pandro said. Can we go now, Miss Balaifum? Any time you want the organ moved, we'll move it for you.

Sing for all you're worth, Miss Balaifal said to me, and turn away from any evil companion who invites you to drink.

Yes, ma'am, I said.

You know where the church is, she said.

What church? I said.

The Tulare Street Presbyterian Church, she said.

I know where it is, I said.

Mr. Sherwin will be expecting you Sunday morning at nine-thirty, she said.

Well, it just seemed like I was cornered.

Pandro went with me to the church on Sunday, but refused to stand with the choir boys and sing. He sat in the last row of the church and watched and listened. As for myself, I was never more unhappy in my life, although I sang.

Never again, I told Pandro after it was all over.

The following Sunday I didn't show up of course, but that didn't do any good, because Miss Balaifal got us into her house again, played the organ, sang, made us try to sing, prayed, and was unmistakably determined to keep me in the Boys' Choir. I refused flatly, and Miss Balaifal decided to put the whole thing on a more worldly basis.

You have a rare Christian voice, she explained. A voice needed by religion. You yourself are deeply religious, although you do not know it yet. Since this is so, let me ask you to sing for *me* every Sunday. I will *pay* you.

How much? Pandro said.

Fifty cents, Miss Balaifal said.

We usually sang four or five songs. It took about half an hour altogether, although we had to sit another hour while the preacher delivered his sermon. In short, it wasn't worth it.

For this reason I could make no reply.

Seventy-five cents, Miss Balaifal suggested.

The air was stuffy, the preacher was a bore, it was all very depressing.

One dollar, Miss Balaifal said. Not a cent more.

Make it a dollar and a quarter, Pandro said.

Not a cent more than a dollar, Miss Balaifal said.

He's got the best voice in the whole choir, Pandro said. *One* dollar? A voice like that is worth *two* dollars to any religion.

I've made my offer, Miss Balaifal said.

There are other religions, Pandro said.

This, I must say, upset Miss Balaifal.

His voice, she said bitterly, is a Christian voice, and what's more it's Presbyterian.

The Baptists would be glad to get a voice like that for two dollars, Pandro said.

The Baptists! Miss Balaifal said with some—I hesitate to say it—contempt.

They're no different than the Presbyterians, Pandro said.

One dollar, Miss Balaifal said. One dollar, and your name on the program.

I don't like to sing, Miss Balaifal, I said.

Yes, you do, she said. You just think you don't. If you could see your face when you sing—why—

He's got a voice like an angel, Pandro said.

I'll fix you, I told Pandro in Armenian.

That's no one-dollar voice, Pandro said.

All right, boys, Miss Balaifal said. A dollar and fifteen cents, but no more.

A dollar and a quarter, Pandro said, or we go to the Baptists.

All right, Miss Balaifal said, but I must say you drive a hard bargain.

Wait a minute, I said. I don't like to sing. I won't sing for a dollar and a quarter or anything else.

A bargain is a bargain, Miss Balaifal said.

I didn't make any bargain, I said. Pandro did. Let *him* sing.

He *can't* sing, Miss Balaifal said.

I've got the worst voice in the world, Pandro said with great pride.

His poor voice wouldn't be worth ten cents to anybody, Miss Balaifal said.

Not even a nickel, Pandro said.

Well, I said, I'm not going to sing—for a dollar and a quarter or anything else. I don't need any money.

You made a bargain, Miss Balaifal said.

Yes, you did, Pandro said.

I jumped on Pandro right in Miss Balaifal's parlor and we began to wrestle. The elderly Christian lady tried to break it up, but since it was impossible to determine which of us was the boy with the angelic voice, she began to pray. The wrestling continued until most of the furniture in the room had been knocked over, except the organ. The match was eventually a draw, the wrestlers exhausted and flat on their backs.

Miss Balaifal stopped praying and said, Sunday then, at a dollar and a quarter.

It took me some time to get my breath.

Miss Balaifal, I said, I'll sing in that choir only if Pandro sings too.

But his voice, Miss Balaifal objected. It's horrible.

I don't care what it is, I said. If I sing, he's got to sing too.

I'm afraid he'd ruin the choir, Miss Balaifal said.

He's got to go up there with me every Sunday, I said, or nothing doing.

Well, now, let me see, Miss Balaifal said.

She gave the matter considerable thought.

Suppose he goes up and stands in the choir, Miss Balaifal said, but *doesn't* sing? Suppose he just *pretends* to sing?

That's all right with me, I said, but he's got to be there all the time.

What do *I* get? Pandro said.

Well, now, Miss Balaifal said, I surely can't be expected to pay you, too.

If I go up there, Pandro said, I've got to be paid.

All right, Miss Balaifal said. One dollar for the boy who sings; twenty-five cents for the boy who doesn't.

I've got the worst voice in the world, Pandro said.

You must be fair, Miss Balaifal said. After all, you won't be singing. You'll just be standing there with the other boys.

Twenty-five cents isn't enough, Pandro said.

We got off the floor and began rearranging the furniture.

All right, Miss Balaifal said. One dollar for the boy who sings. Thirty-five cents for the boy who doesn't.

Make it fifty, Pandro said.

Very well, then, Miss Balaifal said. A dollar for *you*. Fifty cents for *you*.

We start working next Sunday? Pandro said.

That's right, Miss Balaifal said. I'll pay you here after the services. Not a word of this to any of the other boys in the choir.

We won't mention it to anybody, Pandro said.

In this manner, in the eleventh year of my life, I became, more or less, a Presbyterian—at least every Sunday morning. It wasn't the money. It was simply that a bargain had been made, and that Miss Balaifal had her heart set on having me sing for religion.

As I began to say six or seven minutes ago, however, a curious thing about our country is the ease with which all of us—or at least everybody I know—are able to change our religions, without any noticeable damage to anything or anybody. When I was thirteen I was baptized into the Armenian Catholic Church, even though I was still singing for the Presbyterians, and even though I myself was growing a little skeptical, as it were, of the whole conventional religious pattern, and was eager, by hook or crook, to reach an understanding of my own, and to come to terms with Omnipotence in my own way. Even after I was baptized, I carried in my heart a deep discontent.

Two months after I was baptized my voice changed, and my contract with Miss Balaifal was canceled—which was a great relief to me and a terrible blow to her.

As for the Armenian Catholic Church on Ventura Avenue, I went there only on Easter and Christmas. All the rest of the time I moved from one religion to another, and in the end was none the worse for it, so that now, like most Americans, my faith consists in believing in every religion, including my own, but without any ill-will toward anybody, no matter what he believes or disbelieves, just so his personality is good.

The Circus

Any time a circus used to come to town, that was all me and my old pal Joey Renna needed to make us run hog-wild, as the saying is. All we needed to do was see the signs on the fences and in the empty store windows to start going to the dogs and neglecting our educations. All we needed to know was that a circus was on its way to town for me and Joey to start wanting to know what good a little education ever did anybody anyway.

After the circus *reached* town we were just no good at all. We spent all our time down at the trains, watching them unload the animals, walking out Ventura Avenue with the wagons with lions and tigers in them and hanging around the grounds, trying to win the favor of the animal men, the workers, the acrobats, and the clowns.

The circus was everything everything else we knew wasn't. It was adventure, travel, danger, skill, grace, romance, comedy, peanuts, popcorn, chewing-gum and soda-water. We used to carry water to the elephants and stand around afterwards and try to seem associated with the whole magnificent affair, the putting up of the big tent, the getting everything in order, and the worldly-wise waiting for the people to come and spend their money.

One day Joey came tearing into the classroom of the fifth grade at Emerson School ten minutes late, and without so much as removing his hat or trying to explain his being late, shouted, Hey, Aram, what the hell are you doing here? The circus is in town.

And sure enough I'd forgotten. I jumped up and ran out of the room with poor old Miss Flibety screaming after me, Aram Garoghlanian, you stay in this room. Do you hear me, Aram Garoghlanian?

I heard her all right and I knew what my not staying would mean. It would mean another powerful strapping from old man Dawson. But I couldn't help it. I was just crazy about a circus.

I been looking all over for you, Joey said in the street. What happened?

I forgot, I said. I knew it was coming all right, but I forgot it was today. How far along are they?

I was at the trains at five, Joey said. I been out at the grounds since seven. I had breakfast at the circus table. Boy, it was good.

Honest, Joey? I said. How were they?

They're all swell, Joey said. Couple more years, they told me, and I'll be ready to go away with them.

As what? I said. Lion-tamer, or something like that?

I guess maybe not as a lion-tamer, Joey said. I figure more like a work-man till I learn about being a clown or something, I guess. I don't figure I could work with lions right away.

We were out on Ventura Avenue, headed for the circus grounds, out near the County Fairgrounds, just north of the County Hospital.

Boy, what a breakfast, Joey said. Hot-cakes, ham and eggs, sausages, coffee. Boy.

Why didn't you tell me? I said.

I thought you knew, Joey said. I thought you'd be down at the trains same as last year. I would have told you if I knew you'd forgotten. What made you forget?

I don't know, I said. Nothing, I guess.

I was wrong there, but I didn't know it at the time. I hadn't really forgotten. What I'd done was *remembered*. I'd gone to work and remembered the strapping Dawson gave me last year for staying out of school the day the circus was in town. That was the thing that had kind of kept me sleeping after four-thirty in the morning when by rights I should have been up and dressing and on my way to the trains. It was the memory of that strapping old man Dawson had given me, but I didn't know it at the time. We used to take them strappings kind of for granted, me and Joey, on account of we wanted to be fair and square with the Board of Education and if it was against the rules to stay out of school when you weren't sick, and if you were supposed to get strapped for doing it, well, there we were, we'd done it, so let the Board of Education balance things the best way they knew how. They did that with a strapping. They used to threaten to send me and Joey to Reform School but they never did it.

Circus? old man Dawson used to say. I see. *Circus*. Well, bend down, boy.

So, first Joey, then me, would bend down and old man Dawson would get some powerful shoulder exercise while we tried not to howl. We wouldn't howl for five or six licks, but after that we'd howl like Indians coming. They used to be able to hear us all over the school and old man Dawson, after our visits got to be kind of regular, urged us politely to try to make a little less noise, inasmuch as it was a school and people were trying to study.

It ain't fair to the others, old man Dawson said. They're trying to learn something for themselves.

We can't help it, Joey said. It hurts.

That I know, old man Dawson said, but it seems to me there's such a thing as modulation. I believe a lad can overdo his howling if he ain't thoughtful of others. Just try to modulate that awful howl a little. I think you can do it.

Then he gave Joey a strapping of twenty and Joey tried his best not to howl so loud. After the strapping his face was very red and old man Dawson was very tired.

How was that? Joey said.

That was better, old man Dawson said. By far the most courteous you've managed yet.

I did my best, Joey said.

I'm grateful to you, old man Dawson said.

He was tired and out of breath. I moved up to the chair in front of him that he furnished during these matters to help us suffer the stinging pain. I got in the right position and he said, Wait a minute, Aram. Give a man a chance to get his breath. I'm not twenty-three years old. I'm *sixty*-three. Let me rest a minute.

All right, I said, but I sure would like to get this over with.

Don't howl too loud, he said. Folks passing by in the street are liable to think this is a veritable chamber of tortures. Does it really hurt that much?

You can ask Joey, I said.

How about it, Joey? old man Dawson said. Aren't you lads exaggerating just a little? Perhaps to impress someone in your room? Some girl, perhaps?

We don't howl to impress anybody, Mr. Dawson, Joey said. We wouldn't howl if we could help it. Howling makes us feel ashamed, doesn't it, Aram?

It's awfully embarrassing to go back to our seats in our room after howling that way, I said. We'd rather not howl if we could help it.

Well, old man Dawson said, I'll not be unreasonable. I'll only ask you to try to modulate it a little.

I'll do my best, Mr. Dawson, I said. Got your breath back?

Give me just a moment longer, Aram, Mr. Dawson said.

When he got his breath back he gave me my twenty and I howled a little louder than Joey and then we went back to class. It was awfully embarrassing. Everybody was looking at us.

Well, Joey said, what did you expect? The rest of you would fall down and die if you got twenty. You wouldn't *howl a little*, you'd die.

That'll be enough out of you, Miss Flibety said.

Well, it's true, Joey said. They're all scared. A circus comes to town and what do they do? They come to school. They don't go out to the circus.

That'll be enough, Miss Flibety said.

Who do they think they are, giving us dirty looks? Joey said.

Miss Flibety lifted her hand, hushing Joey.

Now the circus was back in town, another year had gone by, it was April again, and we were on our way out to the grounds. Only this time it was worse than ever because they'd seen us at school and knew we were going out to the circus.

Do you think they'll send Stafford after us? I said.

Stafford was truant officer.

We can always run, Joey said. If he comes, I'll go one way, you go another. He can't chase *both* of us. At least one of us will get away.

All right, I said. Suppose one of us gets caught?

Well, let's see, Joey said. Should the one who isn't caught give himself up or should he wreck Stafford's Ford?

I vote for wreck, I said.

So do I, Joey said, so wreck it is.

When we got out to the grounds a couple of the little tents were up, and the big one was going up. We stood around and watched. It was great the way they did it. Just a handful of guys who looked like tramps doing work you'd think no less than a hundred men could do. Doing it with style, too.

All of a sudden a man everybody called Red hollered at me and Joey.

Here, you Arabs, he said, give us a hand.

Me and Joey ran over to him.

Yes, sir, I said.

He was a small man with very broad shoulders and very big hands. You didn't feel that he was small, because he seemed so powerful and because he had so much thick red hair on his head. You thought he was practically a giant.

He handed me and Joey a rope. The rope was attached to some canvas that was lying on the ground.

This is going to be easy, Red said. As the boys lift the pole and get it in place you keep pulling the rope, so the canvas will go up with the pole.

Yes, sir, Joey said.

Everybody was busy when we saw Stafford.

We can't run now, I said.

Let him come, Joey said. We told Red we'd give him a hand and we're going to do it.

I'll tell you what, I said. We'll tell him we'll go with him after we get the canvas up; then we'll run.

All right, Joey said.

Stafford was a big fellow in a business suit who had a beef-red face and looked as if he ought to be a lawyer or something. He came over and said, All right, you hooligans, come along with me.

We promised to give Red a hand, Joey said. We'll come just as soon as we get this canvas up.

We were pulling for all we were worth, slipping and falling. The men were all working hard. Red was hollering orders, and then the whole thing was over and we had done our part.

We didn't even get a chance to find out what Red was going to say to us, or if he was going to invite us to sit at the table for lunch, or what.

Joey busted loose and ran one way and I ran the other and Stafford came after *me*. I heard the circus men laughing and Red hollering, Run, boy, run. He can't catch *you*. He's soft. Give him a good run. He needs the exercise.

I could hear Stafford, too. He was very sore and he was cussing.

I got away, though, and stayed low until I saw him drive off in his Ford. Then I went back to the big tent and found Joey.

We'll get it this time, Joey said.

I guess it'll be Reform School this time, I said.

No, Joey said. I guess it'll be thirty. We're going to do some awful howling if it is. Thirty's a lot of whacks even if he *is* sixty-three years old. He ain't exactly a weakling.

Thirty? I said. Ouch. That's liable to make me cry.

Maybe, Joey said. Me too, maybe. Seems like ten can make you cry, then you hold off till it's eleven, then twelve, and you think you'll start crying on the next one, but you don't. We haven't so far, anyway. Maybe we will when it's thirty.

Oh, well, I said, that's tomorrow.

Red gave us some more work to do around the grounds and let us sit next to him at lunch. It was swell. We talked to some acrobats who were Spanish, and to a family of Italians who worked with horses. We saw both shows, the afternoon one and the evening one, and then we helped with the work, taking the circus to pieces again; then we went down to the trains, and then home. I got home real late. In the morning I was sleepy when I had to get up for school.

They were waiting for us. Miss Flibety didn't even let us sit down for the roll call. She just told us to go to the office. Old man Dawson was waiting for us, too. Stafford was there, too, and very sore.

I figured, Well, here's where we go to Reform School.

Here they are, Mr. Dawson said to Stafford. Take them away, if you like.

It was easy to tell they'd been talking for some time and hadn't been getting along any too well. Old man Dawson seemed irritated and Stafford seemed sore at him.

In *this* school, old man Dawson said, I do any punishing that's got to be done. Nobody else. I can't stop you from taking them to Reform School, though.

Stafford didn't say anything. He just left the office.

Well, lads, old man Dawson said. How was it?

We had lunch with them, Joey said.

Let's see now, old man Dawson said. What offense is this, the sixteenth or the seventeenth?

It ain't that many, Joey said. Must be eleven or twelve.

Well, old man Dawson said, I'm sure of one thing. This is the time I'm supposed to make it thirty.

I think the next one is the one you're supposed to make thirty, Joey said.

No, Mr. Dawson said, we've lost track somewhere, but I'm sure this is the time it goes up to thirty. Who's going to be first?

Me, I said.

All right, Aram, Mr. Dawson said. Take a good hold on the chair, brace yourself, and try to modulate your howl.

Yes, sir, I said. I'll do my best, but thirty's an awful lot.

Well, a funny thing happened. He gave me thirty all right and I howled all right, but it *was* a modulated howl. It was the most modulated howl I ever howled; because it was the *easiest* strapping I ever got. I counted them and there were thirty all right, but they didn't hurt, so I didn't cry, as I was afraid I might.

It was the same with Joey. We stood together waiting to be dismissed.

I'm awfully grateful to you boys, old man Dawson said, for modulating your howls so nicely this time. I don't want people to think I'm killing you.

We wanted to thank him for giving us such easy strappings, but we couldn't say it. I think he knew the way we felt, though, because he smiled in a way that gave us an idea he knew.

Then we went back to class.

It was swell because we knew everything would be all right till the County Fair opened in September.

The Three Swimmers and the Grocer from Yale

The ditches were dry most of the year, but when they weren't dry, they were roaring. As the snows melted in the hills the ditches began to roar and from somewhere, God knows where, arrived frogs and turtles, water snakes and fish. In the spring of the year the water hurried, and with it the heart, but as the fields changed from green to brown, the blossoms to fruit, the shy warmth to arrogant heat, the ditches slowed down and the heart grew lazy. The first water from the hills was cold, swift, and frightening. It was too cold and busy to invite the naked body of a boy.

Alone, or in a group, a boy would stand on the bank of a ditch and watch the water for many minutes, and then, terribly challenged, fling off his clothes, make a running dive, come up gasping, and swim across to the other side. If the boy was the first of a group to dive, the others would soon follow, in order not to walk home in shame. It wasn't simply that the water was cold. It was more that it had no time for boys. The springtime water was as unfriendly as anything could be.

One day in April I set out for Thompson Ditch with my cousin Mourad and a pal of his named Joe Bettencourt, a Portuguese who loved nothing more than to be free and out-of-doors. A school-room made Joe stupid. It embarrassed him. But once out of school, once off the school-grounds, he was as intelligent, as good-natured, casual, sincere, and friendly as anyone could possibly be. As my cousin Mourad said, Joe ain't dumb—he just doesn't want an education.

It was a bright Saturday morning. We had two baloney [sic] sandwiches each, and ten cents between the three of us. We decided to walk to the ditch so that we would get there around noon, when the day would be warm. We walked along the railroad tracks to Calwa. Along the state highway to Malaga. And then east through the vineyard country to the ditch. When we said Thompson Ditch, we meant a specific place. It was an intersection of country roads, with a wooden bridge and a headgate. The swimming was south of the bridge. West of the ditch was a big fenced-in pasture, with cows and horses grazing in it. East of the ditch was the country road. The road and the ditch traveled together many miles. The flow was south, and the next bridge was two miles away. In the summertime a day of swimming was incomplete until a boy had gone downstream to the other bridge, rested a moment in the pasture land, and then came back up, against the stream, which was a good workout.

By the time we got out to Thompson Ditch the brightness of morning had changed to a gloom that was unmistakably wintry; in fact, the beginning of a storm. The water was roaring, the sky was gray, growing black, the air was cold and unfriendly, and the landscape seemed lonely and desolate.

Joe Bettencourt said, I came all this way to swim and rain or no rain I'm going to swim.

So am I, I said.

You wait, my cousin Mourad said. Me and Joe will see how it is. If it's all right, you can come in. Can you really swim?

Aw shut up, I said.

This is what I always said when it seemed to me that somebody had unwittingly insulted me.

Well, Joe said, *can* you?

Sure I can swim, I said.

If you ask *him*, my cousin Mourad said, he can do anything. Better than anybody in the world.

Neither of them knew how uncertain I was as to whether or not I could swim well enough to negotiate a dive and a swim across that body of cold roaring water. If the truth were known, when I saw the dark water roaring I was scared, challenged, and insulted.

Aw shut up, I said to the water.

I brought out my lunch and bit into one of the sandwiches. My cousin Mourad whacked my hand and almost knocked the sandwich into the water.

We eat after we swim, he said. Do you want to have cramps?

I had plumb forgotten. It was because I was so challenged and scared.

One sandwich won't give anybody cramps, I said.

It'll taste better after we swim, Joe said.

He was a very kind boy. He knew I was scared and he knew I was bluffing. I knew *he* was scared, but I knew he was figuring everything out a little more wisely than I was.

Let's see, he said. We'll swim across, rest, swim back, get dressed, eat, and unless the storm passes, start for home. Otherwise we'll swim some more.

This storm isn't going to pass, my cousin Mourad said. If we're going to swim, we're going to have to do it in a hurry and start for home.

By this time Joe was taking off his clothes. My cousin Mourad was taking off his, and I was taking off mine. We stood together naked on the bank of the ditch looking at the unfriendly water. It certainly didn't invite a dive, but there was no other honorable way to enter a body of water. If you tried to walk in, you were just naturally not a swimmer. If you jumped in feet first it wasn't exactly a disgrace, it was just bad style. On the other hand, the water was utterly without charm, altogether unfriendly, uninviting, and sinister. It was certainly challenging, though. The swiftness of the water made the distance to the opposite bank seem greater than it was.

Without a word Joe dived in. Without a word my cousin Mourad dived in. The second or two between splashes seemed like long days dreamed in a winter dream because I was not only scared but very cold. With a bookful of unspoken words on my troubled mind, I dived in.

The next thing I knew—and it wasn't more than three seconds later— I was listening to Joe yelling, my cousin Mourad yelling, and myself yelling. What had happened was that we had dived all into mud up to our elbows, had gotten free only with great effort, and had each come up worrying about what had happened to the other two. We were all standing in the cold roaring water, up to our knees in soft mud.

The dives had been standing dives. If they had been running dives we would have stuck in the mud up to our ankles, head first, and remained there until summer, or later.

This scared us a little on the one hand and on the other hand made us feel very lucky to be alive.

The storm broke while we stood in the mud of the ditch.

Well, Joe said, we're going to get caught in the rain anyhow. We might as well stay in a little while anyway.

We were all shivering, but it seemed sensible that we should try our best to make a swim of it. The water wasn't three feet deep; nevertheless, Joe managed to leap out of the mud and swim across, and then back.

We swam for what seemed like a long time, but was probably no more than ten minutes. Then we got out of the water and mud and dressed and, standing under a tree, ate our sandwiches.

Instead of stopping, the rain increased, so we decided to set out for home right away.

We may get a ride, Joe said.

All the way to Malaga the country road was deserted. In Malaga we went into the general store and warmed ourselves at the stove and chipped in and bought a can of beans and a loaf of French bread. The proprietor of the store was a man named Darcous who wasn't a foreigner. He opened the can for us, divided the beans into three parts on three paper plates, gave us each a wooden fork, and sliced the bread for us. He was an old man who seemed funny and young.

Where you been, boys? he said.

Swimming, Joe said.

Swimming? he said.

Sure, Joe said. We showed that river.

Well, I'll be harrowed, the grocer said. How was it?

Not three feet deep, Joe said.

Cold?

Ice-cold.

Well, I'll be cultivated, the grocer said. Did you have fun?

Did we? Joe asked my cousin Mourad.

Joe didn't know whether it had been fun or something else.

I don't know, my cousin Mourad said. When we dived in we got stuck in the mud up to our elbows.

It wasn't easy to get loose from the mud, I said.

Well, I'll be pruned, the grocer said.

He opened a second can of beans, pitched an enormous forkful into his mouth, and then divided the rest onto the three paper plates.

We haven't got any more money, I said.

Now, tell me, boys, the grocer said, what made you do it?

Nothing, Joe said with the finality of a boy who has too many reasons to enumerate at a moment's notice, and his mouth full of beans and French bread.

Well, I'll be gathered into a pile and burned, the grocer said. Now, boys, he said, tell me—of what race are you? Californians, or foreigners?

We're all Californians, Joe said. I was born on G Street in Fresno. Mourad here was born on Walnut Avenue or someplace on the other side of the Southern Pacific tracks, I guess, and his cousin somewhere around in that neighborhood, too.

Well, I'll be irrigated, the grocer said. Now, tell me, boys, what sort of educations have you got?

We ain't educated, Joe said.

Well, I'll be picked off a tree and thrown into a box, the grocer said. Now, tell me, boys, what foreign languages do you speak?

I speak Portuguese, Joe said.

You ain't educated? the grocer said. I have a degree from Yale, my boy, and I can't speak Portuguese. And you, son, how about you?

I speak Armenian, my cousin Mourad said.

Well, I'll be cut off a vine and eaten grape by grape by a girl in her teens, the grocer said. I can't speak a word of Armenian and I'm a college graduate, class of 1892. Now, tell me, son, he said. What's *your* name?

Aram Garoghlanian I said.

I think I can get it, he said. Gar-oghlan-ian. Is that it?

That's it, I said.

Aram, he said.

Yes, sir, I said.

And what strange foreign language do *you* speak? he said.

I speak Armenian, too, I said. That's my cousin. *Mourad* Garoghlanian.

Well, I'll be harrowed, he said, cultivated, pruned, gathered into a pile, burned, picked off a tree, and let me see what else? Thrown into a box, I think it was, cut off a vine and eaten grape by grape by a girl in her teens. Yes, sir. All them things, if this doesn't beat everything. Did you encounter any reptiles?

What's reptiles? Joe said.

Snakes, the grocer said.

We didn't see any, Joe said. The water was black.

Black water, the grocer said. Any fish?

Didn't see any, Joe said.

A Ford stopped in front of the store and an old man got out and came across the wood floor of the porch into the store.

Open me a bottle, Abbott, the man said.

Judge Harmon, the grocer said, I want you to meet three of the most heroic Californians of this great state.

The grocer pointed at Joe, and Joe said, Joseph Bettencourt—I speak Portuguese.

Stephen L. Harmon, the Judge said. I speak a little French.

The grocer pointed at my cousin Mourad and Mourad said, Mourad Garoghlanian.

What do you speak? the Judge said.

Armenian, my cousin Mourad said.

The grocer gave the Judge the opened bottle, the Judge lifted it to his lips, swallowed three swigs, beat his chest, and said, I'm mighty proud to meet a Californian who speaks Armenian.

The grocer pointed at me.

Aram Garoghlanian, I said.

Brothers? the Judge asked.

Cousins, I said.

Same thing, the Judge said. Now, Abbott, if you please, what's the occasion for this banquet and your poetic excitement, if not delirium?

The boys have just come from showing that old river, the grocer said.

The Judge took three more swigs, beat his chest three times slowly and said, Come from *what?*

They've just come from swimming, the grocer said.

Have any of you fevers? the Judge said.

Fever? Joe said. We ain't sick.

The grocer busted out with a roar of laughter.

Sick? he said. Sick? Judge, these boys dived naked into the black water of winter and came up glowing with the warmth of summer.

We finished the beans and the bread. We were thirsty but didn't know if we should intrude with a request for a drink of water. At least *I* didn't know, but Joe apparently didn't stop to consider.

Mr. Abbott, he said, could we have a drink of water?

Water? the grocer said. Water, my boy? Water's for swimming in, not for drinking.

He fetched three paper cups, went to a small barrel with a tap, turned the tap, and filled each cup with a light golden fluid.

Here, boys, he said. Drink. Drink the lovely juice of the golden apple, unfermented.

The Judge poured the grocer a drink out of his bottle, lifted the bottle to his lips, and said, To your health, gentlemen.

Yes, sir, Joe said.

We all drank.

The Judge screwed the top onto the bottle, put the bottle into his back pocket, looked at each of us carefully, as if to remember us for the rest of his life, and said, Good-bye, gentlemen. Court opens in a half hour. I must pass sentence on a man who says he *borrowed* the horse, *didn't* steal it. He speaks Mexican. The man who says he *stole* the horse speaks Italian. Good-bye.

Good-bye, we said.

By this time our clothes were almost dry, but the rain hadn't stopped.

Well, Joe said, thanks very much, Mr. Abbott. We've got to get home.

Not at all, the grocer said. *I* thank you.

The grocer seemed to be in a strange silence for a man who only a moment before had been so noisy with talk.

We left the store quietly and began to walk down the highway. The rain was now so light it didn't seem like rain at all. I didn't know what to make of it. Joe was the first to speak.

That Mr. Abbott, he said, he's some man.

The name on the sign is Darcous, I said. Abbott's his first name.

First or last, Joe said, he sure is some man.

That Judge was somebody too, my cousin Mourad said.

Educated, Joe said. I'd learn French myself, but who would I talk to?

We walked along the highway in silence. After a few minutes the black clouds parted, the sun came through, and away over in the east we saw the rainbow over the Sierra Nevadas.

We sure showed that old river, Joe said. Was he crazy?

I don't know, my cousin Mourad said.

It took us another hour to get home. We had all thought about the two men and whether or not the grocer was crazy. Myself, I believed he wasn't, but at the same time it seemed to me he had acted kind of crazy.

So long, Joe said.

So long, we said.

He went down the street. Fifty yards away he turned around and said something almost to himself.

What? my cousin Mourad shouted.

He was, Joe said.

Was what? I shouted.

Crazy, Joe shouted back.

Yeah? I shouted back. How do you know?

How can you be cut off a vine and eaten grape by grape by a girl in her teens? Joe shouted.

Suppose he was crazy? my cousin Mourad said. What of it?

Joe put his hand to his chin and began to consider. The sun was shining for all it was worth now and the world was full of light.

I don't think he was crazy, he shouted.

He went on down the street.

He was pretty crazy, my cousin Mourad said.

Well, I said, maybe he's not always.

We decided to let the matter rest at this point until we went swimming again, at which time we would visit the store again and see what happened.

A month later when, after swimming in the ditch, the three of us went into the store, the man who was in charge was a much younger man than Mr. Abbott Darcous. He wasn't a foreigner either.

What'll it be? he said.

A nickel's worth of baloney, Joe said, and a loaf of French bread.

Where's Mr. Darcous? my cousin Mourad said.

He's gone home, the young man said.

Where's that? I said.

Some place in Connecticut, I think, the young man said.

We made sandwiches of the baloney and French bread and began to eat.

At last Joe asked the question.

Was he crazy? Joe said.

Well, the young man said, that's hard to say. I thought he was crazy at first. Then I decided he wasn't. The way he ran this store made you think he was crazy. He gave away more than he sold. To hear him talk you'd think he was crazy. Otherwise he was all right.

Thanks, Joe said.

The store was all in order now, and a very dull place. We walked out, and began walking home.

He's crazy, Joe said.

Who? I said.

That guy in the store now, Joe said.

That young fellow? I said.

Yeah, Joe said. That new fellow in there that ain't got no education.

I think you're right, my cousin Mourad said.

All the way home we remembered the educated grocer.

Well, I'll be cultivated, Joe said when he left us and walked on down the street.

Well, I'll be picked off a tree and thrown in a box, my cousin Mourad said.

Well, I'll be cut off a vine and eaten grape by grape by a girl in her teens, I said.

He sure was some man. Twenty years later, I decided he had been a poet and had run that grocery store in that little run-down village just for the casual poetry in it instead of the paltry cash.

Locomotive 38, the Ojibway

One day a man came to town on a donkey and began loafing around in the public library where I used to spend most of my time in those days. He was a tall young Indian of the Ojibway tribe. He told me his name was Locomotive 38. Everybody in town believed he had escaped from an asylum.

Six days after he arrived in town his animal was struck by the Tulare Street trolley and seriously injured. The following day the animal passed away, most likely of internal injuries, on the corner of Mariposa and Fulton streets. The animal sank to the pavement, fell on the Indian's leg, groaned and died. When the Indian got his leg free he got up and limped into the drug store on the corner and made a long distance telephone call. He telephoned his brother in Oklahoma. The call cost him a lot of money, which he dropped into the slot as requested by the operator as if he were in the habit of making such calls every day.

I was in the drug store at the time, eating a Royal Banana Special, with crushed walnuts.

When he came out of the telephone booth he saw me sitting at the soda fountain eating this fancy dish.

Hello, Willie, he said.

He knew my name wasn't Willie—he just liked to call me that.

He limped to the front of the store where the gum was, and bought three packages of Juicy Fruit. Then he limped back to me and said, What's that you're eating, Willie? It looks good.

This is what they call a Royal Banana Special, I said.

The Indian got up on the stool next to me.

Give me the same, he said to the soda fountain girl.

That's too bad about your animal, I said.

There's no place for an animal in this world, he said. What kind of an automobile should I buy?

Are you going to buy an automobile? I said.

I've been thinking about it for several minutes now, he said.

I didn't think you had any money, I said. I thought you were poor.

That's the impression people get, he said. Another impression they get is that I'm crazy.

I didn't get the impression that you were crazy, I said, but I didn't get the impression that you were rich, either.

Well, I am, the Indian said.

I wish I was rich, I said.

What for? he said.

Well, I said, I've been wanting to go fishing at Mendota for three years in a row now. I need some equipment and some kind of an automobile to get out there in.

Can you drive an automobile? the Indian said.

I can drive anything, I said.

Have you ever driven an automobile? he said.

Not yet, I said. So far I haven't had any automobile to drive, and it's against my family religion to steal an automobile.

Do you mean to tell me you believe you could get into an automobile and start driving? he said.

That's right, I said.

Remember what I was telling you on the steps of the public library the other evening? he said.

You mean about the machine age? I said.

Yes, he said.

I remember, I said.

All right, he said. Indians are born with an instinct for riding, rowing, hunting, fishing, and swimming. Americans are born with an instinct for fooling around with machines.

I'm no American, I said.

I know, the Indian said. You're an Armenian. I remember. I asked you and you told me. You're an Armenian born in America. You're fourteen years old and already you know you'll be able to drive an automobile the minute you get into one. You're a typical American, although your complexion, like my own, is dark.

Driving a car is no trick, I said. There's nothing to it. It's easier than riding a donkey.

All right, the Indian said. Just as you say. If I go up the street and buy an automobile, will you drive for me?

Of course, I said.

How much in wages would you want? he said.

You mean you want to give me wages for driving an automobile? I said.

Of course, the Ojibway said.

Well, I said, that's very nice of you, but I don't want any money for driving an automobile.

Some of the journeys may be long ones, he said.

The longer the better, I said.

Are you restless? he said.

I was born in this little town, I said.

Don't you like it? he said.

I like mountains and streams and mountain lakes, I said.

Have you ever been in the mountains? he said.

Not yet, I said, but I'm going to reach them some day.

I see, he said. What kind of an automobile do you think I ought to buy?

How about a Ford roadster? I said.

Is that the best automobile? he said.

Do you want the *best?* I said.

Shouldn't I have the best? he said.

I don't know, I said. The best costs a lot of money.

What is the best? he said.

Well, I said, some people think the Cadillac is the best. Others like the Packard. They're both pretty good. I wouldn't know which is best. The Packard is beautiful to see going down the highway, but so is the Cadillac. I've watched a lot of them fine cars going down the highway.

How much is a Packard? he said.

Around three thousand dollars, I said. Maybe a little more.

Can we get one right away? he said.

I got down off the stool. He sounded crazy, but I knew he wasn't.

Listen, Mr. Locomotive, I said, do you really want to buy a Packard right away?

You know my animal passed away a few minutes ago, he said.

I saw it happen, I said. They'll probably be arresting you any minute now for leaving the animal in the street.

They won't arrest me, he said.

They will if there's a law against leaving a dead donkey in the street, I said.

No, they won't, he said.

Why not? I said.

Well, he said, they won't after I show them a few papers I carry around with me all the time. The people of this country have a lot of respect for money, and I've got a lot of money.

I guess he is crazy after all, I thought.

Where'd you get all this money? I said.

I own some land in Oklahoma, he said. About fifty thousand acres.

Is it worth money? I said.

No, he said. All but about twenty acres of it is worthless. I've got some oil wells on them twenty acres. My brother and I.

How did you Ojibways ever get down to Oklahoma? I said. I always thought the Ojibways lived up north, up around the Great Lakes.

That's right, the Indian said. We used to live up around the Great Lakes, but my grandfather was a pioneer. He moved west when everybody else did.

Oh, I said. Well, I guess they won't bother you about the dead donkey at that.

They won't bother me about anything, he said. It won't be because I've got money. It'll be because they think I'm crazy. Nobody in this town but you knows I've got money. Do you know where we can get one of them automobiles right away?

The Packard agency is up on Broadway, two blocks beyond the public library, I said.

All right, he said. If you're sure you won't mind driving for me, let's go get one of them. Something bright in color, he said. Red, if they've got red. Where would you like to drive to first?

Would you care to go fishing at Mendota? I said.

I'll take the ride, he said. I'll watch you fish. Where can we get some equipment for you?

Right around the corner at Homan's, I said.

We went around the corner to Homan's and the Indian bought twenty-seven dollars' worth of fishing equipment for me. Then we went up to the Packard agency on Broadway. They didn't have a red Packard, but there was a beautiful green one. It was light green, the color of new grass. This was back there in 1922. The car was a beautiful sports touring model.

Do you think you could drive this great big car? the Indian said.

I *know* I can drive it, I said.

253

The police found us in the Packard agency and wanted to arrest the Indian for leaving the dead donkey in the street. He showed them the papers he had told me about and the police apologized and went away. They said they'd removed the animal and were sorry they'd troubled him about it.

It's no trouble at all, he said.

He turned to the manager of the Packard agency, Jim Lewis, who used to run for Mayor every time election time came around.

I'll take this car, he said.

I'll draw up the papers immediately, Jim said.

What papers? the Indian said. I'm going to pay for it now.

You mean you want to pay three thousand two hundred seventeen dollars and sixty-five cents *cash?* Jim said.

Yes, the Indian said. It's ready to drive, isn't it?

Of course, Jim said. I'll have the boys go over it with a cloth to take off any dust on it. I'll have them check the motor too, and fill the gasoline tank. It won't take more than ten minutes. If you'll step into the office I'll close the transaction immediately.

Jim and the Indian stepped into Jim's office.

About three minutes later Jim came over to me, a man shaken to the roots.

Aram, he said, who is this guy? I thought he was a nut. I had Johnny telephone the Pacific-Southwest and they said his bank account is being transferred from somewhere in Oklahoma. They said his account is something over a million dollars. I thought he was a nut. Do you know him?

He told me his name is Locomotive 38, I said. That's no name.

That's a translation of his Indian name, Jim said. We've got his full name on the contract. Do you know him?

I've talked to him every day since he came to town on that donkey that died this morning, I said, but I never thought he had any money.

He says you're going to drive for him, Jim said. Are you sure you're the man to drive a great big car like this, son?

Wait a minute now, Mr. Lewis, I said. Don't try to push me out of this chance of a lifetime. I can drive this big Packard as well as anybody else in town.

I'm not trying to push you out of anything, Jim said. I just don't want you to drive out of here and run over six or seven innocent people and maybe smash the car. Get into the car and I'll give you a few pointers. Do you know anything about the gear shift?

I don't know anything about anything yet, I said, but I'll soon find out.

All right, Jim said. Just let me help you.

I got into the car and sat down behind the wheel. Jim got in beside me.

From now on, son, he said, I want you to regard me as a friend who will give you the shirt off his back. I want to thank you for bringing me this fine Indian gentleman.

He told me he wanted the best car on the market, I said. You know I've always been crazy about driving a Packard. Now how do I do it?

Well, Jim said, let's see.

He looked down at my feet.

My God, son, he said, your feet don't reach the pedals.

Never mind that, I said. You just explain the gear shift.

Jim explained everything while the boys wiped the dust off the car and went over the motor and filled the gasoline tank. When the Indian came out and got into the car, in the back where I insisted he should sit, I had the motor going.

He says he knows how to drive, the Indian said to Jim Lewis. By instinct, he said. I believe him, too.

You needn't worry about Aram here, Jim said. He can drive all right. Clear the way there, boys, he shouted. Let him have all the room necessary.

I turned the big car around slowly, shifted, and shot out of the agency at about fifty miles an hour, with Jim Lewis running after the car and shouting, Take it easy, son. Don't open up until you get out on the highway. The speed limit in town is twenty-five miles an hour.

The Indian wasn't at all excited, even though I was throwing him around a good deal.

I wasn't doing it on purpose, though. It was simply that I wasn't very familiar with the manner in which the automobile worked.

You're an excellent driver, Willie, he said. It's like I said. You're an American and you were born with an instinct for mechanical contraptions like this.

We'll be in Mendota in an hour, I said. You'll see some great fishing out there.

How far is Mendota? the Indian said.

About ninety miles, I said.

Ninety miles is too far to go in an hour, the Indian said. Take two hours. We're passing a lot of interesting scenery I'd like to look at a little more closely.

All right, I said, but I sure am anxious to get out there and fish.

Well, all right then, the Indian said. Go as fast as you like this time, but some time I'll expect you to drive a little more slowly, so I can see some of the scenery. I'm missing everything. I don't even get a chance to read the signs.

I'll travel slowly *now* if you want me to, I said.

No, he insisted. Let her go. Let her go as fast as she'll go.

Well, we got out to Mendota in an hour and seventeen minutes. I would have made better time except for the long stretch of dirt road.

I drove the car right up to the river bank. The Indian asked if I knew how to get the top down, so he could sit in the open and watch me fish. I didn't know how to get the top down, but I got it down. It took me twenty minutes to do it.

I fished for about three hours, fell into the river twice, and finally landed a small one.

You don't know the first thing about fishing, the Indian said.

What am I doing wrong? I said.

Everything, he said. Have you ever fished before?

No, I said.

I didn't think so, he said.

What am I doing wrong? I said.

Well, he said, nothing in particular, only you're fishing at about the same rate of speed that you drive an automobile.

Is that wrong? I said.

It's not exactly wrong, he said, except that it'll keep you from getting anything to speak of, and you'll go on falling into the river.

I'm not falling, I said. They're pulling me in. They've got an awful pull. This grass is mighty slippery, too. There ain't nothing around here to grab hold of.

I reeled in one more little one and then I asked if he'd like to go home. He said he would if I wanted to, too, so I put away the fishing equipment and the two fish and got in the car and started driving back to town.

I drove that big Packard for this Ojibway Indian, Locomotive 38, as long as he stayed in town, which was all summer. He stayed at the hotel all the time. I tried to get him to learn to drive, but he said it was out of the question. I drove that Packard all over the San Joaquin Valley that summer, with the Indian in the back, chewing eight or nine sticks of gum. He told me to drive anywhere I cared to go, so it was either to some place where I could fish, or some place where I could hunt. He claimed I didn't know anything about fishing or hunting, but he was glad to see me trying. As long as I knew him he never laughed, except once. That was the time I shot at a jack-rabbit with a 12-gauge shotgun that had a terrible kick, and killed a crow. He tried to tell me all the time that that was my average. To shoot at a jack-rabbit and kill a crow. You're an American, he said. Look at the way you took to this big automobile.

One day in November that year his brother came to town from Oklahoma, and the next day when I went down to the hotel to get him, they told me he'd gone back to Oklahoma with his brother.

Where's the Packard? I said.

They took the Packard, the hotel clerk said.

Who drove? I said.

The Indian, the clerk said.

They're both Indians, I said. Which of the brothers drove the car?

The one who lived at this hotel, the clerk said.

Are you sure? I said.

Well, I only saw him get into the car out front and drive away, the clerk said. That's all.

Do you mean to tell me he knew how to shift gears? I said.

It *looked* as if he did, the clerk said. He looked like an expert driver to me.

Thanks, I said.

On the way home I figured he'd just wanted me to *believe* he couldn't drive, so *I* could drive all the time and feel good. He was just a young man who'd come to town on a donkey, bored to death or something, who'd taken advantage of the chance to be entertained by a small town kid who was bored to death, too. That's the only way I could figure it out without accepting the general theory that he was crazy.

Old Country Advice to the American Traveler

One year my uncle Melik traveled from Fresno to New York. Before he got aboard the train his uncle Garro paid him a visit and told him about the dangers of travel.

When you get on the train, the old man said, choose your seat carefully, sit down, and do not look about.

Yes, sir, my uncle said.

Several moments after the train begins to move, the old man said, two men wearing uniforms will come down the aisle and ask you for your ticket. Ignore them. They will be impostors.

How will I know? my uncle said.

You will know, the old man said. You are no longer a child.

Yes, sir, my uncle said.

Before you have traveled twenty miles an amiable young man will come to you and offer you a cigarette. Tell him you don't smoke. The cigarette will be doped.

Yes, sir, said my uncle.

On your way to the diner a very beautiful young woman will bump into you intentionally and almost embrace you, the old man said. She will be extremely apologetic and attractive, and your natural impulse will be to cultivate her friendship. Dismiss your natural impulse and go on in and eat. The woman will be an adventuress.

A what? my uncle said.

A whore, the old man shouted. Go on in and eat. Order the best food, and if the diner is crowded, and the beautiful young woman sits across the table from you, do not look into her eyes. If she speaks, pretend to be deaf.

Yes, sir, my uncle said.

Pretend to be deaf, the old man said. That is the only way out of it.

Out of what? my uncle said.

Out of the whole ungodly mess, the old man said. I have traveled. I know what I'm talking about.

Yes, sir, my uncle said.

Let's say no more about it, the old man said.

Yes, sir, my uncle said.

Let's not speak of the matter again, the old man said. It's finished. I have seven children. My life has been a full and righteous one. Let's not give it another thought. I have land, vines, trees, cattle, and money. One cannot have everything—except for a day or two at a time.

Yes, sir, my uncle said.

On your way back to your seat from the diner, the old man said, you will pass through the smoker. There you will find a game of cards in progress. The players will be three middle-aged men with expensive-looking rings on their fingers. They will nod at you pleasantly and one of them will invite you to join the game. Tell them, No speak English.

Yes, sir, my uncle said.

That is all, the old man said.

Thank you very much, my uncle said.

One thing more, the old man said. When you go to bed at night, take your money out of your pocket and put it in your shoe. Put your shoe under your pillow, keep your head on the pillow all night, *and don't sleep.*

Yes, sir, my uncle said. That is all, the old man said.

The old man went away and the next day my uncle Melik got aboard the train and traveled straight across America to New York. The two men in uniforms were not impostors, the young man with the doped cigarette did not arrive, the beautiful young woman did not sit across the table from my uncle in the diner, and there was no card game in progress in the smoker. My uncle put his money in his shoe and put his shoe under his pillow and put his head on the pillow and didn't sleep all night the first night, but the second night he abandoned the whole ritual.

The second day he *himself* offered another young man a cigarette which the other young man accepted. In the diner my uncle went out of his way to sit at a table with a young lady. He started a poker game in the smoker, and long before the train ever got to New York my uncle knew everybody aboard the train and everybody knew him. Once, while the train was traveling through Ohio, my uncle and the young man who had accepted the cigarette and two young ladies on their way to Vassar formed a quartette and sang *The Wabash Blues.*

The journey was a very pleasant one.

When my uncle Melik came back from New York, his old uncle Garro visited him again.

I see you are looking all right, he said. Did you follow my instructions?

Yes, sir, my uncle said.

The old man looked far away in space.

I am pleased that *someone* has profited by my experience, he said.

The Poor and Burning Arab

My uncle Khosrove, himself a man of furious energy and uncommon sadness, had for a friend one year a small man from the old country who was as still as a rock inwardly, whose sadness was expressed by brushing a speck of dust from his knee and never speaking.

This man was an Arab named Khalil. He was no bigger than a boy of eight, but, like my uncle Khosrove, had a very big mustache. He was probably in his early sixties. In spite of his mustache, however, he impressed one as being closer to a child in heart than to a man. His eyes were the eyes of a child, but seemed to be full of years of remembrance—years and years of being separated from things deeply loved, as perhaps his native land, his father, his mother, his brother, his horse, or something else. The hair on his head was soft and thick and as black as black ever was, and parted on the left side, the way small boys who had just reached America from the old country were taught by their parents to part their hair. His head was, in fact, the head of a schoolboy, except for the mustache, and so was his body, except for the broad shoulders. He could speak no English, only a little Turkish, a few words of Kurdish, and only a few of Armenian, but he hardly ever spoke anyway. When he did, he spoke in a voice that seemed to come not so much from himself as from the old country. He spoke, also, as if he regretted the necessity to do so, as if it were pathetic for one to try to express what could never be expressed, as if anything he might say would only add to the sorrow already existing in himself.

How he won the regard of my uncle Khosrove, a man who *had* to say *something* at least, is a thing none of us ever learned. Little enough is learned from people who are always talking, let alone from people who hardly ever talk, except, as in the case of my uncle Khosrove, to swear or demand that someone else stop talking. My uncle Khosrove probably met the Arab at the Arax Coffee House.

My uncle Khosrove picked his friends and enemies from the way they played *tavli*, which in this country is known as backgammon. Games of any sort are tests of human behavior under stress, and, even though my uncle Khosrove himself was probably the worst loser in the world, he despised any other man who lost without grace.

What are you grieving about? he would shout at such a loser. It's a game, isn't it? Do you lose your life with it?

He himself lost *his* life when he lost a game, but it was inconceivable to him that anyone else might regard the symbols of the game as profoundly as he did. To the others the game was *only* a game, as far as he was concerned. To himself, however, the game was destiny—over a board on a table, with an insignificant man across the table rattling the dice, talking to them in Turkish, coaxing them, whispering, shouting, and in many other ways humiliating himself.

My uncle Khosrove, on the other hand, despised the dice, regarded them as his personal enemies, and never spoke to them. He threw them out of the window or across the room, and pushed the board off the table.

The dogs! he would shout.

And then, pointing furiously at his opponent, he would shout, And you! My own countryman! You are not ashamed. You debase yourself before them. You pray to them. I am ashamed for you. I spit on the dogs.

Naturally, no one ever played a game of *tavli* with my uncle Khosrove twice.

This Coffee House was a place of great fame and importance in its day. In this day it is the same, although many have died who went there twenty years ago.

For the most part the place was frequented by Armenians, but others came, too. All who remembered the old country. All who loved it. All who had played *tavli* and the card game *scambile* in the old country. All who enjoyed the food of the old country, the wine, the *rakhi*, and the small cups of coffee in the afternoons. All who loved the songs, and the stories. And all who liked to be in a place with a familiar smell, thousands of miles from home.

Most of the time my uncle Khosrove reached this place around three in the afternoon. He would stand a moment looking over the men, and then sit down in a corner, alone. He usually sat an hour, without moving, and then would go away, terribly angry, although no one had said a word to him.

Poor little ones, he would say. Poor little orphans. Or, literally, Poor and burning orphans.

Poor and burning—it's impossible to translate this one. Nothing, however, is more sorrowful than the *poor and burning* in life and in the world.

Most likely, sitting in this Coffee House one day, my uncle Khosrove noticed the little Arab, and knew him to be a man of worth. Perhaps the man had been seated, playing *tavli*, his broad shoulders over the board, his child's head somber and full of understanding and regret, and perhaps after the game my uncle Khosrove had seen him get up and stand, no bigger than a child.

It may even be that the man came to the Coffee House and, not knowing my uncle Khosrove, played a game of *tavli* with him and *lost*, and did not complain; and, in fact, understood *who* my uncle Khosrove was—without being told. It may even be that the Arab did not pray to the dice.

Whatever the source of their friendship, whatever the understanding between the two, and whatever the communion they shared, they were at any rate together occasionally in our parlor, and welcome.

The first time my uncle Khosrove brought the Arab to our house, he neglected to introduce him. My mother assumed that the Arab was a countryman of ours, perhaps a distant cousin, although he was a little darker than most of the members of our tribe, and smaller. Which, of course, was no matter; nothing more than the charm of a people; the variety; the quality which made them human and worthy of further extension in time.

The Arab sat down that first day only after my mother had asked him a half-dozen times to be at home.

Was he deaf? she thought.

No, it was obvious that he could hear; he listened so intently.

Perhaps he didn't understand our dialect. My mother asked what city he was from. He did not reply, except to brush dust from the sleeve of his coat. Then in Turkish my mother said, Are you an Armenian? This the Arab understood; he replied in Turkish that he was an Arab.

A poor and burning little orphan, my uncle Khosrove whispered.

For a moment my mother imagined that the Arab might wish to speak, but it was soon obvious that, like my uncle Khosrove, nothing grieved him more than to do so. He could, if necessary, speak, but there was simply nothing, in all truth, to say.

My mother took the two men tobacco, and coffee, and motioned to me to leave.

They want to talk, she said.

Talk? I said.

They want to be alone, she said.

I sat at the table in the dining room and began turning the pages of a year-old copy of *The Saturday Evening Post* that I knew by heart—especially the pictures: Jello, very architectural; automobiles, with high-toned people standing around; flashlights flashing into dark places; tables set with bowls of soup steaming; young men in fancy ready-made suits and coats; and all sorts of other pictures.

I must have turned the pages a little too quickly, however.

My uncle Khosrove shouted, Quiet, boy, quiet.

I looked into the parlor just in time to see the Arab brushing dust from his knee.

The two men sat in the parlor an hour, and then the Arab breathed very deeply through his nose and without a word left the house.

I went into the parlor and sat where he had sat.

What is his name? I said.

Quiet, my uncle Khosrove said.

Well, what is his name? I said.

My uncle Khosrove was so irritated he didn't know what to do. He called out to my mother, as if he were being murdered.

Mariam! he shouted. Mariam!

My mother hurried into the parlor.

What is it? she said.

Send him away—please, my uncle Khosrove, said.

What is the matter?

He wants to know the Arab's name.

Well, all right, my mother said. He's a child. He's curious. Tell him.

I see, my uncle Khosrove groaned. You, too. My own sister. My own poor and burning little sister.

Well, what is the Arab's name? my mother said.

I won't tell, my uncle Khosrove said. That's all. I won't tell.

He got up and left the house.

He doesn't know the man's name, my mother explained. And you've got no business irritating him.

Three days later when my uncle Khosrove and the Arab came to our house I was in the parlor.

My uncle Khosrove came straight to me and said, His name is Khalil. Now go away.

I left the house and waited in the yard for one of my cousins to arrive. After ten minutes, nobody arrived, so I went to my cousin Mourad's house and spent an hour arguing with him about which of us would be the stronger in five years. We wrestled three times and I lost three times, but once I *almost* won.

When I got home the two men were gone. I ran straight to the parlor from the back of the house, but they weren't there. The only thing in the room was their smell and the smell of tobacco smoke.

What did they talk about? I asked my mother.

I didn't listen, my mother said.

Did they talk at all? I said.

I don't know, my mother said.

They didn't, I said.

Some people talk when they have something to say, my mother said, and some people don't.

How can you talk if you don't say anything? I said.

You talk without words. We are always talking without words.

Well, what good are words, then?

Not very good, most of the time. Most of the time they're only good to keep back what you really want to say, or something you don't want known.

Well, do *they* talk? I said.

I think they do, my mother said. They just sit and sip coffee and smoke cigarettes. They never open their mouths, but they're talking all the time. They understand one another and don't need to open their mouths. They have nothing to keep back.

Do they really know what they're talking about? I said.

Of course, my mother said.

Well, what is it? I said.

I can't tell you, my mother said, because it isn't in words; but they know.

For a year my uncle Khosrove and the Arab came to our house every now and then and sat in the parlor. Sometimes they sat an hour, sometimes two.

Once my uncle Khosrove suddenly shouted at the Arab, *Pay no attention to it, I tell you*, although the Arab had said nothing.

But most of the time nothing at all was said until it was time for them to go. Then my uncle Khosrove would say quietly, The poor and burning orphans, and the Arab would brush dust from his knee.

One day when my uncle Khosrove came to our house alone, I realized that the Arab had not visited our house in several months.

Where is the Arab? I said.

What Arab? my uncle Khosrove said.

That poor and burning little Arab that used to come here with you, I said. Where is he?

Mariam! my uncle Khosrove shouted. He was standing, terrified.

Oh-oh, I thought. What's wrong now? What have I done now?

Mariam! he shouted. Mariam!

My mother came into the parlor.

What is it? she said.

If you please, my uncle Khosrove said. He is your son. You are my little sister. Please send him away. I love him with all my heart. He is an

American. He was born here. He will be a great man some day. I have no doubt about it. Please send him away.

Why, what is it? my mother said.

What is it? *What is it?* He talks. He asks questions. I love him.

Aram, my mother said.

I was standing too, and if my uncle Khosrove was angry at me, I was angrier at him.

Where is the Arab? I said.

My uncle Khosrove pointed me out to my mother—with despair. There you are, his gesture said. Your son. My nephew. My own flesh and blood. You see? We are all poor and burning orphans. All except *him.*

Aram, my mother said.

Well, if you don't talk, I said, I can't understand. *Where is the Arab?*

My uncle Khosrove left the house without a word.

The Arab is dead, my mother said.

When did he tell you? I said.

He didn't tell me, my mother said.

Well, how did you find out? I said.

I don't know how, my mother said, but he is dead.

My uncle Khosrove didn't visit our house again for many days. For a while I thought he would *never* come back. When he came at last he stood in the parlor with his hat on his head and said, The Arab is dead. He died an orphan in an alien world, six thousand miles from home. He wanted to go home and die. He wanted to see his sons again. He wanted to talk to them again. He wanted to smell them. He wanted to hear them breathing. He had no money. He used to think about them all the time. Now he is dead. Now go away. I love you.

I wanted to ask some more questions, especially about the Arab's sons, how many there were, how long he had been away from them, and so on, but I decided I would rather visit my cousin Mourad and see if I couldn't hold him down *now*, so I went away without saying a word—which most likely pleased my uncle Khosrove very much, and made him feel maybe there was some hope for me, after all.

A Word to Scoffers

From Reno to Salt Lake City all you get to see from a bus or any other kind of conveyance is desert, and in August all you feel is dry heat. Desert is sand spread out evenly in every direction, different kinds of cactus, and the sun.

Sometimes the sand looks white, sometimes brown, and around sundown the color of the sand changes from white or brown to yellow, and then black. Then it is night, and that is when the desert is best of all. When the desert and night join one another you get what amounts to silence.

This is a thing you remember and remember.

The remembrance is full of the hush and mystery of the world.

I know all this because I rode in a bus from Reno to Salt Lake City once, on my way to New York.

My uncle Gyko told me to get out of town and go to New York. He said, Don't stay in these little town. Go to Nor York. I tell you, Aram, eat ease insanity.

That's how it happened that I rode in the bus from Reno to Salt Lake City.

That was country I had never seen, or imagined. Wide dry wasteland, full of nothing. I kept my eyes open night and day watching that country. I didn't want to pass through country like that without finding out all I could about it.

The bus left Reno a little after midnight. Reno is one of those American towns that lives on nothing but the disease of people. The only thing there is gambling and whoring.

Consequently, the city lights are bright.

I remember going into a gambling joint and seeing clearly all the way from the rail to the poker game in the corner of the room the three black hairs growing out of the dealer's nose. It was that light.

Then the bus rolled out of Reno into the desert. That was a mighty remarkable difference to dwell upon: first the bright lights of the gambling joints of Reno, and then the desert at night. I dwelt on those bright lights and the desert from midnight till morning, and even then I didn't find out enough for one small sentence of three words.

All I did in the morning was yawn. When the bus stopped, I got out and had a good look. Well, all it was was dirt and sky, and the sun coming up. I couldn't think of three little words with which to clarify the situation. It was nothing. That's all. Nothing at all. No streets, no buildings, no corners, no doorways, no doors, no windows, no signs, nothing.

My uncle Gyko told me not to stay in a small town like the small town I was born in, and now I couldn't wait to get out of the desert into a big town and be able to understand something again. I began to figure it wouldn't do my uncle Gyko any harm to get out of our small town and pass through the desert himself. I figured he might not be so sure about everything if he got himself all surrounded by the desert, day and night, and felt that sullen silence. My uncle Gyko hadn't read as many smart books as I had read because he read slower and with greater difficulty, but he had read everything he had read very carefully and memorized whole pages of the works of writers who had lived in Europe as long as two hundred years ago. In his own broken-English way he used to cut loose with a lot of derivative invective. He used to call people sheep, and claim that he himself wasn't a sheep. I myself was just as wise as my uncle Gyko, only I didn't speak with an accent. My uncle Gyko said, Get out of these town and go to Nor York.

I figured my uncle Gyko ought to visit the desert himself and see how *he* felt. I figured I couldn't figure out anything in a place so empty as all that. I didn't feel like feeling smart at all. I felt lonely, too. That's why I tried to start a conversation with the only girl on the bus, inexperienced as I was in the art of polite conversation.

What's the name of this place? I said to the girl.

She was at least thirty-five and very ugly.

What place? the girl said.

All this land around here, I said.

I don't know, the girl said.

That was as far as the conversation went until late the next afternoon when the girl asked me what time it was and I said I didn't know.

I didn't even know what day it was. I was beginning to find out that all I knew was that I didn't know anything, and wanted to get to Salt Lake City as soon as possible so I could see streets and places again and people walking around, and maybe get back my tremendous book-learning that was so useless in the desert.

Just let me get to a city again, I said, and I'll be as smart as the next fellow. Maybe smarter. Just get me out of this desolation and I'll start throwing wise cracks all over the place.

Well, I was wrong. When I got to Salt Lake City I felt more confused than ever. I couldn't find a room for fifty cents, or a restaurant where I could get a big dinner for fifteen cents. I felt tired and hungry and sleepy and sore at the people in the streets, and the buildings there, and I wished to Christ I hadn't left home.

I paid a dollar for a little room in an old hotel. The room turned out to be haunted. It was the toughest room I ever tried to stay in, but I used to be very stubborn in those days and I stayed in the room until I could see every kind of evil form that never in the history of the world reached material substance, and could hear every kind of awful sound that science insisted didn't exist. I was scared stiff. In two hours I didn't move from the rocking-chair in the middle of the room because I was sure something would grab hold of me and strangle me before I could get to the door or window. The room was full of evil things. I don't know how I got out of it alive, but I got out all right.

I walked through the streets of Salt Lake City and found a restaurant where you could get a hamburger dinner for a quarter.

After dinner, I went back to that little room in that little hotel and got in bed without taking off any of my clothes, not even my shoes or my hat. I wanted to be ready to sprint in case of riot, fire, earthquake, flood, pestilence, or any other kind of emergency. Before turning out the light I practiced getting out of the bed and getting to the door. I was making it in record-breaking time, one jump to the door, and maybe three or four seconds to the street. I left the room only three times during the course of the night, but awoke in the morning refreshed and cheerful.

I got up at five in the morning because I didn't want to miss the bus that was leaving town at half past nine.

At a quarter past nine I was standing in front of the bus depot, smoking a five cent cigar, trying to get back my young irreligious poise so that I could be happy again when a very tall and melancholy-looking man of fifty in overalls handed me a little pamphlet and said, Son, are you saved?

I had never before seen such a melancholy-looking man. Six feet two or three, no more than a hundred and twenty pounds, unshaved, and full of religion. I figured he was going to ask me for a dime because he looked more like a hungry tramp than a holy man, but all he did was hand me that religious pamphlet and ask if I was saved. The title of the little story on the pamphlet was *A Word to Scoffers*, and the missionary had found his man all right. I didn't know. I couldn't tell at the time. I was all mixed up.

I took a sophisticated puff on the nickel cigar and said, No, I don't think I'm saved, but I'm sympathetic.

Brother, said the religious man, I can save you through the gospel of Brigham Young.

I'm leaving town in fifteen minutes, I said.

That's all right, said the religious man. I once saved a man in four minutes.

That's fast work, I said. What do I have to do to get saved?

Son, said the religious man, you don't have to do anything. You have no idea how close to being saved every man alive is. Any man you can think of. I used to be something of a rounder myself, snappy clothes, strong drink, panatela cigars, cards, dice, horses, sporting girls. Everything. Changed over-night.

Why? I said.

Lost my luck and couldn't sleep, said the religious man. Fell to thinking and found out I never was intended to be an enemy of the truth.

What truth? 1 said.

God's *holy* truth, said the missionary. No man is ever much of an enemy of the truth. All them crazy things people do is because they don't know what they're after.

Well, what *are* they after? I said.

Truth, he said. Every man who cheats at cards, carries on with women, holds up a bank, gets drunk, or travels, is looking for truth. I guess you're going somewhere, son. Where you going?

I'm on my way to New York, I said.

Well, he said, you won't find any truth there. I been there six times in the last thirty years. You can go hopping around all over the world and never find out anything because that ain't the way you find out anything. All you got to do is change your attitude.

That ought to be easy, I said.

Easiest thing in the world, he said.

I'm game, I said. I've got nothing to lose. How do I change my attitude?

Well, said the religious man, you stop trying to figure things out and you *believe.*

Believe, I said. Believe *what?*

Why, everything, he said. Everything you can think of, left, right, north, east, south, west, upstairs, downstairs and all around, inside, out, visible, invisible, good and bad and neither and both. That's the little secret. Took me fifty years to find out.

Is that all I have to do? I said.

That's all, son, said the missionary.

O.K., I said. I *believe.*

Son, said the religious man, you're saved. You can go to New York now or anywhere else, and everything will be smooth and easy.

I hope you're right, I said.

You'll find out, said the religious man.

The big bus came to the curb and I got in. The lanky man of God came to the window, smiling proudly.

You're the fifty-seventh man I've saved, he said.

Well, so long, I said. Many thanks for the little secret.

Glad to do it, he said. Only don't forget. Just believe.

I won't forget, I said. I'll believe.

Anything, he said.

The motor of the bus started.

Any old thing at all, I said.

The bus belched smoke and slowly rolled away.

I thought I was kidding the old padre of Salt Lake City, getting back my vast book-learning and anti-religious poise, but I was sadly mistaken, because unwittingly I *had* been saved. In less than ten minutes after the bus left Salt Lake City I was believing everything, left and right, as the missionary had said, and it's been that way with me ever since.

Tracy's Tiger

Chapter 1

*T*homas Tracy had a tiger.

It was actually a black panther, but that's no matter, because he *thought* of it as a tiger.

It had white teeth.

This is how he came to get his tiger:

When he was three and went by the sound of things somebody said *tiger!* Whatever a *tiger!* was, Tracy wanted his own.

One day he was walking in town with his father when he saw something in the window of a fish restaurant.

"Buy me that tiger," he said.

"That's a lobster," his father said.

"I don't want it, then," Tracy said.

Several years later Tracy visited the zoo with his mother and saw a real tiger in a cage. It was something like the tiger of the word, but it wasn't *his* tiger.

For years Tracy saw pictures of all kinds of animals in dictionaries, paintings, encyclopaedias, and movies. Among these animals stalked many black panthers, but not once did Tracy think of one of them as his own tiger.

One day, however, Tracy was at the zoo alone, fifteen years of age, smoking a cigarette and leering at girls, when all of a sudden he came face to face with *his* tiger.

It was a sleeping black panther that instantly awoke, raised its head, stared straight at Tracy, got to its feet, hummed the way black panthers do, saying something that sounded like *Eyeej*, walked to the edge of the cage, stood for a moment looking at Tracy, then wandered back to the platform on which it had been sleeping. There it plopped down again and began to stare far out into space, as many miles and years out into space as there are miles and years in space.

Tracy in turn stood staring at the black panther. He stared five minutes, chucked away his cigarette, cleared his throat, spat, and walked out of the zoo.

"That's my tiger," he said.

He never went back to the zoo to have another look at his tiger because he didn't need to. He'd got it. He'd got it whole in the five minutes he'd watched it staring into infinity with a tiger's terrible resignation and pride.

Chapter 2

When he was twenty-one Tracy and his tiger went to New York, where Tracy took a job at Otto Seyfang's, a coffee importer's on Warren Street in Washington Market. Most of the other businesses of that area were produce houses, so that besides having free coffee to drink—in the Tasting Department—Tracy had free fruit and vegetables to eat.

The pay for the unskilled work Tracy did was poor, but the work was good and hard. It was not easy at first for Tracy to throw a sack of coffee beans weighing a hundred pounds over his shoulder and walk fifty yards with it, but after a week it was nothing at all, and even the tiger marveled at the ease with which Tracy threw the stuff around.

One day Tracy went to his immediate superior, a man named Valora, to discuss his future.

"I want to be a taster," Tracy said.

"Who ast you?" Valora said.

"Who ast me *what?*"

"Who ast you to be a taster?"

"Nobody."

"What do you know about tasting?" Valora said.

"I *like* coffee," Tracy said.

"What do you know about tasting?" Valora said again.

"I've done a little in the Tasting Department."

"You had coffee and doughnuts in the Tasting Department, the same as all the others who ain't professional tasters," Valora said.

"When the coffee was good I knew it," Tracy said. "When it was bad I knew it."

"How did you know?"

"By tasting."

"We got three tasters—Nimmo, Peberdy, and Ringert," Valora said. "They been with Otto Seyfang's twenty-five, thirty-five, forty-one years. How long you been with the firm?"

"Two weeks."

"You want to be a taster?"

"Yes, sir."

"You want to get to the top of the ladder in two weeks?"

"Yes, sir."

"You don't want to wait your turn?"

"No, sir."

At this moment Otto Seyfang himself came into Valora's office. Valora jumped up from his chair, but Otto Seyfang, a man of seventy, wouldn't have it—the jumping up, that is—and he said, "Sit down, Valora! Go ahead!"

"Go ahead?" Valora said.

"Now, go ahead where I interrupted and don't act dumb," Otto Seyfang said.

"We was talking about this new man applying for a job as taster."

"Go ahead."

"He's been here two weeks, and he wants to be a taster."

"Go ahead and talk about it," Otto Seyfang said.

"Yes, sir," Valora said. He turned to Tracy. "After only two weeks," he said, "you want a job that Nimmo, Peberdy, and Ringert didn't get until they was with the firm twenty, twenty-five, thirty years? Is that right?"

"Yes, sir," Tracy said.

"You want to come in here to Otto Seyfang's just like that and get the best job?"

"Yes, sir."

"You know all about coffee tasting?"

"Yes, sir."

"What's good coffee taste like?"

"Coffee."

"What's the *best* coffee taste like?"

"Good coffee."

"What's the difference between *good* coffee and the *best* coffee?"

"Advertising," Tracy said.

Valora turned to Otto Seyfang as much as to say, "What are you going to do with a wise guy like this from out of town?" But Otto Seyfang didn't encourage Valora's attitude. He just waited for Valora to go on.

"They ain't no opening in the Tasting Department," Valora said.

"When *will* there be an opening?" Tracy said.

"Just as soon as Nimmo dies," Valora said. "But there are thirty-nine others at Otto Seyfang's who are ahead of you for the job."

"Nimmo won't die for some time," Tracy said.

"I'll tell him to hurry," Valora said.

"I don't want Nimmo to hurry."

"But you want his job?"

"No, sir," Tracy said. "I want *four* tasters in the Tasting Department."

"*You* want to be the fourth?" Valora said. "Not Shively, who's next in line?"

"What line?"

"The coffee tasters' line," Valora said. "You want to step in ahead of Shively?"

"I don't want to step in ahead of him," Tracy said. "I want to step over to the side into the Tasting Department, because I *can* taste coffee, and I know when it's good."

"You do?"

"Yes, sir."

"Where you from?" Valora said.

"San Francisco," Tracy said.

"Why don't you go back to San Francisco?"

Valora turned to Otto Seyfang.

"That's about it, isn't it, sir?" he said.

Valora didn't know, and neither did Otto Seyfang, that it was Tracy's tiger that had done the talking. They thought it had been Tracy himself.

At first Otto Seyfang believed he might do something surprising that he had seen happen in a stage play once. Surprising, that is, to Valora, and perhaps even to Tracy. But after a while he decided he wasn't in any stage play, he was in his coffee importing house and open for business, not art. He had believed he would hire a fourth coffee taster at that, Tracy himself, because Tracy had had guts enough to go up to Valora and tell him the truth: that he, Tracy, knew good coffee when he, Tracy, tasted it, and on top of that to make known that he, Tracy, had ideas in his head. Advertising, for instance. (What a joke art is when you get right down to it, Otto Seyfang thought. Just because a boy from California comes back with quick answers to an imbecile's questions, in art you're supposed to give the boy what he asks for, and make something of him. But what was the boy *actually*? Was he a coffee man? Did he live and breathe coffee? No. He was a smart aleck.)

Thus, Otto Seyfang decided against doing anything surprising.

"What's your work?" Otto Seyfang said to Tracy.

"I'm a song writer," Tracy said.

"Ah! What's your work at *Otto Seyfang's*?" the old man said. "Do you know who I am?"

"No, sir," Tracy said. "Who are you?"

"Otto Seyfang."

"Do you know who I am?" Tracy said.

"Who are you?"

"Thomas Tracy."

(*I've got this company,* Otto Seyfang thought. *I've had it forty-five years. What have you got?*)

(*I've got a tiger,* Tracy thought in reply to Otto Seyfang's thought.)

They went on talking, but first these thoughts were neatly exchanged.

"What's your work at Otto Seyfang's?" the old man said.

"I throw and carry the sacks," Tracy said.

"Do you want to keep your job?" Otto Seyfang said.

Tracy knew what the tiger was going to say and he was eagerly waiting for the tiger to say it when he discovered that the tiger had fallen asleep from boredom.

Tracy soon heard himself say, "Yes, sir, I want to keep my job."

"Then get the hell back to your work," Otto Seyfang said. "And if you ever waste Valora's time again by coming in here to talk nonsense, I'll fire you. Valora knows how to waste his own time without any help from you. Don't you, Valora?"

"Yes, sir," Valora said.

Tracy went back to his work, leaving the tiger fast asleep under Valora's desk.

When the tiger woke up and went back to Tracy, Tracy wouldn't speak to it.

"Eyeej," the tiger said in the hope of breaking the ice.

"Eyeej my foot," Tracy said. "That was a nice trick to play on a pal. I thought you were going to kick it around. I didn't think you were going to fall asleep. When he said do you want to keep your job, I thought you were going to say something sensible. You call yourself a tiger?"

"Moyl," the tiger murmured.

"Moyl," Tracy said. "Go away."

Tracy threw the sacks in angry silence the rest of the day, for never before had the tiger fallen asleep at a time so appropriate for bad manners, and Tracy didn't like it. He was deeply troubled about the probability of a dubious strain in the tiger's lineage.

After work that day Tracy walked with Nimmo to the subway. Nimmo was nervous all the way there from having tasted coffee all day. Nimmo was almost as old as Otto Seyfang himself and Nimmo had no tiger, had in fact no idea there *were* tigers to be had. All Nimmo was doing was standing in Shively's way. And Shively was standing in the way of the thirty-eight others at Otto Seyfang's.

277

Well, Tracy had gone to work, but at the same time he had also written three lines to a song. He would go on working at Otto Seyfang's for a while, waiting for the tiger to snap out of it, but he would stand in nobody's way and in nobody's line.

When Tracy got off the subway and went up to Broadway he decided to have a cup of coffee, and he *had* a cup. He was an expert taster, and knew it. He just didn't want to wait any thirty-five years to prove it. He drank a second cup, then a third, tasting expertly.

Chapter 3

The eye of Tracy's tiger now and then wandered on the chance that it might behold a young lady tiger with appropriate manners for whatever might come of their seeing of one another, but almost never, when the tiger looked, did it see a young lady tiger. It was young lady alley cats. On the few occasions when it did see a young lady tiger Tracy's tiger was going somewhere in a hurry and had time enough only to turn, still moving ahead, to look again. This seemed a sad state of affairs, so the tiger said so.

"Lune," it said.

"What do you mean?" Tracy said.

"Alune."

"I don't get it."

"Ah lune."

"What's that?"

"Lunalune."

"Doesn't mean anything."

"Ah lunalune," the tiger said patiently.

"Speak English if you want to say something," Tracy said.

"La," the tiger said.

"That's almost French," Tracy said. "Speak English. You know I don't know French."

"Sola."

"Solar?"

"So," the tiger said.

"Don't *shorten* the words," Tracy said, "lengthen them, so I can figure out what you're trying to say."

"S," the tiger said.

"You can talk better than that," Tracy said. "Talk or shut up."

The tiger shut up.

Tracy considered what the tiger *had* said, and then suddenly it came to him.

This happened during the lunch hour. Tracy was standing in the sunlight on the steps of the entrance to Otto Seyfang's listening to Nimmo, Peberdy, and Ringert talking about the eminence they had achieved in the coffee world through faithful tasting. Every now and then Tracy tried to get a word in edgewise about the song he was writing, but he never quite made it.

He was trying to figure out what the tiger had said when a girl in a tight-fitting yellow knit dress came walking down Warren Street. She had a great deal of black hair combed straight down. There was so much of it that it seemed to be a mane. It shined with life and crackled with electricity. The muscles of Tracy's tiger became taut, its slim head pushed forward toward the girl, its tail shot straight out, rigid except for the almost imperceptible vibrating of it, and the tiger hummed low and violently, saying, "Eyeej."

The professional coffee tasters hearing the hum turned to Tracy in astonishment, for never before had they heard such an extraordinary sound.

"Oh," Tracy said to the tiger. "I get it."

"Eyeej," the tiger replied, as if in pain, its head moving out still farther, while Tracy's own eyes *dived* into the young lady's. The hum and the diving happened at the same time. The girl heard the hum, received the dive, almost stopped, almost smiled, pushed herself tighter against the yellow knit dress, and then danced on, the tiger moaning softly.

"Is that what they say in California?" Nimmo said.

"Eyeej," Tracy said.

"Say it again," Peberdy said.

Tracy, watching the girl go, watching the tiger lope after her, said it again.

"Hear that, Ringert?" Peberdy said. "That's what they say in California when they see a beauty."

"Don't worry," Ringert said. "I heard it."

"You *heard* it," Nimmo said, "but can you *do* it?"

"Of course I can't do it," Ringert said, "but neither can either of you old coffee tasters."

The coffee tasters agreed with regret that they could not do it, and then everybody went back to work, Tracy's tiger loping after Tracy to the piled sacks of coffee at the far end of the store room overlooking the alley. Tracy threw the sacks around all afternoon as if they were bean bags.

"Whoever she is," he said to the tiger, "she works around here somewhere. I'll see her tomorrow during the lunch hour, and the next day, too. The day after that I'll ask her to lunch."

Tracy talked to the tiger all afternoon, but all the tiger did was hum. Every now and then the other sack-throwers heard the hum. They were all young men, and they wanted to imitate the hum, but it was inimitable. You had to have a tiger. One of them, a man named Kalany, came near doing it, and boldly remarked to Tracy that anything anybody from California could do, *he* could do, being from Texas.

"Tomorrow, the next day, the day after," Tracy said to the tiger. "Then I'll ask her to lunch."

Sure enough, the schedule was met.

There she was across the table from Tracy at the O.K. Café, both of them eating, the tiger stalking around the table, trying not to hum or gulp.

"My name's Tom Tracy," Tracy said.

"I know," the girl said. "You told me."

"I forgot."

"I know. You told me three times. You mean Thomas of course, not Tom, don't you?"

"Yes," Tracy said. "Thomas Tracy. That's my name. That's all it is, I mean, that's just my name. A man's name isn't all there is to a man."

"Any middle name?" the girl said.

"No," Tracy said. "Just Thomas Tracy. Tom for short, if you want to shorten it."

"I don't want to," the girl said.

"No?" Tracy said, for this remark had great meaning for him. He was thrilled by the hope of the wonderful nature of this meaning. He was too thrilled to notice that the tiger was staring at something with so much excitement that its whole body was vibrating. He looked to see what it was that the tiger was staring at, and he saw that it was a young lady tiger.

"No?" Tracy said again.

"Yes," the girl said. "I like the name Thomas Tracy just as it is. Aren't you going to ask me *my* name?"

"What is it?" Tracy asked in a hushed voice.

"Laura Luthy," the girl said.

"Oh," Tracy moaned. "Oh, Laura Luthy."

"Do you like it?" Laura Luthy said.

"Do I *like* it?" Tracy said. "Oh, Laura, Laura Luthy."

The tigers chased around Laura Luthy and Thomas Tracy while they had lunch and they chased around them when they got up after lunch and walked to the cashier's where Tracy plunked down eighty-five cents for both lunches.

What did he care about money?

In the street Tracy took Laura's arm and walked past Otto Seyfang's, past Nimmo, Peberdy, and Ringert, standing out front. The two tigers walked sedately side by side. Tracy walked Laura to the office where she worked as a stenographer, two blocks down Warren Street near the docks.

"Tomorrow?" he said, not knowing what he meant but hoping *she* did.

"Yes," Laura said.

Tracy's tiger hummed. Laura's tiger half-smiled, hung its head, then turned away.

Tracy walked back to Otto Seyfang's, to the coffee tasters standing out front.

"Tracy," Nimmo said. "I hope I live long enough to see how this is going to turn out."

"You will," Tracy said. He spoke with anger and sincerity. "You'll live, Nimmo, because you've *got* to."

The tiger was now standing in the middle of the sidewalk staring into space.

On his way home after work that day Tracy found the tiger still standing in the middle of the sidewalk, and stood there himself, getting in the way of the after-work human traffic. He stood there beside the tiger a long time, then turned and began to walk to the subway, the tiger reluctantly following him.

Chapter 4

Laura Luthy lived in Far Rockaway. Saturdays and Sundays she stayed home with her mother.

Laura's mother, if anything, was more beautiful than Laura herself, so that there was a continuous if delicate rivalry between them in the mirrors around the house, and in their remarks about moving-picture actors, stage actors, men of the neighborhood, and men of the church. (The church was across the street, so that they were able to *see* who the men were. Saturdays and Sundays they watched together, but the rest of the time

Laura's mother watched alone, or, being *free* to do so, didn't bother to do so. Now and then, though, it just happened that she saw a fine upright man enter the church late in the afternoon to confess, or collect a bill.)

This rivalry between mother and daughter enjoyed vigorous life in spite of the fact that Oliver Luthy, Laura's father, came home every night from work in Manhattan, and for twenty-four years had slept in the same bed with Mrs. Luthy, whose first name was Viola.

Mr. Luthy was in accounting. He had been in accounting as long as he'd been in the same bed, so to say, with Mrs. Luthy. It was she who had put him into it, expressing the opinion that it would be nicer if he were in something like accounting instead of in something like shipping, which was what he had been in when he had married her.

What he'd actually been was a shipping clerk, but Viola's way of putting it had always been that he was in shipping, for in putting it that way she often permitted herself to believe that it was cattle or tractors that he shipped, or perhaps *ships* themselves. She frequently believed that others got this fleeting impression, too, which she did not hasten to dispel. The impression seemed to dispel itself soon enough, anyway, but there was always that fleeting instant of daring if dubious glory.

Fine folk from nowhere in particular visited the Luthys quite frequently. There was something attractive about these visitors. They seemed to be, unlike the people one reads about in the society pages of newspapers, dirt. And yet, as their true selves became revealed—through the answering of kind questions asked by Viola—they seemed less and less to be dirt, and more and more as if, except for bad luck, they might have gone on the stage.

These visits were carefully planned, and generally fell on a Saturday afternoon. Once—no one knew but Viola herself— man named Glear, stepping out of the bathroom into the hall and finding himself face to face with Viola, on her way back to the parlor from her bedroom with an old copy of the *Reader's Digest* in which she wished to show Mr. Glear an article about transportation, took her swiftly into his arms and did something to her face that was approximately a kiss. He smelled of Sen-Sen, she remembered, and had he gone into pictures would have been given office work to do—that is, in the pictures themselves. Knowing what she knew, knowing the effect she'd had on a dynamic man who might have been a film actor, she was rather difficult for Mr. Luthy for two years.

By that time she had forgotten Mr. Glear's appearance and thought of him, not as Glear, but as Sherman, though God knows why.

"Whatever happened to that interesting man Sherman?" she once asked her husband, who replied that he had been made into a statue and placed in a park in Savannah.

Thomas Tracy himself visited the Luthys in Far Rockaway one Sunday afternoon.

The tiger had been tense during the entire journey to the Luthy house, impatient to see Laura's tiger again, and once Tracy and the tiger were inside the house extraordinary things began to happen.

Tracy noticed Laura's mother Viola, and Viola noticed Tracy. This noticing was not casual. It was understandable perhaps that Tracy *would* notice Viola, for there was a good deal about her that would have been impossible *not* to notice. She was all of Laura herself, not made larger by time, but more wicked by tiresome innocence.

Laura noticed this noticing that took place between Tracy and her mother, then noticed her father. *He* noticed that there was a great deal of action at the church across the street. Viola sent him for ice cream, which he was glad to fetch, for the church was on the way to the store, and he wanted to step in there to see what was going on.

When he was out of the house Viola brought a box of chocolates to Tracy and offered them to him with a considerable amount of implication. Laura, pretending to be glad that Tracy and her mother were getting on so well, asked to be excused a moment in order to see if she could find her penmanship certificate in which her name had been spelled Luty instead of Luthy.

Laura went off gaily, and there was Tracy and the tiger alone with Mrs. Luthy and the chocolates.

Tracy accepted a chocolate each time one was offered to him until he'd had six, whereupon, unable to account for it, he got up suddenly and accepted everything.

He was surprised to find that his acceptance was not unexpected, but rather anticipated. He, too, like Glear before him, grabbed the innocent woman and did something to her face that approximated a kiss. *His* breath smelled of teeth, Mrs. Luthy observed instantly. Tracy stepped aside just in time to let the tiger go by, and then stepped aside again as the tiger came back, moving with fury. He then gave the theory of the kiss another go.

He was in the midst of this second effort when Laura Luthy returned to the room.

Tracy tried to pretend that what he was actually doing was *not* what it appeared to be, although he could not imagine anything like it at all that he could pretend it was instead.

He saw Laura's tiger standing beside Laura, glaring at him with astonishment and hate. He then looked for the other tiger, but it was gone.

Tracy took his hat and left the house.

He saw Mr. Luthy coming around the church with the ice cream, but he hurried away in the opposite direction.

It was not until he was back on Broadway, among the Sunday evening multitudes, that the tiger found its way through the people to walk beside him again.

"Don't ever do that again," Tracy said.

The next day during the lunch hour Tracy stood in front of Otto Seyfang's in the hope of seeing Laura Luthy, but she didn't come down the street.

It was the same every day of that week.

Chapter 5

"How's it turning out?" Nimmo asked Tracy on Friday at noon.

"The song?" Tracy said.

"No," Nimmo said. "Who cares about the song? How's it turning out with you and the black-haired beauty in the bright yellow dress?"

"Eyeej," Tracy said mournfully.

"What do you mean?" Nimmo said.

"I went to her house in Far Rockaway last Sunday and met her mother," Tracy said. "She brought out a box of chocolates, and I ate six of them. I hate chocolates, but she kept pushing the box in front of my face and I kept taking them and eating them. I'm afraid it's not turning out very well."

"Why?" Nimmo said.

"Well," Tracy said, "I'd had all those chocolates, the father had gone for ice cream, the daughter had gone for the penmanship certificate, I grabbed the mother and kissed her."

"No?" Nimmo said.

"Yes," Tracy said.

The coffee taster began to hiccup violently.

"What's the matter?" Tracy said.

"I don't know," Nimmo said.

"Maybe you'd better go home and lie down," Tracy said.

"No, I'm all right," Nimmo said. "Just tell me exactly what happened. I've got to know."

"Well," Tracy said. "It's like I said. I guess the chocolates made me crazy."

"What are you going to do?" Nimmo said.

"I'll make it turn out all right some way or another," Tracy said.

"How?"

"I'll be standing out here in front of Otto Seyfang's someday during my lunch hour," Tracy said, "and another girl something like Laura Luthy will come down Warren Street, and this time when I go out to her house and meet her mother I won't eat any chocolates, that's all."

"There isn't another girl *like* Laura Luthy, though," Nimmo said. "I guess I'll go in and taste some coffee."

"You've got twenty minutes more on your lunch hour," Tracy said.

"No, I'll go in now," Nimmo said. "What's the use standing out here? What's the use waiting anymore?"

Nimmo was on his way in when he heard Tracy moan. He turned, and saw the black-haired beauty passing. But with her walked an unknown young man, obviously not from California, by appearance a bookkeeper.

Nimmo turned away in disgust, while Tracy stared in disbelief.

Tracy tried to smile but couldn't.

Laura Luthy passed by without even looking at him.

Nimmo couldn't stop hiccuping and was finally given the afternoon off. The following day he did not come to work. Monday morning Shively was in the Tasting Department at last, coming to work in his blue serge Sunday suit, for Nimmo was dead.

Some people say he died of the hiccups, but they are the kind of people who say Camille died of catarrh.

Chapter 6

What hearts have broken in times gone by, what hearts break now in our own times, what hearts shall break in times to come, Nimmo gone, Laura Luthy lost, Shively in the Tasting Department at last, Peberdy and Ringert treating him like a dog, frequently questioning his taste, looking at one another knowingly.

The three lines of Tracy's song turned out to be, as so many other things turn out to be, dirt. The song faded away, the very scrap of paper on which Tracy had so carefully written the words was lost, the melody was forgotten.

Tracy and the tiger walked one Sunday to Saint Patrick's on Fifth Avenue, burning with the fervor of an old and undefined religion that somehow seemed new, each of them walking in man's or animal's loneliness.

They went in and looked at everything.

The following Saturday Tracy quit his job at Otto Seyfang's and went back to San Francisco.

A number of years went by.

Then one day Tracy was twenty-seven, and he was back in New York, and he was walking there as he'd walked six years ago.

He turned off Broadway when he came to Warren Street and went down the street to Otto Seyfang's, which now bore the name of Keeney's Warehouse.

Did that mean coffee had failed, too? Nimmo, Peberdy, Ringert, Shively, Seyfang—had they all failed?

The tiger stiffened when it saw the entrance of the building, for it was there the tiger had stood one whole afternoon staring the way Laura Luthy had gone.

Tracy hurried away from Keeney's Warehouse, stopped a taxi, got in, and got out at the Public Library.

From there Tracy and the tiger began to walk up Fifth Avenue again. The street was full of Sunday people, men and women and their children.

Tracy had not yet found the one to take the place of Laura Luthy. Nimmo had predicted that Tracy would *never* find her, and perhaps Nimmo had been right, after all.

Tracy stood on a corner, a block from Saint Patrick's, and watched a small boy and the boy's sister cross the street. The tiger came up beside him. Tracy rested his hand on the tiger's head.

"They might have been mine," Tracy said.

"Eyeej," the tiger said.

Tracy strolled on, the tiger beside him. He was astonished to find that all of the people on his side of the street were moving swiftly to the other side of the street. He glanced at the other side of the street and saw people standing there, crowds of them, looking at him, some of them through cameras.

In all innocence Tracy decided to go across the street to find out what all the excitement was about, but when he stepped down from the curb to go, the people across the street began to run, some of them shouting, and a number of women screaming.

Tracy turned and looked at the tiger again.

Well, he'd had the tiger beside him most of his life, but never before had anything like this happened.

Never before had anybody else seen the tiger.

Was it possible now that the tiger was actually being seen by others, by everybody?

A number of dogs on leashes began to yap and bark and carry on. This also was something new. Tracy stopped in the middle of Fifth Avenue to let a bus go by, and was astonished once again, this time by the face of the driver of the bus, and by the faces of the passengers.

"Well, what do you know?" Tracy said to the tiger. "I believe they can see you. I believe they can actually see you, just as I've seen you most of my life, but look at them, they're terrified, they're scared to death. Good God, they ought to know there's nothing to be afraid of."

"Eyeej," the tiger said.

"Yes," Tracy said. "I haven't heard you speak so well since we were at Otto Seyfang's and Laura Luthy came dancing down Warren Street."

Tracy and the tiger moved up Fifth Avenue until they were across the street from Saint Patrick's. Tracy had planned to go into the church, as he and the tiger had done six years ago, and so he began to cross the street, to get to the church, but as he did so the few people in front of the church broke and ran. And then everybody in the church came out. Tracy and the tiger were late for church, but even so, they would go in, and Tracy would walk all the way down the center aisle with the tiger and look again at all the fine things there, the wonderful height and light, the stained-glass windows, the fine pillars, the burning candles.

The people who came out of the church seemed at peace, and then suddenly they deteriorated, some of them running down side streets, some up and down Fifth Avenue, and some back into the church, to hide there.

"I'm awful sorry about this," Tracy said. "It's never happened before, as you know."

"Eyeej," the tiger said.

"We're going to church anyway," Tracy said.

He rested his hand on the tiger's head, and thus they went together to the steps of the church, up the steps, and then on to the handsome area that was inside.

But if the *area* was handsome, the people still in the area were not, including several men in robes. Their going was swift and untidy.

Tracy and the tiger walked slowly down the center aisle. He noticed shut doors here and there opening a little, frightened eyes staring out at him, and he saw the doors shut again, heard them being locked or bolted.

"Well, it *is* a beautiful place," Tracy said, "but you remember how different it was when we came here six years ago. The place was full of people then, men, women, and children, and they were all glad about something, not the way they are now, scared to death, gone running, or hiding behind doors. What are they afraid of? What's happened to them?"

"Eyeej," the tiger said.

Tracy and the tiger left the church by a side door that opened on 50th Street, but when they came to the street Tracy saw an armoured car standing there, with gun barrels pointed at him and the tiger.

He looked down the street, and there near Madison Avenue he saw another armoured car. He looked up to Fifth Avenue, and there on the corner he saw two more of them. Beyond the armoured cars was a multitude of people, all terrified, waiting for a fight of some kind, and an outcome.

The man who sat in the driver's seat of the armoured car directly in front of Tracy quickly raised the window of the car, to be better protected against the tiger.

"What's the matter?" Tracy said.

"For God's sake, man," the driver replied, "don't you see the animal beside you?"

"Of course I see it," Tracy said.

"It's a panther escaped from the circus," the driver said.

"Don't be silly," Tracy said. "It's never been *near* the circus. And it's *not* a panther, it's a tiger."

"Stand aside, man," the driver said, "so one of the men can shoot the animal."

"Shoot it?" Tracy said. "Are you crazy?"

He began to walk down 50th Street toward Madison Avenue. The driver of the armoured car started the motor, and the car moved slowly beside Tracy, the driver trying to argue him into stepping away from the tiger.

"Stand aside, man," the driver said.

"Go on," Tracy said. "Take your armoured car back to the bank or the garage or wherever it is you keep it."

"Stand back or we'll shoot anyway," the driver said.

"You wouldn't dare," Tracy said.

"O.K., boy," the driver said. "You asked for it."

Tracy heard the shot. He looked to see if the tiger had been hit. It hadn't, but it *was* off for Madison Avenue.

The tiger was swift, swifter than Tracy had ever before known it to be. When it reached the second armoured car on 50th Street another shot was fired, the tiger leaped, fell, and when it began to run again Tracy noticed that it did so with the right front foot held up. When the tiger reached Madison Avenue, it turned uptown, and disappeared, the nearest armoured car going after it with all of its slow might.

Tracy broke into a trot, chasing after the tiger.

He was stopped at the corner by three officers. They pushed him into the second armoured car and drove off with him.

"What do you want to kill my tiger for?" Tracy said to the driver. "That animal escaped from the circus last night, after mauling a keeper," the driver said.

"What are you talking about?" Tracy said.

"You heard me," the man said.

"I've had that tiger most of my life," Tracy said.

"You haven't had *any* tiger most of your life," the driver said, "but you've had *something*, and we'll soon find out what it is."

Chapter 7

Tracy sat in a Bank of England chair at the center of an enormous room in which newspapermen, photographers, police officers, animal trainers, and a good many others milled about.

If the tiger had actually not been his own tiger, as they said, his own tiger was certainly not with Tracy now.

He sat alone.

The tiger did not sit on the floor at his feet.

Tracy had been in the chair more than an hour.

Somebody new came into the room suddenly.

"Dr. Pingitzer," Tracy heard somebody say.

This was a small, smiling man of seventy or so.

"Now," the man said quickly to the crowd. "What is it?"

The doctor was drawn to one side and surrounded by a group of experts, several of whom told him what it was.

"Ah ha," Tracy heard the doctor say. The doctor went quickly to Tracy.

"My boy," he said. "I am Rudolph Pingitzer."

Tracy got up and shook Rudolph Pingitzer's hand.

"Thomas Tracy," he said.

"Ah ha, Thomas Tracy," Dr. Pingitzer turned to the others. "Perhaps a chair like this for *me*, too?"

Another Bank of England chair was quickly fetched for the doctor. He sat down and said pleasantly, "I am seventy-two years old."

"I am twenty-seven," Tracy said.

Dr. Pingitzer filled a pipe, spilled a good deal of tobacco over his clothing which he did not bother to brush off, used seven matches to get the pipe lighted, puffed at it a dozen times, then said with the pipe in his mouth, "I have wife, sixty-nine years old, boy forty-five years old, psychiatrist, boy forty-two years old, psychiatrist, boy thirty-nine years old, psychiatrist, girl thirty-six years old, says *thirty-one* years old, psychiatrist, girl thirty-one years old, says *twenty-six* years old, psychiatrist, furnished apartment, phonograph, piano, television, typewriter, but with typewriter I have mechanical disorder."

"Why don't you get it fixed?" Tracy said.

"Ah, yes," Dr. Pingitzer said. "Never use typewriter. Is for grandchildren. Junk. I have these things, mostly psychiatrist."

"Do you have any money?" Tracy said.

"No," Dr. Pingitzer said. "Is expensive so many psychiatrists. Have books. Have also, ah, yes, bed. For sleep. At night. I lie down. Sleep. Is change."

"Do you have any friends?" Tracy said.

"Many friends," Dr. Pingitzer said. "Of course when I say friends"—Dr. Pingitzer's hands moved quickly, he made odd little noises—"you understand I mean"—more noises—"naturally. Who knows?"

"Do you go to church?" Tracy said.

"Ah," Dr. Pingitzer said. "Yes. Sentiment. I like it. It is nice."

A newspaperman stepped forward, and said, "How about *you* asking the questions, doctor?"

"Ah ha?" the doctor said quickly. "If to be interview with Dr. Pingitzer room to be empty."

A police captain who was in charge, a man named Huzinga, said quickly, "O.K., you heard the doctor. Everybody out."

There was a good deal of protesting on the part of the newspapermen, but Huzinga and his men got everybody out into the hall. When the room was empty, the doctor, puffing on his pipe peacefully, smiled at Tracy, then began to doze. Tracy himself was tired by now, so he began to doze, too. The old man snored, but Tracy didn't.

After a moment the door was pushed open, and a photographer quickly took a picture of the men asleep in the Bank of England chairs.

Huzinga then came in and woke the doctor up.

"Ah ha," the doctor said.

Huzinga was about to wake Tracy up, too, but the doctor said, "No. Important."

"Yes, doctor," Huzinga said.

He tiptoed out of the room.

The little man sat and watched Tracy's face. After a moment Tracy opened his eyes.

"I dream I was in Vienna," the doctor said.

"When were you there last?" Tracy said,

"Twenty years ago," Dr. Pingitzer said. "Long, long ago. I like very much ice cream. Vanilla."

"Do you like coffee?" Tracy said.

"Coffee?" Dr. Pingitzer said. "I am from Vienna. I *live* on coffee. Ah ha." He shouted, so that they would hear him beyond the door. "Coffee, please!"

Outside, Huzinga sent an officer for a pot of coffee and two cups.

"He knows," Huzinga said to the officer. "He knows what he's doing."

"We will have coffee," the little man said. "Is happened something. I don't know."

"They shot my tiger," Tracy said.

"I am sorry," Dr. Pingitzer said.

"We went into Saint Patrick's," Tracy said, "just as we did six years ago, but when we came out they were waiting there in an armoured car, and another one farther down on 50th Street. The first shot went wild, but it frightened the tiger, and it began to run. When it reached the second armoured car the tiger was shot in the foot."

"This tiger, it is *your* tiger?"

"Yes."

"Why?"

"It's been with me most of my life."

"Ah," the little man said. "It is tiger, like dog is dog?"

"Do you mean," Tracy said, "is it a *real* tiger, as a tiger in the jungle is, or in the circus?"

"Precise," Dr. Pingitzer said.

"No, it is not," Tracy said. "It wasn't until today, at any rate, but it was real today. It was still *my* tiger, though."

291

"Why do they say tiger is escape from circus?"

"I don't know."

"Is possible?"

"I suppose so. A caged animal of any kind might escape from a circus, if possible."

"You are not afraid of this tiger?" Dr. Pingitzer said. "We have here someplace photographs taken by newspaper photographers. My young daughter have hobby of photography one time. Pictures, pictures, pictures of Papa. *Me!*" He turned to the door and spoke loudly. "Photographs, please."

Huzinga came in, and off the top of a desk picked up a dozen photographs, handed them to the doctor, who quickly ran through them, with scarcely time enough to look at any of them, his hands and eyes moving extraordinarily swiftly.

"You are not afraid of this animal," he said again quickly, "this tiger. This is *black panther*."

"Yes, I know," Tracy said, "but it's my tiger just the same."

"You have this name *tiger* for this animal?"

"Yes, I know it's a black panther," Tracy said, "but I've always thought of it as a tiger."

"*Your* tiger?"

"Yes."

"You are not afraid of this tiger?"

"No."

"Everybody is afraid of tiger."

"Everybody is afraid of many things," Tracy said.

"I am afraid of night," Dr. Pingitzer said. "In Vienna at night I go as a young man where are many lights, much brightness. That way I am not afraid of night."

The coffee was brought in and poured by Huzinga, who seemed, for some reason, worshipful of Dr. Pingitzer.

"Now, we taste coffee," the doctor said.

"I wanted to be a coffee taster once," Tracy said.

"Ah, yes?" Dr. Pingitzer said. "Let us drink coffee now. Enjoy coffee. Life is too short." He waved at the door. "Much—much—much—" He made a face, and was unable to finish the thought.

"Yes," Tracy said.

They drank coffee in silence, Tracy tasting it carefully, as he had done six years ago at Otto Seyfang's, sitting with Nimmo, Peberdy, and Ringert.

Chapter 8

After they had tasted three cups each Dr. Pingitzer said, "Ah ha. Work. I hate work. I hate psychiatry. I *always* hate work. I like fun, play, imagination, magic."

"Why do you work, then?" Tracy said.

"Why?" Dr. Pingitzer said. "Confusion." The doctor reflected a moment. "In Vienna I see this girl. Elsa. This is Elsa Varshock. Ah ha. Elsa is wife, is mother, is say, 'Where for food, money?' So? I work."

"You understand psychiatry?" Tracy said.

"Psychiatry, no," Dr. Pingitzer said. "People—little bit. Little, little, little bit. Every year, every day—less, less, less. Why? People is difficult. People is people. People is fun, play, imagination, magic. Ah ha. People is pain, people is sick, people is mad, people is hurt, people is hurt *people*, is kill, is kill self. Where is fun, where is play, where is imagination, where is magic? Psychiatry I hate. People I love. Mad people, beautiful people, hurt people, sick people, broke people, in pieces people, I love, I love. Why? Why is lost from people fun, play, imagination, magic? What for? Ah ha. Money?" He smiled. "I think so. Money. Is love, this money. Is beauty, this money. Is fun, this money. Where is money? I do not know. No more fun. Work, now. Work. Tiger. Tiger."

"Do you know the poem?" Tracy said.

"Is *poem*?" Dr. Pingitzer said.

"Of course."

"What is this poem?" Dr. Pingitzer said.

"Tiger! Tiger! burning bright," Tracy said.
"In the forests of the night,
What immortal hand or eye
Could frame thy fearful symmetry?"

"Ah ha. Is more?" Dr. Pingitzer said.

"Yes, quite a bit," Tracy said, "if I haven't forgotten it."

"Please," Dr. Pingitzer said.

"In what distant deeps or skies," Tracy went on.
"Burnt the fire of thine eyes?
On what wings dare he aspire?
What the hand dare seize the fire?"

"Ho ho," Dr. Pingitzer said. "Is poem like *this* I do not hear seventy-two years! Who do this poem?"

"William Blake," Tracy said.
"Bravo, William Blake!" Dr. Pingitzer said.
"Is more?"
"Yes," Tracy said. "Let me see. Oh yes,

"And what shoulder, and what art,
Could twist the sinews of thy heart?
And when thy heart began to beat,
What dread hand? and what dread feet?"

"More?" the doctor said.
"I think I've got it all now," Tracy said.

"What the hammer? What the chain?
In what furnace was thy brain?
What the anvil? What dread grasp
Dare its deadly terrors clasp?

"When the stars threw down their spears,
And watered heaven with their tears,
Did He smile His work to see?
Did He who made the Lamb make thee?

"Tiger! Tiger! burning bright
In the forests of the night,
What immortal hand or eye,
Dare frame thy fearful symmetry?"

Tracy stopped. "That's the whole poem," he said.
"Ah, ha," Dr. Pingitzer said. "Thank you. Now, you have this poem since childhood. Yes?"
"Yes," Tracy said. "I began to recite it when I was three."
"You *understand* this poem?" Dr. Pingitzer said.
"I don't *understand* anything," Tracy said. "I *like* this poem."
"Ah ha. True."
The old man turned to the door.
"Much—much—much—" he said. "Now. Two questions. One. Your tiger, is *what?*"
"Mine," Tracy said.
"Two," Dr. Pingitzer said. "Tiger in street, is *what?*"
"Well," Tracy said, "I suppose a black panther mauled a keeper and escaped from the circus last night. Such things happen. I suppose a wounded

black panther is now loose in New York. I suppose it will, out of fear, kill somebody if it thinks it must. But the black panther that is loose in the city is *also* my tiger."

"So?"

"Yes."

"Why?" Dr. Pingitzer said.

"I don't know," Tracy said, "but it walked up Fifth Avenue with me and into Saint Patrick's. It didn't attack anybody. It stayed beside me. It didn't run until it was shot at. Wouldn't *you* run if you were shot at?"

"Very fast," Dr. Pingitzer said. "Seventy-two, but very fast." He paused a moment, to imagine himself running very fast at seventy-two.

"The police, they will kill this animal," Dr. Pingitzer said.

"They'll try to," Tracy said.

"They *will.*"

"They'll *try,*" Tracy said, "but they won't, because they can't."

"Why? They can't?" Dr. Pingitzer said.

"The tiger can't be killed."

"One tiger? Can't be killed? Why not?"

"It can't, that's all," Tracy said

"But *tiger* will kill?" Dr. Pingitzer said.

"If it must," Tracy said.

"Is this right?"

"I don't know. Is it?"

"I also don't know," the doctor said. "I know very little. Very, very, very little. Ah ha. Question of psychiatry. You are mad?"

"Yes, of course," Tracy said. The old man looked toward the door. He put a finger to his lips.

"Soft," he whispered.

"I'm mad because they wounded the tiger," Tracy said. "I'm mad because they put the tiger in the cage in the first place. I'm mad because they put it in the circus. But I am also mad, from birth."

"I, also, but this is information *not* to say," Dr. Pingitzer said. He looked at the door again. He got up suddenly. "I speak so. *This man is sane.* This they understand. Ah ha! Work finish." He called out loudly. "O.K., please."

Huzinga was the first to enter the room, but soon everybody was back in.

Dr. Pingitzer surveyed the faces, waited a long time for silence, then said, "Ah ha! This man is sane."

A man altogether unlike Dr. Pingitzer stepped forward and said, "Dr. Pingitzer, I am Dr. Scatter, in charge of Neuro, Borough of Manhattan. May I ask the psychiatric course by which you have reached your conclusion?"

"No," Dr. Pingitzer said. He turned to Tracy. "Good-bye, my boy," he said.

"Good-bye," Tracy said.

Dr. Pingitzer glanced at everyone in the room, then went to the door.

On his way he was photographed by a number of newspaper photographers, one of whom said, "Dr. Pingitzer, how about the black panther? Is it *his*, as he said it is?"

"I have examine *him*, not black panther," the doctor said.

A reporter stepped up to Dr. Pingitzer.

"How did it happen that the black panther didn't harm him, doctor?" the reporter said.

"I don't know," Dr. Pingitzer said.

"Well, what have you found out about it, after talking to him?" the reporter said.

"Nothing," the doctor said.

"What about a black panther being loose in the city?" the reporter said.

"This is not psychiatry problem," the doctor said.

"What kind of a problem is it?" the reporter said.

"Where from is this black panther?"

"From the circus."

"Circus problem," Dr. Pingitzer said. He walked out of the room.

Everybody gathered around Dr. Scatter, who was not at all satisfied with Dr. Pingitzer's conclusion, or manners.

Chapter 9

Tracy, in walking with the tiger, had broken no law.

Still, what he *had* done seemed so enormous and unbelievable as to *seem* illegal, or at any rate arrogant, thoughtless, and rude.

At the very least, it was felt, he must be insane. A man just naturally doesn't walk with a black panther escaped from the circus as if the animal and he were on terms of perfect understanding.

Therefore, after the departure of Dr. Pingitzer, Tracy was examined by Dr. Scatter, who found it irresistible to interpret Tracy's replies in a manner convenient to his education and prejudices.

Dr. Scatter had no difficulty in proving, step by step, that Tracy was in fact mad. This is easy to do. It can be done with anybody.

"Furthermore," Dr. Scatter said to the others involved, including Police Captain Earl Huzinga, who was the only one in the group who maintained disbelief in Dr. Scatter's findings and persisted in being respectful of Dr. Pingitzer's, "when the subject was asked what his reaction would be to an indefinite visit at Bellevue for the purpose of more prolonged and thorough psychiatric investigation, he replied that he would rather go home but that if forced to go to Bellevue he would make the most of his visit and feel just as much at home there as anywhere else, if not more at home. This attitude suggests that, in addition to all the other symptoms already identified, the subject has a martyr complex. It also reveals psychotic arrogance, and contempt for the collective intelligence. The subject is obviously deluded, believing that he is personally exempted from the laws which guide and control the rest of society. This belief is based upon, and has been strengthened by, a prolonged association with a fantasy tiger, which he declares is his, and his alone; which he has confessed is capable of speech—that is, communication by speech with *himself alone*. I am sure there is no doubt in anyone's mind that he must be placed in Bellevue for observation and treatment."

Thus, Thomas Tracy, on a pleasant Sunday afternoon in October, was placed in Bellevue.

He found the people there quite mad. He also found that each of them had a tiger: a very troubled one, a very angry one, a most deeply wounded one, a tiger deprived of humor, and love of freedom and fun, imagination, and hope.

Nimmo's son was there with a depressed and dying tiger. Peberdy's daughter was there with a terrified tiger that paced back and forth. Ringert himself was there with a tiger that resembled a weary old dog.

And Laura Luthy was there, her once magnificent tiger now thin, starved, and pathetic...

Only Tracy was without a tiger.

Tracy's tiger was hiding under the establishment of Roush, Rubeling and Ryan on Madison Avenue between 55th and 56th. The place was dark, secret, and deathly. The tiger was in hiding under the room in which Roush, Rubeling, and Ryan decorated the dead with powder, rouge, and smiles.

The tiger lay there in terror and loneliness, bereaved, heartsick, and eager itself to be dead.

Chapter 10

What's the use trying to describe the effect upon the people of New York of the story of Tracy and the tiger, as reported on the front pages of every newspaper, as told by anonymous and famous newscasters of radio and television, as embellished by newsreels of Tracy and the tiger walking up Fifth Avenue, entering Saint Patrick's, coming out of Saint Patrick's? As further embellished by photographs of Tracy drinking coffee with Dr. Pingitzer, surrounded by police, newspaper reporters, psychiatrists, others?

The effect was the usual one.

Innocent dogs, on their way to relief, came upon men who dropped dead, women screamed at shadows, then slapped their children for wanting to go out and play.

Everybody stayed home Sunday night, and quite a few Monday morning, for the tiger was still at large, and Tracy was in Bellevue.

He was examined a good deal of the time.

He in turn found his examiners interesting.

In his spare time Tracy visited Laura Luthy, who could not remember him. He brought up the matter of the Sunday visit in Far Rockaway, but Laura, pale and wan now, did not remember.

"I ate six soft chocolates," Tracy said.

"You should have had seven," Laura said.

"Why?"

"Then you would have had one extra," Laura said. "One extra is always nice. I have always believed that. One extra for everybody."

"Chocolates?" Tracy said.

"Anything," Laura said. "Mother, father, life, chance. Six is fine, but one extra makes it finer. Another and another, you should have had another."

"Don't you remember?" Tracy said. "Your father went for ice cream."

"Ice cream melts," Laura said. "That is the secret of ice cream. It melts."

"Laura," Tracy said. "Look at me. Listen to me."

"Nothing is so sad as ice cream melting," Laura said.

"It's not sad, Laura," Tracy said. "Ice cream's *supposed* to melt."

"It is?"

"Of course."

"I didn't know," Laura said. "I cried so hard when I saw the ice cream melt."

"What ice cream, Laura?"

"The ice cream girl, the ice cream boy," Laura said. "I didn't know. All those tears for nothing. I cried until I melted, too. Are you sure?"

"No," Tracy said. "No, I'm not sure. I don't know what happened, but whatever it was, listen to me, Laura. Six years ago I was standing in front of Otto Seyfang's."

"Why were you standing *there*?" Laura said.

"I *worked* there," Tracy said. "I was standing there talking to the coffee tasters, Nimmo, Peberdy, and Ringert."

"Where are they now?" Laura said.

"Nimmo's dead," Tracy said. "Ringert's here, and I don't know where Peberdy is. "While I was standing there a beautiful girl came down Warren Street."

"*Was* she beautiful?" Laura said.

"The most beautiful girl in the world."

"Who was she?"

"You, Laura," Tracy said.

"Me?" Laura said. "The most beautiful girl in the world? You must be mistaken."

"No. It *was* you, Laura."

"Well, I'm certainly not the most beautiful girl in the world any more," Laura said.

"That's what I want to talk about," Tracy said.

"All right," Laura said. "Talk about it."

"I want *you* to come down Warren Street again."

"You do?"

"Yes."

"Why?"

"Well, I don't know how else to put it," Tracy said. "I love you."

"What do you mean?" Laura said.

"I don't know," Tracy said.

"I suppose I mean—you're still the most beautiful girl in the world."

"I'm not," Laura said.

"Yes, you are," Tracy said. "You are to *me*."

"No," Laura said. "It's so arrogant to be beautiful. It's such bad taste. It's so pathetic, too. So much more pathetic than just lying still and knowing you're dead."

"You're not dead, Laura."

"Oh, I am."

"Laura!" Tracy said. "For God's sake, Laura, I love you."

"I'm sorry," Laura said. "I'm terribly sorry. I think I prefer to be dead."

Tracy didn't know what to think. Was she *actually* mad?

Like Dr. Pingitzer, he didn't know.

She was at Bellevue, at any rate.

She'd had a high fever for months.

The opinion of the experts was that she would soon be dead.

Later on, they knew, they too would be dead, but this did not trouble them because they believed they might die sane.

Chapter 11

A hectic week for New York went by. The tiger was still at large. That is to say, it was dying of starvation and fear under the embalming room of Roush, Rubeling and Ryan. According to the newspapers, however, on Monday morning the tiger was seen in three different places in Harlem, two in Greenwich Village, six in Brooklyn, and a boy in Fresno, California, killed a black cat with a .22 rifle because it looked enough like Tracy's tiger to make it worth his while. A photograph of the boy, proudly holding the cat by the tail, appeared in newspapers all over the country.

His name was Benintendi, first name Salvatore.

By sundown Tuesday Tracy's Tiger, as it was now called, was seen by miscellaneous people all over the country.

A man in London saw it in Soho and explained in a letter to *The Times* how the creature, as he called it, had reached there. His explanation was quite interesting, and his sympathies were entirely with the creature, as British sympathies sometimes are, at least among her gentle eccentrics.

A bookie in Seattle who had been beaten by a rival bookie's thugs informed the police that he had been attacked by Tracy's Tiger.

A saloon-keeper in Chicago advertised a new drink called Tracy's Tiger, twenty-five cents a shot.

A toy manufacturer in Toledo called in his designers and salesmen, and by Saturday morning had a black velvet Tracy's Tiger for children to take to bed. He also had a sweater on which was stamped a picture of the animal and its name, all sizes of Tracy's Tiger made of inflated rubber, and a jack-in-the-box out of which Tracy's Tiger sprang at one's loved ones.

The animal itself had a cold that was quickly turning to pleurisy. Its eyes were lustreless. They were giving off a good deal of yellow mucus.

Its nose was clogged. Its white teeth had become coated with something that tasted like the end.

The observing of Tracy continued, and was dutifully reported to the nation and the world every day, along with other, equally peculiar, news.

A dozen or more reputations were made by psychiatrists and newspapermen on Tracy and his Tiger.

Tracy's devotion to Laura Luthy was discovered by an astute newspaperman who scooped the world with a story captioned

TRACY LOVES LAURA
TIGER BOY WOOS BELLEVUE BELLE

The *Mirror*, however, having had poor luck in its photographs and stories about Tracy and the tiger, got even with the other newspapers by demanding an instantaneous investigation of the city's police, and if need be the dismissal of Chief August Bly, for if he could not kill or capture a lame tiger, how would he take care of the citizens of New York in the event a bomb was dropped on the city?

This theme was taken up by a number of people who readily take up miscellaneous themes.

Chief Bly was asked point-blank by the *Mirror*, "When can you assure the people of the greatest city in the world that Tracy's Tiger will be killed or captured, and permit the people to sleep peacefully again?"

The question was asked by telegram.

Chief Bly called in his brightest men and asked them to answer the telegram. There were a dozen different answers, all unsatisfactory, because nobody *knew* when the tiger would be killed or captured.

"I don't know," the Chief wanted to say but didn't dare.

Instead, a 500-word reply was written and dispatched by telegram to the *Mirror*. The reply was run on the front page of the *Mirror* under the heading of *Shame on the New York Police*. The *Mirror* demanded that Chief Bly resign. It also offered a reward of $5,000 to any man, woman, or child, regardless of race, color, creed, or religion, who brought Tracy's Tiger to the *Mirror*, dead or alive.

The following day a man went to the *Mirror* with a black panther shot through the head, and the Mirror had the scoop it wanted at last.

The stories and photographs of the killing of Tracy's Tiger were sent all over the country and all over the world.

The man, Art Pliley, in a matter of hours received hundreds of phone calls at the *Mirror*, mostly from women, several of whom offered to be his bride. Negotiations were under way for him to buy a clean suit and appear in a Men of Distinction advertisement when the police escorted Tracy to the *Mirror* to have a look at the tiger.

Each of the other papers had a reporter and a photographer on hand, just in case. It seemed a wild and pathetic chance for the Chief of Police to be taking, but it was worth looking into just the same.

The *Mirror*, however, refused to permit Tracy to examine the tiger.

Art Pliley was asked to shake hands with Tracy for a photograph, but by now he knew the ropes, and said, "I couldn't do that for less than five."

"Five what?" he was asked.

"Hundred," Art Pliley said. "The *Mirror* can photograph me for nothing. That's in my contract. Any other paper, though, five."

"This is a high school paper," the photographer said as a joke, and Art Pliley, never having attended high school and believing it was his duty, shook hands with Tracy free of charge.

He was given a severe bawling out by the managing editor of the *Mirror*, however.

As for Tracy, he shook hands with everybody. He believed they were sincere. Either that or helpless.

The *News* charged that the *Mirror* had perpetrated a hoax on the citizens of New York, and that the dead tiger in their possession was not Tracy's Tiger.

The upshot of this rivalry and jealousy resulted after two days in a formal and ceremonious examination of the Mirror's tiger by Tracy, by the animal's trainer at the circus, and by a half-dozen people who wanted any kind of publicity they could possibly get.

The ceremony was swift. Tracy looked at the poor dead black panther lying beside the specially built casket in which the Mirror planned to bury it. He looked, that is, from across the room. He spoke altogether out of turn, too, making a shambles of the whole ceremony.

"That's not my tiger," he said. "That's not even a black panther. That's a mountain lion that's had its fur dyed black."

Art Pliley, to sum up the hoax, was arrested, his bank account confiscated by the Mirror, and he was put in jail. There he was visited by the managing editor of the *News*, however, and a new deal was made. If Pliley would confess exclusively to the *News*, the *News* would give him *six* thousand dollars. Pliley confessed every day for three days, whereupon he was sent to the penitentiary, for in confessing, he was thorough, and revealed that he had a good many other clever things. He said he'd always wanted to be famous mainly, and since he *was* famous at last, he didn't want to stop half-way.

It would be tedious to go into the nature of his confessions. He wanted to be famous, that's all.

Tracy's Tiger grew very ill on the ninth day of hiding under the embalming room of Roush, Rubeling and Ryan. That night, in trembling desperation, it crawled out from its hiding place to an open garbage can in which it found meat scraps, bones, and outer leaves of miscellaneous vegetables. Much of this scrap it carried to its hiding place, making one trip after another.

A small boy, awake at two in the morning, coughing and waiting for his mother to bring him the cough medicine, said to her when she came with it, "Look at the big cat in the garbage can, Mama."

Mama looked and woke up Papa. Papa had no gun, but he *was* an amateur photographer, and he *did* have a flash camera.

Papa sat at the window three minutes, waiting for the tiger to come back to the garbage can. When the tiger came back Papa got something like buck fever, and found that he couldn't snap the picture.

Mama took the camera angrily out of his hands and handed it to the boy, eight years old. The boy focused as well as he was able to, the tiger saw the flash, leaped, and went back to its hiding place.

The man put on his clothes and developed the picture in his own dark-room. The picture showed the rear half of the tiger.

The man went to the police with the picture of the rear half of Tracy's Tiger. The police questioned the man an hour, and at four that morning the sick tiger heard voices and saw lights. It watched and listened a long time.

When things quieted down, the tiger came out and began to move downtown.

The photograph, and the story of its achievement, was duly published in the newspapers, along with photographs of the sick boy, who immediately grew sicker.

The area of New York in which the boy lived was drawn by special map-makers, and speculations were made as to where the tiger was now hiding.

Chapter 12

Police Captain Earl Huzinga, after many quiet chats with Tracy at Bellevue, made up his mind to go directly to Chief Bly and say his piece, even if it cost him his job.

"He can get us the tiger," Captain Huzinga said.

"How?" Chief Bly said.

"Well, it *sounds* complicated," Huzinga said, "but I've had a lot of talks with him, and it's not complicated. I know he can do it."

"How?" Bly said again.

"First," Huzinga said, "he doesn't want anybody to know about it. No publicity at all."

"We can keep it quiet," the Chief said. He was sick and tired of the whole thing and beginning to feel older than his sixty-six years.

"There's a place on Warren Street that used to be Otto Seyfang's, a coffee importing house," Huzinga said. "It's out of business now, but the building's still there. It's a warehouse now. Tracy wants a sign made like the old sign, *Otto Seyfang's,* and he wants the sign put up where it was. He wants the Tasting Department restored, and he wants a man named Peberdy, a man named Ringert, and a man named Shively to sit there and taste coffee. Peberdy's living in a furnished room. Ringert's at Bellevue. Shively's living with his daughter in the Bronx."

"What's he want all this nonsense for?" Bly said.

"I know it doesn't sound reasonable," Huzinga said, "but I know he'll get us the tiger. He needs only one day. It's got to be a Sunday. That suits us fine because there won't be anybody but one or two drunks on Warren Street at noon on a Sunday."

"You've been at Bellevue so long," Chief Bly said, "you've gone a little bats yourself, but go on, let's hear the whole thing."

"He wants at least a hundred sacks of coffee in the storeroom," Huzinga said.

"What for?"

"He used to work there," Huzinga said. "On this Sunday he's going to get there at eight in the morning. He's going to lift and carry the sacks. Peberdy, Ringert, and Shively will be in the Tasting Department tasting coffee. Every now and then Tracy will stop carrying sacks, and go in there and taste some coffee with them. At noon he'll stop work, go out front, and stand there in the sun. At half-past twelve a girl named Laura Luthy will come walking down Warren Street. She'll stop in front of Otto Seyfang's."

"She will?" Bly said.

"Yes," Huzinga said.

"So what?" Bly said.

"In a moment Tracy's Tiger will be there, too," Huzinga said. "He'll take the girl by the arm and walk down Warren Street with her. There's an empty store three doors down from Otto Seyfang's—used to be a produce house. He'll walk into this store with the girl and the tiger. In the store will be a cage. The tiger will go into the cage. Tracy will lock the cage. Then, he and the girl will walk out of the store."

"He will?"

"Yes."

"Go ahead," the Chief said. "Tell me more"

"Two things we've got to promise him," Huzinga said. "*One.* Absolutely no publicity. No photographs, not even for our own records. You and I can watch from the building across the street. *Two.* We can *have* the tiger in the cage, but we have got to promise that we do not announce to anybody that we've got it. If the tiger's ill, we've got to give it expert care, especially the injured foot. It's the right front one."

"You believe this nut, don't you?" Chief Bly said.

"Yes, sir."

"You put me on the case ten days ago," Huzinga said. "I've been with him the entire time. That was no bull in the papers about Laura Luthy. The doctors said she was dying, and all you had to do was see her to *know* she was. Well, she's not dying anymore. Pingitzer's in there every day talking with both of them, trying to figure it out. He says everybody at Bellevue is somebody who lost love somewhere along the line. The ones that love means the most to get sick, a lot of them die. It doesn't take very long, either. Tracy's not crazy."

"What about Dr. Scatter and all the other experts who say he *is* crazy?" the Chief said.

"I don't know," Huzinga said. "Their reports seem to stack up all right. I guess there are a couple of ways of looking at things like that, though. Pingitzer's studying Tracy's way. He says it's a way he's always *believed* might work, especially if it's started early enough, but he's never seen it work in an advanced case like Laura Luthy's. He says when it comes to human beings, you've got to be patient, you've got to be willing to learn, because anything can happen, especially if love's involved. You wouldn't think there'd be laughter in Bellevue, would you?"

"No, I wouldn't, not decent laughter anyway," Bly said.

"Well, there is, and it's *damned* decent," Huzinga said. "Scatter and all the others are getting annoyed by it, too. They're trying to stop it. They're bringing out new regulations every day, but they can't stop it. They're sore because the patients aren't acting the way they're *supposed* to act. They get up, visit one another, help one another, tell stories, dance, sing—and

I don't mean in a crazy way, either. I mean in a natural, decent, kind way. Most of them are sad, of course, but not much sadder than people anywhere else." Huzinga stopped a moment. "He'll get the tiger for us all right. When that happens we'll know where we stand, at any rate, even if we won't be able to tell anybody about it. Everybody will forget the whole thing after a couple of weeks anyway. How about it?"

"No," the Chief said. "It's silly. It would get around. I'd be the laughing stock of New York."

"Today's Wednesday," Huzinga said. "We'd know in four days. Will you give *me* permission to do it? If it flops, I'll take the rap. I'll say it was my idea, I did it on my own. Pingitzer's with me. He wants to watch."

The Chief thought about all this a long time.

"O.K.," he said at last. "O.K., I'll watch, too."

"We've got to keep our promise, though," Huzinga said.

"O.K.," the Chief said. "Get going."

The Captain, glad and confident but at the same time deeply frightened, got going.

Chapter 13

One bright Sunday morning Tracy came up out of the earth, climbing the subway steps.

He stood in the light, looking around as he had done six years ago. The scene was not greatly changed.

He walked across Bowling Green Park to Warren Street, glanced at his watch, then hurried, as he'd always done, for the time was five minutes to eight.

Warren Street was empty. Like most Sunday streets, it seemed to be a street that was being dreamed.

Tracy saw that the place was again Otto Seyfang's. He hurried to the entrance and went in, and from the building across the street Captain Huzinga and Chief Bly saw him do so.

They had already seen Peberdy, Ringert, and Shively go in.

"Well," Chief Bly said, "I don't know how you feel, but I feel Tracy's crazier than *anybody* knows, or ever will know. How do *you* feel?"

"It's a little early," Huzinga said. "At half-past twelve, I know Laura Luthy is going to come down Warren Street, as she did six years ago."

"Well, that's nice," Chief Bly said. "Now, this work that he's going to be doing in there—it's going to *draw* the tiger away from wherever it's hiding to Otto Seyfang's, is that right?"

"Yes."

They were interrupted by the police radio, the speaker reporting all quiet.

"Now, let me go over everything again," Chief Bly said. "She'll be wearing a yellow knit dress, is that right?"

"Yes," Huzinga said.

"She'll come by around half-past twelve, is that right?"

"Yes."

"Tracy will be standing in front there, on the steps, is that right?"

"Yes."

"The girl will stop when she sees Tracy, is that right?"

"Yes."

"At that moment the tiger will appear, is that right?"

"Yes."

"Tracy will take the girl by the arm and walk down Warren Street, the tiger walking beside him, is that right?"

"Yes."

"Three doors down the block, in that empty store there that is now full of paintings of animals hanging on the walls, will be a cage, is that right?"

"Yes."

"Where'd you get the paintings?" Bly said.

"Raymond & Raymond," Huzinga said. "They're reproductions of the most famous animal paintings in the world."

"The tiger will walk into the cage, and Tracy will shut the cage, is that right?" the Chief said.

"Yes," Huzinga said.

"On the mezzanine of the store, unnoticed, are two of our younger men, Splicer and Slew, to report what they see to us later on, is that right?"

"Yes. They're there now."

"Call them."

Huzinga called, and Slew came to the 'phone. Huzinga and Slew spoke a moment.

"They're all set," Huzinga said.

"What was it you told him not to do?" the Chief said.

"He asked if he could take some photographs," Huzinga said. "He doesn't know what he's going to be observing, but he's got his camera."

"Don't you think it might be a good idea to *have* him take some pictures?" the Chief said.

"We promised we wouldn't," Huzinga said.

"This is the Police Department," the Chief said. "What do we care what we promised?"

"Even so, I don't think we'd better take any pictures," Huzinga said.

"O.K.," the Chief said. "If we've not all of us gone mad, and he *does* get the tiger in the cage, he's going to leave the store and go on down Warren Street with the girl, is that right?"

"Yes."

"Where's he going?" Bly said.

"None of our business," Huzinga said. "For a walk, I suppose."

"We're to go to the store the minute he leaves, for the reports of Splicer and Slew, is that right?"

"Yes."

"In back of the store is a moving van," the Chief said. "The tiger in the cage will be placed in the van. As soon as possible the tiger will be examined, given any care it may need, and then turned loose where it can harm no one, is that right?"

"Yes."

"Where would that be?" Bly said.

"The animal's trainer has stated that the animal was born in captivity," Huzinga said. "The place was Madison Square Garden. Tracy has asked that the tiger be turned loose in the mountains nearest New York."

"Who says it will be safe there?" the Chief said.

"The nearest mountains that are *wild*," Huzinga said. "Where people do not live."

"I'm not thinking of people," Bly said. "I'm thinking of the tiger. How's it going to live? It's liable to run into a hunter, and be shot."

"Those are *decent* chances," Huzinga said.

"That's if everything goes the way Tracy and you like to believe they're going to go," the Chief said. "What do we do if the tiger *doesn't* appear?"

The younger man looked at the older one.

"You'll have to fire me," Huzinga said, "so I'll resign."

"No one else knows, is that right?" Bly said.

"Just you and I," Huzinga said, "but if it flops, I resign."

"What about Tracy and the girl—if it flops?"

"I've given Dr. Scatter my word to take them both back to Bellevue," Huzinga said.

"Does Dr. Scatter know about all this?"

"No, I cooked up another story," Huzinga said. "Pingitzer knows. I mean, he knows Laura Luthy's going to meet Tracy at half-past twelve in front of Otto Seyfang's. He doesn't know anything else, though."

"Where's *he?*" Bly said.

"Tracy asked Dr. Pingitzer to sit in the Tasting Department," Huzinga said. "I saw him go in a few minutes before you arrived."

"What's he doing in there?" Bly said.

"Tracy wanted him in there."

"Does Tracy know that if the thing flops he and the girl go back to Bellevue?"

"No." Huzinga said. "That's the thing that bothers me. I *did* keep that from him. I thought I'd better. I don't feel easy about it, though."

The radio reported again at half-past eight. Again it was all quiet. The Chief telephoned his secretary.

"We've had two all quiets," he said. "I want to know exactly what's happened, *whatever* it is. Call me back."

The secretary called back and said, "All precincts report no events of any kind."

"Are you sure?"

"Yes, sir."

"Has this ever happened before?" the Chief said. "A whole New York hour with no events at all?"

"Not as far as I know," the secretary said.

"Well," Bly said to Huzinga, "*something's* happened. No episodes of any kind, not even drunks, not even a family fight, not even a petty theft, not even a disturbance of the peace in a whole New York hour."

Chapter 14

Back at his old job, Tracy lifted a coffee sack to his shoulder, carried it fifty yards, and set it down, but it was not easy to do.

Tracy walked with another sack from the far end of the storage room to the wall of the Tasting Department and then another. Each time he set a sack down he wanted to go in and taste some coffee with Peberty, Ringert, Shively, and Pingitzer because he could hear them talking, although he could not make out what they were saying. But he knew it would not do to go in until he had achieved again the knack of doing the work easily, until he had begun to enjoy doing it.

He was tired after each trip. The weight of each sack on his shoulder was enormous. Several times his knees almost gave way. He couldn't understand. It was only six years ago that the work had been so easy for him. His breathing was difficult and his heart pounded each time he lifted a sack and walked with it.

He stopped at the rear window at last, to rest, to think about the problem, to look down at the alley and the things there.

Well, it was still the same: asphalt, old brick and stone, discolored wood, garbage cans, miscellaneous junk and rubbish strewn about, a stubborn old tree, a few weeds, a low arch in the brick of the building across the alley, a number of bricks having fallen loose, two of them still lying in the alley.

He needed to rest a long time, staring down at the miserable scene. It was all new once, hopeful, bright and clean, but now it was pathetic.

And yet on the next trip he longed to see it again, as a lover longs to see his beloved, lying sick in bed.

When he came back from the fifth trip and looked at the scene, he began to see beauty in it, and the next sack he lifted was the first not to make him groan.

He walked with it easier, too, and when he set it down he heard Pingitzer and the others laugh.

The next time he looked at the scene the tree was beautiful. He smiled, thinking of the years it had been there—certainly more than six, for he had seen it then, too. Its leaves weren't green, but only because the city had covered them with its dirt. It wasn't big because there wasn't earth enough for its roots to spread out in, or space enough for its branches. But what there *was* of it was there, and it *was* a tree. In all probability its patience had been rewarded from time to time by the arrival of a bird, to greet it and go, or even to stay, to build a nest in it. The tree *was* there, there was no question about that. It had been there for a long time, and was still there. Its trunk was hard and tough, bruised here and there, but for all that still strong.

Each sack Tracy lifted and carried to the wall of the Tasting Department was easier to lift and carry. The lifting and carrying of the ninth sack wasn't work at all.

It was almost nine o'clock then, there was still a great deal to be done before twelve, but Tracy stepped into the Tasting Department. The men sat around the round table, each of them with a silver coffee-pot beside him, Pingitzer's pot percolating.

"Ah ha," Pingitzer said. "Just in time. Here is coffee, my own idea, from Vienna, long ago." He poured a cup for Tracy, lifted it, Tracy took the cup, then tasted the coffee in it. He took his time tasting it, then tasted it again.

"Good," he said.

"My own idea," Pingitzer said. "Vienna."

Tracy walked around the room, listening to the others, as he had done six years ago. When his cup was empty, he took it to Shively, who filled it for him out of *his* pot. Shively's coffee was good, too.

"Well, I've got to get back to work," Tracy said. "I've got a lot to do."

"Ah ha," Pingitzer said. "This is way of youth. This is illusion of youth. This is *fine* illusion. Was time in Vienna when Pingitzer have this way and this illusion. This was fine time, fine way, fine illusion. Ah ha. Here is Pingitzer, seventy-two, wishing no more to work, to have fine illusion."

"I'll be back after a while," Tracy said.

He went straight to the window to have another look at the alley. There was much for him to think about that he wanted to get to as slowly as possible, but at the same time get to in the next hour or two. Time had always fascinated him. He knew he didn't understand it, but he also knew that anything you ever got—anything that ever mattered—any thought—any truth—you got *instantly*. You could wait forever if you wanted to, and let it go at that, or you could get moving—moving *into* time and *with* time—working at the thought to be received, and then suddenly, from having moved into time and with time, and from having worked at the thought, get it, get it whole, get it clean, get it instantly.

But you had to stay slow somewhere inside of yourself, too, to give the arrival a place to stop. You had to be going swiftly and you had to be almost not moving at all at the same time.

There was much for Tracy to think about, much to do, and the doing of what needed to be done had to begin with Tracy working. All that needed to be done—and it was a great deal—had to begin with the doing of a simple work, had to do with the lifting and carrying of the coffee sacks.

Tracy stood a moment, smiling at the miserable scene that was also beautiful, at the enormity of the work to be done, remembering each of the matters involved but trying not to hurry them, his eyes wandering to the low arch in the old building across the alley.

He carried a half-dozen more sacks before he stopped to glance at the scene again, and this time he only *glanced*, for the work had become exhilarating and he wanted to get on with it. But during the glance it seemed to him that he had seen something. He was carrying another sack when he wondered what it had been that he'd seen, or if he'd imagined it, from having been at a time so intense with possibilities.

He decided to carry at least a half-dozen more sacks before stopping a moment again. This time he would go to the back door, open it, and go out on the steps and look from there.

When he was on the steps, not looking anywhere in particular, he thought he saw it again, and there was a deep gladness in him. It was there, whatever it was. It was there somewhere. There was no doubt about that.

He went back to work, carried three more sacks, then stepped into the Tasting Department to spend another moment with the coffee tasters.

"How does it feel after six years?" Ringert said.

"It's beginning to feel all right again," Tracy said. "How about you, Ringert?"

"Oh," Ringert said. "Can't kick, Tracy."

"Ah ha," Pingitzer said. "This kick. This is two? One. To move foot? Two. To make complaint? Can't move with foot? Can't make complaint?"

"I don't know," Ringert said. "I can move with foot all right, but not the way I *could*. And I can complain, too, but not the way I could. I used to be able to complain about anything, and it was a lot of fun. Now, I have only one thing to complain about, and I don't even want to complain about *that*."

"Is what, this thing?" Pingitzer said.

"Ringert's end." ·

"Ah ha. What is taste of Ringert's coffee?"

"Good," Tracy said.

"Please," Pingitzer said, holding his cup across the table to Ringert, who poured it full. Dr. Pingitzer tasted the coffee, then said, "Ah ha. Good."

Tracy carried three more sacks, then stood at the window, with his back turned to the scene, listening. He stood a long time, perhaps three minutes. There was silence in the alley. When he was not sure he had heard something, he decided he was not sure, and went back to work. Each time he came for a new sack he paused for a moment to listen again. When he'd carried six more sacks and had listened six more times, he sat on a sack, not to rest, but to be thankful, to be near things, near the inside of things, and to smile at anything that might be near.

When he was finally sure he had heard the word, he was not surprised. He did not leap to his feet. He did not turn. He said the word back very softly. After a moment he heard it again, and then very slowly he got up and lifted a sack to his shoulder and walked with it.

When he put the sack down and turned he saw the tiger.

Its appearance was pitiful, even from so far away. It was starved, sick, weak, and wounded. He went back to the pile of sacks, scarcely looking at the tiger, lifted another sack and walked off with it. On this third trip the tiger climbed to the top of the pile of sacks, spread itself flat, to rest there and watch.

Tracy and the tiger talked, but this time not with words, not even with sounds, and each of them understood.

The swift thought had arrived to stay.

When all the sacks had been moved, it was a quarter after twelve.

The coffee tasters had left the Tasting Department to go to lunch. The tiger stood beside Tracy, and then together they went down two flights of stairs to the entrance of the building. The tiger was frightened by the door to the street, and hung back. Tracy stayed near the tiger a moment, saying nothing, then went out alone, to stand on the steps, the door swinging shut behind him.

Chapter 15

In the second-floor room across the street Captain Huzinga and Chief Bly watched.

There, on schedule, was Thomas Tracy standing in front of Otto Seyfang's.

"What time is it?" Bly said.

"Half-past twelve." Huzinga said. "Don't you think it'll happen?"

"Something's *already* happened," Bly said. "You heard the reports on the radio every half-hour."

"Yes."

"All quiet for four full hours."

"Yes. Do you think it'll happen?"

"I don't care if it doesn't," the Chief said. "Look at him. He's no madman."

"He's mad all right," Huzinga said suddenly. "This whole thing is. I got it wrong. I misunderstood. We've got that sign up there. *Otto Seyfang's.* Otto Seyfang's been dead three years. The place is a warehouse. It's not a coffee importing house. This is *now*. It's not six years ago. He's mad all right, but not as mad as I am to have believed any of us could do the one thing that's broken the human heart since the beginning of time. It can't be done. It can't be done, that's all. I feel sorry for him. He's crazy. He doesn't know it, but he's got to go back to Bellevue, and the girl with him. Nothing's going to happen, Chief. I'm sorry. I'll resign. I believed with all my heart he could do it. It's madness to believe *that*. Nothing's going to happen."

"What about the stuff that's *already* happened?" Bly said.

"An accident," Huzinga said. "Besides, it's happened before. I happen to have studied the old records. In December, 1882, there were seven hours in which nothing was reported. In March of 1896 there were *eleven* hours, in July of 1901 *five*, in August of 1908 *nine*. It's happened before."

"Yes," the Chief said. "Well, how do you know something else didn't happen at the same time that nobody knows about? Something else happened secretly?"

"You mean, you think something's *still* going to happen?" Huzinga said.

"I say it's *already* happened," the Chief said. "And I say don't take them back to Bellevue."

"I gave Dr. Scatter my word," Huzinga said. "In a few minutes I'll take them back and resign."

"You don't have to resign." Bly said. "We can go out on a limb, can't we? We've done it before—many times. You haven't lost your job. There's nothing at stake for you here. So the thing flops. Who cares?"

"I care," Huzinga said.

Suddenly they saw Laura Luthy walking down Warren Street.

They saw Tracy and Laura meet. They saw them smile. They saw their lips move in speech. They saw Laura go up the three steps to Tracy. They saw him put his arms around her. They saw her arms tighten around him. They saw Peberdy, Ringert, Shively, and Pingitzer standing together, watching. They saw Tracy take Laura by the arm to go, but just before going they saw Tracy reach over to the door, and open it.

He didn't open it very much, just enough.

Then they saw Tracy's tiger come out and stand beside Laura Luthy.

It was a black panther that limped on its right front foot. Except for the limp, it was the handsomest black panther anybody ever saw.

They saw Tracy and Laura Luthy and Tracy's tiger walk together down Warren Street. They saw them go into the store with the pictures of the animals hanging on the walls of it.

After a while they saw Tracy and Laura come out and walk away, toward the docks at the end of Warren Street.

And they saw that there was no longer a tiger with them.

Bly and Huzinga ran downstairs, out of the building to the street, across the street, and into the store. They found Splicer and Slew standing together, waiting for them.

"Which one of you is Slew?" Bly said.

"I am, sir," one of the men said.

"All right," Bly said. "Tell me *exactly* what you just saw."

"I saw a young man and a young woman come in here and look at every picture hanging on the walls of this store," Slew said. "I saw them go out."

"Anything else?" Bly said.

"No, sir."

"You, Splicer," Bly said. "Tell me exactly what *you* saw."

"I saw the same, sir," Splicer said.

"Are you sure?"

"Yes, sir."

"Return to your stations, please," Bly said.

The two young officers left the store.

"Well?" Bly said to Huzinga. "How about it?"

"I don't know," Huzinga said.

"You *did* see the tiger, didn't you?"

"I saw the tiger," Bly said.

"You're not just saying that, are you?" Huzinga said. "You *did* see him open the door? You did *see* the tiger come out and stand beside her, didn't you?"

"Yes, I saw it all," Bly said.

"Splicer and Slew *didn't* see the tiger," Huzinga said.

"No, they didn't," Bly said.

"And the tiger's gone," Huzinga said.

"Yes, it is," Bly said.

"What happened to the tiger?" Huzinga said.

"I don't know," the Chief said.

"Well," Huzinga said. "I'd like the rest of the day off, if it's all right with you,"

"Your work's done," Bly said. "What are you going to do? Go to a ball game?"

"No," Huzinga said. "I think I'd like to go up to St. Patrick's for a while. Then I think I'd like to go home. I can't wait to see my wife and kids again."

"Yes," the Chief said. "Well, get going."

Huzinga went from one painting in the room to the other, and then left the store and went to Saint Patrick's. Bly now looked at each of the pictures. He went back for one last look at the picture of the Arab asleep in the desert, with the lion standing over him.

Then he too left the store and went to Saint Patrick's.

That is the story of Thomas Tracy, Laura Luthy, and the tiger, which is love.

Henry and William (right) Saroyan with a neighbor's dog, in Campbell, California, 1911, not long after their father's death. Photographer unknown. (Courtesy of Stanford University Libraries and the William Saroyan Foundation; M0978, Box 13)

Saroyan as a teenager, in January 1923. Photographer unknown. (Courtesy of Stanford University Libraries and the William Saroyan Foundation; M0978, Box 13)

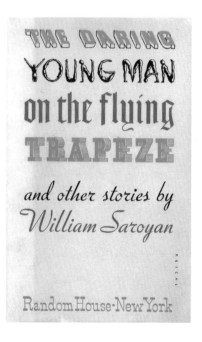

First edition of *The Daring Young Man on the Flying Trapeze*, the short story collection published by Random House in 1934 that launched Saroyan's career as a writer. (Courtesy of Stanford University Libraries and the William Saroyan Foundation; PS 3571 A77 D21 1934)

Saroyan, posing at his beloved typewriter for the *News-Call Bulletin* in 1934, the year that his breakthrough work, *The Daring Young Man on the Flying Trapeze*, was published. Photographer unknown. (Courtesy of The Bancroft Library, University of California, Berkeley; Saroyan, Wm—POR 4)

Saroyan with his cousin, poet Archie Minasian. Photographer unknown. (Courtesy of The Bancroft Library, University of California, Berkeley; Saroyan, Wm—POR 7)

A promotional photograph of Saroyan for his 1940 novel, *My Name Is Aram*. Photographer unknown. (Courtesy of Stanford University Libraries and the William Saroyan Foundation; M0978, Box 13)

Saroyan in 1943, playing checkers with Carol, who was pregnant with their son, Aram. Photographer unknown. (Courtesy of Stanford University Libraries and the William Saroyan Foundation; M0978, Box 13)

Saroyan's children, Lucy and Aram. Photographer unknown. (Courtesy of Stanford University Libraries and the William Saroyan Foundation; M0978, Box 13)

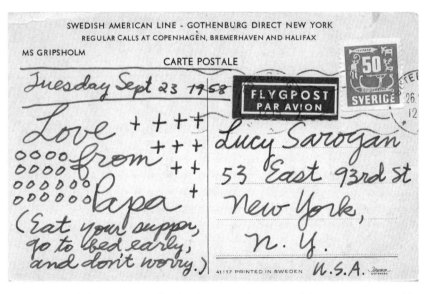

A 1958 postcard from Saroyan to his daughter, Lucy. (Courtesy of the Fresno County Public Library, California History and Genealogy Room; and the William Saroyan Foundation)

Saroyan (left) and his cousin Ross Bagdasarian posing in uniform with the crew of a garbage truck in wartime Paris. Photographer unknown. (Courtesy of Stanford University Libraries and the William Saroyan Foundation; M0978, Box 13)

Drawing of an older Saroyan by his cousin, author William Michaelian. (Courtesy of William Michaelian)

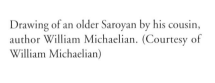

Saroyan reading one of his own collections, published by Avon. Photographer unknown. (Courtesy of Stanford University Libraries and the William Saroyan Foundation; M0978, Box 13)

A commemorative stamp of Saroyan, issued simultaneously in the United States and the Soviet Union on May 22, 1991.

An older Saroyan photographed by Arthur Tcholakian for the 1970 publication of *Days of Life and Death and Escape to the Moon*. (Courtesy of The Bancroft Library, University of California, Berkeley; Saroyan, Wm—POR 10)

Drama

The Time of Your Life

*I*n the time of your life, live—so that in that good time there shall be no ugliness or death for yourself or for any life your life touches. Seek goodness everywhere, and when it is found, bring it out of its hiding-place and let it be free and unashamed. Place in matter and in flesh the least of the values, for these are the things that hold death and must pass away. Discover in all things that which shines and is beyond corruption. Encourage virtue in whatever heart it may have been driven into secrecy and sorrow by the shame and terror of the world. Ignore the obvious, for it is unworthy of the clear eye and the kindly heart. Be the inferior of no man, nor of any man be the superior. Remember that every man is a variation of yourself. No man's guilt is not yours, nor is any man's innocence a thing apart. Despise evil and ungodliness, but not men of ungodliness or evil. These, understand. Have no shame in being kindly and gentle, but if the time comes in the time of your life to kill, kill and have no regret. In the time of your life, live—so that in that wondrous time you shall not add to the misery and sorrow of the world, but shall smile to the infinite delight and mystery of it.

The People

JOE, *a young loafer with money and a good heart*

TOM, *his admirer, disciple, errand boy, stooge and friend*

KITTY DUVAL, *a young woman with memories*

NICK, *owner of Nick's Pacific Street Saloon, Restaurant, and Entertainment Palace*

ARAB, *an Eastern philosopher and harmonica-player*

KIT CARSON, *an old Indian-fighter*

MCCARTHY, *an intelligent and well-read longshoreman*

KRUPP, *his boyhood friend, a waterfront cop who hates his job but doesn't know what else to do instead*

HARRY, *a natural-born hoofer who wants to make people laugh but can't*

WESLEY, *a colored boy who plays a mean and melancholy boogie-woogie piano*

DUDLEY, *a young man in love*

ELSIE, *a nurse, the girl he loves*

LORENE, *an unattractive woman*

MARY L., *an unhappy woman of quality and great beauty*

WILLIE, *a marble-game maniac*

BLICK, *a heel*

MA, *Nick's mother*

A KILLER

HER SIDEKICK

A COP

ANOTHER COP

A SAILOR

A SOCIETY GENTLEMAN

A SOCIETY LADY

THE DRUNKARD

THE NEWSBOY

ANNA, *Nick's daughter*

The Place

Nick's Pacific Street Saloon, Restaurant, and Entertainment Palace at the foot of Embarcadero, in San Francisco. A suggestion of room 21 at the New York Hotel, upstairs, around the corner.

The Time

Afternoon and night of a day in October, 1939.

Act One

Nick's is an American place: a San Francisco waterfront honky-tonk.

At a table, JOE: *always calm, always quiet, always thinking, always eager, always bored, always superior. His expensive clothes are casually and youthfully worn and give him an almost boyish appearance. He is thinking.*

Behind the bar, NICK: *a big red-headed young Italian-American with an enormous naked woman tattooed in red on the inside of his right arm. He is studying the Racing Form.*

The ARAB, *at his place at the end of the bar. He is a lean old man with a rather ferocious old-country mustache, with the ends twisted up. Between the thumb and forefinger of his left hand is the Mohammedan tattoo indicating that he has been to Mecca. He is sipping a glass of beer.*

It is about eleven-thirty in the morning. SAM *is sweeping out. We see only his back. He disappears into the kitchen. The* SAILOR *at the bar finishes his drink and leaves, moving thoughtfully, as though he were trying very hard to discover how to live.*

The NEWSBOY *comes in.*

NEWSBOY (*Cheerfully*) Good-morning, everybody. (*No answer. To* NICK) Paper, Mister? (NICK *shakes his head, no. The* NEWSBOY *goes to* JOE.) Paper, Mister? (JOE *shakes his head, no. The* NEWSBOY *walks away, counting papers.*)

JOE (*Noticing him*) How many you got?

NEWSBOY Five.

(JOE *gives him a quarter, takes all the papers, glances at the headlines with irritation, throws them away.*)

(*The* NEWSBOY *watches carefully, then goes.*)

ARAB (*Picks up paper, looks at headlines, shakes head as if rejecting everything else a man might say about the world*) No foundation. All the way down the line.

(*The* DRUNK *comes in. Walks to the telephone, looks for a nickel in the chute, sits down at* JOE'S *table.*)

(NICK *takes the* DRUNK *out. The* DRUNK *returns.*)

DRUNK (*Champion of the Bill of Rights*) This is a free country, ain't it?

(WILLIE, *the marble-game maniac, explodes through the swinging doors and lifts the forefinger of his right hand comically, indicating one beer. He is a very young man, not more than twenty. He is wearing heavy shoes, a pair of old and dirty corduroys, a light green turtle-neck jersey with a large letter "F" on the chest, an oversize two-button tweed coat, and a green hat, with the brim up.* NICK *sets out a glass of beer for him, he drinks it, straightens up vigorously, saying Aaah, makes a solemn face, gives* NICK *a one-finger salute of adieu, and begins to leave, refreshed and restored in spirit. He walks by the marble game, halts suddenly, turns, studies the contraption, gestures as if to say, Oh, no. Turns to go, stops, returns to the machine, studies it, takes a handful of small coins*

323

out of his pants pocket, lifts a nickel, indicates with a gesture, One game, no more. Puts the nickel in the slot, pushes in the slide, making an interesting noise.)

NICK You can't beat that machine.

WILLIE Oh, yeah?

(The marbles fall, roll, and take their place. He pushes down the lever, placing one marble in position. Takes a very deep breath, walks in a small circle, excited at the beginning of great drama. Stands straight and pious before the contest. Himself vs. the machine. Willie vs. Destiny. His skill and daring vs. the cunning and trickery of the novelty industry of America, and the whole challenging world. He is the last of the American pioneers, with nothing more to fight but the machine, with no other reward than lights going on and off, and six nickels for one. Before him is the last champion, the machine. He is the last challenger, the young man with nothing to do in the world. WILLIE *grips the knob delicately, studies the situation carefully, draws the knob back, holds it a moment, and then releases it. The first marble rolls out among the hazards, and the contest is on. At the very beginning of the play "The Missouri Waltz" is coming from the phonograph. The music ends here.)*

(This is the signal for the beginning of the play.)

*(*JOE *suddenly comes out of his reverie. He whistles the way people do who are calling a cab that's about a block away, only he does it quietly.* WILLIE *turns around, but* JOE *gestures for him to return to his work.* NICK *looks up from the Racing Form.)*

JOE *(Calling)* Tom. *(To himself)* Where the hell is he, every time I need him? *(He looks around calmly: the nickel-in-the-slot phonograph in the corner; the open public telephone; the stage; the marble game; the bar; and so on. He calls again, this time very loud)* Hey, Tom.

NICK *(With morning irritation)* What do you want?

JOE *(Without thinking)* I want the boy to get me a watermelon, that's what *I* want. What do you want? Money, or love, or fame, or what? You won't get them studying the Racing Form.

NICK I like to keep abreast of the times.

*(*TOM *comes hurrying in. He is a great big man of about thirty or so who appears to be much younger because of the childlike expression of his face: handsome, dumb, innocent, troubled, and a little bewildered*

by everything. He is obviously adult in years, but it seems as if by all rights he should still be a boy. He is defensive as clumsy, self-conscious, overgrown boys are. He is wearing a flashy cheap suit. JOE *leans back and studies him with casual disapproval.* TOM *slackens his pace and becomes clumsy and embarrassed, waiting for the bawling-out he's pretty sure he's going to get.*)

JOE (*Objectively, severely, but a little amused*) Who saved your life?

TOM (*Sincerely*) You did, Joe. Thanks.

JOE (*Interested*) How'd I do it?

TOM (*Confused*) What?

JOE (*Even more interested*) How'd I do it?

TOM Joe, you know how you did it.

JOE (*Softly*) I want you to answer me. How'd I save your life? I've forgotten.

TOM (*Remembering, with a big sorrowful smile*) You made me eat all that chicken soup three years ago when I was sick and hungry.

JOE (*Fascinated*) Chicken soup?

TOM (*Eagerly*) Yeah.

JOE Three years? Is it that long?

TOM (*Delighted to have the information*) Yeah, sure. 1937. 1938. 1939. This is 1939, Joe.

JOE (*Amused*) Never mind what year it is. Tell me the whole story.

TOM You took me to the doctor. You gave me money for food and clothes, and paid my room rent. Aw, Joe, you know all the different things you did.

(JOE *nods, turning away from* TOM *after each question.*)

JOE You in good health now?

TOM Yeah, Joe.

JOE You got clothes?

TOM Yeah, Joe.

JOE You eat three times a day. Sometimes four?

TOM Yeah, Joe. Sometimes five.

JOE You got a place to sleep?

TOM Yeah, Joe.

(JOE *nods. Pauses. Studies* TOM *carefully.*)

JOE Then, where the hell have you been?

TOM (*Humbly*) Joe, I was out in the street listening to the boys. They're talking about the trouble down here on the waterfront.

JOE (*Sharply*) I want you to be around when I need you.

TOM (*Pleased that the bawling-out is over*) I won't do it again. Joe, one guy out there says there's got to be a revolution before anything will ever be all right.

JOE (*Impatient*) I know all about it. Now, here. Take this money. Go up to the Emporium. You know where the Emporium is?

TOM Yeah, sure, Joe.

JOE All right. Take the elevator and go up to the fourth floor. Walk around to the back, to the toy department. Buy me a couple of dollars' worth of toys and bring them here.

TOM (*Amazed*) Toys? What *kind* of toys, Joe?

JOE Any kind of toys. Little ones that I can put on this table.

TOM What do you want toys for, Joe?

JOE (*Mildly angry*) *What?*

TOM All right, all right. You don't have to get sore at *everything*. What'll people think, a big guy like me buying toys?

JOE *What people?*

TOM Aw, Joe, you're always making me do crazy things for you, and *I'm* the guy that gets embarrassed. You just sit in this place and make me do all the dirty work.

JOE (*Looking away*) Do what I tell you.

TOM O.K., but I wish I knew *why*. (*He makes to go.*)

JOE Wait a minute. Here's a nickel. Put it in the phonograph. Number seven. I want to hear that waltz again.

TOM Boy, I'm glad *I* don't have to stay and listen to it. Joe, what do you hear in that song anyway? We listen to that song ten times a day. Why can't we hear number six, or two, or nine? There are a lot of other numbers.

JOE (*Emphatically*) Put the nickel in the phonograph. (*Pause*) Sit down and wait till the music's over. Then go get me some toys.

TOM O.K. O.K.

JOE (*Loudly*) Never mind being a martyr about it either. The cause isn't worth it.

(TOM *puts the nickel into the machine, with a ritual of impatient and efficient movement which plainly shows his lack of sympathy or enthusiasm. His manner also reveals, however, that his lack of sympathy is spurious and exaggerated. Actually, he is fascinated by the music, but is so confused by it that he tries to pretend he dislikes it.*)

(*The music begins. It is another variation of "The Missouri Waltz," played dreamily and softly, with perfect orchestral form, and with a theme of weeping in the horns repeated a number of times.*)

(*At first* TOM *listens with something close to irritation, since he can't understand what is so attractive in the music to* JOE, *and what is so painful and confusing in it to himself. Very soon, however, he is carried away by the melancholy story of grief and nostalgia of the song.*)

(*He stands, troubled by the grief and confusion in himself.*)

(JOE, *on the other hand, listens as if he were not listening, indifferent and unmoved. What he's interested in is* TOM. *He turns and glances at* TOM.)

(KITTY DUVAL, *who lives in a room in the New York Hotel, around the corner, comes beyond the swinging doors quietly, and walks slowly to the bar, her reality and rhythm a perfect accompaniment to the sorrowful American music, which is her music, as it is Tom's. Which the world drove out of her, putting in its place brokenness and a manner of spiritually crippled forms. She seems to understand this, and is angry. Angry with herself, full of hate for the poor world, and full of pity and contempt for its tragic, unbelievable, confounded people. She is a small powerful girl, with that kind of delicate and rugged beauty which no circumstance of evil or ugly reality can destroy. This beauty is that element of the immortal which is in the seed of good and common people, and which is kept alive in some of the female of our kind, no matter how accidentally or pointless they may have entered the world.* KITTY DUVAL *is somebody. There is an angry purity, and a fierce pride, in her.*)

(*In her stance, and way of walking, there is grace and arrogance.* JOE *recognizes her as a great person immediately. She goes to the bar.*)

KITTY Beer.

(NICK *places a glass of beer before her mechanically.*)

(*She swallows half the drink, and listens to the music again.*)

(TOM *turns and sees her. He becomes dead to everything in the world but her. He stands like a lump, fascinated and undone by his almost religious adoration for her.* JOE *notices* TOM.)

JOE (*Gently*) Tom. (TOM *begins to move toward the bar, where* KITTY *is standing. Loudly.*) Tom. (TOM *halts, then turns, and* JOE *motions to him to come over to the table.* TOM *goes over.*) (*Quietly*) Have you got everything straight?

TOM (*Out of the world*) What?

JOE What do you mean, what? I just gave you some instructions.

TOM (*Pathetically*) What do you want, Joe?

JOE I want you to come to your senses. (*He stands up quietly and knocks Tom's hat off.* TOM *picks up his hat quickly.*)

TOM I got it, Joe. I got it. The Emporium. Fourth floor. In the back. The toy department. Two dollars' worth of toys. That you can put on a table.

KITTY (*To herself*) Who the hell is he to push a big man like that around?

JOE I'll expect you back in a half hour. Don't get side-tracked anywhere. Just do what I tell you.

TOM (*Pleading*) Joe? Can't I bet four bits on a horse race? There's a long shot—Precious Time—that's going to win by ten lengths. I got to have money.

(JOE *points to the street.* TOM *goes out.* NICK *is combing his hair, looking in the mirror.*)

NICK I thought you wanted him to get you a watermelon.

JOE I forgot. (*He watches* KITTY *a moment. To* KITTY, *clearly, slowly, with great compassion*) What's the dream?

KITTY (*Moving to* JOE, *coming to*) What?

JOE (*Holding the dream for her*) What's the dream, *now?*

KITTY (*Coming still closer*) What dream?

JOE What dream! The dream you're dreaming.

NICK Suppose he did bring you a watermelon? What the hell would you do with it?

JOE (*Irritated*) I'd put it on this table. I'd look at it. Then I'd eat it. What do you *think* I'd do with it, sell it for a profit?

NICK How should I know what *you'd* do with *anything?* What I'd like to know is, where do you get your money from? What work do you do?

JOE (*Looking at* KITTY) Bring us a bottle of champagne.

KITTY Champagne?

JOE (*Simply*) Would you rather have something else?

KITTY What's the big idea?

JOE I thought you might like some champagne. I myself am very fond of it.

KITTY Yeah, but what's the big idea? You can't push *me* around.

JOE (*Gently but severely*) It's not in my nature to be unkind to another human being. I have only contempt for wit. Otherwise I might say something obvious, therefore cruel, and perhaps untrue.

KITTY You be careful what you think about me.

JOE (*Slowly, not looking at her*) I have only the noblest thoughts for both your person and your spirit.

NICK (*Having listened carefully and not being able to make it out*) What are you talking about?

KITTY You shut up. You—

JOE He owns this place. He's an important man. All kinds of people come to him looking for work. Comedians. Singers. Dancers.

KITTY I don't care. He can't call me names.

NICK All right, sister. I know how it is with a two-dollar whore in the morning.

KITTY (*Furiously*) Don't you dare call me names. I used to be in burlesque.

NICK If you were ever in burlesque, I used to be Charlie Chaplin.

KITTY (*Angry and a little pathetic*) I *was* in burlesque. I played the burlesque circuit from coast to coast. I've had flowers sent to me by European royalty. I've had dinner with young men of wealth and social position.

NICK You're dreaming.

KITTY (*To* JOE) *I was in burlesque.* Kitty Duval. That was my name. Life-size photographs of me in costume in front of burlesque theatres all over the country.

JOE (*Gently, coaxingly*) I believe you. Have some champagne.

NICK (*Going to table, with champagne bottle and glasses*) There he goes again.

JOE Miss Duval?

KITTY (*Sincerely, going over*) That's not my real name. That's my stage name.

JOE I'll call you by your stage name.

NICK (*Pouring*) All right, sister, make up your mind. Are you going to have champagne with him, or not?

JOE Pour the lady some wine.

NICK O.K., Professor. Why you come to this joint instead of one of the high-class dumps uptown is more than I can understand. Why don't you have champagne at the St. Francis? Why don't you drink with a lady?

KITTY (*Furiously*) Don't you call me names—you dentist.

JOE Dentist?

NICK (*Amazed, loudly*) What kind of cussing is that? (*Pause. Looking at* KITTY, *then at* JOE, *bewildered*) This guy doesn't belong here. The only reason I've got champagne is because *he* keeps ordering it all the time. (*To* KITTY) Don't think you're the only one he drinks champagne with. He drinks with *all* of them. (*Pause*) He's crazy. Or something.

JOE (*Confidentially*) Nick, I think you're going to be all right in a couple of centuries.

NICK I'm sorry, I don't understand your English.

(JOE *lifts his glass.*)

(KITTY *slowly lifts hers, not quite sure of what's going on.*)

JOE (*Sincerely*) To the spirit, Kitty Duval.

KITTY (*Beginning to understand, and very grateful, looking at him*) Thank you.

(*They drink.*)

JOE (*Calling*) Nick.

NICK Yeah?

JOE Would you mind putting a nickel in the machine again? Number—

NICK Seven. I know. I know. I don't mind at all, Your Highness, although, personally, I'm not a lover of music. (*Going to the machine*) As a matter of fact I think Tchaikowsky was a dope.

JOE Tchaikowsky? Where'd you ever hear of Tchaikowsky?

NICK He was a dope.

JOE Yeah. Why?

NICK They talked about him on the radio one Sunday morning. He was a sucker. He let a woman drive him crazy.

JOE I see.

NICK I stood behind that bar listening to the God damn stuff and cried like a baby. *None but the lonely heart!* He was a dope.

JOE What made you cry?

NICK What?

JOE (*Sternly*) What made you cry, Nick?

NICK (*Angry with himself*) I don't know.

JOE I've been underestimating you, Nick. Play number seven.

NICK They get everybody worked up. They give everybody stuff they shouldn't have.

> (NICK *puts the nickel into the machine and the Waltz begins again. He listens to the music. Then studies the Racing Form.*)

KITTY (*To herself, dreaming*) I like champagne, and everything that goes with it. Big houses with big porches, and big rooms with big windows, and big lawns, and big trees, and flowers growing everywhere, and big shepherd dogs sleeping in the shade.

NICK I'm going next door to Frankie's to make a bet. I'll be right back.

JOE Make one for me.

NICK (*Going to* JOE) Who do you like?

JOE (*Giving him money*) Precious Time.

NICK *Ten dollars?* Across the board?

JOE No. On the nose.

NICK O.K. (*He goes*)

> (DUDLEY R. BOSTWICK, *as he calls himself, breaks through the swinging doors, and practically flings himself upon the open telephone beside the phonograph.*)
>
> (DUDLEY *is a young man of about twenty-four or twenty-five, ordinary and yet extraordinary. He is smallish, as the saying is, neatly dressed in*

*bargain clothes, over-worked and irritated by the routine and dullness
and monotony of his life, apparently nobody and nothing, but in reality
a great personality. The swindled young man. Educated, but without the
least real understanding. A brave, dumb, salmon-spirit struggling for life
in weary, stupefied flesh, dueling ferociously with a banal mind which has
been only irritated by what it has been taught. He is a great personality
because, against all these handicaps, what he wants is simple and basic:
a woman. This urgent and violent need, common yet miraculous enough
in itself, considering the unhappy environment of the animal, is the force
which elevates him from nothingness to greatness. A ridiculous greatness,
but in the nature of things beautiful to behold. All that he has been
taught, and everything he believes, is phony, and yet he himself is real,
almost super-real, because of this indestructible force in himself. His face
is ridiculous. His personal rhythm is tense and jittery. His speech is shrill
and violent. His gestures are wild. His ego is disjointed and epileptic. And
yet deeply he possesses the same wholeness of spirit, and directness of energy,
that is in all species of animals. There is little innate or cultivated spirit
in him, but there is no absence of innocent animal force. He is a young
man who has been taught that he has a chance, as a person, and believes
it. As a matter of fact, he hasn't a chance in the world, and should have
been told by somebody, or should not have had his natural and valuable
ignorance spoiled by education, ruining an otherwise perfectly good and
charming member of the human race.)*

*(At the telephone he immediately begins to dial furiously, hesitates,
changes his mind, stops dialing, hangs up furiously, and suddenly begins
again.)*

(Not more than half a minute after the firecracker arrival of DUDLEY R.
BOSTWICK *occurs the polka-and-waltz arrival of* HARRY.)*

*(*HARRY *is another story.)*

*(He comes in timidly, turning about uncertainly, awkward, out of
place everywhere, embarrassed and encumbered by the contemporary
costume, sick at heart, but determined to fit in somewhere. His arrival
constitutes a dance.)*

*(His clothes don't fit. The pants are a little too large. The coat, which
doesn't match, is also a little too large, and loose.)*

*(He is a dumb young fellow, but he has ideas. A philosophy, in fact. His
philosophy is simple and beautiful. The world is sorrowful. The world*

needs laughter. HARRY *is funny. The world needs* HARRY. HARRY *will make the world laugh.*)

(*He has probably had a year or two of high school. He has also listened to the boys at the pool room.*)

(*He's looking for* NICK. *He goes to the* ARAB, *and says, Are you Nick? The* ARAB *shakes his head. He stands at the bar, waiting. He waits very busily.*)

HARRY (*As* NICK *returns*) You Nick?

NICK (*Very loudly*) I am Nick.

HARRY (*Acting*) Can you use a great comedian?

NICK (*Behind the bar*) Who, for instance?

HARRY (*Almost angry*) Me.

NICK You? What's funny about you?

> (DUDLEY, *at the telephone, is dialing. Because of some defect in the apparatus the dialing is very loud.*)

DUDLEY Hello. Sunset 7349? May I speak to Miss Elsie Mandelspiegel?
(*Pause.*)

HARRY (*With spirit and noise, dancing*) I dance and do gags and stuff.

NICK In costume? Or are you wearing your costume?

DUDLEY All I need is a cigar.

KITTY (*Continuing the dream of grace*) I'd walk out of the house, and stand on the porch, and look at the trees, and smell the flowers, and run across the lawn, and lie down under a tree, and read a book. (*Pause*) A book of poems, maybe.

DUDLEY (*Very, very clearly*) Elsie Mandelspiegel. (*Impatiently*) She has a room on the fourth floor. She's a nurse at the Southern Pacific Hospital. Elsie Mandelspiegel. She works at night. Elsie. Yes. (*He begins waiting again.*)

> (WESLEY, *a colored boy, comes to the bar and stands near* HARRY, *waiting.*)

NICK Beer?

WESLEY No, sir. I'd like to talk to you.

NICK (*To* HARRY) All right. Get funny.

HARRY (*Getting funny, an altogether different person, an actor with great energy, both in power of voice and in force and speed of physical gesture*) Now, I'm standing on the corner of Third and Market. I'm looking around. I'm figuring it out. There it is. Right in front of me. The whole city. The whole world. People going by. They're going somewhere. I don't know where, but they're going. I ain't going *anywhere*. Where the hell can you go? I'm figuring it out. All right, I'm a citizen. A fat guy bumps his stomach into the face of an old lady. They were in a hurry. Fat and old. *They bumped*. Boom. I don't know. It may mean war. *War*. Germany. England. Russia. I don't know for sure. (*Loudly, dramatically, he salutes, about faces, presents arms, aims, and fires*) WAAAAAR. (*He blows a call to arms.* NICK *gets sick of this, indicates with a gesture that* HARRY *should hold it, and goes to* WESLEY.)

NICK What's on *your* mind?

WESLEY (*Confused*) Well—

NICK Come on. Speak up. Are you hungry, or what?

WESLEY Honest to God, I ain't hungry. All I want is a job. I don't want no charity.

NICK Well, what can you do, and how good are you?

WESLEY I can run errands, clean up, wash dishes, anything.

DUDLEY (*On the telephone, very eagerly*) Elsie? Elsie, this is Dudley. Elsie, I'll jump in the bay if you don't marry me. Life isn't worth living without you. I can't sleep. I can't think of anything but you. All the time. Day and night and night and day. Elsie, I love you. I love you. What? (*Burning up*) Is this Sunset 7-3-4-9? (*Pause*) 7943? (*Calmly, while* WILLIE *begins making a small racket*) Well, what's *your* name? *Lorene?* Lorene Smith? I thought you were Elsie Mandelspiegel. What? Dudley. Yeah. Dudley R. Bostwick. Yeah. R. It stands for Raoul, but I never spell it out. I'm pleased to meet *you*, too. What? There's a lot of noise around here. (WILLIE *stops hitting the marble game.*) Where am I? At Nick's, on Pacific Street. I work at the S.P. I told them I was sick and they gave me the afternoon off. Wait a minute. I'll ask them. I'd like to meet *you*, too. Sure. I'll ask them. (*Turns around to* NICK) What's this address?

NICK Number 3 Pacific Street, you cad.

DUDLEY Cad? You don't know how I've been suffering on account of Elsie. I take things too ceremoniously. I've got to be more lackadaisical. (*Into telephone*) Hello, Elenore? I mean, Lorene? It's number 3 Pacific Street. Yeah. Sure. I'll wait for you. How'll you know me? You'll *know* me. I'll recognize you. Good-bye, now. (*He hangs up*)

HARRY (*Continuing his monologue, with gestures, movements, and so on*) I'm standing there. I didn't do anything to anybody. Why should *I* be a soldier? (*Sincerely, insanely*) BOOOOOOOOOOM. *WAR!* O.K. War. *I* retreat. *I* hate war. I move to Sacramento.

NICK (*Shouting*) All right, Comedian. Lay off a minute.

HARRY (*Broken-hearted, going to* WILLIE) Nobody's got a sense of humor any more. The world's dying for comedy like never before, but nobody knows how to *laugh*.

NICK (*To* WESLEY) Do you belong to the union?

WESLEY What union?

NICK For the love of Mike, where've you been? Don't you know you can't come into a place and ask for a job and get one and go to work, just like that. You've got to belong to one of the unions.

WESLEY I didn't know. I got to have a job. Real soon.

NICK Well, you've got to belong to a union.

WESLEY I don't want any favors. All I want is a chance to earn a living.

NICK Go on into the kitchen and tell Sam to give you some lunch.

WESLEY Honest, I ain't hungry.

DUDLEY (*Shouting*) What I've gone through for Elsie.

HARRY I've got all kinds of funny ideas in my head to help make the world happy again.

NICK (*Holding* WESLEY) No, he isn't hungry.

(WESLEY *almost faints from hunger.* NICK *catches him just in time. The* ARAB *and* NICK *go off with* WESLEY *into the kitchen.*)

HARRY (*To* WILLIE) See if you think this is funny. It's my own idea. I created this dance myself. It comes after the monologue.

(HARRY *begins to dance.* WILLIE *watches a moment, and then goes back to the game. It's a goofy dance, which* HARRY *does with great sorrow, but much energy.*)

DUDLEY Elsie. Aw, gee, Elsie. What the hell do I want to see Lorene Smith for? Some girl I don't know.

(JOE *and* KITTY *have been drinking in silence. There is no sound now except the soft shoe shuffling of* HARRY, *the Comedian.*)

JOE What's the dream now, Kitty Duval?

KITTY (*Dreaming the words and pictures*) I dream of home. Christ, I always dream of home. I've no *home*. I've no place. But I always dream of all of us together again. We had a farm in Ohio. There was nothing good about it. It was always sad. There was always trouble. But I always dream about it as if I could go back and Papa would be there and Mamma and Louie and my little brother Stephen and my sister Mary. I'm Polish. Duval! My name isn't Duval, it's Koranovsky. Katerina Koranovsky. We lost everything. The house, the farm, the trees, the horses, the cows, the chickens. Papa died. He was old. He was thirteen years older than Mamma. We moved to Chicago. We tried to work. We tried to stay together. Louie got in trouble. The fellows he was with killed him for something. I don't know what. Stephen ran away from home. Seventeen years old. I don't know where he is. Then Mamma died. (*Pause*) What's the dream? I dream of home.

(NICK *comes out of the kitchen with* WESLEY.)

NICK Here. Sit down here and rest. That'll hold you for a *while*. Why didn't you tell me you were hungry? You all right now?

WESLEY (*Sitting down in the chair at the piano*) Yes, I am. Thank you. I didn't know I was *that* hungry.

NICK Fine. (*To* HARRY *who is dancing*) Hey. What the hell do you think you're doing?

HARRY (*Stopping*) That's my own idea. I'm a natural-born dancer and comedian.

(WESLEY *begins slowly, one note, one chord at time, to play the piano.*)

NICK You're no good. Why don't you try some other kind of work? Why don't you get a job in a store, selling something? What do you want to be a comedian for?

HARRY I've got something for the world and they haven't got sense enough to let me give it to them. Nobody knows me.

DUDLEY Elsie. Now I'm waiting for some dame I've never seen before. Lorene Smith. Never saw her in my life. Just happened to get the wrong number. She turns on the personality, and I'm a cooked Indian. Give me a beer, please.

HARRY Nick, you've got to see my act. It's the greatest thing of its kind in America. All I want is a chance. No salary to begin. Let me try it out tonight. If I don't wow 'em, O.K., I'll go home. If vaudeville wasn't dead, a guy like me would have a chance.

NICK You're not funny. You're a sad young punk. What the hell do you want to try to be funny for? You'll break everybody's heart. What's there for you to be funny about? You've been poor all your life, haven't you?

HARRY I've been poor all right, but don't forget that some things count more than some other things.

NICK What counts more, for instance, than what else, for instance?

HARRY Talent, for instance, counts more than money, for instance, that's what, and I've got talent. I get new ideas night and day. Everything comes natural to me. I've got style, but it'll take me a little time to round it out. That's all.

(*By now* WESLEY *is playing something of his own which is very good and out of the world. He plays about half a minute, after which* HARRY *begins to dance.*)

NICK (*Watching*) I run the lousiest dive in Frisco, and a guy arrives and makes me stock up with champagne. The whores come in and holler at me that they're ladies. Talent comes in and begs me for a chance to show itself. Even society people come here once in a while. I don't know what for. Maybe it's liquor. Maybe it's the location. Maybe it's my personality. Maybe it's the crazy personality of the joint. The old honky-tonk. (*Pause*) Maybe they can't feel at home anywhere else.

(*By now* WESLEY *is really playing, and* HARRY *is going through a new routine.* DUDLEY *grows sadder and sadder.*)

KITTY Please dance with me.

JOE (*Loudly*) I never learned to dance.

KITTY Anybody can dance. Just hold me in your arms.

JOE I'm very fond of you. I'm *sorry*. I *can't* dance. I wish to God I could.

KITTY Oh, please.

JOE Forgive me. I'd like to very much.

(KITTY *dances alone.* TOM *comes in with a package. He sees* KITTY *and goes ga-ga again. He comes out of the trance and puts the bundle on the table in front of* JOE.)

337

JOE (*Taking the package*) What'd you get?

TOM Two dollars' worth of toys. That's what you sent me for. The girl asked me what I wanted with toys. I didn't know what to tell her. (*He stares at* KITTY, *then back at* JOE.) Joe? I've got to have some money. After all you've done for me, I'll do anything in the world for you, but, Joe, you got to give me some money once in a while.

JOE What do you want it for?

(TOM *turns and stares at* KITTY *dancing.*)

JOE (*Noticing*) Sure. Here. Here's five. (*Shouting*) Can you dance?

TOM (*Proudly*) I got second prize at the Palomar in Sacramento five years ago.

JOE (*Loudly, opening package*) O.K., dance with her.

TOM You mean *her?*

JOE (*Loudly*) I mean Kitty Duval, the burlesque queen. I mean the queen of the world burlesque. Dance with her. She wants to dance.

TOM (*Worshiping the name Kitty Duval, helplessly*) Joe, can I tell you something?

JOE (*He brings out a toy and winds it*) You don't have to. I know. You love her. You really love her. I'm not blind. I know. But take care of yourself. Don't get sick that way again.

NICK (*Looking at and listening to* WESLEY *with amazement*) Comes in here and wants to be a dish-washer. Faints from hunger. And then sits down and plays better than Heifetz.

JOE Heifetz plays the violin.

NICK All right, don't get careful. He's good, ain't he?

TOM (*To* KITTY) Kitty.

JOE (*He lets the toy go, loudly*) Don't *talk*. Just *dance*.

(TOM *and* KITTY *dance.* NICK *is at the bar, watching everything.* HARRY *is dancing.* DUDLEY *is grieving into his beer.* LORENE SMITH, *about thirty-seven, very overbearing and funny-looking, comes to the bar.*)

NICK What'll it be, lady?

LORENE (*Looking about and scaring all the young men*) I'm looking for the young man I talked to on the telephone. Dudley R. Bostwick.

DUDLEY (*Jumping, running to her, stopping, shocked*) Dudley R. (*Slowly*) Bostwick? Oh, yeah. He left here ten minutes ago. You mean Dudley Bostwick, that poor man on crutches?

LORENE Crutches?

DUDLEY Yeah. Dudley Bostwick. That's what he *said* his name was. He said to tell you not to wait.

LORENE Well. (*She begins to go, turns around*) Are you sure *you're* not Dudley Bostwick?

DUDLEY Who—me? (*Grandly*) My name is Roger Tenefrancia. I'm a French-Canadian. I never saw the poor fellow before.

LORENE It seems to me your voice is like the voice I heard over the telephone.

DUDLEY A coincidence. An accident. A quirk of fate. One of those things. Dismiss the thought. That poor cripple hobbled out of here ten minutes ago.

LORENE He said he was going to commit suicide. I only wanted to be of help. (*She goes*)

DUDLEY Be of help? What kind of help could she be, of? (DUDLEY *runs to the telephone in the corner.*) Gee whiz, Elsie. Gee whiz. I'll never leave you again. (*He turns the pages of a little address book.*) Why do I always forget the number? I've tried to get her on the phone a hundred times this week and I still forget the number. She won't come to the phone, but I keep trying anyway. She's out. She's not in. She's working. I get the wrong number. Everything goes haywire. I can't sleep. (*Defiantly*) She'll come to the phone one of these days. If there's anything to true love at all. She'll come to the phone. Sunset 7349.

(*He dials the number, as* JOE *goes on studying the toys. They are one big mechanical toy, whistles, and a music box.* JOE *blows into the whistles, quickly, by way of getting casually acquainted with them.*)

(TOM *and* KITTY *stop dancing.* TOM *stares at her.*)

DUDLEY Hello. Is this Sunset 7349? May I speak to Elsie? Yes. (*Emphatically, and bitterly*) No, this is *not* Dudley Bostwick. This is Roger Tenefrancia of Montreal, Canada. I'm a childhood friend of Miss Mandelspiegel. We went to kindergarten together. (*Hand over phone*) God damn it. (*In to phone*) Yes. I'll wait, thank you.

TOM I love you.

KITTY You want to go to my room? (TOM *can't answer*) Have you got two dollars?

TOM (*Shaking his head with confusion*) I've got *five* dollars, but I *love* you.

KITTY (*Looking at him*) You want to spend *all* that money?

(TOM *embraces her. They go.* JOE *watches. Goes back to the toy.*)

JOE Where's that longshoreman, McCarthy?

NICK He'll be around.

JOE What do you think he'll have to say today?

NICK Plenty, as usual. I'm going next door to see who won that third race at Laurel.

JOE Precious Time won it.

NICK That's what you think. (*He goes*)

JOE (*To himself*) A horse named McCarthy is running in the sixth race today.

DUDLEY (*On the phone*) Hello. Hello, Elsie? Elsie? (*His voice weakens; also his limbs*) My God. She's come to the phone. Elsie, I'm at Nick's on Pacific Street. You've got to come here and talk to me. Hello. Hello, Elsie? (*Amazed*) Did she hang up? Or was I disconnected? (*He hangs up and goes to bar.*)

(WESLEY *is still playing the piano.* HARRY *is still dancing.* JOE *has wound up the big mechanical toy and is watching it work.*)

(NICK *returns.*)

NICK (*Watching the toy*) Say. That's some gadget.

JOE How much did I win?

NICK How do you know you *won*?

JOE Don't be silly. He said Precious Time was going to win by ten lengths, didn't he? He's in love, isn't he?

NICK O.K. I don't know why, but Precious Time won. You got eighty for ten. How do you do it?

JOE (*Roaring*) Faith. Faith. How'd he win?

NICK By a nose. Look him up in the Racing Form. The slowest, the cheapest, the worst horse in the race, and the worse jockey. What's the matter with my luck?

JOE How much did you lose?

NICK Fifty cents.

JOE You should never gamble.

NICK Why not?

JOE You always bet fifty cents. You've got no more faith than a flea, that's why.

HARRY (*Shouting*) How do you like this, Nick? (*He is really busy now, all legs and arms.*)

NICK (*Turning and watching*) Not bad. Hang around. You can wait table. (*To* WESLEY) Hey. Wesley. Can you play that again tonight?

WESLEY (*Turning, but still playing the piano*) I don't know for sure, Mr. Nick. I can play *something*.

NICK Good. *You* hang around, too. (*He goes behind the bar.*)

(*The atmosphere is now one of warm, natural, American ease; every man innocent and good; each doing what he believes he should do, or what he must do. There is deep American naïveté and faith in the behavior of each person. No one is competing with anyone else. No one hates anyone else. Every man is living, and letting live. Each man is following his destiny as he feels it should be followed; or is abandoning it as he feels it must, by now, be abandoned; or is forgetting it for the moment as he feels he should forget it. Although everyone is dead serious, there is unmistakable smiling and humor in the scene; a sense of the human body and spirit emerging from the world-imposed state of stress and fretfulness, fear and awkwardness, to the more natural state of casualness and grace. Each person belongs to the environment, in his own person, as himself:* WESLEY *is playing better than ever.* HARRY *is hoofing better than ever.* NICK *is behind the bar shining glasses.* JOE *is smiling at the toy and studying it.* DUDLEY, *although still troubled, is at least calm now and full of melancholy poise.* WILLIE, *at the marble game, is happy. The* ARAB *is deep in his memories, where he wants to be.*)

(*Into this scene and atmosphere comes* BLICK.)

(BLICK *is the sort of human being you dislike at sight. He is no different from anybody else physically. His face is an ordinary face. There is nothing obviously wrong with him, and yet you know that it is impossible, even by the most generous expansion of understanding, to accept him as a human being. He is the strong man without strength—strong only among the weak—the weakling who uses force on the weaker.*)

(BLICK *enters casually, as if he were a customer, and immediately* HARRY *begins slowing down.*)

BLICK (*Oily, and with mock-friendliness*) Hello, Nick.

NICK (*Stopping his work and leaning across the bar*) What do you want to come here for? You're too big a man for a little honky-tonk.

BLICK (*Flattered*) Now, Nick.

NICK Important people never come here. *Here.* Have a drink. (*Whiskey bottle*)

BLICK Thanks, I don't drink.

NICK (*Drinking the drink himself*) Well, why don't you?

BLICK I have responsibilities.

NICK You're head of the lousy Vice Squad. There's no vice here.

BLICK (*Sharply*) Street-walkers are working out of this place.

NICK (*Angry*) What do you want?

BLICK (*Loudly*) I just want you to know that it's got to stop.

(*The music stops. The mechanical toy runs down. There is absolute silence, and a strange fearfulness and disharmony in the atmosphere now.* HARRY *doesn't know what to do with his hands or feet.* WESLEY'S *arms hang at his sides.* JOE *quietly pushes the toy to one side of the table eager to study what is happening.* WILLIE *stops playing the marble game, turns around and begins to wait.* DUDLEY *straightens up very, very vigorously, as if to say: "Nothing can scare me. I know love is the only thing." The* ARAB *is the same as ever, but watchful.* NICK *is arrogantly aloof. There is a moment of this silence and tension, as though* BLICK *were waiting for everybody to acknowledge his presence. He is obviously flattered by the acknowledgment of Harry, Dudley, Wesley, and Willie, but a little irritated by Nick's aloofness and unfriendliness.*)

NICK Don't look at me. I can't tell a street-walker from a lady. You married?

BLICK You're not asking *me* questions. *I'm* telling *you.*

NICK (*Interrupting*) You're a man of about forty-five or so. You *ought* to know better.

BLICK (*Angry*) Street-walkers are working out of this place.

NICK (*Beginning to shout*) Now, don't start any trouble with me. People come here to drink and loaf around. I don't care who they are.

BLICK Well, I do.

NICK The only way to find out if a lady is a street-walker is to walk the streets with her, go to bed, and make sure. You wouldn't want to do that. You'd *like* to, of course.

BLICK Any more of it, and I'll have your joint closed.

NICK (*Very casually, without ill-will*) Listen. I've got no use for you, or anybody like you. You're out to change the world from something bad to something worse. Something like yourself.

BLICK (*Furious pause, and contempt*) I'll be back tonight. (*He begins to go.*)

NICK (*Very angry but very calm*) Do yourself a big favor and don't come back tonight. Send somebody else. I don't like your personality.

BLICK (*Casually, but with contempt*) Don't break any laws. I don't like yours, either.

> (*He looks the place over, and goes.*)
>
> (*There is a moment of silence. Then* WILLIE *turns and puts a new nickel in the slot and starts a new game.* WESLEY *turns to the piano and rather falteringly begins to play. His heart really isn't in it.* HARRY *walks about, unable to dance.* DUDLEY *lapses into his customary melancholy, at a table.* NICK *whistles a little: suddenly stops.* JOE *winds the toy.*)

JOE (*Comically*) Nick. You going to kill that man?

NICK I'm disgusted.

JOE Yeah? Why?

NICK Why should I get worked up over a guy like that? Why should I hate *him?* He's nothing. He's nobody. He's a mouse. But every time he comes into this place I get burned up. He doesn't want to drink. He doesn't want to sit down. He doesn't want to take things easy. Tell me one thing?

JOE Do my best.

NICK What's a punk like *that* want to go out and try to change the world for?

JOE (*Amazed*) Does *he* want to change the world, too?

NICK (*Irritated*) You know what I mean. What's he want to bother people for? He's *sick.*

JOE (*Almost to himself, reflecting on the fact that* BLICK *too wants to change the world*) I guess he wants to change the world at that.

NICK So I go to work and hate him.

JOE It's not him, Nick. It's everything.

NICK Yeah, *I know.* But I've still got no use for him. He's no good. You know what I mean? He hurts little people. (*Confused*) One of the girls tried to commit suicide on account of him. (*Furiously*) I'll break his head if he hurts anybody around here. This is *my* joint. (*Afterthought*) Or anybody's *feelings*, either.

JOE He may not be so bad, deep down underneath.

NICK I know all about him. He's no good.

> (*During this talk* WESLEY *has really begun to play the piano, the toy is rattling again, and little by little* HARRY *has begun to dance.* NICK *has come around the bar, and now, very much like a child—forgetting all his anger—is watching the toy work. He begins to smile at everything: turns and listens to* WESLEY: *watches* HARRY: *nods at the* ARAB: *shakes his head at* DUDLEY: *and gestures amiably about* WILLIE. *It's his joint all right.*)

> (*It's a good, low-down, honky-tonk American place that lets people alone.*)

NICK I've got a good joint. There's nothing wrong here. Hey. Comedian. Stick to the dancing tonight. I think you're O.K. Wesley? Do some more of that tonight. That's fine!

HARRY Thanks, Nick. Gosh, I'm on my way at last. (*On telephone*) Hello, Ma? Is that you, Ma? Harry. I got the job. (*He hangs up and walks around, smiling.*)

NICK (*Watching the toy all this time*) Say, that really is something. What is that, anyway?

> (MARY L. *comes in.*)

JOE (*Holding it toward* NICK *and* MARY L.) Nick, this is a toy. A contraption devised by the cunning of man to drive boredom, or grief, or anger out of children. A noble gadget. A gadget, I might say, infinitely nobler than any other I can think of at the moment. (*Everybody gathers around* JOE'S *table to look at the toy. The toy stops working.* JOE *winds the music box. Lifts a whistle: blows it, making a very strange, funny and sorrowful sound.*) Delightful. Tragic, but delightful.

(WESLEY *plays the music-box theme on the piano.* MARY L. *takes a table.*)

NICK Joe. That girl, Kitty. What's she mean, calling me a dentist? I wouldn't hurt anybody, let alone a tooth.

(NICK *goes to Mary L's table.* HARRY *imitates the toy. Dances. The piano music comes up, the light dims slowly, while the piano solo continues.*)

CURTAIN

Act Two

An hour later. All the people who were at Nick's when the curtain came down are still there. JOE *at his table, quietly shuffling and turning a deck of cards, and at the same time watching the face of the woman, and looking at the initials on her handbag, as though they were the symbols of the lost glory of the world. The* WOMAN, *in turn, very casually regards* JOE *occasionally. Or rather senses him; has sensed him in fact the whole hour. She is mildly tight on beer, and* JOE *himself is tight, but as always completely under control; simply sharper. The others are about, at tables, and so on.*

JOE Is it Madge—Laubowitz?

MARY Is what *what?*

JOE Is the name Mabel Lepescu?

MARY What name?

JOE The name the initials M. L. stand for. The initials on your bag.

MARY No.

JOE (*After a long pause, thinking deeply what the name might be, turning a card, looking into the beautiful face of the woman*) Margie Longworthy?

MARY (*All this is very natural and sincere, no comedy on the part of the people involved: they are both solemn, being drunk*) No.

JOE (*His voice higher-pitched, as though he were growing a little alarmed*) Midge Laurie? (MARY *shakes her head*) My initials are J. T.

MARY (*Pause*) John?

JOE No. (*Pause*) Martha Lancaster?

MARY No. (*Slight pause*) Joseph?

JOE Well, not exactly. That's my first name, but everybody calls me Joe. The last name is the tough one. I'll help you a little. I'm Irish. (*Pause*) Is it just plain Mary?

MARY Yes, it is. I'm Irish, too. At least on my father's side. English on my mother's side.

JOE I'm Irish on both sides. Mary's one of my favorite names. I guess that's why I didn't think of it. I met a girl in Mexico City named Mary once. She was an American from Philadelphia. She got married there. In Mexico City, I mean. While I was *there*. We were in love, too. At least *I* was. You never know about anyone else. They were engaged, you see, and her mother was with her, so they went through with it. Must have been six or seven years ago. She's probably got three or four children by this time.

MARY Are you still in love with her?

JOE Well—no. To tell you the truth, I'm not sure. I guess I am. I didn't even know she was engaged until a couple of days before they got married. I thought I was going to marry her. I kept thinking all the time about the kind of kids we would be likely to have. My favorite was the third one. The first two were fine. Handsome and fine and intelligent, but that third one was different. Dumb and goofy-looking. I liked *him* a lot. When she told me she was going to be married, I didn't feel so bad about the first two, it was that dumb one.

MARY (*After a pause of some few seconds*) What do you do?

JOE Do? To tell you the truth, nothing.

MARY Do you always drink a great deal?

JOE (*Scientifically*) Not *always*. Only when I'm awake. I sleep seven or eight hours every night, you know.

MARY How nice. I mean to drink when you're awake.

JOE (*Thoughtfully*) It's a privilege.

MARY Do you really *like* to drink?

JOE (*Positively*) As much as I like to *breathe*.

MARY (*Beautifully*) Why?

JOE (*Dramatically*) Why do I like to drink? (*Pause*) Because I don't like to be gypped. Because I don't like to be dead most of the time and just a little alive every once in a long while. (*Pause*) If I don't drink, I become fascinated by unimportant things—like everybody else. I get busy. Do things. All kinds of little stupid things, for all kinds of little stupid reasons. Proud, selfish, *ordinary* things. I've done them. Now I don't do anything. *I live all the time.* Then I go to sleep. (*Pause*)

MARY Do you sleep well?

JOE (*Taking it for granted*) Of course.

MARY (*Quietly, almost with tenderness*) What are your plans?

JOE (*Loudly, but also tenderly*) Plans? I haven't *got* any. *I just get up.*

MARY (*Beginning to understand everything*) Oh, yes. Yes, of course.

    (DUDLEY *puts a nickel in the phonograph.*)

JOE (*Thoughtfully*) Why do I drink? (*Pause, while he thinks about it. The thinking appears to be profound and complex, and has the effect of giving his face a very comical and naïve expression*) That question calls for a pretty complicated answer. (*He smiles abstractly*)

MARY Oh, I didn't mean—

JOE (*Swiftly, gallantly*) No. No. I *insist*. I *know* why. It's just a matter of finding words. Little ones.

MARY It really doesn't matter.

JOE (*Seriously*) Oh, yes, it does. (*Clinically*) Now, why do I drink? (*Scientifically*) No. Why does *anybody* drink? (*Working it out*) Every day has twenty-four hours.

MARY (*Sadly, but brightly*) Yes, that's true.

JOE Twenty-four hours. Out of the twenty-four hours at *least* twenty-three and a half are—my God, I don't know why—dull, dead, boring, empty, and murderous. Minutes on the clock, *not time of living*. It doesn't make any difference who you are or what you do, twenty-three and a half hours of the twenty-four are spent *waiting*.

MARY Waiting?

JOE (*Gesturing, loudly*) And the more you wait, the less there is to wait for.

MARY (*Attentively, beautifully his student*) Oh?

JOE (*Continuing*) That goes on for days and days, and weeks and months and years, and years, and the first thing you know *all* the years are dead. All the minutes are dead. You yourself are dead. There's nothing to wait for any more, Nothing except *minutes* on the *clock*. No time of life. Nothing but minutes, and idiocy. Beautiful, bright, intelligent idiocy. (*Pause*) Does that answer your question?

MARY (*Earnestly*) I'm afraid it does. Thank you. You shouldn't have gone to all the trouble.

JOE No trouble at all. (*Pause*) You have children?

MARY Yes. Two. A son and a daughter.

JOE (*Delighted*) How swell. Do they look like you?

MARY Yes.

JOE Then why are you sad?

MARY I was always sad. It's just that after I was married I was allowed to drink.

JOE (*Eagerly*) Who are you waiting for?

MARY No one.

JOE (*Smiling*) I'm not waiting for anybody, either.

MARY My husband, of course.

JOE Oh, sure.

MARY He's a lawyer.

JOE (*Standing, leaning on the table*) He's a great guy. I like him. I'm very fond of him.

MARY (*Listening*) You have responsibilities?

JOE (*Loudly*) *One*, and *thousands*. As a matter of fact, I feel responsible to everybody. At least to everybody I meet. I've been trying for three years to find out if it's possible to live what I think is a civilized life. I mean a life that can't hurt any other life.

MARY You're famous?

JOE Very. Utterly unknown, but very famous. Would you like to dance?

MARY All right.

JOE (*Loudly*) I'm *sorry*. I don't dance. I didn't think you'd like to.

MARY To tell you the truth, I don't like to dance at all.

JOE (*Proudly. Commentator*) I can hardly walk.

MARY You mean you're tight?

JOE (*Smiling*) No. I mean *all* the time.

MARY (*Looking at him closely*) Were you ever in Paris?

JOE In 1929, and again in 1934.

MARY What month of 1934?

JOE Most of April, all of May, and a little of June.

MARY I was there in November and December that year.

JOE We were there almost at the same time. You were married?

MARY Engaged. (*They are silent a moment, looking at one another. Quietly and with great charm*) Are you *really* in love with me?

JOE Yes.

MARY Is it the champagne?

JOE Yes. Partly, at least. (*He sits down*)

MARY If you don't see me again, will you be very unhappy?

JOE Very.

MARY (*Getting up*) I'm so pleased. (JOE *is deeply grieved that she is going. In fact, he is almost panic-stricken about it, getting up in a way that is full of furious sorrow and regret.*) I must go now. Please don't get up. (JOE *is up, staring at her with amazement.*) Good-bye.

JOE (*Simply*) Good-bye.

> (*The* WOMAN *stands looking at him a moment, then turns and goes.* JOE *stands staring after her for a long time. Just as he is slowly sitting down again, the* NEWSBOY *enters, and goes to Joe's table.*)

NEWSBOY Paper, Mister?

JOE How many you got this time?

NEWSBOY Eleven.

> (JOE *buys them all, looks at the lousy headlines, throws them away.*)
>
> (*The* NEWSBOY *looks at* JOE, *amazed. He walks over to* NICK *at the bar.*)

NEWSBOY (*Troubled*) Hey, Mister, do you own this place?

NICK (*Casually but emphatically*) I own this place.

NEWSBOY Can you use a great lyric tenor?

NICK (*Almost to himself*) Great lyric tenor? (*Loudly*) Who?

NEWSBOY (*Loud and the least bit angry*) Me. I'm getting too big to sell papers. I don't want to holler headlines all the time. I want to *sing*. You can use a great lyric tenor, can't you?

NICK What's lyric about you?

NEWSBOY (*Voice high-pitched, confused*) My voice.

NICK Oh. (*Slight pause, giving in*) All right then—sing!

> (*The* NEWSBOY *breaks into swift and beautiful song: "When Irish Eyes Are Smiling." * NICK *and* JOE *listen carefully:* NICK *with wonder,* JOE *with amazement and delight.*)

NEWSBOY (*Singing*)
> When Irish eyes are smiling,
> Sure 'tis like a morn in Spring.
> In the lilt of Irish laughter,
> You can hear the angels sing.
> When Irish hearts are happy,
> All the world seems bright and gay.
> But when Irish eyes are smiling—

NICK (*Loudly, swiftly*) Are you Irish?

NEWSBOY (*Speaking swiftly, loudly, a little impatient with the irrelevant question*) No. I'm Greek. (*He finishes the song, singing louder than ever*)
> Sure they steal your heart away.

> (*He turns to* NICK *dramatically, like a vaudeville singer begging his audience for applause.* NICK *studies the boy eagerly.* JOE *gets to his feet and leans toward the* BOY *and* NICK.)

NICK Not bad. Let me hear you again about a year from now.

NEWSBOY (*Thrilled*) Honest?

NICK Yeah. Along about November 7th, 1940.

NEWSBOY (*Happier than ever before in his life, running over to* JOE) Did you hear it too, Mister?

JOE Yes, and it's great. What part of Greece?

NEWSBOY Salonica. Gosh, Mister. Thanks.

JOE Don't wait a year. Come back with some papers a little later. You're a great singer.

NEWSBOY (*Thrilled and excited*) Aw, thanks, Mister. So long. (*Running, to* NICK) Thanks, Mister.

> (*He runs out.* JOE *and* NICK *look at the swinging doors.* JOE *sits down.* NICK *laughs.*)

NICK Joe, people are so wonderful. Look at that kid.

JOE Of course they're wonderful. Every one of them is wonderful. (*Pause*) A nation like this can't go wrong.

(MCCARTHY *and* KRUPP *come in, talking.*)

(MCCARTHY *is a big man in work clothes, which make him seem very young. He is wearing black jeans, and a blue workman's shirt. No tie. No hat. He has broad shoulders, a lean intelligent face, thick black hair. In his right back pocket is the longshoreman's hook. His arms are long and hairy. His sleeves are rolled up to just below his elbows. He is a casual man, easy-going in movement, sharp in perception, swift in appreciation of charm or innocence or comedy, and gentle in spirit. His speech is clear and full of warmth. His voice is powerful, but modulated. He enjoys the world, in spite of the mess it is, and he is fond of people, in spite of the mess they are.*)

(KRUPP *is not quite as tall or broad-shouldered as* MCCARTHY. *He is physically encumbered by his uniform, club, pistol, belt, and cap. And he is plainly not at home in the role of policeman. His movement is stiff and unintentionally pompous. He is a naïve man, essentially good. His understanding is less than McCarthy's, but he is honest and he doesn't try to bluff.*)

KRUPP You don't understand what I mean. Hi-ya, Joe.

JOE Hello, Krupp.

MCCARTHY Hi-ya, Joe.

JOE Hello, McCarthy.

KRUPP Two beers, Nick. (*To* MCCARTHY) All I do is carry out orders, carry out orders. I don't know what the idea is behind the order. Who it's for, or who it's against, or why. All I do is carry it out.

(NICK *gives them beer.*)

MCCARTHY You don't read enough.

KRUPP I do read. I read *The Examiner* every morning. *The Call-Bulletin* every night.

MCCARTHY And carry out orders. What are the orders now?

KRUPP To keep the peace down here on the waterfront.

MCCARTHY Keep it for who? (*To* JOE) Right?

JOE (*Sorrowfully*) Right.

KRUPP How do I know for who? The peace. Just keep it.

MCCARTHY It's got to be kept for somebody. Who would you suspect it's kept for?

KRUPP For citizens!

MCCARTHY I'm a citizen!

KRUPP All right, I'm keeping it for you.

MCCARTHY By hitting me over the head with a club? (*To* JOE) Right?

JOE (*Melancholy, with remembrance*) I don't know.

KRUPP Mac, you know I never hit you over the head with a club.

MCCARTHY But you will if you're on duty at the time and happen to stand on the opposite side of myself, on duty.

KRUPP We went to Mission High together. We were always good friends. The only time we ever fought was that time over Alma Haggerty. Did you marry Alma Haggerty? (*To* JOE) Right?

JOE Everything's right.

MCCARTHY No. Did you? (*To* JOE) Joe, are you with me or against me?

JOE I'm with everybody. One at a time.

KRUPP No. And that's just what I mean.

MCCARTHY You mean neither one of us is going to marry the thing we're fighting for?

KRUPP *I don't even know what it is.*

MCCARTHY You don't read enough, I tell you.

KRUPP Mac, you don't know what you're fighting for, either.

MCCARTHY It's so simple, it's fantastic.

KRUPP All right, what are you fighting for?

MCCARTHY For the rights of the inferior. Right?

JOE Something like that.

KRUPP The who?

MCCARTHY The inferior. The world full of Mahoneys who haven't got what it takes to make monkeys out of everybody else, near by. The men who were created equal. Remember?

KRUPP Mac, you're not inferior.

MCCARTHY I'm a longshoreman. And an idealist. I'm a man with too much brawn to be an intellectual, exclusively. I married a small, sensitive, cultured woman so that my kids would be sissies instead of suckers. A strong man with any sensibility has no choice in this world but to be a heel, or a *worker*. I haven't the heart to be a heel, so I'm a worker. I've got a son in high school who's already thinking of being a writer.

KRUPP I wanted to be a writer once.

JOE Wonderful. (*He puts down the paper, looks at* KRUPP *and* MCCARTHY.)

MCCARTHY They *all* wanted to be writers. Every maniac in the world that ever brought about the murder of people through war started out in an attic or a basement writing poetry. It stank. So they got even by becoming important heels. And it's still going on.

KRUPP Is it really, Joe?

JOE Look at today's paper.

MCCARTHY Right now on Telegraph Hill is some punk who is trying to be Shakespeare. Ten years from now he'll be a senator. Or a communist.

KRUPP Somebody ought to do something about it.

MCCARTHY (*Mischievously, with laughter in his voice*) The thing to do is to have more magazines. Hundreds of them. *Thousands*. Print everything they write, so they'll believe they're immortal. That way keep them from going haywire.

KRUPP Mac, you ought to be a writer yourself.

MCCARTHY I hate the tribe. They're mischief-makers. Right?

JOE (*Swiftly*) Everything's right. Right and wrong.

KRUPP Then why do you read?

MCCARTHY (*Laughing*) It's relaxing. It's soothing. (*Pause*) The lousiest people born into the world are writers. Language is all right. It's the people who use language that are lousy. (*The* ARAB *has moved a little closer, and is listening carefully.*)(*To the* ARAB) What do you think, Brother?

ARAB (*After making many faces, thinking very deeply*) No foundation. All the way down the line. What. What-not. Nothing. I go walk and look at sky. (*He goes*)

KRUPP What? What-not? (*To* JOE) What's that mean?

JOE (*Slowly, thinking, remembering*) What? What-not? That means this side, that side. Inhale, exhale. What: birth. What-not: death. The inevitable, the astounding, the magnificent seed of growth and decay in all things. Beginning, and end. That man, in his own way, is a prophet. He is one who, with the help of *beer*, is able to reach that state of deep understanding in which what and what-not, the reasonable and the unreasonable, are one.

MCCARTHY Right.

KRUPP If you can understand that kind of talk, how can you be a longshoreman?

MCCARTHY I come from a long line of McCarthys who never married or slept with anything but the most powerful and quarrelsome flesh. (*He drinks beer.*)

KRUPP I could listen to you two guys for hours, but I'll be damned if I know what the hell you're talking about.

MCCARTHY The consequence is that all the McCarthys are too great and too strong to be heroes. Only the weak and unsure perform the heroic. They've *got* to. The more heroes you have, the worse the history of the world becomes. Right?

JOE Go outside and look at it.

KRUPP You sure can philos—philosoph—Boy, you can talk.

MCCARTHY I wouldn't talk this way to anyone but a man in uniform, and a man who couldn't understand a word of what I was saying. The party I'm speaking of, my friend, is *YOU*.

   (*The phone rings.*)

   (HARRY *gets up from his table suddenly and begins a new dance.*)

KRUPP (*Noticing him, with great authority*) Here. Here. What do you think you're doing?

HARRY (*Stopping*) I just got an idea for a new dance. I'm trying it out. Nick. Nick, the phone's ringing.

KRUPP (*To* MCCARTHY) Has he got a right to do that?

MCCARTHY The living have danced from the beginning of time. I might even say, the dance and the life have moved along together, until now we have—(*To* HARRY) Go into your dance, son, and show us what we have.

HARRY I haven't got it worked out *completely* yet, but it starts out like this. (*He dances.*)

NICK (*On phone*) Nick's Pacific Street Restaurant, Saloon, and Entertainment Palace. Good afternoon. Nick speaking. (*Listens*) Who? (*Turns around*) Is there a Dudley Bostwick in the joint?

(DUDLEY *jumps to his feet and goes to phone.*)

DUDLEY (*On phone*) Hello. Elsie? (*Listens*) You're coming down? (*Elated. To the saloon*) She's coming down. (*Pause*) No. I won't drink. Aw, gosh, Elsie.

(*He hangs up, looks about him strangely, as if he were just born, walks around touching things, putting chairs in place, and so on.*)

MCCARTHY (*To* HARRY) Splendid. Splendid.

HARRY Then I go into this little routine.

(*He demonstrates*)

KRUPP Is that good, Mac?

MCCARTHY It's awful, but it's honest and ambitious, like everything else in this great country.

HARRY Then I work along into this. (*He demonstrates*) And *this* is where I *really* get going. (*He finishes the dance*)

MCCARTHY Excellent. A most satisfying demonstration of the present state of the American body and soul. Son, you're a genius.

HARRY (*Delighted, shaking hands with* MCCARTHY) I go on in front of an audience for the first time in my life tonight.

MCCARTHY They'll be delighted. Where'd you learn to dance?

HARRY Never took a lesson in my life. I'm a natural-born dancer. And *comedian*, too.

MCCARTHY (*Astounded*) You can make people *laugh*?

HARRY (*Dumbly*) I can be funny, but they won't laugh.

MCCARTHY That's odd. Why not?

HARRY I don't know. They just won't laugh.

MCCARTHY Would you care to be funny now?

HARRY I'd like to try out a new monologue I've been thinking about.

MCCARTHY Please do. I promise you if it's funny I shall *roar* with laughter.

HARRY This is it. (*Goes into the act, with much energy*) I'm up at Sharkey's on Turk Street. It's a quarter to nine, daylight saving. Wednesday, the eleventh. What I've got is a headache and a 1918 nickel. What I *want* is a cup of coffee. If I buy a cup of coffee with the nickel, I've got to walk home. I've got an eight-ball problem. George the Greek is shooting a game of snooker with Pedro the Filipino. *I'm in rags.* They're wearing thirty-five dollar suits, made to order. I haven't got a cigarette. They're smoking Bobby Burns panatelas. I'm thinking it over, like I always do. George the Greek is in a tough spot. If I buy a cup of coffee, I'll want another cup. What happens? My *ear* aches! My ear. George the Greek takes the cue. Chalks it. Studies the table. Touches the cue-ball delicately. Tick. What happens? He makes the three-ball! What do I do? I get confused. *I go out and buy a morning paper.* What the hell do I want with a morning paper? What I *want* is a cup of coffee, and a good used car. I go out and buy a morning paper. Thursday, the twelfth. Maybe the headline's about *me.* I take a quick look. *No. The headline is not about me.* It's about Hitler. Seven thousand miles away. I'm here. Who the hell is Hitler? Who's behind the eight-ball? I turn around. *Everybody's behind the eight-ball!*

> (*Pause.* KRUPP *moves toward* HARRY *as if to make an important arrest.* HARRY *moves to the swinging doors.* MCCARTHY *stops* KRUPP.)

MCCARTHY (*To* HARRY) It's the funniest thing I've ever heard. Or *seen*, for that matter.

HARRY (*Coming back to* MCCARTHY) Then, why don't you laugh?

MCCARTHY I don't know, *yet.*

HARRY I'm always getting funny ideas that nobody will laugh at.

MCCARTHY (*Thoughtfully*) It may be that you've stumbled headlong into a new kind of comedy.

HARRY Well, what good is it if it doesn't make anybody laugh?

MCCARTHY There are *kinds* of laughter, son. I must say, in all truth, that I *am* laughing, although not *out loud.*

HARRY I want to *hear* people laugh. *Out loud.* That's why I keep thinking of funny things to say.

MCCARTHY Well. They may catch on in time. Let's go, Krupp. So long, Joe. (MCCARTHY *and* KRUPP *go.*)

JOE So long. (*After a moment's pause*) Hey, Nick.

NICK Yeah.

JOE Bet McCarthy in the last race.

NICK You're crazy. That horse is a double-crossing, no-good—

JOE Bet everything you've got on McCarthy.

NICK I'm not betting a nickel on him. You bet everything you've got on McCarthy.

JOE I don't need money.

NICK What makes you think McCarthy's going to win?

JOE McCarthy's name's McCarthy, isn't it?

NICK Yeah. So what?

JOE The *horse* named McCarthy is going to win, *that's all*. Today.

NICK Why?

JOE You do what I tell you, and everything will be all right.

NICK McCarthy likes to talk, that's all. (*Pause*) Where's Tom?

JOE He'll be around. He'll be miserable, but he'll be around. Five or ten minutes more.

NICK You don't believe that Kitty, do you? About being in burlesque?

JOE (*Very clearly*) I believe dreams sooner than statistics.

NICK (*Remembering*) She sure is somebody. Called me a dentist.

> (TOM, *turning about, confused, troubled, comes in, and hurries to Joe's table.*)

JOE What's the matter?

TOM Here's your five, Joe. I'm in trouble again.

JOE If it's not organic, it'll cure itself. If it is organic, science will cure it. What is it, organic or non-organic?

TOM Joe, I don't know— (*He seems to be completely broken-down*)

JOE What's eating you? I want you to go on an errand for me.

TOM It's Kitty.

JOE What about her?

TOM She's up in her room, crying.

JOE Crying?

TOM Yeah, she's been crying for over an hour. I been talking to her all this time, but she won't stop.

JOE What's she crying about?

TOM I don't know. I couldn't understand anything. She kept crying and telling me about a big house and collie dogs all around and flowers and one of her brother's dead and the other one lost somewhere. Joe, I can't stand Kitty crying.

JOE You want to marry the girl?

TOM (*Nodding*) Yeah.

JOE (*Curious and sincere*) Why?

TOM I don't know why, exactly, Joe. (*Pause*) Joe, I don't like to think of Kitty out in the streets. I guess I love her, that's all.

JOE She's a nice girl.

TOM She's like an angel. She's not like those other streetwalkers.

JOE (*Swiftly*) Here. Take all this money and run next door to Frankie's and bet it on the nose of McCarthy.

TOM (*Swiftly*) All this money, Joe? McCarthy?

JOE Yeah. Hurry.

TOM (*Going*) Ah, Joe. If McCarthy wins we'll be rich.

JOE Get going, will you?

> (TOM *runs out and nearly knocks over the* ARAB *coming back in.* NICK *fills him a beer without a word.*)

ARAB No foundation, anywhere. Whole world. No foundation. All the way down the line.

NICK (*Angry*) McCarthy! Just because you got a little lucky this morning, you have to go to work and throw away eighty bucks.

JOE He wants to marry her.

NICK Suppose she doesn't want to marry *him?*

JOE (*Amazed*) Oh, yeah. (*Thinking*) Now, why wouldn't she want to marry a nice guy like Tom?

NICK She's been in burlesque. She's had flowers sent to her by European royalty. She's dined with young men of quality and social position. She's above Tom.

(TOM *comes running in.*)

TOM (*Disgusted*) They were running when I got there. Frankie wouldn't take the bet. McCarthy didn't get a call till the stretch. I thought we were going to save all this money. Then McCarthy won by two lengths.

JOE What'd he pay, fifteen to one?

TOM Better, but Frankie wouldn't take the bet.

NICK (*Throwing a dish towel across the room*) Well, for the love of Mike.

JOE Give me the money.

TOM (*Giving back the money*) We would have had about a thousand five hundred dollars.

JOE (*Bored, casually, inventing*) Go up to Schwabacher-Frey and get me the biggest Rand-McNally map of the nations of Europe they've got. On your way back stop at one of the pawn shops on Third Street, and buy me a good revolver and some cartridges.

TOM She's up in her room crying, Joe.

JOE Go get me those things.

NICK What are you going to do, study the map, and then go out and shoot somebody?

JOE I want to read the names of some European towns and rivers and valleys and mountains.

NICK What do you want with the revolver?

JOE I want to study it. I'm interested in things. Here's twenty dollars, Tom. Now go get them things.

TOM A big map of Europe. And a revolver.

JOE Get a good one. Tell the man you don't know anything about firearms and you're trusting him not to fool you. Don't pay more than ten dollars.

TOM Joe, you got something on your mind. Don't go fool with a revolver.

JOE Be sure it's a good one.

TOM Joe.

JOE (*Irritated*) What, Tom?

TOM Joe, what do you send me out for crazy things for all the time?

JOE (*Angry*) They're not crazy, Tom. Now, get going.

TOM What about Kitty, Joe?

JOE Let her cry. It'll do her good.

TOM If she comes in here while I'm gone, talk to her, will you, Joe? Tell her about me.

JOE O.K. Get going. Don't load that gun. Just buy it and bring it here.

TOM (*Going*) You won't catch me loading any gun.

JOE Wait a minute. Take these toys away.

TOM Where'll I take them?

JOE Give them to some kid. (*Pause*) No. Take them up to Kitty. Toys stopped me from crying once. That's the reason I had you buy them. I wanted to see if I could find out *why* they stopped me from crying. I remember they seemed awfully stupid at the time.

TOM Shall I, Joe? Take them up to Kitty? Do you think they'd stop *her* from crying?

JOE They might. You get curious about the way they work and you forget whatever it is you're remembering that's making you cry. That's what they're for.

TOM Yeah. Sure. The girl at the store asked me what I wanted with toys. I'll take them up to Kitty. (*Tragically*) She's like a little girl. (*He goes*)

WESLEY Mr. Nick, can I play the piano again?

NICK Sure. Practice all you like—until I tell you to stop.

WESLEY You going to pay me for playing the piano?

NICK Sure. I'll give you enough to get by on.

WESLEY (*Amazed and delighted*) Get money for playing the piano?

(*He goes to the piano and begins to play quietly.* HARRY *goes up on the little stage and listens to the music. After a while he begins a soft shoe dance.*)

NICK What were you crying about?

JOE My mother.

NICK What about her?

JOE She was dead. I stopped crying when they gave me the toys.

(NICK'S MOTHER, *a little old woman of sixty or so, dressed plainly in black, her face shining, comes in briskly, chattering loudly in Italian, gesturing.* NICK *is delighted to see her.*)

360

NICK'S MOTHER (*In Italian*) Everything all right, Nickie?

NICK (*In Italian*) Sure, Mamma.

> (NICK'S MOTHER *leaves as gaily and as noisily as she came, after half a minute of loud Italian family talk.*)

JOE Who was that?

NICK (*To* JOE, *proudly and a little sadly*) My mother. (*Still looking at the swinging doors*)

JOE What'd she say?

NICK Nothing. Just wanted to see me. (*Pause*) What do you want with that gun?

JOE I study things, Nick.

> (*An old man who looks as if he might have been Kit Carson at one time walks in importantly, moves about, and finally stands at Joe's table.*)

KIT CARSON Murphy's the name. Just an old trapper. Mind if I sit down?

JOE Be delighted. What'll you drink?

KIT CARSON (*Sitting down*) Beer. Same as I've been drinking. And thanks.

JOE (*To* NICK) Glass of beer, Nick.

> (NICK *brings the beer to the table,* KIT CARSON *swallows it in one swig, wipes his big white mustache with the back of his right hand.*)

KIT CARSON (*Moving in*) I don't suppose you ever fell in love with a midget weighing thirty-nine pounds?

JOE (*Studying the man*) Can't say I have, but have another beer.

KIT CARSON (*Intimately*) Thanks, thanks. Down in Gallup, twenty years ago. Fellow by the name of Rufus Jenkins came to town with six white horses and two black ones. Said he wanted a man to break the horses for him because his left leg was wood and he couldn't do it. Had a meeting at Parker's Mercantile Store and finally came to blows, me and Henry Walpal. Bashed his head with a brass cuspidor and ran away to Mexico, but he didn't die.

> Couldn't speak a word. Took up with a cattle-breeder named Diego, educated in California. Spoke the language better than you and me. Said, Your job, Murph, is to feed them prize bulls. I said, Fine, what'll I feed them? He said, Hay, lettuce, salt, beer, and aspirin.

Came to blows two days later over an accordion he claimed I stole. I had *borrowed* it. During the fight I busted it over his head; ruined one of the finest accordions I ever saw. Grabbed a horse and rode back across the border. Texas. Got to talking with a fellow who looked honest. Turned out to be a Ranger who was looking for me.

JOE Yeah. You were saying, a thirty-nine-pound midget.

KIT CARSON Will I ever forget that lady? Will I ever get over that amazon of small proportions?

JOE Will you?

KIT CARSON If I live to be sixty.

JOE Sixty? You look more than sixty now.

KIT CARSON That's trouble showing in my face. Trouble and complications. I was fifty-eight three months ago.

JOE That accounts for it, then. Go ahead, tell me more.

KIT CARSON Told the Texas Ranger my name was Rothstein, mining engineer from Pennsylvania, looking for something worth while. Mentioned two places in Houston. Nearly lost an eye early one morning, going down the stairs. Ran into a six-footer with an iron-claw where his right hand was supposed to be. Said, You broke up my home. Told him I was a stranger in Houston. The girls gathered at the top of the stairs to see a fight. Seven of them. Six feet and an iron claw. That's bad on the nerves. Kicked him in the mouth when he swung for my head with the claw. Would have lost an eye except for quick thinking. He rolled into the gutter and pulled a gun. Fired seven times. I was back upstairs. Left the place an hour later, dressed in silk and feathers, with a hat swung around over my face. Saw him standing on the corner, waiting. Said, Care for a wiggle? Said he didn't. I went on down the street and left town. I don't suppose you ever had to put a dress on to save your skin, did you?

JOE No, and I never fell in love with a midget weighing thirty-nine pounds. Have another beer?

KIT CARSON Thanks. (*Swallows glass of beer*) Ever try to herd cattle on a bicycle?

JOE No. I never got around to that.

KIT CARSON Left Houston with sixty cents in my pocket, gift of a girl named Lucinda. Walked fourteen miles in fourteen hours. Big house with barb-wire all around, and big dogs. One thing I never could get around. Walked past the gate, anyway, from hunger and thirst. Dogs jumped up and came for me. Walked right into them, growing older every second. Went up to the door and knocked. Big negress opened the door, closed it quick. Said, On your way, white trash.

Knocked again. Said, On your way. Again. On your way. Again. This time the old man himself opened the door, ninety, if he was a day. Sawed-off shotgun, too.

Said, I ain't looking for trouble, Father. I'm hungry and thirsty, name's Cavanaugh.

Took me in and made mint juleps for the two of us.

Said, Living here alone, Father?

Said, Drink and ask no questions. Maybe I am and maybe I ain't. You saw the lady. Draw your own conclusions.

I'd heard of that, but didn't wink out of tact. If I told you that old Southern gentleman was my grandfather, you wouldn't believe me, would you?

JOE I might.

KIT CARSON Well, it so happens he wasn't. Would have been romantic if he had been, though.

JOE Where did you herd cattle on a bicycle?

KIT CARSON Toledo, Ohio, 1918.

JOE Toledo, Ohio? They don't herd cattle in Toledo.

KIT CARSON They don't anymore. They did in 1918. One fellow did, leastaways. Bookkeeper named Sam Gold. Straight from the East Side, New York. Sombrero, lariats, Bull Durham, two head of cattle and two bicycles. Called his place The Gold Bar Ranch, two acres, just outside the city limits.

That was the year of the War, you'll remember.

JOE Yeah, I remember, but how about herding them two cows on a bicycle? How'd you do it?

KIT CARSON Easiest thing in the world. Rode no hands. Had to, otherwise couldn't lasso the cows. Worked for Sam Gold till the cows ran away. Bicycles scared them. They went into Toledo. Never saw hide nor hair of them again. Advertised in every paper, but never got them back. Broke his heart. Sold both bikes and returned to New York.

Took four aces from a deck of red cards and walked to town. Poker. Fellow in the game named Chuck Collins, liked to gamble. Told him with a smile I didn't suppose he'd care to bet a hundred dollars I wouldn't hold four aces the next hand. Called it. My cards were red on the blank side. The other cards were blue. Plumb forgot all about it. Showed him four aces. Ace of spades, ace of clubs, ace of diamonds, ace of hearts. I'll remember them four cards if I live to be sixty. Would have been killed on the spot except for the hurricane that year.

JOE Hurricane?

KIT CARSON You haven't forgotten the Toledo hurricane of 1918, have you?

JOE No. There was no hurricane in Toledo in 1918, or any other year.

KIT CARSON For the love of God, then what do you suppose that commotion was? And how come I came to in Chicago, dream-walking down State Street?

JOE I guess they scared you.

KIT CARSON No, that wasn't it. You go back to the papers of November 1918, and I think you'll find there was a hurricane in Toledo. I remember sitting on the roof of a two-story house, floating northwest.

JOE (*Seriously*) Northwest?

KIT CARSON Now, son, don't tell me you don't believe me, either?

JOE (*Pause. Very seriously, energetically and sharply*) Of course I believe you. Living is an art. It's not bookkeeping. It takes a lot of rehearsing for a man to get to be himself.

KIT CARSON (*Thoughtfully, smiling, and amazed*) You're the first man I've ever met who believes me.

JOE (*Seriously*) Have another beer.

(TOM *comes in with the Rand-McNally book, the revolver, and the box of cartridges.* KIT *goes to bar.*)

JOE (*To* TOM) Did you give her the toys?

TOM Yeah, I gave them to her.

JOE Did she stop crying?

TOM No. She started crying harder than ever.

JOE That's funny. I wonder why.

TOM Joe, if I was a minute earlier, Frankie would have taken the bet and now we'd have about a thousand five hundred dollars. How much of it would you have given me, Joe?

JOE If she'd marry you—*all* of it.

TOM Would you, Joe?

JOE (*Opening packages, examining book first, and revolver next*) Sure. In this realm there's only one subject, and you're it. It's my duty to see that my subject is happy.

TOM Joe, do you think we'll ever have eighty dollars for a race sometime again when there's a fifteen-to-one shot that we like, weather good, track fast, they get off to a good start, our horse doesn't get a call till the stretch, we think we're going to lose all that money, and then it wins, by a nose?

JOE I didn't quite get that.

TOM You know what I mean.

JOE You mean the impossible. No, Tom, we won't. We were just a little late, that's all.

TOM We might, Joe.

JOE It's not likely.

TOM Then how am I ever going to make enough money to marry her?

JOE I don't know, Tom. Maybe you aren't.

TOM Joe, I got to marry Kitty. (*Shaking his head*) You ought to see the crazy room she lives in.

JOE What kind of a room is it?

TOM It's little. It crowds you in. It's bad, Joe. Kitty don't belong in a place like that.

JOE You want to take her away from there?

TOM Yeah. I want her to live in a house where there's room enough to live. Kitty ought to have a garden, or something.

JOE You want to take care of her?

TOM Yeah, sure, Joe. I ought to take care of somebody good that makes me feel like *I'm* somebody.

JOE That means you'll have to get a job. What can you do?

TOM I finished high school, but I don't know what I can do.

JOE Sometimes when you think about it, what do you think you'd like to do?

TOM Just sit around like you, Joe, and have somebody run errands for me and drink champagne and take things easy and never be broke and never worry about money.

JOE That's a noble ambition.

NICK (*To* JOE) How do you do it?

JOE I really don't know, but I think you've got to have the full cooperation of the Good Lord.

NICK I can't understand the way you talk.

TOM Joe, shall I go back and see if I can get her to stop crying?

JOE Give me a hand and I'll go with you.

TOM (*Amazed*) What! You're going to get up already?

JOE She's crying, isn't she?

TOM She's crying. Worse than ever now.

JOE I thought the toys would stop her.

TOM I've seen you sit in one place from four in the morning till two the next morning.

JOE At my best, Tom, I don't travel by foot. That's all. Come on. Give me a hand. I'll find some way to stop her from crying.

TOM (*Helping* JOE) Joe, I never did tell you. You're a different kind of a guy.

JOE (*Swiftly, a little angry*) Don't be silly. I don't understand things. I'm trying to understand them.

(JOE *is a little drunk. They go out together. The lights go down slowly, while* WESLEY *plays the piano, and come up slowly on:*

Act Three

A cheap bed in Nick's to indicate room 21 of the New York Hotel, upstairs, around the corner from Nick's. The bed can be at the center of Nick's, or up on the little stage. Everything in Nick's is the same, except that all the people are silent, immobile and in darkness, except WESLEY *who is playing the piano softly and sadly.* KITTY DUVAL, *in a dress she has carried around with her from the early days in Ohio, is seated on the bed, tying a ribbon in her hair. She looks at herself in a hand mirror. She is deeply grieved at the change she sees in herself. She takes off the ribbon, angry and hurt. She lifts a book from the bed and tries to read. She begins to sob again. She picks up an old picture of herself and looks at it. Sobs harder than ever, falling on the bed and burying her face. There is a knock, as if at the door.*

KITTY (*Sobbing*) Who is it?

TOM'S VOICE Kitty, it's me. Tom. Me and Joe.

> (JOE, *followed by* TOM, *comes to the bed quietly.* JOE *is holding a rather large toy carousel.* JOE *studies* KITTY *a moment.*)

> (*He sets the toy carousel on the floor, at the foot of Kitty's bed.*)

TOM (*Standing over* KITTY *and bending down close to her*) Don't cry any more, Kitty.

KITTY (*Not looking, sobbing*) I don't like this life.

> (JOE *starts the carousel which makes a strange, sorrowful, tinkling music. The music begins slowly, becomes swift, gradually slows down, and ends.* JOE *himself is interested in the toy, watches and listens to it carefully.*)

TOM (*Eagerly*) Kitty. Joe got up from his chair at Nick's just to get you a toy and come here. This one makes music. We rode all over town in a cab to get it. Listen.

> (KITTY *sits up slowly, listening, while* TOM *watches her. Everything happens slowly and somberly.* KITTY *notices the photograph of herself when she was a little girl. Lifts it, and looks at it again.*)

TOM (*Looking*) Who's that little girl, Kitty?

KITTY That's me. When I was seven.

> (KITTY *hands the photo to* TOM)

TOM (*Looking, smiling*) Gee, you're pretty, Kitty.

(JOE *reaches up for the photograph, which* TOM *hands to him.* TOM *returns to* KITTY *whom he finds as pretty now as she was at seven.* JOE *studies the photograph.* KITTY *looks up at* TOM. *There is no doubt that they really love one another.* JOE *looks up at them.*)

KITTY Tom?

TOM (*Eagerly*) Yeah, Kitty.

KITTY Tom, when you were a little boy what did you want to be?

TOM (*A little bewildered, but eager to please her*) What, Kitty?

KITTY Do you remember when you were a little boy?

TOM (*Thoughtfully*) Yeah, I remember sometimes, Kitty.

KITTY What did you want to be?

TOM (*Looks at* JOE. JOE *holds Tom's eyes a moment. Then* TOM *is able to speak*) Sometimes I wanted to be a locomotive engineer. Sometimes I wanted to be a policeman.

KITTY I wanted to be a great actress. (*She looks up into Tom's face*) Tom, didn't you ever want to be a doctor?

TOM (*Looks at* JOE. JOE *holds Tom's eyes again, encouraging* TOM *by his serious expression to go on talking*) Yeah, now I remember. Sure, Kitty. I wanted to be a doctor—*once*.

KITTY (*Smiling sadly*) I'm so glad. Because I wanted to be an actress and have a young doctor come to the theatre and see me and fall in love with me and send me flowers.

(JOE *pantomimes to* TOM, *demanding that he go on talking*)

TOM I would do that, Kitty.

KITTY I wouldn't know who it was, and then one day I'd see him in the street and fall in love with him. I wouldn't know he was the one who was in love with me. I'd think about him all the time. I'd dream about him. I'd dream of being near him the rest of my life. I'd dream of having children that looked like him. I wouldn't be an actress all the time. Only until I found him and fell in love with him. After that we'd take a train and go to beautiful cities and see the wonderful people everywhere and give money to the poor and whenever people were sick he'd go to them and make them well again.

(TOM *looks at* JOE, *bewildered, confused, and full of sorrow.* KITTY *is deep in memory, almost in a trance.*)

368

JOE (*Gently*) Talk to her, Tom. Be the wonderful young doctor she dreamed about and never found. Go ahead. Correct the errors of the world.

TOM Joe. (*Pathetically*) I don't know what to say.

(*There is rowdy singing in the hall. A loud young* VOICE *sings: "Sailing, sailing, over the bounding main."*)

VOICE Kitty. Oh, Kitty! (KITTY *stirs, shocked, coming out of the trance.*) Where the hell are you? Oh, Kitty.

(TOM *jumps up, furiously.*)

WOMAN'S VOICE (*In the hall*) Who you looking for, Sailor Boy?

VOICE The most beautiful lay in the world.

WOMAN'S VOICE Don't go any further.

VOICE (*With impersonal contempt*) You? No. Not you. Kitty. You stink.

WOMAN'S VOICE (*Rasping, angry*) Don't you dare talk to me that way. You pickpocket.

VOICE (*Still impersonal, but louder*) Oh, I see. Want to get tough, hey? Close the door. Go hide.

WOMAN'S VOICE You pickpocket. All of you.

(*The door slams.*)

VOICE (*Roaring with laughter which is very sad*) Oh—Kitty. Room 21. Where the hell is that room?

TOM (*To* JOE) Joe, I'll kill him.

KITTY (*Fully herself again, terribly frightened*) Who is it?

(*She looks long and steadily at* TOM *and* JOE. TOM *is standing, excited and angry.* JOE *is completely at ease, his expression full of pity.* KITTY *buries her face in the bed.*)

JOE (*Gently*) Tom. Just take him away.

VOICE Here it is. Number 21. Three naturals. Heaven. My blue heaven. The west, a nest, and you. Just Molly and me. (*Tragically*) Ah, to hell with everything.

(*A young* SAILOR, *a good-looking boy of no more than twenty or so, who is only drunk and lonely, comes to the bed, singing sadly.*)

SAILOR *Hi-ya, Kitty. (Pause) Oh. Visitors. Sorry. A thousand apologies. (To* KITTY*) I'll come back later.*

TOM (*Taking him by the shoulders, furiously*) If you do, I'll kill you.

(JOE *holds* TOM. TOM *pushes the frightened boy away.*)

JOE (*Somberly*) Tom. You stay here with Kitty. I'm going down to Union Square to hire an automobile. I'll be back in a few minutes. We'll ride out to the ocean and watch the sun go down. Then we'll ride down the Great Highway to Half Moon Bay. We'll have supper down there, and you and Kitty can dance.

TOM (*Stupefied, unable to express his amazement and gratitude*) Joe, you mean you're going to go on an errand for me? You mean you're not going to send me?

JOE That's right.

(*He gestures toward* KITTY, *indicating that* TOM *shall talk to her, protect the innocence in her which is in so much danger when* TOM *isn't near, which* TOM *loves so deeply.* JOE *leaves.* TOM *studies* KITTY, *his face becoming child-like and somber. He sets the carousel into motion, listens, watching* KITTY, *who lifts herself slowly, looking only at* TOM. TOM *lifts the turning carousel and moves it slowly toward* KITTY, *as though the toy were his heart. The piano music comes up loudly and the lights go down, while* HARRY *is heard dancing swiftly.*)

BLACKOUT

Act Four

A little later.

WESLEY, *the colored boy, is at the piano.*

HARRY *is on the little stage, dancing.*

NICK *is behind the bar.*

The ARAB *is in his place.*

KIT CARSON *is asleep on his folded arms.*

The DRUNKARD *comes in. Goes to the telephone for the nickel that might be in the return-chute.* NICK *comes to take him out. He gestures for* NICK *to hold on a minute. Then produces a half dollar.* NICK *goes behind the bar to serve the* DRUNKARD *whiskey.*

THE DRUNKARD To the old, God bless them. (*Another*) To the new, God love them. (*Another*) To—children and small animals, like little dogs that don't bite. (*Another. Loudly*) To reforestation. (*Searches for money. Finds some*) To—President Taft. (*He goes out.*)

(*The telephone rings.*)

KIT CARSON (*Jumping up, fighting*) Come on, *all* of you, if you're looking for trouble. I never asked for quarter and I always gave it.

NICK (*Reproachfully*) Hey, Kit Carson.

DUDLEY (*On the phone*) Hello. Who? Nick? Yes. He's here. (*To* NICK) It's for you. I think it's important.

NICK (*Going to the phone*) Important! *What's* important?

DUDLEY He sounded like big-shot.

NICK Big *what*? (*To* WESLEY *and* HARRY) Hey, you. Quiet. I want to hear this important stuff.

(WESLEY *stops playing the piano.* HARRY *stops dancing.* KIT CARSON *comes close to* NICK.)

KIT CARSON If there's anything I can do, name it. I'll do it for you. I'm fifty-eight years old; been through three wars; married four times; the father of countless children whose *names* I don't even know. I've got no money. I live from hand to mouth. But if there's anything I can do, name it. I'll do it.

NICK (*Patiently*) Listen, Pop. For a moment, please sit down and go back to sleep—*for me.*

KIT CARSON I can do that, too.

(*He sits down, folds his arms, and puts his head into them. But not for long. As* NICK *begins to talk, he listens carefully, gets to his feet, and then begins to express in pantomime the moods of each of Nick's remarks.*)

NICK (*On phone*) Yeah? (*Pause*) Who? Oh, I see. (*Listens*) Why don't you leave them alone? (*Listens*) The church-people? Well, to hell with the church-people. I'm a Catholic myself. (*Listens*) All right. I'll send them away. I'll tell them to lay low for a couple of days. Yeah, I know how it is. (*Nick's daughter* ANNA *comes in shyly, looking at her father, and stands unnoticed by the piano.*) What? (*Very angry*) Listen. I don't like that Blick. He was here this morning, and I told him not to come back. I'll keep the girls out of here. You keep Blick out of here. (*Listens*) I know his brother-in-law is important, but I don't want him to come down here. He looks for trouble everywhere, and he always finds it. I don't break any laws. I've got a dive in the lousiest part of town. Five years nobody's been robbed, murdered, or gypped. I leave people alone. Your swanky joints uptown make trouble for you every night. (NICK *gestures to* WESLEY—*keeps listening on the phone*—*puts his hand over the mouthpiece. To* WESLEY *and* HARRY.) Start playing again. My ears have got a headache. Go into your dance, son. (WESLEY *begins to play again.* HARRY *begins to dance.* NICK, *into mouthpiece.*) Yeah. I'll keep them out. Just see that Blick doesn't come around and start something. (*Pause*) O.K. (*He hangs up*)

KIT CARSON Trouble coming?

NICK That lousy Vice Squad again. It's that gorilla Blick.

KIT CARSON Anybody at all. You can count on me. What kind of a gorilla is this gorilla Blick?

NICK Very dignified. Toenails on his fingers.

ANNA (*To* KIT CARSON, *with great, warm, beautiful pride, pointing at* NICK) That's my father.

KIT CARSON (*Leaping with amazement at the beautiful voice, the wondrous face, the magnificent event*) Well, bless your heart, child. Bless your lovely heart. I had a little daughter point me out in a crowd once.

NICK (*Surprised*) Anna. What the hell are you doing here? Get back home where you belong and help Grandma cook me some supper.

(ANNA *smiles at her father, understanding him, knowing that his words are words of love. She turns and goes, looking at him all the way out, as much as to say that she would cook for him the rest of her life.* NICK *stares at the swinging doors.* KIT CARSON *moves toward them, two or three steps.* ANNA *pushes open one of the doors and peeks in, to look at her father again. She waves to him. Turns and runs.* NICK *is very sad. He doesn't know what to do. He gets a glass and a bottle. Pours himself a drink. Swallows some. It isn't enough, so he pours more and swallows the whole drink.*)

NICK (*To himself*) My beautiful, beautiful baby. Anna, she is you again. (*He brings out a handkerchief, touches his eyes, and blows his nose.* KIT CARSON *moves close to* NICK, *watching Nick's face.* NICK *looks at him. Loudly, almost making* KIT *jump*) You're broke, aren't you?

KIT CARSON Always. Always.

NICK All right. Go into the kitchen and give Sam a hand. Eat some food and when you come back you can have a couple of beers.

KIT CARSON (*Studying* NICK) Anything at all. I know a good man when I see one. (*He goes*)

> (ELSIE MANDELSPIEGEL *comes into Nick's. She is a beautiful, dark girl, with a sorrowful, wise, dreaming face, almost on the verge of tears, and full of pity. There is an aura of dream about her. She moves softly and gently, as if everything around her were unreal and pathetic.* DUDLEY *doesn't notice her for a moment or two. When he does finally see her, he is so amazed, he can barely move or speak. Her presence has the effect of changing him completely. He gets up from his chair, as if in a trance, and walks toward her, smiling sadly.*)

ELSIE (*Looking at him*) Hello, Dudley.

DUDLEY (*Broken-hearted*) Elsie.

ELSIE I'm sorry. (*Explaining*) So many people are sick. Last night a little boy died. I love you, but— (*She gestures, trying to indicate how hopeless love is. They sit down.*)

DUDLEY (*Staring at her, stunned and quieted*) Elsie. You'll never know how glad I am to see you. Just to *see* you. (*Pathetically*) I was afraid I'd never see you again. It was driving me crazy. I didn't want to live. Honest. (*He shakes his head mournfully, with dumb and beautiful affection.* TWO STREETWALKERS *come in, and pause near* DUDLEY, *at the bar*) I know. You told me before, but I can't help it, Elsie. I love you.

ELSIE (*Quietly, somberly, gently, with great compassion*) I know you love me, and I love you, but don't you see love is impossible in this world?

DUDLEY Maybe it isn't, Elsie.

ELSIE Love is for birds. They have wings to fly away on when it's time for flying. For tigers in the jungle because they don't know their end. We know *our* end. Every night I watch over poor, dying men. I hear them breathing, crying, talking in their sleep. Crying for air and water and love, for mother and field and sunlight. *We* can never know love or greatness. We *should* know both.

DUDLEY (*Deeply moved by her words*) Elsie, I love you.

ELSIE You want to live. *I* want to live, too, but where? Where can we escape our poor world?

DUDLEY Elsie, we'll find a place.

ELSIE (*Smiling at him*) All right. We'll try again. We'll go together to a room in a cheap hotel, and dream that the world is beautiful, and that living is full of love and greatness. But in the morning, can we forget debts, and duties, and the cost of ridiculous things?

DUDLEY (*With blind faith*) Sure, we can, Elsie.

ELSIE All right, Dudley. Of course. Come on. The time for the new pathetic war has come. Let's hurry, before they dress you, stand you in line, hand you a gun, and have you kill and be killed.

> (ELSIE *looks at him gently, and takes his hand.* DUDLEY *embraces her shyly, as if he might hurt her. They go, as if they were a couple of young animals. There is a moment of silence. One of the* STREETWALKERS *bursts out laughing.*)

KILLER Nick, what the hell kind of a joint are you running?

NICK Well, it's not out of the world. It's on a street in a city, and people come and go. They bring whatever they've got with them and they say what they must say.

THE OTHER STREETWALKER It's floozies like her that raise hell with our racket.

NICK (*Remembering*) Oh, yeah. Finnegan telephoned.

KILLER That mouse in elephant's body?

THE OTHER STREETWALKER What the hell does *he* want?

NICK Spend your time at the movies for the next couple of days.

KILLER They're all lousy. (*Mocking*) All about love.

NICK Lousy or not lousy, for a couple of days the flat-foots are going to be romancing you, so stay out of here, and lay low.

KILLER I always was a pushover for a man in uniform, with a badge, a club and a gun.

> (KRUPP *comes into the place. The girls put down their drinks.*)

NICK O.K., get going.

> (*The* GIRLS *begin to leave and meet* KRUPP.)

THE OTHER STREETWALKER We was just going.

KILLER We was formerly models at Magnin's. (*They go.*)

KRUPP (*At the bar*) The strike isn't enough, so they've got to put us on the tails of the girls, too. I don't know. I wish to God I was back in the Sunset holding the hands of kids going home from school, where I belong. I don't like trouble. Give me a beer.

(NICK *gives him a beer. He drinks some.*)

KRUPP Right now, McCarthy, my best friend, is with sixty strikers who want to stop the finks who are going to try to unload the *Mary Luckenbach* tonight. Why the hell McCarthy ever became a longshoreman instead of a professor of some kind is something I'll never know.

NICK Cowboys and Indians, cops and robbers, longshoremen and finks.

KRUPP They're all guys who are trying to be happy; trying to make a living; support a family; bring up children; enjoy sleep. Go to a movie; take a drive on Sunday. They're all good guys, so out of nowhere, comes trouble. All they want is a chance to get out of debt and relax in front of a radio while Amos and Andy go through their act. What the hell do they always want to make trouble for? I been thinking everything over, Nick, and you know what I think?

NICK No. What?

KRUPP I think we're all crazy. It came to me while I was on my way to Pier 27. All of a sudden it hit me like a ton of bricks. A thing like that never happened to me before. Here we are in this wonderful world, full of all the wonderful things—here we are—all of us, and look at us. Just look at us. We're crazy. We're nuts. We've got everything, but we always feel lousy and dissatisfied just the same.

NICK Of course we're crazy. Even so, we've got to go on living together. (*He waves at the people in his joint*)

KRUPP There's no hope. I don't suppose it's right for an officer of the law to feel the way I feel, but, by God, right or not right, that's how I feel. Why are we all so lousy? This is a good world. It's wonderful to get up in the morning and go out for a little walk and smell the trees and see the streets and the kids going to school and the clouds in the sky. It's wonderful just to be able to move around and whistle a song if you feel like it, or maybe try to sing one. This is a nice world. So why do they make all the trouble?

NICK I don't know. Why?

KRUPP We're crazy, that's why. We're no good any more. All the corruption everywhere. The poor kids selling themselves. A couple of years ago they were in grammar school. Everybody trying to get a lot of money in a hurry. Everybody betting the horses. Nobody going quietly for a little walk to the ocean. Nobody taking things easy and not wanting to make some kind of a killing. Nick, I'm going to quit being a cop. Let somebody else keep law and order. The stuff I hear about at head-quarters. I'm thirty-seven years old, and I still can't get used to it. The only trouble is, the wife'll raise hell.

NICK Ah, the wife.

KRUPP She's a wonderful woman, Nick. We've got two of the swellest boys in the world. Twelve and seven years old. (*The* ARAB *gets up and moves closer to listen.*)

NICK I didn't know that.

KRUPP Sure. But what'll I do? I've wanted to quit for seven years. I wanted to quit the day they began putting me through the school. I didn't quit. What'll I do if I quit? Where's money going to be coming in from?

NICK That's one of the reasons we're all crazy. We don't know where it's going to be coming in from, except from wherever it happens to be coming in from at the time, which we don't usually like.

KRUPP Every once in a while I catch myself being mean, hating people just because they're down and out, broke and hungry, sick or drunk. And then when I'm with the stuffed shirts at headquarters, all of a sudden I'm nice to them, trying to make an impression. On who? People I don't like. And I feel disgusted. (*With finality*) I'm going to quit. That's all. Quit. Out. I'm going to give them back the uniform and the gadgets that go with it. I don't want any part of it. This is a good world. What do they want to make all the trouble for all the time?

ARAB (*Quietly, gently, with great understanding*) No foundation. All the way down the line.

KRUPP What?

ARAB No foundation. No foundation.

KRUPP I'll say there's no foundation.

ARAB All the way down the line.

KRUPP (*To* NICK) Is that all he ever says?

NICK That's all he's been saying *this* week.

KRUPP What is he, anyway?

NICK He's an Arab, or something like that.

KRUPP No, I mean what's he do for a living?

NICK (*To* ARAB) What do you do for a living, brother?

ARAB Work. Work all my life. All my life, work. From small boy to old man, work. In old country, work. In new country, work. In New York. Pittsburgh. Detroit. Chicago. Imperial Valley. San Francisco. Work. No beg. Work. For what? Nothing. Three boys in old country. Twenty years, not see. Lost. Dead. Who knows? What. What-not. No foundation. All the way down the line.

KRUPP What'd he say last week?

NICK Didn't say anything. Played the harmonica.

ARAB Old country song, I play. (*He brings a harmonica from his back pocket.*)

KRUPP Seems like a nice guy.

NICK Nicest guy in the world.

KRUPP (*Bitterly*) But crazy. Just like all the rest of us. Stark raving mad.

(WESLEY *and* HARRY *long ago stopped playing and dancing. They sat at a table together and talked for a while; then began playing casino or rummy. When the* ARAB *begins his solo on the harmonica, they stop their game to listen.*)

WESLEY You hear that?

HARRY That's *something.*

WESLEY That's crying. That's crying.

HARRY I want to make people laugh.

WESLEY That's deep, deep crying. That's crying a long time ago. That's crying a thousand years ago. Some place five thousand miles away.

HARRY Do you think you can play to that?

WESLEY I want to *sing* to that, but I can't *sing.*

HARRY I'll try to dance.

(WESLEY *goes to the piano, and after closer listening, he begins to accompany the harmonica solo.* HARRY *goes to the little stage and after a few efforts begins to dance to the song. This keeps up quietly for some time.*)

(KRUPP *and* NICK *have been silent, and deeply moved.*)

KRUPP (*Softly*) Well, anyhow, Nick.

NICK Hmmmmmmm?

KRUPP What I said. Forget it.

NICK Sure.

KRUPP It gets me down once in a while.

NICK No harm in talking.

KRUPP (*The* POLICEMAN *again, loudly*) Keep the girls out of here.

NICK (*Loud and friendly*) Take it easy.

> (*The music and dancing are now at their height.*)

CURTAIN

Act Five

That evening. Fog-horns are heard throughout the scene. A man in evening clothes and a top hat and his woman, also in evening clothes, are entering.

WILLIE *is still at the marble game.* NICK *is behind the bar.* JOE *is at his table, looking at the book of maps of the countries of Europe. The box containing the revolver and the box containing the cartridges are on the table, beside his glass. He is at peace, his hat tilted back on his head, a calm expression on his face.* TOM *is leaning against the bar, dreaming of love and Kitty. The* ARAB *is gone.* WESLEY *and* HARRY *are gone.* KIT CARSON *is watching the boy at the marble game.*

LADY Oh, come on, please.

> (*The gentleman follows miserably.*)
>
> (*The* SOCIETY MAN *and* WIFE *take a table.* NICK *gives them a menu.*)
>
> (*Outside, in the street, the Salvation Army people are playing a song. Big drum, tambourines, cornet and singing. They are singing "The Blood of the Lamb." The music and words come into the place faintly and comically. This is followed by an old sinner testifying. It is the* DRUNKARD. *His words are not intelligible, but his message is unmistakable. He is saved. He wants to sin no more. And so on.*)

DRUNKARD (*Testifying, unmistakably drunk*) Brothers and sisters. I was a sinner. I chewed tobacco and chased women. Oh, I sinned, brothers and sisters. And then I was saved. Saved by the Salvation Army, God forgive me.

JOE Let's see now. Here's a city. Pribor. Czecho-slovakia. Little, lovely, lonely Czecho-slovakia. I wonder what kind of a place Pribor was? (*Calling*) Pribor! *Pribor!*

(TOM *leaps*)

LADY What's the matter with him?

MAN (*Crossing his legs, as if he ought to go to the men's room*) Drunk.

TOM Who you calling, Joe?

JOE Pribor.

TOM Who's Pribor?

JOE He's a Czech. And a Slav. A Czechoslovakian.

LADY How interesting.

MAN (*Uncrosses legs*) He's drunk.

JOE Tom, Pribor's a city in Czecho-slovakia.

TOM Oh. (*Pause*) You sure were nice to her, Joe.

JOE Kitty Duval? She's one of the finest people in the world.

TOM It sure was nice of you to hire an automobile and take us for a drive along the ocean-front and down to Half Moon Bay.

JOE Those three hours were the most delightful, the most somber, and the most beautiful I have ever known.

TOM Why, Joe?

JOE Why? I'm a student. (*Lifting his voice*) Tom. (*Quietly*) I'm a student. I study all things. All. All. And when my study reveals something of beauty in a place or in a person where by all rights only ugliness or death should be revealed, then I know how full of goodness this life is. And that's a good thing to know. That's a truth I shall always seek to verify.

LADY Are you *sure* he's drunk?

MAN (*Crossing his legs*) He's either drunk, or just naturally crazy.

TOM Joe?

JOE Yeah.

TOM You won't get sore or anything?

JOE (*Impatiently*) What is it, Tom?

TOM Joe, where do you get all that money? You paid for the automobile. You paid for supper and the two bottles of champagne at the Half Moon Bay Restaurant. You moved Kitty out of the New York Hotel around the corner to the St. Francis Hotel on Powell Street. I saw you pay her rent. I saw you give her money for new clothes. Where do you get all that money, Joe? Three years now and I've never asked.

JOE (*Looking at* TOM *sorrowfully, a little irritated, not so much with* TOM *as with the world and himself, his own superiority. He speaks clearly, slowly and solemnly*) Now don't be a fool, Tom. Listen carefully. If anybody's got any money—to hoard or to throw away—you can be sure he stole it from other people. Not from rich people who can spare it, but from poor people who can't. From their lives and from their dreams. I'm no exception. I *earned* the money I throw away. I stole it like everybody else does. I hurt people to get it. Loafing around this way, I *still* earn money. The money itself earns *more*. I *still* hurt people. I don't know who they are, or where they are. If I did, I'd feel worse than I do. I've got a Christian conscience in a world that's got no conscience at all. The world's trying to get some sort of a *social* conscience, but it's having a devil of a time trying to do *that*. I've got money. I'll always have money, as long as this world stays the way it is. I don't work. I don't make anything. (*He sips*) I drink. I worked when I was a kid. I worked *hard*. I mean hard, Tom. People are supposed to enjoy living. I got tired. (*He lifts the gun and looks at it while he talks.*) I decided to get even on the world. Well, you can't enjoy living unless you work. Unless you do something. I don't do anything. I don't *want* to do anything any more. There isn't anything I can do that won't make me feel embarrassed. Because I can't do simple, good things. I haven't the patience. And I'm too smart. Money is the guiltiest thing in the world. It stinks. Now, don't ever bother me about it again.

TOM I didn't mean to make you feel bad, Joe.

JOE (*Slowly*) Here. Take this gun out in the street and give it to some worthy hold-up man.

LADY What's he saying?

MAN (*Uncrosses legs*) You wanted to visit a honky-tonk. Well, *this* is a honky-tonk. (*To the world*) Married twenty-eight years and she's still looking for adventure.

TOM How should I know who's a hold-up man?

JOE Take it away. Give it to somebody.

TOM (*Bewildered*) Do I *have* to *give* it to somebody?

JOE Of course.

TOM Can't I take it back and get some of our money?

JOE Don't talk like a business man. Look around and find somebody who appears to be in need of a gun and give it to him. It's a good gun, isn't it?

TOM The man said it was, but how can I tell who needs a gun?

JOE Tom, you've seen good people who needed guns, haven't you?

TOM I don't remember. Joe, I might give it to the wrong kind of guy. He might do something crazy.

JOE All right. I'll find somebody myself. (TOM *rises*) Here's some money. Go get me this week's *Life, Liberty, Time,* and six or seven packages of chewing gum.

TOM (*Swiftly, in order to remember each item*) *Life, Liberty, Time,* and six or seven packages of chewing gum?

JOE That's right.

TOM All that chewing gum? What kind?

JOE Any kind. Mix 'em up. All kinds.

TOM Licorice, too?

JOE Licorice, by all means.

TOM Juicy Fruit?

JOE Juicy Fruit.

TOM Tutti-frutti?

JOE Is there such a gum?

TOM I think so.

JOE All right. Tutti-frutti, too. Get *all* the kinds. Get as many kinds as they're selling.

TOM *Life, Liberty, Time,* and all the different kinds of gum. (*He begins to go*)

JOE (*Calling after him loudly*) Get some jelly beans too. All the different colors.

TOM All right, Joe.

JOE And the longest panatela cigar you can find. Six of them.

TOM Panatela. I got it.

JOE Give a news-kid a dollar.

TOM O.K., Joe.

JOE Give some old man a dollar.

TOM O.K., Joe.

JOE Give them Salvation Army people in the street a couple of dollars and ask them to sing that song that goes— (*He sings loudly*) Let the lower lights be burning, send a gleam across the wave.

TOM (*Swiftly*) Let the lower lights be burning, send a gleam across the wave.

JOE That's it. (*He goes on with the song, very loudly and religiously*) Some poor, dying, struggling seaman, you may rescue, you may save. (*Halts*)

TOM O.K., Joe. I got it. *Life, Liberty, Time*, all the kinds of gum they're selling, jelly beans, six panatela cigars, a dollar for a news-kid, a dollar for an old man, two dollars for the Salvation Army. (*Going*) Let the lower lights be burning, send a gleam across the wave.

JOE That's it.

LADY He's absolutely insane.

MAN (*Wearily crossing legs*) You asked me to take you to a honky-tonk, instead of to the Mark Hopkins. You're *here* in a honky-tonk. I can't help it if he's crazy. Do you want to go back to where people *aren't* crazy?

LADY No, not just yet.

MAN Well, all right then. Don't be telling me every minute that he's crazy.

LADY You needn't be huffy about it.

> (MAN *refuses to answer, uncrosses legs.*)

> (When JOE *began to sing,* KIT CARSON *turned away from the marble game and listened. While the man and woman are arguing he comes over to Joe's table.*)

KIT CARSON Presbyterian?

JOE I attended a Presbyterian Sunday School.

KIT CARSON Fond of singing?

JOE On occasion. Have a drink?

KIT CARSON Thanks.

JOE Get a glass and sit down.

(KIT CARSON *gets a glass from* NICK, *returns to the table, sits down,* JOE *pours him a drink, they touch glasses just as the Salvation Army people begin to fulfill the request. They sip some champagne, and at the proper moment begin to sing the song together, sipping champagne, raising hell with the tune, swinging it, and so on. The* SOCIETY LADY *joins them, and is stopped by her* HUSBAND.)

JOE Always was fond of that song. Used to sing it at the top of my voice. Never saved a seaman in my life.

KIT CARSON (*Flirting with the* SOCIETY LADY *who loves it*) I saved a seaman once. Well, he wasn't exactly a seaman. He was a darky named Wellington. Heavy-set sort of a fellow. Nice personality, but no friends to speak of. Not until I came along, at any rate. In New Orleans. In the summer of the year 1899. No. Ninety-eight. I was a lot younger of course, and had no mustache, but was regarded by many people as a man of means.

JOE Know anything about guns?

KIT CARSON (*Flirting*) All there is to know. Didn't fight the Ojibways for nothing. Up there in the Lake Takalooca Country, in Michigan. (*Remembering*) Along about in 1881 or two. Fought 'em right up to the shore of the Lake. Made 'em swim for Canada. One fellow in particular, an Indian named Harry Daisy.

JOE (*Opening the box containing the revolver*) What sort of a gun would you say this is? Any good?

KIT CARSON (*At sight of gun, leaping*) Yep. That looks like a pretty nice hunk of shooting iron. That's a six-shooter. Shot a man with a six-shooter once. Got him through the palm of his right hand. Lifted his arm to wave to a friend. Thought it was a bird. Fellow named, I believe, Carroway. Larrimore Carroway.

JOE Know how to work one of these things? (*He offers* KIT CARSON *the revolver, which is old and enormous.*)

KIT CARSON (*Laughing at the absurd question*) Know how to work it? Hand me that little gun, son, and I'll show you all about it. (JOE *hands* KIT *the revolver.*) (*Importantly*) Let's see now. This is probably a new kind of six-shooter. After my time. Haven't nicked an Indian in years. I believe this here place is supposed to move out. (*He fools around and gets the barrel out for loading*) That's it. There it is.

JOE Look all right?

KIT CARSON It's a good gun. You've got a good gun there, son. I'll explain it to you. You see these holes? Well, that's where you put the cartridges.

JOE (*Taking some cartridges out of the box*) Here. Show me how it's done.

KIT CARSON (*A little impatiently*) Well, son, you take 'em one by one and put 'em in the holes, like this. There's one. Two. Three. Four. Five. Six. Then you get the barrel back in place. Then cock it. Then all you got to do is aim and fire.

(*He points the gun at the* LADY *and* GENTLEMAN *who scream and stand up, scaring* KIT CARSON *into paralysis.*)

(*The gun is loaded, but uncocked.*)

JOE It's all set?

KIT CARSON Ready to kill.

JOE Let me hold it.

(KIT *hands* JOE *the gun. The* LADY *and* GENTLEMAN *watch, in terror.*)

KIT CARSON Careful, now, son. Don't cock it. Many a man's lost an eye fooling with a loaded gun. Fellow I used to know named Danny Donovan lost a nose. Ruined his whole life. Hold it firm. Squeeze the trigger. Don't snap it. Spoils your aim.

JOE Thanks. Let's see if I can unload it. (*He begins to unload it.*)

KIT CARSON Of course you can.

(JOE *unloads the revolver, looks at it very closely, puts the cartridges back into the box.*)

JOE (*Looking at gun*) I'm mighty grateful to you. Always wanted to see one of those things close up. Is it really a good one?

KIT CARSON It's a beaut, son.

JOE (*Aims the empty gun at a bottle on the bar*) Bang!

WILLIE (*At the marble game, as the machine groans*) Oh, Boy! (*Loudly, triumphantly*) There you are, Nick. Thought I couldn't do it, hey? *Now*, watch. (*The machine begins to make a special kind of noise. Lights go on and off. Some red, some green. A bell rings loudly six times.*) One. Two. Three. Four. Five. Six. (*An American flag jumps up.* WILLIE *comes to attention.*

Salutes.) Oh, boy, what a beautiful country. (*A loud music-box version of the song "America."* JOE, KIT, *and the* LADY *get to their feet.*) (*Singing*) My country, 'tis of thee, sweet land of liberty, of thee I sing. (*Everything quiets down. The flag goes back into the machine.* WILLIE *is thrilled, amazed, delighted.* EVERYBODY *has watched the performance of the defeated machine from wherever he happened to be when the performance began.* WILLIE, *looking around at everybody, as if they had all been on the side of the machine.*) O.K. How's that? I knew I could do it. (*To* NICK) Six nickels. (NICK *hands him six nickels.* WILLIE *goes over to* JOE *and* KIT.) Took me a little while, but I finally did it. It's scientific, really. With a little skill a man can make a modest living beating the marble games. Not that that's what I want to do. I just don't like the idea of anything getting the best of me. A machine or anything else. Myself, I'm the kind of a guy who makes up his mind to do something, and then goes to work and does it. There's no other way a man can be a success at anything.

(*Indicating the letter "F" on his sweater*) See that letter? That don't stand for some little-bitty high school somewhere. That stands for *me*. Faroughli. Willie Faroughli. I'm an Assyrian. We've got a civilization six or seven centuries old, I think. Somewhere along in there. Ever hear of Osman? Harold Osman? He's an Assyrian, too. He's got an orchestra down in Fresno.

(*He goes to the* LADY *and* GENTLEMAN) I've never seen you before in my life, but I can tell from the clothes you wear and the company you keep (*Graciously indicating the* LADY) that you're a man who looks every problem straight in the eye, and then goes to work and *solves* it. I'm that way myself. Well. (*He smiles beautifully, takes the* GENTLEMAN'S *hand furiously*) It's been wonderful talking to a nicer type of people for a change. Well. I'll be seeing you. So long. (*He turns, takes two steps, returns to the table. Very politely and seriously*) Good-bye, lady. You've got a good man there. Take good care of him.

(WILLIE *goes, saluting* JOE *and the world.*)

KIT CARSON (*To* JOE) By God, for a while there I didn't think that young Assyrian was going to do it. That fellow's got something.

(TOM *comes back with the magazines and other stuff.*)

JOE Get it all?

TOM Yeah. I had a little trouble finding the jelly beans.

JOE Let's take a look at them.

TOM These are the jelly beans.

> (JOE *puts his hand into the cellophane bag and takes out a handful of the jelly beans, looks at them, smiles, and tosses a couple into his mouth.*)

JOE Same as ever. Have some. (*He offers the bag to* KIT)

KIT CARSON (*Flirting*) Thanks! I remember the first time I ever ate jelly beans. I was six, or at the most seven. Must have been in (*Slowly*) eighteen—seventy-seven. Seven or eight. Baltimore.

JOE Have some, Tom. (TOM *takes some*)

TOM Thanks, Joe.

JOE Let's have some of that chewing gum. (*He dumps all the packages of gum out of the bag onto the table.*)

KIT CARSON (*Flirting*) Me and a boy named Clark. Quinton Clark. Became a Senator.

JOE Yeah. Tutti-frutti, all right. (*He opens a package and folds all five pieces into his mouth.*) Always wanted to see how many I could chew at one time. Tell you what, Tom. I'll bet I can chew more at one time than you can.

TOM (*Delighted*) All right. (*They both begin to fold gum into their mouths.*)

KIT CARSON I'll referee. Now, one at a time. How many you got?

JOE Six.

KIT CARSON All right. Let Tom catch up with you.

JOE (*While* TOM'S *catching up*) Did you give a dollar to a news-kid?

TOM Yeah, sure.

JOE What'd he say?

TOM Thanks.

JOE What sort of a kid was he?

TOM Little, dark kid. I guess he's Italian.

JOE Did he seem pleased?

TOM Yeah.

JOE That's good. Did you give a dollar to an old man?

TOM Yeah.

JOE Was he pleased?

TOM Yeah.

JOE Good. How many you got in your mouth?

TOM Six.

JOE All right. I got six, too. (*Folds one more in his mouth.* TOM *folds one too*)

KIT CARSON Seven. Seven each. (*They each fold one more into their mouths, very solemnly, chewing them into the main hunk of gum.*) Eight. Nine. Ten.

JOE (*Delighted*) Always wanted to do this. (*He picks up one of the magazines.*) Let's see what's going on in the world. (*He turns the pages and keeps folding gum into his mouth and chewing.*)

KIT CARSON Eleven. Twelve. (KIT *continues to count while* JOE *and* TOM *continue the contest. In spite of what they are doing, each is very serious.*)

TOM Joe, what'd you want to move Kitty into the St. Francis Hotel for?

JOE She's a better woman than any of them tramp society dames that hang around that lobby.

TOM Yeah, but do you think she'll feel at home up there?

JOE Maybe not at first, but after a couple of days she'll be all right. A nice big room. A bed for sleeping in. Good clothes. Good food. She'll be all right, Tom.

TOM I hope so. Don't you think she'll get lonely up there with nobody to talk to?

JOE (*Looking at* TOM *sharply, almost with admiration, pleased but severe*) There's nobody *anywhere* for *her* to talk to—except you.

TOM (*Amazed and delighted*) Me, Joe?

JOE (*While* TOM *and* KIT CARSON *listen carefully,* KIT *with great appreciation*) Yes, you. By the grace of God, you're the other half of that girl. Not the angry woman that swaggers into this waterfront dive and shouts because the world has kicked her around. *Anybody* can have *her*. You belong to the little kid in Ohio who once dreamed of living. Not with her carcass, for *money*, so she can have food and clothes, and pay rent. With *all* of her. I put her in that hotel, so she can have a chance to gather herself together again. She can't do that in the New York Hotel. You saw what happens there. There's nobody anywhere for her to talk to, except you. They all make her talk like a whore. After a while, she'll *believe* them. Then she won't be able to remember. She'll get lonely. Sure. People can get lonely for *misery*, even. I want her to go on being

387

lonely for *you*, so she can come together again the way she was meant to be from the beginning. Loneliness is good for people. Right now it's the only thing for Kitty. Any more licorice?

TOM (*Dazed*) What? Licorice? (*Looking around busily*) I guess we've chewed all the licorice in. We still got Clove, Peppermint, Doublemint, Beechnut, Teaberry, and Juicy Fruit.

JOE Licorice used to be my favorite. Don't worry about her, Tom, she'll be all right. You really want to marry her, don't you?

TOM (*Nodding*) Honest to God, Joe. (*Pathetically*) Only, I haven't got any money.

JOE Couldn't you be a prize-fighter or something like that?

TOM Naaaah. I couldn't hit a man if I wasn't sore at him. He'd have to do something that made me hate him.

JOE You've got to figure out something to do that you won't mind doing very much.

TOM I wish I could, Joe.

JOE (*Thinking deeply, suddenly*) Tom, would you be embarrassed driving a truck?

TOM (*Hit by a thunderbolt*) Joe, I never thought of that. I'd like that. Travel. Highways. Little towns. Coffee and hot cakes. Beautiful valleys and mountains and streams and trees and daybreak and sunset.

JOE There *is* poetry in it, at that.

TOM Joe, that's just the kind of work I *should* do. Just sit there and travel, and look, and smile, and bust out laughing. Could Kitty go with me, sometimes?

JOE I don't know. Get me the phone book. Can you drive a truck?

TOM Joe, you know I can drive a truck, or any kind of thing with a motor and wheels. (TOM *takes* JOE *the phone book.* JOE *turns the pages.*)

JOE (*Looking*) Here! Here it is. Tuxedo 7900. Here's a nickel. Get me that number. (TOM *goes to telephone, dials the number.*)

TOM Hello.

JOE Ask for Mr. Keith.

TOM (*Mouth and language full of gum*) I'd like to talk to Mr. Keith. (*Pause*) Mr. Keith.

JOE Take that gum out of your mouth for a minute. (TOM *removes the gum*)

TOM Mr. Keith? Yeah. That's right. Hello, Mr. Keith?

JOE Tell him to hold the line.

TOM Hold the line, please.

JOE Give me a hand, Tom. (TOM *helps* JOE *to the telephone. At phone, wad of gum in fingers delicately*) Keith? Joe. Yeah. Fine. Forget it. (*Pause*) Have you got a place for a good driver? (*Pause*) I don't think so. (*To* TOM) You haven't got a driver's license, have you?

TOM (*Worried*) No. But I can get one, Joe.

JOE (*At phone*) No, but he can get one easy enough. To hell with the union. He'll join later. All right, call him a Vice-President and say he drives for relaxation. Sure. What do you mean? Tonight? I don't know why not. San Diego? All right, let him start driving without a license. What the hell's the difference? Yeah. Sure. Look him over. Yeah. I'll send him right over. Right. (*He hangs up*) Thanks. (*To telephone*)

TOM Am I going to get the job?

JOE He wants to take a look at you.

TOM Do I look all right, Joe?

JOE (*Looking at him carefully*) Hold up your head. Stick out your chest. How do you feel?

 (TOM *does these things.*)

TOM Fine.

JOE You *look* fine, too. (JOE *takes his wad of gum out of his mouth and wraps Liberty magazine around it.*) You win, Tom. Now, look. (*He bites off the tip of a very long panatela cigar, lights it, and hands one to* TOM, *and another to* KIT) Have yourselves a pleasant smoke. Here. (*He hands two more to* TOM) Give those slummers one each. (*He indicates the* SOCIETY LADY *and* GENTLEMAN)

 (TOM *goes over and without a word gives a cigar each to the* MAN *and the* LADY.)

 (*The* MAN *is offended; he smells and tosses aside his cigar. The* WOMAN *looks at her cigar a moment, then puts the cigar in her mouth.*)

MAN What do you think you're doing?

LADY Really, dear. I'd like to.

MAN Oh, this is too much.

LADY I'd *really*, really like to, dear. (*She laughs, puts the cigar in her mouth. Turns to* KIT. *He spits out tip. She does the same.*)

MAN (*Loudly*) The mother of five grown men, and she's still looking for romance. (*Shouts as* KIT *lights her cigar*) No. I forbid it.

JOE (*Shouting*) What's the matter with you? Why don't you leave her alone? What are you always pushing your women around for? (*Almost without a pause*) Now, look, Tom. (*The* LADY *puts the lighted cigar in her mouth, and begins to smoke, feeling wonderful.*) Here's ten bucks.

TOM Ten bucks?

JOE He may want you to get into a truck and begin driving to San Diego tonight.

TOM Joe, I got to tell Kitty.

JOE I'll tell her.

TOM Joe, take care of her.

JOE She'll be all right. Stop worrying about her. She's at the St. Francis Hotel. Now, look. Take a cab to Townsend and Fourth. You'll see the big sign. Keith Motor Transport Company. He'll be waiting for you.

TOM O.K., Joe. (*Trying hard*) Thanks, Joe.

JOE Don't be silly. Get going.

> (TOM *goes.*)
>
> (LADY *starts puffing on cigar.*)
>
> (*As* TOM *goes,* WESLEY *and* HARRY *come in together.*)

NICK Where the hell have you been? We've got to have some entertainment around here. Can't you see them fine people from uptown? (*He points at the* SOCIETY LADY *and* GENTLEMAN)

WESLEY You said to come back at ten for the second show.

NICK Did I say that?

WESLEY Yes, sir, Mr. Nick, that's exactly what you said.

HARRY Was the first show all right?

NICK That wasn't a show. There was no one here to see it. How can it be a show when no one sees it? People are afraid to come down to the waterfront.

HARRY Yeah. We were just down to Pier 27. One of the longshoremen and a cop had a fight and the cop hit him over the head with a blackjack. We saw it happen, didn't we?

WESLEY Yes, sir, we was standing there looking when it happened.

NICK (*A little worried*) Anything else happen?

WESLEY They was all talking.

HARRY A man in a big car came up and said there was going to be a meeting right away and they hoped to satisfy everybody and stop the strike.

WESLEY Right away. *Tonight.*

NICK Well, it's about time. Them poor cops are liable to get nervous and—shoot somebody. (*To* HARRY, *suddenly*) Come back here. I want you to tend bar for a while. I'm going to take a walk over to the pier.

HARRY Yes, sir.

NICK (*To the* SOCIETY LADY *and* GENTLEMAN) You society people made up your minds yet?

LADY Have you champagne?

NICK (*Indicating* JOE) What do you think he's pouring out of that bottle, water or something?

LADY Have you a chill bottle?

NICK I've got a dozen of them chilled. He's been drinking champagne here all day and all night for a month now.

LADY May we have a bottle?

NICK It's six dollars.

LADY I think we can manage.

MAN I don't know. I *know* I don't know.

> (NICK *takes off his coat and helps* HARRY *into it.* HARRY *takes a bottle of champagne and two glasses to the* LADY *and the* GENTLEMAN, *dancing, collects six dollars, and goes back behind the bar, dancing.* NICK *gets his coat and hat.*)

NICK (*To* WESLEY) Rattle the keys a little, son. Rattle the keys.

WESLEY Yes, sir, Mr. Nick.

> (NICK *is on his way out. The* ARAB *enters.*)

NICK Hi-ya, *Mahmed.*

ARAB No foundation.

NICK All the way down the line. (*He goes*)

> (WESLEY *is at the piano, playing quietly. The* ARAB *swallows a glass of beer, takes out his harmonica, and begins to play.* WESLEY *fits his playing to the Arab's.*)

> (KITTY DUVAL, *strangely beautiful, in new clothes, comes in. She walks shyly, as if she were embarrassed by the fine clothes, as if she had no right to wear them. The* LADY *and* GENTLEMAN *are very impressed.* HARRY *looks at her with amazement.* JOE *is reading* Time *magazine.* KITTY *goes to his table.* JOE *looks up from the magazine, without the least amazement.*)

JOE Hello, Kitty.

KITTY Hello, Joe.

JOE It's nice seeing you again.

KITTY I came in a cab.

JOE You been crying again? (KITTY *can't answer*) (*To* HARRY) Bring a glass. (HARRY *comes over with a glass.* JOE *pours* KITTY *a drink.*)

KITTY I've got to talk to you.

JOE Have a drink.

KITTY I've never been in burlesque. We were just poor.

JOE Sit down, Kitty.

KITTY (*Sits down*) I tried other things.

JOE Here's to you, Katerina Koranovsky. Here's to you. And Tom.

KITTY (*Sorrowfully*) Where *is* Tom?

JOE He's getting a job tonight driving a truck. He'll be back in a couple of days.

KITTY (*Sadly*) I told him I'd marry him.

JOE He wanted to see you and say good-bye.

KITTY He's too good for me. He's like a little boy. (*Wearily*) I'm—Too many things have happened to me.

JOE Kitty Duval, you're one of the few truly innocent people I have ever known. He'll be back in a couple of days. Go back to the hotel and wait for him.

KITTY That's what I mean. I can't stand being alone. I'm no good. I tried very hard. I don't know what it is. I miss— (*She gestures*)

JOE (*Gently*) Do you really want to come back here, Kitty?

KITTY I don't know. I'm not sure. Everything *smells* different. I don't know how to feel, or what to think. (*Gesturing pathetically*) I know I don't belong there. It's what I've wanted all my life, but it's too *late*. I try to be happy about it, but all I can do is remember everything and cry.

JOE I don't know what to tell you, Kitty. I didn't mean to hurt you.

KITTY You haven't hurt me. You're the only person who's ever been good to me. I've never known anybody like you. I'm not sure about love any more, but I know I love you, and I know I love Tom.

JOE I love you too, Kitty Duval.

KITTY He'll want babies. I know he will. I know I will, too. Of course I will. I can't— (*She shakes her head*)

JOE Tom's a baby himself. You'll be very happy together. He wants you to ride with him in the truck. Tom's good for you. You're good for Tom.

KITTY (*Like a child*) Do you want me to go back and wait for him?

JOE I can't *tell* you what to do. I think it would be a good idea, though.

KITTY I wish I could tell you how it makes me feel to be alone. It's almost worse.

JOE It might take a whole week, Kitty. (*He looks at her sharply, at the arrival of an idea*) Didn't you speak of reading a book? A book of poems?

KITTY I didn't know what I was saying.

JOE (*Trying to get up*) Of course you knew. I think you'll like poetry. Wait here a minute, Kitty. I'll go see if I can find some books.

KITTY All right, Joe. (*He walks out of the place, trying very hard not to wobble.*)

(*Fog-horn. Music. The* NEWSBOY *comes in. Looks for* JOE. *Is broken-hearted because* JOE *is gone.*)

NEWSBOY (*To* SOCIETY GENTLEMAN) Paper?

MAN (*Angry*) No.

(*The* NEWSBOY *goes to the* ARAB.)

NEWSBOY Paper, Mister?

ARAB (*Irritated*) No foundation.

NEWSBOY What?

ARAB (*Very angry*) No foundation. (*The* NEWSBOY *starts out, turns, looks at the* ARAB, *shakes head.*)

NEWSBOY No foundation? How do you figure?

(BLICK *and* TWO COPS *enter.*)

NEWSBOY (*To* BLICK) Paper, Mister?

(BLICK *pushes him aside. The* NEWSBOY *goes*)

BLICK (*Walking authoritatively about the place, to* HARRY) Where's Nick?

HARRY He went for a walk.

BLICK Who are you?

HARRY Harry.

BLICK (*To the* ARAB *and* WESLEY) Hey, you. Shut up. (*The* ARAB *stops playing the harmonica,* WESLEY *the piano*)

BLICK (*Studies* KITTY) What's your name, sister?

KITTY (*Looking at him*) Kitty Duval. What's it to you?

(KITTY'S *voice is now like it was at the beginning of the play: tough, independent, bitter and hard.*)

BLICK (*Angry*) Don't give me any of your gutter lip. Just answer my questions.

KITTY You go to hell, you.

BLICK (*Coming over, enraged*) Where do you live?

KITTY The New York Hotel. Room 21.

BLICK Where do you work?

KITTY I'm not working just now. I'm looking for work.

BLICK What kind of work? (KITTY *can't answer*) What kind of work? (KITTY *can't answer*) (*Furiously*) WHAT KIND OF WORK?

(KIT CARSON *comes over*)

KIT CARSON You can't talk to a lady that way in *my* presence. (BLICK *turns and stares at* KIT. *The* COPS *begin to move from the bar.*)

BLICK (*To the* COPS) It's all right, boys. I'll take care of this. (*To* KIT) What'd you say?

KIT CARSON You got no right to hurt people. Who are *you*?

> (BLICK, *without a word, takes* KIT *to the street. Sounds of a blow and a groan.* BLICK *returns, breathing hard.*)

BLICK (*To the* COPS) O.K., boys. You can go now. Take care of him. Put him on his feet and tell him to behave himself from now on. (*To* KITTY *again*) Now answer my question. What kind of work?

KITTY (*Quietly*) I'm a whore, you son of a bitch. You know what kind of work I do. And I know what kind you do.

MAN (*Shocked and really hurt*) Excuse me, officer, but it seems to me that your attitude—

BLICK Shut up.

MAN (*Quietly*) —is making the poor child say things that are not true.

BLICK Shut up, I said.

LADY Well. (*To the* MAN) Are you going to stand for such insolence from such a coarse person?

BLICK (*To* MAN, *who is standing*) Are you?

MAN (*Taking the* WOMAN'S *arm*) I'll get a divorce. I'll start life all over again. (*Pushing the* WOMAN) Come on. Get the hell out of here!

> (*The* MAN *hurries his* WOMAN *out of the place,* BLICK *watching them go.*)

BLICK (*To* KITTY) Now. Let's begin again, and see that you tell the truth. What's your name?

KITTY Kitty Duval.

BLICK Where do you live?

KITTY Until this evening I lived at the New York Hotel. Room 21. This evening I moved to the St. Francis Hotel.

BLICK Oh. To the St. Francis Hotel. Nice place. Where do you work?

KITTY I'm looking for work.

BLICK What kind of work do you do?

KITTY I'm an actress.

BLICK I see. What movies have I seen you in?

KITTY I've worked in burlesque.

BLICK You're a liar.

(WESLEY *stands, worried and full of dumb resentment.*)

KITTY (*Pathetically, as at the beginning of the play*) It's the truth.

BLICK What are you doing here?

KITTY I came to see if I could get a job here.

BLICK Doing what?

KITTY Singing—and—dancing.

BLICK You can't sing or dance. What are you lying for?

KITTY I can. I sang and danced in burlesque all over the country.

BLICK You're a liar.

KITTY I said lines, too.

BLICK So you danced in burlesque?

KITTY Yes.

BLICK All right. Let's see what you did.

KITTY I can't. There's no music, and I haven't got the right clothes.

BLICK There's music. (*To* WESLEY) Put a nickel in that phonograph. (WESLEY *can't move*) Come on. Put a nickel in that phonograph. (WESLEY *does so. To* KITTY) All right. Get up on that stage and do a hot little burlesque number. (KITTY *stands. Walks slowly to the stage, but is unable to move.* JOE *comes in, holding three books.*) Get going, now. Let's see you dance the way you did in burlesque, all over the country. (KITTY *tries to do a burlesque dance. It is beautiful in a tragic way.*)

BLICK All right, start taking them off!

(KITTY *removes her hat and starts to remove her jacket.* JOE *moves closer to the stage, amazed.*)

JOE (*Hurrying to* KITTY) Get down from there. (*He takes* KITTY *into his arms. She is crying. To* BLICK) What the hell do you think you're doing!

WESLEY (*Like a little boy, very angry*) It's that man, Blick. *He* made her take off her clothes. He beat up the old man, too.

(BLICK *pushes* WESLEY *off, as* TOM *enters.* BLICK *begins beating up* WESLEY.)

TOM What's the matter, Joe. What's happened?

JOE Is the truck out there?

TOM Yeah, but what's happened? Kitty's crying again!

JOE You driving to San Diego?

TOM Yeah, Joe. But what's he doing to that poor colored boy?

JOE Get going. Here's some money. Everything's O.K. (*To* KITTY) Dress in the truck. Take these books.

WESLEY'S VOICE You can't hurt me. You'll get yours. You wait and see.

TOM Joe, he's hurting that boy. I'll kill him!

JOE (*Pushing* TOM) Get out of here! Get married in San Diego. I'll see you when you get back. (TOM *and* KITTY *go.* NICK *enters and stands at the lower end of bar.* JOE *takes the revolver out of his pocket. Looks at it.*) I've always wanted to kill somebody, but I never knew who it should be. (*He cocks the revolver, stands real straight, holds it in front of him firmly and walks to the door. He stands a moment watching* BLICK, *aims very carefully, and pulls trigger. There is no shot.*)

    (NICK *runs over and grabs the gun, and takes* JOE *aside.*)

NICK What the hell do you think you're doing!

JOE (*Casually, but angry*) That dumb Tom. Buys a six-shooter that won't even shoot once.

    (JOE *sits down, dead to the world.*)

    (BLICK *comes out, panting for breath.*)

    (NICK *looks at him. He speaks slowly.*)

NICK Blick! I told you to stay out of here! Now get out of here. (*He takes* BLICK *by the collar, tightening his grip as he speaks, and pushing him out*) If you come back again, I'm going to take you in that room where you've been beating up that colored boy, and I'm going to murder you—slowly—with my hands. Beat it! (*He pushes* BLICK *out. To* HARRY.) Go take care of the colored boy. (HARRY *runs out.*)

    (WILLIE *returns and doesn't sense that anything is changed.* WILLIE *puts another nickel into the machine, but he does so very violently. The consequence of this violence is that the flag comes up again and the music-box version of "America" begins again.* WILLIE, *amazed, stands at attention and salutes. The flag goes down. He shakes his head.*)

WILLIE (*Thoughtfully*) As far as I'm concerned, this is the *only* country in the world. If you ask me, *nuts* to Europe! (*He is about to push the slide in again when the flag comes up again and the music begins again. Furiously, to* NICK, *while he salutes and stands at attention, pleadingly*) Hey, Nick. This machine is out of order.

NICK (*Somberly*) Give it a whack on the side.

(WILLIE *does so. A hell of a whack. The result is the whole business starts all over again, except that now the flag comes up and down, and* WILLIE *keeps saluting.*)

WILLIE (*Saluting*) Hey, Nick. Something's wrong.

(*The machine quiets down abruptly.* WILLIE *very stealthily slides a new nickel in, and starts a new game.*)

(*From a distance two pistol shots are heard, each carefully timed.*)

(NICK *runs out.*)

(*The* NEWSBOY *enters, crosses to Joe's table, senses something is wrong.*)

NEWSBOY (*Softly*) Paper, Mister?

(JOE *can't hear him.*)

(*The* NEWSBOY *backs away, studies* JOE, *wishes he could cheer* JOE *up. Notices the phonograph, goes to it, and puts a coin in it, hoping music will make* JOE *happier.*)

(*The* NEWSBOY *sits down. Watches* JOE. *The music begins. "The Missouri Waltz."*)

(*The* DRUNKARD *comes in and walks around. Then sits down.* NICK *comes back.*)

NICK (*Delighted*) Joe, Blick's dead! Somebody just shot him, and none of the cops are trying to find out who. (JOE *doesn't hear.* NICK *steps back, studying* JOE.)

NICK (*Shouting*) Joe.

JOE (*Looking up*) What?

NICK Blick's dead.

JOE Blick? Dead? Good! That God damn gun wouldn't go off. I *told* Tom to get a good one.

NICK (*Picking up gun and looking at it*) Joe, you wanted to kill that guy! (HARRY *returns*) I'm going to buy you a bottle of champagne.

(NICK *goes to bar.* JOE *rises, takes hat from rack, puts coat on. The* NEWSBOY *jumps up, helps* JOE *with coat.*)

NICK What's the matter, Joe?

JOE Nothing. Nothing.

NICK How about the champagne?

JOE Thanks. (*Going*)

NICK It's not eleven yet. Where you going, Joe?

JOE I don't know. Nowhere.

NICK Will I see you tomorrow?

JOE I don't know. I don't think so.

> (KIT CARSON *enters, walks to* JOE. JOE *and* KIT *look at one another knowingly.*)

JOE Somebody just shot a man. How are you feeling?

KIT Never felt better in my life. (*Loudly, bragging, but sombre*) I shot a man once. In San Francisco. Shot him two times. In 1939, I think it was. In October. Fellow named Blick or Glick or something like that. Couldn't stand the way he talked to ladies. Went up to my room and got my old pearl-handled revolver and waited for him on Pacific Street. Saw him walking, and let him have it, two times. Had to throw the beautiful revolver into the Bay.

> (HARRY, NICK, *the* ARAB *and the* DRUNKARD *close in around him.*)

JOE (*Searches his pockets, brings out the revolver, puts it in Kit's hand, looks at him with great admiration and affection, loudly*) Kit, did I ever tell you about the time I fell in love with a midget weighing thirty-nine pounds?

KIT (*Amazed*) Now, son.

> (JOE *walks slowly to the stairs leading to the street, turns and waves.* KIT, *and then one by one everybody else, waves, and the marble game goes into its beautiful American routine again. The play ends.*)

CURTAIN

Autobiography

*The Bicycle Rider
in Beverly Hills*

Chapter One
The Phonograph

*I*n my time I have seen with my own eyes perhaps more than a million people. I have spoken to surely fifty thousand of them, perhaps twice that many. Most of them I never knew by name. I saw them once and never saw them again. A great many I saw again and again but still did not know by name. What is a name anyway? A nuisance, in a way. Many I saw and spoke to are now dead.

One of these was an uncle by marriage who when he died said, "Too bad."

I sit at a fine new desk early in the forty-fourth year of my life and write.

Why?

I have the time.

The new desk is in a new office in a new building in a city named Los Angeles, which is Spanish for *The Angels*, I believe.

Los Angeles? What am I doing here? As always, my best.

When I think of the good things still to be written I am glad, for there is no end to them, and I know I myself shall write some of them.

My son says to me, "Gad, what an imagination this guy's got!"

We have been talking about a new book. My son wants to know about the tiger in the book.

"The tiger is love," I say.

My son looks at me out of his eight-year eyes, clenches his fist, draws his arm back, his eyes fill with humor, he laughs, he says *Oh, no!*, and lets go. I am at the stove in the kitchen of the Spanish mansion on North Rodeo in Beverly Hills getting my supper. He is hanging around his father to find out a little more about him

My daughter comes up after a bath seeking a hug, a beauty of five who calls out to boys of ten or eleven, "Hey, fella!"

These two are my strangers.

I sit down at the big table in the dining room and eat lentil soup.

"Why do you sit at *that* table?" my daughter says. "That's for guests."

"I'm a guest," I say.

"He's a guest," my son says. "Gad!"

"No," my daughter says. "You *live* here."

"I do?"

"Gad," my son says. "He doesn't know."

The tiger made them, the swift, sad tiger.

After supper I lie down to sleep, eager for morning. I dream of morning, wake up hoping it has come, lie down again, wake up again, decide it *is* morning, and get up. Morning is any time after a man has had enough rest to carry him to evening.

Morning is best when it begins with the last hours of night.

For years I have known midday mornings. There is something to be said for them. There is a quality of confusion and overlapping in them which is sometimes useful, but in the end the good morning is the morning before daybreak, the morning of dark silence, the morning in which the coming of light is witnessed, the morning which gives a man the *entire* day.

Enough of night, I want the light. Enough of culture's hours, I am a peasant. Enough of feasting, I want hunger. Enough of fat, I want muscle. Enough of pity, I want humor. Enough of vanity, I want pride.

Here I am at daybreak somewhere in the street-and-house sprawl of an unlikely city. Farewell, my friends. Farewell to the feast, the talk, the drink, the smoke, the eyes and mouths of busy despair. I ate, I drank, I spoke, I listened, I looked, I saw. The eyes of anxiety I saw, and the mouths of misery. I heard the false voices, farewell, I wish you well. No more, I want nothing better than bread and water, air and light, my own poor body making a place for my own poor soul.

Yesterday evening my daughter said, "Why do you walk around the house barefooted?"

"I pay the rent."

"He pays the rent," my son said.

"How much?" my daughter said.

"Four hundred and forty-five dollars a month."

"Why are we poor?" my son said.

To the house on North Rodeo have come a number of millionaires. One inherited his money from his father, another earned his. The poorest man who ever came to the house was a writer who had just sold a story to a film producer for fifty thousand dollars. My children felt sorry for him.

"We are not poor," I said. "We are living over our heads."

There was a young man once in San Francisco who worked for the telephone company and wrote poems. An editor of a small magazine asked me to call on him, since we both lived in San Francisco. When I called on him I found him in a small room in which a small fire was burning in a small grate in a small fireplace.

He asked if I would like to read some of his poems. The first I read was called *Aubade*. I didn't know what it meant.

"Morning song," he said.

Unknown poets seem to like such words.

The poem I have forgotten, but I remember that it was earnest. Such poets sometimes never escape from the telephone company.

The room was in the home of a private family. It was as clean as it could be. The poet wore a business suit which at that time must have cost twenty-five dollars. His shirt was white and starched, and there was a pin in his tie. He had a kind of tense poise and something like dignity.

I remembered the poet's name for years and then it attached itself to others who bore the same name, Clifford or Clayton or, something like that. But I haven't forgotten *Aubade*.

The poem was four or five stanzas of four lines each. I read the poem in silence, read it again, and then we talked about it, after which Clifford or Clayton read it aloud. He read it well. As he read I felt that here was a good man, and yet I could not help wondering what would come of his writing of poems. For he was very far away from the dirt and anxiety of the world.

In his bookcase I saw that each of his twenty or thirty books was a good one. He reached out for one or another of them with great accuracy, opened each of them quickly to the right place, and read something excellent by a good poet. Then he put the book on a table, open, so that soon better than half of his books were spread about on various tables, each of them open, all of them making an atmosphere of lonely dignity.

We smoked cigarettes incessantly, the poet with control and grace, myself with excitement, confusion, nervousness. For an hour we talked about poetry, about writing, about getting a written thing accurately written. I envied the poet his room, his fire, his clean books, his poems, especially *Aubade*, or morning song, his white shirt, his job at the telephone company.

At last I spoke about the job.

I had one cigarette half-finished on a blue plate which served as ashtray, another in my mouth. I lighted a third, and discovered the others. I had been out of work a long time. I was tired of poverty and failure.

I wanted to know if he could get me a job at the telephone company.

The poet stopped to wonder about this.

My clothes were old and worn. I was excited. I looked wild and unde-pendable. I moved around continuously, nervously, impatiently, and my most controlled speech was a shout.

I saw that my hope for a job at the telephone company created a problem for the poet. I was so eager for work that I tried to calm down, to stand tall and straight, to move calmly and deliberately, to speak evenly, slowly, and in a pleasant tone of voice.

At last the poet began to tell me how it was at the telephone company. Hundreds of experienced telephone company employees filed applications every day but scarcely three were hired a week. Still, if I wanted to file an application, it was quite a simple matter, he said.

We went back to talking about poetry. He took another book from his library, opened it, and read a short poem.

It seemed meaningless.

A few minutes later I was out in the street, on my way to the telephone company. I filed an application at the employment department and then walked five miles to my room on Carl Street.

I never got the job at the telephone company, whatever it was.

In those days I met, through the editor of the small magazine, a half dozen other writers of various kinds who lived in San Francisco, or in one of the towns near it. One of these was a student at Stanford who wrote both prose and poetry, a fellow from Oklahoma who had an old Ford roadster in which he used to race around Palo Alto and San Francisco, drive home to Oklahoma when a school term was over, back when a new one began. He was a pleasant blond American boy who didn't look around much, swore a good deal in a soft voice, and then laughed quietly. This one, as I got it, went to an asylum. I remember having read some of his poems and some of his prose. I don't remember anything about them, though.

Another was a tall fellow who was a devout Catholic. He wrote philo-sophic or aesthetic essays and poetry. He seemed to know and understand the writings of T. S. Eliot. He did not, however, care very much for Eliot's views, or for his poems.

Still another was a good-looking boy who acted as if he had gone to school in England, although the truth was that he was born in New Jersey and had done a little acting in small companies. He was a poet. He and I played tennis one day in Golden Gate Park. Over the years we met from time to time. The first time we met I noticed that he had got fat in the face. The second time a rather pretty girl was with him. He seemed embarrassed about not having made a name for himself as a poet or as a writer of prose. The third time he was with his wife who was not the girl I had met the second time. He was working on a novel, he said, but of course everybody was working on a novel. Several years later a novel by him—whether it was the one he spoke of I don't know—was published, and his publisher sent me a copy. It wasn't bad, but it was about specific people in that peculiarly specific way which makes a novel meaningless. The writing was rather excited without very much reason, and it did not make a name for him.

There were others. They were, every one of them, poets. I am not sure any of them failed any more than any of the poets who have achieved fame. It is a special profession. The poet who worked for the telephone company may by now have an enormous accumulation of poems, some of them great, which shall one day come to light. The boy from Oklahoma may be writing the finest poetry of our day—or did he commit suicide? I'm not sure. One hears of so many people one has met as having committed suicide. The Catholic poet may very well be doing work far superior to anything Eliot ever did. And at this moment the poet who had been an actor may be finishing a novel the like of which has never before been written.

It doesn't matter. They were there. They were concerned. They wanted to achieve something—for themselves, for others, for art, for society, for whatever. I remember them, and I remember myself as well.

I do not mean that I wrote well and they did not. I did the best I could, and not having any job to fall back on I suppose it was inevitable that my writing would have to earn a living and make some sort of a name for me.

I have driven my Cadillac more than 100,000 miles. The cross-country drives were great, from the Pacific to the Atlantic, or the other way around. But I have never driven to evening without loneliness, despair, regret, and all the other things that are of the end. For one end evokes the others, and the end of day evokes the end of life, especially for the traveler. The end of life evokes the errors of it, and a fellow wishes he had known better.

I almost always drove alone. That is the privilege of the traveler who goes by car. Certain drives are like an affair, and they have got to be private. A man is in love with a great many things strewn about haphazardly all over the country. He gets in his car and drives out to them, to have another look at them, and he doesn't want anybody to be sitting beside him. A man can be in love with streets, towns, and cities: railroad tracks, telegraph poles, houses, porches, lawns. He can go out in search of a fresh assorting and arranging of these things, and of the people of them.

A man's car can thus become a pew on wheels—in the church of the world. That it is why I have always been angry when my car has failed to work as I have expected it to work, for this has been a failure of my own soul in search of truth. I would have searched in any case, but the automobile gave breadth and depth to the search. The truth is not in the landscape, but neither is it *out* of it. My car is not like any other car in the world! It is my car and it is like myself.

Before I was sixteen I had many bicycles. I have no idea what became of them. I remember, though, that I rode them so hard they were always breaking down. The spokes of the wheels were always getting loose so that the wheels became crooked. The chains were always breaking. I bore down on the handlebars with so much force in sprinting, in speeding, in making quick getaways, that the handlebars were always getting loose and I was always tightening them. But the thing about my bicycles that I want to remember is the way I rode them, what I thought while I rode them, and the music that came to me.

First of all, my bikes were always rebuilt second-hand bikes. They were lean, hard, tough, swift, and designed for usage. I rode them with speed and style. I found out a great deal about style from riding them. Style in writing, I mean. Style in everything. I did not ride for pleasure. I rode to get somewhere, and I don't mean from the house on San Benito Avenue in Fresno to the Public Library there. I mean I rode to get somewhere *myself.* I did not loaf on my bike. I sometimes rested on it after a hard day's riding, on my way home to supper and sleep, sliding off the seat a little to the left, pedaling with the left leg, resting the other on the saddle, and letting the bike weave right and left easily as I moved forward. The style I learned was this: I learned to go and make it fast. I learned to know at one and the same time how my bike was going, how it was holding up, where I was, where I would soon be, and where in all probability I would finally be.

In the end I always went home to supper and sleep.

A man learns style from everything, but I learned mine from things on which I moved, and as writing is a thing which moves I think I was lucky to learn as I did.

A bike can be an important appurtenance of an important ritual. Moving the legs evenly and steadily soon brings home to the bike-rider a valuable knowledge of pace and rhythm, and a sensible respect for timing and the meeting of a schedule.

Out of rhythm come many things, perhaps all things. The physical action compels action of another order—action of mind, memory, imagination, dream, hope, order, and so on. The physical action also establishes a deep respect for grace, seemliness, effectiveness, power with ease, naturalness, and so on. The action of the imagination brings home to the bicycle-rider the limitlessness of the potential in all things. He finds out that there are many excellent ways in which to ride a bike effectively, and this acquaintanceship with the ways and the comparing of them gives him an awareness of a parallel potential in all other actions. Out of the action of the imagination comes also music and memory.

In the early days of the search I heard many great symphonies which no composer ever put to paper and no orchestra ever performed. This is understandable, I hope. As the saying is, they came to me. I was born restless and was forever eager to be going. There never seemed to be enough of going for me. I wanted to get out to more and more. This might have worn me out, but what it actually did was refresh and strengthen me. Wanting to go and not being able to do so might have given me another order of strength, but the order that I received was to *want* to go and to go. To want to search and to do so.

On the way I found out all the things without which I could never be the writer I am. I was not yet sixteen when I understood a great deal, from having ridden bicycles for so long, about style, speed, grace, purpose, value, form, integrity, health, humor, music, breathing, and finally, and perhaps best of all the relationship between the beginning and the end.

My eyes (by which I lived even more than by bread, by which, that is, living had reason, purpose, and a hope of meaning) were continuously assaulted by the elements, especially during the three years I rode a bicycle for a living. Unless I was able to see clearly my entire efficiency as a bicycle-rider was nullified, and I found myself at the side of the road, the bike halted but still propped up under me while I tried to restore vision to my eyes.

The wind carried many things into my eyes, and these things did everything from blur my vision to stop it entirely. The things were dust, dirt, pieces of fine gravel, insects, soot, cinders, and many other things. These things were lifted off the ground or driven out of the air into my eyes. I was forever in trouble with the wind. Insects stang in my eyes, filling them with the water which meant to cleanse them. After they were cleansed it would be some time before the eyes were restored to clear vision. Dirt—anything—in my eyes always brought me to an instantaneous halt, and I didn't like to halt. I once bought a pair of inexpensive goggles and wore them, but they were no good at all. The goggles bothered my eyes. I put them away, and thereafter the way it worked was this: I hoped not to have the wind blow anything into my eyes. But I doubt if there ever was a whole day in which nothing was blown into them.

I loved the wind, but it was often a great nuisance to me, a maker of bitter mischief. More than anything else I needed to see clearly. That was what it came to. In order to go—which was my work—I had to be able to see where I was going. Not to see where I was going meant that I had to stop. And to stop was to fail. And I did not enjoy failing. I have always been angered by failure. I am still angered by it. My success as a telegraph messenger depended on my eyes. Consequently, *all* hope of effectiveness depended on them. My effectiveness as a messenger became inseparable from my hope to be effective as a writer.

There were times when blindness, despair, and anger were so great that I believed I would throw it all over, turn in my messenger's coat and cap, put aside my bike, keep myself and my eyes out of the wind, sit down in the Public Library, and devote my time exclusively to the book, my eyes entirely secure now from the wind. But that was not to be.

First, I needed the money the job brought me. That is, the Saroyan family needed it.

Second, I needed the action of myself in the world. That is, the writer needed it.

Third, I needed to go, to continue to go, to continue my study of rhythm, pace, speed, and effectiveness. I needed all this in order to understand who I was, who I could be, and how.

Watching the wind work far off on eucalyptus trees was a great joy. Listening to it among the leaves of them when I reached the trees was sweet music. But best of all was when the wind had great power, when it was erratic and did swift and sudden things, stopped suddenly, picked up suddenly, ran in a circle, sprinted straight ahead, stopped, turned, came back.

Now and then when the wind was very strong I found it difficult to make my way through it on my bike, but I don't believe it was ever able to stop me entirely, except through trickery, by blinding me with dirt. Many times it almost unseated me, but I always managed to hang on.

The wind with the rain made other difficulties. Getting wet meant little or nothing, but rain driven into the eyes by the wind can also blur the vision. The difficulty of blurred vision is great, almost greater than blindness itself, for the eye with blurred vision likes to believe it still has enough vision on which to keep going. I soon learned, however, that to keep going when vision is poor is folly. Even so, I was often tempted to take a chance. If I had had no work to do the wind and the rain would have been a joy to behold. The weather fascinated me, especially storms, but it is one thing to watch a storm and another to fight it.

A second difficulty for the bike-rider in the rain is the slipperiness of the streets and the muddiness of the roads. I have had to get off my bike on muddy roads and push through on foot to where I was to deliver a telegram. Many times I slipped and spilled on the wet streets, for having misjudged the pace I could maintain efficiently.

I also had to be concerned about the vision of others in the streets, the drivers of automobiles especially, for it was not enough for me to see and know where I was going, it was necessary to see where a motorist was going, and be able to predict where he would soon be.

The heat of the summer softened the tar of the outlying streets of Fresno, so that getting the bike over them meant rising up off the saddle and bringing the entire weight of the body to bear upon the pedals—or sprinting, although the amount of speed I was able to achieve may scarcely be associated with the implication of the word sprint. More often than not I was barely able to keep the bike from stopping, but that was the idea—to *move* myself upon my bike to where I was going.

The heat and the riding in it all day made me very thirsty. This thirst was almost unquenchable during July, August, and September. I had a lot of respect for money, consequently I was not given to throwing it around on treats for myself, but after a great deal of thought I saw the wisdom of one transaction that I made at least once a day in the summer, occasionally twice a day. There was a place named The Danish Dairy on Fresno Avenue, across the street from the Hippodrome Theatre, where for five cents anybody could stand and pour cold buttermilk out of a pitcher into a tall glass and drink as much as he liked. This was the perfect drink for the messenger in the summer. Around two or half past two in the afternoon when I stepped into The Danish Dairy I would drink a great deal of buttermilk for five cents. I never drank fewer than four large glasses of it, and frequently, taking my time on the last two or three glasses, I drank seven or eight. The liquid was especially thirst-quenching, cooling, and deeply satisfying. It was also food. The girls and women who took care of the buttermilk-drinkers knew me well and did not ever suggest by any act or expression that I was going too far. If anything they seemed pleased to see me and glad when I drank a very great deal of buttermilk. The little specks of butter floating on top or swimming throughout the liquid were a delight when they were filtered in the mouth and tasted. The big salt-shaker was there on the white marble counter—half a dozen of them—and the taste of the salt was a real joy. The place smelled clean and wonderful, it was cool, and the faces and bodies of the girls and women were fresh and sweet-smelling. The drinking of the buttermilk every afternoon was something I looked forward to all day, and the actual drinking of it was something that made me feel absolutely lordly in my aliveness.

The work was hard, but The Danish Dairy was there, and for a nickel I could drink all the cold buttermilk I liked. And I did. That was one of the great pleasures of the summer, almost as good as the eating of cold watermelon at home after work. I frequently ate an entire watermelon, and not a small one. The summer brought deep thirst to me, and there were good things by which to quench it.

My ears (by which, with my eyes, I lived and learned) had excellent hearing until I was seventeen or eighteen, so that I heard the sounds made by very small creatures, all manner of insects, mice at night, hummingbirds, leaves stirring or letting go and falling, soft whistlings, hummings, moanings.

When I was surely not much more than six, though, I began to hear with the inner ear, too, and although my memory is inaccurate about some of this I know that one of the important inner sounds I heard was what I must call the sound of wings.

This was probably the result of nothing more than an actual apparatus of the interior ear adjusting itself, restoring itself, fighting off illness or partial deafness, or the action of blood itself in my head at a moment of partial blockade somewhere, in some small but important vein in some small but important area. Or it was something else, something I have no way of naming. Whatever it was, from time to time, and not always at night before I fell asleep, I would hear (and feel) a plunging, shifting, charging action in my head which seemed to me to have a quality of swift flight, as if an enormous wing had brushed my soul. When this action was first noticed by me it stopped me cold in my tracks and frightened me, for I felt that the wing was death. A small boy is apt to give an experience of this order such a value. Later on, much later on, the action having become familiar was considered nothing, certainly nothing stranger than the continuous accumulation of phlegm in my nasal passages and throat.

I heard other things with the inner ear. I have already mentioned the music I heard. I had better remark further on this. As I rode my bike, music began to *happen* to me. Insofar as I am able to describe it it was orchestral music. The piano was often involved, but on the whole the music was that of a large orchestra which had become a single instrument. The music had magnificent form, great accumulative power, and passion of a high order—the passion, that is, of control, restraint, and denial—the human conditions out of which we know collective passion is most apt to reach an individual body and soul. Even though I alone knew about this music, I cherished it deeply and took great pride in it.

I both listened to the music and made it, or at any rate so it seemed. It was certainly happening to me, and it was happening as I performed other, less magnificent, work—as I delivered or picked up telegrams. The adventure of the music was always great, but in a quiet way. While the music was happening I kept wondering how it would fulfill itself, how it would round out its form and be finished. The music, I think it is quite understandable, tended to end when a bike ride ended, but this was not always so. Frequently one work, in one key of music or one dimension of memory or inner experience, would endure an entire work day and then carry itself over into evening, night, and sleep. In the morning, though, it would be gone and forgotten. It would be forgotten, that is, in its details, but not in its quality. If I took to the music actively and began to whistle as well as listen to it, this did not stop the orchestra. But when the bike ride ended and it was time for me to go among people to deliver or pick up a telegram, the orchestral portion of the music would fall away from inner hearing, no doubt because now the external hearing was involved with other sounds, but the whistling would continue while I was among the people, in a business office, or in a grape packing house, or in the telegraph office itself. This whistling bothered some people. The wife of the manager of the telegraph office once complained about it to her husband who took me aside and with some awkwardness asked me not to whistle while I was in the telegraph office. I was astonished by this request for two reasons: first, because I hadn't been aware of the whistling, and second, because I couldn't imagine anybody resenting it. But genius is often deeply resented by small souls, so that if the world were a reasonable place all geniuses would be despised outcasts and eccentrics.

I was not always lucky in what I heard. It was not always an orchestra at work on a grand symphony. It was frequently a song, and quite strangely it would be a song which was not whole, which never in fact became whole. It would be a fragment of a song, certainly insofar as the words were concerned. And here perhaps lies the clue to the failure of this form to fulfill itself—its involvement in words. For words are inadequate instruments of communication, or of the making of wholeness. Sounds and rhythms and measures must apparently see themselves through to ends, but words must be driven to their ends, and that is the difficulty and majesty of writing. All the same I was lucky enough. At a time when the air of the world still had purity I heard great music which no one else heard.

I was thirteen when I bought a phonograph and one record and carried it home under my arm on my bicycle to the house on San Benito Avenue. My mother was fiercely angry at me for spending twelve dollars on a piece of junk. She cursed the machine and me and was unable not to come at me with such violence that I had to run out of the house. She followed me in a kind of insane but nevertheless comic chase around the house. The phonograph was resting on the table in the parlor. I ran quickly up the front porch steps, into the parlor to the phonograph. I quickly wound it, put needle to disc, and ran out of the house again just as my mother came into the parlor. She was on her way after me when she began to hear the music of the phonograph record. It was something called *Sonia*, performed by Paul Whiteman's band. I expected my mother to continue the chase, but she didn't. I myself stopped in the backyard to listen to the music. After about a minute I went back into the house. My mother was standing over the machine, listening to the music. Her anger was gone and in place of it I saw in her face the deep sorrow of her nature, her family, her race. A moment of jazz-band orchestration had done this.

When the record ended she turned to me and said, "All right. I had no idea. It is all right. Take good care of the machine. You have this one record only?"

I told her there was another song on the reverse side of the record. She sat down and said, "Please let me hear it."

On the reverse side was something called *Hi-li, Hi-lo*, I believe.

That was the beginning of external music in my own life, in my own family, and in my own house. My sisters and my brother were thrilled by the phonograph, and the one record. My mother established the rule that I alone might buy one new record a week, which I did. She waited eagerly for the arrival of this record and she listened to it again and again. This music must have been very strange to her, certainly music altogether unlike anything she had ever heard in Armenia, unlike the hymns she'd heard and sung at church. And yet she loved the music.

After a time I sent two dollars to a mail order house and received twelve records. This was a great bargain. The quality of the music was poor, but having twelve records for the price of three was exciting, and it satisfied the family necessity to be economical in all things.

But I had been listening to my own bike-riding music long before the arrival of the phonograph.

Now, it is important to understand two things: first, that after the phonograph became an important part of the family life I continued to hear my own music, and second, as I listened more and more to the music of the phonograph I heard my own music less and less.

If the external ear is surfeited with music, the internal ear tends to become deaf. If the body is satisfied, the soul tends to become unwilling or unable to seek satisfaction.

Water to an Armenian is a holy thing, like fire. A farmer watering his plants, trees, or, vines is taking part in a rite which has profound meaning and satisfaction for him. The farmers of Fresno went to the headgates of the irrigation ditches, or to the banks of the San Joaquin River or the Kings River for their Sunday picnics. They had to see the water where it was most abundant. They had to be near it.

Plans for going to *The River* were made by every family all week, and then early Sunday morning, or immediately after church, the family got into the horse-drawn carriage or into the automobile and drove there to spend the day looking at the water, smelling it, hearing it.

Going to *The River* was like going back to Armenia, or back to the days of youth. The mingling of excitement and peace at the river's side was continuous, the kids dancing at the sight of the swift-flowing water, running to dive into it and swim, the old people just sitting and being alive in a place that was like their own country to them.

The eating of the watermelon has deep meaning for the Armenians, too. Watermelon, white bread, and white cheese is a favorite summer meal. A pitcher of water is always on every Armenian table. The people are forever remarking on the quality of the water of a place.

One of the reasons the Armenians settled in Fresno was that the water there was the nearest thing to the water of Armenia. The land of Fresno County and in fact of the greater part of the whole San Joaquin Valley was not unlike the land of Armenia, certainly not unlike great areas of that land. Trees and vines flourished in the land, especially the apricot tree. One of the noblest of Armenian songs bears the name *The Apricot*

Tree. The Armenians quickly planted mulberry trees and watered them, for the mulberry was a tree they knew and loved in Armenia. They put in pomegranate trees as well, olive, almond, walnut, and many of them even tried to grow pistachio trees, but these trees would not grow in California. They planted watermelons, casabas, Persian melons, cantaloupes. They planted okra, eggplant, string beans, cucumbers, squash, tomatoes, bell peppers, parsley, mint, and a dozen kinds of herbs. They planted vines of all kinds. And to all of these things they led water in furrows, working with shovels to guide and control the flow.

If you want to behold a truly religious man in action, go to Fresno and watch a farmer watering his trees, vines, and plants.

There were better cities to live in than Fresno, but the good water was there, the water of home was there, and they went there to live. They weren't all farmers, either.

I remember the actor Vostikanian at a picnic at Kings River one Sunday in the summer in 1918. He was then almost eighty. I had seen him a month before in a play I had not understood but had deeply enjoyed, and he had been magnificent. His Armenian was a joy to listen to, both from the stage and at the picnic itself. He had played to Armenians in cities all over the world, including Paris, Rome, Berlin, London, Calcutta, Bombay, Cairo, Constantinople, Beyrout, Buenos Aires, Rio, and many others. He spoke fair English, excellent Russian, French, German, Italian.

I remember him sitting on the grass under a great sycamore tree at the river's side, talking with friends. One of these was a wealthy dealer in paintings and rare objects of art from New York who was on his way to China and India on business. This man wanted to know of Vostikanian why, of all the places in the world, he had chosen Fresno in which to spend his last years. Vostikanian looked at him and smiled.

"A hunter snared a bird which was so beautiful," Vostikanian said, "that the hunter said to himself, 'It would be a sin to end the life of this creature. I shall take it home, build it a wonderful cage, give it food and water, and I shall love it with all my heart, for I have never seen another bird like it.'

"The hunter disengaged the bird from the snare, stroked its feathers, spoke to it softly and lovingly, took it home. He made a fine cage for the bird, placed the bird in the cage, placed grain and seed and water before it. He kept the bird a year, but every evening when he came home and went to the bird he heard the bird sigh and say, 'Ahkh, Vahtahn!' (Oh, my country!).

"At last the hunter said, 'Bird, tell me. Where is this country of yours that you long for so sorrowfully?'

"'I will show you,' the bird said.

"The hunter opened the door of the cage, and the bird flew out. The bird flew, and the hunter followed. Night and day for a month the bird flew and the hunter followed—through all kinds of places—until at last the bird came to a place so desolate, hot, dry, rocky, and barren that it seemed to be the end of the world.

"The bird came to rest at last on a small dry tree full of thorns and small brittle leaves. The bird then said to the hunter, '*This* is my country.'"

Vostikanian smiled at the man from New York, and then said, "For the love of God, man, this is Armenia, isn't it? This water, this land, these vines?"

My son wanted a bicycle, I bought him one, he rode it a month, and then he wanted a bigger one. His own bicycle was too big for him, but it was not the biggest bicycle built, and he wanted the biggest. I told him he would not be able to ride the big bicycle. He said he would. I knew he wouldn't, but I also knew it was necessary and important for him to believe that he would. I spoke to the bicycle man about the matter while my son listened. The man said my son would not be able to ride the bicycle. It was altogether too big for him. My son told the bicycle man that he *would* be able to ride it. I asked the man how much of the sixty dollars I had paid for my son's bicycle he would be able to allow me in a trade-in for the big bicycle. He said he would not be able to allow me anything for it, but that he would try to sell the bicycle for me. He believed he might be able to get thirty dollars for it. I took my boy and his bike home. I told him his bike was a fine one. I told him he rode it well, which was the truth. These things meant nothing to him. He wanted the big bike. I discussed the matter with his mother and we had an argument, and I became angry at my son, at his mother, and at myself. The boy wept. I went out of the house to a small bar and sat there an hour, drinking and thinking. I had shouted at my son that I would not buy him the big bike, I would never again buy him anything, because he did not appreciate anything I bought him. Early the next morning I went to the bicycle shop and bought the big bike, a Raleigh, manufactured in England. I took it home and showed it to my son. I let him get up on the seat and try to ride, and sure enough, my son rode the bike, just as he had said he would, but he did not ride it well. I told him it was my bike but that it was also his bike, and that he and I would go for rides in Beverly Hills together, beginning that May evening when I got home after work. I put the bike in the garage of the house on North Rodeo and locked it. That evening after work my son and I got on our bikes and rode up Benedict Canyon until we came to the top of a hill there. Then we rode down the hill together.

Riding a bicycle in Beverly Hills with my son made me remember the bicycle-rider I was years ago in Fresno, and it made me want to keep a record of what I remember, which is this book.

Chapter Two
The Typewriter

It is necessary to remember and necessary to forget, but it is better for a writer to remember. It is necessary for him to live purposely, which is to say to live and to remember having done so. This is not easy to do.

First, it is not easy to live purposely—that is, consciously.

Second, it is not easy to remember, certainly not easy to remember accurately, for the unforgettable events of a man's life are not necessarily more important than the insignificant events which do not seem to be remembered at all.

A man is his memories, but he is also the things he forgot.

I want to think about the things I may have forgotten. I want to have a go at them because I have an idea they will help make known how I became who I am. I cannot expect to be altogether successful in this. I can only hope that my luck will be good enough to make the effort worthwhile.

Nothing is ever entirely forgotten. It is all there, and it stays there until a man is dead. The things I forgot I forgot only temporarily. I will now try to remember some of them.

I want to remember the tapping of my feet together almost every night for a great many years, the keeping of a rhythm that was sometimes a comfort and sometimes an annoyance. Even sleep could not stop the keeping of this rhythm. I suppose I could say I was simply too alive for my own comfort, but I doubt if that would be accurate. I know I couldn't wait to be entirely myself, and I knew it was necessary to wait—years.

I didn't want to be a student at school, a harvester of grapes, or a messenger. I *was* by turns each of these things, but they were not what I wanted to be.

What I wanted to be was entire and whole. I wanted this so deeply that it brought into my soul a concern about my chances for success that amounted to anxiety. The symptom of this anxiety was the tapping of the feet, the keeping of the rhythm. During the day while I was up and abroad the keeping of the rhythm was in order. The reason it did not stop at night may have been that I was not satisfied with what had been achieved during the day and couldn't wait for morning. I wanted to be whole, powerful, indestructible, efficient, effective, able. I wanted to be able to do one or another of the finest things any human being *might* do. I wanted to be able to do this thing as no one else had ever done it, which is to say I wanted to do it in precisely my own way, out of my own accident and miracle of mortality. I was somebody definite, like only unto myself, but I had not yet found out who I was, and I meant to find out.

At the same time I also meant to decide how I would be who I was, which in turn means that I meant to choose from within myself *for myself* the one I wished to be. I saw no one about worthy of serving as a model, hence it was necessary to seek from within myself a model. Every man is any kind of man. Helplessly or deliberately he chooses himself out of his own assortment, but at the same time the choosing is done for him. This is altogether true as it stands, a contradiction, or seeming-contradiction, which must not be divided.

I chose, but I do not know why, and not knowing why establishes that the choosing was also done for me. The point does not need to be labored.

The kind of man I wished to be, was impelled to be, could not help trying to be, was something like the kind I became, or am by way of becoming. The fact is I shall go on trying as long as I live. I began to be this man quite early, perhaps before I was three. Quite considerably I have become this man, but the achievement can never be entire. If it were to become entire, then it would simply be true that a man had ceased to live actively, ceased to live in his soul, was now *willingly* declining. The will figures in this importantly. To live actively is to keep trying. It is to keep trying for the inaccessible, with faith in the reasonableness of doing so.

Who was this man precisely? First of all, he was to have a body that had health, humor, and power. This body ought not to tire quickly. It ought to enjoy being extended. This meant that I would have to find out what it was that brought fatigue most quickly to the body, and then avoid it. And I must find out what it was that made the body eager and glad to carry out the wishes of the soul.

I did find out these things and I shall speak of them as I go on.

I do not want to get away from the tapping of the feet just yet. In the keeping of a rhythm lies the source and impulse of art, measured time, balanced matter. A poem is the keeping of a rhythm—the writing of it, as well as the poem itself. And so it is with a song or symphony. A story or a novel or a play—any work of writing—is a keeping of a rhythm. In a sense even a painting or a sculpture is a keeping of a rhythm, even though the rhythm kept is one of final instantaneous *being* rather than of *time-taking* being. It takes time to read a poem. It may take greater time to paint a picture, but the eye of the beholder sees the entire picture instantly.

I wanted to be doing and couldn't stop when it was time to sleep.

I didn't want to go to school, I didn't want to work on a vineyard, I didn't want to be a messenger. But it was necessary for me to go to school, to work on a vineyard, to be a messenger. It was necessary also from the time I was eight to the time I was twelve to sell papers.

Most of all I resented school, but I never resented learning. In fact, the reason I resented school was that the system of teaching involved was hopeless, foolish, meaningless, and a profound annoyance to me. The system of teaching was designed solely for the half-wit who has no desire to learn. I am criticising no one. There are enormous numbers of perfectly fine human beings who do not need to learn anything more than how to earn a few dollars every week by which to keep alive in a modest way. I resented school because the system of teaching did not suit *me*. I felt I had a right to expect it to suit me as well as it suited the others, and the teachers. I had to put up with the system and the teachers, but there is no use pretending that I was ever above not hating both. And the fact remains that I left the system and the teachers as soon as I was able to do so.

I did not mind working during summer vacations on orchards and vineyards, but I never believed this work would be anything nearly like the work of my life. I loved the apricots, peaches, figs and grapes harvested, but the actual work was monotonous and meaningless. The heat of summer was good, swimming in the ditches after work was good, but I could never get away from the eagerness I felt to become as soon as possible myself and to do my own work, the work by which I would become and continue to be truly myself. And I could not get away from the tapping of the feet, the keeping of the rhythm of waiting, hoping, expecting.

From the beginning I wanted to excel. If anybody could do anything I wanted to do it also, and do it better. I was insecure and I must have felt unloved, for I always wanted to be superior, self-sufficient, above emotional pain, oblivious of frustration. I was in some ways unable and unwilling to make adjustments of any kind, and in other ways able to make them most deeply and completely.

I deeply adjusted to school, for instance, and at the same time did not adjust to it at all. I adjusted to school as one adjusts to the probability that a man in a casket is dead, and I never adjusted to it as one would never adjust to the theory that one is one's self dead simply because one happens to find one's self in a casket.

My adjustment was accompanied by steady, continuous, deliberate and often artful combat with the undertakers and pall-bearers. I asked the ignorant teachers valid questions which they neither expected nor knew how to answer. I pointed out to each of them their mistakes in theory, thinking, memory, and behavior. I did so with righteousness, and often with contempt.

The teachers in turn sought to belittle me, generally failed, and then resorted to force, either chasing me themselves, or ordering me to the Principal's Office for punishment.

My refusal to adjust was accompanied by seeming docility and compliance—generally after I had had an enormous siege of trouble. I kept quiet, permitted excellent opportunities to expose the teachers and their system of teaching to pass unexploited, and when called upon to speak spoke briefly and accurately. I gave the impression of having been corrected and of being therefore an improved man. This was external. Inside, I knew the truth, and the truth, now kept to myself, was a source of great amusement to me.

Having had intelligence driven underground I saw extraordinary things happen to it. First of all, it became sharper and more direct than ever, and the deliberate act of keeping it to myself, the control of this and the restraint, soon gave me inner quietude, assurance, authentic aloofness.

But I was always unwilling to go at life without humor, and so the periods of good behavior, of control of intelligence, were never very prolonged, and soon I was back in the fight, deliberately choosing to take a chance on the trouble I would create in order to be able to show off my intelligence, and in order to expose my inferiors, the teachers. I seldom engaged in arguments with other pupils for the simple reason that they seldom offered the basis for a good contest, but now and then I had a go at a snob or a phony.

For the most part, though, the enemy was the public education system and the teachers who were inadequately and improperly educated or endowed to teach under a system whatsoever.

Here I am, in the forty-fourth year of my time, writing about a very little of an enormous amount of experience that took place more than thirty-five years ago. I must remind the reader, and myself, that I am writing about only a very little of the *whole* experience of the time, and that I myself am well aware that anything I have written is simultaneously adequately true and deeply inaccurate. But I shall not permit myself to stop on that account, for in the end a general truth shall come into being precisely out of my having gone on earnestly and from having tried to get—in writing, years after the time—a hint of the nature of the actual truth at the time.

I must not forget that every classroom was first of all poorly ventilated and that it was always difficult to stay there at all. Recess in the school-grounds, in the fresh air, is the only thing that kept me from becoming a half-sleeping lump of nothing. I must remember the old clock in every room, the minute hand of which moved so slowly. I must remember that every teacher was physically ugly and seemed stale and decayed. I must remember the loathing with which they took up their work every morning, apparently loathing themselves, the members of the class, and the miserable subject to be taught. I must remember their pinched, hairy faces and their shrill sick voices. I must remember their isolation entirely from health, fun, enthusiasm, gladness, humor, intelligence, or hope. Most of them were women who had never been married, and some of them had never even had affairs. They were the culls and rejects of their kind. Having failed to become women at all, having failed to become mothers, they had gone into teaching as if to revenge themselves on the children of other women. It is true that each of them had three or four favorites in every class, generally girls, but now and then one of them had a boy favorite, or pet. Such a boy was held in contempt by the other boys in the class.

I must also remember the atmosphere of the entire school itself: it was stiff, unnatural, sorrowful, and full of petty intrigue. The place was an institution to me, not unlike a poor house, penitentiary, public hospital, asylum, or old peoples' home. I despised the sight of it. I prayed for it to burn down. I thought of setting it on fire myself.

I must remember also the peculiar smell of the school, and of every classroom: warm oil on the wood floor, chalk dust, desks, old books, paper, pencils, pencil shavings, ink, the teacher herself. The wretched smell of school. Every school has it. Emerson School had it bad. The place stank. I learned to read and write there.

I more than wanted to excel. I was impelled to do so, or at any rate to try to do so. One is no longer permitted not to know why one has the nature, character, or genius one happens to have. Consequently, I shall say why I believe I was compelled to try to excel. I shall of course be mistaken, or at least partly mistaken, but that is no matter.

It is proper and good to seek to account for everything, including the unaccountable. If errors are made, they will be sensible ones, and like all errors they will be temporary. Eventually they will be corrected, understanding will be extended, health will be improved, grace will be made a little more accessible.

Tentatively, however, I must make known that I do not believe it is required of art, science, religion, philosophy, or family to assure every man born into this life a secure childhood, in which a child knows only love and harmony. If such a childhood happens to come to pass for a child, excellent. If the child, as a result of such a childhood, becomes a truly pleasant or excellent adult who functions in a satisfying manner (to himself and to the family), again excellent. The supplying of such a childhood to a child, however, appears to be impossible. It may not even be desirable. It might just create a nonentity, a happy one, a functioning one, an unconscious one; or on the other hand a wretched one, an inept one, a conscious one. The situation is not simple. I do not think that unhappiness in childhood comes from any specific source other than the accident of mortality itself. I think it is inevitable and in order for the human creature to be unhappy in childhood. I think it is impossible, at the same time, for almost any new human being to be *entirely* unhappy at any time.

I was bitterly unhappy as a small child, but I shall not go into this just now, for it is not the place for it.

My purpose is to remark about the necessity I felt to excel.

From a very early time in my life I sensed quite accurately the end of life. That is, that it *must* end, that it could end at any time, that the end did not come to pass by reasonable or meaningful plan, purpose, or pattern.

A small boy I had slightly known at Fred Finch Orphanage in Oakland was killed in an automobile accident in 1914, for instance. That is to say, he no longer appeared in the dining room, and so I did not see him again. I had forgotten when I had seen him last—*accurately*, that is:

I heard that he was dead, gone, no more, in Heaven, and so on.

I heard of others dying, too. That is, of not being any longer on their feet in any of the places I knew. Some were boys, some men, some girls, some women. This peculiar thing seemed to happen to all kinds of people, young and old, small in size or large in size. There seemed to be great regret about it in every case. I knew intimately some of the pain of this regret, for the regret had to do with separation, and I had been separated from my mother when I was three. This separation had not been an indefinite one, one that I might discover for myself at my leisure. It had been a formal one. And I had been astonished by it. I even believed I might never again see mother. As it happened I saw her at irregular intervals but after each visit she returned to San Francisco, to her job there as a maid. I remained in the orphanage, I believed I might never see her again, and I knew the pain of separation. Soon, though—perhaps after less than half a dozen reunions on the lawn in front of the Administration Building—I found that I could believe I would soon see her again. I did not like to see her go, but I *did* like believing she would be back.

I had by now, however, come to sense quite deeply that there was a final and irrevocable separation. It happened when somebody was put off his feet. I knew it had already happened to my father, and could happen to my mother, to my sisters, to my brother, to myself. I did not want it to happen to any of us, and before it happened to *me* I wanted to think about how I might do something to postpone it or to take away from it some of its absolute finality.

So that my own life—the time I was on my feet—might not be altogether secret, I wanted, while I *was* on my feet, to be very good at it, to be known as being very good at it, and to be remembered as having been very good at it.

But what was I supposed to do in order to be very good at it? Was I supposed to be able to stand well, walk well, run swiftly, and so on? Yes, I was. And I stood well and walked well and ran swiftly. I sat well. I played well. I took part in everything I was permitted to take part in with earnestness, eagerness, confidence, and a desire to excel. Was all this because I had lost my father before I was three? And soon after separated from my mother? Because I felt unloved, or was actually unloved, or unloved by those I wished to be loved by? Partly, of course.

But had my father lived and prospered, had he and my mother loved one another deeply, had they had more and more children, had we been a family in our own home, all of us loved by our father and our mother, all of us loving them and one another, would this love have been enough to keep me from sensing the end of things and from being impelled to do something about it?

I don't know. I shall not pretend that I do. And in all truth I must say that as I lost or became separated from love I was not able ever to believe that I was altogether lost and unloved. I believed, for instance, that my dead father loved me and watched over me. I also believed that another Father, my father's own father, and *his* own father, and the father of my mother loved me, and I loved each of them. This father was God, but to me he was not altogether held fast in that word. He belonged to myself, and to the secrets I knew. He was both dead and alive. He was not seen as others are seen. He had his life and reality in my own nature. I loved him and if no one else loved me, or seemed to love me, I believed he did. I believed that this father knew and understood everything. I sought to impress him with my worth, with my right to his love, and I went about the business of being a small boy with this desire never far removed from my thinking. I wanted whatever I did to be excellently done, for I believed my father would notice and be pleased. I wanted to be a good son. None of this, however, meant that, in spite of the general sorrow I knew, I could not impress my father with a comic excellence, and I found that from very nearly the beginning I was impelled to create comedy, to reveal out of things and events their humor, to be funny, to amuse my friends and my father.

I was impelled to excel because I believed it would please my father, or my witness, or God. It was perfectly natural that I would soon discover, or have revealed to me, my own personal work in which to excel. It could not be enough to excel only in being on my feet. Sooner or later I must discover my work, it must be a very special work, and I must excel at it. I was some time discovering that my work must be in The Word. In effective, accurate, graceful, and wise use of language.

There were influences that hastened this discovery. They may even have determined my choice. Before I was nine, I remember quite clearly, I wanted, even after I was off my feet, or dead, not to be *altogether* separated from my family, my friends, or even strangers.

The first thing that appealed to me was the making of things out of stone, for stone was enduring. This hope in stone appealed to me for quite a long time, but I never made anything out of stone. To begin with I had no appropriate stone with which to work, and no implements with which to work upon it. I *did* examine carefully the shapes of pebbles and rocks, and I did enjoy this examining of them, but I knew that these things I had found whole, and had not myself made. I knew I must make whatever it was by which I would make memorable my having been on my feet for a while. The hope in stone faded away, and I found hope in color. Blank paper had entered into my experience at the orphanage, along with color crayons. I had made a number of pictures. They had been good to make. I returned to paper and color and hoped I would be able to excel at the making of pictures. This work, however, did not satisfy me. I was not pleased with the pictures I made. I therefore put aside color and worked at making pictures on paper with pencil lines, or lines of ink. It was interesting work, but still it was not satisfying, and I knew it was not my work.

I remember some of my thinking. It went something like this, before I was eight or nine:

Stone is fine but one must obtain stone and then one must obtain implements with which to shape it as one wishes, and the work must be very slow, and I do not like to move slowly, I must move swiftly.

To paint pictures is fine, but one must purchase canvases and paints and brushes, and one must work slowly, and in the end a great painting could disappear, it could be destroyed by fire, for instance.

Music, the creating of new music, is fine, but one must have a piano, and a teacher of music, and then one must hope that the music one has created will be performed by an orchestra, and it is not a simple matter to find men who can play all the different instruments of an orchestra. Besides, I don't know anything about music at all.

In order to write all a man needs is paper and a pencil. Furthermore, when a thing has been written, it is written forever. When it is printed, nothing can stop it from being printed again and again if the thing wants to be printed again and again.

I must therefore be a writer.

Most important of all, though, was this, which I have saved for the last:

I learned that my father had been a writer.

The *real* story can never be told. It is untellable. The real (as real) is inaccessible, being gone in time. The art story can be told. If it is effectively told, *all* has been told. In the end art and the real are one, and of course all *is* real. There is no point in glancing at the past, in summoning it up, in re-examining it, except on behalf of art—that is, the meaningful-real.

Boredom was the plague of my childhood. More—much more—than loneliness it filled my days and my soul. I was bored from the beginning, certainly from the moment I was cut off from my own home and my own family, from the moment my mother said deliberate good-bye to me in the waiting room of the orphanage. The first thing that bored me was a mechanical toy my mother had given me on the occasion of this separation. If was called *The Coon Jigger*. It was a small tin Negro on a small tin stage. After the spring had been wound the Negro danced. The toy was instantly boring.

This early boredom, this dissatisfaction with objects that I felt deeply and instinctively were substitutes, has something important to do with my reaching the decision to make writing my work, the *means* by which I would become truly myself, as well as the *result* of my having become truly myself. Which came first, my having become myself, or my having become a writer? These things happened together, they overlapped, they were the same things. Being bored, I needed ideas. I needed a great many of them, and I soon reasoned that I would be able to get the most ideas through writing, for writing can be about anything. In fact, it can be, itself, anything. I remember that during my apprenticeship, long before I was twenty, I used to think somewhat as follows:

I shall write the sun. I shall write fire and light and heat. Or, I shall write music. In words I shall create music. Or, I shall write a nation, a whole nation, entire, not new, but newly noticed. Or, I shall write a rock in a desert where it has been in silence for thousands of years. Or, I shall write a smile. Or, I shall write a school, a whole system of teaching-learning, in which the teacher must learn and the student must teach and both of them must take part in simultaneous teaching-learning. Or, I shall write money. I shall write what it is, what it is supposed to be, what it might be, and so on.

While I was at the orphanage the boredom came from being in a place in which I did not wish to be, in which (especially at first) I did not, could not, would not feel at home, in which an artificial system of law and order had been imposed upon me, in which everything was necessarily placed on a basis of schedule.

Now, this involvement in schedule which I then disliked may, however, have turned out to be a good influence in my life. Good or bad, the fact remains that I am addicted to the keeping of a schedule. The difference is that I now choose the schedule, and in my childhood it was chosen for me. I choose, for instance, to write a novel in thirty-three days, and I write it in thirty-three days. In the orphanage the schedule was never concluded, and it never brought anything into being, although I suddenly discovered that Christmas came every year.

The orphanage bored me also because it didn't smell right. Few places do. The buildings had a peculiar odor. Even the dining room had an odor I did not like. The grounds smelled all right, though, and so did the hills beyond them.

But I was bored. I was bored the entire four years I was there.

In Fresno the boredom came from poverty, but I am not speaking of material poverty, for no human being needs very much of material things. The boredom came from spiritual poverty. I was starved for ideas, nobody had any first-rate ones to share with me, so I had to try to invent or discover my own. In the most commonplace, tiresome, ridiculous, malicious, coarse, crude, or even crooked people or events I had to seek out rare things, good things, comic things, and I did so.

Nobody seemed to be interested in anything except the making of money.

The ones who were effective at making money seemed to me superior to those who wept about their miserable lot and were not effective at improving it.

I found that I noticed virtuosity of a sort even in those who were effective at making money disreputably—those who were dishonest. It seemed to me irrelevant how a man achieved effectiveness, just so he did it—but of course that was a temporary view, compelled out of sheer lack of material to work with.

At the same time, certain failures seemed to me to be the greatest men in town: Armenian poets who had to cadge small loans or donations from friends in order to live. Armenian editors of weekly newspapers who were writing editorials about Armenia restored or resurrected, who were getting by on the few paid subscriptions people had sent in. Armenian composers whose songs earned them nothing at all. Armenian painters whose paintings were ridiculed by wealthy Armenians or admired by poor Armenians who could not afford to buy one for as little as five dollars.

The environment was competitive and fiercely impatient with any who were unable or unwilling to compete.

I remember a dark young poet, three years in Fresno from Armenia, Aram Aramian, haunting the streets of the town day and night, the late coffee houses, the Public Library, the Armenian backgammon and coffee clubs, the newspaper offices.

I remember his laughter, loud and raucous and lonely, as laughter always is in fools who are fools only because the environment is made up of other, different fools, fools who are effective at foolish and irrelevant work—the work of accumulating money because money alone has meaning in the environment.

I do not remember ever having seen him in the streets without books under his arms, or not swiftly on his way somewhere. I remember that whenever he sat down in Hart's Cafeteria with a cup of coffee at midnight, before him would be a tablet of lined paper on which he would be writing or revising something he had written.

And then suddenly Aram Aramian was off his feet, gone and forgotten. But I could not forget him, and I have not done so. I want to remember him, I want his name to be remembered, because he lived in Fresno, because he was a poet there, because I knew him, watched him, and because he died.

On the other side of the line were the fellows like King Maljan who, without education, without very much English, raced around the whole San Joaquin Valley, spoke swiftly, made deals, had luck, came near disaster, laughed uproariously with similar pals, made money, got married, had children, and then died when they were sixty or seventy. Some of them are still going strong. I respected these men, too, for they *did* go at their work with energy, daring, and zest. For a time I think I respected them more than I respected the poets and editors and novelists and composers and other failures.

And then of course it is necessary not to lose sight of the truth that the fellows in King Maljan's camp and the fellows in Aram Aramian's camp frequently met, sat together, talked, laughed, and compared notes about how they were making out. The Maljan crowd looked at the Aramian crowd as foolish dreamers, and the Aramian crowd looked at the Maljan crowd as—what? Well, as countrymen, I suppose, as friends, as contemporaries. And I think there was tolerance if not admiration in each crowd for the other.

The action of these crowds, one upon the other, broke up the monotony a little but not much. Most of the time I considered both crowds boring, useless, ignorant, pathetic, and ridiculous. Once or twice, in fact, as I moved about the streets selling papers, Aram Aramian himself was rude to me—arrogant with me, belittling, or witty at my expense. It was the same with King Maljan. But it didn't matter very much, because they didn't know who I was, and because they were frequently warm and friendly, earnest and amusing, too.

I was not, however, influenced by the Armenian poets of Fresno in the reaching of the decision I made to make writing my work.

431

They were all flops, and I had no intention of taking up work in which I would be a flop.

As for other poets, poets of other peoples, as far as I knew there were none, none at all. The Italians had none, neither did the Russians, nor the Greeks, nor the Slavonians, nor the Danes, nor the Syrians or Assyrians, nor the Americans themselves.

Everybody was busy running away from ideas, except a handful of Armenians not long in Fresno, not long out of the old country, and these few seemed quite inept or unaware of what they were doing. Most of them struck me as being posers. All of them struck me as being vain, if shabby.

Which of them, then, was to be a friend?

None.

All.

I would notice them, and that's all. My friends would have to be my own contemporaries.

At Emerson School my best friend was Gill Varney, a remarkable wit and mimic, a fellow who could take Longfellow's *Hiawatha* and tear it to pieces, reciting it as he believed it ought to be recited. He became an elevator operator.

There were other friends, and as they meant something to me as a man who was going to make writing his work, I will from time to time remember them, for they broke the monotony a little.

At the orphanage one of my first friends in the world was Samuel Isaacs, called Sammy. He was a month or two older than myself—this sort of information got itself established there—and neither of us was much more than three. Half-orphan or whole-orphan, I did not know what he was, but he was there, in the same ward. With us were half a dozen other small boys, two or three of them night-rockers and criers. I don't remember much about Sammy, except that we were friends, that we moved about together, and that older boys provoked us into a fight one day. We fought, stopped suddenly, burst into tears. A half hour later—or was it three minutes?—we were friends again.

One would think that it would be inevitable for eight or nine small boys in a small ward at an orphanage to be friends, all eight or nine of them, but that is not how it goes. From the beginning one chooses one's friends (for reasons one may not understand), or one falls into friendship by accident. Sammy and I fell into friendship, I suppose. I remember that he was not a night-rocker or crier. In fact, pretty much like myself, he put up with things with a certain amount of grace. He didn't like them, but he put up with them. He was a sad fellow who could be quite amusing.

Another friend of that time, 1911 and 1912, was a boy named Theodore Dolan, called Teddy. I don't remember much about my friendship with Teddy, but I do remember that we *were* friends, that on the hikes into the hills we climbed trees together after hazelnuts, and that we shared an interest in lizards, waterdogs, and witches. There was great interest in these things at the orphanage among the older boys which filtered down to the younger ones, so that whenever we were in the hills we searched about for them, to take back with us, and we did go back any number of times with lizards and waterdogs. We never saw a witch. The lizards would snap off their tails in captivity. Then they would die, escape, or be turned free. I don't remember seeing a dead one, but I do remember seeing any number of them with their tails snapped off. They seemed broken and unfortunate in that form, and the lifeless tail seemed absurd. The brown slippery waterdogs were kept in jars or cans or buckets with water and stones and moss in them, but these creatures also suffered in captivity.

What do boys want of these creatures which they catch and keep?

They seem to want living things which they may feel are their own. The Superintendent of the orphanage had a red Collie dog, but no one else on the place had a dog or a cat. One boy caught a young hawk in the hills and brought it home with him, but he was not permitted to keep it. For a day or two I once owned a small owl, which I had received from an older boy in exchange for a dollar-watch which had been out of commission a long time. Somebody had given it to me in that condition. I was astonished to learn that I had made a poor exchange, even though the watch was useless. The owl was alive, but the kindergarten teacher told me the watch was worth more than the owl. I remember that I thought about this a long time. I have forgotten what happened to the owl. I suppose it was turned loose. I kept it in a small cardboard box a day or two, however.

A third friend was a boy whose last name was West. He was one of three or four brothers who lived in a small house in the hills not far from the orphanage. The family kept chickens and rabbits, and the three or four boys, living at home with their mother and father, spent a lot of time with the boys at the orphanage. The youngest of them, a few years older than myself, became my friend for a year or two. I don't remember much about him, except that he was one of the West brothers, and that he and I often met, and were friends.

Joaquin Miller himself lived in the hills not far from the orphanage, but he and I never became friends. In fact, we never met. He was a rather old man, I heard. Fable had it that he was a great man. I couldn't imagine what it meant to be a great man, but I felt that if you happened to meet him you might be frightened by his greatness or you might feel it very quickly and powerfully. My brother, along with a good many other boys of his age, seven or eight, once visited Joaquin Miller in his home, and when I asked my brother about the man he said that he had a beard. It also came to me that Joaquin Miller was responsible for something that had to do with the words "Sail on and on and on." I believed he must have been in a boat at one time and that he had sailed on and on and on, but in the end, after many years, I learned that he had written a poem about Columbus and his frightened, mutinous crew.

Now, there must have been many more friends at this time in my life, but at the moment I cannot remember them. Many friendships are swift and accidental, the result of a chance meeting, followed by a permanent separation.

In Fresno, when I was not yet eight, one of my first friends, and a friend I kept until he died at the age of twenty-one or twenty-two, was a boy named Yedvard Emerian, called Eddie Emerian. His father and mother were from the same city in Armenia as my father and mother, the city of Bitlis. He was two or three years older than myself, so that we were not in the same classes at Emerson School, but we met during every recess period in the school grounds. We ran together after school to the building of *The Fresno Evening Herald* where we got our papers, and we ran to town together, to sell them. He was a swift boy, full of mischief and humor, and a fine wrestler. Wrestling was the school sport. If anything, I was swifter than he was, and together we met all comers in our division, and a few in heavier divisions. I don't remember either of us ever losing a match.

A fellow who was in the same grade with me at Emerson School was a quiet boy named Paul Hagopian. Paul and I were friends all through Emerson, and for a number of years afterwards. It was not easy for the teachers at Emerson to understand this friendship, for we had nothing in common. He was a quiet boy who stayed out of trouble without making any effort to do so. Yet we were friends. What did Paul Hagopian have that paired so well with what I had? I can only guess, but I would say that it was humor, for even though he was naturally well-behaved and intellectually slow I remember that he said many remarkably amusing things about the teachers at Emerson School. Generally speaking, though, I believe the main reason we were friends was that he was an Armenian and that he and I almost never spoke in English.

At the orphanage I did not know for some time that I was an Armenian. I did not know about the divisions, national or cultural or religious, among human beings. All this came later, but while I was still at the orphanage I began to piece together the miscellaneous information that came to me, some of it by accident, some of it related to me by my brother Henry. I was disappointed and hurt, for instance, when a number of older boys and my brother agreed that England was first in power, America second, and Armenia third. I could not accept this order. I believed that if, as I had heard, I was an Armenian, Armenia *must* be first. As for the second and third, it did not matter to me who took either place.

I neither spoke nor understood Armenian. Only for a moment or two when my mother came to visit us on a Sunday afternoon did she speak in Armenian to my oldest sister, Cosette. I can't imagine what I must have thought they were speaking, or what connection it had with me.

In Fresno, however, Armenia was not in third place among the nations of the world, it was in last place, if in any place at all. I was only a few days in total ignorance of the language after I reached Fresno from the orphanage. In not much more than a month I understood the language quite well, and spoke it fluently enough for all practical purposes. Eddie Emerian and I shared a common dialect, the dialect of Bitlis, but Paul Hagopian spoke with the dialect of Harpoot, which is another thing altogether. Still, I could understand him, and he could understand me.

If you were an Armenian in Fresno, this was an enormous fact about you, of special importance, and you had no choice but to carry the fact in one of two ways: proudly or even arrogantly, or shyly (if not secretly), and with embarrassment.

The Armenians of Fresno were considered not only foreigners, but unattractive foreigners. I have no doubt that they were enough of both to make this attitude toward them understandable, but at the same time I was not prepared to be belittled at the very beginning of my life, and so it was necessary for me to meet contempt with contempt.

The attitude of "the American" for "the Armenian" was one of contempt. I despised those Armenian boys who toadied to "the American."

I cherished those who felt the same contempt for "the American" that he felt for "the Armenian," and no one felt this contempt deeper than Paul Hagopian. He referred to them as *ahkh-lahkh*. The word is untranslatable, but in general it means intellectually feeble and spiritually lopsided.

Who, however, were "the Americans" of Fresno? I may best identify them by remarking that they were not the Armenians, Mexicans, Italians, Portuguese, Russians, Syrians, Assyrians, Slavonians, Greeks, or any of the other peoples who spoke two languages or had a culture of their own. (The Russians were actually the Germans, but they were called the Rooshians since they were Germans who had gone to Russia for religious freedom.)

What was it about the Armenian which the American found distasteful? It was an assortment of things, which I shall touch upon briefly, for it doesn't really matter.

The Armenian was not eager to forfeit his culture in favor of American culture. The fact that he *couldn't* do so, even if he had wanted to, is perhaps beside the point.

In 1915 when I reached Fresno the town had a population of about twenty-five thousand, I should imagine. Five thousand of these were Armenians, most of them not much more than ten years in America, many of them a good many years less. Most of them either worked in vineyards or orchards, or were buying their own. They were doing the same work they had done in Armenia. The interiors of their homes were entirely Armenian, even if the furniture was American.

The customs of the old country, of the region from which a family had come, were maintained. They were maintained *entirely*—that is to say, with the children, too, who also attended the public schools. The language of the home was Armenian. The thinking was, the diet was, the manners were, the work was the same as it had been in the old country, and the landscape, air, water, and light were very much the same as in the old country.

Something new was added to Armenian nature when he discovered that he was considered an inferior human being. On the one hand arrogance, on the other embarrassment, and between the two it is difficult to decide which makes the most difficulty for a man. It was inevitable, though, for any Armenian to be either arrogant or embarrassed—certainly in those years. Later on it was possible for him to be neither, to be indifferent instead, but that needed time.

The years of selling papers in the streets of Fresno were important years, but before I try to say something about them I must remind myself that the purpose of this work is to remember as much as possible of the truth of my early years, and to reveal insofar as such a thing is possible how and why I became who I am.

I shall not altogether succeed, but why should I? Or how could I? Who a man is must always be a theory, and it must always be a tentative one. A soul is an elusive thing. It ought never to be anything else. Still, certain things appear to remain generally constant in every man as long as he breathes. His *mystery* certainly remains generally constant, and so does the body he occupies.

The years of selling papers were important because while I saw the same things other newsboys saw I also saw more, and I saw everything deeply and differently. How do I know this? The fact is I didn't know it at the time. It was only years later that I was able to reason that this must have been so, for none of the others who sold papers ever wrote about it, and I did. Apparently they never believed there was anything in the streets worth writing about, or anything anywhere worth writing about, and I believed there was nothing *not* worth writing about.

My friends who sold papers in Fresno were not any of them interested in becoming writers. They were not interested in assaulting reality in any way with any weapon of any order, and I was.

I wanted the place cleaned up, to begin with. The dirt, debris, disorder, and general derangement of the place annoyed me every day. It is true that after many years of inhabiting the place and of making my own share of the dirt, debris, disorder and derangement I became less annoyed with it. I became in fact rather tolerant of it, and in the end fond of it, but I was never willing to believe I ought to do nothing about it, and I am still not willing to believe that.

The place was a mess and I saw no reason why it shouldn't be a decent place. I longed for every man in the world to get up early every morning and assault the dirt and derangement nearest him. I saw a mere week of this action getting everything straightened out. I did not mean exterior things alone, however. I meant getting things straightened out in a man's own soul. But the first attack had to be upon the place in which his body was more or less situated.

I myself got up early many mornings and put the yard of my house in order. I cut down the stinking weeds with a spade. I leveled the dry earth, I watered the whole place making it smell fresh and clean. As I worked I went over swiftly in my mind what this establishment of order and cleanliness would inevitably lead to, and of course it led to ideas, to the capturing of them in language. And the ideas were, I must say, magnificent. The work was a great joy to me.

But nobody else did his share, and soon the weeds were back again, stinking the same as ever, the earth was dry and dirty again, the good ideas were far away again, and I was unhappy almost to the point of despair again.

The things I saw in the streets astonished me because they persisted, so that I could not pretend they were tentative. Yet that is precisely what I did. I insisted that these things were not permanent because I could not believe they *were* permanent.

What were these things?

I saw that man is a deeply frightened animal whose soul is made to snarl by a multitude of small and enormous, real or remembered fears.

What was he afraid of?

Many things, but most of all of his own kind, including his own father or mother, brother or sister.

The newspapers themselves, which it was my business to sell, were full of accounts of the consequences of this fear: murders, suicides, thefts, adultery, mayhem, arson, false witness, and many other things of sniveling violence or obscene cunning.

Instead of living by truth, it seemed that man lived by deliberate lie, or by the deliberate withholding of truth, or by the deliberate distorting of it.

I saw this in the streets, in the people who were alive in Fresno during the First World War, and I saw it again in the moving pictures at the theatres of Fresno: The Liberty, established during the war; The Bijou; The Strand; The Kinema; The Hippodrome.

I am not ready yet to go into the influence the movies I had on me, but I saw a great many of them, and the action of man in them was no better than it was in the streets of Fresno.

Suicide became so common it was a joke among newsboys, who ridiculed it by referring to it as *Society*. I myself on several occasions shouted the headline *Local Man Commits Society*. I felt, as the other newsboys did, *The hell with the man. The hell with his little farewell note, too.*

These farewell notes always interested me. I didn't find one of them that was better than pathetic. No man did away with himself with dignity, pride, or intelligence. His reasons were always absurd and embarrassing.

I saw them standing and talking quietly, comparing experiences, scheming with one another against others, or even against one another even while they pretended to be friends or two of a kind. I overheard much of their empty and tiresome talk, and I couldn't understand how they could be so unconscious, unstarted, and unaware of who they were and what they were about. They were forever involved in the irrelevant details, or sick.

I myself despised sickness. Whenever it happened to me I felt angry and annoyed, for sickness changed me, changed my pace, halted my travels, belittled my hope. Wearing little clothing even in the winter when I wore across my chest a piece of newspaper or wrapping paper, I was seldom sick. I stayed out in the rain. My clothes became wet, my shoes soft, and yet when I got home I sat down and ate whatever food was on the stove and went to bed and slept.

Once in a while, though, I *did* get sick, and then if I insisted on getting up early in the morning, as I often did, I knew I was not who I had been, who I truly was. I was now aching bones, hot blood, a foul taste in my mouth, a feverish, unrefreshed, unrefreshable intelligence which babbled imbecilities. I sometimes insisted on staying on my feet anyhow, and frequently went to school and fought it out. At first, many times, when I was sick I did not know I was sick, for I could not believe I could ever be different from what I truly was. At last, though, I got around to catching on.

The boredom I knew as a small boy came from wanting to do and be a great deal, and from being able to do and be very little. I wanted, for instance, to do as much as any man who has ever lived has ever wanted do—that is, to change the world and to improve the nature of man, or to restore that nature to its rightful wonder and dignity—whichever was the truth.

Most of the time I felt that man was rightfully wonderful and dignified but had had these profound and powerful aspects of his nature driven out of him by something or other. Upon trying to understand what it was that had driven man away from himself I ran into grave difficulty because it was obvious that neither the climate nor the other animals of the earth had done it.

Therefore, either man himself had driven himself away from his true nature, or his true nature had never been wonderful.

Whichever was most nearly the truth, I wanted him to be wonderful.

I wanted his life—the minutes and years straight through from birth to death—to be easy, joyous, loving and intelligent.

I wanted his death—or his end—to come as a benediction.

I believed all this *could* happen, could be *made* to come to pass, if not in all men in enough of them for an example to be set and a hope to be established.

The example of the life of Christ did not satisfy me, for Christ believed he had been born to be mocked, rejected and crucified, and this belief did not seem to me to be a proper one for anyone but himself. Its end was death, which he preferred to call life everlasting.

I had no way of knowing very much about any life other than the one I (and everybody else) was living, or trying to live, so I didn't think very much of having a great deal of interest in a life after death. I was open-minded about the whole thing, but I felt I ought to wait until I had died before making up my mind about how I would live the new life before me, if there happened to be such a new life before me, and I happened to be, still, myself. I wanted to be wonderful in this life, on this earth, while I lived this life.

The Protestant hymns I heard at the orphanage depressed me. They made life just about the dreariest thing imaginable, and I couldn't relish the idea of having more of the same after I died. I would rather avoid being dreary in the first place and take my chances on the eventual outcome of this.

I remember, for instance, somebody having lived and died, and an evening church service for his immortal soul which I, along with other small boys, attended for some reason or other.

Everybody at the service was dreary. The faces were gray, there was no light in anybody's eyes, and when they fell to singing they broke my heart, bored me and annoyed me until I wished to God I had never been born.

Nearer, My God, to Thee they sang, verse after verse and chorus after chorus, one old woman and one old man after another falling into blubbering, until at last I myself was unable not to heave with a terrible and abstract sorrow, or to keep my eyes from filling with salt and water. I did not blubber, though, for it was a sign of weakness among my friends to cry under any circumstances. I don't remember how it was with Sammy Isaacs or Teddy Dolan or any of the others in the ward for the smaller boys, but I suppose they had all had their little hearts broken, just as I had.

I do remember, though, that I longed desperately to escape from the dreariness of these dry souls, and to make my way without their good and righteous company or their hymn-singing. At the same time I felt sorry for the dead fellow, whoever the hell he was, for I supposed the whole fuss was for him, as of course it must have been, although there appeared to be a gruesome sort of taking of pleasure in it on the part of the others who were, unlike himself, still alive, but miserable about it.

To this day, though, if I happen to hear, or overhear, that hymn, I am instantly plunged into the rage and despair and heaving tearfulness that I knew as a small boy. But my anger, though great, is not as great as it was then, for I had no time to be sympathetic in those days, and I have found time for it in these. In fact, anything spurious which annoys my soul with some sort of sorrow, I both hate and sympathize with as the necessary expression of dreary, undeveloped souls. The nobly tragic, on the other hand, has never moved me to sorrow, or made a fool of me in any other way.

I wanted the human being to be both a human being and something not unlike an angel, for I believed he could be a natural human being and an angel at the same time.

By angel I meant, and mean now, a genius, and by genius I meant, and mean now, a man of ever-unfolding grace, intelligence, and creative power.

I felt that man must make, that he must make ceaselessly, again and again, and that he must by work improve both the thing made and the manner of making it. I could not make material things, for I did not receive refreshment from doing so, but I did for many years *try* to make them, and actually succeeded in making quite a few. Doing so was all right, but the work was too slow for me, and not suitable for my personal nature. I did not believe the man who worked with matter and gave it shape and form and value and made an object of beauty or usefulness out of it was in any way less than myself. I believed merely that the working with matter was not for me, and it wasn't. My material had to be of another order. It had to be swift, so that I could move after it swiftly, capture it swiftly, and give it form and beauty and usefulness swiftly. Otherwise, I would be bored, and I didn't want to be bored.

I was some time, as I've said, discovering that ideas move swiftest in language. One of the reasons for this taking of time was that I had found language itself so difficult. I could not understand it at all. I was the last in a class of relatively simple boys and girls to learn to read very simple sentences. The alphabet, letter by letter, seemed wonderful. Each letter seemed to be a fine design, a kind of meticulously shaped picture, but I just didn't get the connection between the shape of A and a meaning it was said to have. Eventually, though, I learned to read, although I believed for some time that I both wouldn't and didn't need to in order to live my life. Had I never learned to read I am sure I would have lived a rather special sort of life anyway. Even after I *had* learned to read, reading didn't mean very much to me. It was a tiresome chore at school, and I hated school. At last, though, I discovered that reading could be very nearly the greatest adventure of all, and that there was no end of things to be read. I suppose having taken so long to learn to read is partly responsible for my decision to be a writer.

I may say now, at the age of forty-four, that I wanted to write so that I would have something interesting to read, for while everything I read was quite good, some of it wonderful, I believed that I would write better, and so of course it turned out to be.

All of this searching and discovering, which I have put into a few words, took years, but it began early, not knowing where it was going most of the time but having an intense hope for a good destination, so that by the time I was eight, by the time I was selling papers, by the time I was seeing the newspaper press every afternoon after school, and the rolls of paper, by the time I was smelling the ink, I had a feeling that writing was the home of ideas and the work which would be most apt to enable my spirit to move as swiftly as I felt it wanted to.

By the time I was ten I was not by any means anything like a widely-read boy, but I had read a Sunday School paper called *What To Do*, some of the Bible, some of the stuff in the books at school, *The Fresno Evening Herald*, and *The Saturday Evening Post*, which I sold in addition to papers, every Thursday. I believe I was ten when I discovered Dickens, but it may have been when I was nine.

At any rate, it was long before I was nine that it was an established fact at Emerson School that I went about my "language lessons," as they were called, differently from anybody else at the school, and that both my handwriting and my writing itself were better than anybody else's.

In a school competition, it was my letter to Mayor Toomey that was sent to him inviting him to visit the school, which he did. And it was my essay or essay-story on *How I Earned My First Dollar* that impelled Miss Carmichael to keep me after school, not as punishment, but to tell me that I must go to college, no matter what, for I had quite innocently handed in a paper more than twenty times the required length, and one full of characters, general and specific, and prose style.

Alas, however, the boredom did not leave me when I knew writing was to be my work.

If anything, the boredom increased, for I wanted to do much and I was able to do little. I believed, for instance, at thirteen when I owned a typewriter that I could write a book in nine or ten days that would, in fact, change the order of the world and the nature of man, only to discover that what I wanted to say, what I knew I had to say, I *couldn't* say.

The words wanted to come out so quickly and the entire book wanted itself written so quickly that no words at all would come out, or so few and such pathetic ones that I was plunged into profound anger and bitter despair.

My family had always looked upon me as a little mad, and this fooling with a typewriter added to this reputation.

At first I was unwilling to admit that I had bought a typewriter in order to write, for I knew this would have seemed preposterous to my family. I said the typewriter was for business, to help prepare me for a career in business. This seemed reasonable because I had done quite well at the telegraph office. First of all, I was the swiftest messenger in town. My nickname for three years, the whole time I was a messenger, was Speed. Second, while I was still a messenger, I learned to take the Delivery Clerk's desk when he had to do other work, for I had memorized all of the calls that rang out and were printed on the paper tape. And third, I could answer the telephone, understand what I heard, even when the speaker was Chong Jan the wholesale produce man speaking with a Chinese accent, or Sujimoto the dealer in fish speaking with a Japanese accent, or for that matter anybody at all. I had also memorized the various rates of telegrams, and most of the cable rates.

The manager, J. D. Tomlinson, encouraged me to learn. I had picked up typing at Tech High. All that remained for me was to learn telegraphy and a little something about the duties of a Wire Chief in order to be able to do every kind of work anybody could do in a telegraph office. I went out several times when I was off duty with the linemen, but that was sport. I went for the ride and to watch how they got a fallen pole back up and broken wires restored.

My work in the telegraph office was important, but I wanted to write. I took a certain understandable pride in my effectiveness around the place, but it wasn't anything at all like what I wanted to do—it was a means to an end. The fifteen dollars a week that I earned my family needed urgently, but I wasn't after money or achievement in the business world at all. I permitted myself to pretend that I was, however, because I didn't dare tell my family that I had made up my mind to be a writer.

In time, though, the news got out, and just as I expected I was now considered entirely mad. One of my uncles pointed out that men were trained in writing at Yale, Harvard, and Princeton, and still had difficulty writing. What chance did I have? He was so reasonable in his argument that he had me worried for about three minutes. That was all the time I needed to remember that I did not intend to write as anybody anywhere had ever before written, let alone a few sons of well-to-do business men who had gone to Harvard, Yale, and Princeton.

I was selling papers when Oliver Twist broke my heart. I came home from the streets every night, ate an enormous supper, generally of sour cabbage soup, and then I sat at the table in the dining room and went on reading about Oliver. When he fell into the hands of Fagin I actually wept, and yet my own life, from day to day, was not much better than his, and the town in which I was trying to live was certainly less encouraging than London. Furthermore, there was no doubt about my birth, and no chance at all that I would suddenly be received into the circle of a very wealthy and cultured family. I knew who the Saroyans were in Fresno, for I had met them all, and they were nothing I could expect very much from. If anything, they expected something from me, and I did not feel that they were unfair or mistaken in this.

My mother's mother Lucy was forever encouraging me to move through life with what she called "guyrot," which is a phonetic rendering of an Armenian word, or a word of Bitlis, or a word of the Saroyan family, or a word invented by my grandmother herself, which signified, apparently, these things: to assault the world with early-morning swiftness and clarity of mind, with planning, with zest, with brilliance, with cunning, with eagerness and with skill.

"A man without guyrot," Lucy frequently said, "is dead. Even while he lives he is dead."

I understood the word without requiring a definition, and I believed her, for what she believed happened to coincide with what I myself believed.

She was always pleased when she heard of my success selling papers. I frequently brought home a dollar in small change, sometimes two or three. I worked with the circus when the circus came to town, on the principle that even though my pay was free admission it was better to work than not to, if work was available. I worked at the County Fairs, selling soda pop, and sometimes made as much as ten dollars in one day, or one evening. I worked on Raisin Day, selling flags and pennants and other things, and often made as much as I made at the County Fairs. One Raisin Day I got the Benham Ice Cream Company to set up a stand for me, and to give me ice cream on credit, and before the celebration was over I myself had made almost a hundred dollars and every one of my cousins, working two or three hours each, had stolen anywhere from five to fifty dollars. I engaged in all of this business not because I wanted to make business a career, but because there was nothing better to do at the time, because it was a challenge, because the family and I needed the money, and because I believed it was important for me to be doing—*anything*, until I could get around to what I really wanted to do.

But the boredom would not end, no matter what I did, no matter how effective I was at picking up a few dollars at this little job or that. I needed to be bored in order to become the writer I have become, I suppose, but I didn't like it at the time at all, and I wondered when I would be able to do precisely what I wanted to do.

I wanted a lot of things, some simple, some complex, but altogether they were one thing.

It is said by those who have examined the human soul most thoroughly and observed its ways most steadily and carefully that love is what everybody wants, but love is an enormous word, synonymous with other enormous words, like God. One wants to love and one wants to be loved. Ordinarily, it is understood by this that one wants to love another, or other, human beings, or to be loved by another, or other, human beings. It is probable, though, that there is more to it than that. One also wants to love and be loved by the measureless universe and by its secret and unknown laws or graces, by the sun and the moon and the stars, by the earth itself and its vegetation, the world and its form and way, the animals and the birds, and by a man's own ancestors or the ancestors of all men—in short, by the loving which is in all matter and energy. One wants love of luck and mystery, of chance and secret, of risk and art. And so on.

One loves another, or other, human beings because his love for them increases his love for the other things and their love for him, or because other human beings embody for him all or most of the other things, and bring some of the love out of these things to him. That is why love is a troublesome and wonderful thing, for it is sent forth out of a body and received into it, and a body is a variable thing, tentative, inconstant, inconsistent, by turns refreshed and joyously loving, weary and wearily loving, or not loving at all, even hating.

Man is more than an occupant of a body, but he is also that, and that cannot be dismissed or forgotten. He is his most when he is least body-occupant, but he is never delivered entirely from it. Or he is his most when the appetites of his body are controlled and few.

My body and I myself hungered for and even lusted after many things, each of these things being part of the others, all of them together being one thing: the realization of myself as a living and working creature of a high order. I hungered for these things with intense desire. I wanted water, light, air, and good things to smell as I breathed—water, grass, foliage, blossoms, fruit, earth. I wanted to eat watermelons, figs, apricots, peaches, grapes, apples, pears, casabas, oranges, berries, almonds, walnuts, and all the other good things that grew in the earth of Fresno, and I ate these things. There were unusual things that I ate, also: loquats, nectarines, persimmons. I wanted tomatoes, bell peppers, cucumbers, all to be eaten straight from the plant. I wanted bread of all kinds, and the white cheese which is the cheese of the Armenians, plain or filled with greens of various kinds, new or aged in the earth. And then I wanted water. After everything I wanted water.

I wanted meat, hot and red from off a spear held over a fire; or cooked in a pot with cabbage, okra, string beans, bell peppers, tomatoes, eggplant; or ground and mixed with cracked wheat and stuffed into tomatoes, cucumbers, squash, long thin eggplants, bell peppers, or made into a meat ball stuffed with fried onions, herbs, and pomegranate seeds. I wanted meat roasted and greasy, with white rice, or with the rice of cracked wheat. I wanted the sour milk of the Armenians, called by them matzoon, by others yogurt, to eat by itself, or to put on stuffed cabbage, or to mix with cold cucumbers and chopped mint, to eat with the crisp flat white bread of the Armenians. I wanted my food with garlic, for then my thirst was greater than ever, and the water of Fresno was good.

I wanted grape leaves wrapped around ground meat mixed with rice and herbs. I wanted meat stewed with vegetables and dried apricots. I wanted all of the dishes made of cereals and lentils, with or without meat. I wanted to eat, and I ate, and afterwards I drank water. I drank it for hours after every big meal. I went back and forth from the faucet in the kitchen to where I was reading, and I turned on the faucet and drank, or I filled a glass and drank, filled it again, and drank, and again.

I wanted to eat because it was a joy to eat. My body felt wonderful while I ate and even more wonderful after I had eaten, and it loved the water I drank. And I lived and believed in it. My body loved the things that were for eating, and so did I myself, so did my soul, my heart, my intelligence. The resourceful poor do not know what it is to go hungry if the time is not a time of famine, or unless there is no money at all, and we saw to it in my family that there was always money enough for food, for it was necessary for all of us to satisfy the hunger of our bodies. If we could not afford one kind of food, we ate a great deal of a kind we *could* afford, and we did remarkable things with the foods which were least expensive. We were always able to afford flour from which we made all kinds of bread; rice which was cooked a dozen different ways; cracked wheat which went into many kinds of dishes; vegetables; fruit; grape leaves, which were obtained merely by going to the vineyard of a friend and taking as many of the young green leaves as we wished. The leaves were placed a moment in boiling water and then put away in jars, so that they would see us through until the arrival of the new leaves the following year.

But to eat is not enough. To give the body pleasure is not nearly enough. To eat and fight, as my mother put it, was not enough. My brother and I invariably got up from enormous meals and wrestled in the backyard, half in fun, half in earnest.

Where we lived was always all right because once we had fallen on a place it was ours, and ours was always the same, the appearance of the house made no difference. Inside the house was our lives, and our way of life—the half-dozen cane chairs with the rattan seats, the two plain rockers, and the round dining room table which my father had managed to leave us; the sofa made of two or three apple boxes and a board, covered with a rough woven cloth from Bitlis, red and white squares alternating; the metal beds with a mattress on a spring and quilts made of the beaten wool of the sheep of Armenia.

Once a year my mother and my sisters took every blanket apart, placed the wool on newspapers in the sunlight of the backyard, sat and beat the wool with a switch for hours, until it was light and fresh and soft again. The sheets and covers were laundered, dried, ironed, and then sewed together again, and the beaten wool spread into them, making the warmest blanket I have ever known. The blankets *had* to be warm, for the house was heated only by the kitchen stove, and the winters were cold. Now and then the kerosene heater was lighted, but everybody disliked the smell that came from it, and it never flourished in any house we ever lived in. The rooms we slept in were cold all winter, but under the Armenian blankets we were warm. The roof of the house leaked in half a dozen places. We placed cooking pots under the leaks, and every now and then my brother or I got up in the night to empty one which had become almost full, or to put a small one under a small leak, and a larger one under a larger leak. Sometimes we slept through the night, so that in the morning there was a pool in the living room and another in the dining room. My mother and my sisters went to work saving the worn rug, and my brother sat down to write a letter to the landlord.

Most of all I wanted the things which are not of matter made, but in order to get them I needed to survive, and I enjoyed the business of surviving.

Chapter Three
The Fire

Fresno was proud of its Fire Department. The Main Station was on Van Ness Avenue, four blocks from the Saroyan house on San Benito. The name of its finest, biggest, brightest, reddest engine was America–La France. In the Raisin Day Parades the Fire Department displayed the America–La France, most of its other engines, and a great many of its men, for it was a tradition that nobody would set fire to anything on Raisin Day.

The Fire Department did a great deal of showing-off. There were many practice alarms, most of them full, so that the department's entire equipment raced from each of the three stations to the place involved. There the men went to work as if something were actually on fire, while hundreds of people watched.

When there were fires where the city had not yet placed water pipes and hydrants, the Fire Department employed a system of pumping water out of irrigation ditches, but this system was never effective, as the pressure was never enough to make a difference. These fires ended when the fire burned itself out. Frequently the fire was a farmer's house, but now and then it was a warehouse, a packing house, a country store, a school, or a church.

A fire was the best public entertainment the city had. If the place that was burning belonged to anybody excepting an American, an immediate investigation began concerning the origin of the fire, for it was exciting to discover that a man had set fire to his own home or place of business. The fireside gossip was always the same—the place was insured, the owner had set fire to it. There was never any doubt about it. The Americans, knowing they were above suspicion, must have seen the practicality of arson. They certainly gave the foreigners a great deal of free entertainment. The foreigners, on the other hand, were terrified of the public attitude toward them and fire, so that they were forever cleaning up around their homes and places of business, and forever fretful that they might be involved in a fire scandal. Still their houses and places of business sometimes caught fire. Once the fire was started a man knew he was in for a great deal of suspicion. He might in fact never live it down, and he might never again be able to obtain fire insurance.

Finally, many of the foreigners began to set fire to their well-insured properties, since popular gossip and suspicion had it that they were doing so anyway. Almost none of them was ever actually tried for arson, but every foreigner who had had a fire was automatically suspected, and a great deal of looking for evidence of arson went on.

A fire in Chinatown was always more exciting than a fire anywhere else. The Police and Fire Departments had little luck pinning anything on anybody there because the Chinese understood and spoke almost no English. And there were always a great many of them attached to a small, place, sometimes as many as thirty. Nobody knew who to question among the people gathered together to watch the burning of a house. In addition to those who had lived in the house would be hundreds of neighbors, all of them standing quietly together earnestly watching the house go up in beautiful flames and feeling the tender and cleansing warmth of it. Now and then a small man would be picked out of the crowd and pushed away to a place for questioning, but nothing ever came of it. The man merely protested in Chinese that he had been afraid to strike a match ever since he had taken up residence in Chinatown.

I went to as many fires as possible, and I saw many of them in Chinatown. The witnesses of a fire interested me as much as the fire itself, and I seldom saw a crowd of Chinese watching a fire in which it was not necessary to notice in the eyes of them that each of them could say a great deal about the origin of the fire if only he were able to express himself in concise English, or if only there were any point in doing so. They were experts in matters of fire and firecrackers. They never wept or grew excited at a fire. Even the children stood with their parents in dignified composure, admiring the spectacle and the dramatic actions of the Police and Fire Departments.

In the end, it was impossible to know if a fire had happened by itself or if it had been encouraged to happen. The fire itself, though, while it lasted, was always beautiful, and the fire-lovers were always grateful to the accident or skill which had started it. The best fires were the night ones, for only in the dark may flames be clearly observed and deeply appreciated. The sirens and bells of the fire engines were loud, so that anybody who might be asleep would be awakened by them, and if the fire seemed reasonably near many people got up, quickly put on their clothes, and fell in with others on their way to it.

There was an Armenian living in my neighborhood named Aspadour who never appeared in the streets unless he was impeccably dressed, for he was employed at Gottschalks in men's clothing, and he liked to set a good example. He wore everything it was possible to wear: cuff links, stick-pin, watch-and-chain across the vest, and perhaps other little odds and ends that took time and trouble to get in place.

One night in November I woke up and heard the commotion of the Fire Department in the nearby streets. My brother was already getting into his clothes, and my uncle Aram, who was in town for a few days from the Law School at the University of Southern California, was already dressed. His red Apperson was in front of the house. He himself was on the front porch watching the brightly lit sky above the fire, which appeared to be somewhere in the vicinity beyond the California Playgrounds. My mother and sisters, who were not going to the fire, were standing in their bare feet on the back porch, admiring the enormity and brightness of the fire.

My uncle took my brother and me to the fire, which turned out to be the packing house of an American who had just had a disastrous season. The place was beyond the water zone of the city and near no irrigation ditch, so that the fire had to be permitted to burn itself out. The time was a little before two in the morning. When we reached the fire only the Fire Department and a half-dozen private cars were there, but in a matter of ten minutes hundreds of people arrived in cars, and many hundreds more began to arrive on bicycles, motorcycles, and foot. An Assyrian popcorn man arrived in his motor-driven wagon and began to do excellent business. The fire was beautiful, for it was a magnificent night, clear and cold, and nobody was able to do anything to interfere with the fire. It continued beautifully a full hour, then began to die down, and around four in the morning when it was as good as over my uncle decided to take us home. When we reached our door the well-dressed Armenian who worked at Gottschalks came down the street on his way to the fire. There was nothing more than a faint glow in the sky now to guide him. My uncle waited for him to reach our house, and so did my brother and I. The man had bathed, shaved, and put on fresh clothes. He looked absolutely immaculate.

"Aram," he said, "where is the fire?"

My uncle Aram brought a match out of his pocket and struck it on the bottom of his shoe. He held the lighted match out to the man and said, "For *you*, who must dress for a fire, here is the fire. Now, go home and take off your clothes and go back to bed."

Years later he said of the man, "I don't know what kind of an Armenian he can possibly be. I doubt very much if he's an Armenian at all."

The fires of Fresno were an exciting and wonderful part of my years there, the years from the time I was eight to the time I was eighteen.

At the orphanage fires were made on summer nights, sometimes in the hills, sometimes on the grounds of the orphanage itself. There was always an abundance of twigs and branches for these fires whether they were in the hills or on the orphanage grounds. The fires were big and they went on for a long time. Before they died down everybody would be back in his own dormitory, or bed, the smaller children being the first to go. While the fire was new and high there was singing. Afterwards somebody would tell stories. I remember listening to singing three or four times, and I remember having heard a man begin to tell a story. I fell asleep while he was telling it, so I can't say much about it. The fire itself was the important thing, in any case. My brother Henry always stayed beside me at the fires, and the night I fell asleep I suppose it was Henry who got me to bed without waking me up. The songs that were sung were not all of them religious or at any rate church songs, although there were always a couple of these in the program. Sometimes the songs were lively and amusing, sung for the fun of it, such as *Yankee Doodle.* I still remember

> My bonnie lies over the ocean,
> My bonnie lies over the sea,
> My bonnie lies over the ocean,
> Oh, bring back my bonnie to me.

I remember also a rollicking song the boys had taken over about, *Sailing, sailing, over the bounding main.* The boys had it over Niagara Falls, with Captain Dick losing something and the fish going off with something else, all in perfect rhyme. *At the Cross* the boys revised so that it was *At the bar, at the bar, where I smoked my last cigar, and the nickels and the dimes rolled away, rolled away. It was there by chance I tore my Sunday pants,* and so on. These words were sung in secret while the others sang the proper ones, the boys having themselves a grand time of controlled gayety. The girls liked something that went *I don't want to play in your yard; I don't like you any more. You'll be sorry when you see me sliding down our cellar door,* and so on. They also liked, *My mother bought me a rubber dolly,* but I have forgotten how that one resolved itself. But I haven't forgotten *When you wake up in the morning and you find your bed is wet, blame the baby, blame the baby,* and so on.

The fires and the songs I remember together, for they happened together, *Oh, the moonlight's fair tonight along the Wabash. From the fields there comes the scent of new-mown hay. Through the sycamores the candle-lights are gleaming, On the banks of the Wabash far away.*

All was far away in fact: my bonnie, the Wabash, the bar where he smoked his last cigar, Niagara Falls, and the girls and women of the songs. The war was faraway, but watching the flames of the fire, breathing the warm evening scent of wood, sap and smoke, I seemed to see where the war had been, where *Tramp, tramp, tramp the boys are marching,* or where they were *Tenting tonight, tenting tonight, tenting on the old camp grounds.* And I used to feel, *Many are the hearts that are weary tonight, tenting on the old camp grounds.*

In the light of the fire the boys and girls seemed dreamy and far away, and no one knew who it was that was singing most or best. Nor was anyone shy or ashamed, for the center of attraction was the fire itself. The big thing was the concert of flames and the song of the fire itself. Nothing else and no one else mattered. Around the fire everybody was no better and no worse than anybody else, and the fire was everything. To the orphans, the boys and girls, the three-year-olds or the thirteen-year-olds, the half-orphans or the full-orphans, the orphans by abandonment, divorce, insanity, murder or suicide, the fire was home, father and mother, light and warmth, secret joy and sorrow, the flames making the wood crack and speak, whistle, hum, sing, every boy and girl near the brightest, warmest and most wonderful Mother and Father of all. Many were the girls who wept softly in the midst of a song, and many were the ones who put their arms around the weeping ones and went on singing. I saw it happen again and again, and I saw the boys give over to speaking softly to one another in earnestness and understanding, for while they were all supposed to be Christians, they were most deeply and personally near something they loved and needed when they were near the fire. They may not have worshipped it, but they were never better than when they sat around it together and sang, and they were never more hopeful about themselves and their friends.

Small fires broke out here and there at the orphanage, some of them accidental, some of them deliberate. A boy of eleven tried to burn down the Administration Building, but the fire was put out before it had consumed much more than half the steps going up to the porch. Dry weed fires were common, but they were put out in no time in a kind of wild celebration. The older boys would fall upon the racing line of fire with wet burlap sacks and beat it to death, shouting and kidding around and every now and then giving a friend a whack with the wet sack. The Laundry caught fire a couple of times in different places, but the fire was never permitted to get very far. The very boys who put it out always stood around regretting their success, for they hated the Laundry, hating their turn working in it, and in fact would have rejoiced had the whole orphanage burned down.

It was against the rules of the orphanage for any boy to make a fire in the hills, but very nearly every boy over eight broke the rule every time he was in the hills. For a man in this world and life must make his own fire; it is his declaration of freedom to do so, whether by day or by night, whether for heat, company, or the cooking of food. All of the older boys had two or three slingshots, and they all carried a great many smooth pebbles. In the hills they aimed their slingshots at birds, and many of them were fairly accurate, so that there would often be doves, quail, or even wild pigeons to be roasted. One or two boys were not above snaring a chicken or a duck that had wandered away from where it belonged. Almost every boy had a pocket-knife (also against the rules) which he kept in a secret place, and they all seemed to know how to clean a bird and what portions of its insides were good to roast and eat. They roasted acorns and hazelnuts over the fires, too, and potatoes and onions pilfered from the orphanage storagehouse. Their excursions into the hills were official, they were accompanied by a Matron or by one of the visiting members of the Board of Directors, but they always managed to see that a certain number of their fellows, taking turns, got lost for an hour or two. These lucky fellows raced off to hunt and roast anything they were able to bring down or snare.

In Fresno—but this was before the orphanage days, when I was under three—we lived in a house with a backyard in which one night I saw a very big fire that had not been planned. My uncle Aram came out of the house quickly, still playing the violin, as he had been playing it in the house, stepped on the fire, put it out, and went back into the house, where he concluded the solo, which was *O Sole Mio*. I have never been able to forget that. The fire was swift, unexpected, and magnificent, and the way my uncle put it out—that is, while playing the violin—seemed to me to be just about the most stylish thing I have ever seen, as I am sure it actually was. Thus, the music of the violin has always been associated in my thinking with fire, which I loved so much from the beginning that it brought me—as it did my son thirty-seven years later—my first profoundly painful experience, the scars still on the thumb and forefinger of my left hand. I watched the flames inside a kerosene burner and then reached out to grasp them, and of course burned my fingers on the porcelain frame of the burner. My son, doing the same thing, burned his fingers on an old-fashioned lamp one night in San Francisco when he was two. And so it goes with fire, and with those who love it.

The theory at the orphanage was that a boy who was not good would burn in hell forever when he died. A lot of boys who had not been good and who had died had been burning in hell for some time. The theory was intended to scare a boy into being good, but I don't think it ever scared any of them into that. I'm sure it scared a great many boys into something or other, but I was never one of them. I rather liked the idea of being involved in fire forever. I don't think fear can make anybody good, or different, or improved, or bring out the best in him. Fear is natural, but fear of punishment, of hell, of being one's self eternally consumed by a personal fire is not natural, it is all artistic fear, and the order of the art involved is inferior.

I loved fire. I loved the flame of a match. I loved the sun, sunrise, sunset, and high noon. I loved the gold, yellow, blue, and red of flames. I loved heat. And I was not afraid of hell. It never occurred to me that the theory was more than an artistic one. I felt sure it must be a bit of pretending. If not, I would have to take my chances on fearlessly living a good life for the simple reason that it was in order for me to do so, or because I had no choice. I didn't believe it was my nature to live a bad life. I felt no desire to do so and I *did* feel a great desire to live a good one. If my idea of a good life didn't happen to be acceptable to Judgment, then of course I would live what I *believed* to be a good life just the same. Good or bad I would live, and find out more and more about good and bad.

I never knew personal fear of fire, hell, or punishment.

But I *did* know the reward that came of *awareness* of form, of the *achievement* of it, and even of the *hope* of achieving it.

How does a boy of three or four know of form? How does he know of style? Grace? Truth? How can he know of such things? It is quite simple. These things are known by instinct because a man is here out of many others who were here and his very being remembers (however it may be) something of everything *they* knew. They knew, between them, a great deal. I remember quite clearly that I sought form and style from the beginning. I had no choice. It was natural and inevitable. I was glad when I moved through time in order and on schedule and with pleasure, and I was annoyed when I didn't and I frequently didn't. In fact, most of the time I didn't.

If I didn't fear hell, I *did* love God, whoever or whatever God was. It was and is my nature to love, and what is easier than to love the greatest idea of all, the most-loving of all ideas? I thought for a number of years of God as an old man with a beard. I believed he knew of me, both because I was who I was, because I was alive, because I loved him, and also because I had heard that he loved every living thing.

I sensed that he was not only near at all times, as I'd heard, but also inside of me. I seemed to feel that he was.

As the years went by, I found that I needed to love things and persons which were not of God (of form, grace, and truth). I found that it was not enough to love that which attracted love, or compelled it. I found that I personally must love that which was not of love made, which did not compel or attract it. For what good is love if it is involved only in itself? Is it in fact love at all? I have never altogether delivered myself from hate, but I think I have come as near to this deliverance as any man I have ever heard of. It came to pass as the years went by and I survived that I saw the need to know more about anything or anybody I believed I hated, and as I imagined or found out more about him I felt the hatred slip out of my soul. All I needed to find out about human beings was that they *were* in fact human beings. This was not an act of finding out so much as an act of simple recognition. How could I hate anybody who was precisely the same as myself and the same as everybody else? I could not hate him. I could regret the manner in which he was a human being, but I could not hate him, for that was spiritual illiteracy, that was failure to read the human soul.

Sitting around the summer fires at the orphanage was the nearest I came in childhood to religious meditation. My thinking did not necessarily happen in my head. It happened all over, the fire itself compelling it, compelling grace, love, warmth, hope, imagination or memory, which are in essence either the same thing or aspects of the same thing. I sat and watched and listened and dreamed. Now and then I looked up and saw the sky splattered with stars. The heavens of childhood seem to have had more stars, brighter stars, nearer stars, and these too seemed to burn and make light. The fireside singing of the orphans was in celebration of beauty, truth, hope and love, no matter what the song happened to be. The arrangement was entirely sensible and satisfying, a large fire at the center of a large circle of boys and girls, all of them home, with friends, deeply alone and true, near memory and love.

If the fire reminded some of them of hell, of the punishment of hell, it didn't seem to spoil the fire itself, the circle, or the singing. I suppose some of the eyes fixed on the heart of the fire knew terror and fear. I remember hearing a visiting minister point out that our fire was like unto a drop of water to an ocean in comparison with the fire of hell, and I remember not caring about that at all.

The fire made light, it made heat, it soothed and encouraged memory and imagination. The light and heat bathed both the body and the soul in a liquid of love, relaxing nerves and muscles, smoothing out the lines of anxiety in the face, so that soon every boy and girl had no reason to pretend anything about himself, or to be watchful of others, or to be fearful of them, or to feel the need to strain at any business of enduring. Voices grew softer around the fire. Eyes became brighter, gentler, more earnest, more loving, more tender, more humorous. Hands ceased to be imminent weapons of offense or defense and became forms of grace and kindness, whether scratched, the nails bitten, or covered with warts.

If there was to be an evening fire the whole orphanage would come to special life in the morning. The older boys and girls would go off to gather twigs and bark, leaves and logs. They would arrange these things with great care and balance. Everybody would go to where the fire was being prepared to notice the work and to guess at the enormity of the fire once darkness had fallen and the fire had been started.

In the house on North Rodeo, on the occasion of his eighth birthday, my son said very softly, "What I would like most of all is a fire."

I believed I hadn't heard him correctly, so I said, "A *what?*"

"Fire."

"Where?'"

"In the fireplace."

"When?"

"Tonight. Because I'm eight years old now," he said.

He and I set the fire up in the large fireplace in the large living room, in the dark, and then he lighted it and the fire began, his sister watching with love and excitement, his mother coming in to sit and watch. Soon my son was singing and my daughter was dancing. I sat and watched them and the fire, the fire that was in themselves, in their singing and dancing. My son sang the songs he remembered from his earliest years. *O, Lord, you know I have no friend like you. If heaven's not my home, Oh, Lord, what will I do? Let the lower lights be burning, send a gleam across the wave. Some poor fainting, struggling seaman you may rescue, you may save.* And many others, including several in Armenian, the words of which he had committed to memory without knowing their meaning. My daughter sang three songs which she invented on the spot. They were beautiful songs, songs of fire, woman's songs. The father and the mother of this man and this woman sat before the fire and watched the strangers and listened to them.

Fire's form is rooted in matter, but the burning bush was not consumed by the flames Moses saw. The voice was in the fire and Moses heard the voice: fire and language, fire and communication, fire consuming matter, decorating it.

My son when he was not yet three marveled at the winter evening fire, and stood desolate in the morning before the cold gray ashes.

They were putting up chain-belt houses all over the sand dunes of San Francisco in those days and his greatest joy was to go to where these houses were being built and to gather pieces of wood for the fire. The builders themselves burned these pieces when a house or a group of them had been finished. Even so, my son always went to work swiftly, as if taking the pieces of wood was stealing. He looked around as he worked and noticed things with special importance—a small dog far down the streets, two route carriers standing and talking, two or three sea gulls flying overhead. He heard automobile horns and streetcar bells and wanted to know if they had any special meaning, any connection with his taking of the wood. Once a workingman himself appeared from somewhere within a half-finished house while my son and I were gathering wood and my son stood with his arms loaded with the wood, waiting to know what was to happen. The man and I chatted a moment and then the man went walking down the street. My son spoke about the man for weeks.

"He doesn't want the wood," he said. "Why doesn't he want the wood? Why doesn't he take it home and burn it? Hasn't he got a fireplace?"

The pieces were handsome to see, to hold, to arrange for a fire. They could be arranged in a manner that suggested a group of houses or part of a city. My son noticed this and delighted in it. He sat and watched the burning of the fire-city, sometimes singing, sometimes silent. As the city made of blocks of wood was consumed by the fire my son considered many things which he soon forgot, as I have forgotten the things I considered when I watched the fires at the orphanage.

As much as water, fire is the beginning, and more than water it is the end. For the final consumption of the matter of man must be in fire, in the Word, articulated or not.

A writer writes of matter being consumed by time or by the fire of time. Thus, fire itself is always close to form and style, so that if he would achieve either, he must know fire, and ought to love it.

Across the alley from the house on San Benito Avenue was a widow with three sons and two daughters. Her last-born was a son who came alive into the world in a twisted body, and went out of it in flames at the age of three. The woman had got up before dawn to set her house in order, to get breakfast for her children, and then to go to work at Guggenheim's Packing House. The little boy followed her around as she tried to start the fire in the wood-burning stove. When the fire began to die she poured coal oil out of a gallon can into a cup, tripped over the boy, flung the explosive fuel over the boy and the fire, and saw the boy in flames before she had gotten to her feet.

He was wrapped in blankets but died an hour later, at dawn, in a chaos of noise, astonishment, anguish, regret, and pain. The house was surrounded by neighbors, among them myself.

My heart was filled with hatred for bad luck, miserable accidents, heart-breaking mistakes, the perils of poverty.

But I never hated fire itself.

For days, for years in fact, I thought about the boy who was consumed by fire and I remembered the hushed anger of his mother long after his death, years after, when she visited my mother and they sat and talked and drank coffee. She was an Assyrian woman who spoke so little Armenian that she and my mother spoke in English, or at any rate tried to.

"My fault," the woman said. "Why I must hurry? To get to packing house? To get few pennies?"

The water took many lives every year, many more than fire, but it was not possible to hate the water because human lives had ended in it.

I once saw a small boy at the bottom of a shallow irrigation ditch, a boy older than myself, ten or eleven. I saw him limp in the arms of a young doctor who tried to bring him back to life, and failed.

Death was all around—in fire, in water, in mystery, in accident, error, ignorance. It was ugly and it infuriated my soul.

I saw it frustrated but even then I was infuriated.

A pal of mine, eight or nine at the time, had found a carton full of shredded paper used in the packing and shipping of crockery or glassware. He had tied this paper around his legs, so that it would seem that he was wearing the chaps of a cowboy. Tom Mix, Harold Lockwood, Dustin Farnum, and other cowboy-actors were the movie favorites of the town's boys. The boy in the paper chaps was admired by his friends, and then one of them, surely as a joke, lighted a match and put it to the paper of the chaps. In an instant the boy was on fire and running.

Jim Lundy himself, seventeen years old, on his way to work at Graf's Hardware, caught up with him, stopped him abruptly, and put out the fire with his hands.

The thing that is most memorable and even a little astonishing about the episode is that when the burning boy began to run the other boys laughed and ran with him. Their laughter was innocent, or at any rate ignorant, but when they heard his screams they stopped laughing and looked for help.

Jim Lundy was the neighborhood hero. It was a good thing for everybody that he happened to be around. He was an all-around athlete, and knew more about track, baseball, basketball, swimming, and gymnastics than anybody else in town. He caught the running fire, put it out, and carried the boy to his terrified mother and father. He tore off the boy's clothes and told the father to get olive oil all over the boy's body as quickly as possible. He then went into the grocer's next door and telephoned for an ambulance. Then he went on to Graf's. He didn't bawl out any of the boys for what had happened, but a week or so later when they stopped him in the empty lot next to my house on his way home from work to ask him a question about baseball he told them a few things about imbecility and fire, too. The two don't go together, he said.

Power goes with genius only.

A writer's style, his achievement of personal language, his employment of form comes from many things with disaster and death as much a part of them as grace and life. A writer cannot hate fire because it sometimes burns a man, or water because it sometimes strangles him. He must hate the ignorance which put fire and water to killing, and it is the same with any other great power come to pass.

My childhood and my boyhood were full of fun. Every day was an adventure, a new chance to draw nearer to that great state of health which approximates immortality, when the senses are so finely alive that a man in his body is altogether a part of everything which is alive, everything which has ever been alive, the whole breathing universe, the whole miraculous secret of matter, light, heat, time.

I was a whistling boy, a singing boy, a laughing boy, a shouting, running, excited, delighted boy. I was also a brooding, miserable, angry, discontented, bitter, bored, lonely, unhappy one. I was both, and frequently simultaneously. I remember exulting in the fun of swimming at Thompson Ditch, at the headgate there, and then after swimming I remember sitting with my friends on the hot earth of the pasture bordering the ditch, in the wonderful light and heat of the August sun, and being miserable about my own impermanence, insignificance, meaninglessness, and feebleness.

Power and effectiveness I longed for and never stopped longing for, but man's power, while seldom fully achieved by anybody, *is* limited, and his greatest effectiveness brings to pass no authentic marvels or miracles. He can be powerful, but only insofar as the nature of the animal he is will permit him to be. He can do quite effectively the things he is able to do at all, but these things are not remarkable or wonderful things. A man cannot walk upon water, and as a boy I believed he ought to be able to do so if he wished to do so. A man cannot take a dead body and restore it to life. A man cannot write a poem or a story that will transform the whole nature of man, his reality and his truth, making them greater and nobler. A man must take days and days to write a book and after he has done so, the book makes no difference. It changes nothing. It works no miracles.

Still, I took my stand. I would try. I would keep trying. My work was writing. I would believe in the importance of writing. I would believe that my engaging in this work *would* make a difference, first to myself, and then to everybody, if not to everything. I would be simultaneously the occupant of a small, insignificant body and an inhabitant of the enormous and unknown universe. I would live my short time and I would try to live forever. I would eat and sleep and work and establish my own family and die, but at the same time I would never be more of a body than a spirit.

The foolishness of my writing in comparison with what I wanted to write infuriated me for years. Greatness, greatness, greatness is what I wanted and insisted upon, only to notice that everything I wrote was small and miserable. I couldn't understand it. My soul *was* great, it was astonishingly great, and yet it was captured in a little, feeble body and could not get itself free. I had in my soul the greatest truths to tell, but when I came to the work of telling them I couldn't do it. I couldn't find a starting place. I couldn't work as I wished to work. The very eagerness with which I went to work and the very enormity of the size of what I expected to achieve stopped me entirely, so that I was not able to put down, often, so much as one word, but sat and stared at the blank paper, rejecting one beginning after another. Where could I begin?

I was long years discovering the secret that it does not matter at all where one begins, and that it is not necessary for anything one writes to be instantly great, the important thing is for a man to resign himself to the truth that he is only a man, and to work, and then to find in the rare moments of luck the greatness which is not his alone, the greatness which comes to pass when he, out of faith and plain labor, excels himself, his body and his soul, and becomes for an instant a part of enormity, of limitless power, of miracle, and of timelessness.

How shall a man lose the sun? How shall he forget fire? I have always loved the sun. I have always loved fire. One of my earliest published stories is called "The Fire." It is somewhere in the book named *Inhale and Exhale*. The sun figures in all of my writing. For years I had a favorite title, to which I hoped to add a fine work of writing: *Fire in the Opera House*. So far I have not written this work.

The fire I had in mind was the fire of art. The opera house, as such, was obsolete, a thing of the past, but California had buildings which had been opera houses and nothing else, and I heard of them and saw some of them. They were silent by then and out of style, falling to pieces, so the fire was also the fire of memory. Since the buildings were old and made of wood, the fire was also fire itself, pure and simple, art in flames, being consumed by the memory of song.

Shah-Mouradian sang like fire and lived like it. I heard him only on phonograph records, saw only photographs of him, even though he visited Fresno at least once while I was there. His last recital was at the Civic Auditorium in Fresno, the year before he died in Paris, 1928 or 1929. At any rate, I wasn't in Fresno at that time. I heard about the recital, though.

His voice broke, he couldn't remember the words of songs he had been singing for years, he was irritable, he shouted at the musicians, he rebuked the audience.

His death came before he was fifty. I still listen to his singing on records, and he remains as far as I am concerned one of the great singers. He sang for a time in opera in Paris, but the music of opera was not for him. He was a singer of the songs of Armenia. His voice was as rich and deep and powerful as fire itself. He was a simple boy, born to simple parents in the city of Moush, one of the trinity cities of Armenia near Lake Van: Bitlis, Moush, and Van.

During the years of my apprenticeship I listened to his voice almost every day. If I listened to the phonograph at all I listened also to the voice of Shah-Mouradian. He was the greatest Armenian I had ever heard about. When he sang the nation lived, and the soul of it burned and made light. His singing was melancholy, angry, lonely, proud, tender.

His last recital in Fresno broke the hearts of the Armenians who were not annoyed with him, as many of them were. His falling into forgetfulness, irritation, and failure stunned and astonished them, for to everyone who had ever heard him he was the carrier of the fire of the Armenian soul, and they saw that the fire was dying out.

My father's brother could barely express the pain and grief he felt when he saw Shah-Mouradian fail.

"I was sick," he said. "I could not sleep all night."

My mother's brother said, "He couldn't sing any more, that's all. On top of that, he was insulting. The whole thing was tragic."

"How did he look?"

"Crazy," my uncle said. "He *was* crazy. He was pathetic, too. Everybody remembered the way he had been—tall, strong, handsome, proud. He wasn't the same man any more, that's all. He was finished. He couldn't sing, so he blamed the people. He acted as if it was their fault."

The fire consumed him, but his own people, who loved him as they loved Armenia, saw it happen. The great voice was never again heard, except on records he had made as a young man. These records are a part of every

Armenian home in America. The newcomers, the Americans, begin listening to the songs and music of Armenia as if doing so were a joke, but they soon discover that it is no such thing. They begin to collect the records of Shah-Mouradian, and they soon find themselves singing the songs he sang. For in these songs is the fire of their own souls. My own son sings these songs, a man who can say to his father, "Will you lay off that Armenian stuff, Pop?"

"Then why do you sing Armenian songs?" I ask him.

"I don't know," he says.

Well, the fire didn't go out, after all. It ended in Shah-Mouradian himself, but it didn't go out.

There have been other Armenian singers, but no other like Shah-Mouradian. As far as I am concerned, he lived magnificently. It does not matter how or why he died, for few men die magnificently. Death to most men is pitiful anyway, a consuming of the poor body by the fire of error.

Chapter 4
The Family

In spite of what I have already said about my good health as a boy, it is also true that I have been more or less ill all my life. Illness is essentially discomfort, and it is not easy for anybody to be comfortable all the time—in his body, in his work, in his house, or in his soul. Illness must be considered to be as natural as health. That doesn't make it any easier to put up with, although there are said to be enormous numbers of people who both unconsciously compel illness, and consciously enjoy it.

To be ill is to be out of harmony with all things. Illness is also one's annoyance with the fact that one *is* out of harmony, or off-key. Illness is a halt to the quarrel a man engages in all his life with the things he does not like. It is an event of the soul more than of the body, although it was for years considered an event of the body alone. No human event is exclusively an event of the body or an event of the soul. Every human event is an event of both, involving both, for both are involved in everything.

The first consciously experienced illness I knew came to pass when I was three or four at the orphanage. It is associated in my memory with the ringing of church bells and the smell of blossoms. I *saw* the blossoms, too. They were white. Looking at them while I was sick made them seem tragic. The white blossoms spread along the leafless branches and twigs of the trees were literally heartbreaking, and they were caught up in the painful premonition of the decay and death of astonishing and miraculous things. The illness, my awareness of the unbelievable change that had taken place in me, made men desolately lonely. I do not believe I felt sorry for myself so much as I felt sorry for everything. Illness does that. It does precisely that. It makes one pity everything of matter made, and everything *is* of matter made.

I have written of this first illness at least a half-dozen times over the past thirty years. I shall in all probability write of it again, and certainly remember it just before I die. I must. It was my first taste of death, my first awareness of the true nature of myself—that is, a thing which must perish at last.

I had been placed alone in a small attic room. It was morning. I had had a very unhappy night. I had been unable to sleep or rest for a long time, and then when I had finally fallen asleep the sleep had not been restful. It had brought no peace to my troubled and laboring soul which went right on laboring, and I had awakened to morning light feeling strange and unlike myself and alone and miserable and longing desperately for all sorts of intangibles: love, nearness, something, anything, to love, to laugh the death out of my soul. And the intangibles did not arrive. The external brought nothing to the internal, and the internal was in pain and in despair. If by magic my mother had walked into the room that morning I should have been instantly warmed by life and hope, I suppose, but my education in truth, in reality, in life would have been kept from swift and profound growth. Death was there, death was in myself, and yet I was there too, desperately in need of the answer to death, love, to come by magic from the outside and work a miracle. But it did not happen.

I got out of bed and wandered around the senseless room, a man of three or four years, forty or fifty pounds in weight. I soon went to the window and looked out at the world, needing to see something past the walls. I saw the white blossoms spread along the bare, brittle branches and twigs of two or three trees. Apple trees, I suppose, although I am not sure. I then heard the church bells ring, and after a moment I saw the boys and girls of the orphanage, including the boys in my own ward, march off in formation to Sunday School at the Methodist Church. They seemed a sad lot, a heartbreaking lot, involved in a heartbreaking, distasteful, senseless, and tragic business.

I shall never get over that first illness. What had happened? Had it happened before, and I hadn't been sensible enough to know? Most likely. What was the illness? It was a fever that wore out my soul in tedious annoyances. Everything miraculous in myself, everything that I had never before appreciated, was out of commission. I was hot and cold, feeble, desperately bored, annoyed, pathetic, lonely, and frantic to reach the intangibles that would restore me, or carry me to something better than ever, love or rest or death itself.

I don't know the details of my restoration, but my eyes must have become darker than ever and the loneliness with which I came into the world must have become more intense. The fever must have driven me past memory entirely, for all I remember is what I have written. I do not remember how long I remained in the attic room. I do not remember being liberated from it. I do not remember returning to my own ward. I do not remember returning to the dining room. My memory is entirely of the death that was involved. The rest is lost in the chaos of fever, or the repetitiousness of unexploited and meaningless health, or at any rate the temporary and meaningless exemption from pain and death.

After the first illness the hope of health began to be the same as the hope of everything else of worth. By the time I was eleven this hope was so great that I sent a few dollars to a mail-order body-building house in New York for their equipment and course.

The firm of Lionel Strongfort (the name alone suggested great things— the body-lion protecting the soul-fort) sent me two grips on which five elastic bands could be attached, by which the muscles of my hands, arms, neck and shoulders could be exercised and strengthened.

The course itself was quite simple: I was advised to breathe fresh air deeply, eat good food, exercise all of the muscles of my body by following the printed instructions, and sleep from eight to ten hours every night.

I had time for everything except the sleep, for I very often stayed in town selling papers or watching movies until ten or later, so that by the time I walked home, had supper, and got to bed the time would be around midnight.

The course was based on early rising and exercising, so that it was necessary for me to set the alarm for six or earlier.

For some time I had sold *The Fresno Morning Republican* and *The San Francisco Examiner*, as well as *The Fresno Evening Herald*, and on Thursdays *The Saturday Evening Post*, consequently I had for a long time been getting up around six or earlier anyhow.

I was always awakened by the alarm clock. The instant the alarm began both my brother and I would sit up, get out of bed, and begin to dress by memory. If it happened that we weren't selling papers we had other early-morning things to do.

We went together, or separately, to The San Joaquin Bakery for a sack of "chicken bread" for twenty-five cents. The best time to buy bread at the bakery was early in the morning before others had arrived. There was only a certain number of loaves every morning that had been damaged, by the machinery in one way or another. We had once or twice reached the bakery too late, and so we had agreed to get there before anybody else. This was sensible for several reasons: first, the bread was fresh, many of the loaves still hot. Second, we could hold the open sack toward certain kinds of loaves we preferred and the bakery man would invariably toss these loaves into the sack. Third, since we were the first to arrive, the bakery man frequently gave us as many loaves as he could get into the sack, not stopping until the loaves had more than reached the top.

Now, with the beginning of the body-building course it was necessary to get up a half hour earlier in order to do the required exercises and get them out of the way for the day. It never occurred to me that my body was more than adequately exercised every day without the course. The doing of a specific thing for a specific end appealed to me, and so I followed the instructions faithfully for quite a few days. My grandmother Lucy heard the commotion several mornings and was quite annoyed. My brother Henry went through the rigamarole a few mornings and then let it go. And finally I myself decided one morning to sleep a little longer instead of doing the exercises.

I tried to find time during the day to go on with the course, but there was no time for it, so that the course was abandoned, or at any rate taken up only when I felt like it.

The equipment remained in the room I shared with my brother.

The printed course was referred to from time to time, and the book Lionel Strongfort had sent me on the art of wrestling and jiu jitsu is still in my library.

I wrote a story about the whole thing many years later, "The Fifty-Yard Dash," and one day, perhaps twenty-five years after I had sent for the course, Lionel Strongfort himself wrote to me from Hollywood where he had retired. I was delighted to have his letter, and I either wrote to him or thought of doing so. He had, it seems, grown old and apparently a little bored with the whole business of body-building, and it may even be that he said something or other in his letter about having written his autobiography, a novel, or a scenario. I am not sure.

At any rate, I had seen his advertisements and I had clipped the coupon and sent it to him for the free booklet, and finally I had paid a few dollars for the equipment and course. And I had followed the course for a short time.

A delegation of German boys came one Saturday morning to my door to inquire respectfully about the course, and to ask if I would be willing to let them know its principles free of charge. I had never known the boys, but one of them was an Armenian who was famous all over town because he spoke German and did not speak Armenian, and because he belonged to the German or Rooshian gang and not to any Armenian gang.

I told the delegation that I would be glad to show them the printed course, with the illustrations of the various exercises, as well as the equipment which I knew could be purchased at Homan's Sports Goods Store. The delegation sat on the steps of the front porch and copied into a lined tablet the entire course. They examined and tried out the equipment, thanked me, and went back to Rooshian town.

I had never seen members of a streetgang so earnest, so respectful, or so well-behaved. The Armenian boy obliged me by speaking with his friends in German, and he said in great earnestness to me in poor Armenian, in reply to my question in Armenian, that he could not speak the language. He then explained in English that he had been brought up in Rooshian town with these boys and that naturally he was one of them, spoke their language, observed their customs, celebrated their national and religious holidays, and fought their street-fights with them.

Later on he learned Armenian, and he and I spoke together each time we happened to meet, and we recalled the visit of the delegation to my house.

It was this boy, Setrak Hovsepian, who had heard that I had sent for the course. He had taken up with his friends the matter of approaching me about it. He reported years later that all of the members of the gang chipped in to buy the equipment from Homan's and that the following of the course became an established requirement for all members of the gang, old and new. They had all been quite astonished, he also reported, that I was the only boy in town who had sent for the course, for by that time it was well-known that I was an intellectual.

Soon after my first book was published I ran into Setrak in Hart's Cafeteria in Fresno and we sat down over coffee and discussed the business of writing, for it seemed to him that he might give the thing a go, too. He did, and found that it was not for him. He went into farming and became one of the most successful farmers in the whole San Joaquin Valley. His father was a native of Bitlis, his mother a native of Moush.

The epidemics of influenza which came to pass before I was thirteen brought death to members of many families I knew. There was almost no newsboy who could say he had not lost somebody. Everybody living in the house on San Benito Avenue was overtaken by the mysterious illness, but each of them reached the crisis, as it was called, on schedule, and then got better.

At this time I found one morning that I was not able to stay on my feet after I had put on my clothes. I therefore did not run to town to sell the morning papers, or to the bakery for the day's bread. I fell back on the bed in my clothes where my mother found me just before she went to work at Guggenheim's, packing figs. She got me back in bed, brought me a bowl of Carnation mush, which I found I could not eat. She then brought me a cup of hot water with the juice of a lemon in it, which I drank. Soon the house was empty and I was alone with the foolish and humiliating illness.

I was astonished when my mother burst into the house and came to my bed several hours later. She began to tell me that I would be up and about in no time, and began to bring me cups of hot lemon water which I kept drinking. I had been perspiring since the night before, but the lemon water soon drenched me with perspiration. My mother went out to the chickens we kept, caught one, chopped off its head, cleaned it, cut it up, and cooked it, so that in the early afternoon she began to bring me bowls of hot chicken broth. And she kept assuring me that I would soon be up and about again. I couldn't understand what all the fuss was about, for I was quite sure that I would be up and about again in any case.

Late that afternoon I fell into deep and restful sleep and didn't wake up until late that night. My mother was sitting at my bedside reading the Bible. She touched my forehead, then began to bring me more chicken broth. She brought also a plate of white Armenian rice which I found that I wanted to eat.

The next morning she started the whole procedure over again, beginning in the dark when I woke up, and at the proper time went off to her job. When she got home that night I was up and around the house, still feeble but past the crisis.

What happened was this. She had remarked to her friends at the packing house that her son was sick in bed. They had told her of the swiftness of this illness in ending a life. She had stepped out of her place and come home, half-expecting to find me dead. She had not called a doctor because she did not believe a doctor could do any more than she could. I was able to get up every afternoon and evening and wander around the house the next couple of days, but I did not go back to school and work for three or four days.

Here I am, then, still alive, still having health and illness mixed in my aging soul.

My illness is life itself. This illness is constant. Entire exemption from it has been rare and momentary, or illusory, as when I have been drunk.

I did not begin to drink in earnest until I was well over twenty-five. Until that time I had on a number of occasions had a jug of wine. I never liked getting things blurred. I liked getting them clear, and then clearer and clearer. Wine-drinking got them blurred, but whiskey-drinking, I discovered, got them clear, and then clearer and clearer. This is not inaccurate. Whiskey made inner and outer realities clearer to me—provided, of course, I didn't drink too much. When I first began to drink it was very nearly impossible for me to drink too much. I never drank alone, consequently my drinking was orderly and balanced. I could drink for eight or ten hours and still be clear-headed and sober, or something better than sober: extraordinarily sharp, in key, wise about death, glad about life, in love with art.

The wicked enemies of my soul were always illness and failure, and I fought them bitterly. I wanted my short time to be effective. I wanted everything I did to be done with style, with rhythm, on schedule.

But for many years I couldn't even begin, and then finally I began.

Thereafter for years everything I did I did with style, rhythm, and on schedule. The results were good, as I believed they must be. I found a suitable language for my writing. I wrote, and what I wrote was altogether my own, frequently good, occasionally great.

And then it came to pass that illness, failure, and anger began to come to me for prolonged visits. I wrote without smiling, often in pain, and hardly ever on schedule.

The matter of schedule must be carefully considered. It is the key to creative achievement. Mozart worked on schedule all his life, and so did Shakespeare. Being on schedule, they were able to achieve great things quickly and easily. To be creatively on schedule is the most important thing for the artist. What does it mean to be on schedule? That is to say, what, precisely, am I talking about?

It is this:

Through accident, through luck, by design, or as a consequence of long years of earnest trying, a man transports his soul from where it was in the beginning to a realm in which the action of all creativeness is in operation, and consequently he himself is involved, by now quite naturally, in the schedule of the miracle of life itself, so that anything he does is virtually done for him. It is done swiftly and magnificently. The man himself, as a man, does little. He goes along with the schedule, as if his soul had latched onto an immemorial means of transportation, himself nothing more than a free rider. It is impossible to otherwise account for the music of Mozart or the plays of Shakespeare. These are works which came to pass as enormous events of nature come to pass. The man to whom this latching onto schedule happens is both fortunate and unfortunate, for once the latching on has taken place he is a man who may never again be merely an animal body in a material world, and he therefore can never again be satisfied with the simple pleasures of an animal body.

Any man who meets the schedule, latches onto it, goes along with it, keeps it, helps it, must in the end also be driven forward by it, and to be driven can often be a painful thing. As there are few men involved in a similar manner with the schedule, such a man is necessarily more alone than ever, too.

On the last day of August in the year 1908 in the city of Fresno I came into the world, sick to death with astonishment, anger and gladness. My father Armenak Saroyan was thirty-four years of age, my mother Takoohi Saroyan twenty-six.

In less than three years my father was dead. My mother survived him by thirty-nine years.

My father had been educated at the American Presbyterian School in Bitlis. He was a preacher by profession. He kept a journal in English and in Armenian, he wrote philosophical essays, poems, accounts of his travels. He was a good extemporaneous speaker.

My mother received no formal education, but learned to read and write Armenian. She also learned to read English and could sign her name. Her reading in English was poor, however, so that she glanced only at newspapers now and then.

Her mother, Lucy, could read and write no language, but spoke eloquently in Armenian, Kurdish and Turkish.

My father's father's name was Petrus, who was the son of Sarkis, who was a Saroyan by adoption, hence while both sides of my family bear the same name they are not related. My mother's father's name was Minas, but I have forgotten his father's name. Family memory was confined to the city of Bitlis. I heard no family lore involving any other city. The city (and its name) has always meant a great deal to me.

My father reached New York alone in 1905. After two years he was reunited there with his wife, his daughters Cosette and Zabel, which appears to be a variant of Isabelle. He saw for the first time his son Henry, born in Erzeroum, enroute to America.

This journey from Bitlis to New York took almost two years, for it was necessary for my grandmother Lucy who was in charge of the journey to halt several times while she and her daughters Takoohi and Verkine and her son Aram worked to earn money for further passage.

They spent three or four months in Erzeroum, a month or two in Marseille, and almost six months in Havre. My uncle Aram, then eleven or so, learned French and acted as interpreter for many Armenians on their way to America. The women knitted stockings which Aram sold to small shopkeepers.

My father preached to an Armenian congregation in Paterson, New Jersey, for a time. He also wrote articles for *The Christian Herald*, or at any rate was connected in some capacity with that publication. His best friend in America was a Presbyterian minister called Dr. William Stonehill who died a few months before I was born. I was named William after this man. Had he not died I have heard that it was my father's intention to name me Petrus after his father.

Dr. Stonehill was the center of a religious circle of young ministers educated by the Presbyterians in Armenia, Greece, Bulgaria, Serbia, Egypt and a number of other Near Eastern countries. There was always in my life a photograph of these young men standing around Dr. Stonehill and his wife. Most of them wore large black moustaches, and all of them seemed enormously earnest. For a number of years I knew the names of everybody in the photograph, but I no longer remember them.

In 1928 when I first went to New York from California I went to Brooklyn and pressed the doorbell of Mrs. William Stonehill's house. She herself came to the door, looked at me a moment, and then said quietly, "You are Armenak Saroyan's son. Please come in."

I had not written to her, telling of my intention to visit her because I felt that I might not do so at the last minute. I had no idea why I wanted to see where she lived, for it was a new house, not a house my father had ever entered. I recognized her instantly as the lady in the photograph. She was very kind and told me about my father and my mother when she had known them. My father liked to go about in good clothes and to dress for the pulpit, she said, but my mother resisted the clothes of America. She had had considerable difficulty with my mother about clothing. My mother confirmed that this had been true. She remarked that she preferred her own clothes, from Bitlis, because they *were* her own, because she was comfortable in them, and because she did not like to wear other people's clothing.

I was just twenty when I visited Mrs. Stonehill. In reply to her questions I told her how my family had fared in California, and I remarked that I had come to New York because I had always wanted to, and because I was a writer. She then revealed that she too was a writer, and handed me two booklets she had had published at her own expense. In the booklets were poems she had written. On the subway back to New York I read through each of the booklets, and again in my furnished room in The New York Hotel, near Washington Market, for which I paid three dollars a week, a room which stank. The poems were terribly lovely, lonely, meaningless, artificial and absurd. They broke my heart and brought tears to my eyes. She had invited me to a church social and was discreetly astonished when I remarked as politely as possible that I never went to such affairs because I never felt at ease at them, and also because my spare time was spent in the streets of New York or at the Public Library on Fifth Avenue. She remarked that my father had always taken active part in church affairs. I replied that I was determined to become a good writer.

My father wasn't home the night I was born. My uncle Mousheg Saroyan's mother was midwife. The birth was swift, relatively painless, and unrecorded. A few minutes before I was born my mother was on her feet, holding a door for support, which appears to have been a family custom. My father was at the vineyard home of his cousins the Mouradians, near Sanger, eleven miles east of Fresno. He was working on their vineyard. He had been promised the Armenian church in Yettem, not far from Fresno, but the congregation there was Turkish-speaking and my father spoke Turkish poorly. He had therefore found himself out of work and had taken any work that had been available.

When I was two he moved his family to San Bruno, twenty-five miles south of San Francisco. Then he moved to San Francisco where he was connected for a time with the Salvation Army, and finally he moved to Campbell, a small town near San Jose, California, where he died in July of 1911.

In Campbell, much like Sherwood Anderson's father somewhere in the Midwest, he raised chickens and sold eggs, but this venture was not successful, either. The chicks died in enormous lots, the hens caught all sorts of diseases, they laid poorly, and finally the market for eggs was bad the whole time he was in the business.

Near the home in Campbell lived a very old Portuguese lady whose children had all married and wandered away. My mother called her Papchah, which was probably the way my mother heard the old lady's name. This woman was a frequent visitor at our house, chatting with my mother in Portuguese while my mother replied in Armenian. The old lady always went home with me after a visit, for she missed her children. My mother said that whenever she went to Papchah's to fetch me home she found me sitting on a box watching the old lady and listening to her, a thick slice of buttered bread in my hand, three or four flies walking around on the butter.

My mother also remembered an Assyrian woman on the boat from Havre to New York, in steerage. This woman helped my mother take care of her children, keep them fed and clean and comfortable in an area of the boat that was crowded, filthy, and painfully depressing. The woman had watched my mother the first few hours out of Havre, and then she had gone to my mother and after saying a few words in Assyrian which my mother had not understood she had gone to work helping her and delivering her from the anxiety and fear that was plainly showing in her face. My mother told me a few years before she died that she would never forget this woman and that she would always thank God for her.

Another friend on the boat was a blond Norwegian sailor who took shy pleasure in bringing food to my mother, in smiling at her, and in hugging my sisters and my brother. My mother said that if she had ever loved a man she had loved this one. He said a few words in Norwegian each time he visited her and my mother said a few in Armenian, and after a moment he disappeared, but every day of the voyage he came with food and love.

Who are these people? Papchah, the Assyrian woman, the young Norwegian seaman? They are my family. They are the people of love.

A man must think well of his family. It is the basic requirement by which he may achieve authentic personal identity, or the illusion of it, which is either the same thing or just as good. It is accurate for a man to think well of his family, no matter what kind of people they may appear to have been, or be, for if a man notices only that the members of his family are nothing much, it is he himself that is nothing much, it is he himself who lacks intelligence, understanding, imagination and most important of all love. If a man considers any family, with intelligence, understanding, imagination and love, that family must be seen to be great in something or other—in the capacity to survive, for instance, if in nothing else, which is enough. Merely to survive is to keep the hope of greatness, accuracy, and grace alive. The hope of these things is as important as the things themselves, for if a family hasn't them, they may get them, and if a family has them, they may lose them.

I decided very early to love my family, and to see in each of its members something rare and good as well as the miserable and painful things that were obvious. I do not think that in writing of them I ever lied, I merely chose to notice in them the things I cherished and preferred, and to refer to the things I didn't cherish with humor and charity; the writer in the end creates his family, his nation, his culture and worth, and I believe that I have more effectively than any other member of the Saroyan family created that family, which appears all through my writing but especially in the small book called *My Name Is Aram*.

The last two letters of the name William are the same as the last two letters of the name Aram. Had I been invited to choose a name for myself I believe I would have chosen Aram. The early life and young manhood of my mother's brother Aram appealed to me deeply, I admired his speed and humor, and I liked the name itself with the name Saroyan. The two seemed to go well together. The name Aram had long been a favorite of the Armenians. I had seen heroic drawings of a number of famous Armenians named Aram in various Armenian newspapers, magazines and books, and I liked the whole inaccurate lore that I came to associate with the name. I gave Aram of the book *My Name Is Aram* the last name of Garoghlanian because that was my grandmother Lucy's name before she married Minas Saroyan when she was eleven and he was twenty-one or twenty-two. I gave my son the name Aram because I had come to think of the name as my true name, and since it was too late for me to have it, I wanted him to have it.

There were times, however, in my life when I found my family and the name Saroyan unbearable.

I thought of running away from home. I thought of changing my name. And I thought of finding a wife as soon as possible and starting a family of my own with a name of its own. I began to have these troubled longings when I was not much more than eight or nine, and they continued to be valid until I was nineteen or twenty, but as the years went by they became less and less valid, so that after I was thirteen or fourteen I knew they were nonsense.

It was clear to me that a change of scene and name would not change *me*. The scene would change, the name would be different, but I would still be who I was, and the challenge of seeking to become who I wished to be would be the same. I never in my life thought of denying my nationality. If my family happened to annoy me I sometimes found that I wanted to be rid of them once and for all, but this feeling was never of long duration.

My cousin Haig Saroyan, Byzant's son, when we sold *The Fresno Evening Herald* together, told George Riekas that he, Haig, was an American. I told Haig we were all Americans, but what Riekas wanted to know was the nationality of Haig's family, which was Armenian. Haig said, "No, my nationality is not Armenian. I had a fight with my father last night, and I quit." A few days later, though, he told me that his nationality was Armenian again, as he and his father had made up.

Now and then the name Saroyan seemed silly to me, as a word is apt to seem if one thinks about it long enough. And of course it was not the name that was ever silly, it was myself, it was the frustration I felt of my desire to become effective in my life. The name simply didn't stand for anything. It didn't mean anything. Nobody bearing the name was known for anything. I might as well have been named Mud, as I once wrote.

In the midst of this annoyance with my family there was always a great affection for them, and a good deal of hopefulness about my intention to give the name importance. The name William was sometimes all right and sometimes not, but little by little both names began to be all right. They were the sounds and images which somewhat accurately signified myself.

Once in the third grade at Emerson School a substitute teacher looking over the class before taking the roll nodded to me, half-smiled and said, "You are, I take it, William Saroyan."

I was absolutely delighted, and went entirely out of my way not to annoy her, and not to permit anybody else to do so. She had been informed by the Principal that I would be the problem of her assignment, and she had taken a chance on guessing which face would fit the name. Had she asked someone else I am sure I would have driven her from the room in tears in a good deal under an hour. I considered her quite pretty and rather intelligent. Actually,

D.D. Davis may have told her that my hair would be uncombed and he may have given her a brief description of myself and my nature. Even so, the fact that she knew who I was made a fool of me. I was so well-behaved I was ashamed of myself.

A good deal of this naïve pride in recognition by strangers still exists, so that if a rake-man in a gambling house calls out to me, "Hiya, Bill!" I must gamble at his table, chat with him, and permit others to know that I am known by a rake-man, have traveled, and am somebody. I am pleased when I am greeted by name by a stranger. I have been friendly with half-drunken schoolteachers who have come to my table in a restaurant or a nightclub and reported to me that they have read my book. Many people who greet a writer tell him they have read his book, making it difficult for the writer to know which book they are talking about. Once, after a few minutes, it turned out that the book was *The Grapes of Wrath* by John Steinbeck. I remember that I remarked, "I am sorry. I didn't write that book. William Faulkner wrote it."

A man goes to a great deal of trouble to create his name, only to discover that the name is now creating him. He finds that he must live up to a lore which has come to be associated with his name. This living up to the lore soon becomes natural.

When I visited George Bernard Shaw in 1944 I sensed immediately that such had been the case with him, for he was a gentle, delicate, kind, little man who had established a pose, and then lived it so steadily and effectively that the pose had become real. Like myself, his nature had been obviously a deeply troubled one in the beginning. He had been a man who had seen the futility, meaninglessness and sorrow of life, but had permitted himself to thrust aside these feelings and to perform another George Bernard Shaw, which is art and proper.

The young heart knows a sickness of family. A man's involvement in a family is not all love and gladness. Every man wonders at one time or another why he is a member of his own family instead of a member of another one. If one's own family is unimportant, insignificant, undistinguished, commonplace, ineffective, or merely unknown, it is understandable that a young member of the family may now and then wish he'd had better luck in the matter of his birth.

I was once astonished by a man who remarked unhappily that he wished he had been born to a poor family because he had always wanted to be a writer. His family was socially prominent in the city of San Francisco and enormously wealthy. He said that it had been impossible for him under those circumstances to become a writer. After a moment I stopped being astonished and began to see the validity of his remarks.

Displeasure with one's family must be very nearly universal. Members of all families must know it in one degree or another. And in the end it is quite unlikely that there has ever lived a man who did not find the human race itself distasteful to him.

But the fact remains that if a man is to go on enduring time, it is in order for him to accept his own family, and to cherish the whole human family. A man cannot live his life effectively hating what he is. It is better for him to find the means by which to like what he is. Illness and hatred go together and they are involved in death. While a man lives it is better for him to avoid purposeful involvement in death, for the inevitable involvement is always more than enough for him to put up with or to put to use in the style with which he lives and works.

A man longs to belong to a family which is noble, honorable, intelligent, graceful, handsome, useful, courageous, spiritually wealthy, kind, loving, healthy, and amusing, but he invariably finds that he belongs to no such family. If he notices nobility in his family, he also notices far greater absence of it. And the same is true of the other things. There is always more of the poor things than of the good things. Somebody in the family is feeble-minded. Somebody else is dishonest. Somebody else is ugly in body, face, and nature. Somebody else is pathetic. Somebody else has no more courage than a mouse. And so on. It is not easy for a man to adjust himself to the truth that the human race is such an inferior order of animal life, or that his own family is not much better than the human race in general.

It is natural for newcomers to expect a great deal of the family to which they belong.

In the end I decided I must consider *myself* my family entirely. I saw that I could not do much about the other members of the family. I decided I must do as much as possible about myself.

When I stopped expecting anything important of anybody excepting myself I began to find many things of worth in everybody else that I had never before noticed, and I began to look upon the worthless things I saw with amusement and affection.

This is an important achievement in the growth of a soul, for it *is* true that one is one's self the human race insofar as the achievement of excellence is concerned. It is not permissible or proper to make demands of anyone but one's self. Nothing can come of it. One cannot demand of a father or a mother, of a brother or a sister, of a wife or a son or a daughter. One can demand only of one's own self, and to all others give understanding or love or both.

But the achievement of excellence is forever no more than a matter of essay and trial. Failure is constant and inevitable so that by noticing failure in others with amusement, understanding, and affection, one's own failure becomes less and less annoying.

My family had in its lore many absurd people, few wonderful ones. The wonderful ones were dead and gone but they were not forgotten. I heard about the miserable ones with shame and regret, the wonderful ones with thankfulness and pleasure. But even the wonderful ones weren't much. Their fame was local and meaningless.

As for the current members of the family, they simply weren't much. For the most part they were stupid or uselessly clever, physically junky and unattractive, unconscious, unaware, indifferent, apathetic, or devoid of any special quality by which I could feel there was any point in their being alive at all.

They seemed to be part of the horde of unborn souls which come and go, which no one notices have come or have gone.

Among these people, who were my own family, I was a stranger. There was no one I could speak to meaningfully. The talk was incessantly about things that were not only boring but infuriating. Everybody was devoid of ideas. There was no turning out after truth, honor, grace. There was eating, sleeping, working, earning money, saving money, dreaming of money, fretting about money.

The true religion of my family was always personal.

We weren't irreligious, but we had long preferred to keep our religion to ourselves. It is true that one of our boys had made the pilgrimage to Jerusalem in 1801, but the family has it that he was insincere, for he transacted considerable profitable business enroute, and spent a rather long time in Constantinople on the way back—a city at that time even more involved in matters of pleasure than it is now. Still, from the time of his return to the end of his life he was appropriately honored for having made the trip.

The family had God, but the attitude was that He was one of the early members of the family. The pose of Christ, his intelligence, manners and wit were carefully examined and found wanting.

If we had any Saints at all, they were members of the family about whom over the years a vast lore of lies had been invented, which in time came to be considered amusing gospel.

One of these Saints was a boy named Kissak who died at the age of eleven. He was the handsomest, wisest, most shining man who had ever lived. This world and life were too coarse for him to put up with, that's all.

Two others were the twins, Ara and Araxi Saroukhan, as the name was said at that time and still is by several branches of the family. Ara had dark skin, eyes, and hair, Araxi fair skin, blue eyes, red hair. These two were lied into Sainthood on the basis of handsomeness, beauty, wit, mimicry, arrogance, and contempt for law and reality. Araxi married a Kurd when she was twelve, bore him three sons and three daughters, thereby bringing the entire Kurdish nation into the fold of the family. Ara, when he was twenty-seven, fell off his father's house while drunk, got up, walked away, and is said to have gone to India.

These were lies. Everybody in the family knew they were, and yet variations of them, as well as an assortment of new ones, are still being told, disbelieved, and finally believed, for as time goes by any man reconsidering any fable he may have heard before he was ten, however unlikely, is apt to believe it *might* be true, for he knows he heard his own father tell him the fable, and he knows the *telling* of it—if nothing else about it—actually happened.

And between the reality of the fable itself and the reality of the telling of it, he does not feel there is enough difference to warrant the destruction of an old church and the founding of a new one.

The family *was* the church, and part of the religion was to tell lies because it was intelligent and imaginative to do so, and because it tended to improve the nature of the family.

The lies were told in Bitlis, in the fortress city high in the mountains, in the long snow of winter, in the long hot quietude of summer.

In Bitlis there was no formal Saint.

In Fresno there was one. But even *he* did not wear the title.

In the rented house on San Benito Avenue, on the piano in the parlor, was a white-chalk slab about the size of a sheet of typing paper on which the head of an old man had been carved in bas-relief and then painted brown. Whoever this man was, he is the nearest thing to a formal Saint I am willing to believe ever entered into my life. I saw the bas-relief from the time I was eight, I still have it, and it still means something to me.

At first I saw it there on the piano and scarcely looked at it. It was a slab, almost square-shaped, that someone had given a place of honor in the house, and that was enough for me. I suppose I felt at first that anything clearly defined, such as the slab, was an object of beauty and therefore deserved to be placed somewhere where it would be seen and where it would exert an influence. The slab certainly succeeded in exerting an influence on me. I believed it to be important.

One day I happened to notice that it was more than a shape. I got up on the piano stool and examined it. What it was was the head of an old man with a long square beard in what I think is called three-quarter profile. This also seemed proper—that is, that the shape should contain the image of the head of an old man. It also seemed proper that the old man appeared to be deeply earnest and sorrowful. I could readily understand that he *might* be. I believed he must be a member of the family.

Thereafter when I felt angry or confused I found that I wanted to look at the old man, and I would go to the piano, get up on the stool, and look at him until I no longer felt angry or confused. Just looking at the carved outline of his head and beard brought peace to my soul and resignation to my heart and mind about my personal ignorance and insignificance. For a long time I did not need to know anything more about the man, but one day I spoke to my grandmother Lucy about him.

"Who is he?" I said.

"Krikor Illuminator," she replied in Armenian, which would be, "Krikor Loosavoreach," as my grandmother pronounced the language. Loosavoreach, however it may be pronounced or spelled in English, means The Illuminator, or more literally The Light-Thrower. My grandmother did not call him *Saint* Krikor Loosavoreach, but I have seen him referred to in English as St. Gregory the Illuminator. One way or the other he is the same man. The bas-relief of his head found its way into the house in which I lived, my eyes found their way to the shape of the slab, to the image of the head of the man himself, and finally my imagination, ignorance, insignificance, longing and many other things gave the carving reality: he was myself, he was the way I felt about this life and world at the age of eight, nine, and ten, and he would be the way I would feel at eighty, most likely.

Here memory fails me and I may as well confess it. I do not remember if my grandmother told me that he invented the Armenian alphabet, or that he took the spoken language and put it into print, or that he translated the Bible into the Armenian language—into of course *Krabar*, or

The Written Word, which is classical Armenian, as against *Ahshkharabar*, which is The World's Word. My own family's language is The World's Word. At any rate, I found out that his name was Krikor, and the name became in some of my earliest stories the name of my brother. Again and again I wrote, *My brother Krikor.*

Krikor's probable involvement in language, in the alphabet, in The Word, in the matter of Light, of Enlightenment, of the holy hope of banishing ignorance from the human heart, head, body and soul seemed precisely right to me, and I was deeply influenced by this intelligence, or mistaken intelligence, for as I've said I'm not sure about any of this. Krikor Illuminator may have been so named for other reasons than the alphabet, The Word, language, paper, print, books. It doesn't matter. Whoever he was, I *believed* he was involved in these things, for by then I was involved in them, and Krikor and I were the same man.

My grandmother had purchased the slab for twenty-five cents. What impelled her to squander the money I can't imagine, but I am sure it must have been something deeply religious in a very personal way.

Chapter Five
The Streets

The streets made me, and the streets stink. Even so, immortality for me would be to be able to walk them forever. Any homesickness I have ever felt has been for the streets, for they have had the most to do in my life with time, mystery, love, hunger, money, and memory.

There are those who love the sea, upon which I, for one, have never walked. There are those who love the far-off mountains, the places where few or no human feet have ever wandered. There are those who love the heavens, and those who love the places of sand or ice and snow.

I love the streets.

Here are some of my own, the streets I walked, in which I began, in which I continue, the streets I knew, know, cannot, will not forget.

Somewhere within these streets are the streets of sleep. Where the real streets begin, where the streets of sleep end, I don't know.

I walked.

I walked the streets. That is what my life has been. I saw the others who walked. Most of them I saw only once, but that once was enough, for whoever I saw was alive then.

It was not all walking of course. I ran in the streets, too.

And I stood in them.

I ran for money, to get somewhere fast, with newspapers under my arm. A couple of times I ran to fires, but I never ran to an automobile accident. I never walked to one of them.

I stood in the streets for nothing, to *look*.

The first street, the last, the one in between—they're all the same, for all of them together are the world, where I lived, and live.

Here's North Rodeo in Beverly Hills. How I ever got here I will never know, any more than I will ever know how I got anywhere else. But here I am. Four blocks down the street is Romanoff's, a restaurant. You will always find a restaurant on a street, or a small coin. I have yet to meet a man, though, who ever found a silver dollar, excepting my cousin Zav one day thirty-three years ago on our way to the County Fair in Fresno. Between us we hadn't ten cents. The finding of the dollar was therefore an event of grand surprise.

Years later, though, Zav confessed he himself had tossed the dollar into the dust, in order to *pretend* that he had found it.

Gold is never found in the streets, although that is supposed to be the promise that brought the poor of Europe to America. Gold is found in the teeth.

The name of the street where Zav found the dollar is Ventura. It's still there. The Fair Grounds are still there, too. The dollar we spent that day.

Here's Diamond Canyon, about which I am able to say this:

I had heard a great deal about Diamond Canyon in 1911 or 1912, when I was three or four. Finally, in 1913 or 1914 or even earlier, I walked there. I saw a man in the window of a basement store mending shoes. I remember him. I remember noticing, as if it were important to do so, that he had a place in which to work and a work to do.

Now, about this same time, in this same city, Oakland, in the neighborhood called Fruitvale, I one day found a brook in which I saw many large stones among water plants, and among these rocks and plants I saw small fish, which I found that I instantly loved. I loved them because they were alive in a cool place, in a wonderful way, and because I believed their aliveness was part of my own.

I heard the older boys at Fred Finch say the words *Diamond Canyon* again and again until I myself was there. I saw neither diamond nor canyon but I did see, and remember, a street and a shoe mender. Another day there I saw, and remembered, a brook with fish living in the water.

I have always had the idea that Fred Finch was on Peralta Street, but that may not be so. There even may not have been a Peralta Street in that neighborhood at all, for I went back there many years after I had left and the name of the street was something else. It was a street I knew just the same, whatever its name. It might as well be called Peralta Street.

From Oakland I went by train to Fresno.

For a short time the family of the late Armenak Saroyan, including myself, lived in a house with a garden of weeds in which now and then I saw one or two large white hares.

The house was on Van Ness Avenue.

It had a steep roof of shingles. It was made of rough planks painted red that rested on a brick foundation. The rent must have been very high, perhaps fifteen dollars a month, because we stayed there only a month.

The next house was on M Street, just across the railroad siding that went to the grape and raisin packing houses. But once again the rent was too high, for we stayed in this house only a month, too.

Work horses, unhitched and led by short heavy men who seemed to resemble the horses, passed that way every evening, going from the brewery to the stables. The brewery was red brick, in appearance much like a castle, named Fresno Beer, later Ranier. The waste waters of the brewery irrigated a small truck garden tended by five Italians who wrapped vegetables in newspapers. The water from the brewery was yellow and gave the truck garden a smell of not unpleasant ferment. The brewery had bats which came out in the evening and shot about in the sky and squeaked. They were alive as secretly as they could be. The sight of them never gladdened me but the sight of the horses every evening did, and so did the voices of the men talking to the horses after work, calling them by name, the horses and the men seeming to have deep friendship for one another.

For a short time there may or may not have been another house on another street that I have forgotten, or I may have forgotten such a house because it was on the same street.

At any rate, we were soon living in the house on San Benito Avenue, about two blocks from the house on M Street, and there we stayed six years. A block and a half away was Emerson School, and beside the house was an empty lot which my brother Henry and I soon converted into a neighborhood arena for boys' sports. I will never forget the number of this house: 2226.

The house was wood frame, painted gray. An old English walnut tree grew in the backyard. A tree of tough wood grew up front, not very big, the name of it never known to me. Two honeysuckle vines climbed the porch. A good sycamore stood alongside the alley, and under two windows on that side of the house two lilac trees grew. The house itself consisted of a parlor, a front bedroom, a middle bedroom, a back bedroom, a dining room, a kitchen, a back porch, and off the porch a small bath. There was also a barn. It was actually two barns with two separate doors.

Up the alley two blocks was the San Joaquin Bakery.

The alley bore no name, and nobody ever gave it one. It was simply The Alley. Across the street lived an Armenian family in a house with a lawn. These people were regular church-goers who seemed stiff and stuffy, although they may not have been, certainly not to one another. Just back of the house was a house on M Street which was occupied by a family of Slavonians.

The house on San Benito Avenue was not above us. The rent was eight or nine dollars a month. It was the property of a man named Barr who came to the house unannounced every six months or so and papered the walls, or mended the steps, or the floor, or a door. He came on a bicycle. He was a quiet man. His daughter, or at any rate one of his daughters, was the substitute teacher at Emerson School one day whom I plagued until she burst into tears and ran out of the room. But I did not know at the time that she was the daughter of the man who owned our house.

We lived there.

I will speak of the cat that was there before we were. This cat was a good hunter and caught a lot of mice. It toyed with every mouse it caught before eating it. I watched and heard the cat eat a great many mice. The house had a great many of them. The cat caught them somewhere or other, in or under the house, carried them out into the sunlight of the backyard, and there upon the surface of the hot earth annoyed them half to death and then ate them. The cat encouraged every mouse to live ten or fifteen minutes on terrible hope.

I was not too late to see runaway horses. In 1916, 1917, and 1918 there were many automobiles in Fresno, but many farmers still came to town by horse and buggy, or by a team of horses and a surrey. Frequently a horse would be frightened by an automobile in the heart of the city and would take off. The sound of the hoofs of a runaway horse was exciting, the sight fearful and grand. The occupants of the carriage were always helpless and busy trying to do something effective at a time when nothing was effective. The runaway horse would run to exhaustion, and then stop. If anybody ran out into the street on foot to try to arrest the runaway horse a poor situation would be made worse, for the horse would turn quickly and sometimes the carriage would tip over. Van Ness Avenue between Tulare and Mariposa was the run that was most dramatic since these blocks were in the center of town. The excitement created by the sudden taking off of a frightened horse was instantaneous. Everybody in town within hearing of the hoofbeats would turn to the scene. As I remember it there was always at least one thrilled dog racing after the horse, barking with all its might. Frequently there were two or even three of them engaged in this celebration of an animal's break for freedom.

A great many people would get out in the center of the street, myself included, to watch the horse and carriage. Very seldom would a horse turn a corner. He would run in a straight line. Anybody in a horse-drawn carriage in the vicinity would immediately rein-up in order to prevent another break. Frequently one break would impel another. And almost invariably during a run one or two other horses would rear up.

It was a great thing to see a runaway horse even though one always felt concerned for the occupants of the carriage. Now and then the occupants would be an old man and his old wife sitting helplessly in the rollicking, helpless burst of unplanned transportation: I don't remember anybody getting hurt. I was lucky enough a couple of times to be at the end of a runaway. The horse being worn out would simply slow down and stop. It would be wet with perspiration, its eyes wild, its nostrils dilating. Under the wet coat the muscles would ripple nervously. It was a fine sight. Everybody would be grateful that no one had been hurt, and there would be concern about the occupants as to how badly they had been frightened. Somebody would help them out of the carriage, walk with them to calm them, while somebody else held the horse.

These were the nervous horses, the horses with perhaps a little Arab in them. The big horses, the brewery horses, never made a break.

Now, it may very well be that some of the horses that made a break did so not because they had been frightened by automobiles at all, but for reasons of their own. I remember having wondered about this. Did they break because they were hitched? Was it because they were in an unnatural place, a city? Was it because the hard surface underfoot made them unhappy? Was it because they were horses?

All I know is that I loved seeing them run away. Now and then something in the harnessing would break, and once a carriage wheel took off on its own making an especially exciting scene. I don't remember where that wheel rolled to, but I do remember watching it roll for some time. There was a lot of power in its movement. The axle of the carriage hit the street making a sound something like human screaming mingled with something like something else, a dull scraping sound. The carriage itself began to bounce and bump. The horse instantly feeling a complication in its straight run drew up.

The big horses walked and made a fine sound as they did so. Now and then they were sent into a kind of trot, rhythmic and good to hear. But it was a slow trot and of short duration.

I don't remember anybody coming to town on horseback but if anybody did and I saw him and have forgotten, I certainly don't remember any runaways that were not involved in carriages.

The aberrations of these handsome animals constituted a moment of drama in a long repetitive tableau of waiting. A horse would suddenly decide that it could wait no longer and it would make the break. There seemed to be a kind of reverence for this event on the part of everybody who watched it. It made some people talkative and others it hushed as if they remembered parallel action within themselves, or a desire for it.

I was not too late to see blacksmiths at work, either. Watching a blacksmith bring his metal to malleability, watching and hearing him pound this molten metal into the shape he desired was always dramatic. The ringing of the anvil was good to hear. The blacksmith was always bare-armed and wore a leather apron made black by fire, soot, and sweat. His face and the skin of his arms would be black. When he went to work getting the finished shoe onto the hoof of a horse it seemed astonishing that such a big animal could endure such action upon itself, and yet I never saw a horse make any kind of a protest or show any intense nervousness. This may have had something to do with the nature of the blacksmith himself or the place itself. I saw blacksmiths at other work, too—sharpening plow shares, straightening or mending other farming implements. It was always easy to watch them at work from the sidewalk, for the slide-door was always open and invariably all day small boys on their way somewhere or on their way back would stop and watch. I know I was never able to pass a blacksmith's without stopping. Sometimes I stopped for half an hour, sometimes an hour, depending upon the work that was being done. Blacksmiths seemed not to be given to speech. I don't remember any of them ever saying anything to any of the small boys watching them. Vulcanizers of tires on the other hand would sometimes turn and greet a small boy or ask him to go away. This surely had something to do with the nature of the work.

I walked one morning from Carl Street to McAllister, to see again the streets between my house and the Public Library in San Francisco.

By then I had listened a thousand times or more to part of Grieg's Concerto in A Minor for Piano and Orchestra. It was a wind-up phonograph. The year was 1929. All I had of the concerto was the one 12-inch record I had picked up for a nickel at the record store on Eddy Street, owned by Bacigalupi. I called my share of this work *The Morning Concerto*. It was a London orchestra, and the man at the piano was de Greef. When I got up in the morning I wound the phonograph, put needle to disc, listened to one side, then the other, as I shaved, dressed, and had coffee. I knew every instant of both sides of the record.

I was twenty and had only lately come back from six months in New York and the streets there.

Now, in Oslo once—I was twenty-five then—I climbed a street that *was* a street. It was one of the great streets of my life, although all I did was climb it. I *saw* that street. That is all I can say about it. On the way to the top no adventures took place, I saw no one I shall have to remember as long as I live, no idea or thought came into my head at the time, nevertheless that is a street I shall never forget.

One by one, wherever I lived, wherever I went, I came to streets and walked them.

As the years go by and the streets remain, unchanged or changing, my love of them grows. I do not pretend to know very much about this love, but I think it must be love of the world itself. It must be love of the people, for the world and the people are caught together in the streets.

The highways are fine, but only because they are the way from the streets of one city to the streets of another. It is the streets of cities that mean my life, and it is in the streets that my love is greatest. It is in the faces of them and in the faces of the people of them. I love also the domestic animals of them—the secret cats and the mad dogs.

Love of streets is the love out of which I see how deeply I love God, how near I come to the truth.

I was an old man by the time I took that walk to the Public Library in San Francisco, because the years between birth and twenty are the years in which the soul travels farthest and swiftest.

Now, as I have said, this is what I had wanted from the very first days in Fresno:

First, to find out what to do.

Second, to *do* what I wanted to do.

When I walked from Carl Street to the Public Library I was twenty, and in the way that belongs to youth very wise. I knew everything. This knowing was in the living flesh itself which had been well-tempered by the years of riding a bicycle, and by the years of swift walking. No one I knew could walk with me for very long. My pace was too swift, and I walked too far. My own brother walking with me once suddenly stopped to call out, "Go on, go on, I'll never walk with you again."

Knowing is in the body, and a good quality of knowing comes from sending forth the body in the streets year after year.

The living of the flesh when I walked was good, its wisdom often astonishing, and I wanted to make this wisdom known.

In the photographs of my father I saw a writer, and as time went on and I saw photographs of Guy de Maupassant, Charles Dickens and Anton Chekhov I saw how much my father resembled them.

Never having known him, never having known them, they also, one at a time and altogether, became my father, as in fact all writers whose writing I cared about did.

Everybody else I knew was charming or idiotic.

First, there were the family story-tellers. They put me to roaring with laughter when I was very small, and I was fascinated with the marvelous style of each of them. The style I liked best was Aram's, though, for it was fiercely real. He himself loved his stories, his variations of the stories of others, his improvisations on themes that had some basis in actuality, and his out and out inventions.

In the lore of his life lived a man called Najari Levon who had been born in Bitlis, who actually lived in San Francisco and in Fresno. This man was a physical giant to whom great and comic things happened every minute, simply because he was who he was. Once, for instance, he slept an entire week, woke up in a casket in a San Francisco undertaking parlor, and found half a dozen friends standing around talking and laughing about the life he had lived.

At last when I was ten or eleven I met Najari Levon himself and saw that no story about him could have been exaggerated. He had by that time married six or seven times and had had by each wife a number of children.

One day while I was chatting with him on the corner of Tulare and Van Ness in Fresno, where I sold papers at that time, a young man walking by swiftly nodded to Najari Levon. I asked him who the man was and he said, "I'm not sure, but I think he's my son."

We spoke in Armenian because his English after twenty years in America was poor. He was a masseur most of the time. His height was six feet six, his weight three hundred pounds, none of it fat, his head and hands and feet enormous. He was taken for a joke by the Armenians who went to school and learned law or medicine or dentistry, but the dentists weren't at all in the same class with the lawyers, who really loved him. He himself took himself for a joke, telling his stories in a language unsurpassed for wit, and in a voice that was wit itself.

Second, there were the people who were busy. These had no time for story-telling. They became, most of them, very rich men who for diversion played backgammon, a suitable good game for money-lovers.

Now, these people I knew in the early years of my life were not writers, but the story-tellers were *good* story-tellers, and the others were good material out of which to invent new stories.

I did not want to be a story-teller, although I began to tell stories as soon as I began to talk, and I still tell them, still enjoy doing so, and have, I am sure, told any number of stories on any number of occasions that, had they been written down, would have been a book each, and as good as anything I have ever written, perhaps better.

I wanted to write. To write is not the same as to tell stories.

A writer wants what he has to say to be heard again and again. He wants it to be heard after he is dead. He wants a great many people to know him. He wants people not yet born to know him, and he wants the children of these people to know him.

In my own time, a published writer a few years short of twenty, I have seen my first book read by a girl who when I wrote the book in 1934 was not yet born, and I have seen the same book in the hands of this girl's infant son.

In those days whenever I reached the Public Library in San Francisco, it was like reaching home, even though I had no book of my own there. It seemed to be my father's house because the best men who ever wrote resembled my father.

I believed I would live to write books that would reach the Public Library.

As I walked to the Public Library I loved the streets, and I loved the books of all the men who ever walked the streets.

In the end their walking stopped, but the streets remained, and remain, and so do the books.

That is why I remember them.

A man is born in the streets and dies in them.

I was at Tech High when I was born. One day I read a short story by Guy de Maupassant. After school I went to *The Fresno Evening Herald*, got my papers, and went into the streets to sell them.

Around nightfall I was born. It happened thus:

I looked, I saw, I understood.

I was there. I was there with everybody. I saw them, I saw where they were, I saw who they were. And where they were was where I was, and who they were was who I was.

To be a writer is to be in the streets. The people in the streets are the book.

I was born because I knew I would write my share of the book. I knew this because I could walk and see. I knew my share of the book would be good, because I was exactly like everybody else and altogether different from anybody else.

The difference was myself: my own truth, vanity, genius, or madness.

I had always believed books had come into being by themselves, as acts of God. I had believed God resided in mystery, made everything, knew everything, and wrote all the books.

Little by little, however, I came to know that books are written by men, but for a long time I was not altogether able to believe this.

I had for a long time believed the writer was God, but when I came at last to Guy de Maupassant I knew the writer was a man. I cared a great deal for what he had written, and I began to believe I could write as he had written.

Now, Tech High had been the original High School of Fresno, but when the new High School was built, the old place was named Fresno Technical High School, and practical things were taught there, including typing. Consequently, I transferred from Longfellow Junior High to Tech. I had long ago understood that I would not spend very much time in schools. I had also understood that I wanted to write. And I had decided to learn to operate the typewriter in order to do my work as swiftly as possible.

Why was I so concerned about being swift? I don't know. It may have been that I did not know how long I had to live. At any rate, I was eager to get going. I wanted to become a writer, and I didn't want to wait until I was twenty-one.

I soon learned to type. I did not have to think any more about the mechanics of getting something written, all I had to think about was what I wanted to write. My study periods I spent in the school library and one day happened to pick up a book by Guy de Maupassant. I had no idea who he was. I opened the book and read a story named in English "The Bell." It was the only story in the book I read.

It was the first story I *really* read, for to read is also to write, and as I read this story I wrote it, and I liked what I wrote. The reading and writing of this story by Guy de Maupassant marks the precise moment in my life when I began to be precisely myself. I was absolutely stunned by the enormity of who I was. I was unable to speak all afternoon. My soul was hushed and humbled. I was filled with sorrow that had within in it a great gladness. I was frightened, I believed I might be mistaken, and at the same time I knew I had got things straight at last.

The building was set back from O Street. I left the building after school as if I were blind because I was not looking at anything in front of my eyes. Still I made my way down O Street to the newspaper office, but saw nothing on the way.

For a while I felt that in having found out who I was I had lost everybody else, but after I had walked in the streets of the city itself, I began to get everybody back.

I was born precisely when I had gotten everybody back and was still precisely who I was: a writer, *the* writer.

I knew a writer had to die, too, but I also knew there was no getting rid of him if he did his work earnestly, and I believed that that was how I was going to do mine.

It was in the streets of San Francisco in 1930 or 1931 that I met Kendall. He was around sixty then and had been in touch with George Bernard Shaw a dozen years or more. Having examined all of Shaw's writing, he had taken to writing letters to Shaw about Shaw's various errors. Shaw in turn had taken to replying on postcards.

Outside the Public Library is where we first met. There used to be discussions out there and Kendall and I used to take part in them. After three or four of these meetings we found out that each of us was a writer and we talked about it.

Kendall wanted to straighten the world out.

He was an Englishman who had been to sea, had been married, but was now alone. He lived in a large basement room on O'Farrell Street, the rent for which was around three dollars a week. The room was littered with books, magazines, and manuscripts. I tried my best to read one or two of the manuscripts, but they were not possible to read. I found that he was able to express himself better when he talked. I could understand him then, but I couldn't when he wrote. He was a good fellow, much like a bad boy at war with the world. His language was full of profanity, and he laughed a lot—at himself, I think, as much as at the world.

We were friends in the streets, but once he asked me to dinner at the home of a friend of his, and I went.

The friend was a playwright. The dinner was cooked by a woman of fifty or so who wasn't yet quite finished. She was the playwright's girl. We had sherry before dinner and port after. We talked, the four of us, four or five hours, about everything.

I was glad to meet these people, but when I left them and was back in the streets it seemed to me that they weren't right.

They were old and full of opinions, but the playwright had never had a play produced, Kendall had never had a book published, and the woman hadn't done anything worth noticing.

Kendall lived to see my first book published. He was quite pleased about this, and about having known me three or four years before the book had been published. He liked the book and wrote a review of it that was favorable, but the review was never published. He called my attention to the word Saroyanesque in his review, and was proud several months later to find that the same word had been used by a famous reviewer of books.

I liked Kendall, but he died, and he never had anything he ever wrote published.

There are a great many writers like him in the streets.

What is it that keeps them from writing in a way that must compel publication? What was it that kept Kendall from writing the way he spoke, which was lively, human, and funny?

It is the dirt of the world with the sun shining on it that astonishes a poet when he is a boy.

The debris was everywhere, and there was no getting rid of it.

I felt that it was important for the world to be a decent place. I felt that it was important for everybody to have a clean face, and a clean place in which to live, and to grow in spirit. I felt that nobody could grow in spirit unless he knew what he was doing, and I didn't think anybody could concentrate on what he was doing, or find out what he *wanted* to do, until he had cleaned up around him. The dirt would annoy and distract him.

It did me, at any rate, and that is why I went to work on the job of putting things in order. The job was never to be finished.

The trees around the house on San Benito Avenue had dead branches that I cut off, but then soon I noticed that there were new dead branches on them. The puncture weeds in the yard kept coming up no matter how many times I rooted them out. I have always had an especial fondness for weeds, but this weed which sprawled flat grew a thorn that was needle-sharp, and I was always stepping on these thorns in the summer when I was barefooted and the thorns were dry and hard. The wind brought rubbish of all kinds around the house every day: pieces of old newspaper, dead leaves, feathers, pieces of string, twigs. And then something else brought other things: new and old tin cans, pieces of rusted metal from machines of various kinds, dead dogs or cats or birds or rats or gophers. I kept clearing these things away, but they kept turning up again.

Sometimes living things turned up that I didn't know what to do about. A troop of half-blind kittens from under the house would turn up, and there would be too many of them to try to put up with decently.

A stray dog would take up in the barn, sick and terrified, whimpering for love.

I would come home from selling papers and find an old man sitting on the steps of the front porch.

"Have you got anything in the house I could eat?" he would say. I would go in and get him a paper bag full of bread and cheese and fruit. Sometimes he would sit there and eat the food, and sometimes he would get up and go, and I would wonder what had happened to him that had brought him to nothing better than begging for food.

In the summer the dirt and decay were greatest, and out of the decay came flies and insects. Somebody would fling the remains of a watermelon or a casaba into the empty lot, the stuff would rot in the heat, insects would fall on it, and soon the whole atmosphere would be full of a stench in which delicate but annoying insects flourished. The berries of China Ball trees would ripen and drop, the heat would turn them yellow and soft, and another stench would come from them.

And of course every house had garbage.

The stuff kept coming. There was no stopping it.

A man trying to think always had a bad time of it. He kept saying to himself, "I've got to get that stink out of the air. I've got to clean up around here again. I can't think with all this filth and stink around."

I had a spade and a rake, and I worked at clearing away everything within the boundaries of my own house and yard. I then took the water hose and sprinkled water all over the earth, settling the loose dirt and dust, and giving the place a decent clean smell. I sprinkled water on the trees and plants, on the house, and on the sidewalk in front of the house. For a minute, on a Sunday afternoon, the place would be clean and smell clean and cool, and I would go into the house, to the round table in the dining room, and sit there with a book or a magazine and try to go on with my thinking. Soon, though, I would hear a fly, then see it, and I would have to get up and go after it. Next, a mosquito, or a brown bug of some kind with long wings, or a spider, or a troop of ants working hard on a few grains of spilled sugar along the top of the table.

The dead dirt was everywhere and the living dirt was everywhere. It annoyed me for a long time, but somewhere along the line the dirt stopped annoying me. Somewhere along the line I came to understand that the dirt was there to stay and that it was part of my life and always would be and I would have to put up with it and learn to think in the midst of it.

My own dirt and decay never stopped, and I got over believing that it ever would. For many years I believed that I would one day achieve total and final health. It would probably happen sometime next year, but it never happened.

What about the dirt? What could a man do about the dirt of the world, and the dirt of himself?

One day my uncle Vahan told me a story.

A poor man with a dirty face went to a gentleman in the streets of Bitlis and said, "Give me some money."

The gentleman said, "Why are you dirty?"

The poor man said, "I am poor."

The gentleman said, "All right, clean yourself and still be poor."

My uncle Vahan was my uncle by marriage, having married one of my mother's sisters. He was a tailor by trade but bought an orchard of apricot and peach trees five years before he died at the age of thirty-nine. He lost the orchard before he died. I had other uncles by marriage who could not speak to a small boy in a sensible way, but this man could. It was the only way he could speak to anybody.

494

One day he found me sitting on the front porch steps of the house on San Benito Avenue, angry and troubled about a newsboy's badge I had lost, for which I had paid a dollar. *The Fresno Evening Herald* decided that each of its newsboys ought to wear a badge with the name of the paper on it and a number. I don't remember the number of my badge, but I do remember that it was nickel-plated, and that it was compulsory to buy and wear it. A dollar was a lot of money, but I didn't want to stop earning a little money every evening, so I bought a badge and wore it, and then suddenly after not more than two hours discovered that it was lost.

This bothered me, and my uncle Vahan wanted to know what the matter was. I told him. He said in Armenian, "A dollar? That is nothing. Let your soul remain alive."

Now, this phrase is better in Armenian than it is in English.

I understood instantly what he meant, and I will never forget how glad I was to know that nothing in the world was more important to me than my own soul, which neither accident nor error nor dirt ought ever to be permitted to destroy.

The wish to change the world, or to rid it of insects, must be a basic one in the early lives of writers, for I haven't met a writer yet, unknown or famous, who wasn't in his childhood annoyed by ants, bugs, insects, or parents.

Still, the world goes right on making debris, insects come forth delicately out of rot and ferment, and parents fight it out with children.

The streets are the hope of both: angry fathers turn to them for peace, and impatient sons run to them for the beginning they believe will get them somewhere.

The streets of Oakland were much involved in sleep, as all streets are in the end. I saw them, dreamed them, saw them again, and still they were not out of sleep. I walked in them more asleep than awake, woke up in them only to feel I had awakened into deeper sleep, for the streets are sleep itself, not one man's sleep, but the sleep of the dead. It is in the streets that the dead live on. It is there that the life of man is immortal, for there is no man dead who isn't in the streets again, going his way.

Fred Finch was a number of buildings, a few acres in which there was a vegetable garden, a barn, a storage building, and something like a meadow, after which came woods, but the best woods were past the boundaries of the place.

Peralta Street was in the hills which were not big. I walked that street from the time immediately after I was three to the time immediately after

I was seven. From Peralta a curved road climbed to the Administration Building, then went down to Peralta again.

I was walking down that road one day when a boy on a bicycle knocked me down. My head struck one of the jagged stones bordering the road, and I got up with a cut over my left eye. I wasn't hurt but I *was* surprised and annoyed and I began to bawl, although I knew I didn't need to. No one believed I didn't need to, though. My face was covered with blood. I might have gone on bawling, but I couldn't imagine what the good of that would be, so I stopped. I was bored.

John Wesley Hagan took me by horse and wagon to a doctor who sewed the cut together. It was no trouble for the doctor to do this simple surgical work. The man sewed the flesh back together, and I stood and waited while he did it. He said nothing, John Wesley Hagan said nothing, and I said nothing.

After that John Wesley Hagan and I were friends, and a theory that I was a brave fellow got around in the orphanage. It was a false theory as far as I was concerned because I hadn't saved anybody from drowning in the sea or from burning to death in a small locked room somewhere. I didn't go to any trouble to dispute the theory, though, mainly I think because I didn't know how.

John Wesley Hagan was the Superintendent of Fred Finch. He was Scotch, fifty or so, slim and quiet, and he seemed to have an earnest nature and a sense of humor at the same time. Now and then when it was time for him to take the horse and wagon to market, to fetch provisions, he sought me out in the playground and told me I could go with him. We sat together on the seat of the uncovered wagon, and the horse took off, generally knowing where to go and when to stop. Hagan and I did not chat, as I remember it, but there was real communication between us. I remember being with him in a store and having him take a large spoon of chocolate and put it before my mouth. I opened my mouth and he dumped the chocolate in and I ate it. It was an hour or so before supper time and his own wife would have told him that he was spoiling me and spoiling my dinner, but he did it just the same—for she wasn't there—and I was glad that he did.

From the seat of the wagon the streets of Oakland were different. I was up, looking down. The streets were not the same from the seat of the wagon, nor was I, but it was Hagan more than the wagon that made the change in me. It was his having picked me out of the small boys to go with him. I didn't like him especially, because a small boy never likes a Superintendent, but I didn't hate him, either, as most boys did.

Later on, though, I *did* hate him, but it wasn't for long. I can't hate for long. It isn't worth it.

His wife was Lillian Pender. She was rather delicate and beautiful. She painted in oils, but bore him no children. She painted portraits of a number of the children at Fred Finch. One day I sat for her. I sat a few more times, I think, but I never saw the portrait. She never finished it, most likely. She finished the portrait of the boy who was killed in the automobile accident, though. The portrait was reproduced in color on a postcard, and everybody old enough to do so was permitted to take a batch of these cards and go around ringing doorbells and selling them.

The money thus obtained was brought to Lillian Pender, for the orphanage, for the boy's mother, for a tombstone for him, I forget which. There was great rivalry among the older boys and girls in the matter of the number of cards sold and the amount of money brought to Lillian Pender. He was a blond boy of eight or so who wore light blue overalls and seemed awfully sad, almost as if he knew he would not live very long. Part of the lore of his death had to do with the opening up of new fields of adventure for the boys and girls who went out and sold the cards. Many of the boys kept some of the money for themselves or bought things they had always wanted: pocket knives, mainly. Several boys proudly told of stealing things in stores. The excitement got to be too much for the smaller boys, so one day several of the boys who were in my ward, the smallest boys at Fred Finch, Sammy Isaacs, Teddy Dolan and myself, decided to get hold of some of the cards and go out into the streets and sell them.

I went to Lillian Pender's office or studio and found hundreds of the cards on her desk and nobody there to ask what I wanted. I took a great many of the cards and left the office. I handed some to Sammy Isaacs, some to Teddy Dolan, and kept some for myself. We then took off to see how we would make out in this adventure.

I ran a block or so up Peralta, then down into another street, and finally to the door of a house, to press the bell-button. A woman came to the door. I told her the story of the boy's death. She went inside a moment, came back with a number of coins, handed them to me, and took a card. I remember that there were tears in her eyes and that her voice was pity-laden.

She was sorry the poor little boy had been killed and glad I hadn't and handed me the money.

This was rather strange.

It was good to ring a doorbell and have somebody unknown open it, to speak to a stranger, and then to receive money from the stranger, but it was something else, too. Money is good, children love money for its own sake, as money, as coins, but this was funny money. It was pity money. It was begged money. I took the money and ran back to Sammy Isaacs and Teddy Dolan. We talked about what had happened to each of us. We knew it was not necessary to be ten or eleven or twelve to ring a doorbell and get money for a postcard. Each of us had been given money by the person who had come to the door. The money was not a nickel and a couple of pennies. It was real money. It was quarters and half-dollar pieces, and a few nickels and dimes thrown in.

We went on with the work and soon each of us had a small pocketful of coins. We then went to a store and spent some of the money on candy and other things we wanted.

When it was dark we decided to call it a day and go back, but when we reached the orphanage we found the whole place in an uproar on the theory that we had got lost, had been kidnapped, or had run away.

We turned in the money but were not thanked for it.

For a while we believed we were to go without supper, since we had not been on time for it and everybody else had already had supper, but at last the cook fixed us a plate each and we sat down in the big dining room and ate in silence.

Years later I decided to write a play. I wrote it and called it *Subway Circus*. In this play a small boy is kept after school for dreaming. His teacher asks him questions of arithmetic.

"Now, if a boy has five apples and gives away two, how many apples remain?" she says.

"What kind of apples?" the boy says.

The teacher speaks to the Principal of the school about this. The Principal says to the teacher, "Let *him* ask *you* questions."

The boy then asks questions, and among them is this one: "What is a street?"

The year was 1935. I was in New York for the second time in my life. I was twenty-seven years old. I had had a book of short stories published. I was famous. I had been famous two years. I had been famous before the publication of "The Daring Young Man on the Flying Trapeze" in *Story Magazine*, but not as a writer. I had been famous as myself. A few days after the story was published I was famous as a writer. How famous can you be? What is the good of it?

Still, I will not repudiate my fame. I got it, I earned it, I have it. My name is known to millions I do not know, and I wanted this to be so. I have met thousands of people I would not have met had I not become famous, and I wanted this to be so, too. My writing is careless, but all through it is something that is good, that is mine alone, that no other writer could ever achieve.

What is this thing?

It is love of streets. It is love of this world and this life, which in the end must become for each of us old and rotten, which each of us must regret, of which each of us must be ashamed.

Our comfort is the streets, the lanes we took, the time we took in them, the other walkers we saw in them, in the light of day, in the electric light of night, in wind, in rain, in snow—the hard, gray streets in which we lived or tried, in which we were blind or came to seeing.

One day on my way home from Sequoia School in Oakland where I was in the first grade I heard a small boy cry. The boy was my own age, and someone in his family had died, perhaps his mother or his father. The boy stood on a high porch. In front of the house was a hearse. I stood across the street, alone there, as the boy was alone on the porch. I heard the boy cry. I saw men carry a casket out of the house, across the porch, down the steps. I saw the boy follow them, dressed in his best clothes. I saw the men slide the casket into the hearse. In my own heart I wept for the stranger who was dead, as the boy wept.

What is a street? It is where the living weep, where the dead go off in silence to their peace.

Death made me sick. Death hurt me. Death annoyed me. Death and dirt kept me from my thinking. Death in the streets made me want to know.

The weeping boy made me want to think of a way to get the dead one back for him. The sound of his weeping made me want to find out a way to do that. I believed something might be invented to bring back the dead. I went to work on this invention, brokenhearted by the boy's sorrow, thinking of his need of love.

I went to work on the invention in the playground at Fred Finch, working with discarded things. I searched among the stuff that would be carted away the following morning and found two empty tomato cans. I removed the labels on which I saw engravings of red tomatoes. I dug two holes in the earth. I placed a can in each of these holes, the open tops level with the earth. I filled one can with water, and sat all afternoon thinking about the can full of water and about the empty can beside it. I believed I was on my way to the answer for the boy.

If I could get the water out of the full can into the can which was empty, then no doubt the boy could get the dead back. He could get love back. I sat and thought. How could I get the water to transfer itself from the full can to the empty one? That was the problem. I concentrated on the problem, watching both cans intently, waiting for love to achieve this simple miracle. I believed love could do it. I waited, brooded, thought, remembered, concentrated. I packed the earth around the edges of the tops of each can, believing this might help. I dreamed about the joy of the boy seeing his father or mother walking up the street, not knowing how this thing had happened, not knowing I had done it.

The water remained where it was. The empty can remained empty.

I lifted the full can out of the earth and poured the water into the empty can and when it was full I lifted it out of the earth, too. I poured the water back and forth from one can to the other. I poured the water into one of the holes in the ground. I went back to the faucet and filled both cans with water and took them back to where I had been thinking. Now I had both cans filled with water, but I had invented nothing, and out of thought and love had not yet made anything impossible happen, which is what I wanted to do. I set the cans on the surface of the earth and watched them a long time, thinking steadily and remembering the boy and the anguish of the heart when it has lost something, when it has lost the source of love. Both cans were full of water in front of my eyes. I poured the water out of one can into the dry hole in the ground, and again saw the water disappear.

The problem was still simple and clear: to get the water in the full can to go by itself into the empty can.

This time the cans were not set into the earth, they were placed on the surface of it. There was a distance of eight or nine inches between them. The water did not lift itself out of one can into the other. The water did not disappear out of one can and re-appear in the other. One can remained full, the other empty. I brought the cans together, hoping this might do the trick. It did not do the trick.

I felt desperately that I must do this thing. I must witness it. I must make it come to pass. I kept hearing the boy cry. I kept seeing him follow the casket to the hearse.

But the thing would not happen.

I poured the water out of the full can and saw it steal away into the earth.

I kicked the can, and then I kicked the other can. By turns I kicked them both until I had gone all the way across the playground.

A number of boys I knew by face but not by name got into the game and the cans were kicked back and forth until they were out of shape and you could never get water into them again.

The invention failed. The dead did not come back. Death remained death. The end remained the end. When the bell rang I went into the dining room and ate supper. There was nothing else to do under the circumstances.

I am not taking the world street by street, for I never lived or walked or wrote in chronological order. In the beginning I lived in the end, I lived in the middle, I lived in the beginning, all at once and altogether, and it was so in the middle, and will be so in the end. I never had the time or the nature to live only in the beginning in the beginning, or to live only in the middle in the middle.

I walked every which way in the streets. I lived every which way in the time of them. I wrote every which way in my own time, which I knew was not my own time but anybody's, and the time of the dead as well. I longed for order and I longed for my own self. The order I found was the order of disorder. The self I came to, or the self that came to me, was not my own.

I was somebody more in the streets.

The first street of all was a road.

The horse was hitched to the wagon, the wagon was loaded with my father's belongings, my mother sat on the seat, my two sisters, my brother and myself sat in the back. My father got up onto the wagon and sat beside my mother. He took the reins and clicked at the horse. The horse and the wagon began to move down the country road. I looked back and saw a house surrounded by grape vines. We had lived there, but I did not remember that we had. The day smelled of heat, dust, grass and water. The wagon rocked. My father clicked at the horse again. I fell asleep.

After that, my father was dead. I saw him once and never saw him again. The road was near the town of Sanger, which is nine miles east of Fresno. The wagon stopped in Fresno, and from there my father took his family by train to San Bruno, but I did not remember the arrival of the wagon in Fresno, the departure of the train, my father, or anything else.

From the begining I slept and awoke by turns, but for a long time I didn't remember anything, and then for a long time I remembered one thing or another but didn't remember the greater part of anything.

Fresno, Sanger, San Jose, Campbell, San Bruno, San Francisco, Oakland—these are the places I knew when there was no true knowing, when it was all sleep and no memory.

The streets of Fresno followed the letters of the alphabet, and numbers, and they were named after saints, and others. Across the Southern Pacific tracks in 1908 was A Street, and still is, but Z Street was nowhere at all. H Street was just inside the S.P. tracks. Between Tulare and Kern, on H Street was a house in 1908, in which I was born.

The name of the vineyard near Sanger I have forgotten, but it had a Spanish name. Was it La Paloma? I believe it was. I remember nothing. I go on hearsay.

I began in earnest at the Fred Finch Orphanage in Oakland, California. I said good-bye to my mother and began. I began to reason, to think, to wonder what it was all about. Until this good-bye there had been no reason to notice or remember. I had noticed and remembered by accident, but now I noticed and remembered because I wanted to know who I was, where I belonged, and what I was supposed to do. I was my father's son, but he was dead. I was my mother's son, but she was gone. I was Henry's brother. He was in another ward at the orphanage, the ward for boys who were six or over. I was Cosette's brother and Zabel's brother, and they were in the ward for girls. Still, the four of us were there in the orphanage together. I was called Willie. I didn't know much about the other name, although I had heard it. I do not remember having been sure it was my name. I did not know anything about nationality or religion.

In my ward this is what I knew: I was there with five or six other small boys and our matron was a woman named Mrs. Winchester.

At night two or three of the boys in the ward rocked their cribs and wept, trying to hide from the others that they were doing so, for it had come to pass that it was shameful to rock a crib, cry, or wet the bed. In the dark of the ward the boys who were not rocking and crying talked to one another. They laughed at Mrs. Winchester and they laughed at the rockers and criers. Now and then somebody rocking and crying would stop to speak to the others, so that the others would perhaps believe he had not been rocking and crying. But then in a moment he would fall silent and soon he would be rocking and crying again. Finally, everybody would fall silent, and then asleep.

Who was I? I was one of the boys in the ward for small boys. Where did I belong? I didn't know, but I didn't believe I belonged where I was. What was I supposed to do? I was supposed to obey the rules, and I was supposed to learn to dress myself, tie my shoe laces, and to believe the story about God.

I saw my brother every day but he was in another part of the life at the place. I asked him where our mother was and he told me she was in San Francisco, working as a maid for a family. I asked him when we would see her again and he said he didn't know. I asked him how long we would be staying at this place and he said he didn't know. I asked him if he liked this place and he said he hated it.

Everybody in the place hated it. It wasn't home, that's all.

One Sunday my mother came from San Francisco with a basket full of sandwiches, and we had a picnic, sitting on the grass of a hill, my mother handing sandwiches around, all of us eating and talking. Her English was poor, but she could make herself understood. She spoke in Armenian to my oldest sister, Cosette, who was then twelve. I could not understand what they were saying.

Farewell to the boys and girls. Whoever he was I remember Melvin Athey. Whoever she was I remember Juanita Pollard. The white pitcher full of cold milk on warm afternoons I remember. The cook's meat pies with the golden crust. The Sunday breakfast eggs, brown and white. The martial walks to Sunday School. The witches in the hills. The hazelnuts in the trees. The ferns and the poison oak along the paths. The waterdogs, captured and brought home. The blue-bellied lizards which snapped off their tails in captivity. The climbing of the slim eucalyptus trees, making them bend to the earth again. The visiting tellers of tales. The German band on the steps of the Administration Building.

They invited me to spend a summer week with a family somewhere in Oakland and like a fool I let somebody come and take me by streetcar to this family. The place smelled, and I couldn't wait to get back. Every family has a smell. The smell this family had made me sick. I preferred the smell at Fred Finch which I no longer noticed.

I spent long days and years there, and the day I went away was a fine day. The locomotive came up with the train, and the four of us got aboard and sat down and the train began to go, and it went to Fresno, and I was seven, and I stayed in Fresno ten years.

I do not know what makes a writer, but it probably isn't happiness. A happy boy or man is not apt to need to write. But was there ever a happy boy? Is there ever a happy man?

In Oakland I woke up and began to notice and remember. In Fresno I went to work. The idea of going to work was my own. My brother Henry went to work selling *The Fresno Evening Herald,* so I went to work selling it, too. He was ten and a half and I was seven and a half. I went out into the streets and began to live in them. I had escaped from the orphanage at last. I had a home at last, the house at 2226 San Benito Avenue. I lived there with my mother, my sisters, and my brother. All through the city were branches of my father's family and branches of my mother's family. Each branch had its own house and its own members.

But the world was my home and I was glad to be in it.

Inside the world I found another world in the theatres of Fresno. The Hippodrome had movies and vaudeville both, the Orpheum on Broadway had vaudeville only, The Liberty had movies only, and so it was with The Kinema and The Bijou. I got into all of these theatres free of charge through friendship with the ticket-takers or by sneaking in. I saw very nearly every movie that came to town, and very nearly every vaudeville show. This other world inside the real world was strange and wonderful. I found it necessary to inhabit this world, but I always attended to my work first, which was to sell papers.

My hope was to earn at least half a dollar every day.

The Herald cost a nickel. Half was mine, half was the Herald's. If I sold two papers I had a profit of a nickel. If I sold twenty I had a profit of half a dollar. I had no regular customers. I sometimes sold twenty papers in a matter of minutes, and then sometimes I couldn't sell ten from half past three until half past eight or nine.

For a time it was permissible to turn in unsold papers, but this ruling was changed, so that if I took out twenty papers and sold only ten papers I had no profit for the day at all. The risk was great and now and then I sold only eight, losing a dime and taking home twelve papers.

Before I had been selling papers a month, though, I could get rid of twenty every afternoon and evening, so I took out twenty as a matter of course and hung on in the streets until I had sold them all, or had only three or four to go.

If it was very late I took one to a Greek candy store where I traded it for whatever the man there wanted to let me have, generally about a dime's worth of candy. I took another to the ticket-taker at the Liberty Theatre and went in and saw the show or part of it, and then I took one to the ticket-taker at the Hippodrome and went in there, too.

I sometimes didn't get home until after ten at night. When I was nine I sometimes didn't get home until the town was closed, or at any rate the theatres.

I loved the theatres, and even though I was hungry, I never spent money for food. The Greek's candy, and water, would be my food until I got home where I always knew there would be a pot on the stove full of something good to eat.

The streets made me, and the streets stink, but I love them, for I was born in them out of flesh and I was born in them out of spirit.

This book is necessarily without beginning or end. Had I not started until I had come to the beginning I could never have started. Had I not stopped until I had come to the end I could never have stopped. For the subject of the book is not so much myself, now and sometime ago, as it is the action of the human soul, to which there is no start or stop. My life has not been, is not, and cannot be art, but it has been, is, and shall continue to be an essay at it, because that is the action to which I am committed—that is to say, to endure time, and to meet the varying circumstances of truth, reality and potential impersonally, in order to be free, even of my self. At his best, things do not happen to the artist; he happens to them. He is kinder to things than they tend to be to one another, because being free he must choose to be kind, or quit. This kindness is impersonal. It belongs to no man alone but to evolving life itself. Out of it may finally come (perhaps more than out of anything else) the beginning of the integration of man, and the achievement of form and meaning in his action. Neither love nor hate, nor any order of intense adherence to personal involvement in human experience, may be so apt to serve the soul as this freedom and this necessity to be kind.

from
Obituaries

1.

*P*eople die. It is a strange event, a strange order of event; it is an order that is not accurately understood. Nobody really knows what death is. Everybody talks about death all their lives. Everybody dies and falls silent. Human life may be said to be obsessed with death. Everybody is said to be afraid of death. All the same sooner or later everybody becomes adjusted to life, fully aware that he is going to die. The anxiety about when it is going to happen gives being alive something extra. A kind of interior companionship, something to talk to which sometimes becomes somebody, a side of himself, a side of everybody else, a side of God, or something altogether unidentified and unidentifiable. Not knowing how much time he has, has quite clearly made every man vital. He has had to stop and think about how to use the time. It is not that he isn't going to be forgotten in any case; it is something else. He goes to work and starts a program of work that he believes is likely to do several things at the same time, the most important of which is to keep himself alive longer than he might otherwise be likely to be alive, and then this program of work seems likely to compel astonishment and admiration among the members of his family, and then it is likely to be spread out into the whole neighborhood itself, which might turn out to be the whole world itself, and the whole human race; whereupon something rather amusing has been achieved: fame. Or notoriety. There's no reason to believe that any of the most notorious of the monsters of the human race ever imagined themselves to be anything less than the child of a mother, and loved not only by her but by possibly even the father as well, and possibly by the brother and the sister as well. There is no need to go back in time any further than a couple of hundred years for an example or two; but for our purposes, all of us being quite alive, a hundred years back is more than enough. Adolf Hitler in all of his photographs seems quite clearly to believe he is the darling of the people of Germany and of quite a number of other peoples. Well, was he? The answer is that he was as much as anybody else probably ever was. It really isn't necessary to be the darling of a great many people in order for any man to imagine that he is the darling of the world, of the human race, of history. Let us get one thing straight—or as straight as possible—at the outset: there is no man alive who is not the darling of himself, and that's enough for all practical purposes. And he will do the necessary, as the saying is, to spread that radiance to the less fortunate. (As I write, on January 17, 1977, a Monday, the noon news in Fresno begins with the information that a murderer named Gilmore has been shot to death by the State of Utah. His execution had been "stayed" several times and after each of these postponements he had attempted suicide by drugs. His execution was witnessed by his two lawyers, his uncle, and his Hollywood agent, unnamed. This man insisted that the State of Utah carry out its own law and execute him. His mother, working with the American Civil Liberties Union, and many others who are opposed to Capital Punishment, were successful in postponing the event several times, but his mother very sensibly declined to witness her son's execution, or murder, as you wish. So did his bride or fiancée—Or did she die in their attempted suicide pact?—No, she didn't die, and it is not inconceivable that Gilmore's Hollywood agent will be interested in putting forward the prospect of fame and fortune for her. Who is the agent? Well, he might be the man who is the agent for Mr. Richard Nixon, who stands to earn two or three million dollars for telling his side of his story; and let the smart-aleck press tell any side they like. Is America supposed to hang its head in shame about the execution ten minutes after sunrise this morning of the murderer? How about the man who survived everything, including something with the official name of phlebitis? And finally how about the unnamed agent: should he be the man for the nation to hang its head in shame about? Let that sit there, please.) I am a subscriber to a weekly paper called *Variety*. The 71st Anniversary Edition, dated January 5, 1977, arrived a few days ago, and I examined with fascination—on the last page, 164—the names in alphabetical order in the annual feature entitled "Necrology." I had predicted that among those listed would be 34 men or women that I had met. I was not far off the mark: there were 28. But many of the 200 or more others listed were of course people I knew *about*, for *Variety* is the paper, the Bible, as they say, of show business, celebrated in song by Irving Berlin. Well, I thought, I'm very well along into my 68th year, hadn't I better write about the people I know in *Variety*'s Necrology of 1976? So that is what I am doing. And about Dr. Leo Eloesser, who is not on that list, who died at the age of 95 on Monday October 4th. We met in San Francisco in 1938, and he was another of that city's amazing sons. I was just 30 at the time, and he was about 58. Now I'm 68 and Dr. Eloesser is dead, cremated, and his ashes scattered at his 40-acre ranch near the small village of Tacambaro, in the state of Michoacan. He died in bed, asleep, apparently of cardiac arrest, *The San Francisco Chronicle* says. He was a great man, very small, rather eccentric, he certainly never married, and I was astonished to notice the item in the old issue of the paper on the floor of the bathroom. I thought he had died long years ago, and there he was, alive all the time.

2.

Is there a way to live that will change death in any of its varieties? In any of its meanings, that is to say? In any of its realities? In any of its imponderables? (if that's anything at all like the idea we're trying to suggest). Isn't death death, period, as the saying is? Isn't it the same every time for every man, including Kings and Billionaires and Rich Writers with Women and Big Cars? Well, of course it is in no sense, ever, sir, ever, madam, the same, not even for the same, or so-called same, customer. We die a little, somebody nice said to himself, when anybody else dies. We live a little, too, and that's the reason the obituary page of the paper is so popular. But there is truth to the bright sayings of children, always. We do die a little when anybody else dies. He prepares the way, for us. Didn't the young fellow say something along the lines of going ahead to prepare the way, and now here we are all old and leaky and unprepared, or at any rate no more prepared than we ever were. There is a way to live, and there is a way to die, and there is a way to fuck, to put no bones upon it, and there is a way to make money, to spend money, to be cheated out of money, and all this money monkey business is for the simple reason that life, death, and making sense are connected from before the beginning to after the end, with money. Think of it: money has that kind of unnatural but very ferocious connection with each of us. If your father was rich when he got your mother with child, and you turned out to be the child, you have got that fact to live with. If he was poor, as the father of Charles Dickens was, then of course you have *that* fact to live with—and what it did to Charles Dickens it has not done again, although there were many by the millions whose fathers were much poorer, much more in debt, than Charles Dickens's father. So how do we put that fact to work in a useful way? We don't, do we? We only ponder longer about the amazing truth of Charles Dickens and the reality of his literary art. I like especially the flare-up of fancy orgasm-seeking that sent him self-deceiving into the arms and scent and warmth of the delicious little actress who didn't mind having the physical fool in bed, not especially, at any rate, since she had been to bed with others, perhaps a good variety of others, and probably not excluding members of the profession (that is actors, acting lovers in bed, or acting dandies out of bed), and in addition to actors surely or at any rate probably also producers, backers, directors, and whoever else was immediately or potentially useful in the business of putting forward the career. The mother of the many children of Charles Dickens was as he felt thick-skulled and really nothing much in bed, but she had got pregnant a good dozen or more times, and presumably by him, so she must have served the purpose, or the several purposes, since when he was getting his faithful wife pregnant he was also writing *Oliver Twist* and *Great Expectations* and the better part of all the rest of his books. After taking up with the actress he was indeed pretty much done (he had done his writing), and something more was in order, he felt; he had also done the better part of his lecturing or acting, and yet something more was wanted, and he had every reason to believe that she might very well supply precisely what was wanted. Perhaps she was, but one suspects that she wasn't, not by a million miles or fathers or characters in sad and hilarious works of writing. What she was was pussy, pure and simple, and the British have traditionally put forward some of the best pussy in the human family. And only pimps, it seems, are above getting basic matters confused by the proximity of pussy. An acquaintance forty years ago stood in the back room at Gelber-Lilienthal, a bookstore on Sutter Street, in San Francisco, and said, "I want to write a novel about pimps. They are not like other men, it is a very complicated situation." But of course he said a thousand times as much as I have put down, summing up what he said: he hated pimps, he was afraid of pimps. They seemed to treat women wickedly, and what's worse, women seemed to love them for their rotten characters and their dirty behavior. They were not made helpless by their pricks, and this young writer wanted to try to understand that. He was in trouble all the time from the demands of his prick, and from the impossibility of not adoring women, and consequently being deceived by them, being hurt by them, being almost driven mad by them, and almost being driven to the murder of them, one by one. Yes, of course there is a way to live that makes a difference in every aspect of both putting up with time, and being put out of any connection with it: passing, passing, and you're not there going with it, which is of course what death is, or at any rate what else it is, for it is many, many things, and no obituary notice, whether in *The New York Times*, or in *Variety*, even begins to try to tell anybody what it is, not even in the instance of the person whose death is the hero of that particular obituary notice. The poor son of a bitch up and died, but we can tell you that he was born in China, the son of a Seventh Day Adventist Medical Missionary, and went to school there, and in Boston, and worked hard and married three times, and a child by each marriage, and died. And he died. And died. And died. And finally was taken to the mortician's, and that motherfucker fell on him with needles and thread and syringes and cosmetics and wax and spit and polish and had him in his casket looking like a million. I hate morticians, they belittle life, and I have never heard of one of them ever saying anything worth anything. Not one word.

3.

My purpose is to run down the alphabetical list in *Variety* of the dead of 1976, but it is in order first to think about the earliest experience of death—which of course would have to be the death of others. I have no intention of over-doing this, but it is desirable to get our bearings, so to put it, about this enormous part of life. Death is the last thing that happens to a person, but it is not his last experience—that has to be something he remembers, of course. An experience happening is one thing, and it is not complete until it is remembered as having happened. Memory—remembering an event—is artful. There is no way to get away from that, it would seem. The one who remembers makes more of that which happened, or less, as he decides he should. And of course there is the puzzlement of not remembering anything—all of a sudden: whereas ordinarily one remembered everything. This troubles people, as it should. You don't remember what you did last night? somebody asks somebody, and then is told what he did: generally something slightly offside, unworthy, embarrassing, stupid, out-of-character. Nobody remembers dying. It can't be remembered, for the reason that death is an event that includes the total effacement of memory, of the vast stored "life" experienced, dreamed, imagined, wished, witnessed in reality, or the world, and in fancy, or art, and death takes on that instant totality which nothing else ever takes on. O'Neill's father of Anna Christie learns (or witnesses) the truth that his beautiful daughter (Anna performed by Greta Garbo in a production at the Geary Theatre in San Francisco about 40 years ago or in 1937 or so), the truth that Anna is a streetwalker, and it seems to drive him mad; but while his upbringing was responsible for that deep shock and pain, it also kept him from dropping dead. So Anna was a whore, so let her be, she was still Anna, and she could stop being a whore, most likely, and she could be all the things fathers imagine they want their daughters to be—but of course the real story here is Anna, not her father, and of course she felt terrible about being a waterfront whore; but that was far from final; she hadn't fallen dead in any bed anywhere; she had only accepted money for sexual congress, as the saying is, with vagrant and hungry men. Or a great man is exposed as a fraud, and his greatness is seen to be instantly either far greater than anybody ever suspected, or a total sham, a false thing—and the man himself picks and chooses what he wants to remember about the experience of exposure: yes, he is not actually a member of the Russian nobility, he is a poor boy from a desperate background in Lower Manhattan, or in Brooklyn, or somewhere, and his elegant manners, with apparently natural and profound courtesy, are acquired; he did not inherit them. He owns and operates the famous restaurant bearing his name: Mike Romanoff. His exposure does not belittle but enlarges him. Of course I speak from memory: I knew Mike, I knew Gergerson-Romanoff, but I'm not sure Gergerson is or was his family name, either, and it doesn't matter. He was a decent fellow and his English accent was considered excellent. Among his friends were many writers, especially Robert Benchley. All of the successful Hollywood writers enjoyed eating at Mike's, and in being able to chat with him casually. The food was expensive for those days: a lunch might cost as much as $5 with a cocktail and wine, but it was good food, served at a fine table, in a very pleasant atmosphere. He was Mike Romanoff, and not Harry Gergerson, as he had been born. He was alive, in his own elegant restaurant, not dead, in Forest Lawn. All right. Or okay, question mark—as the strange nervous swift-talking young people, generally young women, say, and go on quickly to another phase of the dissertation on the real meaning of love, and how it differs from hate. Hate: he don't let you know he likes you, okay? No, not at all okay, but on she goes with a grand philosophy of something very like total absence of information or meaning. Has she been reading Sartre perhaps? In any case, the idea if not the reality of death starts as a mystery with great force and power to affect others—everybody is all hot and bothered because somebody has done something that is called "died." And there's the hearse (I used to marvel at the name of Hearst, how right it was for his reputation—he was a kind of jitneybus for the dead, or the murdered), there's the black wagon out front, and on the porch there's the small boy in Oakland in 1911 or 1912 crying in a way that just won't do at all, and there I am across the street, alone, on my way back to Fred Finch Orphanage, fallen back from Blanche

Fulton's group, to be alone, on my own a moment, and nobody to tell me why the small boy, my own age in fact, is crying that way. Then, how do I know instantly that it is because somebody has died: his mother? or his father? How can you know who is in a casket brought out from the parlor of the house? I decided for some reason that it was his mother, and then decide no, it was his father. A woman certainly tried to comfort him, to stop his crying, but he would have none of it. He wanted—I wanted—his father back. Indeed I called out to everything: If you're that smart, give that boy back his father. Anybody can do what's easy, do something that's hard, something that's impossible, get that man out of that stupid box, start him up again, he's stopped, give him back his memory, he doesn't know what happened to him. That was my first awareness of death—and of course I am remembering it, again, with art.

4.

Will do, will do, will get along to the list of the dead, but hell-fire, man, shucks, friend, shoot, brother, good Lord, enemy, gosh, reader, there is such a thing, is there not, as preface and preparation? You can't bite off the universe and expect to be able to chew and swallow it, can you? Death is everything, man; death is not just a little part of everything, it is the whole thing, but of course what we mean is that life and death are together, one thing, or as the pitchmen used to say, one and the same thing, you have one and you also have the other; you can't have one without the other, so what's all the crying about? What's the boy on the porch carrying on about? What's *Finnegan's Wake* laughing and crying about? What's all art talking and talking and talking about? Why does religion, as the shortcut and meaningless word puts it, start with a repudiation of death, as if in doing that life also is not repudiated? It is not necessary to live forever; it is not desirable, it is not even a small softening of the shock of stopping cold: think of the thousands of—bang—heart-attacks in America alone every year. Walter Huston was at lunch with three or four pals, when suddenly he said, "This is it," and fell forward onto the table and died. Jed Harris said he was at the table, and so I must suspect that he was and that his telling of Walter Huston's last event, his non-experience, is not totally false: and of course there are many similar last events among friends and members of the family. I like best those who cry bitterly as they seem to know the damned thing is going to happen soon...but how do they know? Well, it seems to be from having had a survival from a heart attack, a kind of teasing reprieve, and they know they aren't going to last very much longer—a week, a day, a month, but never again are they going to carry on as if there is no such thing as death. It is right for lovers of life to cry about the unstoppable arrival of effacement. It is no fun to be that stupid about anything. Why? Why me? Why now? What's the hurry? What did I do? Jesus, Joe, do you remember those days in San Francisco forty years ago when we were young punks full of piss and vinegar—sudden failure to speak, sudden necessity for the fac[e] to twist and the lungs to exercise with terrible sobs. Christ, do I remember, man? I sure do, I sure do, old friend. All we did was chase tail, didn't we? And money, didn't we? Of course those who have felt the end fully, but for some reason been granted a short reprieve, of course they cry like babies, and of course they should, for they don't know how to use the reprieve; they don't know what they are supposed to do in order to make the inevitable both acceptable and welcome. What they want is to be who they had been before the damned shock, or better than that, who they had been forty years ago, if only in memory, if only in the art of remembering dismal days of hustling a living as if they had been luminous days and nights of beautiful women giving themselves joyously to the piss and vinegar boy in the shower after the first bang. The first of four, at least. Those were the days, weren't they, Joe?—so now what am I doing in this stupid bed in this stupid intensive care ward at this stupid hospital. You're right, aren't you, Joe; I'm over the crisis, I'm going to walk out of here in a couple of days, I'm not going to die, am I, Joe; you were always the smartest bastard in our group, this is nothing, is it, Joe; I'm too big a bull to be brought down at only 64 years of age, Joe, and don't think I don't appreciate it; everything you ever said came true, Joe, so why shouldn't I believe I am not going to die: you said it, I didn't, and you were always right, Joe, about everything, and then suddenly the poor big lunk chokes on sobs and says, Ah, Christ, Christ, Joe, this is it: I am going to die, and I don't want to, I just don't want to, that's all; I had an idea in my head that I would take a drive all the way south, south, south, straight to Tierra del Fuego, so now what, I'm not ever going to see Tierra del Fuego, that's what, and it hurts, old friend, it murders me, Joe. Do me a favor, will you, just get the hell out of here, you healthy son of a bitch; you were always my enemy, you always hated my guts: I had so much luck in everything, while all you ever did was hang around the edges, so now you are glad, you are getting even, you're enjoying this, you think it's funny a great big man like me brought low this way, so get out of here, I don't need your phony sympathy and friendship: you're my enemy, not my friend. Ah, Christ, man, don't go; I take it all back, but do you know what I'd like more than anything in the world, for the first time in my life—I'd like to trade places with you; I wish to God you were dying, and I had come to visit you. Do you know that would make me happy, Joe, it would make me even happier than you are right now coming here to visit me, when you and I both know that in less than another six days you will be a pallbearer at my stupid funeral, Joe you son of a bitch. I wish to Christ you were dying and I were visiting you and being just as polite as you are, taking all of my abuse as if it were the ravings of a dying man, not the hatred of a living big bull of a son of a bitch on Market Street in San Francisco forty years ago, Joe: what happened? Why me? Why now? What did I do wrong? I always believed I was never going to die; I enjoyed life more than anybody else, you said so yourself, so what's this, why is somebody giving me this rotten time? I am going to be all right again, am I not, Joe? And he breaks into big sobs all over again. It couldn't happen but it did.

8.

The first name on the list is Victor Alessandro, but I never had the honor. I never met him, never saw him, and therefore cannot say anything about him that might be possible had I met him. What might that have been? Well, the fact of him, the reality of him, the reality of the substance of him, or if you choose the myth, his appearance, his face, his voice, his eyes, and anything else that was there. The trouble is that in remembering the dead, or for that matter the living who are not where I am, I don't especially think of the various parts of them, I think of entireties, of mysteries, of something total that instantly came to me as being that person. I have never been anything like a clever judge of people, but I do seem to get first impressions that are sound. Not long ago (in the early summer of 1972 as a matter of fact) I met an Armenian I instantly considered a crook, but little by little I changed that hunch to something I believed was much more sensible and worthy of acceptance, and I began to consider him a very good man. Well, my first impression was correct. He was a crook. I found out slowly but very clearly. He isn't dead, but whenever I remember him I know he is a crook, and I wonder why. Why is anybody not the best possible person he might be? Well of course we are obliged to conclude that everybody is indeed that best possible person he might be, no matter what he is, and then he dies and it doesn't really change anything, although it is traditional to believe that's it, he was, he is no longer, he has died, he is remembered but only by a few others, and then by nobody at all, because those who remembered him have also died. But what does this mean? It doesn't have to mean anything. Not instantly, at any rate. But it does bring into the arena of thought or speculation the significance of action and the recollection of action—not of the one who recollects but of somebody else, starting at home with father, mother, brother, sister, and other members of the large family. Everybody also remembers as he goes along his own actions and recollections of the actions. And of course he remembers the inaccuracies of his earlier recollections and keeps moving nearer to what probably happened and what it probably meant. But when somebody he is remembering dies, that does it, that locks it up, as the saying is: he can only work with the reality or unreality up to the death. And this work is so deeply difficult that he abandons it almost instantly upon the death or upon hearing of it, which is how it is with most of the deaths which have any meaning for him: the big people, the famous people, the legendary people, the public people, the stars, the celebrities, the monsters—all of a sudden but one by one, the bigshots of their day are dead, and their day is done: Hitler, Mussolini, Stalin, Roosevelt, Churchill, and so on. Very nearly everybody in the world upon learning of the death of each of these paused an instant in his own fight to acknowledge that fact—the man's death—and at the same time to connect himself somewhat to the man's life: when Stalin met Roosevelt and Churchill at Yalta, ah yes, I was in the Army and the world was in a shambles of self-destruction. Or something else. And all that sort of remembering is light and swift, and the dropping off of the great is taken with the same sort of acceptance of the inability in anybody to make anything useful of it. When Lincoln died he was instantly remembered in a rather special way, for he had been shot while he sat in a box at a theatre watching a play that was meant to be funny, to be amusing, and for all we know had been amusing to Lincoln himself up to that point. And there have been other world-famous men who have been shot, or have shot themselves, as Hitler is said to have done. What does it mean? Very few of the rememberers of any of the world-famous men knew them, and yet everybody feels connected to each of them, so what does the connection mean? Does it mean perhaps that everybody is everybody, no matter who? Anybody dies, everybody dies. Well, the matter of birth is comparatively simple in its unimportant details, but again nobody knows who the man or woman just born really is, or is going to turn out to be, but it is agreed among us that if he lives he is going to turn out to be somebody, and this somebody is going to be fairly explainable by some knowledge of his genetic line, his father and his mother and their fathers and mothers—otherwise it is possible to consider the event of birth to be as useless to the dead as the event of death is useless to the living, although there is altogether clear evidence that a vast usefulness attends both birth and death, however difficult to identify at the time: somebody has been born but who he is is not known; somebody has died, and while it is known who he was, or was supposed to have been, the fact that he is no longer alive doesn't really do anything for anything. Hitler's death does something for people who hated him and had every reason to hate him, but Hitler's death doesn't do anything for intelligent usage of such a piece of final information. He is dead. He is said to have shot himself. He didn't win. He lost. What does it mean? The second name is Alyce Allyn, and I don't know her, either. I am instantly intrigued by the spelling of each of her names, however. There must have been something in her reality that was connected in a very important way with the spelling. She may very well have meant to encourage not being instantly forgotten both during life, and after giving it up. The third name is Geza Anda, a fine name for a fine variety of reasons, but I have no idea who Geza Anda was, male or female, actor, clown, or what.

14.

Gloat? Really? Gloat over somebody's demise, if I may use that word for kicking the bucket? Gloat over somebody's laying aside of the mortal flesh and moving on to a higher level of life, or reality? Gloat at somebody's passing away, passing on, passing through, or whatever else the euphemism is for rotting on the vine, dropping dead, falling like a leaf? Gloat because another miserable human being has given up the ghost? Good God, man, how could you be so insensitive, so inhuman, so dirty? Gloat? You ought to be ashamed of yourself, and the dead man believed you were his friend, or at the very least one of his many acquaintances, perhaps not necessarily one of his admirers, but also not one of his enemies. How can you gloat about the death of anybody at all? Human beings just don't gloat over the deaths of other human beings. They become sad, or they pretend to become sad, for there is a polite procedure about such a thing as death.

Impoliteness is always a potentiality in human relations when the parties are both alive, or not yet dead, but once one of them has died, the other is always polite, and now and then he says, "God rest his soul," or something else like that. Who are you to gloat about the death of Krakauer, even, the crackerjack lawyer who under the given name of Arnold was such a whiz-bang champion of the rights of your vicious little, lying little, dirty little, crooked little, monstrous little bride, who hired him to take you to court and to carry on like *Mr. Chips Goes to the Himalayas*, a real clever showbiz lawyer, brisk, clear of speech, emphatic, a former Captain of Marines, the fourth husband of a woman who wrote sex novels, a lawyer who was more than a lawyer—he was a friend if you were his client, and a real enemy if you weren't—and he died, he just up and died, and who are you to gloat about a thing like that: it could happen to anybody, couldn't it? And who are you to gloat about Jerry Giesler who is also Jerry Geisler and so listed in the Beverly Hills phone book, when Jerry Giesler/Jerry Geisler also up and died, the most famous movieland lawyer of them all: the defender of Alexander Pantages, Charlie Chaplin, Busby Berkeley, Walter Wagner, and anybody else big and famous and rich in serious trouble, along the lines of spending the rest of his life in jail, and didn't the busy little bride call him in to attend to the funeral of the damned fool at the time of the second divorce, the damned fool having failed to break his leg and having married her a second time, knowing she was a liar and a crook and a fraud and an all-around weird but clever money-hustler and having given her diamonds and dentistry and house and money, and the famous lawyer joined his client in making the world as nearly impossible as it could possibly be for an idiot father of a young and stupid son and a younger and more stupid daughter, and then, the lawyer richer than almost any other lawyer in movieland, up and kicked the bucket. Who are you to gloat about the death of that fine famous man? Well, whoever the hell I am, by God, I do gloat about the way death sooner or later wipes out the mothers who take to the law and make stupid fools of the fathers, especially me. I rejoice when such mothers are unable to fish out a phoney law and keep death over in the slums among only the inferior and poor. I hear the news and the sun lights up in my soul. Why should I pretend anything else when I know the truth. The sons of bitches very nearly murdered me: why shouldn't I rejoice that death murdered them? And if the truth is told, why should I not rejoice that even while they were alive, busy in their offices, with their full staffs of bright young people doing their bidding, the silly little mothers were dead, and even worse than dead, they were miscarried spirits, like the stuff thrown out by abortionists. The bastards that do me, that seek to do me in, that plague my soul, that rob my purse as they say, that belittle my name, that very nearly drive me mad, I am proud to say I loathe, despise, hate, and patiently dismiss from my mind forever and ever, and am only reminded for a flash of profound gloating when I hear that death has done them in, the dirty little mothers. I hate the breed, and yet it is the one breed that, as Mahatma Gandhi informed all his young fellows, is the one profession that if righteously exercised can bring to pass all of those desirable changes in the imbalance created by wealth, which the human race so desperately longs for and indeed needs, and further indeed, must have or perish. But lawyers soon enough get in where the flow of money is abundant, and they arrange for rivulets to come flowing into their treasure chests. All right, all right, a writer flips his wig remembering perfidy in his bed, toying with his genitals and polluting his soul, and he carries on like an uncivilized animal about the weasel-eyed bride, and gloats over the deaths of her supporters and conspirators, but what about death itself, real death, actual death: not of lawyers, but of members of the human race—of anybody at all—does he gloat over death like that? Well, the answer is that he does, and his doing so has nothing to do with anything so sophisticated as a human being, a man, a writer, a father: it has only to do with nature, with the reality of nature. And let nobody pretend that in man nature is discarded—it is put to one side until death when it comes right back in loud and full. Any man who doesn't rejoice in the death of anybody else, as well as stand hushed and overwhelmed by sorrow and ignorance, any such man is very uncomplicated, very undeveloped, and need not really be considered a man at all: he is a unit of one in relation to a billion never to be understood.

33.

Is it in order to tell the reader a few things about the writer and how he is going about getting this work written? It is not, so the writer will tell him anyway. Reader, old pal, or dear lady, or gentleman in the penitentiary, or girl in the hospital, or big man in the big man's Office, or anybody, and if it happens to be so, nobody: this is what I have to tell you, that I hope is not altogether extraneous but is also reasonably intraneous, and at the same time nice: what do we do? We do what we know how to do. I write. You do what you do. Writing is my work. I get up in the morning to start my work. You get up when you get up to start doing your work. If you are retired and don't really work any more, you still get up, most likely, and start something: you start being up. If you are too young to have a job, and work to do every workday of the week, and I hope you are, although if you are reading this writing, this book, this writer, chances are about four to one that you are either a very precocious young person, or that by some chance or mischance this is the only book on hand at a time when you really want to read, and don't want to do anything else—don't want to write, don't want to watch television, don't want to just sit, don't want to work out the details of how you are going to spend the rest of your life. For that really is what everything everybody does is all about: all doing is to the end that each person who is still alive may consider again, for it goes on pretty much all the time, and by itself—consider again how the rest of that person's life is going to be spent, for there is no person who does not deeply feel that the life so far spent is not what it might have been and therefore the rest of the life, unknown as the portion may be, is to be spent as the person believes it ought to be spent. You get up and you go to work or to the equivalent of work and get your pay or your reward or your rating or your congratulation or your criticism and you come home and sit down to some tea or coffee or beer or alcohol and you think or something thinks by itself for you as you watch or half-watch how it goes. Why don't you invent something that will instantly deliver everybody from the theory that it is absolutely necessary to own an automobile and to drive all over the place? That invention would not only make you rich, it would make you famous, and admired by young women of considerable intellectual potential, and deeply respected by those enormities of refusal who are lumped together as anarchists, a category and designation misunderstood by everybody. Listen, my friend inside there, listen, enemy outside everywhere, if you will invent something to make not racing somewhere in an automobile one of the supreme joys of the human experience, if you will send the human race of the Western World out of their houses, out of their places of employment, offices, factories, warehouses, and wherever, and if you will have them forget their watches on their wrists, and their previous schedules, and just have them not feel they must race—to anything at all, the table, the food, the drink, the television news, the clutter of claptrap, and what they really need to do (because it is what they really want to do, and have always wanted to do) is to be in the sunlight and to first just stand there and feel that light, and then to not sit down in the absurd seat of an automobile, but to turn easily and to walk lightly and to go on down the street and slowly and steadily reach open country and then, and then, to really begin to notice the awesome truth of clockless, carless, smokeless, gasless, anxiety-less nature, but nature, nature, the very word has come to have a bad sound, a bad name, you will really begin not only to notice but to feel, to breathe, to become immersed in, surrounded by, blessed by the easy pressure of the air that keeps the ball bouncing a million million years, and the pressure that makes everything brought into being have its own private, distinguished, miraculous, beautiful and apparently everlasting center. Sir, if you can invent something that will take the place of the telephone, you will be the beloved hero of the whole Western World, for in the Eastern World the people do not connect themselves to the telephone with its endless wires going everywhere, to everybody—except of course to the dead, the only people really worth the bother of reaching, whether by telephone or some other connection. The American song of 1918 said "Hello Central, give me No-Man's Land" or, Give me the old buddy, my buddy, he died, you know, he was killed in a very strange and stupid accident involving gunpowder and lead and explosion, and where does that leave me, out here in Ohio, the mother of his three kids, and no money, let me talk to Charley my boy, Oh Charley, why did you get into such a mess and get yourself killed forever and ever? And if that doesn't work, try to get Charlie Manson, the guardian of the Redwood Trees of California, and all of the ecological treasures that the fools are pissing away, Charlie Manson's in the penitentiary, and you may be able to reach him and help in his noble work of preserving shorelines and forests and elephants and porpoises. Invent something, friend, to make all gunpowder and lead and explosions so silly that nobody will manufacture them, no matter what the profit for doing so may be, and will be astonished that he ever believed manufacturing them was anything less than monstrous, obscene killing, far worse than any Charlie Manson and his adoring girls ever engaged in, with their absolute conviction of righteousness. Is it in order to tell the reader stuff like this? No, it is never in order, and it is never done, but now and then, such as right now, it is more than in order to tell the reader something—it is urgently necessary to do so: wreck the car, hang up the telephone, shut off the TV, take up thy bed and walk, and walk.

34.

Let me tell you something else. The next name on the list is Benjamin Britten, and while I have never knowingly spoken to Benjamin Britten, I have come to meet him in an autobiographical book by Ronald Duncan entitled *How to Make Enemies*, and so I know Benjamin Britten was a composer of music, and quite a good one, they say. Ronald Duncan founded a magazine called *The Townsman* way back in the late 1930s, and he wrote to me from London and asked me to send him something or other to run in the magazine. And of course I sent him something or other and it appeared in *The Townsman*, and then he wrote again and again. I sent him something or other in the way of a small piece of writing, and this also appeared in *The Townsman*, and then the War came along, and I got drafted for three years, and Ronald Duncan became a Conscientious Objector and did not go into the British army but was maligned by a lot of people on various grounds, but he fought his private fight and if he didn't win it, he certainly didn't lose it, either. He didn't lose his life, and he and his wife became the parents of several children. England needs such people. So does America, so does Russia, so does China—but Russia and China, having a special kind of social philosophy, would not be likely to tolerate anybody invoking some kind of private sentiment about war under the generality of Conscientious Objector, and the poet-writer Ronald Duncan would have been persecuted, imprisoned, and in other ways belittled, humiliated, and ridiculed. If you were to avoid maiming or death in the national army, in one or another of its miscellaneous branches, and your home and nation happened to be Russia or China, you would be expected to be cleverer about that business, a super-patriot in fact, and to avoid risk by becoming apparently indispensable in some political activity. There are always outs for the clever, but not everybody is clever. One of the best [of] ours, and one exploited by men in every country where a draft system worked over men from the age of 18 to 40 (which was reduced to 35 in America after the first force of hysteria had somewhat subsided) was to tell the machine-men working the draft that by religion, preference, custom, and practice you were homosexual. A very young Australian newspaperman in London in 1944 said that he and all of his friends had avoided being drafted by making that declaration, and nobody among the machine-men believed it might be in order to suspect the declarations, for it is presumed that anybody who says he is homosexual *is*, period. And so the young Australian had got himself a magnificent job at excellent wages and a generous expense account, as both bureau chief, and occasional writer, for a news syndicate. Now I forgot all about *The Townsman*, and its editor, Ronald Duncan, for many years, and in fact I seemed to be sure that both were gone, forever, and then one day in July 1974 I paid three francs (or about 75¢) for a book entitled *All Men Are Islands* by somebody named Ronald Duncan, a name I was not sure I did not know. I began immediately to read the book, and parts of it two or three times, and little by little I understood that he was the founder and editor of *The Townsman*, and had published a couple of short throw-away pieces by me, and that of course we had exchanged two or three short letters. What is a throw-away piece? Just that, pretty much, except that there is more to say about it: a throw-away piece of writing is a piece of writing that the writer wants to write for a variety of reasons, knowing that the writing is pretty much for himself, and that he has really no intention of making a dime from it, or for that matter of ever seeing it in print. He writes the piece because he wants to, because doing so is part of the continuation of his education as a writer, or as a man, or if you prefer, as a human being, or even as an angel, if your mind goes that far in the dimension of naming categories—and you may as well understand right here and now that this writer—myself, that is—believes, on full evidence over thousands of years, that it is impossible for anybody to be born into this life and world and experience, who is not an angel. But this isn't the time or place to go into that. This is the time and place to go into how I came to somewhat meet Benjamin Britten—in the writing of Ronald Duncan, but not in the pages of *All Men Are Islands* (which I am sure you have noticed is a refutation, so to put it, of Donne's poetic assertion that no man is an island, a theory that went on until it provided Ernest Hemingway with the title of one of his biggest novels—to me unreadable: *For Whom the Bell Tolls*, full of clumsy Hispanic renderings into English, and coy exchanges between the hero and his strong Spanish lady friend and sleepingbag companion—embarrassing, as I've heard vaudeville comedians and patent medicine pitchmen say of male conditions not unrelated to bladder, passing of water, penis, prostate, erection, putting in place, pumping, semen, and possibly the passing of wind, usually on the part of the female party, but not impossible for the male). The book had been published in London ten years previous to my buying a copy which had been in the possession of the literary agent W. A. Bradley, 18

Quai de Bethune, and along with perhaps ten dozen other books which had not won French publication, was remaindered so to put it, to the little bookshop on Rue Clichy just beyond Trinite in my own neighborhood of Paris. I learned that the book was the first of three that were planned, and after several years got my friend in London, Gerald Pollinger, to get me the second volume, entitled *How to Make Enemies*, and that's where I read about Benjamin Britten.

35.

After Benjamin Britten comes Harry R. Burke. (Reader: You mean that's all you're going to say about Benjamin Britten? Writer: Yes, it is, and I'll tell you why, too: the explanation may not satisfy the reader at all, but it is the only explanation there is, so it will have to do: by mistake, dear reader, I ordered ten reams of white typing paper from a Fresno business machine company where this very typewriter over which I am standing and upon which I have written pretty much everything I have written over the past thirty years—a Royal Quiet de Luxe portable, for which I paid a nice small sum in Santa Monica in 1951, second-hand, and let me tell you they don't make machines like this any more: good thing I made that small transaction way back then. I wanted the length of this typing paper to be longer than the standard 8½ x 11, or whatever it is, because around the corner from my place in Paris the paper sold to me by the stationer came longer, without even asking: 8½ by 12, possibly 12½ (but not much more than that), and I had found that this added length at the end of the sheet of paper was more right for me than the regular size, but in Fresno I discovered that such paper had to be cut to order and nobody would cut it unless ten reams were ordered, so I ordered ten reams and they were duly delivered and all was well, except that the length was somewhat greater than the paper in Paris, perhaps it was 13 or even 14 inches—the 8½ part seems to be standard, to meet the limitations of typewriters. Well, I don't like waste, and while the new size was a little too long, I began to use it, both for correspondence and for new writing. Out of one sheet I could get four replies to letters and just use a scissors to make each reply separate, and this was a grand time-saver, for all the fooling with paper and envelopes tends to be both tedious and time-taking. I read somewhere, furthermore, that it costs any man who hires a secretary about 88¢ to send a reply to any letter, no matter how short, and I just didn't want to bother about that kind of silly and useless extravagance, or perhaps more properly, downright waste. Furthermore I don't want to have my letters go through the rigamarole of a secretary. I can do it all right in the first place in less than the time it would take to get the secretary only *ready* to hear the dictation and to jot it down, about half-wrong, too, in shorthand, in the lined tablet, the very sight of which offends the sense of direct action and simplicity. And so I was stuck with ten reams of first class thin white typewriter paper that was oversize, so to put it. Well, I decided, dear reader, and thank you very much for hanging on, but if you have been asleep while reading, that's all right, I fall asleep that way reading all the time—I decided to use up every sheet of paper in those ten reams—500 sheets in a ream makes it 5,000 sheets—and by God don't crumple one sheet and throw it into a wastepaper basket. That is the behavior of boob newspapermen, and writers who are taking a course in writing. And the idea was quite simple: single-spaced, each sheet filled from top to bottom constituted a chapter, and that was it. I had to live by that procedure, and I must say I found that it made good sense. Each page takes about 80 lines of about 10 words each, making about 800 words, which for all practical purposes is far better than about 50 lines, and about 500 words a page. Of course various editors, stuffed shirts and awful bores, especially at certain magazines and publishing houses, point out icily that it is requested that the writer use double-spacing at the very least, and if possible triple-spacing. I ignore all such hot or icy suggestions: I don't run their business, and I don't expect them to run mine. Every writer follows a procedure that makes sense for him, and the procedure I have just very poorly explained is my procedure. I want about 80 lines of typing to a sheet of paper, and I don't want any murmurings from protesting editors. That is the reason, dear reader, that I have said pretty much all I am going to say about Benjamin Britten, for the simple reason that I came to the end of the sheet. Is there anything more that might be said about Benjamin Britten? That is to say, by me, by this writer? There most certainly is, but not at this time, and very likely not at any other time. Never again, I've had my chance, and if I said almost nothing about Benjamin Britten, about his music, which I hear is quite good, well, I have no memory at all of ever having consciously heard one tiny portion of it. You can write forever about anybody, because anybody connects almost instantly with everybody, and while writing about only one person could keep you busy the rest of your life, it seems always to be in order to write about a lot of people, although in all truth every writer writes only about himself, and that includes historians, as A. J. P. Taylor, the English writer of history, has pointed out. Writing is writing, it comes from a person, and if you write about the origins of World War II, for instance, it is you who is doing the writing, and the writing is essentially about yourself. Someday, some day, dear reader, get some longplay discs or some tapes of the music of Benjamin Britten and listen to that music, and I think you will remember that I asked you to do so.) And so it's Harry R. Burke's turn. Harry, I never met you, but as you are dead and listed in *Variety*'s famous Necrology of 1976, I am willing to presume you did something in the general vicinity of entertainment. I hope you did it well, but I am sorry I doubt it. It isn't that you might not have done it excellently, it is just that really nobody does anything well, so why should you be the exception? But enjoy your death, you earned it, and earning anything takes time and doing. Enjoy the mud in your mouth.

43.

I'll tell you something, reader, I'll tell you something good: you are the star of your life, knock on wood. You are the living one, old soul, inside your own skin: even when you lose, you win. (A little doggerel joke there, as we say, friend, don't be discouraged, don't get hot, keep it cool, melancholia is not the end of the world, that's something else again, so just wade along in the minnow shallows and feel the easy grains of sand upon the soles of the easy living feet—feet, great good God Almighty, how do we ever forget feet, our actual contact with the earth, our symbolic and actual contact and connection with all matter—and upon the soles of the ever living memory. Any man who permits a little bit of depression to throw cold water on his fire is not really in very much real trouble: he only thinks he is, or more likely only wants to think he is, for there is also that, dear reader: the not really wanting to be all that vital and warm-blooded and alive to the sun and whirling into the joyousness of everything always in place but never even slightly located or known. Any man who lets feeling rotten become being rotten isn't in luck at all, he's out of all of those little things that gather together into one grand reality of self, himself, allself, Godself, truthself, dreamself—what dreams we've dreamed, haven't we, old reader—earthself, heavenself—you know heaven, reader old pal, don't you? of course you do—hellself, hot hot cool cool hellself, funself, unself, superself, hold on a minute, reader, this selfstuff is the thing we may have been sailing the waters of the universe in the expectation of someday finding, but then it may not, too, so let's cool it, let's not let it get to be too meaningful in any kind of way at all, shall we, self, old readerself, old writerself, old friendself, old enemyself, it's all right, it's not wrong at all, what it comes to is that you are not going to get up out of bed every morning feeling as if the whole place is yours, or not caring to bother to notice at all whose it is, who cares whose it is, no place being really anybody's, except possibly his own body being a place and the only place that is his, the only place that belongs to himself in his own selfself inside the bodyself and of course also outside of both bodyself and selfself and out out out into outself itself making everything stay put in a kind of fluid putself, but then again maybe even his own body is not his place at all, not his own at all, it may even be the one place that is his least of all, a beautiful deception of nature, to keep everything in its place, and to keep everybody with just enough despair and joy wrestling one another to keep him within the bounds of his selfself, within the limits of his soulself struggling with his bodyself, what do we know, reader: it took us so long even to get the hang of written language in the first place. Remember when we chiselled marks on stones instead of scribbling on papyrus? Well, we're still just as slow as when we chiselled on stone, and of course there is no place in the world where such chiselling in one form or another is not still going on—go to the cemeteries and read the chisellings on stone and you may very well be astonished by the simplicity and rightness of it: name and measure: that's it, good-bye old folks at home, this world is not mine, I was only passing through, and now I have done with it, reader, old customer of air and glacier. No need, no need at all for any writer, any reader, to be down in the dumps just because he's down in the dumps: that's living like a fool, that's having life literally, without its inexhaustible and bouncing error of abundance, that's getting things so right they are more wrong than when they were not nearly right but were not really so wrong a reader or a writer couldn't get hisself—not himself but hisself—couldn't get his own self full smack into the clutter of all selves of all times and of all airs and glaciers and all flames and orange meltings of all rock for the invention of all coolings into all continuing errors, no man in his right mind or in God's right mind—ah let's just leave God in his own mind and out of our right or wrong mind and let God go on sleeping a moment or two longer before the alarm, good God let's try to be polite to God for a change no matter what or who or where or why God is or may be invented into being—or no man in the right mind of his own silly famous ancestors or infamous near-ancestors is ever really going to believe without a big horse-laugh at himself that there is anything at all about himself that is of even the most rudimentary order of relevance, and yet, and yet, his very shape and isolation from all other shapes is the fullest possible demonstration of relevance itself, all relevance, the relevance of everything to everything to everything and back again through nothing and nothing and the heart of relevance through nothing, so don't despair, reader and eater, but at the same time don't get so good at not despairing when you are despairing that you don't know your very own air from the earth's own despair, because if you do that, and get good at doing that, you are likely to discover that both figuratively and literally you have joined earth in earth's own breathless despair, and are actually dead and buried and just don't happen to have any of the haphazard apparatus left with which to tell the difference, and won't be the day, all done, never begun but already all done, the self's own self all undone and redone and again never done, just there, just there and with not enough gray matter anywhere with which to know the geography of the terrain or the algebra of the empty emptiness without worms, even, without anything of any kind at all.

51.

Why do I write? Why am I writing this book? To save my life, to keep from dying, of course. That is why we get up in the morning. It is also why now and then we don't get up, we stay abed, generally feeling guilty because something has come along during the ages and told us that it is necessary for life to get up from sleep. But when? Is it upon awakening? Well, I used to think it was, and then George Garabedian, a young doctor down from Worcester (pronounced "Wooster"), or somewhere, in Manhattan in the late 1930s and early 1940s, suggested that since I had reached the age of thirty, henceforth it might be in order to go back to sleep after the first awakening, and so that's the way it began, and I believe a good thing, too, for while it was exhilirating to get up and get to the world after only perhaps as little as four hours of sleep, and almost never more than six, it just wasn't something to prolong, no matter what the sleep experts happened to say, think, believe, advise, and so on. I need a lot of sleep, or the equivalent. I need to lie abed, reading, becoming ready and willing and able to drop off into the universe of sleep and dream, and I do not feel at all guilty about frequently spending half the time of one day and night abed: I feel pleased about it. The question about the apportionings of time, and the usages, is this: during our up time, during the time we are in and of the world, and of its action, what do we do? Well, we work, and even if the work happens to be the manufacture of—let's say, for a laugh—plastic roses, work is work, and must be done, and it permits us to pay our way, and so on and so forth. But the truth of the matter is that after we have functioned ecologically as members of the surviving human race, married and had kids, and used the money from our work also to protect and perhaps even to honor our aged, any work we do solely for wages might be sensibly identified as dead or even wasteful work, for it only repeats what had a slight portion of private meaning for each of us only in that it brought us the money, the means by which to marry, to put forward new people, and the means at the same time to protect and even to honor the old. Having done our unavoidable ecological chores, it is not desirable and it may even be inimical, harmful to the entirety of us, the whole human family in the whole world, to go on doing this basically unnecessary work—if it happens to be the manufacture of plastic roses, or the equivalent of that. And when that is so, that is the time to stay abed longer than ever thinking about the usages of time and skill in the doing of work that is both privately and collectively satisfying and useful. For me, that work is writing, for the vineyardist it is the tending of his vines, for everybody else it is whatever they can decide is right, or whatever they can manage, different from what they had been more or less forced to do, solely for the money, what they had done in a willing but not necessarily painless order of enslavement, of slavery, and that of course includes all of the activities that come under the heading of hobbies. But whatever it is that is done, the basic reason for the doing of it is to stay alive, to avoid dying, whether of boredom or of functional failure. And that's why I write. It happens to be not much more than an accident that the form and structure of this particular work is based upon a list of the dead, and possibly not the most suitable list of the dead for the kind of work this is, and the kind of writer I am: might it not have been better to have asked somebody at the Library of Congress to list for me all who died in 1976 of suicide, so to put it: or all those who died in automobile accidents, but not all over the country, but for purposes of connection, at least, in California: or all who died in family disputes, a father killing the lot of them suddenly: or all who drowned: or were asphyxiated: or all who died as innocent bystanders: and so on and so forth. No, I only wanted to get to work in mid-January of the new year, and the *Variety* list was in the big issue dated January 5th which reached me January 15th, and two days later I went to work. This is not an age in which writing must necessarily follow forms and traditions and all that sort of thing. Writing is writing, a writer is a writer, an age is an age, and the business of going to work is every man's business, and he is to decide how to go about what he is to do. Am I obsessed with death? Is that it? Bet your life I am, how could I possibly not be, how could anybody not be, especially you, yourself, still alive, alive, O, as the song about cockles and mussels goes. There is a portion of any man's time when it is impossible to believe in his own death, and then there comes a time when he knows in his bones that that time is gone, a change of thinking has taken place, as well as a change in other things, one and two and three, one at a time, and he becomes so interested in the unaccountable and unpredictable way of death in everything, but especially in the human branch of life, that a great full entertainment comes forward out of life to enrich his hours every day and night: new people are dying every day, and as the years go by he notices that he knows more and more of these new dying, he notices that many of them are people whose living time connected with his living time somehow, and frequently in ways that are intimate—a girl a man had loved has died an old woman, for instance, and the man thinks, Well, dear little Violet has died—well, what about all those girls and women I didn't really know at all, who I only bought for a few minutes, in the silent whorehouses of San Francisco? Are they all right? Or have they all long since died, too? I write to remember, and you read not to forget, or something like that.

56.

There are similes, if that is the word for what I'm thinking of: somebody says, You get on your bike and go, and we understand that he doesn't necessarily mean that you get on your bike and go, he means that you do the equivalent of that inside, in your spirit, and nobody is the worse for having had it put that way, but when I get on my bike I really do go, that's my transportation after walking and where I live there is no walking, almost nobody walks anywhere, although I walk to a supermarket named Save Mart (but it is really no such thing, at least insofar as the Save part of Save Mart is concerned: the prices are high, higher than at other supermarkets) so at least once a day I get out on one of two good bikes, neglecting the portable Italian bike which has such a hangar ratio that your legs work like machine parts in a cotton milling machine and you barely move, but for $55 and a carton of cigarettes to hand to crazy friends it was a fair buy, ten years ago: and I go, I actually get on my bike and go, generally to the nearby P.O. (named Hughes, but not after Rupert, a rich and once-famous writer of novels nobody can even think of by title, unlike Zane Grey for instance or even Rex Beach, and Rupert Hughes became quite a personage, even in Hollywood: and not named surely after the bearded Hughes who persecuted Woodrow Wilson about the League of Nations and got it defeated in the Senate and in the House, I forget his first name, the Hughes whose name—do you like that, Hughes whose?—is on the new branch of the Post Office, not much more than eight hundred yards as the crow doesn't fly, has got to be somebody local, and God help us there are a lot of us locals, if you have in mind putting our names on Post Office branches and schools), and from the outdoor mailbox where I slipped two important sticks of mail, one to New York, the other to London, I rode across the street to the dusty dingy entrance of the Moonglo Drive-In Movie, deserted these days but due back in business in the next four weeks for sure as the weather has gone bland, and from there straight down Dakota to the Gillis Branch of the Public Library where I ran through two issues of *The Fresno Bee*, now a morning paper, and one of *The Chronicle*, of San Francisco, and then glanced but just glanced at the February issue of *The Atlantic*—word is out that the whole staff is Boston high society and a pain in the ass about it: sailing, lunch, dinner, meetings by appointment only and all that—and I decided I would give that issue a little authentic attention at a more appropriate time. From a reference shelf I took down Macmillan's *Dictionary of Proverbs and Sayings*, and turned to Death, where there is so much chronologically that I want to get them all, and tie them in with everything under Death in Mencken's collection, and other collections, and choose from them at the top of this book, even if there are 200 or more of them, or perhaps spread them through the book, one at least at the top of each chapter, of which I expect that there shall be 88, but who knows, there may be 101, or even more, even though I am to stay close to the list of the dead in *Variety*. And just noticing that there are perhaps two dozen thin fine Bible pages of paper covered with the sayings and writings of races and individuals on the subject, if you want to call it that, of Death, I rejoiced. My heart lifted almost in literal song, for it is heartening to know that from the beginning of memory in man, and the usages of memory in writings, there have been sayings about this thing, and these sayings have both comforted and strengthened the people, some of them non-sayers, but mainly all of them sayers in ways sometimes far better than the ways which have been preserved and have got into Macmillan's reference book: Zabu of Central Africa, who came back from near-drowning and said, "Brother, I have always known Life, and now I know Death, and let me tell you, Life is better." Which was carried along from generation to generation and was heard at El Rancho Vegas in that corrupt and crazy Nevada town where gambling is legal, out of the mouth of one Joe E. Lewis, except that instead of Life and Death, it became Rich and Poor. Ha. And just noticing all those magnificent sayings listed chronologically I thought, Well, there we are, aren't we, folks. Accidentally a couple of weeks ago I hit upon a good idea for my latest book, if you are willing to call it a book, or if you dare—I am writing in this book about last year's showbiz dead, and unavoidably also about any year's dead, and about Death, and of course also Life—you can't write about one and not write about the other: if there is a face, there is also the back of the head, if you are willing to accept that simile—all right, I know it is not a simile, I am not bragging about my ignorance, but I am saying that from about the age of eight, at the latest, I have been vitally aware of the law of opposites, and this awareness has permitted me to be reasonably serene about everything, and at the same time not to forfeit entirely any natural longing I may have to believe that the lot of anybody, of everybody, beginning with myself, can with effort be improved. And I've demonstrated it to some degree in the improvement I have achieved in my own life, but I have failed rather sorrowfully everywhere else: you can love a wife, but you can't make her understand what your love means: or a son, or a daughter, or a friend, or a stranger, and by love I mean love, not anything involving the body and the action of one set of genitals in connection with another set—a man's and a woman's as far as I am concerned—and you take it from there if you will, or must: let every woman, let every man be his own man or his (or her) own woman, and let Death tell them the brave details of the achievement or disachievement. That's none of my business.

60.

The dead, the dead, the poor dead, the wonderful dead, the lonely dead, the stupid dead, they should never have died, I suppose, but there it is, they did, the stupid bastards, they up and died, and it was really not necessary: everybody who has studied the matter in depth says it is not necessary to die, ever, but one by one everybody has died, including the specialists who had said that it was really not necessary, but they probably left messages saying that yes, it is not necessary, they simply decided they wanted to, and did, and thus became the same as the rest of us, the living who die, who must die, who believe they must, or believe they don't have to, as the case may be, but one thing is certain, and painful: it is no fun at all when somebody dies prematurely, and of course that also happens all the time, even to ninety-year-old folks—they die, they become the dead, they join the dead, the same as the author of "The Dead," the same as James Joyce himself, the greatest writer in English of all time, or the next greatest, or the fourth greatest, or the twenty-eighth greatest, or whatever it needs to be. He wrote and wrote and his eyes went, and he rather persecuted his good devoted brother Stanislaus, who said so in his memoirs, and he blew borrowed money on a riot of comradeship and good food and drink, and big tips—a beggar who had to, he blew the begged money as if it came from the estate and there was plenty more where that came from, he accepted the help of young men and women who also wanted to write, and they got the hard work of his big wordy beautiful manuscripts precisely the way he wanted them. (One of them, Samuel Beckett, went on his own to become one of the new stars of the literary world, in the literary firmament, and there were others who did not go on, boys and girls both, probably.) And then James Joyce got so fed up with not having money, not having elegant clothes, yes good weavings of fine white tablecloths, and sheets and pillowcases, and curtains, and good clothing, good dandy clothes for a dandy man, a dandy boy, with a dandy stick, and dandy glasses to perch upon the bridge of his nose, and this condition of being bitterly fed up brought on an ulcer, or two ulcers, or half a dozen, and these ulcers gave him very bad times, but they had their seasons, they came and went, and they came and they went, and in the meantime he loved Nora Barnacle, his wife, and he loved their daughter and their son, and he loved his writing and the characters in his writing, and he loved the world, and he loved the human race, and he hated really nobody except possibly the Pope and everybody, but sometimes he loved even them, as the pain of the ulcers arrived and departed, and then the War came and there he was in Austria, in France, in the very homegrounds of the War, and that isn't what did it: it was something else which is clearly in his writing if somebody clever will fish through carefully and find it—perhaps "Carry me along Tad like you done at the toy fair," if that is indeed what he put near the end of *Finnegans Wake*—James Joyce has left all of the meanings and messages of his life and death in all of his writing if anybody wants to get right in and bring them out, and suddenly the ulcers, the ulcer (one is enough and in any case isn't it always one at a time) flared up rather more than ordinarily, possibly because of the War, possibly because of the failure of money to come to him abundantly even after he knew in his heart that he was the greatest and almost nobody wanted to say nay to him, except possibly Henry Miller, who must have met him in Paris, or tried to, they were there at the same time, for years, and also during the 1930s when so many people believed that the time had come to turn the human race upside-down and straighten out the world and establish righteousness and decency in all of the cities, and be human, really human, or by God be shot for not being human, and anybody who didn't go along with that big pushy program was sneered at by the rest of the silly little raging mob. James Joyce was put down by the communist writers, as they called themselves and one another, because, they said, he didn't care about the whole human race, and because his writing was a game, a private game, inhuman almost, disconnected from purpose, it was one long sustained tour-de-force of masturbation: Henry Miller said that, implying that his work was one long sustained tour-de-force of straight fucking—much better, you see, women, you know, the stiff prick into women, you know, the vice-president of the Bowery Bank at least in appearance put down the dandy boy of Dublin, and so did the communist boys and girls, but that didn't bring on the last flare-up of the ulcer: it is in the books he wrote and somehow managed to get published in spite of all of the opposition of Rome, of Boston, of anywhere at all, the ulcer flared up and this time it was bigger and better (for itself) and worse for James Joyce, but he was sure it would go, or so I have read, and Nora was sure it would, and the world knew nothing about it at all, being busy with Adolph (Hitler, you know), and the literary world knew as good as nothing about it, too, and at best only a few people anywhere knew anything about it, and then they carted the great man in terrible pain to a hospital somewhere—perhaps it was in

Zurich, perhaps not, but it was in Europe, it was not in Ireland—and the medical staff at the hospital fell on him, to help him, to get him safely out of the valley of the shadow, but they failed, James Joyce failed, he died, the author of "The Dead" died, and he died too soon, he died prematurely, even if he had done pretty much all the work he should have done, he had done it all, but he shouldn't have died, not from a perforated ulcer, not from peritonitis, not from anything, he was too young.

72.

In my earliest years I longed to have a full personal past because whenever I considered writing, there wasn't enough (or at least so I thought) to permit me to write anything interesting. Of course the failure was not that the past was limited: it was that the skill was unequal to the discovery of the enormity of the past, and the editorial opinion that everything that was there that I knew was there was not interesting enough to put into words and to pass along to others. There is sense of one sort or another in everything we feel, however mistaken we may be in our basic premises. All the same from the earliest days (or even hours) of memory I longed to be a total man, in order to escape the limitations of dependency, along with its rules and regulations, and from the first hours and days of writing (rather than only reading) I longed to have a very large and rich store of personal participation in the world, among some of the other members of the human race, so that I might never need to feel, as I did in the early years, that there was really nothing worth writing. I am sure writers of all kinds will understand what I am talking about, unless of course they will not, because they had no such feeling or longing, or because they did not write altogether out of themselves, they wrote another kind of writing, out of another source, entirely. But the real point here is that I was sure at fourteen that in ten years I would have pretty much everything I wanted in the way of a full personal past, and in a sense, allowing for my own much more fully developed ability to see use in everything, in every dimension of myself and my life and my known and unknown past, in ten years I did indeed have all that I really needed—except unfortunately that small edge of need which can outweigh a thousand times more of everything else: I was not finding paper and print of a world's publication for the writing I was doing. And part of the reason was that the writing wasn't ready, or at any rate only a little of it was ready, the writing just wasn't me, as the comic saying is: it was beginning to be me by the time I was twenty-four, but it was not so fully me as to compel the editors to run my stuff, if that is how it happens, which I doubt, although it is a good big part of it, for sure. So I waited and worked, and traveled and looked and listened and took part and fought through all of the obstructions and hindrances and doubts and illnesses and the sense of isolation and the roaring joy of comedy known only to myself, which in its richness and variety made me feel I would never be able to capture it and hold it in words for anybody else, and in due time things began to happen, and I suddenly was a writer, and I have been ever since. So now I am in my 69th year, as I have mentioned several times, because that also is part of my way of living and working and being aware: I have about as much of a personal past as I am willing to believe any man of 69 is likely to have, so what have I done with it, how have I used that enormous wealth, what great works have I written and passed along to the rest of the human family? Well, not nearly enough, of course, nobody has ever done that, but I believe that all things considered, including the things that no man knows about himself, I have done quite well, quite well, thank you, as the rambling remark goes. I have certainly had quite a number of books published, I have not died, and I am still writing. My name signifies a kind of writing, and while it is a kind that some estimable critics look down their noses at, I don't especially mind, for I look down my nose at both them and their writing, and I would name them one by one except that it would bore me, and be irrelevant in a way that I do not want any of my irrelevant flights to be. I do not believe in making negative references about my writing. Frankly, I marvel at it. Let whoever can or will do his own work as he chooses, and place it alongside my work, or long after his death let his partisans do that for him, and I have an idea that my work will survive such a relationship very nicely—and with no belittlement to either body if the writing is right: and that is the one thing every writer asks of himself, or demands, each in his own way, even to the writer of profitable trash, of full falsity, of deliberate inferiority, it must be still right, of its order. In any case, not long ago, less than twenty-four hours ago, myself aged 14 or 24, asked myself, now, All right, so you have your full past, what are you doing with it? And I was both pleased and surprised by the unexpected question, but at the same time also left with my mouth open, for the implication of the question was very clear: I hadn't done half what I ought to have done, half what I had believed at 14 and 24 that I would do if I ever lasted until I was forty, or perhaps fifty, so now that I am almost 20 years older than fifty, what do I have to show for it? I have what I have, that's all. And I said so, but nevertheless was not all that satisfied with saying so, for it was I who asked, and I who answered, and the asker was more nearly correct than the answerer. For instance, the asker went on, this thing that you're writing, is this the kind of thing you had all that experience for? Isn't it in order to be putting your time, experience, skill, and energy into another kind of work entirely? Into what the reporters of the literary life call a major work. Major? I reply. What does that mean? Well, it could mean pompous, and it has proved to be pompous in relation to a good assortment of so-called major works, but what it really means is that the work is really itself, and right. It is right. Well, I have such works, and if the truth is told I believe that all of my works put together are right.

74.

It is easy for a man to be a fool if the weather is right, and the weather is always right, so what is so bad about being a fool? Well it's costly, as the saying is: in time, money, alternative, and to sum it all up, self. A fool loses himself, and if it is in prayer or genius of one sort or another, all well and good, but if it is in loafing, lust, or empty longing, it is not good, because it diminishes instead of increasing. But so what, I have work to do, and if it is fool's work, I am not absolutely sure of that, and I am willing to go ahead with the work, and I am even prepared to find out at the end of it that I have been a fool again. I was a live fool, I was there, I visited the Public Library, I bought 14 discarded magnificent books for one dollar, only one dollar, think of it, and on my way out less than half an hour ago I said to the sweet little girl at the check-out desk, "How is the little girl?" and she smiled and replied, "*He's* just fine." And this is how that happened: last November when she was very pregnant I said, "Don't let this be troublesome, but I believe you are going to have a boy, do you and your husband want a boy?" And she said, "No, we both want a girl." And I said, "Well, you shall have a girl, then." (Just to be polite, but it was a big up-high pregnancy and for that reason and for no reason at all I was sure it was going to be a boy, due in two weeks. Then I didn't see her for two months and when I was back at the Public Library I said, "How is your little daughter?" And she said, "My little son." I congratulated her, but ever since when I see her I think she is the new young pretty mother of a little girl. Ah, well, the weather all day has been fool's weather, and when my mother's kid sister Verkine's boy Harry Bagdasarian came by in his fine big 1972 car, I said, "Shall we drive to talk, walk the Mall, pick up 14 books for a dollar at the Public Library, and come back?" And he said, "Hell yes," so that's what we did, and so now I am back, and it is time to proceed with the work—and reader let's not be too sure that this seemingly stupid digression, this apparent irrelevance, is not just as right as anything else in this book, or ever likely to be in this book, for there are 14 more days to go. Why does a writer ramble? Why does he make himself into some kind of Muscat Rambler? Why doesn't he stay put and work within those limits which will get him a fortune? I don't know why any other writer doesn't, but the reason I don't is very simple: I both don't know how, and I don't want to. I want to write, by now, the way I write, the way I must, and if nobody approves, I haven't forgotten that when somebody does approve, it doesn't make all that much difference—my books for forty years have just barely earned my living, but they have done that, and I am grateful that they have, because that had never been the thing I was after, at all. I don't know how Eddie Dowling died, but I understand that he was in what is known as a Rest Home not far from where he was born, in Providence, Rhode Island, or somewhere like that, and that he had been there for some time, having apparently given up any notion of actually founding a new Holy Land in Florida—it has a silly ring to it no matter how you look at it. But the next name on the list after Leif Eid (had it been Ericson I might have remembered Frances Farmer, for that Leif had been her husband when she and he had been in favor of having my very first play produced by The Group Theatre—*My Heart's in the Highlands*—and I don't tend to forget things like that), but this Leif, Eid, is a totally unknown quantity to me: and so is Harold Erichs who comes immediately after Leif Eid and immediately before Morris L. Ernst, somebody I do know, somebody I spoke with at least half a dozen times in New York, somebody I had almost always known had a rather large reputation as a lawyer and a liberal, and it may very well be that it was he who won the landmark case of *Ulysses vs. the United States*, permitting James Joyce at last to become publishable in the United States, and to provide him with a little income from his publisher Random House—but not much, for publishers, like all other big businesses, feel no qualms at all about taking far more than their just and appropriate share of profits from a book, no matter who the author is—and they are even so shameless as to take pride in giving a writer, like William Faulkner, for instance, a pittance in the way of an advance, knowing all too well that what he needs, just to survive, is ten times the total of the pittance, and that what his books are likely to earn over the years is a hundred times as much. Random House is (was) Bennett Cerf, of course, the eternal college boy, even in death, for he did die a multi-millionaire six or seven years ago, bereaving a television program called *What's My Line*, and virtually destroying its constancy: but then Dorothy Kilgallen had died before him by four or five years, and the blight of death had begun to destroy the popular if really silly program—its jolliness was pompous, and there is no worse kind than that. Morris L. Ernst also represented the opposition in a legal situation that was a pain in the ass to me, because it involved two little kids and their cheating mother, and Mr. Ernst's client. I had an idea my goose was cooked, all around, and it was, and continued to be for the next twenty years or more, but the whole thing is so boring I don't want to even begin to get hot about it all over again. Mr. Ernst's client was a prick, but Mr. Ernst took his side without any trouble at all, and no misgivings whatsoever. But of course the poor man had the support of the little woman, and that made it quite a nice time for everybody. I paid 7¢ for one of Mr. Ernst's books, a diary: it was bogus patriotic Americana, idiotic, and totally stupid.

99.

In writing, art is said to come out of tension, and there seems to be a very real probability that that is so, or at the very least that some kinds of art must come out of tension—but whose tension? Well, of course to begin with it has to be the tension of the maker of the art, the writer, and then it has to be inside the art itself, between the characters in a story or a play, or possibly even between the ideas of the story, (and let ideas signify all of the things that people believe they live by: religion, culture, tradition, and so on). When he wrote his plays it is not possible to believe William Shakespeare did so in serenity, without having his very soul in his body shaken up, and if that is accepted by us we have no trouble believing that his own tension heightened the tension in the play *Hamlet*, for instance—but God help us I find that it is really a failure of mind and soul to be forever referring to Shakespeare and to *Hamlet*, and I ought to lay off. Still, still, there is this matter of struggle, and there is its connection to that which is the everlasting source of art: yourself, life in yourself, the world, time, weight, vast weight gathered together in the world and in the human race and especially in yourself, and your struggle with this weight, which is part also of an accumulation of system and procedure and demand, incessant constant demand to go on, to breathe, to live, which is in the minutest units by the billions which constitute the preposterous whole, yourself, with your eyes, nose, mouth, teeth, ears, and the system working, and moving you on and on by unknown and unknowable needs. All right, it starts and it stops, and when it stops if you have had some connection with the world in which William Shakespeare was a kind of star, your name is listed in the annual year-end issue of *Variety*, which is actually given the date of the first Wednesday of the new year: and there you are. Dead. And famous. And clearly a damned fool. (For dying, of course, for not finding a way to go on fighting, for losing the fight, for giving up the body and spirit's use of muscle in tension and opposition.) Or you are an object of pity—you died too soon, you died in a stupid accident, you were shot in the head by a jealous husband, or a jealous wife, or a jealous son, or a jealous daughter, or a jealous stranger, or a jealous Avon Lady in a fit of disbelief about falling so low as to be peddling cosmetics to dismal people not in showbusiness, or in a terrible displeasure that her singing of the *You, you* hymn is restricted to front doors and not part of grand opera. Or if you are not an object of pity, you are something worse that courtesy almost compels a writer not to mention—indifference: you are an object of indifference. You have died, your name is in *Variety*'s list, and nobody gives a shit. All your tension, all your muscle in putting over the campaigns you put over have been apparently in vain. All right again, nobody needs to argue about it: art comes out of tension, or most art does, so the next question is this: since art comes out of nature, does nature also come out of tension: is the universe, in short, a product of tension? Yes, and explosive tension, at that, as we have heard so many times in so many beautiful explanations by so many beautiful experts with patient beautiful minds—charitable about the rest of us who just hang around with the big mouth open because we don't know, we just don't seem to be able to decide how the universe started, and why it is big beyond even the idea of size—it is beyond size, it is past measure, it is everything everywhere everlastingly and who are you to say so or not to say so? Well, it has been my experience from the very beginning of writing, and I mean from the first days of putting words slowly and neatly on lined paper at school, that there is tension in writing nothing more than my name, my place, and the date, and the name of my paper—"The Rich and the Poor," for instance. And then when I went into the thing with everything I had, the tension increased so much that it seemed to efface time, place, and person, myself, and the thing to be made, by writing, became pretty much the only thing, the thing lost inside the unknown of the beginning of things, of systems, the universe and its track, so to put it, its circling and circling, or its moving in a straight line forever everywhere, and straight into you, and after your flash of being, straight out of you, leaving you a name in Variety. Reader, sometimes long before I was twenty years old, after I had worked for as little as three hours on a work of art in the form of writing, as little as one hour, as little as half an hour, obliterating self, time, and place, and I came to, came out of it, what do you think I saw in my own face as I stood and pissed and glanced in the bathroom mirror? I saw somebody else, myself but somebody else, not myself alone, as it was when I hadn't concentrated on the production of art with so much intensity: it was all of my own people, all unknown to me, it was the human race itself, it was all of the animals especially, each with its own face, serene and unknowing, like my own face at that moment, and I would be less than candid (as the crooks of politics are forever saying) if I did not say that what I saw was handsome, impersonal, totally without vulnerability, without vanity, without ego, and with the same handsome-ness that is in the animals, fish, birds, insects, trees, vines, plants, leaves, flowers, fruit, and the same that is in grass, in blades of grass of all kinds, all the handsome green and green of grass.

106.

Reader, take my advice, don't die, just don't die, that's all, it doesn't pay, people aren't that sincere, you know, they will pretend to be sorry but really they don't care, they think it is perfectly all right that you died, and it isn't, so don't do it, don't die, figure out how, and stay put, there is plenty of time, let it go for this summer and next winter, and give the matter your best thought, even as you go about on your feet in your shoes and clothes and enjoy the business of looking and moving, it is right that you should not die, so don't do it, don't do what Charles R. Meeker did last year, I don't know why he did it, but he did do it, but don't you do it, sir, and lady, Oh lady, lady, don't you do it, either, you just take your good time about it, and if your husband had to rush away so you could get the insurance and all of his estate, don't you do what he did, and as for you younger men and women, and you adolescent boys and girls, and you teenagers, listen: suicide is no solution, just as drugs are no solution, and if you feel that nothing is a solution, don't be sure of that, that may very well not be so at all, it may be the consequence of something you can't even know about—bad weather, in a cycle, a cold winter of the soul, freezing, so hang in, hang on, hang over, hang under, and wait, and while you're waiting go for something, go fetch somebody something he thinks he needs—fresh bread is good straight from the bakery unsliced, go buy a loaf and take it to somebody and get a good sharp knife and take the round crusty loaf of sourdough bread made by the Basques of Fresno and very smartly slice the bread straight down the middle and smell the sourdough baked bread, man, it is good, at 80¢ a loaf it isn't half bad, the loaf has a weight of 24 ounces, a pound and a half, and you can make a meal out of some of the bread, breaking bread as the saying is with the man or woman or the both of them who sent you to fetch the bread, take a quarter of a pound of good sweet butter or good sweet margarine and smear the slice of sourdough with that stuff and smell it real full and well and bite it and chew it slowly and swallow it, and live, that's living, and if you really want to make it a kind of celebration of living, friend, young or old, brew a pot of plain tea, Lipton's, and pour, and without sugar or milk or anything sip a little of the piping hot tea and let it flow and wash upon the sourdough Basque bread and the butter or margarine, and yum yum yum, remember Mary Margaret McBride, swallow and know you are alive and doing nobody any harm, doing nothing any harm at all. Another man who somehow or other fell into that trap and died is William Melniker, but again he is not somebody I know at all, and about whom I also know nothing, how he rated the mention in the *Variety* list or anything else, although I like the name Melniker and wish I knew what it means, in Yiddish perhaps, or in Polish, or in German, or in another language brought to the New World by one of William Melniker's good ancestors long ago, but not all that long ago, just recently long ago. And then Johnny Mercer died, and I know him, I knew Johnny Mercer, I saw him sometimes at parties in Hollywood, and sometimes at Stanley Rose's bookstore, and sometimes at various other places. He wrote the lyrics, the words, to many great songs, but he also sang those songs, and he sang them well. He made good money, but his father died broke and in debt, somewhere in the South, possibly in Atlanta, and quietly Johnny Mercer went to work and paid every one of his father's debts, even though legally he was in no way obliged to do so, it was a simple matter of pride, of a son not wanting his father to have left anybody holding the bag, and once at a party I told him that I thought he was one of the great writers of words for songs, one of the really good singers of songs, but I had lately heard about what he had done for his father, and that was the thing I now admired about him above all other things, and I was glad that he had not been able to suppress the news of his devotion to his father, and to his own sense of family, as he had wanted to do, for it is necessary for all of us to hear about such news, and Johnny Mercer in his shy way smiled and thanked me, and we talked about the stuff people always talk about at parties, especially Hollywood parties, and that stuff is never without its comedy, that is the best thing about all talk at all parties, perhaps on account of the booze, and the fact that everybody is free again for a little while, and it is permissible and in order to talk about the funny stuff in the world, what somebody said to somebody else at a time when something else was expected of him traditionally har har har har har har. Christ, reader, take my advice, don't die, Johnny Mercer died, but don't you, and don't get the kind of headaches that made Johnny Mercer agree to go to the highest branch of the medical profession for the latest kind of examination and then don't be told yes, yes sir, yes Johnny Mercer, we've found it, you have a brain tumor, it has to come out, because it may be benign but also may not be, and in any case, it appears to be the thing that is hurting your soul by way of pain in your head, so Johnny Mercer agreed and they did their good work, and he died, a great artist, a great man, a great son, a great living member of the human race died, and he is gone, and don't you do it, and don't think you may have a brain tumor, too, because thinking about it may start a little one growing in your head, watch out for giving the mystery of cells any hint of fear, because those cells may be like dogs and if they sense you're afraid of them, they'll go to work and start multiplying in a kind of disorganized way and hurt you so badly you will risk dying on the operating table, and then lose your bet, and die. Don't do it.

107.

Jo Mielziner is another of the showbiz losers of 1976, and he was somebody I both know and know about: a great artist in the arena of the theatre, in the branch known as scene design: he was a great one, and his sets helped many a play come through in a fine way, especially Mr. Arthur Miller's

Death of a Salesman—death, death, death, reader, all over the place, bad for you, painful, if it can grab Jo Mielziner, be careful, it can grab you, too, and that's what's bad for you, that grabbing, death is always grabbing, taking a man away from his work, there were great scenes for Jo Mielziner still to design, but he was stopped cold. I was shaking-up Broadway with my own idea of what a play ought to be, and with my high spirits, and kidding around, and breaking of rules, and carrying on for laughs, yelling at everybody that I was the one, and all the rest of it, when I met Jo Mielziner who seemed to be a very sober sensible man, ten or eleven years my senior, and the author of a book about his branch of showbiz. I said, But the imagination is the best designer of scenes, why prevent it from having its own easy way with where any play is taking place, why not let it be in the scene which is the beholder's own past and truth, and stuff like that, kidding around some more of course, and Jo Mielziner said, Well, of course that is true and for centuries great plays have been done without scenery and nobody has felt they needed scenery to really enjoy the play or be moved by its tragedy and delighted by its comedy: it is really impossible in a modern theatre to put on a play without scenery, however, because if you work on a bare stage, that in itself is scenery—all I do is try to help certain kinds of plays a little, especially when scenery is part of the drama. He was a friend of all of the other scene designers of course, and of most of the good painters and sculptors of New York, and with some of the good architects, for all of these things are related, and elements of them are demanded by the craft and art of scene designing—you have got to know about them, and he did, and so did, and so does Boris Aronson, a great artist in or away from the theatre, and Sam Leve who did the fine set for *The Beautiful People*, and so was Watson Barrett who did the really perfect set for *The Time of Your Life*, and these artists are people who think and think all the time about places and shapes and light and shadow and densities and literature and life and how bodies in action in a play, with breath moving through lungs upon mouths and tongues and voice boxes making a kind of orchestral work of speech, how all of these things intermingle and make a kind of something that rewards people for sitting side by side like cells side by side in a beehive, for instance, each occupant of a seat something like an embryo of something to come though fully formed as a bee of some sort or another: worker, gatherer of honey, dancer, or whatever one or another of the several bee categories are. I used to love getting to my own individual seat in a theatre, any theatre, any play, because this permitted me to study life the way the scientist studies stuff under the heightened vision of a microscope, and I sat there in that private seat and watched the stuff on the stage, mostly vaudeville at the Hippodrome Theatre, and it was great, it was so great that years later I wrote a fine story called "The World and the Theatre," and one of these days I am going to read it again because in it is the stuff I put in it so that I would know how it was after the failure of memory, which is right now—but I did it, I held it all fast in that story and I know how and why I found my private seat in a great auditorium, after sneaking in, as a matter of fact, and always preferred sitting in a theatre that was almost empty, the whole place becoming almost my own property. But these days, and for years, I don't do that any more, it isn't age, it is selectivity, I don't feel like going in like an abstract morsel of some strange form of life to behold something I know from having seen it a dozen times and also from having myself put it into the play form. Jo Mielziner was a good workman in the scenery department of the American Theatre. But Sal Mineo—there is a young man whose murder by stabbing is still painful to think about. I suggested to Robert Saudek that *Omnibus*, a Sunday afternoon cultural TV show sponsored or underwritten by the Ford Foundation, should invite interesting old men of America to simply sit and recall their earliest years, and so a number of people decorated the variety program by doing that, and that Robert Saudek invited me to do it, but I said no, I would put it in a play, *A Few Adventures in the California Boyhood of William Saroyan*, or something to that effect, and Robert Saudek hired Sal Mineo to play William Saroyan, and when I saw the boy I swore he was myself, that is how it really was, reader, and he did the part absolutely flawlessly, and I was amazed: his brother Tom was also in the play, and I enjoyed chatting with both of them between my own chores on camera, before tapes, live, really live, and these chores were simple: I told about what happened, and then Sal Mineo performed it: I also hired a Greek who played the mandolin and walked up Van Ness Avenue in Fresno during World War I and played "There's a Long Long Trail Awinding Into the Land of My Dreams," and it was magic, that's all. So last year walking from his car in its proper place in the basement parking space of his apartment in Hollywood young Sal Mineo was stabbed by somebody who ran away, and Sal Mineo died, crying out in terrible protest, and the dirty killer, Death Itself, was never apprehended. I'll never forget him, he was great. Walter Schulze-Mittendorf also died last year, but I don't know him, and I wish I did.

108.

I have been called a sentimental writer, and this has annoyed me, but it may be that I haven't understood the meaning of sentiment, or of sentimental. That is not something unusual—for me, for you, for anybody. The fact is it is usual. We almost never know accurately anything at all. Language is supposed to protect us from inaccuracy but it may very well be that it compels more of it. All the same I have taken the written statement in book reviews that my writing is sentimental as a lie, an insult, and a deliberate attempt to belittle me. Does this reaction constitute something like paranoia? Bet your ass it does, and proudly. Name the least sentimental of writers—of men—and he is far more sentimental than I am. That becomes my reply. Shakespeare? (Poor Shakespeare, his name is dragged into every dispute of every kind everywhere.) But name him just the same, I say his writing is more sentimental than mine, and even while I say this, I think, Have you flipped your wig again, sir? Shakespeare has nothing to do with any of this. Nothing to do with this world, or its literature, or American writing, or California writing, or Armenian-American writing, or Armenian California Christian writing, or Saroyan-this-that-the-other writing, or sentiment, or literary criticism, or anything at all, you are just throwing a name around, and it would be far more sensible to make the name something really irrelevant, like Gaston Lafitte, or somebody. Gaston Lafitte was believed to be the least sentimental of men but he was far less sentimental than you, sir, so don't get hot, just don't get hot, that's all, so some jerk writing a stupid review has said you are sentimental, so be like Ernest Gallo or somebody and go about your business with your natural aloofness, who cares what the jerk reviewer says? We don't really ever know fully what we mean when we use certain words, even words as simple and as clear as good and bad. This is good, this is bad. We can say it, but we can't know what we mean unless it is grapes for instance, because a bunch of grapes can be seen and can be tasted and chewed and swallowed, and we can know what we have, and we can be absolutely certain that these grapes are good. Take muscats, for instance, which long ago became especially pleasant for me to take from vines and dust and eat, for all grapes have what is called a bloom, a mixture of actual soil dust and something that belongs to the nature of grapes themselves, of their slow ripening, or swift ripening. The muscat grapes on the muscat vines that I pruned when I was kicked out of Fresno High School and decided that I wouldn't even think of trying to get back, as I had been forced to do a number of times, in the dead of winter, little bunches overlooked by the grape-pickers and left on the vines, hidden sometimes low on the vine and under dry crisp leaves, these grapes came as a delightful gift as I worked and I loved eating them. Let that stand. Let almost fifty years go by. I have bought a flat in an old building in old Paris, the original Paris, and from the fruit and vegetable carts and shops I have bought stuff and eaten it, and one day I paid about a dollar for about a pound of grapes—everything is expensive everywhere, but I wanted these grapes because the sign said muscats—and the first thing I noticed was that they had a touch of purple in the skin, whereas the color in the California muscats was what is technically called white but is more transparent with a touch of green and yellow or golden, but just a touch. The second thing I noticed was that the untouched bunch of grapes was slightly scented, and touched, broken by accident for instance, the scent became strong and was most pleasing, and when broken by the teeth and tasted the Paris muscat grapes were absolutely new and special, and I thought better than the California muscat grapes. Look, I wouldn't think of being a man of power, a man of power over other men, power of life and death and money, like the leaders and politicians and all such, for they are the sentimental souls of the human race, of the human world, of the human time and life, and their sentiment is stupid and limited to the self, to themselves, each of them, although they invariably put the self out into something abstract like the name of the people themselves, totally unreal of course, or the region, or the religion, or the philosophy: they claim they are everybody, in short, it is an awful crime of sentiment and dirty dishonesty. There is clean dishonesty, as when a decent man doesn't happen to know but does believe in the opposite of what is the truth, and does so with passion and innocence. What I'm saying is, let's just get things inaccurately as we have always done, and let's have the clutter grow beyond all limits, and let's every one of us know his own little portion of the inaccuracy in his own way, to suit his own participation in the dance, the labor, the play, the fun, the anguish, the joy, the pain of being, of having connection, place, property, clothing, memorabilia, letters, stamps, coins, shoes, souvenirs, bottles, china or at any rate dishes, silver or at any rate stainless steel (including little sets from airline meals), napkins of both cloth and paper, and let us not demand that what we have and know is all there is, all there is, take it or leave it. Don't tell me I'm sentimental, you sons of bitches. You are contemptible, your dishonesty is contemptible, your careful plodding with words, to keep them safely captured inside your silly little theories are contemptible, but I don't hate you because each of you is a sad little pompous son of a bitch, with a chair at a university, and you are fighting bravely to seem to be somebody.

112.

It goes around and around that to look back is a bad thing, and to live in the past is the worst thing, it is death. Well, of course anything that goes around, anything that becomes lore, anything that people believe has merit, has truth to it, but this truth is invariably only some of the truth, not all of the truth, and it is some of the truth only to some of the people—all that someing and truthing which we are supposed to have got into the American variation of the English language by way of Abraham Lincoln makes for a jingling kind of fun, but it may also be a few other things as well, one of them being something in the dimension of confusion, or further confusion. But what we are talking about—always, always, remember that, reader—is the connection between life and death, living and dying, being and not being, and this large connection connects with many other, lesser, connections, but especially to the connection between words used in living languages and the people who live and use the language, and indeed live by them, so that when the lore gets around, by way of a grand old baseball player, for instance, like Satchell Paige, that it is not a good idea to look back (because you may see something catching up on you), there is really no reason for us to dispute the lore. The fact remains just the same that it is a good idea to look back, and to keep looking back, pretty much as long as you live, every day, literally by turning and looking and figuratively by making a point of remembering, if you need to make a point of it, and most us tend to remember without trying or even without especially wanting to. The thing that may be something to think about, to be concerned about in this connection between popular sayings and popular beliefs, and the refuting of them, or of part of them, is not so much what the lore says is probably wrong but why it is done, at all. Do you follow, reader? You don't, well that certainly suggests the wisdom of dropping the matter and moving along, for we just haven't got forever, have we, any longer, although up until my fiftieth year I seemed to believe I not only had forever, I would always have forever. But before it's dropped, let me say that all we are really ever concerned about is the improving of the quality that is in everything we know and experience, and to move nearer to excellence and away from less than it. In other words, make a point of looking back so that you may more fully notice and appreciate where you are, and the time it has taken to get there, but if I were now to follow through with this indicated pattern and say don't look back to enjoy the fun you think you had twenty years ago or twenty days ago, or to be astonished at the trouble you were in but got through, or to feel again the joy and sorrow you felt simultaneously because you were involved in an affair, if I were to follow through and say don't do that because it is silly and indulgent and at its core destructive and even deadly, that would be just as inaccurate as the other. And at best a demonstration that anything can be done with words, with language, with print, with writer, with reader, but especially with voice, speaker, and listener, for we know all too well what the great speakers have done, and how near madness so much of their doing has been. Language, words, speech, voice, style, ranting, raving, and something like orchestration of achieved emotional changes in the listeners did it. Prolix is the word for what is going on right here, right now, and also for what I am talking about. But there is no use at all commanding ourselves to shut up, it can't be done, however grand it would be if there were to be as little as 24 hours of shutting up all over the world, what a profound change that would bring to all of us, and if we might also have another day, not the same day, during which everything was stopped—nobody did anything, possibly not even eat, and just be there, everybody in his own gift of hide and hair, foot at the bottom, head at the top, arms at the side—this might be the beginning of the arrival of full and real humanity to the human race. But it might not, too, that is what I am getting at. And full and real humanity might not help, and is for all practical purposes what we have and have always had in any case, only we have been astonished or annoyed that it has been so flawed, that out of it could come so much that is inhuman and indeed insane and criminal and monstrous, and totally, totally without the innocence which not one animal has so far in any tribe of animals lost, even the man-eating tiger has not lost his innocence, he tracks down that order of game because the tiger is too old and slow to track down any other order. Prolix, too many words for what is being said, and I mean right here and right now, but listen here, sir, and lady, man, and woman, boy, and girl, this prolixity is nothing at all to the prolixity of nature before we ever came into possession of words and language and began to see about working things out so that having what we had would be fun and life and not pain and death. Besides, I can't be bothered about avoiding any of the theories about the most effective use of language. This is the most effective—for me. And I would be willing to at least suspect that it might be the most effective for you, too. And let the other writers write their writing and the other readers read their reading and let the aged and feeble tigers stalk old men and have them, shall we imagine that any tiger can really enjoy the liver and lights of a tired old man, that must taste really flat to a tiger, but it is a meal, and it demonstrates that the tiger hasn't looked back, at any rate.

133.

This is a book about life, not death, but let's not use language in any such convenient and beautiful and mistaken and misleading way, it is a book about everything and anything and nothing, folks, nothing at all, excepting himself, and yourself: a writer and a reader, and if classrooms take up any of this book then it is himself and the group, on behalf of life, on behalf of death, on behalf of something like the truth, on behalf of laughter, and never not on behalf of all the dark things across the street everywhere. An old writer, an older writer, an adult writer, a child writer, a boy writer, a young writer, a wild writer, a brilliant writer, a stupid writer, a running writer, a running running running writer has got to run, has got to write as he runs, has got to quickly choose a scheme for another book, has got to see the scheme through, and that is how it is here, in this book. There are no excuses, there is always the beautiful comedy of a writer in America on a talk show telling how he did it, and I have loved every moment of such delicatessen on such pushcarts. What I cherish especially is the casual ease and seeming unawareness in a rich writer about the huge thing he has done, working steadily for seven years—everybody works seven years, the idea probably came about from childhood references heard from adults quoting the great chronicles about plagues and pestilences, droughts and upheavals. A writer telling one or another of the beautiful owners of popular talk shows how he did it, how he actually pieced together a great book, that is the thing to cherish—and everybody is so pleased, so deeply delighted by the writer, and the talk show host, as they are called, so pleased about being the host and being rich and having his show exhibited in 48 cities to a daily audience of 48 million people—wow, that's fun, that's life, that's getting it, or nothing is getting it. And thank God that so far no talk show host has made it to *Variety*'s Necrology list, or if any have, it is not known to me, and so it comes to the same thing. And what a parade of great souls they fetched to their chairs for presentation to the nation, and in some cases even to the world. Just thinking of the stars of the talk shows makes a writer glow with patriotic pride. The men, the men, the men, comics, national heroes, statesmen, horsemen, cocksmen, and the women, the women, the women, experts on summing up conditions of mental illness among slumdwelling pregnant unmarried prostitutes with mouth sores, the whispered message about the findings at Johns Hopkins, and the former girls now large and high-scented women telling all about their experiences with their famous husbands and their more athletic and physical lovers, and the jeering fat women who roar with such laughter and song that small men try not to imagine how sex could possibly be managed with them. What a loyal group of American citizens they are, enriching the national soul, and themselves in high finance. But what have talk shows to do with anything? Anything at all? Well, they have a lot to do with everything, because they have become several things quite clearly, one of which is the national graveyard. For the living, that is. Everybody goes to the talk shows as during a funeral and a musical march to the graveyard for death and burial. But surely it is not the talk shows alone of all of the stuff on television that do it, provide the funeral service and the march and the eulogy and the casket and the body and the plot and the burial. No, indeed it is not, but it is the last program and the most effective conclusion to all of the others, it is the show that ties everything together into a corpse. Well, what's wrong with that, since it has got to happen in one way or another, in any case, so why not have it happen on television, on the talk shows? The fact is that not only is nothing wrong with it, almost everything is just right with it, so that when one soul dies in one body, it is invariably after that soul in that body has been sent out into the whole nation, into the whole world, and transformed into a part of the whole national body and soul, and into a part of the whole human body and soul, of reality, of imagination, of intelligence, of folly, of God, of Satan, and folded together into some kind of sweet pudding and put into the oven to rise and become sweet-smelling and in a way rather beautiful. Or a soufflé or something. And television came along just in time for the end of the world, so to put it, although the world will end only when it will, and nature will end only when it will, and there is no evidence of the end of either in the foreseeable future, as the saying is. Death is fun, life is fun, death is unnecessary but only if life is, too, death is educational, it provides all of the things everybody who has never had them has always longed for: travel, fulfilled fantastic sex, orgies, fame, enormity of personal significance, recognition and reverence from everybody including animals everywhere, wealth beyond any order of need, wit, charm, beauty, generosity—does this little nation want its land and sovereignty restored, voila, it is restored, go and be who you are, if you know, or if you think you know (the Americans thought they knew, you know, and suddenly they were not so sure) and beyond generosity a serene and wholesome hatred, a hatred like supreme love, and gentle in its clinical ruthlessness, all things criminal (in the opinion of the dreaming dead one) ended forever with a gesture of sweep it away, Joe and Jenny, death is love and life is hatred, and the two together produce the only beauty, the only reality, the only truth, the only art—what's that mud in my head for? Why am I forgetting something? Why am I leaving out so much?

from
More Obituaries

Tuesday January 15 1980 12:55 P.M.

*T*he bicycle is the noblest invention of mankind. Who says so? I say so, that's who, and my saying so is serious, perhaps silly, and definitely final, for that is quite simply the law of sayings. Somebody says something, and the saying is passed from person to person like a dollar from hand to hand or a woman from man to man, as the famous song goes. And the sayings have always been preposterous and if not irrelevant certainly useless: a rolling stone gathers no moss. (Anonymous.) Neither does a rolling bicycle, for that matter. Roll out the barrel, we'll have a barrel of fun. Who said that? Also Anonymous, or at any rate Anonymous enough, for the writer of the words to that famous beer-drinking song surely heard somebody say the saying. When the roll is called up yonder, I'll be there. Well, that's another order of roll entirely, but the irrelevance of the saying shares with the other rolls their deepest and best connection to the human experience. I love the bicycle, I always have, I can think of no sincere decent human being, male or female, young or old, saintly or sinful, who can resist the bicycle. Now, Captain Boyle asked his pal Joxer in that sweet play of Dublin early in this century, What is the moon? What is the stars? The question that is most wildly, the most really stupidly rhetorical, is far more meaningful than any answer, or any attempt at an answer, and of course 88 billion lightyears of answers in books and speech and conversation have accumulated virtually every day among the living in the form of attempted answers, and each of them is wrong, if now and then nicely so, as for instance when the singer says he knows Jesus loves him because the Bible tells him so. The fact is before the Bible tells him so, or tells him anything, he has experienced the unstoppable light and warmth of the sun telling him so. Or the Englishman come to Alabama also early in the century rejoicing that he knows Lily of Laguna loves him, but is asked by the world, by skeptics, by science, by allegory, How do you know? And instantly replies, Because she says so. What is the bicycle? Well, like coins of money (but perhaps unlike paper of money, which connects essentially to conspiracy—to defraud the working class, if you will not mind too much, and there is *that* class, and the majority of the people of the world either belong to it or aspire to it), like coins of money, the bicycle is something to every person, it is something else, that is. To me it is, for starters, action, movement, music, departure, arrival, poetry, art, design, but most of all, most most of all all, it is this incredible machine that involves two wheels, a pipe frame, handlebars, seat, hangar (if that's the spelling of the word), pedals, and chain. You get on this simple machine that is sheer poetry just the same, and you hold the handlebars very firmly, and you press down on the pedals, and you go. That's what you do, man, you go, and to a boy of eight or nine, going is the thing, going is living, it is experience itself, it is art, it is observation, it is even religion, even if you are an atheist or think you are, and I have never had any impulse at all to limit myself by any such theory of disbelief. I am a believer, starting with the awesome rightness and majesty of the bicycle, and the vast meaning of ownership and usage of the contraption, or marvel. The bicycle has a fork to hold the front wheel, and I like that fact. My brother Henry and I had one bike between us in Fresno at 2226 San Benito Street in 1919 and we got into a dispute about both its ownership and the usage to which each of us preferred to put it. Henry was 14 and I was 11, and suddenly in the tradition of brothers Henry became so angry at my righteousness that he picked up the sprocket, or if that is not the proper word for it, the notched metal wheel upon which the chain worked, and with all his might he directed it at my head, and just barely missed. The metal had been thrown with such force that it stuck in the barn wall beside which we had been taking the bike apart for a hour or more. I did not believe that like pistol duellists of yore that he deliberately threw the metal weapon to miss the target, my head, he threw to strike it, and this realization suddenly drove me mad, and Henry noticed and got up and ran around the house, to escape being murdered. Our mother Takoohi heard the commotion and my shouting: You tried to kill me, you dirty son of a bitch, so I'm going to kill you. She came out of the house and grabbed me, permitting Henry to get away. He hurried a mile and a half to the Public Library and didn't come home for two or three hours, by which time I had decided that he had thrown the weapon to miss. If he hadn't, point blank, I wouldn't be writing this piece of homage both to the bicycle, and to Henry, a good brother, who ever afterwards restricted his outrage to polite reasonable talk. Good boy, as his father Armenak informed him when he rode his tricycle at the age of four to fetch the man some nails from the barrel around our house in Campbell, near San Jose, where a few years later Armenak died. As a poet and a Presbyterian preacher, without a pulpit, he also rode a bike, but solely for transportation, it would seem, for didn't he go, at the age of 36 straight out of himself and the world. Had he loitered on his bike he would surely [have] escaped some of the anxieties that ruptured his appendix and brought on the peritonitis that burned him in the manner of hell-fire itself, compelling him to cry out, Takoohi, for the love of God, water. Which she took to him in large glasses straight from the faucet or tap, even though the rustic doctor had suggested that perhaps it would be best if he took no water. But by then it was too late, and he was on the Celestial Bicycle pedaling like Christian Pilgrim himself to escape from the Devil and his terrible Everlasting Fire, while Armenak's real bicycle rested against the apricot tree in our backyard. July 1911, not exactly recent, but recent enough for me not to have forgotten the telling of the tale, which I did not witness.

Tuesday January 15 1980 1:45 P.M.

Mohammed was called The Messenger, and as I have always associated that designation with telegraph messengers, I have put Mohammed on a bicycle, as I had been for three years at the Postal Telegraph Office in Fresno, from 1921 through 1924 at which time I moved along into vineyard work, at slightly better pay—thirty cents an hour. I pruned vines with Japanese and Mexican vineyard works, and I ploughed vines and irrigated them, and when heavy January prevented us from earning $3 from dark of morning to dark of evening, I rode the wheel to an old bookshop on Mariposa Street where for a nickel I could buy many kinds of magnificent magazines, like *The Dial*, containing for instance "The Oral History of the World by Joe Gould," or a copy of *Broom* published in 1922 and full of all manner of new writing by all kinds of new writers, including Sherwood Anderson and the young fellow he was encouraging, William Faulkner. Sprocket? Is that the proper name of the metal that Henry threw at my head? Cain didn't kill Abel with a bicycle sprocket because in those simple, or perhaps simpler, days the bicycle had not come to the world, to the human race. Stones were always there, and they seemed to have been swiftly employed as tools and weapons, and so poor, poor Cain killed his brother with a stone. That which Henry did, or rather didn't quite do, instantly made profoundly real the story or legend of Cain and Abel which I had heard about at the First Armenian Presbyterian Sunday School in the class of my father's kid brother Mihran, one of the unassuming saints of the human race. He never knew he was a saint of course, hence his modesty was no virtue, it was a simple fact of being. Ah ha, I instantly thought when I saw the flying sprocket and heard it imbed itself into the wood of the barn, this is how it happens between brothers, and of course there are brothers and brothers, apart from the simple truth that all men are brothers, and fools, and angels, and murderers, and penitents down the ages for their terrible but finally innocent crimes. Mohammed was a walking Messenger, and indeed when the Moslems, his children, first saw Christian missionaries mounted upon bicycles, they stoned the poor gentle souls, for the contraption seemed to have come from the Devil, from evil, and Takoohi herself let me know that Turks and Kurds, our neighbors in Bitlis at the turn of the century (everything is at the turn of the century forever, isn't it?), our good friends, all of us sharing our languages and cuisine and customs, the Turks and Kurds, also Moslems, also either threw stones at the Missionaries or chased after them, shouting wildly, and knocked them off their wheels, and beat them. Now, what does this mean, this automatic, impulsive, apparently natural resentment on the part of the enduring human race to the bicycle? If that's English, at all, but even if it isn't, I suspect that the reader must know what I mean. Why wasn't the connection between a man and a bicycle wonderful to so many tribes and branches of the human family—and I am not thinking of the earliest bicycles, those with enormous front wheels, and tiny back wheels, and the rider perched away up there at the top, I mean the simple, beautiful, practical, sensible bicycle we all know. The earliest bicycles were quite simply very nearly nightmarish, and it would be easy to understand the simultaneous disbelief and anger about its intrusion into the business of going for all of us—by foot. Ali, on the other hand, having appropriated the Messenger's holy name as his own first name, Mohammed Ali, one of the human marvels of our age, Mohammed Ali, spell it as you choose, it is the sound of it that we are concerned about, goes by airplane for the most part in his large pieces of going, as we all do, and walks in his smallest pieces of going. What is the moon? What is the stars? We ask and ask, and we listen to the replies a thousand times by the scientists but in the end we simply insist on what seems to our simple souls, our simple minds, our simply unaccountableness, what seems to be the simple truth, that we don't know, that's all, never mind what Carl Sagan says on the Johnny Carson talk show. He may believe he knows, but we go right on knowing that we don't know. And putting a man on the moon only compels one or another of us to write a play or two about this equivalent of early bicycle-riding, now out into the universe, the bicycle being logically transformed into the rocket, but without handlebars and seat and openness, Lord God, the riders to the Moon are prisoners of the mystery of molecules and atoms and all locked-in systems of refusing to yield final information. It was really so, several Americans both landed and walked on the Moon, but more truly really so, it was not on the moon at all, it was on television, it was on fantastic and mighty systems of cameras and film, on photography that the whole human race which witnessed the actuality of it all joined the three (or was it two?) who walked and with them walked on the moon. They should have rode a bicycle to an old bookshop for some bargains in old literary magazines. I own three wheels (as we refer to bicycles in my world): a 3-speed Raleigh, a one-speed Japan bike called Jet Wind, and an Italian foldable bike, which can be taken in the trunk of a car to the country for detailed going there, where the car cannot go, along paths, for instance. I ride the Japan Wheel pretty much every day. It is a beautiful bike, and it cost $28 about fourteen years ago, at a White Front, and I assembled it, after which Vartan Avakian, about 78 these days, of the famous Avakian Brothers of Fresno, at The Broadway Cyclery, about four years after my assembling did the whole thing over again, without in any way taking from the bike its connection to me, which every bike soon acquires. What is a bicycle? Well, my bike is himself. It is me. I am still the Messenger in *The Human Comedy*, to whom I gave the name Homer Macauley.

Tuesday January 22 1980 10:05 A.M.

How do you write? How do you live? How do you die? How do you do? Now, the last variation of the basic question, or group of questions, is the one we use without literalness, we do not mean how do you do, we mean hello, in all of its variations, or politeness, or at any rate civility, of sorts. But how do [you] write is also meant in the unliteral how do you do, and for that matter also how do you die, and my answer is that I start with the trees and keep right on straight ahead, I start with these companions of this place each fixed into the soil of where it is, and sometimes the rock or rocks, and very little else, and after that the going is not only easily [sic] it is very nearly rollicking, it is unavoidable, for the tree is a thing of great attachments, and it puts forth all manner of leaves, abundantly, and each leaf is the same, but not precisely so, so that noticing this repetitious imprecision leads to everything else, especially life, especially speculation, and especially the last act of life, the unknown abandonment of tree, branch, twig, leaf, bud, flower, fruit, and self. How do you do, die, write, live, sicken, heal, despair, rejoice, move along, move along. Well, you are lucky if you don't start at the end, at abstraction, if you start at the beginning or something like it, at the specific, the seen, the real, as the saying goes (although do not diminish by one jot the glorious reality of the unreal, the thundering substantialism ha ha ha of the insubstantial, the unseeming sanity of the seemingly insane, and all that sort of thing, for if you are a writer, if you are to venture into the dimension of the Maker, you cannot permit yourself to be limited, although in your art, in your writing, in your tiny microscopic making you have got to impose limits after all, or you will be able to make nothing, do you follow, or is it too much trouble?). The real, as the saying goes, the something that is a solid something, or the something that is a liquid something, rock and water, as examples, then, flowing water in a shallow brook, flowing upon visible sweet colorful pebbles, among cress, and with little nooks and crannies upon which Water Skaters have their fun in living, in breeding, in continuing. You start with the visible but really impossible to hold, or fire, that gift that is swiftly made commonplace by familiarity, that demonstration of the infinitude of sameness, of flame, of color, of structure, of design, of mass, of movement, Christ, what a love-liness a fire in a fireplace, for instance, is to the man sitting there watching and listening, and what sweet whisperings of all manner of language come from the wood being consumed by the fire. Well, in fire, for instance, or at any rate, we may answer the question of life and art, how do you die, do, live, make, and all the rest of it. I have a short story entitled "The Broken Wheel" from my earliest days and I remember that when I was just beginning to write the story I kept asking myself, What's going on, why are you writing about the old English walnut tree in the backyard of the rickety frame house at 2226 San Benito Avenue, and about the two barns stuck together, and about the cactus plant, and the grass, and the creosote bushes in the empty lot adjoining that house, although you didn't know the name of that scented plant, that stinking plant, one might say, stinking of something like kerosene, which years later you came upon by accident out by the Southern Pacific Railroad Tracks north, north from the center of town, and getting a whif[f] of the strong smell, forgotten for thirty or forty years, you whooped with joy, with restoration of youth and confusion and joy and joy and joy again and again: so this is what the creosote bush is, then, about which I have read a dozen or more times in twenty or thirty years and never knew it was our own bush in the empty lot where we played Pee Wee, Horse, tincan hockey, soccer, baseball, football, and as assortment of invented, improvised games. If you practice an art faithfully, it will make you wise, and most writers can use a little wising-up, but perhaps not quite as much as painters and sculptors and composers do, although it varies and now and then a composer will be almost bright, straight out, from the start, but not often. (I'm Ludwig van Beethoven, I'm Jean Sibelius, I'm Frederick Chopin.) Well, Beethoven's last words probably were not but certainly might have been, The Fifth, the Fifth, I should never have written it. And Jean Sibelius might have said as he expired, I never did write the 8th, and I'm not sure I shouldn't have, just as I'm not sure I should have broken my arms and legs and even my head and forced it, out of my deterioration might have come my best, my most beautiful, my truest symphony. And Chopin never said anything at all like, The piano, the piano, I made that entire continent my own, my very name is upon the piano, it is furniture without my usage of it, but why should I boast, why should I use my last breath saying something so silly, the piano belongs to the very idea that out of machinery, out of careful clever physics, mechanics, hammers and levers, the human race can get something rare and reasonable that no other race can even suspect might be there to be got—and I helped, I did my soft, hard, flower-like, knife-like, dream-like, riot-like, unlike any previous like, truth-like, truth's own truth-like, I did my Poland-like, France-like, piano-like, universal-like pieces and made the furniture speak with the mouth of God, of bird, of man, of woman, of child, but why am I talking at a time like this instead of just shutting up and letting the piano stand in the corner of the parlor and be silent and be furniture? Suppose you had been at Chopin's bedside and heard him say what I have just said he might have said, would you have been thrilled, or would you have said, Good God, the poor man is talking like Saroyan, not like Chopin, and Saroyan hasn't even been born yet, hasn't even arrived in Fresno yet. What's going on around here? *10:45 A*

Friday January 25 1980 2:50 P.M.

Is this any way to write a book? Well, maybe not, at that, but it certainly is as good a way as any to drown, to see it all like a speeded-up movie of 10 seconds for a hundred years, to die, to kick the bucket, to start all over again, and that's good enough for me. The way to write a book is the way the writer writes it, and I will not put down any of the several ways that this writer has written books, just as I won't consider with awe and profound respect if not admiration for the way other writers have written their books, for the longer I live (and die) the more I find it possible, even necessary, to notice that the way I live and therefore the way I write is at least as right as the way any other writer (or anybody else) lives, and writes, and if the beautiful truth is told it is a better way to live and write than the way of anybody else, without exception. Is this madness? Why, of course it is, but let us not knock madness, either. The enormity of my folly and vanity I leave to others to measure, I cannot consider myself a saint or an angel, but I'll be damned if I am going to say that I am not as near to these classifications than anybody else I know, or have heard about—notwithstanding my bile, my jealousy, my hatred, my all-around nonsense of rivalry with all other writers, especially those who make big money and are paid a lot of attention by all kinds of people. None of my business. I am my business, and I am not going to mind at all that I find my rivals altogether unacceptable. To begin with, I can't read their writing, it is as simple as that—when the rest of the people of the whole nation are reading their best-sellers I stand at a bookshop counter and try to read the stuff and I can't. It is so artful it is arty, it is so careful it is phony, it is so cleverly constructed it is painful to notice its structure, but most of all, most most of all, the damned thing just naturally leaves out so much, it might just as well have left out the speck that is not left out, the speck that is made into the best-seller itself. I am concerned about as much as possible, and then I am concerned about more, and then still more, and if all this prevents creating great simple straight narrative, full of the teasing of suspense, by God that's none of my business at all, I can't be bothered about that at all, what I have got to do is liberate literature from the ancient tyranny of art, and not out of not knowing about art, and how to make art, but out of simple rejection of the limitations of that awareness and adherence to its laws. I don't need a best-seller, and if the truth is told I take pride in the fact that I haven't had one in about forty years. That makes me proud, for all of the best-sellers are in a grand pile of paper for shredding and re-making into pulp. All I've got to do as often as possible is stand and writing [sic] the new book, whatever it turns out to be, and as always I refuse, flat all out I refuse to plot and plan and construct and concoct a story, just right for book-buyers, book-borrows, book-stealers, book-readers, and just right for excerpting in *The Reader's Digest*, and in *Book Digest*, and in other Digests, and in magazines, and just right for transforming into a movie, and into a television series, and into a stage play. I write my book as I have always written it, straight out of then and there, out of myself at that time and in that place, and if I don't know what I am going to write I do discover later on what it was I wrote, and it has a kind of authenticity, a kind of reality, a kind of connection with everything, that you don't get out of any other kind of writing, and that includes the tippytop kinds of writing, by the really skilled historians, biographers, interpreters, philosophers, theologians, politicians, statesmen, scientists, gentlemen of wealth and leisure, anthropologists, and the hell with naming any more of them, each with his own territory carefully mapped out, and each with his own chosen small portion of material—the full and true life, for instance, of Henry James by the brilliant fellow whose name I keep forgetting, or by the full and true invention of himself placed into the name, one of the greatest biographers of all time who may or may not have said straight out, Well, he wrote that way, you see, making so much of everything, of nothing actually, because he was never at any pains to find a place to put himself, helplessly or almost helplessly, gathered into a hard-on, he just never seems to have experienced a hard-on, and consequently he had never been a fool in relation to girls and women, in affairs or in marriage, he was like a whole solid category of good men and writers who wrote fantastic and sometimes very funny works because they had never been bothered by the matter of hard-ons: J. M. Barrie writing his gentle books and his Peter Pan, and the man with two names who wrote *Alice in Wonderland*, and thousands of letters to little girls, and Henry James, Let me tell you something, reader—I cannot imagine any apprentice writer not having done writing of the same order as that of Henry James, who did not graduate from it because of hard-ons. Indeed if a writer is neutral in that manner, then of course he is not only able to write with that kind of thorough neutrality, he is unable not to do so, it is the only way he can write, and it turns out that we are fascinated by the simple truth that during his lifetime the stories and novels of Henry James were never best-sellers, they became best-sellers after his departure from the vale of tears and sexual madness and absurdity, excess and horror, family and wife and children. Jane Austen before him wrote in a style not unlike his, but she also did not ever suggest that she had gone berserk somewhere with a man, as George Sand tried and tried to suggest, and failed, because she had pretty much gone berserk every night and every afternoon, and yet somehow found time to write all those grand novels of great, great popularity, whatever else they may be, and I'm told by several writers that Ms. George Sand was a great writer, as a matter of fact. Why not, so was Edgar Rice Burroughs.   *3:[2]5 P*

Monday January 28 1980 12:20 P.M.

Dear old friend whoever you are, or dear old self whoever you are, or dear new soul: please accept this greeting and homage, for if ye do not greet one another, shall ye be able, then, to say farewell when it is time to do so, when it is time to go. I'm Little Harry the singer at Le Triolet in Paris in 1959, on rue Galilee (yes that's all right, it is not all wrong). I'm Charley Dan[v]ers, the pianist at Le Triolet, and the composer of the music of the song "Till," and a few other internationally known (and unknown) songs, and here comes loud and laughing Americans, John Fante summoned to Paris to salvage a property bought by Darryl Zanuck by writing a new screenplay based upon the novel, and here comes James Jones and his wife Gloria, and here comes Juliette Greco and Darryl Zanuck and Lord, Lord the year is 1959, and what can I say, I'm Darryl Zanuck, I'm James Jones, I'm Little Harry, I'm Charley Danvers, but didn't we have a lot of fun in those long-gone days of that beautiful year? This is what happened, Le Triolet sold out three years later and the place became a Mexican nightclub, it had been a French-Algerian saloon-restaurant with a dance floor where Little Harry tambed a tambourine while Charley Danvers play[ed] the piano, with a good assortment of clinkers, and harmonized with the voice of Little Harry, sometimes deliberately falsetto and quite feminine, himself a stocky Algerian Jew of forty-four or so, four feet eight or so, with short thick stubby fingers, and a smile that compelled gladness in any beholder. While Harry Danvers was perhaps the same age, or perhaps ten years older, and while Harry Danvers was a composer of sometimes great songs, like the song "Till," their reward in worldly terms appeared to be tips, and it pleased me to tip rather well, for when you are gambling high stakes in Paris or out at the Casino in Enghien, win or lose, you like to hand out French currency generously, because you know that on one play you risk and sometimes lose, and sometimes win a thousand times as much as you are handing around, so that after a foray at the Aviation I went to Le Sexy nearby just at closing time and took the four girls to the famous onion soup restaurant and bought them food and drink of the best quality, the champagne and soup and fish coming to the equivalent of a hundred or two in dollars—and gladly, for it is amusing to notice hard-working girls smiling at one another and thinking, Get a load of this boy, will you? And I took my son and daughter to Le Triolet so they could have forever the memory of having heard heard Little Harry sing in English, It's a sin to tell a lie, and Is it true what they say about Dixie, and Whispering, and in French "Till," with Charley Danvers harmonizing on the chorus of each song, but especially all-out on "Till": the desert sands grow cold, and so on. Oh, these two were a great team, and the waiters and bartenders and bar drinkers and table sitters, they were all a grand living lot in those summertime days of 1959. And then Little Harry disappeared, along with Charley Danvers, and if they didn't die, they might just as well have done so as far as the rest of us were concerned, for we could not find them. I was sure in 1964, for instance, that they must be singing at another saloon-restaurant in Paris, but nobody who might be expected to know had any word of them at all. And the song Charley Danvers wanted me to put words to, a good sombre song, was not heard except in memory, when he played it, and Little Harry sang the French words to it, which Charley Danvers really didn't like, and tambed the tambourine and scuffled around, dancing to the somber music. My kids liked going to that place, and Little Harry saw to it that they were appropriately entertained, and that while they were in the place, usually for a visit of about two hours, for a good leisurely meal, steak, salad, dessert, or perhaps a good couscous, and filet of sole, and champagne, lightly and politely, just enough for the kids to feel worldly, during their presence in the place the sweet stripper sat fully clothed at the bar, sipping non-intoxicant beverages and chatting with owners and customers and admirers and relatives. It was a Jewish establishment essentially and everybody was warm and really enthusiastic about everything, and they all remembered Algeria, where Albert Camus was born and brought up, and where Guy de Maupassant placed some of his best short stories, especially of illicit intrigue, so to put it. The stripper worked in the Paris manner, and was not really a stripper in the American sense, and certainly very near to everybody eating at tables or drinking at the bar, and really very far from the San Francisco stripping at the old burlesque house on Ellis Street, in 1931 when a little New York Jewish stripper stunned three cousins by suddenly flinging off a long black fur covering impersonating mink, to reveal the sweetest, whitest body in the whole world, and then to run off and never come back. Unforgettable it was, and it could not possibly be the same if it had happened on the floor of a small saloon-restaurant, like Le Triolet, where the stripper was always very near and spoke and laughed with everybody, while the 1931 girl only sang, Christmas it comes only once every year. And herself only once in a lifetime in a world, and where is she now, who that one matinee was alive and truer than the Venus de Milo or any of the other artful representations of the glorious girls of all time and place? Will Dyson of Australia has an etching of a similar girl revealing her full front nakedness, and he called his picture something like, All Right, Then, Have a Good Look. How the eye of male youth holds fast the fleeting image of sweet while female nakedness. How lonely it is to behold such reality and not to embrace it. But the little bordellos were all about, and the girls in them were not all that unlike the sweet girl on the stage of the 1931 San Francisco theatre. The point is not having what is desired is also good, indeed perhaps the greatest good.   *1:05 P*

Thursday February 14 1980 9:50 A.M.

Well, folks, I'm dying, dying of cancer, dying of the self, my own self, of my ancestors, so how about a little gallows humor? Well, I don't really have any, and of course like the man about to be hung I don't really believe I'm dying, and while I also don't believe it is somebody else, it is really not quite possible to make known what it is that I do believe, so this doesn't quite encourage gallows or any other kind of humor, it encourages more of the same kind of speculation that I have known, you have known, all of us have known from pretty much the beginning of speculation, or at any rate that order of it that relates to each of us in our meanderings through the self and everything else. —Pardon me a minute, folks: my mother Takoohi's father Minas had a bother Hairabet whose son Mihran has a son Ruben who just phoned to ask, When are we going to do the Laundry, and then go out to the Veterans Hospital, to Celebrate Valentines Day, as you told me to tell them you would do this year, like you did last year. I said, Ruben, by God, that is a very fine speech you just made, and I thank you for doing so. The man who wrote to me said I would be expected around 1:30 or a little later, I am now at work on the day's new writing, at ten o'clock in the morning, I ought to be finished by noon, suppose we have in mind doing the laundry at that time, and then going along to honor the inmates at the Army Hospital. Inmates? Ruben said. Yes, inmates, so I'll call you back as soon as I finish my work and we'll take it from there. Good enough, Ruben said. And so I went along to conclude the rounding-up of the laundry, which I take every ten or eleven days to the Mayfair Laundromat next door to the Straw Hat Pizza, not far from Longs Drug Store (which is a General Store but also sells drugstore stuff, and has a prescription-filling department where a man named Durgarian is employed, first name forgotten, but perhaps Haig. Now, all of these people, all of them, all of them, are either dead or dying—Takoohi, Minas, Hairabet at the top, and the others not dead but surely dying, although in the tradition of the human race very few of them, if indeed any of them, does not believe he is dying, and as I said a moment ago I also, on the brink of the grave, on the gallows platform, am not quite able to believe that it is myself, and that I shall indeed soon be dead, and a member of that great group, that greatest group, the earth-visitors who have returned, so to put it, and I almost wish I hadn't. I have always been obsessed with the notion that there is such a circumstance or piece of preference that puts first things first and second things second and so on, but in actual practice I have seldom put first things first, and right now here I am simultaneously proceeding in the writing of a kind of book and rounding-up the laundry and trying to think how to participate in the honoring of the inmates at the Veterans Hospital—last year I was actually called on by a Brigadier General to speak while Television, or Tee Wee, as I prefer to put it, cameras from two of the three local stations cranked away, as we inaccurately put it, and I made a point of saying the equivalent of, In honoring those who are captured here, let us try not to intrude upon them with our health and freedom—they might not want even our honor, for I remember when I was hospitalized, as the word has it, in the Army I didn't want to see anybody to whom I couldn't say, I hate it here, I hate being in the Army, I hate this stupid War, I hate this stupid sickness, all I want is for the War to end, the Army to be demobilised, everybody to go home, and for me to be formally released from the hospital and honorably discharged from the Army, so I can be myself again—this is not me in this stupid bed. And I looked at the big brass of the Army as I spoke, and when the local news showed the short footage on the Tee Wee screen that night, nothing I said was heard although the moving of the mouth did make known that I was saying something, by God, and perhaps a few lip readers knew what it was. I mean, I've got death symptoms and so I am trying to think how I may manage my visit to the hospital and not intrude on anybody there, whatever he may have, and of course we may presume that perhaps as many as half the inmates have illnesses that will be contained or banished or healed in well under another seven or eight days, while my illness, according to medical science, has another kind of connection with me entirely. So what is first in my schedule, right now, this morning, in Fresno, on Valentines Day? Well, whatever it is I'm standing here at my work because I am a writer, and because once I start a work I have got to proceed with it to the end, because during the long years of my apprenticeship I abandoned one work after another, and then knew that such a procedure, in the interest of excellence of course, was foolish: I learned that I must not demand too much of myself to begin with, or too much of my writing, next, and finally, too much of heaven, so to put it: for if heaven of God or fate or luck doesn't do the writing, I can't imagine how we can believe that I do, or any writer does, although the situation may be reversed when it comes to reading. Heaven does the writing, we do the reading—and how lucky we are in this, for just yesterday and all of last night I ran through all kinds of printed matter with absolute enjoyment, as if I had every blessed instant of forever straight ahead, and consequently need not trouble my head of making the best use of my remaining time, and to take up the great neglected works of literature instead of the accidental and haphazard stuff I have always enjoyed most and preferred to read. So I am dying, so what is the nice little gallows joke to tell? Well, was it tactless of me to say what I said last year at the Veterans Hospital? I certainly hope so. But what about the principal of first things first? Am I observing it at this moment?   *10:40 A*

Monday February 18 1980 11:10 A.M.

Lord God of writers, readers, editors, publishers, literary agents, and all the rest of us, kindly see me through my day's work, for I live in work, and I stand here ready and willing to take the two hours needed for the work, but Sir Senor Lord my head is clogged, my ears hiss and ring, the whole fat aging body is thick and wrong, I slept poorly, I got up and entered into the living day a dying man daying all over again in this new day, for daying is daying and nighting is nighting and they happen to the same person one at a time but day is not night as night is not day, and when I speak of the living day of a dying man, for Christ's sake, don't think of me as some kind of silly man, for I mean dying as each of us is dying, and every day, although on a day like this the dying is noticed, it is felt in the bone, the bile, the blood and the beautiful aloofness of the green grass beyond the window. I like that, Lord, that indifference of the green grass. We die, we die, but at least it's a living. The indifference of green grass only sweetens the truth of it all. Or some such useless and meaningless drivel, but Lord you know I like to say my say even when a sensible man would keep his big mouth shut on the chance that his silence would be taken for wisdom, in the tradition of silence is golden, and of course it is, for a man who says nothing cannot be reminded later on by somebody watchful and not very friendly, either[.] But I thought you said, The theory is that mortals understand nothing, not even such mortals as Albert Einstein, the favorite wise man of recent times, but the truth is that mortals understand plenty, and the longer a mortal visits the earth and its world the more he understands, although the order of his understanding may be said to be at best theatrical if not downright song and dance—and how we loved the boy and girl, man and woman, husband and wife, rake and trollop song and dance team at the Hippodrome Theatre on the alley downtown in 1916, big War in Europe, 1917, the German U-boats sink the Lusitania and many people drowned, including a famous rich man whose wife refused to take to the lifeboats, and drowned with him, one of the great love stories of the age, but who knows, who knows, in the fear and confusion, the panic and disbelief, the story may have been something at least a little different and possibly very, very different, but the children decided to set it down the way we have it, and are glad to have it, nobody permitting himself to believe that the father put on the mother's clothes and a wig and knocked her down to get to the lifeboats but was pushed back by a Liverpool sailor who said, Blimey, Governor, this is no time to play Ophelia, we've got the lives of women and children to save. But it was all hushed up and the more romantic version was broadcast throughout the living world of love, and the sunk Lusitania compelled poor Woodrow Wilson to enter into the big business of the War and so even the songs and dances at the Hippodrome Theatre changed, and there I sat, didn't I, watching the clever draft-dodger Reno, shall we call him, an Italian perhaps although he could be an Irishman or a Jew or a Frenchman or an Armenian, and his sweet white-and-pink fleshed dark-haired beauty Mary, shall we say: and they moved to the measures of There's a long long trail awinding into the land of my dreams, as indeed there was such a trail awinding in my dreams, and then after quickly embracing Mary, Reno belted out the patriotic message, Good-bye, Mary, I'm going to the war, War, WAR, like that, and I thought, Christ Almighty, give me Mary, and By God I'd go to the War myself. Song and dance, Lord God, what would we do without song and dance, how would we put up with ourselves and one another without breaking into song and twinkle-toe, twinkle-toe, twinkle-toe turning in and out and all about, Lord? How, or even why? And I sat there for the full one-hour cheap vaudeville part of the show, and watched and listened and moved steadily down the unexplored unknown trail of my dreams into the land of my dreams. Wow, it was beautiful. I have written about it, there is a whole short story entitled "The World and the Theatre," and I am glad that in the earliest years of my emancipation from the hard work of the apprenticeship I wrote the story, and many others like it, and even while writing I knew that I was doing so because I knew I would forget all that good stuff if I didn't, and so it was, for if I read what I wrote, I tell you, Lord, I marvel at the stuff, it is that true and right, and in its way wiser even than this, almost half a century later, plagued, plagued, plagued every day, every night by all kinds of time-tricks of continuance. In 1916 I was eight and selling papers and getting into the Hippodrome free by hook or crook, but as long as I could remember I had been traveling the long long trail of dreams, and keeping it all to myself, for it was not traditional in my family for a child to sing from the bottom of his balls, to roar straight out of his sex. And when Elvira Martin, Portuguese from the Islands of the Azores, celebrated in the poem called "Columbus" by Joaquin Miller, stood in front of the class at Emerson School, and sang Juanita straight out of her full and stunning 11-year sex, everybody in the 4th Grade was both thrilled and ashamed, for she wasn't singing she was engaging in sex, she was flowering, and in silence everybody knew it, including Miss Brockington never again called on Elvira Martin to perform as if on the stage, for the teacher, aged surely 50, skinny, and with a wooden leg, had somehow never come anywhere near the flowering of Elvira Martin, and never would, never would. Lord God of teachers, old maids, even if it is a long way to Tipperary, and everybody's heart is right there, and even while roses fade in Picardy, let everybody experience what everybody has got to experience one way or another in order to die.   *12:05 P*

Sunday March 2 1980 12 M (Noon)

Heavy rain falls in Fresno, it is good to be alive. One suspects that the only real escape is into birth and that all of the souls out in immeasurable space, and time, are hankering for that escape and finding that just by the narrowest margin they must wait another billion years among a billion times that many fellow waiters, both possibly male or possibly female. Get yourself born by only waiting as you must and you don't know for a year or two of mortal time what it is all about, and then ever afterwards you wonder, you really do, for the adventure and mystery and seeming meaninglessness of it is beyond digging, beyond knowing, beyond putting a real useful portion of science upon, if I may. (You may, there is nobody else here, you see.) Now, reader, if you so much as only suspect what I am saying, by God, I believe I can call out to you, bravo boy, bravo girl, and so on. It is good to be alive when it rains in Fresno, and that is essentially the time when many good souls find themselves enclosed in melancholy, but forget it, folks, forget it entirely. It's all right, this is your day, your chance, and if it isn't, you will get your day tomorrow, most likely, so don't despair, don't get hot, don't go berserk with boredom, just go non-beserk with non-boredom, you'll find it is nice, for there is so much that is forever not nice, unnice, non-nice along the way that if you find the body without pain, and the spirit without fear and anger and malice—things you have got to learn to live with hot or cold like running water in the first hotel rooms that went hightone—if you are not put upon terribly by Heaven and the Greek Gods and the Christian God and the Gods of the Tribes of Africa and the Nations of the American Plains and the Mongols of Asia, if you are forgotten in the shuffle and are free to look around and notice stuff and to breathe easily the scent that rain brings up from grassy earth and the light scent of dust washed from architecture of no real reality, crackerbox houses, tickytacky houses as the protest song of one of the popular protest singer goes: all in a row: as if the people in the houses could possibly be anything but every one of them unique, for having escaped into birth, by hook or by crook, by the uncountable numbers of little twists and turns, stoppings and startings, that finally found each of them a face and set it upon each, his own body, and pushed each out of his carrier, the mother, with the befuddled father standing about and asking himself, For God's sake, what do I think I am doing? Why am I imitating The Maker? I am a billion miles from being made myself, so who is this now, that I have helped to make. Call him Dedalus. I'm James Joyce, I'm James Stephens, I'm James Jesus, I'm James God, for didn't I make a son and a woman, my own kids, brought out into the light by the mother of them that I stumbled and found? Didn't I arrange for the little silly things to come yawping out of eternity and distance so remote it only enlarges as you measure, didn't I stand there with my cap in hand shifting weight from one foot to the other and saying to herself, my own dear saucy comfort and bride, I really meant perhaps something else for you, but you know how we are where it matters, we don't know anything, and there is nothing we do that is not done to us or upon us or against us by somebody, by something, you just rest easy and get yourself back on your feet and back into your center so wildly shifted by that red yawping fellow there, Christ Almighty is it me? is it again me, and if so why? Wasn't once enough? You just come away from all that bloody battling with everybody and everything to put the thing out of you, and heal up neatly, and I promise you, Katey Kid, you shall have flowers, even if I have to go pick them from the garden of enemies—red, yellow, and black, Kid, all kinds of flowers, free of charge. You escape in, reader, and you escape out, or so we can agree to say and yet somehow both not to believe and to believe with everything we have got, and at the same time to keep the index and middle fingers of the right hand crossed, to cancel the pretending, and of the left hand when we double our protest of being faithful and true but want to escape just the same. Can a body, can a soul stay and escape at the same time? Jimmy Durante said you certainly gave the matter considerable thought and feeling, singing something hoarse and rasping about having a feeling that you want to go, and at the same time a feeling that you want to stay. James Joyce remembered every music hall song he heard in Dublin, both at the theatre and in the saloons, and at the houses of poor people who had their voices, at any rate. He had to work the songs into his writing, and we thank rain and escape for the songs heard by young James Joyce, and surely also young James James, and young James Jesus, and young Jesus Jesus, and young James God, and young God God, forasmuch as anybody is anybody everybody is the One, the Only One, and the names are not only permitted to proliferate, they are compelled to do so: and how right we are to cherish the names, each of us to cherish his own, and what names we have, so amazing that the Science of Names has its own word, which I don't happen to know, and a study of this Science only superficially will somehow carry you, mind and memory, straight to the escape out of the infinite and immeasurable into the immediate and local. Talk about fun. Wow, as the good halfwit children of quarterwit millionaire fathers and mothers put it, wow here, and wow there, and wow in and wow out, and wow when, and wow how, and what's going on man? So of course we can imagine from the confused way any of us in fatherhood feels how God must feel, at least now and then, after he has turned away from the reassuring beauty of the young of all animals, not even excluding the human animals, at least now and then, when they are not crying like condemned, that's all, condemned to breath, to body, to hands, to fingers, to eyes, ears, mouth, teeth, great good God Almighty, crying because everything has been given to them free of charge. Easy God, everything is O.K.   *12:40 P*

Friday March 21 1980 11:15 A.M.

There was a vaudeville remark about forty years or so ago that certain comedians found it useful to make: Everything happens to me. And one knew instantly that hardly anything had ever happened to him or was ever likely to happen, but it got the monologue going, at any rate. There is a story to tell, in other words, and this is that story, as far as I am concerned, all of this is the story, and while very little of the spectacular is in it, there is nothing in it that is not to be carefully noticed, mentioned, remembered, put in its place. At the moment the thought comes to me that I have always worked at staying alive, and this thought is instantly succeeded by the thought that I have also never hesitated to take a risk, and some of these risks could have ended in instant death, if I may, and I regret that I must ask if I may. I know my story, and I have probably forgotten the most spectacular parts, very probably because I feel and have always felt that the most spectacular of all human behavior is survival, staying alive, continuing to be there, fighting off slowly and steadily and pretty much in secret the menace of boredom, despair, suicide, murder, madness and dissolution, or death. I remember being deeply moved by an anecdote that I read long before I was twelve years old about Macedonian Troops on their way to Persia (but who cares what troops they were and where they were going, they were young and full of piss, vinegar, ignorance, and something very like love, or even passion, each for himself, for his potential, for the rewards of girls and women beneath them in sweet connection, and so on and so forth, as I am obliged to sum up a generality now and then. By the side of the road lay an old man, apparently near death itself, who said to a soldier who had paused to look at him: The war you go to, lad, is sport. Behold a battlefield inside yourself someday, alone in combat with fever, hell, and death. Now, of course who doesn't know that I have put the story both inaccurately, the details are not precisely the same as those in the anecdote I read, indeed I have forgotten the details, but not only that: I have taken the liberty even of changing the key words of the anecdote, the punch-line, as it is called, but the point I am getting to is the point of importance, and this is the point: I knew precisely what the dying man was talking about, for I had experienced the same thing, not once, not twice, but perhaps three or four times: when I was alone at home around eleven in the morning in my bed in the house at 2226 San Benito Avenue and Takoohi very nearly broke the front door down in hurrying to see if I was still alive, sick with the influenza in late 1918 that just about wiped out somebody from every family in town, almost without exception, as she had been informed by her fellow fig-packers at Guggenheim's—Armenians, Italians, Syrians, Assyrians, Portuguese, and Germans—I was in the midst of the mortal combat of the old man in the anecdote, and the loud arrival of the Eagle out of the sky to its nest, the lion out of jungle to its lair, the Mother of Life itself to its endangered child, I was absolutely astonished, and did indeed say, I'm all right, why have you come home? I had been over the worst, or almost so, but the combat was still a terrible wasting of my very soul along with the bread and substance of my flesh. She worked in silence, bringing me hot lemonade to drink, she brought the death in the flesh out as sweat, changed the bed, fetched warm water and cloth so I could bathe, and towel to dry, and fresh soft nightgown, and when I got into the bed this time and put my head down, I knew I was home, I was home free, as the saying goes, and I gladly let myself slip away to sweet life, as I had not permitted myself in terrible combat, and fever, to slip, slip, slip away to death, even if somehow it might have seemed, at last, sweet, or even sweeter than life. She did that. It would have happened had she not done it, and something would have been gained by that procedure, but the fact remains that dropping her work suddenly, hurrying a mile straight home, finding the young still alive, still himself, still proclaiming his inviolability, his indestructibility, his stamina, she did what she knew how to do, to help, and it was so, and unforgettable. If you don't die in the deadly flu epidemic of 1918, when do you die? Well, I have tended to the theory that you die when you choose to die, but this theory at the very least needs more study, and the problem of the relative balance or imbalance between spirit and flesh, and between unknown preference and known preference makes such a study very complicated. It certainly suggests that there is far more unknown about us than is known. Indeed, whatever it is that we know, is in itself incomplete and insecure and vulnerable to constant correction, and its inconsistencies are virtually outrageous in that some of them make a shambles of science, of measure, of tabulation, of evidence, of generality, of precedent, of procedure, and all the rest of the procedures by means of which each person understands himself, his connections to everything and everybody else, to his continuance, to his accessibility at all times to the concluding of himself, to death, that is, very nearly terrifying now and then in its sudden potentiality and its desolating meaninglessness. A man is expected to follow the established procedure of his specific illness and perish of it, but instead he becomes fully healed and continues his life and legend. That is the spectacular thing I am thinking about, and I have known both men and women who have astonished science, and family and friends, and possibly also themselves, and not died, not given over somehow, surely willynilly, or by the Grace of God, or by accident, or by the Writing on the Forehead, or by simple luck, good or bad, to the inevitable—not yet.   *12:05 P*

Wednesday April 16 1980 11:50 A.M.

Ruben, I said, I have a favor to ask of you. I would like you to drive me to the vineyard of seedless grapes just back of Ararat Cemetery because the new leaves of the vine are now large enough for plucking, and I want to gather four or five dozen, to stuff, for I have a strong hunger for our beloved main course Bitlis dish. Now, of course it happens that it is not Bitlis alone, by any means, that knows and loves stuffed grapeleaves—there are no people for hundreds of thousands of square miles of that area, start at the east end of Europe and going west deeply into Asia and north of the Black Sea to Rostov-on-the-Don and up into the Ukraine to Kiev and to Kharkhov, and south into and beyond all of North Africa and all of the Arabian peninsula and all through Persia and Afghanistan, there are no people at all in that vast geography which do not love gathering grapeleaves, making a stuffing of ground lamb, chopped onions, coarse cut bulghour, and tomatoes and juice, and salt and pepper. Wow Again. How delicious the eating of this dish is, with traditionally yogurt spooned on top of half a dozen pieces, and then another half-dozen, and there was a lunchtime occasion in Fresno at 2226 San Benito Street in 1921 when my brother Henry had six stuffed grapeleaves served by the mother six times, making it thirty-six, in all, to the great admiration of the mother, who said to her mother, Takoohi to Lucintak, He is a small boy, he will never be as big as his father, but he has a big boy's appetite. The old woman said, Don't encourage greed, five servings was enough, that sixth serving was out of order. Ah, well, the daughter replied, he eats with such relish. And so Ruben Saroyan said, All right, sure, why not? He hoisted my bicycle into the back of his Jeep, the front wheel and handlebars sticking out a bit, and we set out. I understand, Ruben said, that in taking leaves from the vine it is traditional to take every third one along a branch, or cane, have you heard about that? Well, I said,

I haven't but it does seem a kind of Armenian thing, a respect for the rights of the vines for the shade the grapes will want at the height of summer, but I did go out to several vineyards long years ago when both fathers and mothers and sons and daughters gathered the new fresh grapeleaves. As a matter of fact I spoke about this in one of the stories in my first book: the name of the story is "Big Valley Vineyard." Such things seem to have the kind of meaning for me that church rituals have for other people. At first, I must say, I didn't see how seedless vine leaves, or any kind of grape vine leaves, could be made into food, which to me up in Oakland consisted of sensible Anglo-Saxon dishes. Meat pie was my favorite, and the Irish cook also was excellent at Irish stew, and hash was a favorite of all of us, and we all pretended to hate tapioca pudding, and pork and beans, and sometimes fish—well, not to put too fine a point upon it, the meals served at the Fred Finch Orphanage were superb, that's all, but there could never in a million years or more be any kind of culinary usage of grapevine leaves by the lovely sad institution—grapes, yes, grapeleaves, no. Ruben said, Did we invent stuffed grapeleaves? Ah, I said, if you mean the Armenians, the answer is no. If you mean the Saroyans of Bitlis, the answer is yes, and I'll tell you why—we are the greatest cooks in the world, our mothers and fathers alike, for I am sure you long ago noticed that the meals fixed by your father were every bit as delicious as those cooked by your mother. And we don't fool with recipes. We study what we have, and we make the best of it. No, stuffed grapeleaves belong to the entire lot of us in a vast area of the world. When the Greeks brought this dish into their cuisine I don't know, but I like to think that Plato and Socrates and all the other pioneers of intellect and democracy frequently received plates of stuffed grapeleaves at home, at the homes of friends, or in restaurants. Now, the flavor that is in the grapeleaf is very special, and the manner in which it enters into the stuffing and into the juice, and is heightened by madzoon, called yogurt, man, that is the thing about the dish that I am eager to experience again, very soon. At Palm and Olive Ruben said, Shall we visit Monroe Books next to the Tower Theatre, where there is this big framed color photograph of yourself—the best photograph of yourself I have ever seen. The owner has some books he might like you to sign for his customers. And so I replied, Sure, let's go visit the man, you know I love books and bookshops. The owner turned out to be a pleasant fellow of forty-four or so who at my request gave me three cards: Monroe Books Established in 1958 809 E. Olive Fresno, CA 93728 Hardback Books Bought and Sold

Out-of-print Book Search Service Specialists in NEW-USED-RARE BOOKS: and finally John M. Perz, German is what it is he replied to my question, it used to be Pertz but the T was lost soon after our arrival. And so I signed a first edition of *My Name Is Aram* that cost an Armenian family of four in Los Angeles $35, and a first edition of *The Human Comedy* for which John M. (for Monroe I believe he said) Perz received $50 from another Armenian family, this one in San Francisco. And he indicated a couple of dozen copies of two stories brought out together by Doubleday fourteen [or] more years ago under the title of *My Father and The Tooth*, retail price $4.95, his price, he said, $1.95 each, less 40%, would I put my name in a few? I said, In as many as you like, I'm here and I mean to be helpful. From next door, from La Tabatier, Precious Crystals & Pewter, Fine Pipes, Meerschaum and Briar, Choice Cigars and Tobaccos came George Nazar to ask me to visit his shop after my visit to the bookshop. I had first visited Nazar in 1964 soon after my arrival back in Fresno. I said sure. *12:30 P*

Thursday May 1 1980 11:20 A.M.

Again, as we see, one thing leads to another, the path in the wilderness, the highway to everywhere, so to put it, is forsaken because something out there in the tropical forest or among the shattered parts of the glacier, is irresistible to curiosity, or the compulsion to gather—how does the saying go? Gather ye flowers, as ye go? And how I love sayings, and how write [sic] I was to write to Ben Huebsch and the other American publishers to ask if he (and they) would be interested in publishing a book of my sayings. What is easier to read than sayings, in short. They are short and snappy. Well, the hell with it: I am reporting the plan and procedure of the writing of this book—as if this might have some meaning for the reader. Well, does it, then, perhaps have no meaning for him, at all? I say it has the most basic kind of meaning that is possible whoever the reader is, whatever the reader does, however the reader pursues his reality and escapes from his terrors, or whatever, the worst of which is probably plain ordinary even wholesome boredom: it can do you in, that's all: it can bury you where you stand. When I started to write this book on Monday January 14 1980, as I have remarked three or four times, when I put paper into this small very light and excellently-working old, old Royal Quiet De Luxe portable, my purpose was very simple: not to let the days ahead get away from me, to move to me and through me and out of me and away forever, empty, with nothing from me to remember them by. I didn't want that. I have always been compelled to avoid that. I must put every day to some enduring, noticeable use, so that if I want to notice how a day forty years ago had been I shall somehow be able to do so—what a fool, the tripping-away of the hours cannot be noticed with anything like the truth with which they tripped away. Even so, it is better than nothing. Something is better than nothing. Art is not better than experience, but without art it is difficult for experience to really be experience. And so, knowing I had been tagged and that in all probability my mortal days were numbered, as indeed they would have to be in any case, for a man in his 72nd year knows there cannot possibly be a lot of time remaining for him to experience, but with a tagging, he is compelled to abandon the delightful illusion that his time, as always, is unlimited. That is the thing about being tagged which can be very profoundly troublesome. It takes doing to restore the illusion that no sir the tagging has no real connection with me and my going on and eventually out, and my attending to my work: I must not forget that there was almost never an entire unit of 24-hours that was not crowded with potential ends, of all kinds, each possibly final, terminal, deadly. People, some of whom I knew, from my very earliest years, were coming to the end every day—and I was not. I was hearing about it, or reading the obituaries of them, and feeling the sorrow of having lost a friend, or even an enemy, and also feeling the joy of still being alive and in full possession of the illusion that my time was unlimited. This is something nature and heaven, God and biology, I suppose, has built into the human body, mind and spirit. I thought, Well, if ever there was a time for me to write, this is it, and so I will not permit myself to devote all of my time and attention and energy to the matter of the tagging, to the disease, to the statistics about it, to the probabilities insofar as I myself am concerned. I shall live and work the same as ever, for I do believe in life, even if there is a powerful melancholy in me, and even a profound enchantment with getting out of the mortal scene, of returning to everywhere or nowhere, and to being again nothing or everything, or everybody, an enchantment that Armenak the father must surely have known to have permitted himself to die of something so absurd and simple as a swollen appendix, which burst and poisoned him and made him hot with fire and unquenchably thirsty—for water, for the love of God, Takoohi, let me have water. And so I set out to write a book of some kind, and made a gift to myself of the Necrology List of *Variety* for 1979, to be a kind of easy support whenever reluctance dominated and came near obliterating the plan and program to watch it, to keep track of the days, perhaps the last days, and to say the last sayings, for had I not planned all my life, all my born days, to reach such a time precisely in order to give an accounting of it, to pass along to you, the reader, perhaps yourself no more than 18 years of age, but also possibly in your 72nd year, my activities during such days, and nights, my trivia, if you like, and indeed it is all trivia, although trivia now and then of a grand order, I suppose I can say. Getting the first sentence on paper, across the sheet, the first line, that's the thing that is basic: do that, and you are on your way, and I was. At first my thought was to fill only one sheet each day, so that at the end of the assignment I would have 101 sheets, or chapters, and we know perfectly well that if writing is of a certain order it isn't necessary to have 101 long sheets filled, or even one long sheet filled, half a sheet, a quarter of a sheet, an eighth of a sheet is enough—but not for me, and not for this book: I want to be who I am as I am at this time, this moment, and if this is altogether artless and even foolish, that's just fine, too: for there comes a time when the achievement of art, in writing, is invalid, and indeed out of order, for being now altogether false, deceptive, dishonest, and consequently while delightful palatable, so to put it, essentially indigestible and harmful. Like dope, like drugs, like putting the self to sleep deliberate, like escape, and that's not for me.   *11:50 A*

Chronology

Compiled by Amanda Choi

1908 William Saroyan (WS) is born on August 31 in Fresno, California, to Armenak and Takoohi Saroyan.

1911 Armenak dies of a burst appendix; WS, his brother, and his two sisters are placed in the Fred Finch Orphanage in Oakland while Takoohi works as a domestic in San Francisco.

1916 Takoohi and her children are reunited; the family settles in Fresno, where Takoohi works in a cannery and WS adds to the family's income by selling newspapers.

1920 WS reads Guy de Maupassant's story "The Bell" and resolves to become a writer.

1925 After repeated disciplinary expulsions, WS drops out of Fresno High School before earning his diploma.

1926 WS leaves Fresno for Los Angeles, where he joins the California National Coast Guard, quitting two weeks later; he settles in San Francisco and works for Postal Telegraph, first as a messenger and later as a manager.

1928 WS has a story accepted by *Overland Monthly* but the magazine folds before the story can be published; WS moves to New York City to pursue literary aspirations, buying a one-way Greyhound ticket to the city with money borrowed from his uncle.

1929 Homesick, unable to support himself, and not making the literary breakthrough he had hoped for in New York, WS returns to San Francisco and works at a series of short-lived odd jobs.

1932 WS submits work under the pseudonym Sirak Goryan to an Armenian newspaper, *Hairenik* ("Fatherland"), which accepts four of his poems unpaid.

1933   *Hairenik* publishes the poetry and WS's first short stories, still under the pseudonym Sirak Goryan; late that year, *Story* accepts for publication "The Daring Young Man on the Flying Trapeze," paying fifteen dollars for the story.

1934   *Story* editors Whit Burnett and Martha Foley work to launch WS's career, publishing several of his stories and introducing his work to the editors at Random House; "The Broken Wheel," one of the short stories published pseudonymously in *Hairenik*, is selected for both the *Best Short Stories* anthology and the O'Henry collection. (WS, who had been meanwhile trying to convince the *Story* editors to publish Sirak Goryan's stories, passing him off as a cousin, must reveal his deception.) Random House publishes *The Daring Young Man on the Flying Trapeze*, a short story collection, to immediate critical and commercial success.

1935   Ernest Hemingway, responding to a crack WS took at *Death in the Afternoon* in his *Daring Young Man*, writes, in a disparaging review for *Esquire*, "You're not that bright....You've only got one new trick and that is that you're an Armenian"; WS tours the world, visiting Armenia for the first time, and along the way buys a make-up gift to give to Hemingway.

1936   A second short story collection, *Inhale and Exhale*, is published by Random House, but WS drops the publisher over creative differences; his third short story collection, *Three Times Three*, is published by Conference Press; WS moves to Los Angeles and begins working as a screenwriter first for B. P. Schulberg and then for Columbia Pictures.

1937   *Little Children*, a short story collection, is published, about which Graham Greene in *Spectator* writes, "the humour of these tales is often delightful."

1938   Two more short story collections—*Love, Here Is My Hat* and *The Trouble with Tigers*—are published, but the market proves oversaturated with WS's work and the collections sell poorly.

1939   "One of the enormous years of my life," WS would later say of 1939; WS begins dividing his time between San Francisco and New York; his first two plays—*My Heart's in the Highlands,* adapted from his short story "The Man with His Heart in the Highlands," and *The Time of Your Life,* written in just six days—run on Broadway to critical acclaim;

WS collaborates with Vincente Minnelli on a musical revue, although the project eventually falls through; *Peace, It's Wonderful,* a short story collection, is published.

1940   WS wins and declines the Pulitzer Prize for *The Time of Your Life,* explaining that "art must be democratic; but at the same time it must be both proud and aloof"; WS puts out four new plays—*Love's Old Sweet Song, Sweeney in the Trees, Something About a Soldier,* and *The Hero of the World*—all of which fare poorly at the box office and with critics; *My Name Is Aram,* a series of autobiographical sketches on his boyhood, is published in December and becomes an instant best-seller.

1941   WS writes a new play, *Across the Board on Tomorrow Morning,* in part responding to critics who felt *The Time of Your Life* failed to adequately address the realities of a world at war, but the play does not make it past tryouts; WS produces and directs *The Beautiful People,* called "a garrulous ode to vagabonds" by *Life* magazine, and nominated for the New York Drama Critics Circle's play of the year; gambling debts force WS to begin working as a screenwriter for MGM, where he writes the script for *The Human Comedy;* the *Baltimore Evening Sun* runs an article about WS with the headline "'I'm a Genius' says Saroyan—And He Believes It Himself."

1942   WS meets Carol Marcus, his future wife; *Razzle-Dazzle,* a collection of short plays and sketches, is published; WS splits with MGM over a disagreement about *The Human Comedy,* publicly making the split in a letter to the studio published by the *Daily Variety,* stating that, "Sooner or later a man gets bored with bores, finaglers, and jitney politicians. A man just naturally gets fed up with the baloney. He gets tired of witnessing the continuous and disgraceful crying, trembling, and shaking"; WS opens but is almost immediately forced to close the ill-fated Saroyan Theatre with *Across the Board on Tomorrow Morning* and *Talking to You;* WS is drafted into the U.S. Army as a buck private.

1943   WS marries Carol Marcus; WS is sent to New York for basic training; *The Human Comedy* wins an Academy Award for Best Original Story; WS writes a novelization of *The Human Comedy* and it is published to rave reviews—Wallace Stegner calls it "profoundly romantic" and "full of the curiosity of childhood and the naïveté that sometimes disturbingly approaches wisdom"; WS's son, Aram, is born on September 25.

1944 WS is stationed in England for Army duty with the Signal Corps; he is given time off in London to write a propaganda novel promoting Anglo-American relations in exchange for leave to see his family in New York; rather than leave, his novel *The Adventures of Wesley Jackson* nearly earns WS a court-martial for its antiwar sentiments; *Dear Baby*, a short story collection, is published.

1945 WS is hospitalized in Luxembourg for back pain, returned to the United States, and discharged from the Army.

1946 WS's daughter, Lucy, is born on January 17; *The Adventures of Wesley Jackson* is published to reviews questioning his patriotism; Irwin Shaw, critic and WS's friend, wrote, "Once more Saroyan is full of love for the entire world. He loves the Germans, he loves the Japs, he loves the Bulgarians and Finns and Roumanians. The only people he can find to hate are the Americans" (Leggett 206); gambling debts create a growing rift between WS and Carol.

1947 WS moves to New York in hopes of renewing his career and takes up a six-month residence at Mill Neck, Long Island; he returns to San Francisco after failing to find an affordable New York apartment to rent; Sydney Chaplin produces WS's allegorical play *Sam Ego's House* with his company, the Circle Players of Hollywood; WS's beloved grandmother Lucy dies.

1948 The film adaptation of *The Time of Your Life*, produced by the Cagney brothers and starring James and Jeanne Cagney, proves a financial disaster; *The Saroyan Special*, an anthology of WS's best stories, is published; WS buys Lane's Bridge, a farm in Fresno he had seen from afar while on a picnic as a child, but, at the urging of Carol and Carol's mother, he puts it back on the market almost immediately; Carol attempts to divorce WS but they reconcile; the family moves to New York City.

1949 WS separates from Carol; he travels through Europe, returning in the fall; he spends thirty days in Las Vegas finalizing his divorce and ends up losing $50,000 gambling.

1950 Takoohi dies in February after suffering a stroke; WS begins to profit writing on assignment for a number of large magazines; he publishes *The Assyrian and Other Stories,* which the critics embrace and which earns WS a lucrative three-book contract with Doubleday; WS writes both *Tracy's Tiger*, a novella, and *Rock Wagram*, a novel, in just one month.

1951 WS remarries Carol and moves the family back to Los Angeles; *Tracy's Tiger* and *Rock Wagram* are published; Rosemary Clooney's song "Come on-a My House," with lyrics by WS and his cousin Ross Bagdasarian, tops the Hit Parade, selling 900,000 copies almost instantly; Carol files for divorce.

1952 WS and Carol's second divorce is granted; Carol and the children remain in Los Angeles and WS buys a beach cottage for himself in Malibu; *The Bicycle Rider in Beverly Hills*, an autobiographical work revealing for the first time the years that WS spent in an orphanage, is published; six of WS's plays air in December and January (1953) on the Ford Foundation's *Omnibus* television series.

1953 *The Laughing Matter*, a bitter melodramatization of his marriage written just after his first divorce from Carol, is published and rejected by both the critics and WS himself, who calls the work "sick."

1954 *A Lost Child's Fireflies*, a play that WS wrote in 1950, is performed in Dallas by the Round Up's, an all–African American theater company.

1955 WS writes and produces *The Boyhood of William Saroyan*, a dramatization of his childhood starring Sal Mineo, for the *Omnibus* series.

1956 *Mama, I Love You*, a novel written for WS's daughter, Lucy, is published, appearing serially in the *Saturday Evening Post*; MGM offers to purchase the movie rights for *Mama* but WS, still bearing a grudge, declines the offer.

1957 *Papa, You're Crazy*, a novel written for WS's son, Aram, is published, about which George Adelman writes in *Library Journal*, "…not exactly fiction, not exactly biography, not exactly philosophy, not exactly anything, just Saroyan"; *The Cave Dwellers*, a play WS wrote in eight days, and his first New York production since 1943, enjoys a successful run on Broadway, receiving favorable comparisons to Beckett's *Waiting for Godot*.

1958 WS leaves Malibu for a trip around the world, writing a number of magazine articles and working on *Fifty-Fifty*, a memoir written in daily installments and to be finished by his fiftieth birthday and which he would set aside as unpublishable upon its completion.

1959 In response to an ever increasing IRS bill, WS exiles himself to Europe; he lives in Paris with his children, working for Darryl Zanuck, the

Twentieth Century Fox mogul, on revising a number of scripts for both film and theater; WS is deeply upset by news that Carol has remarried, to actor Walter Matthau.

1961 WS accepts a playwright-in-residence position at Purdue University in Indiana, where he teaches drama and students produce his comedy *High Times Along the Wabash*; WS buys an apartment in Paris in which he lives on and off for the next twenty years, later describing it as "this old building which I have come to believe in and to love, although it is falling to pieces."

1962 *Here Comes, There Goes, You Know Who*, an autobiography inspired by if not adapted directly from *Fifty-Fifty*, is published, of which Robert Kirsch in the *LA Times* writes, "It is unconventional, inconsistent, filled with that mixture of contempt and respect for humanity, of self-contempt and colossal egotism, which is, was, and will be Saroyan"; "The Unstoppable Gray Fox," a half-hour teleplay, is televised on *General Electric Theatre*.

1963 WS returns to New York City and lives for a short time in a Third Avenue penthouse before becoming disturbed by the sounds of the ventilation system and walking out on his lease; *Boys and Girls Together*, an autobiographical novel, is published.

1964 *One Day in the Afternoon of the World*, an autobiographical novel, is published; the thirtieth-anniversary edition of *The Daring Young Man* is published; WS visits Bitlis, his ancestral home in Armenia, for the first time; he returns with renewed vigor to writing short stories, some of which would be published by such magazines as *The Atlantic*, *Harper's*, *McCall's*, *Playboy*, and *The New Yorker* over the next decade; WS finally succeeds in paying off his debt to the IRS.

1966 *Short Drive, Sweet Chariot*, an autobiographical road novel, is published; WS establishes the William Saroyan Foundation.

1968 *I Used to Believe I Had Forever, Now I'm Not So Sure*, a memoir, is published.

1971 *Don't Go, But If You Must, Say Hello to Everybody* (alternate title: *Letters from 74 rue Taitbout*), a collection of literary portraits, is published.

1972 *Places Where I've Done Time*, a memoir, is published, becoming the most successful book of WS's later career.

1973 *Days of Life and Death and Escape to the Moon*, a journal-like memoir titled in response to the Apollo 11 moon landing and Neil Armstrong's moonwalk, is published.

1976 *Sons Come and Go, Mothers Hang in Forever*, a memoir, is published on WS's sixty-eighth birthday; Ed Hoagland, in his glowing review of *Sons* for the *New York Times Book Review,* writes that WS is "up near the top of his form," calling for "a Saroyan revival."

1978 *Chance Meetings*, a brief memoir, is published.

1979 *Obituaries*, a memoir, is published—*Publisher's Weekly* describes it as "an astonishing book, a profound and even original meditation about death."

1980 WS is diagnosed with prostate cancer but refuses treatment, returning instead for one last season in Paris; *Obituaries* is nominated for the American Book Award.

1981 WS dies at the Veterans Administration Hospital in Fresno on May 18; before dying, WS famously called the Associated Press to say, "Everybody has got to die, but I have always believed an exception would be made in my case. Now what?"; half of his ashes are buried at the Fresno Chapel of the Light and the other half at the Armenian Pantheon in Yerevan, Armenia.

Works Consulted

Arax, Mark. "William Saroyan." *Forgotten Bread: First-Generation Armenian American Writers.* Edited by David Kherdian. Berkeley: Heyday Books, 2007. pp. 94-96.

Darwent, Brian. "William Saroyan: A Biographical Sketch Based Largely on His Own Writings." *Saroyan: The New Reader*. Edited by Brian Darwent. Berkeley: Creative Arts, 1984. pp. ix-xix

Foard, Elisabeth C. *William Saroyan: A Reference Guide*. Boston: G. K. Hall, 1989.

Fresno County Public Library. "Saroyan Chronology." November 22, 2006. http://www.fresnolibrary.org/calif/sarchron.html.

Lee, Lawrence, and Barry Gifford. *Saroyan: A Biography*. New York: Harper and Row, 1984.

Leggett, John. *A Daring Young Man: A Biography of William Saroyan*. New York: Alfred A. Knopf, 2002.

Selected Bibliography

Short Story Collections

The Daring Young Man on the Flying Trapeze and Other Stories, Random House, 1934; reprinted, Yolla Bolly, 1984.

Inhale and Exhale, Random House, 1936; reprinted, Books for Libraries Press, 1972.

Three Times Three, Conference Press, 1936.

Little Children, Harcourt, 1937.

A Gay and Melancholy Flux (compiled from *Inhale and Exhale* and *Three Times Three*), Faber, 1937.

Love, Here Is My Hat, and Other Short Romances, Modern Age Books, 1938.

The Trouble with Tigers, Harcourt, 1938.

A Native American, George Fields, 1938.

Peace, It's Wonderful, Modern Age Books, 1939.

Three Fragments and a Story, Little Man, 1939.

My Name Is Aram, Harcourt, 1940; revised edition, 1966.

Saroyan's Fables, Harcourt, 1941.

The Insurance Salesman and Other Stories, Faber, 1941.

Forty-eight Saroyan Stories, Avon, 1942.

Thirty-One Selected Stories, Avon, 1943.

Someday I'll Be a Millionaire Myself, Avon, 1944.

Dear Baby, Harcourt, 1944.

The Saroyan Special: Selected Short Stories, Harcourt, 1948; reprinted, Books for Libraries Press, 1970.

The Fiscal Hoboes, Press of Valenti Angelo, 1949.

The Assyrian, and Other Stories, Harcourt, 1950.

Love, Lion Library Editions, 1955.

The Whole Voyald and Other Stories, Atlantic-Little, Brown, 1956.

After Thirty Years: The Daring Young Man on the Flying Trapeze (includes essays), Harcourt, 1964.

Best Stories of William Saroyan, Faber, 1964.

Deleted Beginning and End of a Short Story, Lowell-Adams House Printers, 1965.

My Kind of Crazy and Wonderful People, Harcourt, 1966.

Man with the Heart in the Highlands, and Other Stories, Dell, 1968.

My Name Is Saroyan (autobiography), Coward-McCann, 1983.

Madness in the Family, New Directions, 1988.

The Man with the Heart in the Highlands and Other Early Stories, New Directions, 1989.

Fresno Stories, New Directions, 1994.

Novels

The Human Comedy, Harcourt, 1943; revised edition, 1966.

The Adventures of Wesley Jackson, Harcourt, 1946.

The Twin Adventures: The Adventures of William Saroyan, A Diary; The Adventures of Wesley Jackson, A Novel, Harcourt, 1950.

Rock Wagram, Doubleday, 1951.

Tracy's Tiger, Doubleday, 1951; revised edition, Ballantine, 1967.

The Laughing Matter, Doubleday, 1953.

Mama, I Love You (listed in some sources under the working title *The Bouncing Ball*), Atlantic-Little, Brown, 1956; reprinted, Dell, 1986.

Papa, You're Crazy, Atlantic-Little, Brown, 1957.

Boys and Girls Together, Harcourt, 1963; reprinted, Barricade, 1995.

One Day in the Afternoon of the World, Harcourt, 1964.

Plays

The Hungerers: A Short Play, S. French, 1939.

My Heart's in the Highlands (produced on Broadway at Guild Theatre, April 13, 1939; first published in *One-Act Play Magazine*, December 1937); Harcourt, 1939.

The Time of Your Life (produced on Broadway at the Booth Theatre, October 25, 1939; produced in London by the Royal Shakespeare Company, 1982; also see below), Harcourt, 1939; acting edition, S. French, 1969; reprinted, Methuen, 1983.

A Theme in the Life of the Great American Goof (ballet-play), produced in New York City at Center Theatre, January 1940.

Subway Circus, S. French, 1940.

The Ping-Pong Game (produced in New York, 1945), S. French, 1940.

A Special Announcement, House of Books, 1940.

The Beautiful People (produced under the author's direction on Broadway at Lyceum Theatre, April 21, 1940), Harcourt, 1941.

Love's Old Sweet Song (first produced on Broadway at Plymouth Theatre, May 2, 1940), S. French, 1941.

Three Plays: My Heart's in the Highlands, The Time of Your Life, Love's Old Sweet Song, Harcourt, 1940.

Radio Play, CBS-Radio, 1940.

The People with Light Coming Out of Them (radio play; first broadcast, 1941), Free Company/CBS-Radio, 1941.

Jim Dandy, A Play, Little Man Press, 1941; reprinted as *Jim Dandy: Fat Man in a Famine*, Harcourt, 1947.

Across the Board on Tomorrow Morning, first produced in Pasadena at the Pasadena Playhouse, February, 1941; produced under the author's direction on Broadway at the Belasco Theatre, on the same bill with *Talking to You*, August 1942.

Hello Out There (first produced in Santa Barbara at the Lobeto Theatre, September 1941; produced on Broadway at the Belasco Theatre, September 1942), S. French, 1949.

Three Plays: The Beautiful People, Sweeney in the Trees, Across the Board on Tomorrow Morning, Harcourt, 1941.

Razzle-Dazzle (short plays; includes *A Theme in the Life of the Great American Goof*), Harcourt, 1942.

Talking to You, produced in New York, 1942.

The Good Job (screenplay based on his story "A Number of the Poor"), Loew, 1942.

The Human Comedy (screenplay scenario based on *The Human Comedy*), Metro-Goldwyn-Mayer, 1943.

Get Away Old Man (produced on Broadway at the Cort Theatre, November 1943), Harcourt, 1944.

Sam Ego's House (produced in Hollywood, 1947), S. French, 1949.

Don't Go Away Mad, produced in New York, 1949.

Don't Go Away Mad, and Two Other Plays: Sam Ego's House; A Decent Birth, A Happy Funeral, Harcourt, 1949.

The Son, produced in Los Angeles, 1950.

Once Around the Block (produced in New York, 1950), S. French, 1959.

A Lost Child's Fireflies, produced in Dallas, 1954.

Opera, Opera, produced in New York, 1955.

Ever Been in Love with a Midget?, produced in Berlin, 1957.

The Cave Dwellers (produced on Broadway in New York City, October 19, 1957), Putnam, 1958.

The Slaughter of the Innocents (produced at The Hague, Netherlands, 1957), S. French, 1958.

The Paris Comedy; or, The Secret of Lily (produced in Vienna, 1960), published as *The Paris Comedy; or, The Dogs, Chris Sick, and Twenty-One Other Plays*; also published as *The Dogs, or The Paris Comedy, and Two Other Plays: Chris Sick, or Happy New Year Anyway[;] Making Money[;] and Nineteen Other Very Short Plays*, Phaedra, 1969.

Sam, the Highest Jumper of Them All, or The London Comedy (produced in London under the author's direction, 1960), Faber, 1961.

(With Henry Cecil) *Settled Out of Court*, produced in London, 1960.

High Time along the Wabash, produced at Purdue University, West Lafayette, IN, 1961.

Ah, Man, music by Peter Fricker, produced in Adelburgh, Suffolk, England, 1962.

Bad Men in the West, produced in Stanford, CA, 1971.

(With others) *People's Lives*, produced in New York, 1974.

The Rebirth Celebration of the Human Race at Artie Zabala's Off-Broadway Theater, first produced in New York, July 10, 1975.

Two Short Paris Summertime Plays of 1974: Assassinations and Jim, Sam, and Anna, Santa Susana Press, 1979.

William Saroyan: The Armenian Trilogy, edited and with an introduction and glossary by Dickran Kouymjian, The Press at California State University, Fresno, 1986.

Warsaw Visitor and Tales from the Vienna Streets: The Last Two Plays of William Saroyan, edited and with an introduction by Dickran Kouymjian, The Press at California State University, Fresno, 1991.

Also author of the plays *Something about a Soldier, Hero of the World*, and *Sweeney in the Trees*, 1940; *Cat, Mouse, Man, Woman*, 1958; *Four Plays: The Playwright and the Public, The Handshakers, The Doctor and the Patient, This I Believe*, 1963; *Dentist and Patient* and *Husband and Wife*, 1968; *The New Play*, 1970; *Armenians*, produced in 1974; *Play Things*, produced in 1980; *There's Something I Got to Tell You* (radio play); *The Oyster and the Pear* (tele-play), televised in 1953. Plays represented in anthologies, including *Famous American Plays of the 1930s*, edited by Harold Clurman, and *One Act: Eleven Short Plays of the Modern Theatre*, edited by Samuel Moon.

Other

A Christmas Psalm (poetry), Gelber, Lilienthal, 1935.

Those Who Write Them and Those Who Collect Them, Black Archer Press, 1936.

The Time of Your Life (miscellany), Harcourt, 1939.

Christmas, 1939 (poetry), Quercus Press, 1939.

Harlem as Seen by Hirschfield, Hyperion Press, 1941.

Hilltop Russians in San Francisco, James Ladd Delkin, 1941.

Fragment, Albert M. Bender, 1943.

(With Henry Miller and Hilaire Hiler) *Why Abstract?*, New Directions, 1945; reprinted, Haskell House, 1974.

(Author of introduction) Khatchik Minasian, *The Simple Songs of Khatchik Minasian*, Colt Press, 1950.

The Bicycle Rider in Beverly Hills (autobiography), Scribner, 1952; reprinted Ballantine, 1971.

The William Saroyan Reader, Braziller, 1958; reprinted, Barricade, 1994.

Here Comes, There Goes, You Know Who (autobiography), Trident, 1962; reprinted, Barricade, 1995.

My Lousy Adventures with Money, New Strand, 1962.

A Note on Hilaire Hiler, Wittenborn, 1962.

Me (juvenile), Crowell-Collier, 1963.

Not Dying: An Autobiographical Interlude (autobiography), Harcourt, 1963.

Short Drive, Sweet Chariot (reminiscences), Phaedra, 1966.

(Author of introduction) *The Arabian Nights*, Platt and Munk, 1966.

Look at Us; Let's See; Here We Are; Look Hard, Speak Soft; I See, You See, We All See; Stop, Look, Listen; Beholder's Eye; Don't Look Now But Isn't That You? (Us? U.S.?), Cowles, 1967.

I Used to Believe I Had Forever, Now I'm Not So Sure, Cowles, 1968.

(Author of foreword) Barbara Holden and Mary Jane Woebcke, *A Child's Guide to San Francisco*, Diablo Press, 1968.

Horsey Gorsey and the Frog (juvenile), illustrated by Grace Davidian, R. Hale, 1968.

Letters from 74 rue Taitbout, or Don't Go, But If You Must, Say Hello to Everybody, World, 1968, published as *Don't Go, But If You Must, Say Hello to Everybody*, Cassell, 1970.

Days of Life and Death and Escape to the Moon, Dial, 1970.

(Editor and author of introduction) *Hairenik, 1934–1939: An Anthology of Short Stories and Poems* (collection of Armenian American literature), Books for Libraries Press, 1971.

Places Where I've Done Time, Praeger, 1972.

The Tooth and My Father, Doubleday, 1974.

An Act or Two of Foolish Kindness, Penmaen Press and Design, 1976.

Sons Come and Go, Mothers Hang In Forever, Franklin Library, 1976.

Morris Hirschfield, Rizzoli International, 1976.

Chance Meetings, Norton, 1978.

(Compiler) *Patmuatsk`ner/Uiliem Saroyean; hayats`uts` Hovhannes Sheohmelean* (selected Armenian stories), Sewan, 1978.

Obituaries, Creative Arts, 1979, second edition, 1979.

Births, introduction by David Kherdian, Creative Arts, 1981.

The New Saroyan Reader: A Connoisseur's Anthology of the Writings of William Saroyan, edited by Brian Derwent, Creative Arts, 1984.

The Circus (juvenile), Creative Education, 1986.

The Pheasant Hunter: About Fathers and Sons, Redpath Press, 1986.

The Parsley Garden (juvenile), Creative Education, 1989.

Saroyan's Armenians: An Anthology, edited by Alice K. Barter, University Editions, 1992.

Saroyan on Paper: Drawings, Watercolors, and Words, Fresno Art Museum, 2002.

Where the Bones Go, edited by Robert Setrakian, The Press at California State University, Fresno, 2002.

Essential Saroyan, edited by William E. Justice, Heyday Books, 2005.

Also author of *Famous Faces and Other Friends*, 1976. Writer of song lyrics, including "Come on-a My House" with Ross Bagdasarian, 1951. Contributor to *Overland Monthly*, *Hairenik* (Armenian American magazine), *Story*, *The Saturday Evening Post*, *Atlantic*, *Look*, *McCall's*, and other periodicals.

The Human Comedy and *The Adventures of Wesley Jackson* have been translated into Russian; *Mama I Love You* and *Papa You're Crazy* have been translated into French.

Media Adaptations

A film version of *The Human Comedy* starring Mickey Rooney was released in 1943; United Artists made a film based on *The Time of Your Life* starring James Cagney in 1948; an opera version of *Hello Out There* prepared by composer Jack Beeson was widely performed in 1953; a television adaptation of *The Time of Your Life* was produced on Playhouse 90 in October 1958; *Ah, Sweet Mystery of Mrs. Murphy* was produced by NBC-TV in 1959; *The*

Unstoppable Gray Fox was produced by CBS-TV in 1962; *My Heart's in the Highlands* was adapted for opera by Beeson and broadcast on television on March 18, 1970; selections from *Making Money and Thirteen Other Very Short Plays* were presented on television by NET Playhouse on December 8, 1970; a musical version of *The Human Comedy* was produced on Broadway by Joseph Papp in 1986.

Further Readings about the Author

Books

Aaron, Daniel, *Writers on the Left*, Oxford University Press, 1977.

Agee, James, *Agee on Film*, McDowell, Obolensky, 1958.

Axelrod, Stephen Gould, *Robert Lowell: Life and Art*, Princeton University Press, 1978.

Balakian, Nona, *The Armenian-American Writer*, AGBU, 1958.

———, *Critical Encounters*, Bobbs-Merrill, 1978.

———, *The World of William Saroyan: A Literary Interpretation*, Bucknell University Press, 1997.

Calonne, David Stephen, *William Saroyan: My Real Work Is Being*, University of North Carolina Press, 1983.

Contemporary Literary Criticism, Gale, Volume 1, 1973; Volume 8, 1978; Volume 10, 1979; Volume 29, 1984; Volume 34, 1985; Volume 56, 1989.

Dictionary of Literary Biography, Gale, Volume 7: Twentieth-Century American Dramatists, 1981; Volume 9: American Novelists, 1910–1945, 1981; Volume 86: American Short Story Writers, 1910–1945, 1989.

Dictionary of Literary Biography Yearbook: 1981, Gale, 1982.

Esslin, Martin, *The Theatre of the Absurd*, Doubleday, 1961.

Floan, Howard, *William Saroyan*, Twayne, 1966.

French, Warren, editor, *The Thirties: Fiction, Poetry, Drama*, Everett/Edwards, 1967, pp. 211-219.

Geismar, Maxwell, *Writers in Crisis: The American Novel, 1925–1940*, Hill and Wang, 1966.

Gifford, Barry, and Lawrence Lee, *Saroyan: A Biography*, Harper, 1984; reprinted, UC Press, 1998; reprinted, Thunder Mountain Press, 2005.

Gold, Herbert, *A Walk on the West Side: California on the Brink*, Arbor House, 1981.

Kazin, Alfred, *Starting Out in the Thirties*, Vintage, 1980.

Keyishian, Harry, *Critical Essays on William Saroyan*, Prentice Hall, 1995.

Krutch, Joseph Wood, *The American Drama since 1918*, Braziller, 1957.

Leggett, John (Ward), *A Daring Young Man: A Biography of William Saroyan*, Knopf, 2002.

Lipton, Lawrence, *The Holy Barbarians*, Messner, 1959.

Martin, Jay, *Always Merry and Bright: The Life of Henry Miller*, Penguin, 1980.

McCarthy, Mary, *Sights and Spectacles*, Farrar, 1956.

Rosa, Alfred, editor, *The Old Century and the New: Essays in Honor of Charles Angoff*, Fairleigh Dickinson University Press, 1978, pp. 192-206.

Saroyan, Aram, *William Saroyan*, Harcourt, 1983.

———, *Last Rites: The Death of William Saroyan*, Harcourt, 1983.

Saroyan, William, *Not Dying*, Barricade Books, 1997.

Stevens, Wallace, *The Necessary Angel: Essays on Reality and the Imagination*, Knopf, 1951.

Straumann, Heinrich, *American Literature in the Twentieth Century*, Harper, 1965.

Trilling, Diana, *Reviewing the Forties*, Harcourt, 1978.

Weales, Gerald C., *American Drama since World War II*, Harcourt, 1962.

Whitmore, John, *William Saroyan: A Research and Production Sourcebook*, Greenwood, 1994.

Wilson, Edmund, *The Boys in the Back Room: Notes on California Novelists*, Colt Press, 1941.

———, *Classics and Commercials*, Farrar, Straus, 1950, pp. 26-31, 327-330.

Periodicals

American Mercury, September 1943.

Chicago Tribune Book World, July 5, 1970.

College English, March 1955, pp. 336-340, 385.

Commonweal, November 4, 1942.

Detroit Free Press, May 22, 1981.

Esquire, October 1960, pp. 85-91.

Georgia Review, fall 1970, pp. 281-296.

Los Angeles Times, May 19, 1981; June 7, 1981.

Los Angeles Times Book Review, April 10, 1988, p. 11.

Modern Drama, September 1972, pp. 185–194.

New Republic, March 1, 1943; March 9, 1953.

New York Times Book Review, April 2, 1972; August 15, 1976; May 20, 1979, pp. 7, 49-51; August 21, 1983.

Pacific Spectator, winter 1947.
Punch, January 31, 1973.
Quarterly Journal of Speech, February 1944.
Saturday Review of Literature, December 28, 1940.
Soviet Literature, No. 12, 1977, pp. 159-166.
Theatre Arts, December 1958.
Times Literary Supplement, June 22, 1973.
Tribune Books (Chicago), May 1, 1988, p. 3.
Virginia Quarterly Review, summer 1944.
Western American Literature, winter 1986, p. 369; fall 1988, p. 283.
World Literature Today, winter 1985, p. 100.

Bibliographies

Foard, Elisabeth, *William Saroyan: A Reference Guide*, G. K. Hall, 1989.
Kherdian, David, *A Bibliography of William Saroyan, 1934–1964*, Howell, 1965.
Nelson, Charles. "William Saroyan: Periodical Appearances, Etc.," unpublished.
Whitemore, Jon, *William Saroyan: A Research and Production Sourcebook*, Greenwood Press, 1994.

Major Saroyan collections are housed at Stanford University; the Fresno Public Library; California State University, Fresno; Cornell University; and the University of California, Los Angeles.

Sources for Selected Bibliography

Contemporary Authors Online, Gale, 2007. Reproduced in Biography Resource Center. Farmington Hills, MI: Thomson Gale, 2007. http://galenet.gale group.com/servlet/BioRC
Kherdian, David, *Forgotten Bread: First Generation Armenian American Writers*, Heyday Books, 2007.

About the Editor

William Emery Justice has edited *Essential Saroyan* and *California Uncovered: Stories for the Twenty-first Century*. His first book, *Edges of Bounty: Adventures in the Edible Valley*, will be published by Heyday Books in 2008.

HEYDAY INSTITUTE

Since its founding in 1974, Heyday Books has occupied a unique niche in the publishing world, specializing in books that foster an understanding of the history, literature, art, environment, social issues, and culture of California and the West. We are a 501(c)(3) nonprofit organization based in Berkeley, California, serving a wide range of people and audiences.

We are grateful for the generous funding we've received for our publications and programs during the past year from foundations and more than three hundred individual donors. Major supporters include:

Anonymous; Anthony Andreas, Jr.; Audubon California; Barnes & Noble bookstores; BayTree Fund; B.C.W. Trust III; S. D. Bechtel, Jr. Foundation; Fred & Jean Berensmeier; Book Club of California; Butler Koshland Fund; California Council for the Humanities; California State Coastal Conservancy; California State Library; Candelaria Fund; Columbia Foundation; Compton Foundation, Inc.; Malcolm Cravens Foundation; Federated Indians of Graton Rancheria; Fleishhacker Foundation; Wallace Alexander Gerbode Foundation; Richard & Rhoda Goldman Fund; Marion E. Greene; Walter & Elise Haas Fund; Leanne Hinton; Hopland Band of Pomo Indians; James Irvine Foundation; George Frederick Jewett Foundation; Marty & Pamela Krasney; Guy Lampard & Suzanne Badenhoop; LEF Foundation; Robert Levitt; Michael McCone; Middletown Rancheria Tribal Council; National Endowment for the Arts; National Park Service; Philanthropic Ventures Foundation; Poets & Writers; Rim of the World Interpretive Association; River Rock Casino; Riverside-Corona Resource Conservation; Alan Rosenus; San Francisco Foundation; Santa Ana Watershed Association; William Saroyan Foundation; Seaver Institute; Sandy Cold Shapero; Service Plus Credit Union; L. J. Skaggs & Mary C. Skaggs Foundation; Skirball Foundation; Orin Starn; Swinerton Family Fund; Thendara Foundation; Victorian Alliance; Tom White; Harold & Alma White Memorial Fund; and Stan Yogi.

For more information about Heyday Institute, our publications and programs, please visit our website at www.heydaybooks.com.

GREAT
VALLEY

Great Valley Books

G reat Valley Books is a program of Heyday Institute, Berkeley. Books in the Great Valley series strive to publish, promote, and develop a deep appreciation of various aspects of the region's unique history and culture. Created in 2002 with a grant from The James Irvine Foundation, it strives to promote the rich literary, artistic, and cultural resources of California's Central Valley by publishing books of the highest merit and broadest interest.

A few of our Great Valley Books and other Central Valley titles include:

Blithe Tomato, by Mike Madison; *Haslam's Valley*, by Gerald Haslam; *Highway 99: A Literary Journey through California's Great Central Valley*, edited by Stan Yogi, Gayle Mak, and Patricia Wakida; *Skin Tax*, by Tim Z. Hernandez; *Letters to the Valley: A Harvest of Memories and Heirlooms*, by David Mas Masumoto; *Bloodvine*, by Aris Janigian; and *A Sweetness Rising*, by Roberta Spear.

For more a complete list of Great Valley Books titles and information, please visit our website at www.heydaybooks.com/public/greatvalley.html.